The Cambridge French–English Thesaurus

This is the first ever bilingual thesaurus of its kind. The book is aimed at all English-speaking learners and users of French at intermediate and more advanced levels, and is structured in a uniquely helpful way. The book is arranged thematically rather than alphabetically, with 15 part titles subdivided into a total of 142 subheadings which are further subdivided into topic categories. In each category learners will find synonyms and related French words and phrases of use for writing or speaking about the topic, as well as sayings, metaphors, proverbs, famous quotations or usage notes connected with the topic. Every word, phrase and example has an English translation. Illustrations provide additional help, and there is a special section on conversational gambits. Two alphabetical indexes of more than 8,000 words each, one listing English vocabulary and the other French, help readers find what they're looking for easily.

The Cambridge French–English Thesaurus

Marie-Noëlle Lamy
Open University

Advisory Editor:
Richard Towell

CAMBRIDGE
UNIVERSITY PRESS

Pour Denise Lamy

PUBLISHED BY THE PRESS SYNDICATE OF THE UNIVERSITY OF CAMBRIDGE
The Pitt Building, Trumpington Street, Cambridge CB2 1RP, United Kingdom

CAMBRIDGE UNIVERSITY PRESS
The Edinburgh Building, Cambridge CB2 2RU, United Kingdom
40 West 20th Street, New York, NY 10011–4211, USA
10 Stamford Road, Oakleigh, Melbourne 3166, Australia

First published 1998

Printed in the United Kingdom at the University Press, Cambridge

Typeset in Frutiger 7/8.5 pt

*A catalogue record for this book is available from
the British Library*

Library of Congress cataloguing in publication data

Lamy, Marie-Noëlle, 1949–
The Cambridge French–English thesaurus / Marie Noëlle Lamy;
advisory editor, Richard Towell.
        p.   cm.
Includes index.
ISBN 0 521 56348 8 (hb). – ISBN 0 521 42581 6 (pb)
1. French language – Synonyms and antonyms – Glossaries,
vocabularies, etc. 2. English language – snynoyms and antonyms –
Glossaries, vocabularies, etc. I. Towell, Richard. II. Title.
PC2591.L24 1998
443'.21 – dc21   96–29914 CIP

ISBN 0 521 56348 8 hardback
ISBN 0 521 42581 6 paperback

WD

Contents

Many learners of French understand more vocabulary and phrases than they are able to summon when called upon to speak or write in French. Words may be on the tips of their tongues (*ils ont le mot sur le bout de la langue*), or their pens, but may not materialize when needed. The aim of **The Cambridge French-English Thesaurus** is to fill this need by providing those who wish to add variety and authenticity to their spoken or written French with a reference tool for quick and easy consultation. Organised according to topics, the book can be thought of as a thesaurus, or *dictionnaire analogique,* with a difference: the French language is not presented as a list of words but as a network of ideas. This approach permeates the book, whose specific nature can be summarized in two ways.

Firstly, unlike many thesauri, **The Cambridge French-English Thesaurus** is not limited to listing synonyms but provides information to allow users to select a word or phrase with the right intensity in the right circumstances. Here are two instances:

• You have just seen an excruciatingly boring film. How do you convey your feeling in French? 'Ennuyeux'? This book will help you do better than this. Look up 'boring' in the index: you will be referred to topic category 10.2. There you will find a choice of adjectives, metaphors and stylistic information which will help you express your criticism with maximum impact.

Perhaps the film was plain dull (*ennuyeux comme la pluie*) or it felt endless (*long comme un jour sans pain*), or perhaps it was so dire that your verdict (delivered in the strongest terms to an audience which is robust enough not to take offence) will be: 'C'était horriblement emmerdant!'

• Or suppose that you are trying to translate 'She's really clever!' Look up 'clever' in the index, then consult topic category 59.13 as directed. There you will find a variety of ways of praising her intelligence, depending on the reason for your admiration: is she very brainy (*c'est un cerveau!*),

or do you mean that she's cunning and knowing (*finaude?*, *roublarde?*) or that she wasn't born yesterday (*Elle n'est pas née de la dernière pluie*)? If none of these phrases fit, you could look further afield for instance to 59.2 Competence, 59.3 Competent people, 59.12 Intelligence, or use antonym categories as your source of inspiration, for instance 59.4 Stupidity (*Elle est loin d'être sotte*). In this way, **The Cambridge French-English Thesaurus** builds up several layers of vocabulary around an idea, in order to ensure that users have a full and flexible resource from which to choose.

Secondly, unlike a standard thesaurus, this book offers a translation for every word, phrase and example provided, and specific help for dealing with 'false friends'. Particular care has been taken to provide translations reflecting British English and American English usage, and our thanks go to editorial consultant John Bailie (for UK usage) and to Donna Farina who has carefully analysed the French in order to create appropriate American translations. Thank you also to Paul Heacock for extensive supplementary advice on American usage.

The order of the verb tables in the 'Verb conjugations' section is based on that adopted by *Le Nouveau Bescherelle* (Hatier, 1990), though the tables differ significantly in other ways from the ones reproduced in that book.

Finally, many thanks are due to Adrian du Plessis who provided the original idea for this book and whose support for the project was unfailing, to Liz Walter for contributing in many different ways to its development, and to Clare Orchard for tirelessly editing the typescript.

We hope that **The Cambridge French-English Thesaurus** will be used in many different ways: as an *aide-mémoire*, as a tool for prose translation, as an inspiration for composition, or simply as a means of browsing through the French language for pleasure.

How to use this book

The following examples give a clear indication of the structure of *The Cambridge French-English Thesaurus* and of the most efficient methods of extracting information from the book.

Part title showing which of the 15 general themes is being illustrated.

Subheading title and number, showing one of the subdivisions within the main theme. (There are 142 such subdivisions within the book as a whole).

Topic category with its translation and number.

Cross-reference to a synonym category (sometimes cross-references are to antonym categories, i.e. with opposite meanings).

French headword. All headwords appear in the French index p 283 in alphabetical order, followed by their topic category number.

Part of speech The part of speech is given for the headword wherever possible. See list of parts of speech and other abbreviations p xii.

Verb conjugation number Main verb forms, listed under their number and conjugated, appear p 231.

Wanting

50 Wanting to have, seeking and finding

50.1 *Désir et passion* Desire and passion

see also **45.3 Affection**

désir *nm* **1** [longing for a specified thing] longing *mon désir de verdure/paix* my desire for greenery/peace **2** [used on its own, refers to carnal longing] desire

désirer (6) *vt* **1** [want carnal relations with. Obj: e.g. man, woman] to desire **2** [in shops, restaurants, etc] would like *Je désire une bière, s'il vous plaît.* I would like a beer, please.

passion *nf* [great love of anything, from food to persons] passion *avoir une passion pour qqch* to have a passion for sthg *Elle a une passion pour l'électronique.* She's mad about electronics. *Elle a une passion pour le copain de son frère.* She's besotted with her brother's friend.

Synonyms Differences between synonyms are indicated through glosses showing typical collocation or register.

62.3 *Adjectifs affectueux désignant la grosseur* Terms for fatness: affectionate

joufflu, e *adj* chubby-cheeked.
potelé, e *adj* [describes esp babies] chubby
rondouillard, e *adj* [humorous. Describes adults and implies small stature] tubby

62.4 *Termes péjoratifs et insultes désignant la grosseur* Terms for fatness: unflattering

gros lard! ALSO **gros-plein-de-soupe!** fat slob!
mastodonte *nm* [man or woman. Tall, large and ugly] great hulk
patapouf *nm* [male or female child. Clumsy and fat] fatty

Lexical fields Phrases that relate to each other in some way are grouped together to help find the 'right' way of expressing a particular communicative or translation need.

66.6 *Décrire sa douleur* Describing pain

Ça fait mal! That hurts!
Ça pique! That stings!
Ça brûle! That burns!
Ça (me/le) lance! It's a throbbing pain!
Ça tire! [when a stitch is being removed] It's pulling my skin!
Ça me démange! I've got an itch (there)!
C'est comme si on m'enfonçait des aiguilles. It feels as if needles.were being pushed into me.
aïe! ouch!

Idioms Images, similes, sayings or idioms belonging to a topic (here: parts of the body) are grouped together at the end of the topic.

Locutions Idioms
avoir la tête sur les épaules to be level-headed
avoir les pieds sur terre to have both feet (firmly planted) on the ground
Ça va lui mettre du plomb dans la cervelle [implies that the person spoken of is irresponsible] That'll teach him a thing or two.

Quotations Where a famous quotation is in currency as part of today's culture, it is given, together with details of its provenance, at the end of the topic.

Citation Quotation
Le cœur a ses raisons que la raison ne connaît point. [This line from Blaise Pascal, the 17th-century philosopher, is often quoted. It is due as much to its meaning, excusing irrational behaviour as long as it stems from the heart, as to its poetic form] The heart has its reasons that reason does not recognize.

Near-synonyms in headwords or in examples are indicated by the word ALSO.

faire étalage de, ALSO **étaler** {6} *vt* [pejorative. Obj: knowledge, erudition] to show off

Head translations and example translations All headwords including phrases, idioms and quotations are given one (sometimes two) **head translation.** Examples, each with its **example translation,** show the meanings in context. All head translations are listed in the English index p 241.

difficile *adj* difficult **difficulté** *nf* difficulty
compliqué, e *adj* complicated
délicat, e adj [requiring tact] tricky *Je n'ose pas le lui dire que je ne veux pas d'elle dans mon équipe, c'est délicat.* I daren't tell her that I don't want her on my team, it's tricky.
pénible *adj* [disagreeable and difficult. The translation of this depends on context] unpleasant *Marcher, c'est pénible par cette chaleur.* Walking in this heat is really unpleasant. *Il faut repasser par chez eux, que c'est pénible!* We have to go back via their place, what a drag! *Les enfants ont été pénibles, cet après-midi.* The children were hard work this afternoon.

British and American English All head translations which differ in the British and American varieties of the English language are shown as BrE or AmE. American and British usage is also signalled in example translations where necessary.

rond-point *nm, pl* **ronds-points** BrE roundabout AmE traffic circle
carrefour *nm* crossroads
croisement [implies simpler junction than **carrefour**] *nm* BrE junction AmE crossing

Glosses and explanations Sometimes a translation isn't quite enough to convey the exact meaning. In thoses cases, additional **glosses** help supplement the translation. Where the reality described is so different that no direct translation can be offered, an **explanation** is provided.

le parquet the legal profession
le barreau the bar
juriste *n* lawyer, attorney
avocat, e *n* A lawyer whose work includes advocacy on behalf of a client in a court of law, similar to an English barrister, or in some circumstances a solicitor.
notaire *nm* A practising solicitor whose work does not involve advocacy.

La cuisson à la chaleur Cooking with heat

Grammatical information Verb constructions and other useful grammatical information are given under the topic concerned.

All the cooking verbs below can be used transitively, e.g. *v* + *n*, or preceded by *faire* + *v* + *n*. E.g.: *dorer des oignons* or *faire dorer des oignons.* Both mean: to brown onions. The cooking verbs can also be used intransitively: *pendant que les oignons dorent* while the onions are browning

cuire {82} *vt* and *vi* **1** [obj: all foods except dough-based] to cook
cuire à la vapeur to steam *cuire au bain-marie* to cook in a double-boiler **2** [obj: dough-based foods] to bake
dorer {6}*vt* and *vi* to cook until golden brown

False friends The main false friends that tend to be a source of confusion between English and French speakers are explained and illustrated with examples.

Notoriété *nf* and **notoire** *adj*
Notoriété means fame, and **notoire** means famous. These words do not necessarily have negative connotations in French, but derive their sense from the context: e.g. *Il y avait au village une dentellière dont la notoriété s'étendait à des kilomètres à la ronde.* In the village there was a lacemaker who was famous for miles around. *un ivrogne notoire* a notorious drunkard *un botaniste notoire* a noted botanist

Usage Throughout the book, interesting usages are signalled. They illustrate a variety of aspects of language, including:

– pitfalls for English-speaking users of French.

usage

gueule *nf*
Gueule is the mouth of an animal: *Le chat tenait une souris dans sa gueule.* The cat had a mouse in its mouth. **Gueule** is neutral when referring to animals, but vulgar and pejorative when talking about humans: *Ta gueule!* BrE Shut your gob! AmE Shut your trap!

usage

banlieue *nf* **faubourg** *nm* and **zone** *nf*
The most common translation for *banlieue* is suburb, but in French the word often suggests the deprivation, unemployment and ghettoization more often associated with inner-city areas in Britain and in the United States. *Faubourg* is the outer edge of a town. In large towns the name *faubourg* was given to outlying districts but as the towns extended their boundaries, streets called *faubourg* became part of the city centre, for example *le faubourg Saint-Honoré* in the heart of Paris. *Une zone* is an area designated for a particular purpose, generally specified by the following word, e.g.: *zone industrielle* industrial estate, *zone inondable* area liable to flooding. In large towns the phrase *la zone* refers to a run-down area. In Britain it is associated with the inner city, while in France it tends to be associated with the deprived suburbs.

– socio-cultural information designed to help use vocabulary appropriately.

Conversational gambits Useful phrases to help with conversations and spoken French in general are organised into 43 different **numbered topics**. A selection of **head phrases** can be found under each topic, with **translations** and, if necessary, **glosses**. The gambits have their own table of contents p 209.

103.3 *Pour soutenir l'argumentation de quelqu'un* Supporting someone's point of view

Comme tu dis As you say
Je suis d'accord avec ce que tu dis/avec toi. I agree with what you're saying/with you.
[more formal] **Je partage votre opinion.** I share your views.
Non seulement cela, mais . . . Not only that, but . . .
J'ajouterais que . . . I'd also say that . . .

103.4 *Interruptions* Interrupting

Désolé(e) de vous couper la parole . . . Sorry to butt in . . .
[rather formal] **Excusez-moi de vous interrompre.** Sorry to interrupt you.
[When you feel you cannot get a word in, or someone is dominating the conversation] **(Vous) permettez!** Hang on (a minute)!
Laissez-moi parler! Let me speak!
Laissez-moi terminer! Let me finish!
[when a child is trying to interrupt you] **Je parle!** I'm talking!
Vous n'avez pas répondu à ma question! You didn't answer my question!

List of abbreviations

adj	adjective
adv	adverb
AmE	American English
BrE	British English
esp	especially
inv	invariable
n	noun
nf	noun feminine
nm	noun masculine
pl	plural
obj	object
qqch	quelque chose
qqn	quelqu'un
rel pron	relative pronoun
sb	somebody
sthg	something
subj	subject
usu	usually
v refl	verb reflexive
vi	verb intransitive
vt	verb transitive

1 Shape

1.1 *Formes* Shapes

forme *nf* shape
formes *nf pl* [euphemism. Of girls and women] curves

En forme de is used when an object is manufactured to look like another: *une montre en forme de cœur* a watch in the shape of a heart. **Sous la forme de** refers to an object temporarily used as a way to represent something else: *Ses remerciements sont arrivés le lendemain sous la forme d'un bouquet de roses.* He sent his thanks the next day in the form of a bouquet of roses.

1.2 *Formes en deux dimensions* Two-dimensional shapes

carré *nm* square **carré, e** *adj* square
cercle *nm* circle
circulaire *adj* circular
rond *nm* circle **rond, e** *adj* round
diamètre *nm* diameter
circonférence *nf* circumference

rond *nm* and **cercle** *nm*
Rond is commonly used for any circular shape. *Dessinez un rond et coloriez-le en rouge.* Draw a circle and colour it red. **Cercle** is a slightly more formal term, used when greater precision is needed, especially in geometry.

rayon *nm* radius
angle *nm* angle *angle aigu* acute angle *angle obtus* obtuse angle *angle droit* right angle *angle rentrant* reflex angle
30 degrés ALSO **30•** 30 degrees
rectangle *nm* rectangle
rectangulaire *adj* rectangular

see also **3.6 Près**
coin *nm* and **angle** *nm*
Coin is the everyday term for corners and angular parts of objects. **Angle** is in common usage for parts of objects and street intersections. *La boulangerie est à l'angle de la rue Rimbaud et de l'avenue Poincaré.* The bakery is on the corner of rue Rimbaud and avenue Poincaré. But when familiarity with the streets is implied *coin* is more likely, e.g. *Depuis trente ans, elle prend son pain chez le boulanger du coin.* She's been buying her bread from the bakery on the corner for thirty years. *Coin* is also used in situations where the emotional impact is strong, e.g. *Aïe, je me suis cogné contre le coin du bureau!* Ouch! I banged into the corner of the desk! In geometry, and when greater objectivity or precision is needed, only **angle** is used.

triangle *nm* triangle
triangulaire *adj* triangular
pointe *nf* ALSO **bout** *nm* **pointu** tip *en pointe* wedge-shaped
pointu, e *adj* sharp

pointe *nf* and **point** *nm*
pointe meaning 'pointed end' or 'tip', must not be confused with **point**, a dot or full stop. *La pointe d'un couteau* the pointed end of a knife *un point à l'horizon* a dot on the horizon.

1.3 *Formes à trois dimensions* Three-dimensional shapes

cube *nm* cube
cubique *adj* cubic
pyramide *nf* pyramid
pyramidal, e *adj mpl* **-daux** pyramid-shaped
cône *nm* cone
conique *adj* cone-shaped
sphère *nf* sphere
sphérique *adj* spherical
cylindre *nm* cylindre
cylindrique *adj* cylindrical
spirale *nf* coil
arc *nm* arch

1.4 *Formes décoratives* Shapes used for decoration

motif *nm* [single design, often repeated] pattern *à motifs* patterned
décor *nm* [decorative border or background on linen, chinaware] design
dessin *nm* [usu. figurative] drawing
croix *nf* cross
carreau *nm pl* **-x** check *cravate à carreaux* BrE checked tie AmE checkered tie
rayure ALSO **raie** *nf* stripe *à rayures* striped
rayé, e *adj* striped
à pois [describes material, blouses, dresses] polka-dot

1.5 *Lignes* Lines

ligne *nf* line
trait *nm* [in a drawing] line
droit, e *adj* straight
raide *adj* steep
ondulé, e *adj* wavy
tordu, e *adj* bent
incurvé, e *adj* curved
courbe *nf* curve
parallèle *nf* parallel (line)
parallèle *adj* parallel
diagonale *nf* diagonal line *en diagonale* diagonally
oblique *adj* angled
rangée *nf* row

1.6 *Formes irrégulières* Irregular shapes

bosse *nf* **1** [on the surface of an object] lump **2** [on a person or an animal, after a knock] bump **3** [on sculpture, on tree trunk] bump *un mauvais chemin qui a des creux et des bosses* a rough path with hollows and bumps in it
bosselé, e *adj* [describes the damaged surface of a metal object] dented
informe *adj*, ALSO **sans forme** *adj* [pejorative] shapeless *un vieux chapeau informe* a shapeless old hat
inégal, e *adj mpl* **-gaux** [describes, e.g. surface, ground] uneven

1.7 *Changements de forme* Changing shapes

former {6} *vt* **1** [voluntary action] *Formez une boule avec la pâte.* Shape the dough into a ball. *Formez un cornet avec le papier.* Make the paper into a cone. **2** [involuntary action] to form *Le vent a formé des zig-zags sur le sable.* The wind has formed wiggly lines on the sand.
prendre forme [refers to, e.g. clothes being sewn, model being built, garden being laid out] to take shape *Enfin, ma nouvelle salle de bain prend forme.* My new bathroom is finally taking shape.
prendre des formes [euphemism. Applies to pubescent girls only] to fill out
déformer {6} *vt* [pejorative. Voluntary or involuntary action] to pull out of shape *Ne joue pas avec ton écharpe, tu risques de la déformer.* Don't fiddle with your scarf or you'll pull it out of shape. *Trop d'usage déforme les chaussures.* Shoes lose their shape when worn too much. *Les grossesses lui ont déformé la taille.* Her figure has been ruined by child-bearing.

> *u s a g e*
>
> **déformer** can be used figuratively to describe distortions *Tu déformes la vérité.* You're distorting the truth. *Ne déformez pas ma pensée.* Don't put words into my mouth.

façonner {6} *vt* [obj: malleable substances only] to fashion *Façonnez une étoile avec la pâte.* Fashion the dough into a star.
gonfler {6} **1** *vt* [obj: balloon] to blow up **2** *vi* [subj: e.g. dough, blister] to rise
enfler {6} *vi* [subj: bruised flesh] to swell (up)
plier {15} *vt* **1** [obj: sheet of paper] to fold *Plier suivant les pointillés.* Fold along the dotted line. **2** [reduce the size of an object in order to store it. Obj: blanket, umbrella, garden chair] to fold away **3** [obj: wrist, knee, elbow] to bend
replier {15} *vt* [similar to **plier**, but stresses the fact that the object was laid out flat before the action started] to fold up *Je n'arrive pas à replier la tente.* I can't manage to fold up the tent.
redresser {6} *vt* to straighten (up) *Redressez le parapluie.* Straighten (up) the umbrella. *Redressez (le volant)!* [when driving] Straighten the wheel!
tordre {53} *vt* **1** [obj: e.g. pipe, wire] to bend **2** [obj: wet clothes] to wring
tortiller {6} *vt* [obj: thin strip of paper, ribbon, tie] to twist

2 Position

2.1 *Limites des objets* Boundaries and edges

see also **22.6 Le bord des étendues d'eau**
bord *nm*, ALSO **bordure** *nf* [general term] edge *le bord du trottoir* the curb
border {6} *vt* [be alongside an edge] to line *Des peupliers bordent les deux rives.* Poplar trees line both banks of the river.
limite *nf* **1** [line beyond which an area changes its character or status] boundary **2** *la limite d'âge* the age limit
au delà de beyond
cadre *nm* **1** [of picture] frame **2** [on printed page] box *Inscrivez vos nom, prénom et adresse dans le cadre ci-dessous.* Write your name, first name and address in the box below.
entourer {6} *vt* to surround *le cadre qui entoure le miroir* the frame surrounding the mirror *la campagne qui entoure le village* the countryside surrounding the village
lisière *nf* **de la forêt** edge of the forest
confins *nm pl* [distant part of province, country] edge *Il arriva enfin dans une petite ville aux confins du royaume.* At last he reached a small town at the edge of the kingdom.

> *u s a g e*
>
> *Things with a common border*
> Houses with a wall in common are **maisons contiguës**.
> Neighbouring regions are **régions limitrophes**.
> Adjoining rooms are **pièces attenantes**.

2.2 *Positions* Position

devant *adv* and *nm* in front *fenêtre de devant* front window *le devant de la maison* the front of the house
porte *nf* **d'entrée** front door
derrière *adv* behind *porte de derrière* back door
arrière *adv* and *nm* back *fenêtre donnant sur l'arrière* window overlooking the back *l'arrière de la maison* the back of the house

---

In a queue
Elle est au début ALSO *à l'avant de la queue.* She is at the front of the queue.
Elle est au milieu de la queue. She is in the middle of the queue.
Il est à la fin ALSO *au bout de la queue.* He is at the back of the queue.

On a garment
Les boutons sont devant. The buttons are on the front.
Les boutons sont derrière. The buttons are on the back.
une étiquette sur l'endroit a label on the outside
une étiquette sur l'envers a label on the inside

> *u s a g e*
>
> **extérieur, externe** and **intérieur, interne** *adj*
> **Extérieur** bears the same relation to **externe** as **intérieur** does to **interne**.
> **Extérieur** is commonly used while **externe** belongs to the vocabulary of geometry and science: *l'oreille*

externe the outer ear ; *l'oreille interne* the inner ear. Another special use of **interne** and **externe** (as nouns) is in the context of schools: *les internes et les externes* boarders and day pupils
cercle extérieur ALSO *externe* outer circle
cercle intérieur ALSO *interne* inner circle
l'intérieur de la boîte the inside of the box
l'extérieur de la boîte the outside of the box

centre *nm*, ALSO **milieu** *nm* middle
dehors *adv* outside
dedans *adv* ALSO **à l'intérieur** inside
le haut the top
le milieu [neither top nor bottom] the middle
le bas the bottom
en bas at the bottom
au milieu half-way up
en haut at the top

debout *adv* upright
vertical, e *adj, mpl* **-caux** vertical
horizontal, e *adj, mpl* **-taux** horizontal
à l'envers [describes, e.g. the way a vase, a painting, or a tin with a label, is placed] *adv* upside down
à l'endroit *adv* the right side up

2.3 *Placer dans une position* To place in a particular position

mettre {56} *vt* [general term] to put *Mets ton parapluie là.* Put your umbrella there. *J'ai mis le journal sous mon sac.* I put the newspaper under my bag.
poser {6} *vt* **1** [on a surface] to put (down) *Il posa devant moi une assiette d'olives.* He put a plate of olives in front of me. **2** [install] *poser une moquette* to lay a carpet *poser de l'isolant* to put in some insulating material *poser un miroir* to hang a mirror *poser une étagère* to put up a shelf *poser une moulure autour d'une porte* to fit a moulding round a door *poser une serrure* to fit a lock *poser un compteur électrique* to install an electricity meter
pose ALSO **installation** *nf* installation *1.000 francs pour le programmateur et 500 francs pour la pose* 1,000 francs for the programmer plus 500 installation charges
installer {6} *vt* **1** [set permanently, usu by connecting to a supply] to install *Il n'y a pas de place pour installer une photocopieuse.* There isn't room to install a photocopier. *L'appareil a été livré mais il n'est pas encore installé.* The machine has been delivered but it hasn't been installed yet.
placer {7} *vt* [stresses the exact location] to position *Où voulez-vous que je place cette applique?* Where would you like me to put this wall-light? *Placez le calque sur le modèle.* Place the tracing paper (exactly) over the drawing. *Ils ont placé leurs canons autour de la ville.* They positioned their guns around the town.
monter {6} *vt* [set vertically. Obj: e.g. tent] to set up
disposer {6} *vt* **1** [in a pattern] to set up *disposer un cordon de police autour de la ville* to set up police roadblocks around the town **2** [in an aesthetically pleasing way] to arrange *disposer des verres sur une table* to arrange glasses on a table

3 Direction and distance

3.1 *Directions* Directions

direction *nf* [use this term when you have a direction in mind] direction *en direction de Nantes* towards Nantes *dans la direction opposée* the other way
sens *nm* [use this term when you have a movement in mind] direction *dans le sens de la marche* facing forward *dans l'autre sens* (facing) the other way

u s a g e

The phrases 'to ask for directions', 'to give sb directions' are best translated as *demander son chemin, indiquer le chemin à qqn.*

3.2 *Principales directions* Main directions

devant *adv* in front, ahead *Passez devant.* You go ahead. *Continuez droit devant.* Keep going straight ahead.
derrière *adv* behind *Les autres passent d'abord, mets-toi derrière.* The others go first; you go behind them.
en avant forward
en arrière back(wards) *Il faut que tu retournes en arrière.* You have to go back.
à droite (towards the) right *Tournez à droite.* Turn right.
à gauche (towards the) left *Prenez à gauche.* Go left.
tout droit straight ahead *Si vous allez tout droit, vous verrez la pharmacie.* If you go straight ahead, you'll see the pharmacy.

3.3 *Les points cardinaux* Points of the compass

point *nm* **cardinal** point of the compass
est *nm* east *vers l'est* eastward *un vent qui vient de l'est* an easterly (wind)
ouest *nm* west *vers l'ouest* westward *un vent qui vient de l'ouest* a westerly (wind)
sud *nm* south *vers le sud* southward *un vent qui vient du sud* a southerly (wind)
nord *nm* north *vers le nord* northward *un vent qui vient du nord* a northerly (wind)
midi *nm* south *dans le midi de la France* in southern France
orient [literary term] east *quand on regarde vers l'orient* when you look towards the east
occident *nm* [literary term] west *À l'occident, une nuée s'amoncelait.* Clouds were gathering towards the west.

3.4 *Noms géographiques des points cardinaux* Place names that include points of the compass.

Nord *nm* **1** [in France] Nord (Pas-de-Calais) administrative region *habiter dans le Nord* to live in the Nord **2** [in North America] *le grand Nord* the Far North
Sud *nm* [the southern half of a country or continent] South
Est *nm* ALSO **pays** *nm pl* **de l'Est** [former Soviet bloc countries] eastern countries
Ouest ALSO **Occident** *nm* [developed countries of Western Europe and the United States] West
Orient *nm* (Far) East *le proche Orient* the Near East *le moyen Orient* the Middle East

Locutions Idioms

tous azimuts [informal. Literally: to all points of the compass] in all directions at once *Ils ont de gros budgets, alors ils peuvent se permettre d'envoyer des reporters tous azimuts.* They have huge budgets so they can afford to send reporters in all directions.

Il/elle ne perd pas le nord. He's/She's not lost his/her grip on reality.

3.5 *Distance* Distance

distance *nf* distance *une grande distance* a great distance *à une distance de trois kilomètres* at a distance of three kilometres *C'est à quelle distance d'ici?* How far is it from here?

télé-enseignement *nm* distance teaching

apprentissage *nm* ALSO **études** *nf pl* **par télé-enseignement** distance learning

kilomètre *nm* kilometre

borne *nf* [everyday slang] *C'est à cent bornes d'ici.* It's a hundred kilometres from here.

3.6 *Près* Near

près *adv* close *Le marché n'est pas très près.* The marketplace isn't very close (by). *tout près* very close

près de near *La maison est près de l'église.* The house is near the church.

de près close to *Vue de près, la surface de la roche présente des irrégularités.* Seen up close, the rocky surface looks uneven.

proche *adj* near *la gare la plus proche* the nearest train station *proches voisins* near neighbours *des amis proches* close friends

environs *nm pl* (surrounding) area *Voici la liste des activités sportives que vous pouvez pratiquer dans les environs.* Here's the list of sports activities available in the area. *Ils ont une ferme dans les environs de Sisteron.* They have a farm in the area near Sisteron.

avoisinant, e *adj* neighbouring *dans la campagne avoisinante* in the neighbouring countryside

voisinage *nm* neighbourhood

auprès de [in close proximity to a person. Implies emotional or other bond] near *J'ai fait mes études de musique auprès d'un grand maître.* I studied music with a maestro. *élevé auprès de sa grand-mère* brought up close to his grandmother

local, e *adj mpl* **locaux** local *les journaux locaux* the local papers *la production locale* the local produce

---

Local people and places

The French adjective *local* is not used when describing people. For this purpose use phrases adapted to the context, e.g. *de la région* (to cover a fairly wide area), *du quartier* (in towns) or *du coin* (informal, to mean 'in this area'), as follows.

Toutes les plages de la région sont polluées. All the local beaches are polluted. *un espace vert pour les enfants du quartier* a park for the local children. *Le petit restaurant du coin sert des moules tous les soirs.* The little local restaurant has mussels on the menu every evening.

---

coin *nm* [informal and often pejorative] local area *les gens du coin* local people *On ne trouve rien comme boutiques dans le coin.* You can't find any decent shops around here. *Ils sont en vacances dans un coin paumé.* They're on holiday in some godforsaken place.

s'approcher {6} *v refl* (often + *de*) to move close(r) *' "Approche-toi, petit Chaperon Rouge", dit la grand-mère'. '"Come closer, little Red Riding Hood", said the grandmother.' Ne vous approchez pas du bord, vous pourriez tomber dans la rivière.* Don't go close to the edge, you could fall in the river.

3.7 *Loin* Far

éloigné, e *adj* [describes: e.g. country, relative] distant

lointain, e *adj* **1** (before the noun) [similar to **éloigné**] distant **2** [literary] faraway *les pays lointains* faraway countries

loin *adv* far *C'est loin, la mer?* Is it far to the sea? *Je ne suis pas allé très loin, à cause de mes rhumatismes.* I didn't go very far because of my rheumatism. *venir de loin* to have come far *C'est assez loin d'ici.* It's pretty far from here.

infini *nm* infinity *à l'infini* to infinity *des miroirs qui reproduisent une image à l'infini* mirrors repeating an image to infinity

au loin in the distance

de loin from a distance

s'éloigner de {6} *v refl* (often + *de*) to move (further) away *Éloigne-toi du feu.* Move away from the fire.

4 Arrival and departure

4.1 *Arrivée* Arrival

arrivée *nf* [of a person, a vehicle] arrival *Il faut que tout soit prêt pour l'arrivée des invités.* Everything must be ready when the guests arrive. *J'attendais l'arrivée du train.* I was waiting for the train to arrive.

apparition *nf* [of a new technology, a trend] arrival *Avec l'apparition des moissonneuses-batteuses, l'économie de la région a été complètement transformée.* With the arrival of combine-harvesters, the economy of the area was completely transformed.

entrée *nf* [arrival in a closed space, or in a space bounded by walls, fences, etc] entrance *Son entrée nous a tous surpris.* We were all surprised when he made his entrance. *À l'entrée de la suite présidentielle nous nous sommes tous levés.* When the president and her entourage entered we all got up.

venue *nf* [move affecting the speaker, or the people spoken about] arrival *Nous attendions la venue de l'enfant pour novembre.* We were expecting the baby to arrive in November. *La venue précoce de l'hiver a perturbé les viticulteurs.* The early arrival of winter upset the winegrowers.

Verbes signifiant l'arrivée Verbs expressing arrival

arriver {6} *vi* **1** [reach a destination] to arrive *Laisse-le reprendre son souffle, il vient d'arriver.* Let him catch his breath, he only just got here. *L'avion est arrivé.* The plane has arrived. *Le bébé est arrivé avec un mois d'avance.* The baby arrived one month early. **2** [in response to a call] to come *Oui, on arrive!* Yes, we're coming!

entrer {6} *vi* [implies movement into a closed space or a space bounded by walls, fences etc] **1** [action seen from the point of view of the person, animal or thing which is moving] to go in *Je n'osais pas entrer chez ces inconnus.* I was reluctant to go into the house of these strangers. *Le chien n'a pas le droit d'entrer dans le restaurant.* The dog isn't allowed to go in to the restaurant. *La clé n'entre plus dans le trou: ils ont dû changer la serrure.* The key no longer fits the hole, they must have changed the lock. **2** [seen from the point of view of the stationary person towards whom the movement is made] to come in *Entrez!*

Come in! *Je vais ouvrir mes grilles pour que la camionnette de livraison puisse entrer dans la cour.* I'll open my gates so that the delivery van can come into the yard.

venir {23} *vi* [seen from the point of view of the person towards whom the movement is made] to come *Viens voir!* Come and take a look! *Certains sont venus de loin pour assister au concert.* Some people have come a long way to attend the concert. *Viendras-tu à mon anniversaire?* Will you come to my birthday party? *Pourquoi est-ce que tu ne viens pas plus souvent nous voir?* Why don't you come and see us more often? *Viens, on s'en va.* Come on, we're off.

atteindre {57} *vt* [arrive at something which one has sought] to reach *Après un kilomètre, on atteint le sommet d'où l'on voit un magnifique panorama.* After one kilometre, you reach the top, where there is a superb view.

survenir {23} *vi* [arrive after something has happened, often suddenly. Subj: e.g. person, event] to arrive. *Ils se rhabillaient quand le mari est survenu.* They were putting their clothes back on when the husband arrived. *Il avait vingt ans au moment où la guerre est survenue.* He was twenty when the war started.

advenir {23} *vi* (always with impersonal subject *il*; followed by *que*) [implies that fate took a hand. Literary] to happen *Il advint que les orages gâchèrent les récoltes cette année-là.* It so happened that thunderstorms spoiled the crops that year.

revenir {23} *vi* [seen from the point of view of the person towards whom the movement is made] to come back *Il faudra revenir nous voir!* You must come back and see us! *Il m'a brisé le cœur en partant et je n'attends qu'une chose, qu'il revienne!* He broke my heart when he left and I just can't wait for him to come back (to me).

débarquer {6} *vi* [informal] to show up *C'est à cette heure-ci qu'on débarque?* What a time to show up!

s'amener {9} *v refl* ALSO **se ramener** {9} *v refl* [very informal] to show (up) *Il s'est ramené, il était passé minuit!* He didn't show up until past midnight! *Alors, tu t'amènes?* Get a move on if you're coming.

Locutions Idioms
aller et venir to come and go
des allées et venues ALSO **un va-et-vient** comings and goings
Tout vient à point à qui sait attendre. [proverb] Good things come to those who wait.

4.2 *Départ* Departure

départ *nm* **1** [leaving a place] going (away) *J'attendrai ton départ pour reprendre le travail.* I'll start work again once you've gone (away). *Notre départ n'a pas eu lieu à la date prévue car Isabelle s'était cassé la jambe.* We didn't go away when we were supposed to because Isabelle had broken a leg. *les grands départs* the mass exodus for the holidays (out of the city, at certain times of year) *Le directeur a exigé votre départ.* The director demands that you leave the company. **2** [in a competition] start *prendre un bon/mauvais départ* to get off to a good/bad start

fuite *nf* [absconding, usu because one has done something wrong] running away *être en fuite* to be on the run *prendre la fuite* to run away

faire une fugue [used of children or teenagers] to run away

retraite *nf* **1** [period] retirement *prendre sa* ALSO *partir en retraite* to take retirement *prendre sa retraite avant l'âge* to take early retirement *à leur départ en retraite* when they retired **2** [informal. Money] (retirement)

pension *Maintenant, il touche la retraite.* He's a pensioner now.

Verbs exprimant le départ Verbs expressing departure
partir to leave *Quand est-ce que vous partez pour la piscine?* When are you leaving for the swimming pool? *Le train part à 13 h 30.* The train leaves at 1.30 p.m. *Le directeur part et il ne sera pas remplacé avant deux mois.* The director is leaving and his replacement won't be here for another two months.

To go away
One of the most useful phrases for 'to go away' is *s'en aller.* It is a colloquial phrase, used mostly in the following tenses:

Present	Future	Near future	Imperfect
je m'en vais	je m'en irai	je vais m'en aller	je m'en allais
tu t'en vas	tu t'en iras	tu vas t'en aller	tu t'en allais
il/elle s'en va	il/elle s'en ira	il/elle va s'en aller	il/elle s'en allait
ils/elles s'en vont	ils/elles s'en iront	ils/elles vont s'en aller	ils/elles s'en allaient

In other tenses and in the first and second persons plural, it is normally replaced by *partir*. Thus, instead of *je m'en suis allé*, you will hear *je suis parti*, and instead of *nous nous en allons* you will hear *nous partons*.

---

quitter {6} *vt* **1** [go away from (a place)] to leave *J'ai quitté Paris ce matin à 5 heures.* I left Paris at 5 this morning. *Sur ces mots, elle quitta la pièce.* Having said this, she left the room. *Les soldats quitteront le territoire demain.* The soldiers will be leaving the country tomorrow. **2** [go away from (a person)] to leave (behind) *Ne me quitte pas!* Don't leave me!

abandonner {6} *vt* **1** [stronger than **quitter** 2] to abandon *Il a abandonné sa femme avec deux enfants en bas âge.* He abandoned his wife and two young children. **2** [Obj: e.g. school, office, career] to leave, to give up *J'abandonne la médecine!* I'm giving up medicine!

se sauver ALSO **filer** {6} *vi* **1** [in order to avoid being caught] to run away *Les voleurs se sont sauvés* ALSO *ont filé en entendant la sirène de la patrouille.* The thieves ran away when they heard the police siren. **2** [informal synonym for **partir vite**] to run along *Allez, sauve-toi,* ALSO *file, il est tard et ta mère doit t'attendre!* Go on, run along now, it's late and your mother must be expecting you.

disparaître {64} *vi* [leave for mysterious or suspicious reasons] to disappear *Un beau jour, la femme du boucher a disparu avec la caisse.* One fine day the butcher's wife disappeared with the cash.

déguerpir {19} *vi* [pejorative. Leave after doing something bad] to run off

Locutions Idioms
Il/Elle est parti(e) sans demander son reste [when released from an obligation or an awkward sitation] He/She was only too glad to disappear.
ficher le camp [informal] to bug(ger) off
foutre le camp [very informal. May offend] to fuck off
prendre la clé des champs ALSO **prendre la poudre d'escampette** to make oneself scarce
battre en retraite to beat a retreat

---

usage

Note that *foutre le camp* is used in all the forms of the verb (*Fous le camp!* Fuck off! *Vous allez foutre le camp, oui ou non?* Will you fuck off!)

4.3 *Visites* Visits

see also **41.3 Montrer le chemin**

visite *nf* visit *recevoir la visite de qqn* to be visited by sb *rendre visite à qqn* to visit sb *Pas de photos pendant la visite, s'il vous plaît.* Please refrain from taking photographs during your visit.

visiter {6} *vt* [obj: e.g. cathedral, offices] to visit *Je vais vous faire visiter la maison.* I'll show you round the house.

Visiter

The verb *visiter* cannot be used when referring to people. To translate 'I visited my friends', you have to say *J'ai rendu visite à mes amis*, or *Je suis allé voir mes amis*. Nor is it often appropriate to use it with geographical names. To express 'I visited Burgundy', it is better to avoid the construction *visiter* + place name, and to use, for example, *J'ai fait du tourisme en Bourgogne*. You may use *visiter* transitively, as in English, when talking about enclosed places, e.g. *visiter un château* to visit a chateau, or *visiter des grottes* to visit caves.

---

passer chez qqn ALSO **passer voir qqn** [slightly informal] to drop by sb's place *Passe me voir demain.* Drop by my place tomorrow.

fréquenter {6} *vt* [to visit often] to be on friendly terms with *du temps où je fréquentais leur fils* in the days when I used to be friends with their son *Ils fréquentent beaucoup les Dumard.* They see a lot of the Dumard family.

---

5 Movement

5.1 Apporter et déplacer To bring and to move

apporter {6} *vt* [move an object so that another person may have it] **1** [movement away from the starting position of the person doing the moving] to take *Je lui apporterai mes chaussures à réparer.* I'll take him my shoes to be repaired. **2** [movement toward the recipient of the move] to bring *Il m'apporte toujours des œufs frais quand il vient me voir.* He always brings fresh eggs when he visits me. *Apportez-nous deux cafés, s'il vous plaît.* Could you bring us two coffees, please?

rapporter {6} *vt* [same usage as **apporter**, but implies that the action has happened before] **1** [movement away] to take back *Il ne les a pas bien réparées, rapporte-les lui.* He didn't fix them properly, take them back to him. **2** [movement towards recipient] to bring back *Je te le prête si tu me le rapportes demain.* I'll lend it to you if you bring it back tomorrow.

amener {9} *vt* [move a person, animal or vehicle so that someone may meet the person, or use the vehicle] **1** [movement away from the starting position of the person doing the moving] to take *Je leur amènerai Élodie, ils ne l'ont encore jamais vue.* I'll take Élodie to see them, they haven't met her yet. **2** [movement towards the recipient of the move] to bring *Amène ta soeur dîner avec nous vendredi!* Bring your sister to dinner with us on Friday!

ramener {9} *vt* [same usage as **amener**, but implies the action has happened before] **1** [movement away] to take back *Je te ramènerai chez toi après le cinéma.* I'll take you back home after the movies. **2** [movement towards recipient] to bring back to *Je te ramènerai ici.* I'll bring you back here.

amener and **emmener** You will often hear these two verbs used with an inanimate direct object, i.e.: *J'ai amené mon chapeau pour te le montrer.* I brought my hat to show you. or *Emmène la moutarde dans la cuisine!* Take the mustard into the kitchen! This is not always accepted as correct and the verbs *apporter* and *emporter* are more appropriate in the above contexts. With an animate direct object, however, *amener* and *emmener* are suitable, e.g.: *J'ai amené ma belle-fille pour vous la présenter.* I brought my daughter-in-law to introduce her to you. or *Emmène les petits jouer dans le jardin.* Take the little ones to play in the garden. They are also acceptable with a direct object representing a vehicle: e.g. *Amène la charrette.* Bring the cart.

transporter {6} *vt* [implies organized system for moving objects] to carry *Autrefois on transportait le charbon sur des péniches.* In the old days, barges were used to carry coal. *Regarde les fourmis transporter une feuille morte.* Watch the ants carrying a dead leaf.

déplacer {7} *vt* [change the position of an object, usu temporarily. Obj: e.g. car, chair, lamp] to move (along) *Je n'ai jamais déplacé ce lit: il doit y avoir beaucoup de poussière dessous.* I've never moved that bed; there must be a lot of dust underneath.

manœuvrer {6} *vt* [cause a large wheeled object to move. Obj: e.g. tank, trailer, tractor] BrE to manoeuvre AmE to maneuver

livrer {6} *vt* [move for a payment. Obj: e.g. goods, wardrobe, piano] to deliver

5.2 *Éviter* To avoid

éviter {6} *vt* **1** [take evasive action when faced with something or someone] to avoid *Nous avons évité l'accident de justesse.* We narrowly escaped having an accident. *J'évite les gens qui veulent me vendre quelque chose.* I avoid people who try to sell me things. **2** (often + de) [refrain from] to avoid *Évitez les graisses.* Avoid fatty foods. *Il faut éviter de parler de cela devant eux.* It is better not to mention this in front of them.

échapper {6} *vi* [implies that the thing avoided is annoying, boring, unpleasant or dangerous] *échapper à* to get out of *Tu n'échapperas pas à la corvée de vaisselle.* You won't get out of having to do the washing up.

éluder {6} *vt* [obj: question] to evade

se dérober {6} *v refl* to be evasive *Quand on lui demande des nouvelles de son père, il se dérobe.* When asked about his father he is evasive.

fuir {36} **1** *vi* to run away **2** *vt* [same meaning as **éviter 1**, but implies more fear on the part of the person doing the avoiding] to avoid *Pourquoi est-ce que tu me fuis?* Why are you avoiding me? *Elle fuit les plateaux de télévision.* She avoids television appearances.

5.3 *Pousser et tirer* To push and to pull

pousser {6} *vt* **1** [cause to move away from one] to push *Pousse la porte et entre.* Push the door open and come in. *Il avait poussé des meubles contre la porte pour que nous ne puissions pas entrer.* He had pushed furniture up against the door to prevent us from coming in. *pousser des pions sur un échiquier* to move pawns on a chessboard **2** [propel, usu with some force] to push *C'est pas de ma faute, M'sieur, c'est lui qui m'a poussé!* It's not my fault, sir, he pushed me! *Quelqu'un l'a poussé sous le train.* Someone pushed him under the train.

pousser *vi* to shove *Mais arrêtez de pousser!* Stop shoving, will you!

tirer {6} *vt* **1** [make a vehicle or an object on wheels move] to pull *une remorque tirée par un tracteur* a trailer pulled by a tractor *Le chariot est trop lourd pour que tu le pousses, tourne-le dans l'autre sens et tire-le.* The trolley is too heavy for you to push, turn it the other way and pull it. **2** [implies great force, sometimes brutality] to pull *Aïe, tu me tires les cheveux!* Ouch, you're pulling my hair! **3** [pull behind or towards oneself. Implies that the object or person pulled is resistant and that some force has to be applied] to drag *Il faut tirer les chaises vers la baie vitrée.* Let's drag the chairs towards the window. *Elle me tirait vers l'estrade.* She was dragging me towards the platform.

tirer *vi* (+ *sur*) to pull *Tirez sur la poignée qui se trouve sous le tableau de bord.* Pull the handle that's located under the dashboard.

traîner {6} *vt* [like **tirer 3**, but implies stronger resistance] to drag *La malle était lourde et il a fallu trois personnes pour la traîner jusqu'à la chambre.* The trunk was heavy and it took three people to drag it to the bedroom. *Il a traîné le cadavre de la route à l'étang.* He dragged the corpse from the road to the pond.

remorquer {6} *vt* [like **tirer 1**, but applies to vehicles and ships] to tow *Je vais acheter une voiture plus puissante pour remorquer mon bateau.* I'll buy a more powerful car to pull my boat

tracter {6} *vt* [like **tirer 1**, but this is a technical term applying to vehicles only] to tow

haler {6} *vt* [like **tirer 1**, but applies to boats and ships only] to tow

entraîner {6} *vt* **1** [suggests movement towards an undesirable destination. Subj: esp object, force of nature] to pull *Le pont s'est effondré et les a entraînés dans sa chute.* The bridge collapsed and dragged them down with it. **2** [used in technical contexts] to drive *Une chaîne entraîne la roue dentée.* A chain drives the cogwheel. **3** [get someone involved usu against their better judgment] to drag *Il nous avait entraînés dans une affaire louche.* He'd got us involved in a sordid business.

écarter {6} *vt* **1** [remove from one's path] to push aside *Il fallait écarter les feuillages pour traverser le jardin abandonné.* You had to push the branches aside to get through the overgrown garden. **2** [move] to spread apart *Écartez les bras le plus possible et prenez appui sur la barre.* Spread your arms as far apart as you can and lean on the bar.

enfoncer {7} *vt* [cause to move further down, or deeper into something] to push in(to) *enfoncer une fiche dans une prise* to push a plug into a socket *Il a fallu que j'enfonce mon bras dans le tuyau jusqu'au coude pour récupérer la bague.* I had to plunge my arm into the pipe up to my elbow to get the ring back.

secouer {6} *vt* to shake

presser {6} *vt* [subject to pressure] to squeeze

---

usage

Expressing English nouns of movement
To render into French a number of English nouns like 'a pull', 'a shove', 'a shake', etc, you will need to use French verbs, e.g.:
If the drawer is stuck, give it a pull. *Si le tiroir est coincé, tire dessus.*
I felt a shove. *J'ai senti qu'on me poussait.*
Give the cushion a shake. *Secoue le coussin.*

Locutions Idioms

Faut pas pousser (grand-mère dans les orties) ! [informal] That's going too far!

Tu pousses! [informal] You're going too far!

tirer sur la corde ALSO **ficelle** [pejorative] to (try and) milk the situation

tirer le diable par la queue to live from hand to mouth

5.4 *Porter* To carry

porter {6} *vt* **1** [hold the weight of. Subj: person] to carry *J'ai mal au dos et je ne peux pas porter de valises.* I have a bad back and I can't carry suitcases. *Elle porta l'enfant endormi jusqu'à son lit.* She carried the sleeping child to his bed. **2** [be the support for. Subj: esp tree] to bear *un poirier qui porte des fruits splendides* a pear tree bearing superb fruit

soutenir {23} *vt* [be a support for something so that it does not collapse] to support *une poutre qui soutient le plafond* a beam supporting the weight of the ceiling

supporter {6} *vt* [similar to **soutenir** but implies great weight] to bear the whole weight of *Une seule colonne supporte toute la galerie supérieure.* A single column bears the whole weight of the upper gallery.

Choses faites pour porter Things designed to carry other things

porte-avions *nm inv* aircraft carrier

porte-bagages *nm inv* **1** [in a train, a bus] luggage rack **2** [on a bicycle] carrier

porte-bouteilles *nm inv* **1** [for storing] wine rack **2** [for carrying] crate

porte-cartes *nm inv* card wallet

porte-cigarettes *nm inv* cigarette case

porte-clés *nm inv* key ring

portemanteau *nm, pl* **portemanteaux** coat rack

porte-parapluies *nm inv* umbrella stand

porte-plume *nm inv* penholder

porte-savon *nm, pl* **porte-savons** soap dish

porte-jarretelles *nm inv* suspender belt

5.5 *Lancer et propulser* To throw

jeter {11} *vt* [implies no particular aim or caution when throwing] to throw *Il a jeté un os au chien.* He threw the dog a bone.

lancer {7} *vt* [similar to **jeter** but implies that the object thrown travels a greater distance] to throw

projeter {11} *vt* [uncontrolled; therefore may be dangerous] to throw out, to throw off *un chalumeau qui projette des étincelles* a blowtorch throwing off sparks

envoyer {6} *vt* [suggests that someone will receive the object thrown] to throw *Envoie-moi la balle.* Throw me the ball.

éparpiller {6} *vt* [over a wide area. May imply carelessness or gracefulness] to scatter

propulser {6} *vt* [implies suddenness] to propel

précipiter {6} *vt* [implies speed or force] to hurl *Il l'a précipitée dans l'escalier.* He hurled her down the stairs.

projectile *nm* projectile

5.6 *Avancer et marcher* To go forward and to walk

marche *nf* **1** [activity] walking **2** [time and place where the activity happens] walk *Pendant votre marche, vous découvrirez de nombreuses variétés de fleurs sauvages.*

During your walk you'll discover a great variety of wild flowers.

démarche *nf* [personal way of moving one's feet] gait *une drôle de démarche* a strange way of walking *la démarche assurée d'un marin sur un pont de bateau* the confident gait of a sailor on a ship's deck

allure *nf* [implies way of projecting one's personality] style *Elle entra, avançant d'une allure de reine.* She walked in, moving like a queen.

marcher {6} *vi* to walk

avancer {7} *vi* [implies progress forward] to move (forward) *Avancez jusqu'à la barre, mesdemoiselles.* Walk up to the bar, please, young ladies. *Allez, tu n'avances pas!* Come on, you're so slow!

Ways of translating English verbs of walking
Some English verbs describing ways of walking are best translated into French by using the verbs *aller*, *avancer* or *marcher*, and adding the relevant adverb or phrase, as in the following examples:

avancer sans bruit to creep (forward)
avancer au pas to march (forward)
marcher d'un air dégagé to saunter
marcher sur la pointe des pieds to tiptoe
marcher à quatre pattes [usu describes babies] to crawl (on all fours)
marcher en canard to walk with turned out feet
marcher les pieds en dedans to walk pigeon-toed

Others have a specific French translation, as in the following verbs:
traîner {6} *vi* to loiter
s'attarder {6} *v refl* to linger
s'éclipser {6} *v refl* to slink away
se faufiler jusqu'à {6} *v refl* to sidle up to
ramper {6} *vi* to crawl
s'enfuir {36} *vi* to run off
piétiner {6} *vi* [in snow] to trudge
se pavaner {6} *v refl* to strut
flâner {6} *vi* to stroll
tituber {6} *vi* to stagger
boiter {6} *vi* to limp
ramper {6} **(sur le ventre)** *vi* to crawl on one's belly

5.7 *Courir* To run

see also **81.9 Sport**
courir {33} *vi* [go forward fast on one's legs] to run *J'ai dû courir pour attraper l'autobus.* I had to run to catch the bus. *Soudain il s'est mis à courir.* He suddenly broke into a run. *courir à droite et à gauche* to run (all over the place)

courser {6} *vt* [run in order to catch] to run after *Les gendarmes l'ont coursé jusqu'à la forêt, puis ils ont perdu sa trace.* The police ran after him all the way to the forest, then they lost him.

accourir {33} *vi* [run towards someone or something with intent to help, or to embrace, etc. Emotional charge] to rush (up) *Il y a eu un bruit de freins, suivi d'un choc, et le cycliste a été projeté contre le mur.* There was a screech of tyres, followed by a crash, and the cyclist was thrown against the wall.

Citation Quotation
Rien ne sert de courir, il faut partir à point. [Often quoted line from La Fontaine's *Le lièvre et la tortue*, 1694, praising those who don't do things at the last minute] There is no point in rushing, you must leave on time.

5.8 *Suivre* To follow

suivre {75} *vi* and *vt* to follow *suivre qqn à la trace* to track sb

Citation Quotation
Qui m'aime me suive! [attributed to Francis 1st, attempting to rally his troops around him. Used humorously, to generate an enthusiastic following] If you love me, then follow me!

5.9 *Suivre afin d'attraper* To follow in order to catch

pourchasser {6} *vt* [implies speed. Implies to catch or to drive away] to pursue *Un chien pourchassait le chat dans le jardin.* A dog was pursuing the cat in the garden.

poursuivre {75} *vt* [implies to catch, after an investigation] to hunt *La police le poursuit depuis trois mois.* The police have been hunting him for three months.

poursuite *nf* chase
course-poursuite *nf, pl* **courses-poursuites** [car chase or other eventful chase] chase
filer {6} *vt* [implies secrecy] to tail
filature *nf* tailing *faire une filature* to tail a suspect

5.10 *Personnes qui suivent les autres* People who follow other people

suite *nf* [of a V.I.P.] entourage
fidèle *nm* keen practitioner *Nous sommes des fidèles de la bicyclette.* We use bicycles in preference to anything else. *Ce sont des fidèles des camps naturistes.* They're very keen on nudist camps.
suiveur *nm* [at a bicycle race or car rally] member of the support team
poursuivant, e *n* pursuer
groupie *nf* [of rock star] groupie

5.11 *Sauter et bondir* To jump and to leap

sauter {6} *vi* to jump *Les gens sautaient des fenêtres de la tour en flammes.* People were jumping from the windows of the blazing tower. *sauter par-dessus une barrière* to jump over a fence *sauter à la corde* to skip (rope)
sautiller {6} *vi* [small-scale and repeated jumps] to hop
bondir {19} *vi* [more energetic than **sauter**] to leap
rebondir {19} *vi* to bounce
s'élancer {7} *v refl* to spring (forward)

5.12 *Tomber* To fall

tomber {6} *vi* to fall *Elle a trébuché et elle est tombée.* She tripped and fell. *Attention, tu vas tomber!* Watch out you don't fall!! *Une ardoise est tombée du toit.* A slate fell off the roof. *laisser tomber qqch* to drop sthg
chuter {6} *vi* [similar to **tomber**, but used only with people, esp skiers, skaters, cyclists, etc] to fall
chute *nf* fall *Elle a entraîné la nappe dans sa chute.* She fell dragging the tablecloth with her. *la saison de la chute des feuilles* the season when leaves fall off the trees *à l'âge de la chute des cheveux* at the age when hair falls out
trébucher {6} *vi* to trip *J'ai trébuché sur la marche et je me suis tordu la cheville.* I tripped on the step and twisted my ankle.

faire un tonneau [describes wheeled vehicle] to roll over
s'effondrer {6} *v refl* **1** [fall] to collapse *La tour s'est effondrée.* The tower collapsed. *La route s'est effondrée.* The road caved in. **2** [become prostrate] to collapse *un sportif qui s'effondre après l'effort* an athlete collapsing after too much effort *Elle s'est effondrée quand on lui a appris la nouvelle.* She collapsed when she heard the news.
s'écrouler {6} *v refl* [similar to **s'effondrer**, but used esp of a stack or pile of objects] to collapse. *La pile de livres s'est écroulée.* The heap of books collapsed.
renverser {6} *vt* **1** [obj: e.g., liquid, milk] to spill *J'ai renversé une bouteille de vin sur le tapis.* I spilled a bottle of wine on to the carpet. **2** [obj: e.g. stack, heap] to topple
se renverser {6} *v refl* to be spilled *Le lait s'est renversé.* The milk was spilled.
basculer {6} *vi* [fall and turn upside down at the same time] to topple over *L'homme est resté en équilibre un instant sur le bord du toit, puis il a basculé dans le vide.* The man stayed poised on the edge of the roof for a moment, then toppled over into the void.

5.13 *Venir d'une hauteur* To come down from a height

plonger {8} *vi* **1** [into water] to dive **2** [in order to catch a ball] to dive
se précipiter {6} *v refl* [voluntary] *se précipiter de/sur/sous* to throw oneself off/towards/under *Il s'est précipité du cinquième mais sa chute a été amortie par un arbre.* He threw himself off the fifth floor but his fall was cushioned by a tree.
piquer vers {6} *vi* [subj: e.g. plane] to plunge towards *descendre en piqué* plummeting (towards the ground)
dégringoler {6} *vi* [informal] to fall *Je me suis fait un bleu en dégringolant dans l'escalier.* I got a bruise falling down the stairs.
descendre {53} *vi* **1** to go down **2** *vt* to go down *descendre l'escalier* to go down the stairs
descente *nf* hill *dans la descente* down the hill

Common informal and slang phrases for falling
se casser la figure (slightly informal) to take a bad fall
(se) prendre une pelle ALSO **une bûche** ALSO **un gadin** (informal) to fall flat on one's face
se casser la gueule [very informal] BrE to fall arse over tit AmE ass over teakettle

5.14 *Monter* To go up

monter {6} **1** *vi* to go up *monter au premier étage* to go up to the first floor *monter sur un escabeau* to climb up on a stool **2** *vt* to go up *monter l'escalier* to go up the stairs
montée *nf* hill *dans la montée* up the hill
remonter {6} *vi* **1** [again] to go back up *Vous pouvez remonter dans vos classes maintenant.* You may go back up to your classrooms now. *Je monte et remonte cet escalier cent fois par jour!* I go up and down these stairs a hundred times a day!
grimper {6} *vi* [implies effort] to climb *grimper sur une chaise* to climb up onto a chair
s'élever {9} *v refl* [with apparent lack of effort] to rise (up) *La mouette s'éleva dans les airs.* The gull rose (up) into the sky.
jaillir {19} *vi* [obj: e.g. water jet, fountain] to spurt (up)
ascension *nf* [in mountaineering, ballooning] ascent
escalier *nm* staircase *monter/descendre l'escalier* to go up/down the stairs

marche *nf* stair, step
rampe *nf* banister
palier *nm* landing
ascenseur *nm* BrE lift AmE elevator *prendre l'ascenseur* to take the lift
escalator *nm* ALSO **escalier** *nm* **roulant** escalator

5.15 *Mouvement circulaire* Circular movement

tourner {6} *vi* **1** [follow a circular trajectory] to go (a)round *La Terre tourne autour du soleil.* The Earth goes (a)round the sun. *J'ai tourné autour de l'église, puis j'ai garé la voiture.* I drove (a)round the church, then I parked the car. *Les aiguilles de la pendule tournaient avec une lenteur désespérante.* The hands on the clock went (a)round desperately slowly. **2** [on one's axis] to spin *faire tourner une toupie* to spin a top *La Terre tourne.* The Earth spins (on its axis). *Tourne, pour que je voie si l'ourlet de ta jupe est bien régulier.* Turn round, so I can check that the hem on your skirt is even.
révolution *nf* [in scientific or technical usage] revolution
rotation *nf* [in scientific or technical usage. Around an axis] rotation

Citation Quotation
Et pourtant, elle tourne! [usual translation of Galileo's: 'Eppur, si muove!'] And yet, it does move!

5.16 *Onduler* To wave

onduler {6} *vi* [subj: surface of water, banner, hair, ribbon] to ripple, to sway *Les blés ondulaient sous le soleil de juillet.* The wheat swayed in the July sunshine.
ondulation *nf* **1** [of banner, ribbon. Also, natural shape of hair] wave **2** [artificial shape of hair] crimp *se faire faire des ondulations* to have one's hair crimped
flotter {6} *vi* **1** [be borne up and down on water] to float, to bob *Un bouchon flottait à la surface de l'eau.* A cork bobbed up and down on the water. **2** [wave in the air. Subj: e.g. flag, windsock] to flap

6 Travel

6.1 *Billeterie des transports* Tickets for travel

see also **8.19 La gare**

Billet and **ticket**
On most forms of transport, you require a ticket called *un billet*: e.g. *un billet de train* a train ticket, *un billet d'avion* a plane ticket, *un billet pour prendre le ferry* a ferry ticket. The term *un ticket* is preferred for short trips, such as on a bus, a funicular railway or a river boat.

horaire *nm* **1** [brochure] timetable *Donnez-moi un horaire des trains pour Fontainebleau s'il vous plaît.* Could I have a timetable for trains to Fontainebleau, please? **2** [system] times *Au mois de mai, les horaires des trains changent.* In May train times change.
carte *nf* [giving access to cheaper fares] pass, season ticket *carte orange* monthly season ticket *carte Vermeil* Senior Citizen railcard *carte d'embarquement* boarding pass

On the Paris buses, in the Métro and the R.E.R
In Paris the Métro underground has its own fare system. You normally pay for your journeys with a ticket which you buy singly, or in a booklet, *un carnet (de tickets)* at a Métro station. With a single ticket, you may make as long a journey as you like, providing it's unbroken. These tickets also allow you to travel on the Paris buses, where route maps show you clearly how many tickets you must use, depending on the length of your journey. Underground, the newer, faster, long-distance network called the Réseau Express Régional, or R.E.R, is fully linked to the Métro and you can change from one system to the other at many key stations throughout the capital. Beware, however, as tickets bought for use on the Métro network are not valid on the R.E.R. For this special tickets have to be purchased, on sale at the underground stations.

6.2 *Voyages et déplacements* Journeys and trips

see also **41.3 Montrer le chemin**

voyager {8} *vi* to travel *Je voyage beaucoup pour mon métier.* I travel a lot in my work. *Je préfère voyager en train.* I prefer to travel by train. *Je n'aime pas voyager en avion.* I don't enjoy flying. *Ils sont en voyage en Hollande à l'heure actuelle.* They're travelling around Holland at the moment.

voyage *nm* BrE journey AmE trip *Le Caire–Assouan par le Nil, quel beau voyage!* Cairo to Aswan on the Nile, what a wonderful journey! *partir en voyage* to go on a journey *être en voyage d'affaires* to be on a business trip *faire un voyage d'agrément* BrE to be touring (for pleasure) AmE to go on a pleasure trip

voyageur, -geuse *n* traveller *un grand voyageur* a seasoned traveller

passager, -gère *n* passenger

agence *nf* **de voyages** travel agency

agent *nm* **de voyages** travel agent

récit *nm* **de voyage** [published book by travel writer] travel book

organisateur, -trice *n* **de voyages** BrE tour operator AmE tour organizer

assurance-voyage *nf, pl* **assurances-voyages** travel insurance

traveller *nm* traveller's cheque

gens *nm pl* **du voyage** [people who have non-sedentary lifestyles] travellers

trajet *nm* [shorter than **voyage**. Usu for work] **1** BrE journey AmE trip **2** [place] route *Le trajet de la course est jalonné de publicités pour des marques de bière.* There are advertisements for brands of beer all along the route of the race.

déplacement *nm* [long or short journey, undertaken for work or for official purposes. The term is slightly formal] business trip *Je suis souvent en déplacement.* I'm away (on trips) a lot. *au cours d'un déplacement pour un congrès en Belgique* during a trip to attend a conference in Belgium

frais *nm pl* ALSO **indemnités** *nf pl* **de déplacement** travelling expenses

excursion *nf* [for children, tourists, often to a nature spot] outing

sortie *nf* [implies a treat for people who are normally confined, such as a group of children or older people] outing *la sortie de fin d'année* the end-of-term outing

circuit *nm* **1** [circular] round trip **2** [circular or not, with several points of interest along the route] tour *Faites le circuit des vignobles.* Go on a tour of the vineyards.

itinéraire *nm* [line on a map from starting point to point of arrival] route *carte des itinéraire bis* map with recommended alternative routes (for tourists)

parcours *nm* [like **itinéraire**, but used in the context of a race or rally, etc] route

escale *nf* stopover *faire une escale* to make a stop

station *nf* resort *station balnéaire* seaside resort *station de montagne* mountain resort *station de ski* ski resort *station thermale* spa

lieu *nm,* **-x de villégiature** [slightly formal, used in guides] place to stay

tourisme *nm* tourism

touriste *n* touriste

6.3 *Les bagages* Luggage

valise *nf* suitcase

bagage *nm* (piece of) luggage *mes bagages* my luggage *un seul bagage à main* only one piece of carry-on luggage

malle *nf* trunk

sac *nm* bag *sac de voyage* travel bag *sac de nuit* overnight bag

6.4 *Passer les frontières* Crossing borders

frontière *nf* border *à la frontière* at the border

douanier, -ière *n* customs officer

douane *nf* customs *passer la douane* to go through customs

à l'étranger abroad *aller passer ses vacances à l'étranger* to go abroad for one's holidays

étranger, -gère *n* foreigner

rapatrier {15} *vt* to repatriate

rien à déclarer nothing to declare

quelque chose à déclarer something to declare

Locutions Idioms

Les voyages forment la jeunesse. [proverb] Travel broadens the mind (of the young).

Il/Elle est toujours par monts et par vaux. He's/She's always off on his/her travels.

7 Cars

7.1 *Voitures – parties et accessoires* Cars – parts and accessories

voiture *nf* car

break *nm* BrE estate (car) AmE station wagon

automobile *nf* ALSO **auto** *nf* [formal or slightly old-fashioned term] car

7.2 *L'extérieur de la voiture* The outside of the car

carrosserie *nf* (car) bodywork

roue *nf* wheel *roue de secours* BrE spare (wheel) AmE spare tire

plaque *nf* **d'immatriculation** ALSO **minéralogique** BrE number plate AmE license plate

enjoliveur *nm* hub cap

pare-brise *nm, pl* **pare-brises** BrE windscreen AmE windshield

pare-choc *nm, pl* **pare-chocs** bumper

galerie *nf* roof-rack
essieu *nm pl* **-x** axle
antenne *nf* BrE aerial AmE antenna
capot *nm* BrE bonnet AmE hood
coffre *nm* ALSO **malle** *nf* BrE boot AmE trunk
tuyau ALSO **pot** *nm* **d'échappement** exhaust pipe
pot *nm* **catalytique** catalytic converter
pneu *nm pl* **-x** BrE tyre AmE tire
phare *nm* headlight

7.3 *L'intérieur de la voiture* The inside of the car

levier *nm* **(de changement) de vitesse** BrE gear stick AmE gear shift
ceinture *nf* **de sécurité** safety belt
lave-glace *nm, pl* **lave-glaces** BrE windscreen washer AmE water squirter
rétroviseur *nm* rear(-view) mirror
volant *nm* steering wheel
essuie-glace *nm, pl* **essuie-glaces** BrE windscreen wiper AmE rubber blade
lunette *nf* **arrière** rear window ledge
siège *nm* seat
frein *nm* brake
pédale *nf* pedal
téléphone *nm* **de voiture** carphone

7.4 *Sur le tableau de bord* On the dashboard

tableau *nm, pl* **-x de bord** dashboard
compteur *nm* meter *compteur de vitesse* speedometer *compteur kilométrique* BrE milometer AmE odometer
contact *nm* ignition
jauge *nf* **(d'essence)** BrE petrol gauge AmE gas gauge
clignotant *nm* BrE indicator AmE turn signal *Mets ton clignotant, on va tourner à droite.* Put on your indicator, we're about to turn right.
clé ALSO **clef** *nf* **de contact** ignition key

7.5 *Voitures – conduire* Cars – driving

conduite *nf* **1** [skill] driving **2** [type of car] *une voiture avec conduite à droite* a right-hand drive (car) *conduite intérieure* BrE saloon (car) AmE sedan
conducteur, -trice *n* driver
automobiliste *n* [slightly formal] motorist
pilote *n* [less usual for ordinary motorists. Used mainly for racing cars] (racing car) driver
chauffeur *nm* **1** [in a coach or a bus] driver **2** [paid driver, of a private car] chauffeur
stationnement *nm* **1** [short-term] waiting *Je ne peux pas rester en stationnement ici très longtemps, c'est une aire de livraison.* I can't wait here very long, it's a delivery bay. **2** [longer-term] being parked *J'étais en stationnement devant l'hôtel lorsque . . .* I was parked outside the hotel when . . .
stationner {6} *vi* **1** [short-term] to wait **2** [longer-term] to park
fourrière *nf* BrE car pound *mettre une voiture en* ALSO *à la fourrière* to impound a car
crevaison *nf* BrE puncture AmE flat tire
embouteillage *nm* traffic jam
bouchon *nm* [not necessarily extensive but causing blockages] traffic jam

7.6 *Verbes exprimant les manoeuvres en voiture* Verbs for driving

conduire {82} *vt* and *vi* to drive
dépasser {6} ALSO **doubler** {6} [when vehicles are going in the same direction] *vt* BrE to overtake AmE to pass
croiser {6} *vt* [when vehicles are going in opposite directions] to pass
garer {6} *vt* to park
se garer *v refl* to park
mettre le frein to put the (hand)brake on
changer de vitesse to change gear
passer en première/deuxième vitesse to go into first/second gear
rétrograder {6} *vi* BrE to change down AmE to shift down
mettre son clignotant BrE to indicate AmE to put on a turn signal
faire marche arrière to (go in) reverse
appuyer sur l'accélérateur to put one's foot down (on the accelerator)
accélérer {10} *vi* [in order to overtake, or at the lights] to accelerate
ralentir {19} *vi* to slow down
freiner {6} *vi* to brake
caler {6} *vi* to stall
faire un créneau to back into a parking space
pleins phares BrE with full beams AmE highbeam *mettre ses (pleins) phares* BrE to put one's headlights on full beam AmE to put one's brights on
en codes BrE with dipped headlights AmE on low beams *se mettre en codes* to dip one's headlights

7.7 *Station service* Petrol/Gas station

station *nf* **service** BrE petrol station AmE gas station *une station service sur l'autoroute* BrE a motorway service station AmE highway service station
plein *nm* full tank *faire le plein* to fill up *Le plein, s'il vous plaît.* Fill her up, please. *La voiture vous est livrée avec le plein.* When you take delivery of the car, it has a full tank.
réservoir *nm* BrE petrol tank AmE gas tank
pompe *nf* **à essence** BrE petrol pump AmE gas pump
essence *nf* BrE petrol AmE gas
super *nm* BrE four-star AmE super
sans plomb lead-free
vérifier les pneus BrE to check the tyres AmE tires

7.8 *Réseau routier* Road network

réseau, x *nm* network
rocade *nf* [around a town] bypass
routier, -tière *adj* road *transports routiers* road transport *circulation routière* traffic
panneau *nm* **indicateur, pl** **panneaux indicateurs** road sign
rond-point *nm, pl* **ronds-points** BrE roundabout AmE traffic circle
carrefour *nm* crossroads
croisement [implies simpler junction than **carrefour**] *nm* BrE junction AmE crossing
limitation *nf* **de vitesse** speed limit
ralentisseur *nm* **1** [hump] speed bump **2** [uneven surface] rumble strip
dos *nm* **d'âne 1** [accidental] bump (on the road) **2** [to slow vehicles down] sleeping policeman
passage *nm* **à niveau, pl** **passages à niveau** level crossing
virage *nm* bend

7.9 *Autoroutes* Motorways/Highways

autoroute *nm* ALSO *nf* BrE motorway AmE highway
  autoroute à péage BrE toll motorway AmE toll road
échangeur *nm* (motorway) junction
bretelle *nf* (**d'autoroute**) (motorway) BrE slip-road AmE
  adjoining road
sortie *nf* (**d'autoroute**) (motorway) exit
bande *nf* **centrale** BrE central reservation AmE median
  strip
voie *nf* lane *voie de droite/gauche* right-hand/left-hand
  lane
bande *nf* **d'arrêt d'urgence** (hard) shoulder
borne *nf* **d'appel d'urgence** emergency phone
aire *nf* **de pique-nique** picnic area
péage *nm* toll

7.10 *Routes* Roads

Routes
The term **route** *nf* is used mainly for roads outside towns
or villages, as opposed to **rue** *nf* street, in towns and
villages. However, a road in a small town or village
leading to a neighbouring town or village is sometimes
called *route de* followed by the placename, e.g. *J'habite
au 3, route de Villeneuve*. I live at number 3, Villeneuve
Road.

In the list below, translations are provided to give a general
indication, although it is difficult to be accurate, as
classification systems vary from country to country.

route principale ALSO **à grande circulation** BrE trunk
  road AmE high traffic road
route nationale [shown on road signs as N, followed by
  the number of the road] main road
route départementale [shown on road signs as D
  followed by the number of the road] (smaller) main road
route cantonale [shown on road signs as C followed by
  the number of the road] local road
chemin *nm* non-metalled road
pont *nm* bridge *pont suspendu* suspension bridge

7.11 *Rues* Streets

rue *nf* street *rue piétonne* pedestrianized street
aire *nf* **piétonnière** pedestrian area
passage *nm* **piéton** ALSO **clouté** pedestrian crossing
trottoir *nm* BrE pavement AmE sidewalk
caniveau *nm*, *pl* **-x** gutter
parcmètre *nm* parking meter
feu *nm*, *pl* **-x** lights *au feu rouge* BrE at the lights AmE at a
  red light *Le feu est rouge/orange/vert*. BrE The lights are
  red/amber/green. AmE The light is red/yellow/green.

7.12 *Véhicules divers* Various vehicles

véhicule *nm* vehicle
bicyclette *nf* bicycle
vélo *nm* [extremely common informal word for **bicyclette**]
  bike
V.T.T. *nm* [Vélo Tout Terrain] mountain bike
moto *nf* motorbike
vélomoteur *nm* motorized bicycle
mobylette *nf* ® moped
tram(way) *nm* tramway, tram (car)
camionnette *nf* van
camion *nm* BrE lorry AmE truck

(auto)car *nm* coach
(auto)bus *nm* bus
métro *nm* BrE underground train AmE subway (New York),
  metro (Washington) *le métro parisien* the (Paris) Métro *le
  métro londonien* the (London) Underground
taxi *nm* taxi
pousse-pousse *nm inv* rickshaw
charrette *nf* cart

8 Ships, planes and trains

8.1 *Navires* Ships

navire *nm* [formal or literary] ship *navire marchand*
  merchant ship *navire de haute mer* sea-going ship
bateau *nm*, *pl* **-x** [everyday term] boat, craft *bateau de
  plaisance* pleasure boat
vaisseau *nm*, *pl* **-x 1** [literary] vessel **2** [naval] warship
embarcation *nf* [slightly formal] (small) craft
naval, e *adj*, *mpl* **navals** naval

8.2 *Parties principales des navires* Main parts of ships

cabine *nf* cabin
coque *nf* hull
pont *nm* deck
entrepont *nm* steerage
cale *nf* hold
gouvernail *nm*, *pl* **gouvernails** rudder
hublot *nm* porthole
cheminée *nf* funnel
mât *nm* mast
voile *nf* sail
ancre *nf* anchor
amarre *nf* mooring line
ligne *nf* **de flottaison** waterline
flotteur *nm* float

8.3 *Principaux mouvements de la navigation* Main terms used for movement of ships

navigation *nf* **1** [using boats] sailing, shipping *la
  navigation de plaisance* pleasure sailing *la navigation
  commerciale* merchant shipping **2** [sum total of vessels at
  sea in a particular area] shipping *La Manche est une zone
  de navigation intense*. The English Channel is a very busy
  shipping area. *estuaire interdit à la navigation* estuary
  closed to shipping
naviguer {6} *vi* to sail
accoster {6} *vt* to berth
être à quai to be berthed
être à l'ancre to be (riding) at anchor
larguer les amarres to cast off one's moorings
rompre ses amarres to break one's moorings
corps-mort *nm*, *pl* **corps-morts** mooring buoy
balise *nf* marker buoy
dériver {6} *vi* to drift
mouiller {6} *vi* **1** [stop] to cast anchor **2** [stay] to be
  anchored *mouiller en rade de Brest* to be anchored off
  Brest harbour
faire du cabotage to ply along the coast
voie *nf* ALSO **couloir** *nm* **de navigation** shipping lane
météo *nf* **marine** shipping forecast

8.4 *Naufrages* Shipwrecks

naufrage nm shipwreck *Le 'Malouin' a fait naufrage.* The 'Malouin' was shipwrecked.
naufragé, e n shipwrecked person *Son père fut naufragé.* His father was shipwrecked.
naufrageur, -geuse n [a form of piracy] wrecker
couler {6} vi to sink
sombrer {6} vi [literary synonym for **couler**] to sink
épave nf [ship] wreck

8.5 *Construction navale* Shipbuilding

chantier nm **naval** shipyard
constructeur nm **de navires** shipbuilder
armateur nm (ship)owner
armer {6} vt [subj: shipowner] to fit out
magasin nm **d'articles de marine** ship's chandler's (shop)
radouber {6} vt to refit
en radoub being refitted
sur cales on the stocks
en cale sèche in dry dock

8.6 *Les passagers des navires* Passengers on ships

see also **6.2 Voyages et déplacements**
embarquer {6} vi ALSO **s'embarquer** v refl to go on board
débarquer {6} vi to disembark
passerelle nf gangway
passager nm **clandestin**, **passagère** nf **clandestine** stowaway
être à bord to be on board
passer par-dessus bord to go overboard
avoir le pied marin to have (one's) sealegs, to be a good sailor
avoir le mal de mer to be seasick
marin nm **d'eau douce** landlubber

8.7 *Petites embarcations* Small craft

barque nf BrE rowing boat AmE rowboat
canot nm dinghy *canot de sauvetage* lifeboat
vedette nf launch
voilier nm ALSO **bateau à voiles** BrE sailing ship AmE sailboat
yacht nm (luxury) yacht
hors-bord nm, pl **hors-bords** outboard motor
catamaran nm catamaran
aéroglisseur nm hovercraft

8.8 *Types de gros navires* Types of large ships

paquebot nm liner
ferry nm, pl **ferries** (car-) ferry
navire-citerne nm, pl **navires-citernes** (oil) tanker
navire-hôpital nm, pl **navires-hôpitaux** hospital ship
sous-marin nm, pl **sous-marins** submarine
péniche nf barge

8.9 *Les gens qui travaillent sur les navires* People who work on ships

navigateur, -trice n [suggests an adventurous explorer] sailor
mousse nm cabin boy
pilote nm pilot
marin nm sailor
capitaine 1 [general term] captain **2** [in the BrE merchant navy marine] master
docker nm docker
équipage nm crew
navigant, e n [on, e.g. ferries, person who works on the ship as opposed to personnel in the offices on land] member of the crew *les navigants* the crew
sous-marinier nm, pl **sous-mariniers** submariner
vieux loup de mer [humorous] old sea dog

8.10 *Avions* Aircraft

aviation nf **1** [using aircraft] aviation *l'aviation civile* civil aviation **2** [activity, professional or as a hobby] flying *Il est dans l'aviation.* He flies planes.
aviateur, -trice n [suggests a pioneer] aviator, aviatrix

8.11 *Principaux types d'avions* Main types of aircraft

avion nm BrE aeroplane AmE airplane *avion à réaction* jet *avion à turboréacteur* turbojet *avion de ligne* airliner *avion de chasse* fighter plane
moyen-courrier nm, pl **moyen-courriers** medium-haul aircraft
long-courrier nm, pl **long-courriers** long-haul aircraft
avion-taxi nm, pl **avions-taxis** air taxi
planeur nm glider
avion-cargo nm, pl **avions-cargos** air freighter
appareil nm [slightly formal] aircraft
hélicoptère nm helicopter

8.12 *Parties principales de l'avion* Main parts of the aircraft

poste nm **de pilotage** [for pilot and copilot] cockpit
cabine nf [for passengers] cabin
aile nf wing
fuselage nm fuselage
train nm **d'atterrissage** landing gear
hélice nf propeller
rotor nm rotor
moteur nm engine *moteur à réaction* jet engine
turboréacteur nm turbojet engine
altimètre nm altimeter
manche nm **à balai** [informal] joystick
kérosène nm jet fuel

8.13 *Voler* To fly

voler {6} vi [be transported in the air. Subj: plane, pilot] to fly
prendre l'avion [as a passenger] to fly *Tu vas à Rome en voiture ou tu prends l'avion?* Are you driving to Rome or flying?
décollage nm take-off
décoller {6} vi [subj: plane, pilot, passenger] to take off
s' envoler {6} vi [less technical than **décoller**] to take off

altitude *nf* altitude *Nous volons à une altitude de 12.000 pieds.* Our altitude is 12,000 feet.
mur *nm* **du son** sound barrier *passer le mur du son* to break the sound barrier
supersonique *adj* supersonic
trous *nm pl* **d'air** turbulence

8.14 *Aéroports* Airports

aéroport *nm* airport
aérogare *nm* air terminal
héliport *nm* heliport
piste *nf* **d'atterrissage** runway
hangar *nm* hangar
tour *nf* **de contrôle** control tower
espace *nm* **aérien** airspace
manche *nf* **à air** windsock
balise *nf* beacon

8.15 *Les gens qui travaillent dans les aéroports et les avions* People who work in airports and aircraft

capitaine *nm* captain
pilote *n* pilot
copilote *n* copilot
équipage *nm* crew
personnel *nm* staff *personnel au sol* ground personnel *personnel navigant* cabin crew
hôtesse *nf* **1** [in everyday usage] hostess *hôtesse de l'air* air hostess *hôtesse au sol* ground hostess **2** [in official usage] stewardess, flight attendant
steward *nm* (air) steward
bagagiste *nm* baggage handler
aiguilleur, -lleuse *n* **du ciel** air traffic controller

8.16 *Les chemins de fer* The railways

chemin *nm* **de fer 1** [rail infrastructure] (transport by) rail *le développement du chemin de fer dans l'Angleterre victorienne* the development of rail transport in Victorian England **2** [trains] train(s) *Je préfère voyager en chemin de fer.* I prefer to travel by train.
ferroviaire *adj* rail *les transports ferroviaires* rail transport *tunnel ferroviaire* rail tunnel

8.17 *Les locomotives* Locomotives

locomotive *nf* (train) engine *locomotive à vapeur* steam engine *locomotive diesel* diesel engine
loco *nf* [affectionate slang term] locomotive
bogie *nm* bogie

8.18 *Les rails* The track

rail *nm* **1** [single piece of metal] rail **2** [line] track *Ne traversez pas dans les rails.* Don't walk across the track.
ligne *nf* **de chemin de fer 1** [two rails] BrE railway line AmE railroad line *Tournez à droite après la voie ferrée* ALSO *la ligne de chemin de fer.* Turn left after the railway line. **2** [link] railway line *la voie ferrée* ALSO *la ligne de chemin de fer qui va de Plouarnoz à Trigastel* the railway line that goes from Plouarnoz to Trigastel
aiguillage *nm* (set of) points
cabine *nf* **d'aiguillage** signal box

sémaphore *nm* railway signal
butoir *nm* buffer

8.19 *La gare* The station

gare *nf* (**ferroviaire**) (train) station *Le train de Paris entre en gare.* The Paris train is coming in. *Dépêchez-vous, il est déjà en gare.* Hurry up, it's already standing in the station.
hall *nm* (**de gare**) station concourse *Attends-moi dans le hall.* Wait for me inside the station.
salle *nf* **des pas perdus** [old-fashioned term. Found in large stations] station concourse
buffet *nm* **de la gare** station buffet
quai *nm* (train) platform
voie *nf* **1** [platform] platform *Le train de Chambéry entre en voie 7.* The Chambéry train is arriving at platform 7. **2** [rails] track *Ne traversez pas dans les voies, empruntez le souterrain.* Don't walk across the track, use the underground passage.
tableau *nm*, *pl* **-x** board *tableau des départs* departures board *tableau des arrivées* arrivals board

---

Validating your ticket
In France you are required to punch your own ticket before you're on the train. This is called *composter son billet.* Failure to do so may mean a fine when the inspector asks to see proof that you have paid your fare, even though you can produce the actual ticket. The special punching machine to be used for this purpose is called *un composteur.* These machines can be found in stations and on platforms.

8.20 *Le train* The train

train *nm* train
TGV *nm* [Train à Grande Vitesse] high-speed train
tortillard *nm* [humorous] slow train (on a winding route)
wagon *nm* BrE carriage AmE car
wagon-lit *nm* BrE sleeper AmE sleeping car
voiture *nf* [rail company language for **wagon**] BrE carriage AmE car
compartiment *nm* compartment
couchette *nf* **1** [in a sleeper] BrE couchette AmE berth **2** [foldaway, in an ordinary compartment] bunk
couloir *nm* corridor
place *nf* seat *place dans le sens de la marche* front-facing seat *place dans le sens contraire au sens de la marche* rear-facing seat

8.21 *Personnel des trains* Train staff

chef *nm* **de gare** station manager
chef *nm* **de train** BrE (railway) guard AmE conductor
cheminot *nm* [old-fashioned term] BrE railwayman AmE railroadman
conducteur, -trice ALSO **mécanicien, -cienne** *n* BrE (engine) driver AmE engineer
agent *nm* **de conduite** [official term. Synonym for **conducteur**] BrE (engine) driver AmE engineer
porteur *nm* porter
chauffeur *nm* [in steam engine] BrE boilerman AmE stoker
aiguilleur, -lleuse *n* BrE points operator AmE switches operator

9 Measuring time

9.1 Calendrier et saisons Times, dates and seasons

calendrier nm 1 [list of days] calendar 2 [work plan] diary établir son calendrier pour l'année to plan one's diary for the year

saison nf season la mauvaise saison winter la belle saison summer fruit/temps de saison seasonal fruit/weather

9.2 Les jours de la semaine The days of the week

lundi nm Monday
mardi nm Tuesday
mercredi nm Wednesday
jeudi nm Thursday
vendredi nm Friday
samedi nm Saturday
dimanche nm Sunday
jour nm dans huit jours [8 days] in 8 days' time, [7 days] in a week's time

usage

Un jour férié is a day when offices and shops are closed (frequently but not necessarily a Monday): holiday. **Un jour ouvrable** is one of the six days in the week which aren't a holiday: working day. **Un jour ouvré** is one of the five days in the week which aren't part of the weekend: weekday

Note that the article le is only used with days of the week when you want to indicate that something happens, or used to happen, regularly on that day. Le lundi, il fait son marché. He shops at the market every Monday. Elle ne s'arrêtait de travailler que le dimanche après-midi. She used to stop work on Sunday afternoons only. BUT Nous sommes vendredi aujourd'hui. Today is Friday. Je viendrai lundi prochain. I'll come next Monday.

demain adv tomorrow à demain see you tomorrow
après-demain adv the day after tomorrow
lendemain nm le lendemain the next day le lendemain du 6 juillet the day after the 6th of July sans penser au lendemain without a thought for the morrow les lendemains qui chantent a brighter future
hier adv yesterday
avant-hier adv the day before yesterday
veille nf la veille the day before la veille de son anniversaire the day before his birthday. Nous échangeons toujours les cadeaux la veille de Noël. We always exchange presents on Christmas Eve. C'est une veille de Noël que je l'ai rencontré pour la première fois. I first met him on a Christmas Eve.
semaine nf week la semaine des quatre jeudis [schools used to be off on Thursdays. A week with four Thursdays in it means happiness for schoolchildren and symbolizes something which will never happen] à la petite semaine [describes plans showing no forethought beyond next week] short-sighted
hebdomadaire adj weekly
quinzaine nf BrE fortnight AmE two weeks remis à quinzaine postponed for a fortnight Envoyez-le sous quinzaine. Send it within the fortnight.
huitaine nf period of eight days Envoyez-le sous huitaine. Send it within eight days. dans une huitaine de jours in about eight days
week-end nm weekend
pont nm [days off between a public holiday and a weekend] long weekend faire le pont to have a long weekend

	LUN	MAR	MER	JEU	VEN	SAM	DIM	LUN	MAR	MER	JEU	VEN	SAM	DIM	LUN	MAR	MER	JEU	VEN	SAM	DIM	LUN	MAR	MER	JEU	VEN	SAM	DIM	LUN
JAN	1	2	3	4	5	6	7	8	9	10	11	12	13	14	15	16	17	18	19	20	21	22	23	24	25	26	27	28	29
FEV			1	2	3	4	5	6	7	8	9	10	11	12	13	14	15	16	17	18	19	20	21	22	23	24	25	26	
MAR				1	2	3	4	5	6	7	8	9	10	11	12	13	14	15	16	17	18	19	20	21	22	23			

If today is Wednesday, the 10th January, this is how to locate something which happened or will happen on the Mondays of that month.

1er ça s'est passé il y a eu lundi huit jours
8 ça s'est passé lundi dernier
15 ça se passera lundi prochain
22 ça se passera lundi en huit
29 ça se passera lundi en quinze

9.3 *Les mois de l'année* The months of the year

janvier *nm* January
février *nm* February
mars *nm* March
avril *nm* April
mai *nm* May
juin *nm* June
juillet *nm* July
août *nm* August
septembre *nm* September
octobre *nm* October
novembre *nm* November
décembre *nm* December
mois *nm* month
mensuel, -suelle *adj* monthly

u s a g e

To specify a month, use *en* or *au mois de*, e.g: *En septembre*, ALSO *au mois de septembre, nous irons à Montréal*. We'll go to Montreal in September. To specify a part of the month, use the following:
au début octobre (in) early October
à la mi-octobre (in) mid-October
à la fin octobre (in) late October
For the beginning and the end of a month, a slightly more formal variant is: *au début/à la fin du mois d'octobre* at the beginning/end of October. To denote specific days in the month, use e.g.*Je leur ai écrit le 10 novembre/le 15 janvier*. I wrote to them on the 10th of November/the 15th of January.

9.4 *Les quatre saisons* The four seasons

le printemps *nm* spring *au printemps* in (the) spring
l'été *nm* summer *en été* in (the) summer
l'automne *nm* autumn *en automne* in (the) BrE autumn AmE fall
l'hiver *nm* winter *en hiver* in (the) winter

Locutions Idioms
du jour au lendemain very quickly and without warning
Ne remets jamais au lendemain ce que tu peux faire le jour même ALSO **Il ne faut jamais remettre au lendemain ce qu'on peut faire le jour même.** [proverb] Never put off till tomorrow what you can do today.
Noël au balcon, Pâques au tison. [proverb] If it's warm at Christmas, it'll be cold at Easter.
giboulées ALSO **averses** *nf pl* **de mars** [in France, showers occur earlier than in more northerly countries] April showers
En avril ne te découvre pas d'un fil, en mai fais ce qu'il te plaît. [proverb. April in France, at least in the northern half, is considered too cold a month for people to start wearing spring clothes. This is echoed in the British proverb but the advice is postponed by one month for geographical reasons.] Ne'er cast a clout till May is out.
poisson d'avril! [to mock someone's gullibility on April Fool's Day; often symbolized by sticking a paper fish to the person's back] April fool!

9.5 *Fêtes et grandes dates* Festivals and important dates

Noël *nm* ALSO **la Noël** *nf* Christmas *à Noël* ALSO *à la Noël* at Christmas
Nouvel An *nm* New Year's Day

Season's greetings
To wish someone a happy Christmas, there is a choice of the very common *Joyeux Noël* or the slightly more subdued *Bon Noël*. The greeting which people exchange at the new year, and up until well into January, is usually *Bonne Année* and sometimes (mostly in speech *Bonne Année, bonne santé!*. To extend 'season's greetings' to someone in speech or in writing, the best formula is *Joyeux Noël et Bonne Année*. But those two festivals are also referred to as *Les Fêtes*, so you could say *Passez de bonnes Fêtes*, and write *Joyeuses Fêtes*. The festival day itself is called *le Nouvel An*: e.g. *On va passer le Nouvel An chez Gérard*. We'll spend New Year's Eve at Gérard's. The main celebration takes place on the evening of 31 January, *la Saint-Sylvestre*, and the food and drink consumed on that occasion make up *le réveillon du Nouvel An.*

mardi-gras *nm* BrE Shrove Tuesday AmE mardi gras
le dimanche des Rameaux Palm Sunday
le lundi de Pâques Easter Monday
Pentecôte *nf* BrE Whitsun AmE Pentecost *le lundi de la Pentecôte* Whit Monday *On y est allés un lundi de Pentecôte.* We went there one Whit Monday.
Pâques *nf pl* Easter
le quinze août [formerly an important Catholic festival, now a public holiday] the mid-August public holiday
Ramadan *nm* Ramadan *un jour de Ramadan* a day during Ramadan
la Toussaint ALSO **le jour des morts** All Saints' Day
à la Saint-Glinglin [humorous] never *Ton argent, tu le reverras à la Saint-Glinglin.* If you get your money back, pigs might fly!
Elle va coiffer Sainte-Catherine. [an allusion to the virgin Saint Catherine, traditionally celebrated by spinsters when they reached their 25th birthday] She's 25 on her next birthday and still not married.

9.6 *Périodes* Periods of time

u s a g e

an *nm* and **année** *nf*, **jour** *nm* and **journée** *nf*, **soir** *nm* and **soirée** *nf*, **matin** *nm* and **matinée** *nf*
Each pair is contrasted in the following way: the word in -ée stresses duration while its counterpart refers to the section of time as a unit. The contrast is strongest with **an** and **année**. E.g.:
J'ai trente ans. [a unit for counting years of age] I'm thirty years old.
J'ai habité Lens une année entière. [stresses how long it was or felt] I lived in Lens for a whole year.
Le soir, nous nous promenons sur le front de mer. [an identified unit or part of the day] In the evening we go for a walk along the seafront.
Nous passons notre soirée à nous promener sur le front de mer. [stresses time elapsing within the period] We spend the evening walking along the seafront.
à chaque jour suffit sa peine [emphasises the day as a single, complete unit] sufficient unto the day . . .
Il se plaint à longueur de journée. [focuses on the effect of the complaining on the listener: it feels endless] He complains all day long.

9.7 *Temps et durée* Time and duration

u s a g e

1 The preposition **à** is used to refer to specific times: e.g. *à huit heures* at eight o'clock. The preposition **vers** is used for approximate times: e.g. *vers dix heures* around ten. When speaking about time within a period, use the preposition *pendant*: e.g. *pendant la matinée* (some time) during the morning.
2 You may use either the 12-hour or the 24-hour clock. If you want to speak with precision, use the 24-hour clock. Most people use the 12-hour clock, specifying *du matin* (a.m.), *de l'après-midi* (p.m. until roughly 6 p.m.) or *du soir* (after 6 p.m.). To greet people at different times of the day, say *bonjour* at any time, *bonsoir* any time after dark (and in summer, from approximately 7 p.m.). When leaving, say *au revoir*. Conventional leave-taking, e.g. in shops, may involve saying *bonne journée* when the day is still relatively young, *bonne après-midi* in early afternoon, and *bonne soirée* at the beginning of the evening. Say *bonne nuit* only when you are taking leave of someone late at night or going to bed.

12 heures 12.00 hours
minuit *nm* midnight
midi *nm* midday
six heures six o'clock
six heures du soir six o'clock in the evening
six heures du matin six o'clock in the morning
deux heures two o'clock
deux heures du matin two o'clock in the morning
deux heures de l'après-midi two o'clock in the afternoon

u s a g e

Do not say *de la nuit* when you refer to a specific time at night. The only way the phrase is used is when no time is specified: e.g. *à n'importe quelle heure de la nuit* at all hours (any hour) of the night, *à une heure avancée de la nuit* late at night, *au milieu de la nuit* in the middle of the night. If you want to refer to '10 at night' or '11 at night', say *à 10 heures du soir, à 11 heures du soir*.

9.8 *Lire l'heure* Telling the time

see also **138 (Gambits)**
Il est cinq heures et quart/Il est cinq heures quinze.
BrE It's a quarter past five/It's five fifteen AmE It's a quarter after five.
Il est neuf heures moins vingt-cinq/Il est huit heures trente-cinq.
It's twenty-five to nine/It's eight thirty-five.
Il est neuf heures et demie/Il est neuf heures trente.
It's half past nine/It's nine thirty.
Il est quatre heures moins le quart/Il est trois heures quarante-cinq.
It's a quarter to four/It's three forty-five.
Il est dix heures précises/Il est dix heures pile.
It's ten o'clock precisely.

pendule *nf*, ALSO **horloge** *nf* clock

u s a g e

pendule and **horloge**
Une horloge is usually larger than **une pendule**. Big clocks in stations or streets are **horloges**. *À l'horloge de la gare, il est huit heures.* It's eight by the station clock.

réveil *nm* alarm-clock
radio-réveil *nm*, *pl* **radio-réveils** BrE radio-alarm AmE clock-radio
montre *nf* **de gousset** pocket watch
montre, ALSO **bracelet-montre**, *pl* **bracelets-montres** wristwatch
heure *nf* hour *Cela a demandé quatre heures.* It took four hours. *une demi-heure* half an hour *un quart d'heure* a quarter of an hour *une heure et demie* an hour and a half
minute *nf* minute *une promenade de cinq minutes* ALSO *cinq minutes de promenade* a five-minute walk. *Une minute!* Just a minute! *Oui, (une) minute!* Yes, in a minute!
seconde *nf* second *Attendez-moi une petite seconde!* Wait, a (one) second!
instant *nm* moment. *Un instant!* Just a moment!

9.9 *Périodes plus longues* Longer periods of time

décennie *nf* decade
siècle *nm* century
période *nf* time *en période de guerre* in wartime *à la période des vacances* at holiday time *en période de soldes* while the sales are on *en période scolaire* during the school term
ère *nf* **1** [period since a great event] time *au début de l'ère chrétienne* in early Christian times *en l'an 900 de notre ère* in AD 900 **2** [in geology] era
âge *nm* [period notable for a particular invention or trend] age *l'âge de l'imprimerie* the age of printing

phase *nf* [part of a period] phase *la première phase du projet* phase one of the project

passé *nm* past *dans* ALSO *par le passé* in the past *C'est du passé, n'en parlons plus!* Let bygones be bygones!

présent *nm* present time *vivre dans le présent* to live in the here and now

u s a g e

futur *nm* and **avenir** *nm*
These two words are interchangeable when referring to future events as they affect people in general, but they are used differently in the following ways:
1 When referring to future events of personal import, use **avenir** *Tout mon avenir dépend de leur décision.* My whole future hangs on their decision. **2** Always use **avenir** for this phrase: *à l'avenir* in future. **3** The noun **le futur** is best reserved for general considerations, e.g. *Il faudra inventer de nouvelles méthodes de recyclage dans le futur.* New ways of recycling resources will have to be devised in the future.

9.10 *Adjectifs et adverbes de temps* Adjectives and adverbs dealing with time

passé, e *adj* **1** [neither present nor future] past *le temps passé* the past **2** [recent] last *l'année passée* last year

présent, e *adj* current *Quelle est votre occupation présente?* What is your current job?

à présent 1 [in the current period] nowadays **2** [in the next few minutes or hours] now

futur, e *adj* **1** [to come] future *les jours futurs* days to come **2** [which will become as stated. Before noun] *future maman* mother-to-be *mon futur beau-père* my future father-in-law

à venir next few *les jours à venir* the next few days *les années à venir* the next few years

prochain, e *adj* **1** [of the immediate future] next *Les jours prochains, je compte repeindre ma chambre.* In the next few days, I intend to repaint my room. **2** [before noun. Next in a series] next *Le prochain autobus va au centre ville.* The next bus goes to the town centre.

prochainement *adv* soon

tout à l'heure in a (little) while *À tout à l'heure.* See you in a while.

il y a quelque temps a (little) while ago

actuellement *adv* at the moment *Je n'ai pas beaucoup de travail actuellement.* I don't have a lot of work at the moment. *Actuellement, les gens ne veulent plus acheter sans garantie.* People nowadays will not buy without a guarantee.

en ce moment at the moment

u s a g e

prochain, e *adj*
Prochain used with the name of a day or a month is placed after the noun, e.g. *Nous préparons déjà nos calendriers pour janvier prochain.* We're already getting our calendars ready for next January.

10 Repetition in time

10.1 *Fréquence* Frequency

fréquemment *adv* often

fréquent, e *adj* frequent

de temps en temps every now and then *une fois de temps en temps* once in a while

quelquefois *adv* sometimes

parfois *adv* [slightly more formal than **quelquefois**] sometimes

souvent *adv* often

toujours *adv* always

tout le temps [spoken equivalent to **toujours**] all the time

sans cesse constantly

To show that the situation continues	To show that the situation is habitual
encore/toujours = still	*encore* = always
Je suis encore ALSO *toujours toute tremblante après l'accident.* I'm still shaky after the accident.	*Je suis toujours toute tremblante quand j'entends cette voix.* I always shake when I hear that voice.
Partons pendant qu'il fait encore ALSO *toujours beau.* Let's go while the weather's still nice.	*L'été ici il fait toujours beau.* The weather is always nice here in summer.
When the verb is negative *toujours* = still	When the verb is negative *toujours* = always
On n'a toujours pas payé nos dettes. We still haven't paid off our debts.	*Dans le passé, on n'a pas toujours payé nos dettes.* In the past, we didn't always pay off our debts.

Locution Idiom
C'est toujours le même refrain, ALSO **la même rengaine.** It's the same old story.

à répétition [describes repeated unpleasant occurrences] repeated *Après des grippes à répétition elle a été hospitalisée.* After repeated bouts of flu she was taken to the hospital.

10.2 *Monotonie* Monotony

ennui *nm* boredom

ennuyer {17} *vt* to bore

s'ennuyer *v refl* to be bored *On ne s'ennuie pas ici!* This is fun!

ennuyeux, -yeuse *adj* boring

barbant, e *adj* [informal] dead boring

rasoir *adj inv* [very informal] tedious *Ce que tu peux être rasoir avec ton football!* You're such a bore always going on about football!

mortel, -telle *adj* excruciatingly boring

monotone *adj* [describes: e.g. voice, routine] monotonous **monotonie** *nf* monotony

monocorde *adj* [describes: e.g. voice] toneless

routinier, -nière *adj* [describes: e.g. person, turn of mind] prone to habit

morne *adj* **1** [describes: e.g. face, gait, story] dull **2** [describes: e.g. morning, landscape] dreary

train-train *nm* [pejorative] routine *le train-train quotidien* the daily round *Il a son petit train-train.* He's in a rut.

rebutant, e *adj* [so boring that you do not feel like doing it] off-putting

Locutions Idioms

long comme un jour sans pain [so boring that it seems endless. Describes : e.g. speeches, films, books, evenings] never-ending

ennuyeux comme la pluie [describes : e.g. person, show, job] dull as ditchwater

(en) avoir marre de qqch/qqn [informal] to be fed up with sthg

(en) avoir ras-le-bol de qqch/qqn [more informal than **(en) avoir marre**] to be sick to death of sthg/sb

Citation Quotation

L'ennui naquit un jour de l'uniformité. [a famous verse from a lesser-known early 18th-century fabulist, Houdar de la Motte] Routine breeds boredom.

10.3 *Routine* Routine

routine *nf* [can be slightly pejorative] routine *vérifications de routine* routine checks *s'enfoncer dans la routine* to get stuck in a rut

habitude *nf* habit *C'est devenu une habitude (chez lui).* It's become a habit (with him). *avoir ses petites habitudes* to be set in one's ways *par habitude* through force of habit

habituer {6} *vt* habituer qqn à to get sb used to

s'habituer *v refl* to adjust. *Le chat ne connaît pas encore cette maison, laisse-lui le temps de s'habituer.* The cat's new in this house, give him time to adjust. *s'habituer à qqch/qqn* to get used to sb/sthg

être enclin, e à faire to be inclined to do

avoir tendance à faire to have a tendency to do

quotidien, -dienne ALSO **journalier, -lière** [done every day and therefore routine] *adj* everyday, daily *les préoccupations quotidiennes* everyday concerns *mon trajet quotidien de la maison au bureau* my daily trip to the office *le train-train quotidien* the everyday routine

de tous les jours everyday *la vie de tous les jours* everyday life *des vêtements de tous les jours* everyday clothes.

Locutions Idioms

vivre au jour le jour [by choice] to live from day to day [through penury] to lead a hand-to-mouth existence

gagner son pain quotidien to earn one's daily bread

11 Changes in time

11.1 *Commencer* To start

commencement *nm* [first stage in a process or a period] early stage *Quand on crée une entreprise, les commencements sont toujours difficiles.* The early stages of setting up a new business are always difficult.

début *nm* [like **commencement**, but stresses the point at which things start] start *Pour un roman, il faut un bon début.* A novel needs a really good beginning.

débutant, e *n* beginner *la classe des débutants en français* the beginners' French class *Tu t'es laissé rouler comme un débutant.* [pejorative] You were hoodwinked like a novice. **débutant, e** *adj* novice *quand j'étais un skieur débutant* when I was a novice at skiing

débuter {6} **1** *vi* [to be a beginner at something which will be a lasting activity] to start *À l'époque où j'ai débuté, je n'avais que dix élèves par classe.* When I first started I had only ten pupils to a class. *Elle a débuté à l'Alhambra.* She made her debut at the Alhambra. **2** *vt* [informal. Make a first start at something lasting. Obj: e.g. book, piece of knitting, career, course] to start *Ils viennent de téléphoner qu'ils arrivent: je débute ma sauce.* They've just rung to say they're on their way: I'll start preparing my sauce.

départ *nm* [more dynamic than **début** and **commencement**] start *Il y avait deux mille personnes au départ du marathon.* There were two thousand competitors at the start of the marathon.

démarrer {6} *vi* and *vt* **1** [neutral when referring to vehicles] to start (up) *La voiture a démarré.* The car started. *Démarre le moteur.* Start (up) the engine. **2** [informal when implying the sudden and effective start of any process] to get going *Je démarre mon rôti.* I'll get the roast going. *On démarre?* Shall we get going? *Je suis toujours lent à démarrer le matin.* It always takes me a while to get going in the morning.

démarrage *nm* **1** [neutral. Of a vehicle] starting up **2** [informal. Of a process] getting under way *Le démarrage de la campagne a été un peu lent.* The campaign was a bit slow to get under way.

coup *nm* **d'envoi** [start of a ball game, of a collective undertaking] kick-off *le coup d'envoi de la campagne électorale* the start of the election campaign

Locutions Idioms

Ça remonte à la nuit des temps. It goes back to the ark.

Retour à la case départ! [informal. Describes a fresh start after a failure, as in a board game] Back to square one!

11.2 *Finir* To end

fin *nf* end *à la fin* in the end *sans fin* never-ending

finir {19} *vt* and *vi* (often + de + infinitive) to finish *quand j'aurai fini de lire* when I have finished reading

finir par 1 (+ noun) [describes the action or object which comes last] *Nous finirons par une mousse au chocolat.* We'll finish with chocolate mousse. *Les enfants, ça va finir par des larmes!* BrE Children, it'll end in tears (before bedtime)! **2** (+ infinitive) [describes an action brought about by the accumulation of preceding actions] *Elle a fini par céder.* She gave in in the end. *Leurs disputes finissent par me faire peur!* Now their arguments are beginning to frighten me.

final, e *adj, mpl* **-naux** final **finalement** *adv* finally

terminer {6} *vt* [bring to an end voluntarily] to finish

se terminer *v refl* [same usage as **finir** *vi*] to finish *La fête se terminera vers deux heures.* The party will finish around two.

terminus *nm* [of trains and buses] terminus
terminal *nm* [at airport] terminal
achever {9} *vt* [slightly formal. Obj: work] to finish
achèvement *nm* [slightly formal] end *L'achèvement des travaux est prévu pour l'année prochaine.* The work is scheduled to end next year.
arrêter {6} *vt* [often + *de* + infinitive] to stop *arrêter de fumer* to stop smoking **arrêt** *nm* stop
cesser {6} *vt* and *vi* [more formal than **arrêter**, but can be used in conversation. Often + *de* + infinitive] to stop *Cesse tes âneries!* Will you stop fooling around! *Cessons de nous plaindre.* Let's stop complaining.
dernier, -nière *adj* **1** [final one in a series] last *Louis-Philippe fut le dernier roi de France.* Louis-Philippe was the last king of France. **2** [most recent] latest *Son dernier livre ne vaut rien.* Her latest book is no good. **3** [just past] last *la semaine dernière* last week
dernièrement *adv* lately

> **usage**
>
> **dernier**
> When used with words for intervals of time, **dernier** changes its meaning according to its position: *la semaine dernière* means the week before the current one, but *la dernière semaine des vacances* is the final week of the holidays.

Locutions Idioms
jusqu'au bout to the end
tirer à sa fin [describes the gradual ending of events or periods of time] *La journée tirait à sa fin.* The day was coming to an end.
jusqu'à la fin des temps 1 [biblical] until the end of time **2** [in exaggeration] till kingdom come
C'est la fin des haricots! [informal and often ironic. Used when predicting that a fresh disaster will turn an already difficult situation into a catastrophe] That's the last straw!

Citation Quotation
Et s'il n'en reste qu'un, je serai celui-là. [Victor Hugo's famous line from *Les Châtiments*, 1853, his republican pamphlet directed against the emperor Napoléon III. It is quoted (sometimes humorously) to symbolize proud opposition to tyranny] And if only one remains, I will be that person.

12 Old and new

12.1 *Nouveau* New

> **usage**
>
> **Nouveau** before or after a noun
> **1.** The masculine singular form *nouveau* changes to *nouvel* before a noun beginning with a vowel or a silent 'h': e.g. *un nouvel ami* a new friend, *un nouvel hôpital* a new hospital
> **2.** In most of its meanings *nouveau* comes before the noun. The main exceptions are definition **1** below and a number of set expressions like *pommes de terre nouvelles* new potatoes, *vin nouveau* (this) year's vintage and *art nouveau*, which needs no translation.

nouveau, -velle *adj, mpl* **-x 1** [recent, not old or established] new *Ils ont construit une ville nouvelle dans le désert à l'est du Caire.* They built a new town in the desert to the east of Cairo. **2** [more recent and different from whatever went before] new *les nouveaux pauvres* the new poor *Comment va ton nouveau travail?* How's your new job?
neuf, neuve *adj* **1** [which has not been worn or used by anybody before] new *Je ne peux plus me permettre d'acheter une voiture neuve.* I can no longer afford to buy a new car. **2** [which has not been in existence a long time. Often with **tout**, which adds a positive value judgment] new *La ville s'est dotée d'un tramway tout neuf.* The town gave itself a brand new tramway system. **3** [original] fresh *J'ai tout essayé pour la persuader de ne plus fumer, je n'ai plus d' idées neuves sur la question.* I've tried eveything to persuade her to stop smoking, I've run out of fresh ideas on the matter.
neuf *nm* **1** [in commercial contexts, anything that is not second-hand] new *En vêtements je veux bien porter de l'occasion mais en chaussures j'achète toujours du neuf.* I don't mind wearing second-hand clothes but where shoes are concerned I always buy them new. **2** [state of being new] new *faire du neuf avec du vieux* to create something new out of something old

---

Nouveau and **neuf**
Beware of the difference between *ma nouvelle voiture* my new car (i.e., the car which I have recently acquired) and *ma voiture neuve* my (brand-) new car. If you had just bought a second-hand car, you could say *Ma nouvelle voiture n'est pas une voiture neuve!*

12.2 *Nouveau et intéressant* New and interesting

original, e *adj, mpl* **-naux** original, out of the ordinary *Des myrtilles avec du sirop d'érable, c'est original.* Blueberries with maple syrup, there's an original combination.
original *nm* [often used pejoratively. Someone who has surprising or worrying ideas] eccentric
originalité *nf* originality
novateur, -trice ALSO **innovateur, -trice** *adj* [describes: e.g. idea, artist] innovative
innover {6} *vi* to have a new idea, to have new ideas. *Depuis que nous existons, nous avons toujours innové en matière de technique.* Since our inception we've always been technically innovative. *Cette année pour le feu d'artifice, le conseil municipal a innové: il sera tiré à partir de barques sur la rivière.* This year the local authorities have had a new idea for the fireworks display: it will be set off from boats on the river.
se renouveler {11} *v refl* [produce new ideas or creations] to come up with fresh ideas *un cinéaste qui ne se renouvelle pas beaucoup* a film-maker who has got into a rut

Locution Idiom
C'est tout nouveau tout beau. [this phrase is invariable. It is used ironically to comment on something, a gadget, a love affair, a trend, etc that is exciting because it is new but will soon pall] It's only a nine-day wonder./It's a flash in the pan.

12.3 *Moderne* Modern

moderne *adj* **1** [up-to-date] modern *les techniques modernes de communication* modern communication techniques **2** [in academic contexts, late 19th century onwards] contemporary *l'histoire moderne* contemporary history
moderniser {6} *vt* to modernize
mode *nf* fashion *C'est la mode.* It's fashionable. *à la mode* in fashion *L'orange n'est plus à la mode.* Orange has gone out of fashion. *passer de mode* to go out of fashion

---

False friends **actuel** and **actuellement**
Do not be misled by the similarity between these words and 'actual', 'actually'. In French *actuel* means 'current', and *actuellement* 'today' or 'now'.

---

actuel, -tuelle *adj* current *dans la situation actuelle* in the current situation **actuellement** *adv* these days *Actuellement, il y a des compagnies qui refusent d'assurer une voiture qui couche dehors.* Some insurance companies are now refusing to insure cars that are not parked in a garage at night.
actualité *nf* [in journalism] item of news *C'est la Corée qui fait l'actualité ce soir.* Korea is the main item of news tonight.
d'actualité (used as an adjective) topical *La déontologie médicale est d'actualité.* Medical ethics are topical.
actualités *nf pl* [in journalism] news
contemporain, e *adj* **1** [of our time] contemporary **2** (often + *de*) [belonging to the same period as the person or thing under discussion] contemporary *un peintre contemporain de Fujita* a painter contemporary with Fujita
de pointe [up to date technically] latest *la chirurgie de pointe* the very latest developments in surgical techniques

12.4 *Vieillot* Old-fashioned

see also **33.6 Ancien**
vieillot, -llote *adj* [old-fashioned and slightly ridiculous] dated *C'est écrit dans un style un peu vieillot.* It's written in a rather dated style.
démodé, e *adj* [no longer in fashion. Describes: e.g. clothes, songs, ideas] out of date *Ce style est tellement démodé qu'il revient à la mode.* That style is so out of date that it's coming back into fashion.
dépassé, e *adj* [which has been overtaken by more modern ways of doing things] old hat *Les téléphones à cadran sont plutôt dépassés aujourd'hui.* Telephones with dials are rather old hat nowadays. *Le constat d'adultère, dans un divorce, c'est un peu dépassé.* Establishing adultery in a divorce suit is rather old hat.
suranné, e *adj* [old-fashioned and charming. Describes: e.g. furnishings, photograph frames, clothing style, hairstyle] quaint *J'aimais passer des après-midi dans le salon suranné de ma grand-tante.* I loved to spend afternoons in my great-aunt's charmingly old-fashioned sitting room.
désuet, -suette *adj* **1** [no longer in use. Describes: e.g. habit, phrase] old-fashioned **2** [synonym for **suranné**] quaint
archaïque *adj* [pejorative. From a much earlier age] ancient *un système archaïque pour amener l'eau à l'évier* an ancient system for bringing water to the sink
tomber en désuétude [is used of a fashion, an expression, a style] to become obsolete

13 Being on time

13.1 *Tôt* Early

tôt *adv* early *Il est encore tôt, rendors-toi.* It's still early, go back to sleep! *Pas trop tôt!* BrE Not before time! AmE Not too early!
d'abord *adv* first, in the first place
en avance ahead of schedule
avancer {7} *vi* [subj: e.g. clock, watch] to be fast
matinal, e *adj*, *mpl* **-naux** early (in the morning) *la douceur matinale* the beauty of the morning *Tu es bien matinal aujourd'hui!* You've started early this morning!
hâtif, -tive *adj* [in gardening language] early *chou hâtif* early cabbage
de bonne heure *adv* **1** [in the day] early *Le bus de ramassage scolaire passe de bonne heure.* The school bus comes by early (in the morning). **2** [relative to a particular time] early *Il va falloir que je commence mes plantations de bonne heure.* I'll have to start on my planting early.
né, e *adj* **avant terme** born prematurely

Locutions Idioms
Il/Elle est du matin [informal] ALSO **C'est un/une lève-tôt**. He's/She's an early riser.
Le monde appartient à ceux qui se lèvent tôt. [proverb] The early bird catches the worm.

13.2 *Tard* Late

tard *adv* late *se lever tard* to get up late *Il est tard.* It's late.
retard *nm* delay *Qu'est-ce qui a causé ce retard?* What was the cause of this delay? *livrer des marchandises avec du retard* to deliver goods late *en retard* behind schedule *Le train a du retard.* The train is late. *avoir dix minutes de retard* to be ten minutes late *mettre qqn en retard* to make sb late *se mettre en retard* to make oneself late
à la dernière minute at the last minute
tardif, -dive *adj* **1** [in the day] late *faire du bruit à des heures tardives* to make a noise late at night **2** [relative to a particular time] late *J'ai eu un éveil tardif à la musique.* I didn't become interested in music until late in life.
retardataire *n* latecomer
retarder {6} *vi* **1** [subj: e.g. clock, watch] to be slow
sur le tard *adv* late in life *J'ai eu mon fils sur le tard.* I had my son late in life
avancé, e *adj* late *à une période avancée de ma vie* late in (my) life *à un stade avancé de la maturation du fromage* at a late stage in the cheese ripening process

Locutions Idioms
Il est grand temps. It's high time. *Il est grand temps que tu fasses tes valises.* It's high time you packed your suitcases.
à la onzième heure at the eleventh hour
les ouvriers de la onzième heure those who come along at the last minute (and reap the benefits without any of the effort)

13.3 *Ponctualité* Being on time

ponctuel, -tuelle *adj* **1** [describes: e.g. person] punctual **2** [describes: e.g. event, arrival, departure] timely
à l'heure 1 [at the right time] on time *Le train est à l'heure.* The train is on time. *Tous les vols vers la France sont à l'heure.* All flights to France are running to time.

2 [with plenty of time to spare] *à l'heure pour* in time for *Je suis arrivée à l'heure pour prendre la correspondance de Grenoble.* I got there in time to catch the connection for Grenoble.
à temps [implies urgency] (just) in time, in the nick of time *On allait partir, il est arrivé à temps.* We were about to leave, he arrived in the nick of time.
à l'heure dite at the appointed hour
au jour dit on the agreed day

Locution Idiom
Chaque chose en son temps. All in good time.

13.4 *Prêt* Ready

prêt, e *adj* **1** [prepared and on time] ready *Les valises sont faites, je suis prêt.* The cases are packed, I'm ready. *Il est fin prêt/Elle est fin prête.* He's/She's good and ready.
2 (always + *à*) [willing or prepared to carry out an action] ready to *Il est toujours prêt à rendre service.* He's always ready to help others. *Elle est prête à tout pour sauver son fils.* She's prepared to do anything to save her son. *prêt à l'emploi* ready for use
prêt-à-porter *nm* [trade] ready-to-wear trade **prêt-à-porter** *adj, mpl* **prêts-à-porter** [describes: garment] ready to wear
préparer {6} *vt* **1** [make ready, with idea of transformation or processing. Obj: e.g. recipe, meal, bedroom] to prepare *Comment prépares-tu ta sauce?* How do you prepare the sauce? *Il faut préparer la surface du mur avant de commencer à peindre.* You have to prepare the surface of the wall before you can start painting. **2** [assemble disparate elements] to get ready *préparer les bagages* to get the luggage ready *Tu as préparé tes affaires pour l'école demain?* Are your school things ready for tomorrow?
se préparer *v refl* to get ready *Préparez-vous à défendre le projet face à l'opposition de l'administration.* Be prepared to defend the project in the face of administrative opposition.
apprêter {6} *vt* **1** [same meaning as **préparer**. General term] to make ready *Il ne reste plus qu'à apprêter la salle de réception.* All that needs to be done now is to prepare the reception area. **2** [technical language. Obj: e.g. paper, surface] to apply a finish to **3** [put clothes on someone, usu for an occasion] to dress (up) *Les institutrices avaient apprêté les enfants pour le défilé.* The teachers had dressed the children up for the procession.
s'apprêter *v refl* **1** [same meaning as **se préparer**] to get ready **2** (always + *à*) [be on the verge of] to get ready to *Je m'apprêtais à partir lorsque le téléphone a sonné.* I was getting ready to leave when the phone rang.

Locution Idiom
À vos marques, prêts, partez! Ready, steady, go!

13.5 *Proche – dans le temps* Close – in time

see also **9.10 Adjectifs et adverbes de temps**
d'un moment à l'autre ALSO **d'une minute à l'autre** any minute now
bientôt *adv* [within a short time] soon *J'espère vous revoir bientôt.* I hope to see you again soon. *Elle est bientôt finie, la répétition?* Will the rehearsal be over soon?
tout de suite *adv* immediately
incessamment *adv* any moment now *Le médecin doit passer incessamment.* The doctor will be along any moment now.

sous peu *adv* [within a short time] soon *Je vous envoie votre carte de membre sous peu.* I shall be sending your membership card soon.
à l'instant *adv* [in the past] a minute ago *Tu l'as ratée, elle a téléphoné à l'instant.* You missed her, she rang a minute ago.
dans un instant ALSO **dans une minute** in a minute

13.6 *Remettre à plus tard* To put off until later

reporter {6} *vt* [implies that a new date will be set] to postpone
remettre {56} *vt* (often + *à* followed by new time or date) [same meaning as **reporter**] to put off *La réunion a été remise à demain.* The meeting was put off until tomorrow. *Remettons notre visite à plus tard.* Let's put off our visit until another day.
ajourner {6} *vt* [put off without specifying a new date] to postpone *La réunion a été ajournée.* The meeting was postponed.
retarder {6} *vt* [make something happen later than planned, usu to the participants' disappointment] to put off *Nous avons dû retarder la date du mariage.* We had to put off the wedding day. *Tous les avions en provenance du Canada sont retardés.* There are delays on all flights from Canada.
retard *nm* delay *Il y a eu un retard dans l'ouverture du chantier.* There was a delay in starting the construction.

> ### usage
>
> The false friends **delay** and **délai**
> **Délai** *nm* refers to the length of time allowed for something to happen, without any implication of lateness. So when you're ordering goods or booking services which aren't available immediately, the question *Quels sont les délais?* simply means 'How long will it take?' Other examples: *Je vous donne un délai d'une semaine pour terminer l'inventaire.* BrE I'll give you a week in which to finish stocktaking. AmE I'll give you a week in which to finish taking inventory. *livraison dans un délai de 15 jours* delivery within a fortnight

atermoyer {17} *vi* [pejorative. Make excuses in order to gain time] to procrastinate
atermoiement *nm* [pejorative] procrastination
prolonger {8} *vt* [make something take longer. Obj: e.g. discussions, quarrel, party, vacation] to extend *La grève des trains nous permet de prolonger notre séjour dans la région.* The train strike has enabled us to prolong our stay in the area. *Je ne voudrais pas prolonger la soirée indûment, je travaille demain matin.* I don't want to stay up too late, I'm working tomorrow morning.
prolongations *nf pl* [at football] BrE extra time AmE overtime *jouer les prolongations* BrE to play extra time AmE to play overtime

Locutions Idioms
Demain il fera jour [informal]. Tomorrow is another day.
Il ne faut jamais remettre au lendemain ce que l'on peut faire le jour même. Never put off till tomorrow what you can do today.

13.7 *Rapide* Quick

see also **5.7 Courir, 62.23 Mouvements du corps**
rapide *adj* **1** [implies a relatively high speed. May also imply saving time] quick *une toilette rapide* a quick wash

le flot rapide du torrent the fast flow of the mountain stream

rapidement *adv* vite *On va maintenant de Paris à Londres beaucoup plus rapidement.* The trip from Paris to London is much faster now. *J'ai parcouru le journal rapidement.* I had a quick glance at the newspaper.

rapidité *nf* [of a reaction, a procedure] speed

vite *adv* quick(ly) *Viens vite!* Come quick(ly)! *Je ne cours pas aussi vite que toi.* I can't run as fast as you can. *faire vite* to be quick *Je me suis coupé, apporte-moi du sparadrap, fais vite!* I cut myself, get me some plasters, quickly!

vitesse *nf* [of athletes, vehicles] speed

vif, vive *adj* **1** [with the speed of movement typical of young people] fast **2** [fast and lively] quick-witted

usage

Vite and **rapidement**
Both adverbs are similar in meaning, but there are some situations where they are not interchangeable. When adressing someone urgently, *vite* is used: e.g. *Éteins le gas, vite!* Turn off the gas, quickly!

13.8 *Essayer de faire vite* To try to be quick

se dépêcher {6} *v refl* (often + *de* + infinitive) to hurry *Je me suis dépêchée de rentrer à la maison.* I hurried back to the house. *Dépêche-toi!* Hurry up!

se hâter {6} *v refl* (often + *de* + infinitive) [slightly literary. Synonym for **se dépêcher**] to hurry *Les derniers passants se hâtaient de rentrer avant la pluie.* The last passers-by were hurrying home before the rain.

bousculer {6} *vt* [pejorative] to rush *Ne me bouscule pas, je veux prendre le temps de choisir.* Don't rush me, I want to have time to make my choice.

se précipiter {6} *v refl* **1** [go very fast] to rush *Je me suis précipité chez le médecin.* I rushed to the doctor's. **2** [pejorative. Go too fast for safety, or quality of result] to rush *Ne vous précipitez pas pour rédiger ce rapport, je veux que vous me remettiez un travail de qualité.* Don't rush to get this report out, I want you to submit a high-quality piece of work.

activer {6} *vt* [make happen faster] to hurry *J'ai rajouté du révélateur pour activer le processus.* I added some more developer to hurry the process along.

accélérer {10} *vi* and *vt* [go faster, in a vehicle or in a process] to speed up *un moyen d'accélérer la production* a way of speeding up production

hâte *nf* [undesirable speed, due to having too much to do in too short a time] haste *faire quelque chose à la hâte* to do something in haste

hâtif, -tive *adj* [pejorative. Too fast] hurried *une décision hâtive* a hurried decision *Je te demande pardon de t'avoir mis en cause, j'ai été trop hâtif dans mes jugements.* I apologize for having unjustly accused you, I came to a conclusion too hastily. **hâtivement** *adv* hurriedly

être pressé, e to be in a hurry *Elle est toujours pressée.* She's always in a hurry. *Je ne suis pas pressé de finir ce travail parce qu'après je suis au chômage.* I'm in no hurry to finish this work as I shall be unemployed afterwards. *On n'est pas pressé!* There's no hurry!

précipitation *nf* [pejorative] rush *On a dû partir dans la plus grande précipitation, et on a oublié la moitié de nos affaires.* We had to leave in an incredible rush, and we left half our things behind.

à toute vitesse [informal] flat out *Nous sommes allés à l'hôpital à toute vitesse.* We drove flat out to the hospital.

Phrases for encouraging people to hurry
Dépêchez-vous! Hurry up!
Accélérez! Get a move on!
Vite, il n'y a pas de temps à perdre! Quick, there's no time to lose!
On ne va pas rester là une heure! We haven't got all day!

13.9 *Qui se passe ou qui agit vite* Quick to happen or act

soudain, e *adj* sudden **soudainement** *adv* [slightly formal term], ALSO **soudain** *adv* suddenly

tout à coup *adv* [commonly used phrase] suddenly

brusque *adj* [happening or acting too fast] (too) sudden

instantané, e *adj* instant *Le soulagement va être instantané.* Relief will be instant. *du café instantané* instant coffee **instantané** *nm* snapshot **instantanément** *adv* instantly

immédiat, e *adj* immediate **immédiatement** *adv* immediately

aussitôt *adv* straightaway

aussitôt que *conj* as soon as, immediately *Je suis venu aussitôt que j'ai eu votre appel.* I came immediately (when) I received your call.

Locutions Idioms
Aussitôt dit aussitôt fait. No sooner said than done.
ventre à terre [describes running, or going fast in a vehicle] like greased lightning *Effrayé par la détonation, le cheval est parti ventre à terre.* Frightened by the noise of the explosion, the horse bolted. *Il est revenu ventre à terre avec la lettre.* He came back like greased lightning with the letter.
sans demander son reste [implies swift disappearance to hide guilt] without so much as a by-your-leave

13.10 *Lent* Slow

lent, e *adj* slow *Les progrès sont très lents.* Progress is very slow. *Tu n'as pas encore fini? Que tu es lent!* Haven't you finished yet? How slow you are! **lenteur** *nf* slowness

lentement *adv* slowly *Recommence le mouvement, plus lentement cette fois.* Do the movement again, more slowly this time.

ralentir {19} **1** *vi* to slow down *Le train ralentit, nous entrons en gare.* The train's slowing down, we're coming into the station. *Attention, un piéton, ralentissez!* Watch out for the pedestrian, slow down! **2** *vt* to slow down *La neige nous a ralentis en venant.* The snow slowed us down on the way here.

ralentissement *nm* slowing down *pas de ralentissement de l'activité économique au premier semestre* no slackening of economic activity in the first half of the year

lambiner {6} *vi* [informal and pejorative] to dawdle

Locutions Idioms
Il n'y a pas le feu! What's the big hurry?
C'est lui/elle, la lanterne rouge. He's/She's taking up the rear of the race.
avancer comme un escargot to go at a snail's pace

Citation Quotation
Hâtez-vous lentement. [Latin saying made famous by Boileau in *L'Art poétique*, 1674, where he urges would-be poets to take as much time and trouble as possible whilst keeping at the task. Used as advice to go neither too fast nor too slow] Make haste slowly.

13.11 *Attente* Waiting

attente *nf* wait *une longue/courte attente* a long/short
wait *une demi-heure d'attente* a thirty-minute wait
salle *nf* **d'attente** waiting room
attendre {53} **1** *vi* to wait *faire attendre qqn* to keep sb
waiting **2** *vt* to wait for *Qu'est-ce que tu attends?* What
are you waiting for? *J'attends un taxi.* I'm waiting for a
taxi.
poireauter {6} *vi* [pejorative] to hang around (waiting) *J'ai
poireauté deux heures chez le médecin.* I was kept
hanging around for two hours at the doctor's.

Locutions Idioms
faire le pied de grue ALSO **faire le poireau** to kick one's
heels
poser un lapin à qqn to stand sb up
Ils ne perdent rien pour attendre! They're going to get
what's coming to them!
Tout vient à point à qui sait attendre. [proverb]
Everything comes to him who waits.

14 Animals

14.1 *Animaux de la ferme* Farm animals

Familles d'animaux de la ferme Groups of farm animals
bouc *nm* billy-goat
chèvre *nf* (nanny-)goat
chevreau *nm, pl* **-x** kid
bélier *nm* ram
mouton *nm* sheep
brebis *nf* ewe
agneau *nm, pl* **-x** lamb
canard *nm* (male) duck, drake
cane *nf* (female) duck **caneton** *nm* duckling
cochon *nm* pig
porc *nm* [live animal or meat] pig **porcelet** *nm* piglet
truie *nf* sow
coq *nm* rooster
poule *nf* hen **poulet** *nm* chicken
poussin *nm* chick
dinde *nf* turkey (hen)
dindon *nm* turkey (cock) **dindonneau** *nm, pl* **-x** young turkey
cheval *nm, pl* **-vaux** horse
jument *nf* mare
poulain *nm* foal
pouliche *nf* filly
âne *nm* donkey **ânesse** *nf* female donkey **ânon** *nm* young donkey
mulet *nm* (male) mule
mule *nf* (female) mule
jars *nm* gander
oie *nf* goose **oison** *nm* gosling
bœuf *nm, pl* **bœufs** bullock
taureau *nm, pl* **-x** bull
vache *nf* cow
veau *nm, pl* **-x** calf
génisse *nf* heiffer

Noms collectifs des animaux de la ferme Collective names for farmyard animals
le bétail [animals for meat production] livestock
la basse-cour [includes poultry and rabbits] small farm animals

Locutions Idioms
Il est bête comme un âne. [has no sense] He's really stupid [knows nothing] He knows absolutely nothing.
Il est fort comme un bœuf. He's as strong as an ox.
Il est rouge comme un coq. [through anger] He's scarlet with rage.
Il est sale comme un cochon. He's filthy dirty.
Il est têtu comme une mule. He's stubborn as a mule.

14.2 *Animaux sauvages* Wild animals

tigre *nm* tiger **tigresse** *nf* tigress
léopard *nm* leopard
guépard *nm* cheetah
panthère *nf* panther
girafe *nf* giraffe

girafeau *nm, pl* **-x** ALSO **girafon** *nm* baby giraffe
hippopotame *nm* hippopotamus
rhinocéros *nm* rhinoceros
babouin *nm* baboon
chimpanzé *nm* chimpanzee
gorille *nm* gorilla
grand singe *nm* ape *les grands singes* the big apes
ours *nm* bear **ourse** *nf* she-bear **ourson** *nm* bear-cub
ours polaire polar bear
panda *nm* panda
koala *nm* koala bear
bison *nm* bison
buffle *nm* buffalo
renard *nm* fox **renarde** *nf* vixen **renardeau** *nm, pl* **-x** fox cub
loup *nm* wolf **louve** *nf* she-wolf **louveteau** *nm, pl* **-x** wolf cub
antilope *nf* antelope
zèbre *nm* zebra
lion *nm* lion **lionne** *nf* lioness **lionceau** *nm, pl* **-x** lion cub
éléphant *nm* elephant **éléphante** *nf* she-elephant **éléphanteau** *nm, pl* **-x** elephant calf
singe *nm* monkey **guenon** *nf* female monkey
chameau *nm, pl* **-x** camel **chamelle** *nf* she-camel
kangourou *nm, pl* **kangourous** kangaroo
cerf *nm, pl* **cerfs** red deer
daim *nm* fallow deer
biche *nf* doe
faon *nm* fawn
sanglier *nm* wild boar **laie** *nf* wild sow **marcassin** *nm* baby wild boar

> ### usage
>
> *Shooting and hunting*
> The noun **chasse** *nf* and the verb **chasser** *vi* and *vt* refer to both shooting and hunting. To distinguish between the two, specify **chasse à courre** for hunting and **chasser à courre** for to hunt. For the activity that is done on foot, individually or in a group, use **chasse** (shooting) and **chasser** (to shoot).
> The general term **gibier** *nm* is used for all game, but you can specify **du gibier à poil** (game animals), **du gibier à plumes** (game birds) or **du gibier d'eau** (waterfowl). A different distinction is made between **du gros gibier** (big game) and **du petit gibier**, ALSO **du menu gibier** (which includes mammals and birds)

14.3 *Termes généraux désignant les animaux* General words for animals

bête *nf* creature *Ne fais pas de mal à cette petite bête.* Don't hurt the little creature. *La bête s'apprêtait à bondir.* The creature was about to pounce. *En voilà une grosse bête qui a peur des petites!* Go on, it won't eat you!
bestiole *nf* [used of a small animal or insect when its name is not known] small creature
faune *nf* fauna *la faune de la région* the local wildlife

14.4 *Modes d'alimentation* Feeding habits

mammifère *nm* mammal
omnivore *nm* omnivore **omnivore** *adj* omnivorous
herbivore *nm* herbivore **herbivore** *adj* herbivorous
carnivore *nm*, ALSO **carnassier** carnivore **carnivore** *adj* carnivorous
rongeur *nm* rodent

14.5 *Noms d'animaux sauvages désignant les humains* Names of wild animal used for people

tigresse, ALSO **panthère** *nf* [a fierce, cruel or violently possessive woman] tigress
gorille *nm* **1** bodyguard **2** [as insult] *Une espèce de gorille entra.* A great hulk of a man walked in.
chameau! [insult, directed against a man or a woman] you mean so-and-so!

14.6 *Parties du corps des animaux* Parts of animals' bodies

griffe *nf* claw
queue *nf* tail
sabot *nm* hoof
défense *nf* tusk
moustaches *nf pl* whiskers
museau *nm*, *pl* **-x 1** [of dog] muzzle **2** [of rodent, cat] nose
patte *nf* **1** [of big mammal, bird, insect] leg **2** [of small mammal] paw
poil *nm* **1** [of dog] hair **2** [of cat] fur
fourrure *nf* **1** [of wild animal] fur **2** [long hair, of show animal] coat
pelage *nm* [short or long hair, any animal] coat
aile *nf* wing
plume *nf* feather
corne *nf* horn
bois *nm* antler
échine *nf* [shoulder and back of a mammal] back(bone)
croc *nm* fang *Le chien montrait ses crocs.* The dog bared its fangs.
bec *nm* beak
serre *nf* talon
branchie *nf* gill
écaille *nf* **1** [of fish, of snake] scale **2** [of tortoise] shell *un peigne en écaille* a tortoiseshell comb
carapace *nf* [of tortoise, insect] shell
antenne *nf* feeler
aileron *nm* [of shark] fin
pince *nf* claw

Locutions Idioms
être dans les griffes de qqn to be in sb's power
L'entreprise bat de l'aile ALSO **a du plomb dans l'aile.** [by reference to a wounded bird] The firm is in trouble financially.
Elle l'a pris sous son aile. She took him under her wing.
Il m'a volé dans les plumes. [suggests instant aggression and physical assault, but can also mean verbal attack, often in retaliation] He flew at me.
Elle ne bougeait ni cou ni pattes. [usu out of fear or as a ruse] She was playing dead.

14.7 *Bruits d'animaux* Animal noises

grogner {6} *vi* **1** [subj: e.g. dog] to growl **2** [subj: e.g. pig] to grunt
grognement *nm* **1** [of dog] growl(ing) **2** [of pig] grunt(ing)
gronder {6} *vi* [more aggressive than **grogner**] to growl
grondement *nm* [more aggressive than **grognement**] growl(ing)
siffler {6} *vi* **1** [subj: e.g. blackbird] to sing **2** [subj: e.g. trained parrot] to whistle **3** [subj: e.g. snake] to hiss
sifflement *nm* **1** [of blackbird] song **2** [of macaw] whistle **3** [of snake] hiss(ing)
aboyer {17} *vi* to bark
aboiement *nm* bark(ing)
ronronner {6} *vi* to purr
ronron ALSO **ronronnement** *nm* purr(ing)
bêler {6} *vi* to bleat
bêlement *nm* bleat(ing)
miauler {6} *vi* **1** [gently] to me(o)w **2** [harshly] to caterwaul
miaulement *nm* **1** [gentle] me(o)w **2** [harsh] caterwaul(ing)
rugir {19} *vi* to roar
rugissement *nm* roar(ing)
hennir {19} *vi* to neigh
hennissement *nm* neigh(ing)
braire {61} *vi* to bray
braiement *nm* braying
meugler {6} *vi* to moo
mugir {19} *vi* [more high-pitched and more agitated tham **meugler**] to moo
caqueter {11} *vi* to cluck
caquètement *nm* cluck(ing)
cancaner {6} *vi* to quack
coasser {6} *vi* [subj e.g: frog] to croak
coassement *nm* [of frog] croak(ing)
croasser {6} *vi* to caw
croassement *nm* caw(ing)

14.8 *Mots enfantins pour désigner les bruits d'animaux* Baby words for animal noises

ouah *nm* woof
miaou *nm* BrE miaow AmE meow
coin coin *nm* quack quack
cocorico *nm* cluck cluck
glou glou *nm* gobble gobble
meuh (meuh) *nm* moo

15 Pets and small animals

15.1 *Animaux familiers* Pets

Any pet can be called **animal familier**. The more formal phrase **animal de compagnie** is also used, mainly for cats and dogs.

15.2 *Les chats* Cats

chat *nm*, **chatte** *nf* cat
chaton *nm* [used for males and females] kitten
minet *nm*, **-nette** *nf* [affectionate] puss, pussy(-cat)
minou *nm* [affectionate, male or female] pussy(-cat)
chat *nm* **de gouttière** alley cat
matou *nm* tom (cat)

15.3 *Les chiens* Dogs

chien *nm* dog **chienne** *nf* bitch
chiot *nm* [used for males and females] puppy
cabot *nm* [informal and usu pejorative] *Fais taire ton cabot!* Shut that damn dog up!
clébard *nm* [slang. Usu strongly pejorative] *lui et son clébard!* him and his damn dog!
toutou *nm* [baby talk. Used of or to dogs] doggy
chien-loup *nm*, *pl* **chiens-loups** ALSO **berger** *nm* **allemand** BrE Alsatian AmE German shepherd
caniche *nm* poodle
épagneul *nm* spaniel
cocker *nm* cocker spaniel

15.4 *Autres animaux familiers* Other pets

lapin *nm* (buck) rabbit **lapine** *nf* (doe) rabbit
perroquet *nm* parrot
poisson *nm* **rouge** goldfish
hamster *nm* hamster
gerboise *nf* gerbil
cochon *nm* **d'Inde** [commonly used] ALSO **cobaye** *nm* [when referring to experiments] guinea pig
tortue *nf* tortoise

15.5 *Petits animaux* Small animals

rat *nm* rat **rate** *nf* she-rat **raton** *nm* baby rat
grenouille *nf* frog
souris *nf* mouse **souriceau** *nm*, *pl* **-x** baby mouse
crapaud *nm* toad
limace *nf* slug
fouine *nf* stone marten
hérisson *nm* hedgehog
taupe *nf* mole
furet *nm* ferret
porc-épic *nm*, *pl* **porc-épics** porcupine
loutre *nf* otter
castor *nm* beaver
écureuil *nm* squirrel
chauve-souris *nf*, *pl* **chauves-souris** bat
escargot *nm* snail
blaireau *nm*, *pl* **-x** badger
putois *nm* polecat
lièvre *nm* hare **levraut** *nm* young hare

Locutions Idioms
face de rat! [insult. Implies pointed, mean features] rat-face!
grenouille de bénitier [pejorative. Refers to women and implies narrow-minded piety] self-righteous church-goer
myope comme une taupe [means BrE short-sighted AmE near-sighted, not actually blind] blind as a bat
Il criait comme un putois ALSO **poussait des cris de putois.** He was screeching like a stuck pig.
J'aurais voulu disparaître dans un trou de souris. I wanted the earth to open up and swallow me
aller à une vitesse d'escargot to go at a snail's pace

16 Reptiles, insects and birds

16.1 *Reptiles* Reptiles

reptile *nm* reptile
couleuvre *nf* grass snake
vipère *nf* adder
serpent *nm* snake
lézard *nm* lizard
alligator *nm* alligator
crocodile *nm* crocodile

16.2 *Noms de reptiles désignant les humains* Reptile names used for people

paresseux comme une couleuvre bone-idle
C'est une vraie vipère. He's/She's a really nasty piece of work.
C'est un serpent que j'ai réchauffé dans mon sein. [used humorously] I've been nursing a viper in my bosom.

16.3 *Insectes* Insects

abeille *nf*, ALSO **mouche** *nf* **à miel** bee
araignée *nf* spider
fourmi *nf* ant
fourmiller *vi* {6} (often + *de*) [more pejorative when describing humans] *Les rochers fourmillent de petits insectes.* The rocks are teeming with tiny insects. *La place fourmille de monde.* The square is swarming with people.
fourmilion ALSO **fourmi-lion** *nm*, *pl* **fourmis-lions** anteater
mite *nf* (clothes) moth *un pull mangé aux mites* a moth-eaten sweater
mouche *nf* fly *mouche à vers* bluebottle
moustique *nm* mosquito **moustiquaire** *nf* mosquito net
papillon *nm* butterfly *papillon de nuit* moth
puce *nf* flea **puceron** *nm* aphid
sauterelle *nf* grasshopper

asticot *nm* maggot
chenille *nf* caterpillar
chrysalide *nf* chrysalis
larve *nf* larva
nymphe *nf* pupa
œuf *nm*, *pl* **œufs** egg *la femelle pond ses œufs.* The female lays her eggs.
métamorphose *nf* metamorphosis
se métamorphoser {6} *v refl* (often + *en*) [in common and scientific use. Subj: insect] to go through (different) stages *La chenille se métamorphose en papillon.* The caterpillar turns into a butterfly.

ver *nm* worm *ver blanc* grub, *ver à soie* silkworm *bois piqué aux vers* timber infected with woodworm
véreux, -reuse *adj* [describes: e.g. fruit, berry] worm-eaten

Locutions Idioms
C'est une larve. [pejorative] He's stupid.
J'ai des fourmis dans les jambes. I've got pins and needles in my legs.
Il leur a tiré les vers du nez. He wormed it out of them.
C'est ce qui lui a mis la puce à l'oreille. That's what alerted him to what was going on.

16.4 *Habitat des insectes* Insect habitats

essaim *nm* swarm
fourmilière *nf* anthill *C'est une vraie fourmilière ici!* [many people] The place is swarming with people! [busy people] This is a hive of activity!
ruche *nf* beehive
toile *nf* **d'araignée** spider's web

16.5 *Oiseaux* Birds

see also **14.6 Parties du corps des animaux**
oiseau *nm, pl* **-x** bird *oiseau aquatique* water bird *oiseau de compagnie* cage bird *oiseau de proie* bird of prey *oiseau migrateur* migratory bird
échassier *nm* wader
oisillon *nm* fledgling
nid *nm* nest

autruche *nf* ostrich
colombe *nf* dove
grive *nf* thrush
hirondelle *nf* swallow
mésange *nf* **bleue** blue tit
mésange charbonnière coal tit
paon *nm* peacock
pigeon *nm* pigeon
pivert *nm* woodpecker
rouge-gorge *nm, pl* **rouges-gorges** robin (redbreast)

16.6 *Noms d'oiseaux* Names of birds

aigle *nm* eagle **aiglon** *nm* eaglet
chouette *nf* owl
cigogne *nf* stork
corbeau *nm, pl* **-x** crow
cygne *nm* swan
épervier *nm* hawk
étourneau *nm, pl* **-x** starling
hibou *nm, pl* **-x** [unlike **chouettes**, **hiboux** have crests] owl
martin-pêcheur *nm, pl* **martins-pêcheurs** kingfisher
merle *nm* blackbird **merlette** *nf* female blackbird
moineau *nm, pl* **-x** sparrow
piaf *nm* [informal, mostly Parisian usage] sparrow
roitelet *nm* wren
rossignol *nm* nightingale
tourterelle *nf* turtle dove
vautour *nm* vulture

16.7 *Ce que font les oiseaux* Actions performed by birds

éclore {70} *vi* to hatch
percher {6} *vi* to roost

se percher *v refl* to perch
picorer {6} **1** *vt* [obj: e.g. seed, crumb] to peck at **2** *vi* [subj: bird] to feed
planer {6} *vi* to hover overhead
pondre {53} *vt* and *vi* to lay
s'envoler {6} *v refl* to fly away *Un oiseau s'est envolé.* A bird flew away.
vol *nm* (bird) flight *prendre son vol* to fly away *un vol d'hirondelles* a flight of swallows
voler {6} *vi* to fly
voleter {11} *vi* [subj: young or sick bird] to flutter

Locutions Idioms
à vol d'oiseau as the crow flies *La gare est à dix kilomètres à vol d'oiseau.* The station is ten kilometres away as the crow flies.
pratiquer la politique de l'autruche to hide one's head in the sand
saoûl comme une grive drunk as a lord
Une hirondelle ne fait pas le printemps. [proverb] One swallow doesn't make a summer.
C'est toujours lui le pigeon! [slang] He's a born sucker!
Quelle cervelle de moineau! What a birdbrain!

17 Water animals

see also **14.6 Parties du corps des animaux, 72.11 Pêche et poissonnerie**

17.1 *Poissons* Fish

alevin *nm* [young fish for stocking rivers] *des alevins* fry
aleviner {6} *vt* [obj: river, pond] to stock with young fish
banc *nm* **de poissons** shoal of fish
(menu) fretin *nm* [small fish rejected by angler] small fry
poisson *nm* fish **poissonneux, -neuse** *adj une rivière poissonneuse* a river well stocked with fish

17.2 *Animaux marins* Sea creatures

baleine *nf* whale **baleinier** *nm* whaler
corail *nm, pl* **-raux** coral
banc *nm* **de corail** coral reef
crabe *nm* crab
dauphin *nm* dolphin
méduse *nf* jellyfish
pieuvre *nf* octopus
poulpe *nm* octopus
morse *nm* walrus
otarie *nf* sea-lion
phoque *nm* seal

17.3 *Comparaisons avec les humains* Comparison with human beings

All the similes below are pejorative.
limande *nf* **1** [fish] lemon sole **2** [woman] *Elle est plate comme une limande.* She's as flat as a board.
moule *nf* **1** [animal] mussel **2** [expresses contempt for a person] twit
morue *nf* **1** [fish] cod **2** [slang. Prostitute]] tart
maquereau *nm, pl* **-x 1** [fish] mackerel **2** [slang] pimp
maquerelle *nf* madam
merlan *nm* **1** [fish] whiting **2** [slang] barber
requin *nm* **1** [fish] shark **2** [person] crook

17.4 *Cages des animaux aquatiques* Places for keeping water animals

aquarium *nm, pl* **aquariums 1** [in zoo] aquarium **2** [small, in a house] fish tank
bocal *nm, pl* **-caux** fishbowl
delphinarium *nm, pl* **delphinariums** dolphinarium
vivier *nm* **1** [for fish] fish farm **2** [for lobsters] lobster farm **3** [container, in restaurant] aquarium

Locutions Idioms
Il/Elle est comme un poisson dans l'eau. He's in his/She's in her element.
Le poisson pourrit par la tête. [in hierarchies] The rot starts at the top.
C'est un véritable panier de crabes ici! It's 'dog eat dog' around here!
marcher en crabe to walk sideways
Il y a anguille sous roche. There's something in the wind.
souffler comme un phoque to puff and pant
engueuler qqn comme du poisson pourri [very informal, for comic effect] to call sb all the names under the sun
regarder qqn avec des yeux de merlan frit [phrase used for comic effect] BrE to gawp at sb AmE gawk
J'avalerais la mer et les poissons! I'm parched!
rigoler, ALSO **se marrer comme une baleine** [informal] to laugh one's head off

18 Plants

18.1 *Plantes* Plants

see also **79.1 Agriculture, 80 Jardinage**
végétal *adj, mpl* **-taux** [mostly scientific usage] *la vie végétale* plant life *huile végétale* vegetable oil **végétal** *nm, pl* **-taux** plant **végétalien, -lienne** *adj* and *n* vegan
végétarien, -rienne *adj* and *n* vegetarian

18.2 *Fleurs des champs* Wild flowers

bleuet *nm* cornflower
bouton d'or *nm, pl* **boutons d'or** buttercup
coquelicot *nm* poppy
marguerite *nf* daisy
pensée *nf* pansy
pissenlit *nm* dandelion
souci *nm* marigold *souci des marais* marsh marigold
violette *nf* violet *violette odorante* sweet violet *violette de chien* dog violet

18.3 *Parties des plantes* Parts of plants

épi *nm* [seed-bearing part] *épi de maïs* cob (of sweetcorn) *manger le maïs en épi* to eat corn on the cob *épi de blé* ear of wheat
épine *nf* thorn
feuille *nf* leaf
feuille *nf* **de vigne 1** [on vine] vine leaf **2** [on statues] fig-leaf
fleur *nf* **1** [on plant] flower **2** [on tree] blossom *une fleur de cerisier* a cherry blossom *des cerisiers en fleur(s)* cherry-trees in blossom
graine *nf* seed
racine *nf* root

Locutions Idioms
effeuiller la marguerite 1 [with a daisy] to play BrE 'she-loves-me, she-loves-me-not' AmE love me, love me not **2** [euphemism. Amorous activity taking place outdoors] *pendant qu'il effeuillait la marguerite avec sa petite amie* while he was being romantic with his girlfriend
Ça lui retire une (belle) épine du pied. That's got him out of a nasty spot.
quand je mangerai les pissenlits par la racine [humorous] when I'm dead and gone

To find out whether your beloved loves you, pluck the petals of a daisy one by one and recite: *il (elle) m'aime un peu, beaucoup, passionnément, à la folie, pas du tout.* Repeat until the last petal gives you the answer.

usage

tige *nf* and **sarment** *nm*
Tige refers to stems and stalks. A woody stem is called a *sarment*: e.g. *un sarment de vigne* a vine shoot

18.4 *Des plantes pour décorer* Decorative plants

plante *nf* **verte** ALSO **plante d'appartement** house plant
plante en pot potted plant

usage

bouquet *nm*, **gerbe** *nf*, **botte** *nf* and **brassée** *nf*
Bouquet is used for bunches of flowers of all types.
Gerbe applies to long-stemmed flowers or grasses: *une gerbe de glaïeuls* a bunch of gladioli. A **botte** is a neatly tied and compact bunch: *une botte de foin* a bale of hay *une botte de cresson* a bunch of watercress. **Brassée** suggests a large bunch of recently picked wild or garden flowers: *Elle a posé une brassée de lilas sur le piano.* She placed an armful of lilac blooms on the piano.

18.5 *Des plantes pour la santé* Medicinal plants

see also **68.1 Traitements et médicaments**
herboriste *n* herbalist
plante *nf* **médicinale** medicinal herb
infusion *nf*, ALSO **tisane** herbal tea *boire une infusion de camomille* to have a cup of camomile tea
une cure de [a course of treatment, often involving plants] *Faites une cure de jus de carotte pendant une semaine.* Drink carrot juice for a week.

18.6 *Plantes symboles* Meaning attached to certain plants

chrysanthème *nm* chrysanthemum. Symbolises death and is the most popular flower for taking to a loved one's grave on All Saints' Day.
lis *nm, pl* **lis** lily. Its flower symbolizes the French monarchy.
muguet *nm* lily-of-the-valley. Sold for good luck on street corners on Labour Day (May 1st).

18.7 *Types d'arbres* Types of trees

arbre *nm* tree *arbre fruitier* fruit tree *arbre à feuilles
  caduques* deciduous tree *arbre à feuilles persistantes*
  evergreen (tree)
arbuste *nm* small shrub
arbrisseau *nm, pl* - **x** [smaller than **arbuste**] shrub
buisson *nm* bush
conifère *nm* conifer

18.8 *Parties de l'arbre* Parts of trees

bourgeon *nm* bud *Les arbres sont en bourgeon(s).* The
  trees are in bud.
branche *nf* branch
brindille *nf* twig
tronc *nm* trunk

gland *nm* acorn
pomme *nf* **de pin** pine cone

feuillage *nm* **1** [in temperate climates] foliage **2** [in
  rainforests] canopy
rameau *nm, pl* -**x** [literary, from olive tree or holly bush]
  small branch
sève *nf* sap
souche *nf* stump
sous-bois *nm* **1** [low vegetation] undergrowth **2** [space
  beneath the branches] wood *se promener dans les sous-
  bois* to walk in the woods
branchage *nm* [large, fan-shaped] bough
écorce *nf* bark

18.9 *Arbres poussant ensemble* Trees growing together

forêt *nf* forest
bois *nm* wood *un bois* a wood *les bois autour de la maison*
  the woodland around the house
bosquet *nm* grove
taillis *nm* copse, coppice
maquis *nm* [in Corsica and Provence] scrubland area
pinède *nf* pine grove
oliveraie *nf* olive grove

18.10 *Noms d'arbres à feuilles caduques* Names of deciduous trees

aulne *nm* alder
bouleau *nm, pl* -**x** birch
châtaignier *nm* sweet chestnut
chêne *nm* oak
hêtre *nm* beech
marronnier *nm* chestnut tree *marronnier d'Inde* horse
  chestnut
orme *nm* elm *la maladie des ormes* Dutch elm disease
peuplier *nm* poplar
platane *nm* plane tree
saule *nm* willow *saule pleureur* weeping willow

18.11 *Noms d'arbres à feuilles persistantes* Names of evergreen trees

cyprès *nm* cypress
épicéa *nm* spruce
if *nm* yew

mélèze *nm* larch
pin *nm* pine
sapin *nm* fir

18.12 *Noms d'arbres fruitiers* Names of fruit trees

cerisier *nm* cherry tree
framboisier *nm* raspberry bush
pêcher *nm* peach tree
poirier *nm* pear tree
pommier *nm* apple tree
prunier *nm* plum tree

19 Minerals and metals

19.1 *Pierres précieuses* Precious stones

see also **25.13**
diamant *nm* diamond
opale *nf* opal
rubis *nm* ruby
saphir *nm* sapphire
améthyste *nf* amethyst
émeraude *nf* emerald
perle *nf* pearl

Locutions Idioms
C'est un bijou! [in admiration of a small, neat place or
  object] How cute!
une perle! [usu of efficient domestic staff] a treasure!
payer rubis sur l'ongle to pay cash on the nail

19.2 *Métaux* Metals

métallurgie *nf* metallurgy **métallurgiste** *n* metallurgist
sidérurgie *nf* steel industry **sidérurgiste** *n* steel worker
métal *nm, pl* -**taux** metal
or *nm* gold
aluminium *nm* aluminium
cuivre (rouge) *nm* copper
cuivre (jaune), ALSO **laiton** *nm* brass
acier *nm* steel
étain *nm* **1** [ore] tin **2** [in ornaments and pots] pewter
fer *nm* iron *fer blanc* tin plate
plomb *nm* lead
alliage *nm* alloy
argent *nm* silver
bronze *nm* bronze
fonte *nf* cast iron
mercure *nm* mercury
rouille *nf* rust **rouillé, e** *adj* rusty

usage

Colours and metals
The adjectives **doré, e** and **argenté, e** can refer to the
colour of an object, regardless of what it is made of, or
they can denote the presence of gold or silver in the
object: *des cheveux dorés* golden hair *une pendule
dorée* [colour] a gold-coloured clock [substance] a gold-
plated clock *un cadre argenté* [colour] a silvery frame
[substance] a silver-plated frame

20 States of matter

20.1 *Corps gazeux* Gases

gaz *nm* gas *gaz carbonique* carbon dioxide *les gaz
d'échappement* exhaust fumes
carbone *nm* carbon *daté au carbone 14* radiocarbon dated
oxygène *nm* oxygen
hélium *nm* helium
hydrogène *nm* hydrogen

20.2 *Humidité* Dampness

humidité *nf* **1** [in common usage] dampness *l'humidité de
la cave* the dampness of the cellar **2** [in scientific usage]
humidity *mesurer l'humidité de l'air* to measure the
humidity in the air
humide *adj* **1** [not yet dry] damp *Ne sors pas les cheveux
humides.* Don't go out with damp hair. **2** [unpleasantly
wet] damp *des draps humides* damp sheets
moite *adj* [unpleasantly warm and moist] clammy *J'avais
les mains moites.* My hands were clammy.
moelleux, -lleuse *adj* [soft because of moisture inside]
juicy *blanc de poulet moelleux* nice and juicy chicken
breast
liquide *adj* **1** [dilute. Describes: e.g. pancake batter,
yoghurt] runny **2** [in scientific usage. Not solid or gaseous]
liquid **liquide** *nm* liquid
aqueux, -queuse *adj* [scientific term Describes: e.g.
solution, plant] aqueous
adipeux, -peuse *adj* [same usage as **aqueux**, but describes
human flesh and tissue] adipose

20.3 *Les corps solides et les liquides* Solids and liquids

mouiller {6} *vt* **1** [with a little liquid] to moisten *Mouillez
d'un peu de cognac.* Moisten with a dash of brandy.
2 [with a lot of liquid] *mouiller qqch* to get sthg wet *Ne
marche pas dans la flaque, tu vas mouiller tes chaussures.*
Don't step in the puddle, you'll get your shoes wet.
tremper {6} *vt* **1** [implies temporary soak] to dip **2** [implies
excess water] to drench *Je suis trempé.* I am drenched.
plonger {8} *vt* **1** [deep into liquid] to dip *Il a plongé la
louche dans la soupière.* He dipped the ladle into the
soup bowl. **2** *vi* [subj: e. g. swimmer] to dive
immerger {8} *vt* [more formal than **plonger**] to immerse
immersion *nf* [mostly scientific usage] immersion *un corps
en immersion* an immersed body
arroser {6} *vt* **1** [by pouring, usu in gardening] to water
2 [carelessly, aggressively] to splash *Fais attention de ne
pas m'arroser pendant que je lis!* Be careful not to splash
water over me while I'm reading! **3** [culinary term] to
baste
inonder {6} *vt* [implies excess water on a flat surface] to
flood *Il a inondé le sol de la salle de bains.* He's left the
bathroom floor soaking wet. *des crêpes inondées de rhum*
pancakes swimming in rum

usage

humecter {6} *vt* and **imbiber** {6} *vt*
With **humecter**, the liquid merely touches the surface
of the object, usually the lips, whereas **imbiber** implies
that the liquid permeates a spongy object for culinary or
medicinal purposes. *L'infirmière est obligée de lui
humecter les lèvres régulièrement.* The nurse has to
moisten his lips regularly. *Imbibez les biscuits de rhum.*
Dip the sponge fingers in rum.

20.4 *Mouvements des liquides* Flow of liquids

verser {6} *vt* [obj: esp liquids to be drunk] to pour
se déverser dans {6} *v refl* **1** [subj: e.g. river] to flow into
2 [subj: e.g. duct] to overflow into
gicler {6} *vi* [accidentally, in a single stream] to spurt out
L'eau gicle du tuyau crevé. Water is spurting out of the
burst pipe.
éclabousser {6} *vt* **1** [accidentally] to splash *Une voiture
m'a éclaboussé.* A car splashed me. **2** [purposefully] to
throw water at *Ta sœur m'a éclaboussé!* Your sister threw
water over me!
éclaboussure *nf* splash
ruisseler {11} *vi* [implies liquids flowing fast over a surface]
to run *L'eau ruisselle sur la paroi rocheuse.* Water is
running down the rock face. *Le mur ruisselle d'humidité.*
The wall is running with damp.
dégouliner {6} *vi* [slightly comic, usually accidental] to run
L'omelette lui dégoulinait sur le menton. The omelette
was running down his chin.
suinter {6} *vi* [pejorative, often implies viscous liquids] to
ooze *des murs qui suintent* oozing walls *Le sang suintait
de la plaie.* Blood was oozing out of the wound.

Locution Idiom
trempé jusqu'à la moelle, ALSO **trempé comme une
soupe** [a reference to soaking bread in soups] soaked to
the skin

20.5 *Sécheresse* Dryness

sec, sèche *adj* **1** [no longer moist] *un abricot sec* a dried
apricot *La peinture est sèche.* The paint is dry. **2** [not wet]
dry *la saison sèche* the dry season
sécher {10} **1** *vt* to dry *Sèche tes cheveux.* Dry your hair. **2** *vi*
to dry (out) *On met les raisins à sécher au soleil.* The
currants are left to dry in the sun.
sécheresse *nf* **1** [quality] dryness *la sécheresse du sol* the
dryness of the soil **2** [period] drought
dessécher {10} *vt* [a natural process] to dry (out) *L'air de la
mer dessèche la peau.* The sea air dries out the skin.
assécher {10} *vt* [geographical term. Obj: e.g. marsh, coal
mine] to drain
déshydrater {6} *vt* to dehydrate
se déshydrater *v refl* to become dehydrated
essorer {6} *vt* **1** [obj: e.g. cloth] to wring out **2** [obj: e.g.
salad, herbs] to dry
aride *adj* arid **aridité** *nf* arid conditions
désert *nm* desert
désertique *adj* **1** [geographical term] *les zones désertiques*
desert areas **2** [desert-like] *un paysage désertique* an
empty landscape
à pied sec [walking across an area normally covered in
water] *traverser un ruisseau à pied sec* to walk across the
dry bed of a stream *À marée basse on atteint l'île à pied
sec.* At low tide you can walk out to the island.

20.6 *Feu* Fire

brûler {6} *vi* and *vt* to burn
se brûler *v refl* [receive a burn to a part of the body] to get burned
feu *nm, pl* **-x** [general term for burning material, but not often used for domestic fires] fire *en feu* on fire
incendie *nm* **1** [in a dwelling] fire *C'est un incendie volontaire.* It's arson. **2** [in a vehicle] fire
sinistre *nm* [term used in insurance forms and newspaper reports. Any occurrence causing damage or loss, particularly fire] disaster
brasier *nm* [big fire, lit purposely or accidentally] inferno
flambée *nf* [sudden cheering burst of flames in hearth] blaze *Il fait frais, je vais faire une petite flambée.* It's chilly, I'll light a little fire.
foyer *nm* [one of the smaller burning parts of a large fire] seat of the fire *Tous les foyers sont maintenant éteints.* All the different seats of the fire have been put out now.

Feux et incendies
un feu (de cheminée) a fire
un feu a bonfire
un incendie a (house) fire
un feu de joie a bonfire

20.7 *Effets du feu* Consequences of a fire

brûlure *nf* burn *brûlure du 1er/2ème/3ème degré* 1st/2nd/3rd degree burn
grand(e) brûlé(e) *n* burn(s) victim *service des grands brûlés* burn(s) unit
cendres *nf pl* [in the grate, in an ashtray] ashes
décombres *nm pl* [mixture of rubble and burnt materials after a house fire] debris

20.8 *Faire brûler* To make things burn

mettre le feu à 1 [as arson]] to set on fire *La cigarette a mis le feu aux rideaux.* The cigarette set the curtains on fire. **2** [with intent to destroy, but under control] to burn *mettre le feu à des vieux chiffons* to set fire to some old rags
allumer {6} *vt* to light *allumer un feu de cheminée* to light a fire in a fireplace *allumer un incendie* to start a fire

20.9 *Éteindre le feu* To put out a fire

éteindre {57} *vt* [obj: e.g. flames, fire, candle] to put out
extincteur *nm* **(d'incendie)** fire extinguisher
pompier *nm* fire-fighter
femme *nf* **pompier** fire-fighter
voiture *nf* **de pompiers** fire engine
bouche *nf* **d'incendie** fire hydrant

Locutions Idioms
pas de fumée sans feu no smoke without fire
au feu! fire!

20.10 *L'air* The air

see also **23.4 Sortes de vents** and **23.5 Brouillard et nuages**
air *nm* air *dans l'air* (up) in the air
ciel *nm* sky

cieux *nm pl* [literary] skies
horizon *nm* horizon *à l'horizon* on the horizon
couche *nf* **d'ozone** ozone layer

21 Light

21.1 *Nuit et demi-jour* Darkness and half-light

nuit *nf* [quality of the light after the sun has gone down] dark(ness) *Attendons la nuit.* Let's wait till after dark. *Il fait nuit.* It's dark.
noir, e *adj* [absence of light, whatever the time of day] dark. *Il fait noir pendant une éclipse.* It's dark during an eclipse.
noir *nm* dark *Il a peur dans le noir.* He's afraid of the dark.
obscurité *nf* darkness *dans l'obscurité* in the dark
obscur, e *adj* [more literary than **obscurité**] dark *La pièce est un peu obscure.* The room is a bit dark.
pénombre *nf* **1** [literary word. Positive sense] half-light **2** [negative sense] gloom
demi-jour *nm* [refers to the painterly quality of the light] half-light
clair *nm* **de lune** moonlight
ténèbres *nf pl* [literary. Very dark and rather frightening] darkness
sombre *adj* dark *Il fait sombre.* It's dark.
ombre *nf* **1** [shelter from the sun] shade *à l'ombre d'un platane* in the shade of a plane-tree **2** [shape on a surface] shadow *L'enfant essayait de rattraper son ombre.* The child was trying to catch his shadow. **3** [unlit area] shadows *L'ombre envahissait lentement les rues.* The streets were slowly enveloped in darkness. **4** [poorly lit area] gloom

Locutions Idioms
Il fait noir comme dans un four. It's pitch dark.
On n'y voit pas à trois pas. You can't see your hand in front of your face.
Demain il fera jour. [common saying. We will understand things better tomorrow] Let's sleep on it.

21.2 *Lumière* Light

lumière *nf* [general term] light *à la lumière d'une vieille lampe à huile* in the light of an old oil lamp *allumer/éteindre la lumière* to switch the light on/off

21.3 *Faire de la lumière* To make light

allumer {6} *vt* **1** [obj: e.g. lamp, electrical apparatus] to switch on **2** [obj: e.g. candle, cigarette] to light
éclairer {6} **1** *vt* to shine a light on. *Éclairez le dessous de la voiture pour que je vérifie le pot d'échappement.* Shine the light underneath the car so that I can check the exhaust pipe. **2** *vi La lampe éclaire bien.* The lamp gives a good light.
briller {6} *vi* **1** [emit a bright light] to shine **2** [reflect a light] to be shiny
luire {82} *vi* **1** [with a soft light] to gleam **2** [subj: esp wet surfaces] to glisten
scintiller {6}*vi* [subj: e.g. lurex, distant town lights] to glitter
étinceler {11} *vi* [subj: e.g. eye, tiara] to sparkle

illuminer {6} *vt* [cause light to spread over a surface or across a space] to light up *Le soleil couchant illuminait la falaise.* The setting sun lit up the cliff. *En appuyant sur ce bouton, on illumine tout le jardin.* You can light up the whole garden by pressing this button.
chatoyer {17} *vi* [subj: esp fabrics] to shimmer
clignoter {6} *vi* [subj: e.g. indicator light/turn signal, distant lights] to blink

21.4 *Qualité de la lumière* Quality of light

The adjectives below differ from each other in the same way as the corresponding verbs.
brillant, e *adj* [implies intensity and reflection of light] bright
éclairé, e *adj* [implies an external source of light unless specified] lit
luisant, e *adj* **1** [describes: e.g. polished surface] gleaming **2** [describes: e.g. sealskin] glistening
scintillant, e *adj* glittering
étincelant, e *adj* sparkling
chatoyant, e *adj* shimmering

21.5 *Sortes de lumière* Kinds of light

rayon *nm* **de soleil** [of a knife blade, of a pair of eyes] flash
lueur *nf* [feeble or dull] glow
éclat *nm* [literary. Of a star, of metal, of glass. Implies beauty] shine *briller avec l'éclat du verre* to sparkle like glass
clarté *nf* [poetic. Natural light] light

lampe *nf* lamp *lampe de chevet* bedside lamp *lampe de bureau* table lamp
lampe *nf* **électrique** (electric) torch
phare *nm* **de bicyclette** bicycle lamp
bougie, ALSO **chandelle** [old-fashioned term] *nf* candle
ampoule *nf* **électrique** light bulb

Locutions Idioms
Tout ce qui brille n'est pas or. All that glitters is not gold.
le siècle des lumières [the 18th century, by reference to developments in philosophy during that period] the century of the Enlightenment

Citation Quotation
cette obscure clarté qui tombe des étoiles [line from Corneille's *El Cid*, often quoted as an example of poetic contrast, or oxymoron] the darkened light which falls from the stars

22 Geography and astronomy

22.1 *Géographie physique et humaine* Physical and human geography

géographie *nf* geography
géographe *n* geographer **géographique** *adj* geographical
géologue *n* geologist **géologique** *adj* geological

22.2 *La géographie humaine* Human geography

pays *nm* country
peuple *nm* people *le peuple* the people *un peuple* a people
peupler {6} *vt* to populate *des régions peu peuplées* sparsely-populated areas
France *nf* France
Français *nm* Frenchman **Française** *nf* Frenchwoman
français, e *adj* [Note: the adjective has no capital letter] French *la nationalité française* French nationality
globe *nm* world *la population du globe* the world population
mappemonde *nf* [sphere with world map] globe
carte *nf* **(de géographie)** (geographical) map
monde *nm* world
mondial, e *adj*, *mpl* **-diaux** (of the) world
nation *nf* nation **national, e** *adj*, *mpl* **-naux** national
nationalité *nf* nationality
naturaliser {6} *vt* [to take on the nationality of the country in which one lives] *Il est naturalisé français.* He has taken French nationality.
international, e *adj*, *mpl* **-naux** international
cité *nf* **1** [a term reflecting the personality of a town] town *Marseille est une cité commerçante.* Marseilles is a commercial town. **2** [residences] (workers' housing) estate *la cité universitaire* the University halls of residence
ville *nf* town
village *nm* village
bourg *nm* large village
campagne *nf* countryside *à la campagne* in the countryside
golfe *nm* gulf
île *nf* island
équateur *nm* equator
Pôle *nm* **Sud** South Pole
parallèle *nm* parallel

Citations Quotations
Nous somes ici par la volonté du peuple et nous n'en sortirons que par la force des baïonnettes. [Mirabeau's famous exhortation to the new French Assembly in 1789.] We are here because the people want us to be, and we shall not leave unless driven out by bayonets.
Toute ma vie je me suis fait une certaine idée de la France. [De Gaulle justifying his national vocation in *Mémoires de Guerre*, 1953] All my life I have had my own special concept of France's place in the world.

22.3 *Hauteurs naturelles* Natural elevations

versant *nm* **1** [in low upland] (hill)side **2** [in high mountains] (rock)face
pente *nf* slope
sommet *nm* mountain
volcan *nm* volcano
montagne *nf* mountain
pic *nm* [mostly in the Pyrenees] peak
aiguille *nf* [mostly in the Alps] peak
vallée *nf* valley
vallon *nm* [literary] small valley
altitude *nf* [measurable distance from sea-level] height, altitude
colline *nf* hill
coteau *nm*, *pl* **-x** (hill)side
côte *nf* hill

colline, coteau, côte
Une colline is a hill, sometimes quite large, often visible from a distance. **Un coteau** refers to a slight rise, with only one side visible. **Coteau** is often used of vine-covered hillsides. **Une côte** is more subjective, suggesting the idea of going up or down a slope: *Il y a beaucoup de côtes (à grimper) entre les deux villages.* There are many hills (to climb) between the two villages. **Côte** also forms part of the name of many wines growing on hills: *boire un bon Côte Saint Jacques* to drink a fine Côte Saint Jacques wine.

22.4 *Roches* Rocks

rocher *nm* **1** [angular] rock **2** [rounded] boulder
rocheux, -cheuse *adj* rocky
pierre *nf* stone **pierreux, -rreuse** *adj* stony
caillou *nm, pl* **-x** (small) stone **caillouteux, -teuse** *adj* stony
gravier *nm* stone chipping
galet *nm* pebble *une plage de galets* a pebble beach
fossile *nm* fossil
minerai *nm* ore *du minerai de fer* iron ore
minéral, e *adj, mpl* **- raux** mineral

22.5 *Étendues d'eau* Expanses of water

mer *nf* sea
lac *nm* lake
océan *nm* ocean
réservoir *nm* reservoir
étang *nm* (small) lake
mare *nf* pond
marais *nm* marsh
marécage *nm* marshy area **marécageux -geuse** *adj* marshy

22.6 *Le bord des étendues d'eau* The land bordering a stretch of water

bord *nm* **1** [of a pond] side **2** [of a river] bank *au bord de la rivière* on the bank of the river **3** [of a lake, of the sea] shore *au bord du lac* on the shore of the lake *au bord de la mer* at the seaside
rive *nf* bank *la Rive Gauche* the Left Bank (of the Seine in Paris)
rivage *nm* [of larger lakes, of the sea] shore
littoral *nm* coastline
plage *nf* beach
côte *nm* coast
côtier, -tière *adj* coastal
falaise *nf* cliff
cap *nm* cape

22.7 *Caractéristiques de la mer* Features of the sea

marée *nf* tide *marée haute* high tide *marée basse* low tide *La marée monte.* The tide is coming in. *La marée descend.* The tide is going out.
vague *nf* wave
raz-de-marée *nm inv* tidal wave
algue *nf* (piece of seaweed) *des algues* seaweed

sable *nm* sand **sableux, -euse** *adj* sandy **sablonneux, -nneuse** *adj* [literary. Covered in fine sand] sandy
banc *nm* **de sable** sandbank
dune *nf* sand dune

22.8 *Cours d'eau* Flowing water

ruisseau *nm, pl* **-x** brook
torrent *nm* [in mountains] stream
canal *nm, pl* **-naux** canal
embouchure *nf* mouth
source *nf* source *La Loire prend sa source au plateau de Millevaches.* The source of the Loire is on the Millevaches Plateau.
courant *nm* current

usage

fleuve *nm* and **rivière** *nf* river
A **fleuve** flows into the sea, while a **rivière** flows into another river. *La Seine et la Tamise sont des fleuves.* The Seine and the Thames are rivers.

22.9 *Chutes d'eau* Waterfalls

chute *nf* **(d'eau)**, ALSO **saut** *nm* waterfall *les chutes du Niagara* Niagara Falls *le saut du Doubs* the falls of the river Doubs
cataracte *nf* [like **chute d'eau**, used for a large river] waterfall
cascade *nf* [like **chute d'eau**, used for a small river or a torrent] waterfall

22.10 *Lieux plats* Flat regions

plaine *nf* plain *en plaine* (down) in the lowlands
plateau *nm pl* **-x** plateau
creux *nm* [in a field, a road] dip
faux plat *nm* [term used by cyclists to refer to a stretch of road which looks flat but is in fact uphill] deceptive climb

usage

haut, e *adj*, **haut** *nm* and **bas, basse** *adj*
Many placenames include the adjective **haut** 'high', referring to the upper part of an area or river: *la haute Silésie* Upper Silesia, *la Haute-Loire* the Upper Loire area, *la Haute-Savoie* the French department of Haute-Savoie. The noun **haut** 'height' forms part of the names of hills, real or imagined: *les Hauts de Hurlevent* Wuthering Heights.
Bas, 'low', forms part of many placenames referring to lowlands, lower parts of areas or stretches of rivers: *les Pays-Bas* the Netherlands, *la Basse-Loire* the Lower Loire area.

22.11 *Topologie et zones* Ways of dividing up areas of the world

endroit *nm* [general word for an area of any size] place *L'Égypte, un des plus beaux endroits que j'aie jamais vu !* Egypt, one of the most beautiful places I've ever seen!
coin *nm* [informal word for a place of any size] place *l'épicier du coin* the local grocer *Il n'a jamais quitté son coin de Paris.* He never left his own (small) area of Paris.

les coins de la planète où il y a la guerre those parts of the world where there is war

domaine *nm* [land belonging to a private owner or a government department] estate

environs *nm pl*, ALSO **alentours** *nm pl* surrounding area *C'est dans les environs* ALSO *c'est aux alentours de Fontainebleau.* It's in the area around Fontainebleau.

province *nf* **1** [part of the country which is distant from the capital] *la province* the provinces **2** [in official travel announcements] *dans la direction Paris-province* outward-bound (from Paris)

provincial, e *adj, mpl* **-ciaux** [emotional term with pejorative or nostalgic overtones] provincial.

région *nf* **1** [in geography] area *régions montagneuses* mountainous areas **2** [administrative division in France. With capital letter] region *la Région Champagne-Ardenne* the Champagne-Ardenne administrative region

terres *nf pl* [old-fashioned term] landed estate *Quitter mes terres, jamais!* Leave my land, never!

territoire *nm* [the area under a country's legal jurisdiction] territory

---

usage

banlieue *nf* **faubourg** *nm* and **zone** *nf*
The most common translation for *banlieue* is suburb, but in French the word often suggests the deprivation, unemployment and ghettoization more often associated with inner-city areas in Britain and in the United States. *Faubourg* is the outer edge of a town. In large towns the name *faubourg* was given to outlying districts but as the towns extended their boundaries, streets called *faubourg* became part of the city centre, for example *le faubourg Saint-Honoré* in the heart of Paris.
Une zone is an area designated for a particular purpose, generally specified by the following word, e.g.: *zone industrielle* industrial estate, *zone inondable* area liable to flooding. In large towns the phrase *la zone* refers to a run-down area. In Britain it is associated with the inner city, while in France it tends to be associated with the deprived suburbs.

22.12 *Astronomie* Astronomy

astronomie *nf* astronomy
astronomique *adj* [used literally and figuratively] astronomical
astronaute *n* astronaut
cosmonaute *n* cosmonaut
astronome *n* astronomer

Citation Quotation
Le silence éternel de ces espaces infinis m'effraie. [comment by the 17th-century mathematician and theologian, Blaise Pascal, about a world without a God] The eternal silence of these infinite spaces terrifies me.

22.13 *La science des astres* The science of the stars

astrophysique *nf* astrophysics
astrophysicien, -cienne *n* astrophysicist
trou *nm* **noir** black hole
téléscope *nm* telescope

22.14 *L'univers* The universe

étoile *nf* star *une étoile filante* a shooting star *l'étoile du berger* the evening star
astre *nm* [scientific or literary term] star
soleil *nm* sun
lune *nf* moon
planète *nf* planet
univers *nm* universe
galaxie *nf* galaxy
météore *nm* meteor
comète *nf* comet
la Grande Ourse the Great Bear
la voie lactée the Milky Way

Le système solaire The solar system
Saturne Saturn *l'anneau de Saturne* Saturn's rings
Neptune Neptune
la Terre the Earth
Vénus Venus
Pluton Pluto
Jupiter Jupiter
Mercure Mercury
Mars Mars
Uranus Uranus

---

usage

Planets other than Earth and Venus are masculine, e.g.: *Saturne est impressionnant sur les images du satellite.* Saturn looks impressive on the satellite images. However, the names of all the planets may be used with feminine agreement when the word *planète* is present or assumed in the general context, e.g.: *On n'a pas encore photographié toutes les planètes. Saturne, quant à elle, a fourni de très belles images.* Not all of the planets have been photographed to date, but Saturn has provided some wonderful images.

---

23 Weather and temperature

23.1 *Météorologie et climat* Weather and climate

temps *nm* weather *Quel temps fait-il?* What's the weather like? *Il fait beau (temps).* The weather's lovely. *Il fait mauvais (temps).* The weather's awful.
climat *nm* climate
météorologie *nf* meteorology
météo *nf* [informal. Bulletin] weather report *Qu'a dit la météo?* What did they say on the weather?
couvert, e *adj* [describes: e.g. sky, weather] overcast
dégagé, e *adj* [describes: e.g. sky, weather] clear

23.2 *Verbes indiquant le temps qu'il fait* Verbs describing weather conditions

quel temps fait-il? what's the weather like?
il y a [+ *du, de la* + noun] *Il y a du vent.* It's windy. *Il y a du soleil.* It's sunny. *Il y a de la tempête.* It's stormy. *Il y a du brouillard.* It's foggy.
Il pleut. It's raining.
Il flotte. [very informal] It's pouring.
Il neige. It's snowing.

Il grêle. There's a hailstorm.
Il vente. The wind's blowing.
Il gèle. There's a frost.
Il fait lourd. It (the weather) feels close.

23.3 *Sortes de pluie* Types of rain

pluie *nf* rain
pluvieux, -vieuse *adj* rainy
averse *nf* shower
giboulée *nf* [often associated with March] shower
goutte *nf* **de pluie** raindrop
bruine *nf*, ALSO **crachin** *nm* drizzle
neige *nf* **fondue** sleet
précipitations *nf pl* [scientific term] rainfall

23.4 *Sortes de vents* Types of wind

bise *nf* [cold and unpleasant] north wind
brise *nf* [usually light, warm and pleasant] breeze
coup *nm* **de vent** gust (of wind)
bourrasque *nf* gust (of wind)
courant d'air *nm* draught

23.5 *Brouillard et nuages* Fog and clouds

brouillard *nm* fog
brume *nf* mist
brumeux, -meuse *adj* misty
nuage *nm* cloud
nuageux, -geuse *adj* cloudy

23.6 *Phénomènes climatiques inhabituels* Unusual weather conditions

arc-en-ciel *nm, pl* **arcs-en-ciel** rainbow
orage *nm* [usually over land] storm
tempête *nf* [usually at sea] storm
foudre *nf* lightning
éclair *nm* flash of lightning
tonnerre *nm* thunder *un coup de tonnerre* a clap of thunder
vague *nf* **de chaleur**, ALSO **canicule** *nf* heatwave
inondation *nf* flood
déluge *nm* **1** [rain] downpour **2** [in the Bible] *le Déluge* the Flood
ouragan *nm* hurricane
verglas *nm* (black) ice

Locutions Idioms
un coup de tonnerre dans un ciel serein a bolt out of the blue
par tous les temps in any weather
qu'il pleuve ou qu'il vente [in any weather. Stresses obstinacy of behaviour] come hell or high water
contre vents et marées against all odds

23.7 *Froid* Cold

see also **23 Météorologie et climat**
frais, fraîche *adj* chilly *Il fait frais ce soir.* It's chilly tonight.
froid, e *adj* cold
froid *nm* cold *Il fait un froid de canard.* It's freezing (cold) *prendre froid* to catch a chill
gel *nm* frost

geler {11} *vt* and *vi* [used of the weather and its effects. Obj: e.g. river, pond, washing on the line] to freeze
glacer {7} *vt* [used of the weather. Obj: e.g. ears, cheeks] to freeze
congeler {12} *vi* and *vt* [in a freezer. Obj: e.g. meat, leftovers] to freeze
rafraîchir {19} *vt* and *vi* [mostly used of foodstuffs] to chill. *Mets la bière à rafraîchir.* Put the beer in (the refrigerator) to chill.
se rafraîchir *v refl* to get cooler *Le temps se rafraîchit.* It's getting colder.
refroidir {19} *vi* to go cold. *Mange ou la soupe va refroidir.* Eat or the soup will get cold.
se refroidir *v refl* [subj: temperature] to drop
boule *nf* **de neige** snowball

23.8 *Chaud* Hot

see also **23.1 Météorologie et climat**
chaud, e *adj* **1** [not cold] hot *un repas chaud* a hot meal **2** [at a high temperature] hot *Il a les mains chaudes.* His hands are warm.
chaleur *nf* **1** [temperature] heat **2** [season] *pendant les (grandes) chaleurs* in very hot weather
chauffer {6} **1** *vt Le soleil a chauffé les tuiles.* The sun made the tiles hot. *Le soudeur doit d'abord chauffer le métal.* The welder must first heat the metal. **2** *vi La roche chauffe au soleil.* The rock gets hot in the sun. *Le moteur chauffe.* [from cold] The engine is warming up. [from hot] The engine is overheating.
tiède *adj* **1** [describes: things which should be colder or hotter] lukewarm *J'ai horreur du café tiède!* I hate lukewarm coffee! **2** [at a comfortable temperature] warm *Servez tiède.* Serve while still warm.
tiédeur *nf* (slight) warmth
bouillant, -e *adj* [describes: liquids] boiling hot
brûlant, -e *adj* [describes: solids and liquids] burning hot
torride *adj* [describes: climate] scorching hot
réchauffer {6} *vt* **1** [obj: food] to reheat **2** [by the fireside or stove. Obj: e.g. hands, legs] to warm (up)

24 In the house

24.1 *Architecture* Architecture

Home, at home
When talking about someone's home, use *son appartement* or *sa maison*. If you don't know what sort of accommodation the person has, use *chez lui* or *chez elle*. The question 'where's home?' is translated by *Vous habitez où?*, unless it means 'Where did you grow up?', in which case it is best rendered by *Vous venez d'où?* When I want to talk about the place where I live, the most common phrase is *chez moi*. For example, *Chez moi, je laisse toujours la lumière allumée dans l'entrée le soir.* At home, I always leave the light on in the hallway at night. The phrase *à la maison* can also be used in this context. Thus you could say: *Venez chez moi demain* or *Venez à la maison demain.* Come over to my place tomorrow. *Mon foyer* is the place I call home, and the people and way of life I associate with it, e.g. *Les prisonniers de guerre ont été libérés et sont rentrés dans leur foyer.* The prisoners of war were freed and returned home. When the word *foyer* is accompanied by a complement, it means an institutional home, e.g. *un foyer d'étudiants* a student residence *un foyer de travailleurs immigrés* a hostel for immigrant workers. A retirement home is *une maison de retraite*.

maison *nf* [detached, semi-detached or terraced] house
maison de campagne [second home, in the country] country home
résidence *nf* **secondaire** [more formal than **maison de campagne**. Usu in the country] second home
villa *nf* [big comfortable house, usu in leafy suburb or in seaside resort] detached house
lotissement *nm* [cheap housing built on the edge of a small town or a village] estate
bidonville *nm* [substandard dwellings made of corrugated iron sheets and other makeshift materials] shanty town
taudis *nm* hovel

Describing typical British housing
Because French houses look very different from houses in Britain, there is no real equivalent for 'detached', 'semi-detached' or 'terraced' house in French. However, when describing a detached house, you could use the estate agent's phrase *une maison individuelle*. For a semi-detached pair, you could say *deux maisons mitoyennes* (but note that this only means two houses sharing an interior wall, and does not imply that the two houses look similar). Finally, a terrace could be rendered as *une rue aux maisons mitoyennes* and a terraced house would have to be *une petite maison avec des maisons mitoyennes de chaque côté*. Neither phrase, however, implies that the houses look alike. Most detached houses on the outskirts of towns are commonly referred to as *pavillons*.

pavillon *nm* (detached) house

Une maison individuelle (a detached house)

Les HLM
The initials *HLM* stand for *habitations à loyer modéré* or BrE council dwellings (AmE public housing). They are usually blocks of high-rise flats. The phrase *habiter dans des HLM*, to live on a council-built estate, used to bring instantantly to mind the picture of tower blocks. Now there are many low-rise HLM, and even some estates of detached or semi-detached HLM. An individual flat within an estate can be referred to as *un HLM*.

24.2 *Parties de bâtiments* Parts of buildings

appartement *nm* BrE flat AmE apartment
studio *nm* BrE studio flat AmE studio apartment
duplex *nm* [flat/apartment on two floors] maisonnette
chambre *nf* **de bonne** [traditionally on the top floor of an
 old block of flats in Paris or other large cities, formerly
 maid's quarters, and often used as student digs] BrE
 bedsitter AmE studio apartment
avoir une chambre en ville [said of students who do not
 live in a hall of residence or at home] to have digs in town
loge *nf* [ground-floor room in typical old-fashioned block]
 (porter's) lodge *S'adresser à la loge avant 20 heures.*
 Enquiries before 8 p.m. should be addressed to the porter.
meublé *nm* **1** [house] furnished house **2** [flat] BrE
 furnished flat AmE furnished apartment
pièce *nf* room

château *nm, pl* x (manor house)

> ### *usage*
>
> Avoid *pièce* when talking about someone's room. Use
> *bureau* if you are referring to an office or *chambre* if
> you are referring to a bedroom.

24.3 *Bâtiments hauts* Tall buildings

immeuble *nm* **1** [any large property with several dwellings
 inside] building **2** [purpose-built, rather than a converted
 property high-rise or low-rise] block (of flats)
tour *nf* tower block
building *nm* [very tall, in highly populated cities like New
 York, Hong Kong or in the modern parts of Paris such as
 La Défense] BrE tower block AmE high-rise
gratte-ciel *nm, pl* **gratte-ciels** [term becoming old-
 fashioned] skyscraper
résidence *nf* [group of low-rise or high-rise flats] BrE block
 of flats AmE block of apartments
moulin *nm* **à vent** windmill
château *nm, pl* **-x d'eau** water tower

château-fort *nm, pl* châteaux-forts (castle)

24.4 *Beaux bâtiments historiques* Fine historic buildings

manoir *nm* (country house)

18th C Parisian town house:hôtel particulier (town house)

24.5 *Petits bâtiments* Simple buildings

cabane *nf* **1** [general term] shed **2** [in garden] *cabane (à outils)* garden shed
appentis *nm* lean-to
refuge *nm* [in mountains, for shepherds or tourists] hut
case *nf* [in Africa] hut

fermette *nf* (small converted farm)

mas *nm* ALSO bastide *nf* (farm)

24.6 *Gens qui construisent des bâtiments* People who work on buildings

architecte *n* architect
géomètre-expert *n* (quantity) surveyor
les corps de métier the building trades
électricien, -cienne *n* electrician
couvreur *nm* roof contractor
maçon, -çonne *n* bricklayer
menuisier, -sière *n* joiner
charpentier *nm* carpenter
plombier *nm* plumber

24.7 *Habiter* To live somewhere

see also **24.8 Hébergement**
habiter {6} *vi* [have as one's address or place of usual residence] to live *J'habite (au) 32 rue des Beaux Moulins.* I live at 32, rue des Beaux Moulins. *les gens qui habitent la Suisse* people who live in Switzerland
vivre {76} *vi* [have as one's usual place of residence, esp when talking about countries] to live *Il est venu vivre en France en 1985.* He came to live in France in 1985.
demeurer {6} *vi* [same meaning as **habiter**, but more official term] to reside
loger {8} *vi* [this verb is used esp in the context of short-term rents, student digs, etc] to live *Pour le moment, je loge chez mes parents.* At the moment I'm living with my parents.
s'installer {6} *v refl* **1** [move in for a long or short period. Implies comfort] to settle in *Voilà votre chambre, installez-vous et faites comme chez vous.* Here's your bedroom, settle in and make yourself at home. **2** [move to a place and begin a period of one's life there] to settle *Ils se sont installés à Bruges après la guerre.* They settled in Bruges after the war.
déménager {8} *vi* **1** [from one place to another] BrE to move (house) AmE to move **2** [out of a place] to move out
emménager {8} *vi* to move in

24.8 *Hébergement* Accommodation

see also **24.2 Parties de bâtiments, 24.7 Habiter**
deux-pièces *nm* BrE one-bedroomed flat AmE one-bedroom apartment
trois-pièces *nm* Br/e two-bedroomed flat AmE two-bedroom apartment
logement *nm* **1** [place to live in general] housing *consacrer un tiers de son budget au logement* to spend a third of one's income on housing **2** [home] BrE flat AmE apartment *un logement social* BrE a council flat *Elle a un joli petit logement.* She has a nice little flat.
loger {8} *vi* **1** [provide housing for] to house **2** [provide temporary accommodation for] to put up *La municipalité a construit une résidence pour loger les nouveaux arrivants.* The civic authority built an estate in order to house newcomers to the town.
hébergement *nm* [often temporary due to emergencies or seasonal changes] accommodation
héberger {8} *vt* [similar to **loger** 2] to put up
demeure *nf* [literary] house *de larges avenues bordées de magnifiques demeures* wide avenues lined with magnificent houses *sa dernière demeure* his last resting place
domicile *nm* [official usage] place of residence *livré à domicile* delivered to the home

24.9 *Les gens et les endroits où ils habitent* People and the places where they live

see also **41.15 Posséder**
locataire *n* tenant
propriétaire *n* landlord, landlady
proprio *n* [informal. Owner of accommodation] landlord, landlady
gardien, -dienne *n* [in new or old blocks of flats] porter
concierge *n* [the term is now considered old-fashioned and, by some, offensive. Properly, it refers to the paid warden living in a small tied flat on the ground floor of an old block of flats in Paris or in other large cities] concierge
sans-domicile-fixe *nm*, ALSO **SDF** homeless person
louer {6} *vt* to rent

Locutions Idioms
pendre la crémaillère [a *crémaillère* is a notched metal plate fixed inside an open fireplace, to hang cooking pots from. Putting it in position, as in this phrase, symbolizes the end of the moving-in ritual and the start of life in a new home] to have a housewarming (party)
faire le tour du propriétaire [as a visitor, guest, new owner or tenant] to look around *faire faire le tour du propriétaire à qqn* to show sb around

24.10 *Autour des bâtiments* Around buildings

toit *nm* roof
ardoise *nf* slate
tuile *nf* tile
cheminée *nf* chimney
antenne *nf* **(de télévision)** aerial *(antenne) parabolique* satellite dish
mur *nm* wall
crépi *nm* rendering
gouttière *nf* gutter
fenêtre *nf* window
vitre *nf* windowpane
rebord *nm* **de fenêtre** windowsill
volet *nm* shutter
garage *nm* garage
allée *nf* drive
cour *nf* yard
jardin *nm* garden
grille *nf* gate
pilier *nm* **(de grille)** gatepost
grillage *nm* fence
perron *nm* steps
porte *nf* door *porte d'entrée* front door
boîte *nf* **à lettres** letterbox
huis *nm* door knocker
poignée *nf* **de (la) porte** doorknob
seuil *nm* **de la porte** threshold
digicode *nm* [with keyboard for punching in a code] entry phone

24.11 *Entrées et sorties* Ways in and out

entrée *nf* [access] way in *L'entrée donne sur la rue Fabre.* The entrance is on the rue Fabre.
sortie *nf* [in public places] exit *sortie de secours* emergency exit

à l'intérieur indoors *On mange à l'intérieur ce soir, il fait frais.* Let's eat indoors tonight, it's chilly.
dehors *adv* outdoors *envoyer les enfants jouer dehors* to send the children to play outside

24.12 *Niveaux* Levels

rez-de-chaussée *nm* BrE ground floor AmE first floor
premier étage *nm* BrE first floor AmE second floor
deuxième étage *nm* second floor
balcon *nm* balcony
niveau *nm* [in car parks and car ferry holds] level
sous-sol *nm* basement
grenier *nm* attic

24.13 *À l'intérieur des bâtiments* Inside buildings

entrée *nf*, ALSO **vestibule** *nm* [in house or flat/apartment] hall
hall *nm* [in block of flats/high-rise apartment] lobby
vestiaire *nm* [in house or theatre] cloakroom
couloir *nm* passage

24.14 *D'un niveau à l'autre* Different levels

haut *nm* upstairs *les chambres du haut* the upstairs bedrooms *en haut* upstairs
bas *nm* downstairs *le bureau du bas* the downstairs study *en bas* downstairs
dessous *nm les pièces du dessous* the rooms below *les gens du dessous* the people in the flat/apartment below
dessus *nm les pièces du dessus* the rooms above *les gens du dessus* the people in the flat/apartment above

24.15 *Dans les pièces* Inside rooms

sol *nm* floor
revêtement *nm* **de sol** floor covering
plancher *nm* floorboards
plafond *nm* ceiling
parquet *nm* parquet floor
meuble *nm* piece of furniture *les meubles* the furniture
meubler {6} *vt* to furnish *Ils sont meublés en Louis XV.* All their furniture is Louis XV.

24.16 *Salle de séjour* Living room

This room is also called *le séjour*, *le salon* and sometimes *le living*. In houses or flats where it is not separated from the dining-room, it is called *le salon-salle-à-manger*.

table *nf* table *petite table*, ALSO *table basse* coffee table
buffet *nm* sideboard
chaise *nf* chair
siège *nm* [refers to any kind of chair or armchair] chair *J'ai fait recouvrir tous les sièges du salon.* I've had all the chairs in the living-room re-covered.
canapé *nm*, ALSO **divan**, ALSO **sofa** *nm* sofa
fauteuil *nm* armchair *fauteuil à bascule* rocking chair
coussin *nm* cushion
cheminée *nf* fireplace
rebord ALSO **manteau (de cheminée)** *nm* mantelpiece

foyer *nm* **(de cheminée) 1** [in fireplace] hearth
  2 [administrative term for dwelling currently lived in]
  home *un village de cinq cents foyers* a village with 500
  homes
grille *nf* **de foyer** ALSO **de cheminée** grate
tapis *nm* large rug
carpette *nf* rug
moquette *nf* (wall-to-wall) carpeting
rideau *nm* [outer, made of heavy fabric] curtain
voilage *nm* [inner, made of transparent fabric] BrE net
  curtain AmE sheers
lampadaire *nm* standard lamp
abat-jour *nm inv* lampshade
variateur *nm* **de lumière** dimmer switch
halogène *nm* halogen lamp
étagère *nf* shelf
étagère *nf* **(à livres)**, bookshelf **bibliothèque** *nf*, ALSO
  rayonnages *nm pl* bookshelves
vase *nm* vase

24.17 *Cuisine et ustensiles* Kitchen and kitchen equipment

cuisine *nf* kitchen
évier *nm* sink
bassine *nf* **à vaisselle** BrE washing-up bowl AmE dishpan
égouttoir *nm* dishrack
paillasse *nf* draining board
cuisinière *nf* BrE cooker AmE stove
plaque *nf* **de cuisson** BrE hob AmE stove (top)
four *nm* oven
poêle *nf* **(à frire)** frying pan
casserole *nf* saucepan
cocotte-minute® *nf, pl* **cocottes-minutes** pressure
  cooker
réfrigérateur *nm* refrigerator
frigo *nm* [informal] fridge
congélateur *nm* freezer
plan *nm* **de travail** work surface
planche *nf* **à découper** BrE chopping board AmE cutting
  board
placard *nm* cupboard
ouvre-boîte *nm, pl* **ouvre-boîtes** can opener
robot-ménager *nm, pl* **robots-ménagers** food processor
four *nm* **à micro-ondes**, ALSO **micro-ondes** *nm inv*
  microwave (oven)

24.18 *Petits ustensiles* Small kitchen utensils

bol *nm* [unless specified, e.g. *bol à cidre*, bowl for drinking
  cider. This utensil is the one from which coffee or
  chocolate will be normally drunk at breakfast time] bowl
tasse *nf* cup
carafe *nf* (glass) jug
cruche *nf* (earthenware) jug
plateau *nm, pl* **-x** tray
râpe *nf* **à fromage** cheese-grater
salière *nf* **1** [for grinding] salt mill **2** [container] BrE salt
  cellar AmE salt shaker
poivrier *nm* ALSO **poivrière** *nf* pepperpot
moulin *nm* **à poivre** BrE pepper mill AmE pepper (shaker)

24.19 *Service de table* Tableware

service *nm* **de table** dinner set
verre *nm* glass
petite assiette *nf* side plate
grande assiette *nf* dinner plate
coupe *nf* [for individual portions of icecream or dessert]
  dish
plat *nm* **à légumes** (vegetable) dish
plat *nm* **à viande** (serving) dish
couteau *nm* **à découper** carving knife
fourchette *nf* **à viande** carving fork
serviette *nf* **de table** napkin
nappe *nf* tablecloth
beurrier *nm, pl* **-x** butter dish
petite cuillère *nf*, ALSO **cuiller** *nf* desert spoon
couteau *nm* knife
grande cuillère *nf*, ALSO **cuiller** *nf* soup spoon
fourchette *nf* fork
un couvert est mis a place is set

> ### usage
>
> **couvert** *nm*
> The word **couvert** denotes many different things
> connected with serving at table. **Couvert** is the
> collective word for the set of utensils laid around a
> plate. *Tu as mis les assiettes mais pas les couverts.* You
> set the table but forgot the cutlery. The word also refers
> to the utensils: *le tiroir où je range les couverts* the
> drawer where I keep the cutlery. It can also mean the set
> of utensils, including plates and glasses, on a table which
> has been set: *mettre le couvert* to set the table. Finally, it
> can denote the number of guests attending: *préparer un
> repas de 50 couverts* to prepare a meal for 50 people.

24.20 *Chambre* Bedroom

lit *nm* bed
coiffeuse *nf* dressing table
glace *nf* mirror
commode *nf* chest of drawers
tiroir *nm* drawer
armoire *nf* BrE wardrobe AmE closet

24.21 *Sur le lit* On the bed

literie *nf* [collective term for all sheets, blankets, etc]
  bedding
oreiller *nm* pillow
traversin *nm*, ALSO **polochon** *nm* bolster
taie *nf* case *taie d'oreiller* pillowcase *taie de traversin*
  bolster case
drap *nm* sheet
couverture *nf* blanket *couverture électrique* electric
  blanket
duvet *nm*, ALSO **couette** *nf* BrE duvet AmE comforter
housse *nf* **de couette** BrE duvet cover AmE comforter
  cover
édredon *nm* eiderdown
couvre-lit *nm, pl* **couvre-lits** bedspread
bouillotte *nf* hot-water bottle

24.22 *Sanitaires* Bathroom and toilet

lavabo *nm* BrE (wash) basin AmE sink
vasque *nf* [round-shaped, stylish] BrE (wash) basin AmE
  sink
robinet *nm* BrE tap AmE faucet
bain *nm* BrE bath AmE bathtub
mélangeur *nm* BrE mixer tap AmE faucet
douche *nf* shower
douchette *nf* shower attachment
rideau *nm* **de douche** shower curtain
bonde *nf* BrE plug AmE stopper
tapis *nm* **de bain** bath mat
bidet *nm* bidet
siège *nm* **(des toilettes)** toilet seat *rabattre le siège* to
  lower the seat
réservoir *nm* BrE cistern AmE toilet tank
porte-serviette *nm, pl* **porte-serviettes** BrE towel rail
  AmE towel rack

usage

Toilettes *nf pl*
When you need to mention the toilet, the best phrase is
les toilettes. Note that **les WC** *nm pl* and **les cabinets**
nm pl are both a little informal, and *les cabinets* is a
term often used by or to children. There isn't really a
euphemism in common use, apart from **le petit coin**,
equivalent to 'the smallest room', which is informal.

papier *nm* **toilettes**, ALSO **papier hygiénique** toilet
  paper
rouleau *nm* **de papier toilettes** toilet paper roll
chasse *nf* **d'eau** flush
tirer la chasse [said whether a chain or other mechanisms
  are used] to flush
C'est occupé! It's occupied!

24.23 *Chauffer la maison* Heating the house

chauffage *nm* **1** [system] heating system *chauffage central*
  central heating **2** [device] heater *J'ai apporté un
  chauffage d'appoint.* I've brought an extra heater along.
radiateur *nm* **1** [general term] heater **2** [as in central
  heating] radiator **3** [glowing red] fire *radiateur à gaz* gas
  heater *radiateur électrique* electric heater

24.24 *Hôtels* Hotels

hôtel *nm* hotel
palace *nm* luxury hotel
pension *nf* **1** [system for taking meals in a hotel] *pension
  complète* full board *demi-pension* half board **2** [old-
  fashioned. Cheap hotel] boarding house
motel *nm* motel
chambre *nf* room **chambre à deux lits** ALSO **à deux
  personnes** BrE double room AmE two-person room
chambre à un lit ALSO **à une personne** single room *Vous
  voulez une chambre avec un grand lit ou des lits jumeaux?*
  Would you like a double room with one bed, or a twin-
  bedded room? *chambre avec douche* room with shower
  only
petit déjeuner compris breakfast included
salle *nf* **de bain(s)** bathroom
cabinet *nm* **de toilette** [usu this means a washstand but
  no bath] washing facilities

aller à l'hôtel to go to a hotel *Il est trop tard pour planter
la tente, on va aller à l'hôtel.* It's too late to pitch the tent,
let's go to a hotel.
descendre à l'hôtel [this phrase implies that a reservation
has been made. It also hints at comfort, although not
luxury] to stay at a hotel *Je descends toujours au
Miramare.* I always stay at the Miramare.

25 Clothes, accessories and cosmetics

25.1 *Habillement* Clothes

habillement *nm* clothes *Je dépense beaucoup pour
  l'habillement.* I spend a lot on clothes. *le rayon
  habillement* the clothing department
habit *nm* **1** [any item] piece of clothing *mes habits* my
  clothes **2** [ceremonial] full (ceremonial) dress *un
  académicien en habit* a member of the Académie wearing
  ceremonial dress
vêtements *nm pl* clothes
vêtement *nm* **1** [general term] garment **2** [item worn over
  other clothes, such as a overcoat, mac or cape] coat

25.2 *Parties des vêtements* Parts of clothes

col *nm* collar
manche *nf* sleeve
jambe *nf*, ALSO **jambière** *nf* (trouser) leg
entrejambes *nm* crotch
poche *nf* pocket
poignet *nm* cuff
revers *nm* **1** [on jacket] lapel **2** [on trouser leg] BrE turn-up
  AmE cuff
ourlet *nm* hem
braguette *nf* [on trousers, shorts] BrE flies AmE fly
bouton *nm* button

25.3 *Porter des vêtements* To wear clothes

habiller {6} *vt* to dress *habiller un enfant* to dress a child
  habiller une actrice à la ville comme à la scène to be the
  designer for an actress both on and off stage
s'habiller *v refl* **1** [to cover one's nakedness] to put clothes
  on **2** [for a special occasion] to dress up
déshabiller {6} *vt* to undress
se déshabiller *v refl* to take one's clothes off
mettre {56} *vt* **1** [as an action] to put on *Dépêche-toi de
  mettre ton jeans.* Hurry up and put your jeans on. **2** [as a
  choice of clothing] to wear *Pourquoi tu ne mets jamais
  ton châle?* Why don't you ever wear your shawl?
porter {6} *vt* [similar to **mettre 2**] to wear
passer {6} *vt*, ALSO **enfiler** {6} *vt* [denotes speed] to slip on
essayer {16} *vt* to try on
endosser {6} *vt* [obj: clothes which cover the whole back]
  to put on *endosser un manteau* to put a coat on
étrenner {6} *vt* to wear . . . for the first time
arborer {6} *vt* [indicates that the item is worn with pride]
  to wear *Elle arborait son écharpe de maire.* She was
  wearing her mayor's tricolour sash with some pride.

25.4 *Vêtements courants à porter le jour* Ordinary clothes for day wear

pantalon *nm* [man or woman's] (pair of) trousers *J'ai acheté un pantalon.* I bought a pair of trousers.
veston *nm* [The term is being superseded by **veste**. Man's] jacket
veste *nf* [man's or woman's] jacket
jupe *nf* skirt
robe *nf* dress
costume *nm*, ALSO **complet** *nm* [man's] suit
tailleur *nm* [woman's] suit
gilet *nm* **1** [part of three piece suit, worn by both sexes] BrE waistcoat AmE vest **2** [sleeveless, sometimes made of leather, worn by both sexes over a shirt] BrE jerkin AmE vest
corsage *nm*, ALSO **chemisier** *nm* [woman's] blouse
blouse *nf* [man's or woman's, shaped like a coat] BrE overall AmE coverall
chemise *nf* [man's or woman's] shirt
chemisette *nf* [man's] (short-sleeved) shirt
imperméable *nm* [man's or woman's] raincoat
manteau *nm*, *pl* **-x** [man's or woman's] coat
pardessus *nm* [man's] overcoat
salopette *nf* [man's or woman's; fashion item] (pair of) BrE dungarees AmE overalls
cotte *nf*, ALSO **combinaison** *nf* [divided garment. Man's or woman's] (worker's) overalls
bleu *nm* **de travail** [jacket and trousers. Man's or woman's] (worker's) BrE overalls AmE work clothes
chaussette *nf* [man or woman's] sock

25.5 *Vêtements tricotés* Knitted clothes

pull *nm*, ALSO **pullover** *nm*, ALSO **chandail** *nm*, *pl* **chandails** sweater
tricot *nm* **1** [open at the front] cardigan **2** [for slipping over the head] sweater
gilet *nm* cardigan

25.6 *Sous-vêtements* Underwear

culotte *nf* (pair of) BrE knickers AmE panties
slip *nm* **1** [man's] (pair of) underpants **2** [woman's] (pair of) BrE knickers AmE panties
soutien-gorge *nm*, *pl* **soutiens-gorge** bra
bas *nm* BrE stocking AmE hose
mi-bas *nm*, *pl* **mi-bas** BrE knee-high stocking AmE hose
collant *nm* (pair of) tights
jupon *nm* BrE petticoat AmE slip
combinaison *nf* slip
caleçon *nm* boxer shorts *caleçon long* (pair of) long johns
en petite tenue wearing only one's underwear

25.7 *Vêtements de nuit* Nightwear

pyjama *nm* [man or woman's] (pair of) pyjamas
chemise *nf* **de nuit** [long shirt for men, or any style for women] nightie
nuisette *nf* [very short, for women] nightie
robe *nf* **de chambre** [man or woman's] BrE dressing gown AmE robe

25.8 *Vêtements de sport et de danse* Sports and dance wear

survêtement *nm* track suit
jogging *nm* [the term and the garment are more fashionable than **survêtement**] track suit
justaucorps *nm* [for female or male dancers] leotard
tunique *nf* **(à volant)** [for female dancers] leotard (with a frill)
body *nm* [with fasteners between the legs. Term used in e.g. aerobics] leotard
tutu *nm* tutu
chausson *nm* **de danse** ballet slipper

25.9 *Chaussures* Shoes

chaussure *nf* **1** [various types] shoe **2** [sturdy types] boot
godasse *nf* [commonly used informal, pejorative term] shoe
pompe *nf* [slang] shoe
soulier *nm* [old-fashioned term] shoe
sandale *nf* sandal
sandalette *nf* [for woman or child] small sandal
boucle *nf* buckle
botte *nf* [knee-length] boot
talon *nm* heel *talon haut* high heel *talon aiguille* stiletto heel
lacet *nm* (shoe) lace
tennis *nf* [below the ankle] BrE trainer AmE sneakers
basket *nf* [above the ankle] BrE trainer AmE high-top sneakers
semelle *nf* sole
chaussure de gym gym shoe
pantoufle *nf* BrE slipper AmE house slipper
chausson *nm* BrE slipper AmE house slipper
sabot *nm* BrE clog
botte *nf* **en caoutchouc** [made of rubber] (wellington) boot
cirage *nm* shoe polish
brosse *nf* **à chaussures** shoebrush

25.10 *Couvre-chefs* Headgear

chapeau *nm*, *pl* **-x** *nm* hat
casquette *nf* [flat, made of cloth] cap
turban *nm* turban
casque *nm* [construction worker's or motorbike rider's] helmet *casque intégral* (wraparound) crash helmet
capuchon *nm* hood
serre-tête *nm inv* **1** [man's] headband **2** [woman's] BrE hair band AmE head band
perruque *nf* wig

25.11 *Protection contre le froid et la pluie* For keeping warm and dry

écharpe *nf*, ALSO **foulard** *nm* scarf
fichu, *nm* ALSO **carré** *nm* [as worn by, e.g. country women] headscarf
passe-montagne *nm*, *pl* **passe-montagnes** BrE cagoule AmE windbreaker
gant *nm* glove *une paire de gants* a pair of gloves
châle *nm* shawl
parapluie *nm* umbrella

cartable *nm* (school bag)

25.12 *Sacs et serviettes* Bags and briefcases

sac *nm* **(à main)** BrE handbag AmE purse
serviette *nf*, ALSO **attaché-case** *nm* briefcase
mallette *nf* small suitcase
porte-document *nm inv* document case

25.13 *Accessoires et bijoux* Accessories and jewels

cravate *nf* tie
nœud *nm* bow *nœud papillon* bow tie
ruban *nm* ribbon
ceinture *nf* belt
ceinturon *nm* [man's, military-type] belt
bretelles *nf pl* (pair of) braces
bouton *nm* **de manchette** cufflink *une paire de boutons de manchette* a pair of cufflinks
éventail *nm* fan
badge *nm* badge
bijou *nm*, *pl* **- x** jewel
bijoutier -tière *n* jeweller
bijouterie *nf* jeweller's
joaillier, -llière *n* [specialist in gems] jeweller
joyau *nm*, *pl* **-x** gem

boucle *nf* **d'oreille** earring
pendant *nm* **d'oreille** [dangling] earring
collier *nm* necklace
bague *nf* ring
bracelet *nm* bracelet
broche *nf* brooch

25.14 *Produits de beauté* Cosmetics

produit *nm* **de beauté** [phrase used by advertisers, in shops, etc] cosmetics, beauty products
maquillage *nm* **1** [substance that has been applied] make-up *Tu as du maquillage sur ton col.* There's make-up on your collar. **2** [product] **du maquillage**, ALSO **des produits de maquillage** cosmetics *J'ai laissé tout mon maquillage à côté du lavabo.* I left all my all my make-up next to the sink.
rouge *nm* **à lèvres** lipstick
mascara *nm* mascara
fard *nm*, ALSO **ombre** *nf* **à paupières** eye-shadow
parfum *nm* **1** [pleasant smell] scent **2** [essence] perfume
eau *nf*, *pl* **-x de Cologne** eau de Cologne

---

parfum and **eau de toilette**
Un parfum is more expensive than the same scent sold as *une eau de toilette*, since it is more concentrated.

25.15 *Mouchoirs* Handkerchiefs

mouchoir *nm* handkerchief *mouchoir en papier* tissue
pochette *nf* breast pocket handkerchief

26 Textiles and materials

see also **83.6 Travaux d'aiguille**

26.1 *Textiles* Textiles

textile *nm* **1** [product. Term used in the trade, in shops, etc] material *textile synthétique* ALSO *artificiel* man-made material **2** [trade] textile industry
tissu *nm* [general term] material *Il me faut deux mètres de tissu.* I need two metres of material. *du tissu synthétique* man-made material
tissu-éponge *nm*, *pl* **tissus-éponges** towelling
étoffe *nf* fabric *vêtu d'une étoffe grossière* dressed in coarse cloth *Les fauteuils sont tapissés de riches étoffes.* The armchairs are luxuriously upholstered.
fil *nm* **(à coudre) 1** [for sewing] cotton **2** [piece pulled off material] thread
tisser {6} *vt* to weave *métier à tisser* loom
tisserand, e *n* weaver

26.2 *Tissus courants* Common materials

feutre *nm* felt
nylon *nm* nylon
polyester *nm* polyester
velours *nm* velvet *velours côtelé* corduroy
cuir *nm* leather
daim *nm* suede
lin *nm* linen

toile *nf* cloth
soie *nf* silk
satin *nm* satin
dentelle *nf* lace *des dentelles* lacework

26.3 *Matériaux* Materials

matériau *nm, pl* **-x** material
matière *nf* **première** raw material
caoutchouc *nm* **1** [raw] gum **2** [processed] rubber
latex *nm* latex
vulcanisation *nf* vulcanization
verre *nm* glass
plexiglas *nm* plexiglas
moule *nm* mould
réfractaire *adj* refractory
porcelaine *nf* china
céramique *nf* ceramic
kaolin *nm* kaolin
vernis *nm* glaze
émail *nm, pl* **émaux** enamel
four *nm* kiln
bois *nm* **1** wood *bois tendres* softwoods *bois durs*
  hardwoods **2** [for building] timber
cellulose *nf* cellulose
papier *nm* paper
pâte *nf* **à papier** BrE wood pulp AmE paper pulp
papyrus *nm* papyrus
carton *nm* cardboard *carton bitumé* roofing felt
matières *nf pl* **plastiques** plastics
biodégradable *adj* biodegradable *qui n'est pas biodégradable* non-biodegradable
celluloïde *nm* celluloid
polystyrène *nm* polystyrene *polystyrène expansé*
  expanded polystyrene
polymère *nm* polymer
argile *nf* clay
chaux *nf* lime *chaux vive* quicklime
craie *nf* chalk
marbre *nm* marble
goudron *nm* tar
plâtre *nm* plaster
ciment *nm* cement
placoplâtre *nm* ® plasterboard
aggloméré *nm* chipboard
contreplaqué *nm* plywood

26.4 *Verbes exprimant l'utilisation de matériaux* Verbs describing the use of materials

vulcaniser {6} *vt* to vulcanize
souffler {6} *vt* [obj: glass] to blow
vitrifier {15} *vt* [obj: e.g. glass, enamel] to glaze
émailler {6} *vt* [obj: lid, valve] to enamel
polymériser {6} *vt* to polymerize
goudronner {6} *vt* to tar
enduire {82} *vt* to coat *enduire qqch de vernis* to glaze sthg
  enduire qqch de peinture to paint sthg

27 Repairs, decoration and construction

27.1 *Assembler* To put together

assembler {6} *vt* [general term. May involve various
techniques. Obj: e.g. machine, kit, toy] to put together
rassembler {6} *vt* [put together after the elements have
been separated] to collect (together) *Je vais rassembler
nos affaires.* I'll collect our things (together).
monter {6} *vt* [put together with nails, screws etc. More
technical than *assembler*] to assemble
accrocher {6} *vt* to hook (up) *accrocher une remorque à un
tracteur* to hitch a trailer up to a tractor
mêler {6} *vt* [create a single substance out of two or more
elements] to blend *mêler de l'eau et* ALSO *avec du vin* to
blend water and wine
mélanger {8} *vt* [same meaning as **mêler**, but stresses the
disparity of the original elements] to blend *Mélangez les
dés de carottes, de tomates et de concombre.* Mix
together the diced carrot, tomato and cucumber.
combiner {6} *vt* [put together in particular proportions,
e.g. in cooking, chemistry, etc] to combine *Combinez l'eau
avec le plâtre jusqu'à obtenir une masse pâteuse.* Mix the
water with the plaster until you have a paste.
joindre {58} *vt* [put together edge to edge] to join *le fil de
fer qui joint les deux parties de la clôture* the wire joining
the two sections of the fence
attacher {6} *vt* [usu with string, wire, cable, etc] to tie up
attacher un colis to tie up a parcel *attacher un rosier au
mur* to tie a climbing rose to a wall *attacher un chien à un
arbre* to tie a dog to a tree
lier {6} *vt* [literary. Same meaning as **attacher**] to tie up
lier un bouquet de fleurs avec un ruban de couleur to tie
up a bunch of flowers with a coloured ribbon
coller {6} *vt* to glue (together)
collant, e *adj* sticky
agrafer {6} *vt* to staple (together)
épingler {6} *vt* to pin (together)

27.2 *Séparation* Separation

see also **56.1 Classifier**
séparer {6} *vt* [move a part away from the whole, or move
two parts away from each other] to separate *Séparez le
blanc du jaune* ALSO *le blanc et le jaune.* Separate the yolk
from the white. *séparer deux chiens qui se battent* to
separate two dogs in a fight
séparation *nf* separation *Ils ont tenté de procéder à la
séparation des sœurs siamoises.* They attempted to
separate the Siamese twins.
partager {8} *vt* [implies allocation of resources or duties] to
share (out)
partage *nm* sharing (out)
diviser {6} *vt* **1** [create subsets within a set] to divide *diviser
une équipe en trois groupes* to split a team into three
groups **2** [pejorative Obj: e.g. community, family] to tear
apart
division *nf* dividing (up)

27.3 *Façons de séparer* Ways of separating

écarter {6} *vt* **1** [move parts away from each other, without separating completely] to move apart *écarter une mèche* to move a strand of hair *écarter les rideaux pour mieux voir* to move the curtain aside to get a better look *Écartez doucement le papier qui recouvre le bouquet.* Carefully remove the paper protecting the bouquet. **2** [obj: arms, legs] to spread, to open

déchirer {6} *vt* [separate parts of a woven material, mainly cloth and paper] to tear

arracher {6} *vt* [remove a part of, usu with force] to rip (out)

détacher {6} *vt* [remove carefully, neatly] to undo *détacher ses lacets* to undo one's laces *Détacher en suivant les perforations.* Tear along the dotted line.

27.4 *Réparations et bricolage* Repairs and Do It Yourself

see also **26.3 Matériaux**

réparation *nf* repair *faire une réparation* to make a repair

réparer {6} *vt* and *vi* to repair *J'ai donné mon aspirateur à réparer.* I've sent my vacum cleaner away to be repaired.

bricolage *nm* **1** [activity] DIY **2** [pejorative. Ineffective or ugly repair] rough and ready piece of work

bricoler {6} **1** *vi* to do DIY *Le samedi, je fais du bricolage.* I do DIY on Saturdays. **2** *vt* to do a makeshift job on *Le dossier de la chaise s'est cassé alors je l'ai bricolé comme j'ai pu.* The back of the chair broke, so I fixed it as best I could.

27.5 *Équipement* Equipment

outil *nm* tool *un outil pratique pour dénuder les fils électriques* a handy tool for stripping wires

boîte *nf* **à outils** tool box

sac *nm* **à outils** tool bag

jeu *nm* kit *un jeu de tournevis* a screwdriver kit

perceuse *nf* electric drill

perceuse *nf* **à main** hand drill

scie *nf* saw

ciseau *nm* chisel

ciseaux *nm pl* scissors

pince *nf* pliers

tenailles *nf pl* pincers

marteau *nm*, *pl* **-x** hammer

tournevis *nm* screwdriver

clef *nf* **à molette** BrE (adjustable) spanner AmE wrench

hache *nf* axe

lame *nf* [on axe, knife] blade

poignée *nf* [on axe, knife] handle

clou *nm* nail

vis *nf* screw

écrou *nm* nut

boulon *nm* bolt

27.6 *Peintures et papiers peints* Decorating

peinture *nf* **(en bâtiment)** painting and decorating

peintre *n* **(en bâtiment)** (painter and) decorator

peinture *nf* **1** [material] paint **2** [technique] painting **3** [effect on wall] decoration *Il faut refaire les peintures dans la cuisine.* The kitchen must be redecorated.

rouleau *nm*, *pl* **-x (à peinture)** (paint) roller

pinceau *nm*, *pl* **-x** paintbrush

lait *nm* **de chaux** whitewash *passer un mur au lait de chaux* to whitewash a wall

créosote *nf* creosote

papier *nm* **peint** wallpaper *un rouleau de papier peint* a roll of wallpaper *refaire les papiers peints dans une maison* to redecorate a house

colle *nf* [for wallpaper] wallpaper paste

échelle *nf* ladder

27.7 *Eau et électricité* Water and electricity

eau *nf* water *fermer l'eau* to switch off the water supply

plomberie *nf* [trade, also piping] plumbing

tuyau *nm*, *pl* **-x** [single tube] pipe *un tuyau de plomb* a (length of) lead pipe

canalisation *nf* [tube forming part of the system bringing water to or taking sewage out of a house] *Les canalisations sont à refaire.* The piping needs replacing.

électricité *nf* electricity *avoir l'électricité* to have electricity laid on *refaire l'électricité dans une maison* to have a house rewired

fiche *nf* plug

prise *nf* **1** [fixed, e.g. on wall] socket **2** [this term is often used informally as a synonym for **fiche**] plug

fil *nm* **électrique** (length of) BrE flex AmE electrical wire

rallonge *nf* BrE extension lead AmE extension cord

câble *nm* **électrique** (electric) cable

adaptateur *nm* adapter

fusible *nm* fuse

plombs *nm pl* [informal] fuses *Les plombs ont sauté.* The fuses have blown.

joint *nm* washer

27.8 *Construire et fabriquer* To build and to make

fabriquer {6} *vt* [general term. Create from raw materials] to make *fabriqué en France* made in France

produire {82} *vt* [economic term] to produce *Ils produisent des voitures de sport.* They produce sports cars.

27.9 *Fabrication industrielle* Manufacturing

fabrication *nf* manufacturing

fabricant, e *n* manufacturer *fabricant de meubles/boulons* manufacturer of furniture/bolts

produit *nm* **manufacturé** (industrial) product

usine *nf* [making raw materials or large objects] factory *usine sidérurgique* steel works *usine de composants pour l'aéronautique* aircraft components factory

fabrique *nf* [making consumer products] factory *une fabrique de pipes/gants* a pipe/glove factory *une fabrique d'appareils électro-ménagers* a factory making household electrical appliances

confection *nf* clothes manufacturing

27.10 *Construire des bâtiments* Constructing buildings

construire {82} *vt* [general term. Obj: e.g. house, high-rise building] to build

bâtir {19} *vt* [implies a greater, more complex building than **construire**. Obj: house, palace, cathedral] to build

matériaux *nm pl* **de construction** building materials
chantier nm (**de construction**) building site
entrepreneur *nm* (**en bâtiment**) builder
terrain *nm* **à bâtir** building site
permis *nm* **de construire** BrE planning permission AmE building permit

28 Machines and energy

28.1 *Machines* Machines

machine *nf* **1** [any mechanical object, particularly in an industrial setting] machine *faire qqch à la machine* to do sthg on a machine **2** [domestic. For sewing] (sewing) machine **3** [domestic. For typing] typewriter *tapé à la machine* typed **4** [domestic. For washing] (washing) machine *Donne-moi tes chaussettes, je les mets dans la machine.* Give me your socks, I'll put them in the machine.
appareil *nm* [machine sold complete with outer casing, etc for easier use] appliance
engin *nm* **1** [any equipment, particularly heavy] machine **2** [military] heavy vehicle
machine-outil *nm, pl* **machines-outils** machine-tool
moteur *nm* engine *à moteur* motorized
mécanisme *nm* mechanism
mécanicien, -cienne *n* **1** [who assembles or fixes machines] mechanic **2** [on a train] engine driver
usiner {6} *vt* to machine
usinage *nm* machining

28.2 *Quelques machines industrielles* Some industrial machines

pompe *nf* pump *pompe à air/vide* air/vacuum pump
presse *nf* press *presse hydraulique* hydraulic press
rotative *nf* rotary press
turbine *nf* turbine
réacteur *nm* reactor *réacteur nucléaire* nuclear reactor *réacteur à neutrons* neutron reactor *réacteur convertisseur* converter reactor
chaudière *nf* boiler

28.3 *Énergie* Energy

see also **27.7 Eau et électricité** and **7.7 Station service**
énergie *nf* energy *faire des économies d'énergie* to save energy *un dispositif qui permet de réaliser des économies d'énergie* an energy-saving device
énergétique *adj* [describes: e.g. supplies, policy] energy *les ressources énergétiques de notre pays* the energy resources of our country
alimentation *nf* supply *l'alimentation en électricité/gaz* the electricity/gas supply
combustible *nm* (type of) fuel *Quel combustible utilisez-vous?* What kind of fuel do you use?

Forms of energy
énergie nucléaire nuclear power
énergie éolienne wind power
énergie marémotrice tidal power
énergie solaire solar energy
énergie de remplacement alternative source of energy
énergie hydroélectrique hydroelectric power

gaz *nm* gas

Gas
In remote areas of France, people use bottles of gas, *des bouteilles de gaz*. In towns, gas is laid on and it is referred to as *gaz de ville*. Methane gas, for domestic consumption, is called *gaz naturel*.

charbon *nm* coal
pétrole *nm* oil
vapeur *nf* steam
marcher {6} *vt* to work *marcher au gaz/à l'électricité* to work by gas/electricity *Ça marche à quoi?* What does it run on?

29 Arranging and handling objects

29.1 *Méthodique* Orderly

see also **56.1 Classifier**
méthodique *adj* **1** [describes : e.g. person] methodical **2** [describes: e.g. survey, drawing, process] thorough
ordonné, e *adj* **1** [describes: e.g. room, work, person] organized
impeccable *adj* [describes: e.g. room, apron] spotless
systématique *adj* [describes: e.g. approach, preparation] methodical

29.2 *Méthodique et propre* Methodical and neat

see also **30.1 Propre**
net, nette *adj* neat (and tidy)
soigné, e *adj* [describes: e.g. person, piece of work] neat *Elle est toujours très soignée.* She is always very neat.
briqué, e *adj* [looking as though a lot of effort has gone into cleaning and tidying] spick and span
pimpant, e *adj* [suggests colourfulness and gaiety. Describes esp person's appearance, house, garden] smart

dans l'ordre
A phrase used in French betting systems, when you bet on three horses to win in the order which you name. *Elle a joué Baba, Bismuth et Blaireau gagnants dans l'ordre.* She bet on Baba, Bismuth and Blaireau to take first, second and third place respectively.

Locutions Idioms
tiré, e à quatre épingles [with not a hair out of place or a crease in one's clothing] dressed with the utmost care
sur son trente et un [in best clothes] dressed up to the nines

29.3 *Désordonné* Untidy

désordre *nm* **1** [lack of orderliness] untidiness **2** [things which are not in in any logical or practical order] mess *Il y avait du désordre dans toutes les chambres.* All the bedrooms were in a mess.
en désordre untidy

Dans le désordre
This is a phrase used in French betting systems, which allow bets to be placed on three horses. You name the three first horses without stating the order in which they will pass the post, and you stand to win less than if you had specified the order in which you thought they would win. *Il a joué Pipeau, Pair et Poireau gagnants dans le désordre.* He bet on Pipeau, Pair and Poireau to take the first three places in any order.

désordonné, e *adj* **1** [describes: person's habits] untidy **2** [describes: e.g. movements, actions] uncontrolled
fouillis *nm* [informal. Things heaped together] jumble
pagaille *nf* [informal. Things heaped together or disorganized system] shambles *Depuis qu'ils ont commencé les travaux c'est la pagaille au centre ville.* Since they started the roadworks the town centre has been a shambles.
en l'air [implies unusual and extreme mess, possibly as a result of violent actions] in a mess *Tout était en l'air dans la maison après le passage des cambrioleurs.* Everything in the house was upside down after the burglary.

Locutions Idioms
sens dessus dessous [literally: with its top part underneath] all topsy-turvy
Une chienne n'y retrouverait pas ses petits. [in such a mess that you could never find what you wanted in it, even if you had the instinct of a bitch looking for its young] You couldn't find anything in there in a month of Sundays.

29.4 *Groupes d'objets* Groups of objects

see also **58.3 Grande quantité**
collection *nf* **1** [objects with a feature in common, often valuable] collection **2** [of books, magazines] series
paire *nf* **1** [two objects] pair *une paire de bougeoirs* a pair of candlesticks **2** [one object with two parts] *une paire de jumelles* binoculars *une paire de lunettes* (a pair of) glasses
série *nf* [sequential] series
pile *nf* [objects neatly placed on top of one another] stack *une pile de livres* a stack of books *une pile de bois* a stack of wood
rang *nm* row
tas *nm* **1** [untidy] heap *un tas de vêtements* a heap of clothes **2** [of wood. Can be untidy or neat] heap *un beau tas de bois bien régulier* a nice neat pile of wood

29.5 *Mettre les objets en groupe* To group objects together

empiler {6} *vt* to stack
entasser {6} *vt* [less tidy than **empiler**] to heap up
amasser {6} *vt* [heap up in order to stock up] to accumulate *Ils amassaient leurs provisions dans des caves par crainte des restrictions.* They stockpiled food in cellars, fearing rationing.

Locutions Idioms
en rang d'oignon [lined-up neatly. Sometimes also implies arranged in order of size] in a row. *Toute la famille attendait en rang d'oignon devant la grille du jardin.* The whole family was lined up waiting outside the garden gate.
pêle-mêle higgledy-piggledy *Ils laissent toujours leurs habits pêle-mêle sur le fauteuil.* They always leave their clothes lying higgledy-piggledy on the armchair.

30 The cleanliness of objects

30.1 *Propre* Clean

see also **29.2 Méthodique et propre**
propre *adj* **1** [not dirty] clean **2** [not messy] neat
propreté *nf* cleanliness
impeccable *adj* immaculate *C'est toujours impeccable chez eux.* Their place is always immaculate.
hygiénique *adj* [respecting the rules of hygiene] hygienic

> ### usage
>
> **clair, e** *adj* and **pur, e** *adj*
> *De l'eau claire* is water devoid of any added component. For example, *rincer à l'eau claire* means to rinse in water that is free of any trace of detergent, shampoo, or whatever. *De l'eau pure* is water with no chemicals in it.

Locutions Idioms
propre comme un sou neuf as clean as a new penny

30.2 *Sale* Dirty

sale *adj* dirty *Tes mains sont sales.* Your hands are dirty.
saleté *nf* **1** [dirty appearance] dirtiness *La cuisine était d'une saleté repoussante.* The kitchen was filthy dirty. **2** [small particle] piece of dirt *avoir des saletés sous les ongles* to have dirt under one's nails
salissant, e *adj* [which gets dirty easily] which shows the dirt *Les vêtements blancs, c'est salissant.* White clothes shows the dirt.
crasseux, -sseuse *adj* [informal. Usu describes dirt on people or clothes] (filthy) dirty *Allez vous laver, vous êtes crasseux.* BrE Go and have a wash, you're filthy dirty. AmE Go wash yourself, you're filthy dirty.
crasse *nf* [informal] filth *La crasse recouvrait tous les meubles.* The furniture was filthy.
boueux, -boueuse *adj* [describes: e.g. boot, tyre, rugby shirt, dog] muddy
boue *nf* mud
crotté, e *adj* [covered in mud and dirt from the street This word, in spite of its literal association with *crotte*, 'excrement', is neutral, and is often used in storytelling] covered in muck
dégueulasse *adj* [very informal, commonly used term. Dirty from any kind of source of dirt] filthy

30.3 *Rendre les choses sales* To make things dirty

salir {19} *vt* [obj: e.g. garment, floor] to make dirty, to get dirt on *En sortant la bicyclette du garage, j'ai sali mes gants.* I got dirt on my gloves while taking the bicycle out of the garage.
se salir *v refl* [become covered in dirt or any substance that spoils the clean look of an object] to get dirty *J'habillerai les enfants à la dernière minute pour éviter qu'ils ne se salissent.* I'll dress the children at the last minute so that they won't get dirty. *L'argenterie se salit très vite.* Silver gets dirty very quickly.
polluer {6} *vt* [spoil the environment. Obj: e.g. water, air, river] to pollute

pollution *nf* pollution *la pollution de l'eau* the pollution of water

noircir {19} **1** *vi* to go black **2** *vt* [obj: e.g. face, hands] to make black *L'encre d'imprimerie noircit les doigts.* Printer's ink makes your fingers black.

noir de black with *les yeux noirs de khôl* eyes black with kohl *un mur noir de suie* a wall black with soot

tacher {6} **1** *vi* to stain *Le jus de cassis tache.* Blackcurrant juice stains. **2** *vt* [accidentally] to make a stain on *J'ai taché le tapis en renversant du vin.* I made a stain on the carpet when I spilt some wine.

tache *nf* stain *une tache de jus de tomate* a tomato juice stain

marquer {6} *vi* to leave a mark *Quelqu'un a mis ses doigts sur le miroir et ça a marqué.* Somebody touched the mirror with their fingers and it left a mark.

traînée *nf* smear

Locutions Idioms

sale comme un peigne ALSO **cochon** [used of people] disgustingly dirty

Il n'est pas à prendre avec des pincettes. He's so dirty you wouldn't want to touch him with a bargepole.

30.4 *Le ménage* Housework

laver {6} *vt* [general term] to wash

se laver *v refl* to wash *Le coton se lave facilement.* BrE Cotton washes easily. AmE Cotton cleans easily. *La laine se lave à l'eau tiède.* Wool should be washed in warm water.

nettoyer {17} *vt* [describes any cleaning process] to clean *nettoyer à sec* to dry-clean *faire nettoyer une veste à sec* to have a jacket dry-cleaned

nettoyage *nm* cleaning *nettoyage de printemps* spring-cleaning

nettoyage *nm* **à sec** dry-cleaning

ménage *nm* housework *faire le ménage dans une maison* to do the housework *Ce matin, il faut que je fasse le ménage (dans la maison).* I must do the housework this morning. *Entrez mais ne faites pas attention, le ménage n'a pas été fait.* Come in but don't look, the place is a mess.

femme *nf* **de ménage** cleaner

entretien *nm* [long-term] looking after, upkeep *C'est moi qui m'occupe de l'entretien des parquets dans la maison.* I look after all the parquet floors in the house.

30.5 *Nettoyer avec des liquides* To clean with liquids

see also **30.9 Lavage des vêtements**

nettoyer {17} *vt* [remove dirt by any means. Obj: e.g. floor, table, dish] to clean

laver {6} *vt* [with a liquid. Obj: e.g. floor, table, dish] to wash

tremper {6} *vt* to soak

trempage *nm* [process] soaking

frotter {6} *vt* to scrub

rincer {7} *vt* to rinse

rinçage *nm* [process] rinsing

javelliser {6} *vt* to bleach

eau *nf* **de javel** bleach

javel *nf* [informal] bleach *Passe le carrelage de la salle de bain à la javel.* Clean the bathroom tiles with bleach.

éponge *nf* sponge

éponger {8} *vt* to mop up (with a sponge)

30.6 *Nettoyer les sols* To clean floors

aspirateur *nm* vacuum cleaner *J'ai passé l'aspirateur dans la chambre.* I vacuumed the bedroom.

aspirer {6} *vt* [applies to pieces of fluff, etc. Subj: vacuum cleaner] to suck up *Ça aspire bien.* It's got powerful suction.

lave-pont *nm, pl* **lave-ponts** mop

serpillière *nf* floorcloth *passer la serpillière* to mop (the floor)

balayer {16} *vt* [with a broom] to sweep

balai *nm* broom

balayette *nf* [appliance which goes with dustpan] brush

pelle *nf* dustpan

30.7 *Nettoyer les surfaces* To clean surfaces

brosse *nf* [for soft furnishings and hard surfaces] brush

chiffon *nm* rag

chiffon *nm* **à poussière** [for dusting] cloth *Elle passe le chiffon à poussière sur les meubles toutes les semaines.* She dusts the furniture every week.

plumeau *nm, pl* **-x** feather duster *passer le plumeau* to dust (with a feather duster)

dépoussiérer {10} *vt* [obj: e.g. ornament, mantelpiece] to dust

essuyer {17} *vt* **1** [remove dust or spillage] to wipe (off) **2** [dry after washing] to wipe (down)

encaustiquer {6} *vt* to polish

encaustique *nm* (furniture) polish

brosser {6} *vt* to brush

30.8 *Faire la vaisselle* To wash up

vaisselle *nf* **1** [things to be washed up or that have been washed up] dishes **2** [process] washing-up *faire la vaisselle* BrE to do the washing-up AmE to do the dishes

lave-vaisselle *nm inv* [machine] dishwasher

liquide *nf* ALSO **produit** *nm* **à vaisselle** washing-up liquid

torchon *nm* **(à vaisselle)** drying-up cloth

lavette *nf* BrE dishcloth AmE dishrag

eau *nf* **de vaisselle** BrE washing-up water AmE dishwater

30.9 *Lavage des vêtements* Laundering clothes

see also **30.5 Nettoyer avec des liquides**

lessive *nf* **1** [product, powder or liquid] detergent **2** [action] laundering **3** [clothes needing washing or that have been washed] wash(ing)

lessiver {6} *vt* [term used in instructions. Implies use of water] to launder

blanchissage *nm* [in spite of the word stem *blanc*, this refers to cleaning any colour. It refers to cleaning done by a business or an individual for a customer.] laundering *porter qqch au blanchissage* to have sthg cleaned

buanderie *nf* [old-fashioned term] utility room

machine *nf* **à laver,** ALSO **lave-linge** *nm inv* washing machine

séchoir *nm* **à tambour** tumble-drier

corde *nf* **à linge** clothes line

pince *nf* **à linge** BrE clothes peg AmE clothes pin

adoucissant *nm* BrE fabric conditioner AmE fabric softener

amidon *nm* starch *amidon en bombe* spray starch *passer des cols de chemise à l'amidon* to starch shirt collars

détachant *nm* stain remover

repasser {6} *vt* to iron
fer *nm* **à repasser** iron
planche *nf* **à repasser** ironing board
étendre {53} *vt* [obj: e.g. clothes, laundry] to hang out/up
  Je vais étendre mon ligne. I'll hang out my washing.

31 Closing, enclosing and fastening objects

31.1 *Fermeture* Closing

fermer {6} **1** *vt* [obj: e.g. door, lid, box, cupboard, car, room, shop] to close **2** *vi* [subj: e.g. box, purse, drawer, shop] to close *Ça ferme bien/mal.* It's easy/hard to close.
se fermer *v refl* [subj: e.g. door, car door, eye, bolt] to shut
enfermer {6} *vt* [place someone or something inside so that they cannot get out] to shut in *N'enferme pas le chat dans la maison.* Don't shut the cat in the house.
refermer {6} *vt* [after having opened] to shut (again)
serrure *nf* lock
verrou *nm* bolt
cadenas *nm* padlock
fermé, e *adj* shut
hermétique *adj* tightly shut
scellé, e *adj* sealed
verrouillé, e *adj* bolted

31.2 *Ouverture* Opening

ouvert, e *adj* open
grand ouvert *adj*, *f* **grande ouverte** wide open
entr'ouvert, e *adj* ajar
béant, e *adj* gaping wide
ouvrir {27} **1** *vt* [obj: e.g. door, box, lid, shop] to open **2** *vi* [subj: e.g. shop] to open
s'ouvrir *v refl* [subj: e.g. oyster, box, drawer] to open
réouvrir ALSO **rouvrir** {27} *vt* and *vi* to reopen
clef *nf* ALSO **clé** *nf* key

31.3 *Couvert* Covered

couvert, e *adj* [with a cover, lid or roof on. Describes: e.g. bed, saucepan, market, swimming pool] covered
couvrir {27} *vt* [in order to protect or to hide something] to cover
recouvrir {27} *vt* **1** [completely] to cover *Une épaisse couche de neige recouvrait toute chose dans la campagne.* A thick layer of snow covered the whole countryside. *Il faut que je recouvre tous les meubles avant que les peintres n'arrivent.* I must cover up all the furniture before the painters come. **2** [when renovating furniture] to make new fitted covers for **3** [provide with extra protection. Obj: e.g. book, exercise book] to cover
envelopper {6} *vt* [to protect or to hide something. Subj: esp cloth, paper, plastic] to wrap (up) *Enveloppe bien les sandwiches pour le pique-nique.* Wrap the sandwiches up carefully for the picnic.

étendre {53} *vt* [obj: e.g. layer, coating] to apply, to spread
emballer {6} *vt* [cover completely, usu before an object is posted] to wrap (up) completely
habiller {6} *vt* [technical term used by: e.g. decorators, packagers, etc] to cover *une bouteille habillée avec de la paille* a bottle covered with a sheath of straw
napper {6} *vt* (often followed by *de* + noun) [cooking term. Cover with a thick, decorative layer of sauce] to coat

31.4 *Choses faites pour couvrir* Coverings

couverture *nf* **1** [on roof] roof *Tous les 20 ans, nous sommes obligés de refaire la couverture*. Every 20 years we have to have the roof redone. **2** [of a book] cover **3** [bag for clothes] BrE suit bag AmE garment bag
couvercle *nm* [for saucepan, container] lid
housse *nf* **1** [for piano, furniture, clothes. Loosely fitted to the shape of the object covered] loose cover **2** [for use: e.g. as protection for furniture when decorating] dust sheet, dust cover
protège-cahier *nm*, *pl* **protège-cahiers** [to keep exercise books clean] cover
emballage *nm* packaging

31.5 *Découvert* Uncovered

nu, e *adj* **1** [lacking its usual protective or ornamental cover. Describes: e.g. electric wire, brick, blade] exposed **2** [without clothes] bare
dénudé, e *adj* [describes: e.g. electric wire, tree] bare
nu-tête *adv* without a hat (on)
nu-pieds *adv* barefoot
nu-jambes *adv* barelegged
exposer {6} *vt* [place on show] to bare *exposer ses seins sur une plage* to bare one's breasts on a beach
révéler {10} *vt* [allow to show, for effect] to show off *une robe courte qui révélait des jambes incomparables* a short dress showing off a matchless pair of legs
en plein air [in a place without a roof] in the open *un marché en plein air* an open-air market *piscine de plein air* outdoor swimming pool

31.6 *Cavités et espaces* Cavities and hollow spaces

see also **91.14 Couper des matériaux durs**
espace *nm* space *L'herbe pousse dans les espaces entre les pavés*. Grass grows in the spaces between the paving stones.
cavité *nf* [hollow space, in a solid body] cavity
anfractuosité *nf* [hollow space in rock or cliff] hole *Les enfants aimaient se cacher dans les anfractuosités de la falaise*. The children liked to hide in the holes in the cliffs.
trou *nm* [an opening going right through an object or allowing entry into it] hole *Si tu fais un trou dans le ballon, il va éclater*. If you pierce a hole in the balloon, it will burst.
trouer {6} *vt* to make a hole in *Le chien a réussi a trouer le grillage*. The dog managed to make a hole in the chicken wire.
troué, e *adj* with a hole in it, with holes in it *un collant troué à plusieurs endroits* a pair of tights holed in several places *troué aux coudes* worn out at the elbows
percé, e *adj* [with a very small hole or holes through it] pierced
piquer {6} *vt* to make small holes in *Piquez votre rôti et mettez-y de l'ail*. Make small incisions in your joint and insert garlic in them.

intervalle *nm* [between two objects, two houses, two lines of print] gap
puits *nm* **1** [for drawing water] well **2** [in mining] *puits (de mine)* shaft
fente *nf* [long and narrow] slit
crevasse *nf* **1** [in skin] crack *J'ai des crevasses aux mains*. I have chapped skin on my hands. **2** [on the earth's surface] crack **3** [in ice on: e.g. a glacier] crevasse
orifice *nm* **1** [in the body] orifice **2** [in a wall, hole affording a narrow passage or a view into the space beyond] hole

Locutions Idioms
boire comme un trou to drink like a fish
faire son trou to create a niche for oneself

31.7 *Objets faits pour attacher* Fasteners

épingle *nf* pin *épingle de sûreté* ALSO *à nourrice* safety pin
crochet *nm* [on a door, a lid] hook
agrafe *nf* **1** [on a skirt, a bra] hook **2** [on a document] staple
trombone *nm* (paper) clip
ficelle *nf* string
corde *nf* rope *un bout de corde* a length of rope
fil *nm* **de fer** (metal) wire
ficelle *nf* string *un bout de ficelle* a piece of string
chaîne *nf* chain

32 Usefulness of objects

32.1 *Utilisation* Use

utilisation *nf* [doing something with materials] use *L'utilisation de crèmes protectrices est à recommander lors des premières expositions au soleil*. Use sunscreens until you get accustomed to the sun. *C'est un matériel d'utilisation courante*. This equipment is in general use.
utiliser {6} *vt* [general term] to use *Je n'utilise que des produits biologiques*. I use only organic produce. *Elle a utilisé le tabouret comme pied de table*. She used the stool as a table leg. *À utiliser de préférence avant le 8/9/99*. Use before 8/9/99.
se servir de {35} *v refl* [same as **utiliser**] to use *Apprends-lui à se servir d'une fourchette*. Teach him to use a fork.
usage *nm* **1** [stresses the way and the length of time during which one uses something] use *un vêtement/une machine qui peut encore faire de l'usage* a garment/a machine that can still be of use *Je te prête mon VTT mais fais-en bon usage*. I'll lend you my mountain bike but do look after it. *pour mon usage personnel* for my own use *à l'usage de* for the use of *à usage externe* for external use only *hors d'usage* no longer in use **2** [in language, in society] usage *L'usage veut que . . .* Usage dictates that . . .
user {6} *vi* (always + *de*) *user de patience avec qqn* to be (especially) patient with sb *user d'un stratagème* to employ a stratagem
exploitation *nf* **1** [economic or ecological term] use *L'exploitation des ressources de notre planète doit être repensée*. We must rethink the use to which we put the resources of our planet. *des gisements charbonniers qui ne sont plus en exploitation* disused coalfields. **2** [pejorative] exploiting *Ils se sont enrichis grâce à l'exploitation d'une main-d'œuvre à bon marché*. They grew rich by exploiting cheap labour.

exploiter {6} vt **1** [in mining. Obj: e.g. deposit, coalfield] to work **2** [make good use of. Obj: e.g. possibility, opportunity] to use **3** [pejorative. Obj: e.g. worker, woman] to exploit

abus nm [using illegally or in a way detrimental to health] abuse *l'abus d'alcool* alcohol abuse *commettre un abus de privilèges* to abuse one's privileged position

abuser {6} vi (always + de) to abuse *abuser des somnifères* to abuse sleeping pills *abuser des sanctions pénales* to rely too heavily on custodial sentences

emploi nm [putting a specified object to use] use *On peut critiquer l'emploi de cette illustration pour la couverture du livre.* The use of this picture for the cover of the book is debatable. *Nous conseillons l'emploi d'un abrasif pour le nettoyage du four.* We recommend using a scouring product to clean the oven. *des techniques d'emploi courant* techniques in general use

mode nm **d'emploi** directions for use

prêt, e à l'emploi ready for use

employer {17} vt [obj: e.g. talent, phrase, technique] to use *Il voudrait employer ses connaissances en informatique.* He'd like to use his computer skills. *employer la violence* to use force *employer un langage châtié* to use very polite language

inusité, e adj [term used only when talking about language] not used *Le participe passé du verbe 'paître' est 'pu', mais il est inusité sauf en termes de fauconnerie.* The past participle of the verb 'paître' is 'pu', but is used only in the language of falconry.

32.2 *Contenants* Containers

Names of different containers
Boîtes
une boîte à œufs an eggbox
une boîte à ordures BrE a rubbish bin AmE garbage can
une boîte à pharmacie a first aid kit
une boîte à thé a tea caddy
une boîte de bière a can of beer
une boîte de conserve a tin can (beans, sardines, etc)
une boîte en carton a cardboard box

Bouteilles
une bouteille de vin/d'huile a bottle of wine/oil
une bouteille thermos ® a thermos (flask)
une bouteille de gaz a gas cylinder

Caisses
une caisse à outils a toolbox
une caisse d'emballage a packing crate

Cartons
un carton pour dossiers a box file
un carton à chapeau a hatbox
un carton à chaussures a shoebox
un carton à dessins a portfolio
un carton de 6/12 bouteilles de vin a case (of 6 or 12 bottles) of wine

Casiers
un casier à bouteilles a wine rack
un casier à disques a record rack
un casier à bagages a locker

Écrins et étuis
un écrin à bijoux a jewellery box
un écrin à argenterie, ALSO **un étui à couverts** BrE a canteen AmE a silverware box

un étui à cigarettes a cigarette case
un étui à lunettes a spectacle case
un étui à violon a violin case

Flacons
un flacon (de détachant) a bottle (of stain remover)
un flacon (de parfum) a bottle (of perfume)

Paniers
un panier à bouteilles a bottle carrier
un panier à couverts a cutlery basket
un panier à diapositives a slide holder
un panier à provisions a shopping basket

Paquets
un paquet de bonbons a bag of sweets
un paquet de chips BrE a bag of crisps AmE chips
un paquet de sucre a packet of sugar

Sacs
un sac à dos BrE a rucksack AmE backpack
un sac à pommes de terre a potato sack
un sac en plastique a plastic bag
un sac poubelle BrE a (dust) bin bag AmE garbage bag

Trousses
une trousse à ongles a manicure set
une trousse de toilette BrE a sponge bag AmE cosmetics bag
une trousse (de médecin) a doctor's bag

Others
un bocal a (preserving) jar
un pack de bière a six-pack, a twelve-pack
une poche (plastique) a plastic bag (not a carrier bag from a shop)
un coffret a gift box

Cageots
Cageots are open crates made of wood or plastic, used by wholesalers and greengrocers for handling fruit and vegetables. The word also refers to wooden or cardboard trays holding a large retail quantity of fruit (24 peaches, 10 melons, etc), which you can buy in the summer in shops and supermarkets.

Conditionnements et emballages
Le conditionnement is the process of protecting an item from damage and displaying it to the purchaser. The word applies mainly to foodstuffs and drink. L'emballage refers to the packaging of an object for sale or for dispatch. Similarly, un conditionnement is a package or a form of packaging mostly used for food and drink, whereas un emballage can refer to any piece of packaging: e.g.
Le conditionnement des eaux minérales se fait de plus en plus sous plastique. Plastic is being increasingly used for packaging mineral water. *J'ai jeté l'emballage.* I threw away the packaging.
du papier fort pour l'emballage des manuscrits strong paper to wrap manuscripts in
des vis sous (un) emballage plastique plastic-wrapped screws

Gift-wrapping
Shops selling confectionery, flowers or small consumer goods like books, records, shavers, toys, ties, etc, provide gift-wrapping, sometimes elaborate and always free. The way to ask for this service is e.g.: *Pouvez-vous me faire un paquet-cadeau?* Would you gift-wrap it for me?

32.3 *Utile* Useful

utile *adj* **1** [able to help] useful *se rendre utile* to do something useful **2** [in a position to serve the interests of someone] useful *Cultivez de bon rapports avec le maire, il peut vous être utile un jour.* Keep in with the mayor, he could be useful to you one day.

commode *adj* convenient

par commodité for convenience

pratique *adj* **1** [describes: e.g. gadget, tool, product] handy, convenient *C'est bien pratique, un téléphone sans fil.* A cordless telephone is a very handy thing to have. **2** [describes: e.g. timing, arrangement] convenient *L'école a demandé qu'on vienne chercher les enfants à 16 heures précises mais ce n'est pas très pratique pour les parents qui travaillent.* The school has asked that children be collected no later than 4 p.m. but it's not very convenient for working parents.

convivial, e *adj, pl* **-viaux** [in computing] user-friendly *Tu as vu leur dernière version du SX280? Elle est beaucoup plus conviviale.* Have you seen their latest version of the SX280? It's much more user-friendly.

32.4 *Inutile* Useless

inutile *adj* [describes: e.g. comings and goings, discussion, information, attempts] pointless

inutilisable *adj* [which cannot be used] unusable *Le cadenas est tellement rouillé qu'il est inutilisable.* The padlock is so rusty that it's unusable.

bon à rien *adj* and *nm*, **bonne à rien** *adj* and *nf* good-for-nothing *Ça ne sert à rien.* It's useless. *Il ne sert à rien de . . . * It's useless to . . .

32.5 *Ordures* Rubbish/Garbage

ordures *nf pl* BrE rubbish AmE garbage

déchets *nm pl* waste

papiers *nm pl* **(gras)** litter

égout *nm* sewer *les égouts* the sewerage system

broyeur *nm* [in a domestic kitchen] BrE waste-disposal (unit) AmE garbage disposal

vide-ordures *nm inv* [in block of flats] BrE rubbish chute AmE garbage chute

décharge *nf* **(municipale)** BrE council rubbish dump AmE city dump

grande poubelle *nf* BrE skip AmE dumpster

benne *nf* **(à ordures)** BrE dustcart AmE garbage truck

éboueur *nm* BrE dustman AmE garbage man

poubelle *nf* BrE dustbin AmE garbage can

ramassage *nm* **des ordures** BrE rubbish collection AmE trash collection

32.6 *Éliminer* To get rid of

éliminer {6} *vt* **1** [in a logical process] to eliminate *Éliminons tout de suite l'hypothèse du suicide.* We can eliminate from the start the theory that it was suicide **2** [in politics. Obj: e.g. party, opposition] to suppress **3** [kill for motives of self-interest. Obj: esp political enemy, rival] to do away with

supprimer {6} *vt* **1** [no longer include in one's diet] to avoid *Il faut que vous supprimiez tous les sucres (de votre alimentation).* You must avoid eating anything with sugar in it. **2** [in a round of cuts] to do away with *Ils menacent de supprimer les prêts inter-bibliothèques.* They're threatening to do away with the inter-library loan service.

jeter {11} *vt* to throw (away) *Ces mandarines avariées sont bonnes à jeter!* These rotten mandarins are good only for the dustbin!

jetable *adj* disposable

se débarrasser {6} *v refl* (+ *de*) [obj: something or someone that is felt to be a burden] to get rid of *Je travaillerai toute la matinée s'il le faut, mais je veux me débarrasser de cette corvée!* I'll work all morning if necessary, but I want to get this chore out of the way!

32.7 *Synonymes familiers* Informal words for throwing away

All the informal or strong verbs below can be translated into stronger BrE English by adding 'flipping', 'sodding' or even stronger ' . . . ing' words according to strength of feeling and company present.

ficher en l'air [informal. Usu in the perfect tense] to throw away *Je ne retrouve plus la lettre des impôts, j'espère que je ne l'ai pas fichue en l'air!* I can't find the letter from the tax people, I hope I didn't throw it away!

foutre en l'air [same meaning and usage as **ficher en l'air**, but a much stronger use of language] to chuck out *Fous-moi ces vieilleries en l'air!* Chuck out this load of old crap!

mettre, ALSO **flanquer** [informal], ALSO **foutre** [a very strong but commonly used term] **à la porte** [remove from one's home, or dismiss from a job, often in a violent or abrupt manner] to throw out *J'ai été mis à la porte sans préavis.* I was thrown out without notice. *S'ils recommencent, je les fous à la porte!* If they do it again, I'll throw them out!

balancer {7} *vt* [very informal. Obj: e.g. papers, old furniture] to chuck out

33 Age

33.1 *Bébés* Babies

see also **34.2 Enfants**
bébé *nm* baby *Elle va avoir un bébé à Pâques.* She's having a baby at Easter.
jumeau *nm* [male] twin *des jumeaux* [two males, or one male and one female] twins *vrais jumeaux* identical twins *faux jumeaux* non-identical twins
jumelle *nf* [female] twin *des jumelles* [two females] twins
triplés *nm pl*, **triplées** *nfpl* triplets
quadruplés *nm pl*, **quadruplées** *nf pl* quadruplets

> ### u s a g e
>
> **jumeaux, triplés, quadruplés**
> The masculine plural can refer to boys only, or to any combination where there is at least one boy: *Les triplés, Laura, Tania et Joseph, se portent bien.* The triplets, Laura, Tania and Joseph, are doing well.

33.2 *Avoir un bébé* To have a baby

concevoir {38} *vt* and *vi* to conceive
conception *nf* conception *dès la conception* from the moment the baby is conceived
enceinte *adj f* pregnant *quand j'étais enceinte (de Paul)* when I was pregnant (with Paul) *enceinte de trois mois* three months pregnant
grossesse *nf* pregnancy *au milieu de sa grossesse* in the middle of her pregnancy *une grossesse difficile* a difficult pregnancy
foetus *nm* foetus
embryon *nm* embryo
utérus *nm* [in common and medical usage] womb, uterus *col de l'utérus* neck of the womb
cordon *nm* **ombilical**, *pl* **cordons ombilicaux** umbilical cord
placenta *nm* placenta
travail *nm* **(de l'accouchement)** labour *commencer le travail* to go into labour
naissance *nf* birth *donner naissance (à)* to give birth (to) *Vas-tu assister à la naissance?* Will you be present at the birth? *son poids de naissance* her birth weight

> ### u s a g e
>
> **naître** {65} *vi* and **né, e** *adj*
> The verb **naître** means to be born and can be used in any tense, including the narrative present: *Il naît en 1974, dans une famille aisée.* He was born in 1974 into a well-to-do family. As an adjective, **née** can also be used to specify a woman's maiden name, although this practice is nowadays confined to official documents. The phrase '*né à*' followed by a blank space on an official document means 'birthplace'.

33.3 *Les bébés et la médecine moderne* Babies and modern medicine

avorter {6} *vi* **1** [naturally or voluntarily] to have an abortion **2** [voluntarily] *se faire avorter* to have an abortion **avortement** *nm* abortion
interruption *nf* **volontaire de grossesse** ALSO **IVG** *nf* (planned) abortion
insémination *nf* **artificielle** artificial insemination
mère *nf* **de substitution** surrogate mother
bébé-éprouvette *nm, pl* **bébés-éprouvettes** test-tube baby
FIV, ALSO **fivete** *nf* [spells 'fécondation in vitro'] in vitro fertilization
échographie *nf* ultra-sound scan *on a vu à l'échographie que . . .* we saw on the scan that . . .

33.4 *Gardiens de bébés* People who care for babies

nourrice *nf* [looks after babies and toddlers, usu in their own home] BrE babyminder AmE babysitter
baby-sitter *n, pl* **baby-sitters** baby-sitter
baby-sitting *nm* baby-sitting *faire du baby-sitting* to babysit
adopter {6} *vt* to adopt
adoption *nf* adoption
nourricier, -cière *adj* foster (as adj) *famille nourricière* foster family
garde *nf* custody *avoir la garde d'un enfant* to have custody of a child
droit *nm* **de visite** rights of access
orphelin, e *n* and *adj* orphan

33.5 *Équipement de puériculture* Baby equipment

berceau *nm, pl* **-x** BrE cot AmE crib
moïse *nm*, ALSO **couffin** *nm* Moses basket
porte-bébé *nm, pl* **porte-bébés 1** [made of cloth] baby-sling **2** [wicker basket] Moses (basket) **3** [made of plastic] carry-cot
hochet *nm* rattle
biberon *nm* bottle
tétine *nf* **1** [on bottle] BrE teat AmE nipple **2** [pacifier] BrE dummy AmE pacifier
sucette, ALSO **tétine** *nf* [pacifier] dummy
bavoir *nm* bib
couche *nf*, ALSO **change** *nm* BrE nappy AmE diaper *couche jetable* BrE disposable nappy AmE disposable diaper
épingle *nf* **à nourrice** safety pin
landau *nm* [old-fashioned] BrE pram AmE baby carriage
poussette *nf* BrE pushchair AmE stroller
poussette-cane *nf, pl* **poussettes-canes** [often folding] BrE baby buggy AmE umbrella stroller

33.6 *Ancien* Old

see also **12.4 Vieillot**

âgé, e *adj* **1** [when talking about people] elderly **2** (always + *de*)[when stating someone's age, however young] *un bébé âgé de 18 mois* an 18-month old baby *La victime était âgée de 49 ans.* The victim was 49 years old.

âge *nm* **1** [the number of years a person has lived, or the number of weeks or months when talking about a baby] age *Quel âge as-tu?* How old are you? *quand tu auras mon âge* when you get to my age **2** [fact of aging] age *On change avec l'âge.* People change with age.

> ### u s a g e
>
> **vieux** before or after the noun
> 1. The masculine singular form *vieux* changes to *vieil* before a noun beginning with a vowel or a silent 'h': e.g. *un vieil aspirateur* an old vacuum-cleaner, *un vieil hôtel* an old hotel.
> 2. *Vieux* normally comes before the noun except in phrases like *un vin vieux* a wine that has been aged. The other exception is when *vieux* is followed by one or more other adjectives also describing the noun: e.g. *une voiture vieille et sale* a dirty old car

vieux, vieille *adj* **1** [not young] old *un vieil arbre* an old tree **2** [not new] old *un vieux radiateur qui ne marche plus* an old radiator which no longer works **3** [former] old *Recopiez les vieux documents sur une disquette avant de les effacer de votre disque dur.* Copy the old files onto a floppy disk before you erase them from your hard disk. **4** [in insulting phrases, regardless of the victim's age] *vieil imbécile* old fool *vieille bique* old hag

vieux *nm* **1** [informal for **âgé**. May be used offensively] old man **2** [slang for father] *mon vieux* my old man *Le vieux prenait toujours son café sous les tilleuls.* The old man always took coffee under the lime trees.

vieille *nf* [informal and offensive] old woman *L'enfant arriva près de la fontaine où elle trouva une vieille qui l'attendait.* The child came to the fountain where she found an old woman waiting for her.

vieillesse *nf* [when talking about people or pets] old age

> ### u s a g e
>
> **ancien** before or after the noun
> *Ancien* normally comes before the noun, except when it means 'antique'.
> **ancien, -cienne** *adj* **1** [going back a very long time] ancient *D'anciennes querelles les opposent encore.* They are still fighting old battles. **2** [the one that existed before, as opposed to the current one] former *L'hôtel a été construit à l'emplacement de l'ancienne écurie.* The hotel was built on the spot where the former stables were. *un ancien élève* a former pupil **3** [valuable because it was made a long time ago. Describes: e.g. furniture, instrument, book] antique *des fauteuils anciens* antique armchairs

ancienneté *nf* [refers to time spent in a position] seniority

33.7 Euphémismes pour dire âgé Euphemisms for aged

d'un certain âge getting on a bit

personne du troisième âge BrE old age pensioner AmE retired person

personne du quatrième âge very elderly person

33.8 *Place dans la famille selon l'âge* Ranking within the family according to age

aîné, e *adj* and *n* **1** [the first-born] eldest *Elle a eu son aînée juste après la guerre.* She had her first child just after the war. *Dans ces familles-là, on servait toujours l'aîné en premier.* In those families the eldest brother was always served first **2** [one of several older siblings] elder *Mes aînés m'ont toujours protégé des brimades à l'école.* My older brothers and sisters always protected me against bullying at school. *Les deux aînés sont devenus médecins.* The two elder children became doctors.

cadet *nm* younger brother

cadette *nf* younger sister *Je suis la cadette de Marie.* I'm Marie's younger sister.

cadet, -ette *adj* younger *mon frère cadet* my younger brother

benjamin, e *n* youngest (child) *François est le benjamin* François is the youngest (in the family)

33.9 *Jeune* Young

jeune *adj* **1** [person aged approximately 10 to 20] young **2** [person from a later generation than one's own] younger *Les gens qui sont jeunes peuvent se permettre de travailler douze heures par jour, mais moi j'ai besoin de repos.* Younger people can afford to work a twelve-hour day but I need my rest. **3** [animal or bird that is not fully grown] immature

jeune *nm* young man *Demande au jeune qui est là-bas, il a l'air de connaître le quartier.* Ask the young man over there, he seems to know the area *les jeunes* the young *Nous les jeunes, on veut un avenir correct.* Young people want a proper future.

jeune *nf* young woman

jeunesse *nf* **1** [time of life] youth **2** [group within a population. In this sense, the term tends to be used by people who are not themselves 'young'] the young *Ça plaît à la jeunesse.* Young people like it.

juvénile *adj* **1** [biological term] juvenile *acné juvénile* juvenile acne **2** [used pejoratively. Not sophisticated] immature *humour juvénile* childish humour **3** [used as praise] youthful *fougue juvénile* youthful enthusiasm.

Locutions Idioms
La jeunesse n'a qu'un temps. You're only young once.
Il faut que jeunesse se passe. Youth will have its fling.

33.10 *Inexpérience* Inexperience

inexpérimenté, e *adj* inexperienced

inexpérience *nf*, ALSO **manque** *nm* **d'expérience** inexperience

naïf, naïve *adj* naive **naïf, naïve** *n* naive person **naïveté** *nf* naivety **naïvement** *adv* naively

Locution Idiom
C'est un blanc-bec. [humorous. Term used to tease or talk teasingly about an inexperienced man] He's still wet behind the ears.

34 The family

34.1 *Père et mère* Parents

père *nm* [formal when used as a term of address] father
papa *nm* dad(dy) *Elle peut emprunter la voiture de son papa.* She can borrow her dad's car.
mère *nf* [formal when used as a term of address] mother
maman *nf* BrE mum(my) AmE mom(my)

> ### u s a g e
>
> **parent, e** *n* and *adj*
> In French *un parent* can mean one's father or mother or a relative. Similarly, *mes parents* can be my mother and father, or my relatives. *Nous sommes parents* means 'we're related'. But *une parente* can only be a female relative, not one's female parent.

34.2 *Enfants* Children

enfant *nm* child *Elle est l'enfant de ma cousine.* She's my cousin's child.
fils *nm* son
fiston *nm* [informal] son *Ça va, ton fiston?* How's your boy?
fille *nf* daughter
frère *nm* brother
sœur *nf* sister
frangin, e *n* [informal] [male] brother [female] sister

> ### u s a g e
>
> **frère et sœur**
> This phrase is used to express the idea of siblings: e.g. *Bien que frère et sœur, ils ne se ressemblent pas.* Despite being siblings, they don't look like each other.

34.3 *Grands-parents et petits-enfants* Grandparents and grandchildren

grands-parents *mpl* grandparents *Il voit ses grands-parents paternels et maternels.* He sees both sets of grandparents.
grand-père *nm, pl* **grands-pères** grandfather
grand-mère *nf, pl* **grands-mères** grandmother
mamie, ALSO **mémé, mamé, mémère** *nf* BrE granny AmE grandma
papy *nm,* ALSO **pépé, papé, pépère** *nm* BrE grandad AmE grandpa
petit-fils *nm, pl* **petits-fils** grandson
petite-fille *nf, pl* **petites-filles** granddaughter
petit-enfant *nm, pl* **petits-enfants** grandchildren

> ### u s a g e
>
> **arrière-** *pref*
> To refer to one generation further up or down the family tree, use **arrière-** as a prefix: *mon arrière-petit-fils* my great-grandson, *leur arrière-grand-mère* their great-grandmother

34.4 *Alliance* Marriage

par alliance by marriage *cousin par alliance* cousin by marriage
mari *nm* husband
femme *nf* wife
beau-père *nm, pl* **beaux-pères 1** [father of spouse] father-in-law **2** [second husband of mother] stepfather
belle-mère *nf, pl* **belles-mères 1** [mother of spouse] mother-in-law **2** [second wife of father] stepmother
beau-fils *nm, pl* **beaux-fils 1** [husband of daughter] son-in-law **2** [son of spouse] stepson
belle-fille, *nf, pl* **belles-filles 1** [wife of son] daughter-in-law **2** [daughter of spouse] stepdaughter
gendre *nm* [husband of daughter] son-in-law
bru *nf* [wife of son] daughter-in-law
beau-frère *nm, pl* **beaux-frères** brother-in-law
belle-sœur *nf, pl* **belles-sœurs** sister-in-law
belle-famille *nf* in-laws
veuf *nm* widower **veuve** *nf* widow
demi-frère *nm, pl* **demi-frères 1** [sharing one parent] half-brother **2** [step-parent's son] stepbrother
demi-sœur *nf, pl* **demi-sœurs 1** [sharing one parent] half-sister **2** [step-parent's daughter] stepsister

34.5 *Frères et sœurs des parents, cousins* Uncles, aunts, cousins

oncle *nm* uncle
tonton *nm* [informal. Usu as form of address] uncle
tante *nf* aunt
tata *nf* [informal. Usu as form of address] auntie
neveu *nm, pl* **-x** nephew
nièce *nf* niece
cousin, e *n* cousin *cousin germain* first cousin *cousin(e) issu(e) de germain* second cousin

34.6 *Liens de famille* Family ties

liens *nm pl* **de famille,** ALSO **attaches** *nf pl* **familiales** family ties *J'ai des attaches familiales en Bourgogne.* I have family ties in Burgundy.
arbre *nm* **généalogique** family tree
famille *nf* family *famille nombreuse* large family *famille monoparentale* single-parent family *les gens de ma famille* my folks *Nous ne sommes pas de la même famille.* We're not related.
proche parent, e close relative *La Duchesse de Remouet était une proche parente du Cardinal Viermot.* The Duchess of Remouet was a close relative of Cardinal Viermot.
descendant, e *n* descendant
descendre {53} *vi* (always + *de*) to be descended from *Il descend d'une famille terrienne.* He's descended from a landed family.
progéniture *nf* [humorous] offspring
génération *nf* generation *des immigrés marocains de la première génération* first-generation Moroccan immigrants

ancêtre n, **aïeul** nm, **aïeule** nf, **aïeux** mpl
Ancêtre refers to any relative from the great-grandparents' generation and beyond: e.g. *nos ancêtres les Gaulois* our ancestors the Gauls. **Aïeul, e** is an obsolete word for male or female ancestor, while the plural **aïeux** is current but literary: *des aïeux illustres* illustrious forebears. In the interjection *mes aïeux!* the word is informal and is used for comic effect: e.g. *Mes aïeux, quel embrouillaminis!* My godfathers, what a mix-up!

35 Groups, individuals and gender

35.1 *Gens* People

personne nf person *Joseph est une personne irascible.* Joseph is bad-tempered.
grande personne [children's language] grown-up
humain, e n [as opposed to animal] human (being) *Il arrive que les humains ne se distinguent guère des animaux.* Sometimes human beings are really no different from animals.
individu nm **1** [pejorative] individual. *Deux individus ont été aperçus près du lieu du crime.* Two individuals were seen near the scene of the crime. **2** [member of a society or group] individual *Que peut faire l'individu pour contribuer au bien-être de la collectivité?* What can individuals do to contribute to the well-being of the community at large?
prochain nm [religious overtones] fellow human being, neighbour
particulier, -lière n (private) individual *une réglementation qui s'adresse aux particuliers* regulations aimed at private individuals

35.2 *Les adolescents* Adolescents

adolescence nf adolescence
adolescent, e n adolescent
ado n [slang, short for **adolescent**. Implies difficult or negative attitudes sometimes associated with that age group] teenager
pubère adj pubescent
puberté nf puberty *à (l'âge de) la puberté* at puberty

Gens People
The word *gens* is masculine plural, except when it is preceded by an adjective showing the feminine form, in which case it is feminine plural. Thus *Ce sont des gens merveilleux.* They're marvellous people, but *de bonnes gens* good people, *les vieilles gens* old people, *les petites gens* people of modest means. *Jeunes gens* refers to young people in general, male or female. When you want to specify which sex, use *jeunes hommes* for young men and *jeunes femmes* for young women.

35.3 *Gens vivant ensemble* People living together

see also **36.1 Société et communauté**
communauté nf **1** [group of people in an institution] community *des moines vivant en communauté* monks living in a community **2** [group sharing a similar background, a religion or a set of ideas] community *la communauté islamique de Paris* the Islamic community in Paris **3** [local people] community *Notre petite communauté est prête à accueillir une trentaine de réfugiés.* There is room in our little community for about 30 refugees.
collectivité nf [group of people sharing a project or aim] local people *La mairie n'ayant pas assez de ressources, c'est la collectivité qui a elle-même organisé la crèche.* As the council had no money available, local people got together to organize the creche AmE day care center

35.4 *Termes familiers désignant les hommes* Informal words for referring to men

type nm [used by all generations and social groups] guy
mec nm [more informal then **type**. Used mainly by the younger generation] BrE bloke AmE guy

35.5 *Termes familiers désignant les femmes* Informal words for referring to women

nana nf BrE bird AmE chick
bonne femme nf [patronizing] woman *des bavardages de bonnes femmes* women's talk

35.6 *Masculine* Male

homme nm **1** [male human] man **2** [humans as opposed to animals] mankind *L'homme ne respecte plus la nature.* Mankind has lost respect for nature.
masculin, e adj [having physical or mental qualities seen as male. A term with positive connotations] masculine
masculinité nf masculinity
mâle adj **1** [in biology] male **2** [having male physical qualities. A term which is normally used positively] masculine *une voix mâle* a masculine voice
viril, e adj [having traditional male qualities, esp physical courage] virile
macho adj [informal and pejorative] macho
phallocrate nm male chauvinist
phallo nm [informal] male chauvinist pig

Insulting words for men or women who do not conform to type and look, and sound or behave like the opposite sex are:
hommasse adj [pejorative. Used only of women] butch
efféminé, e adj [pejorative. Used only of men] effeminate

35.7 *Féminin* Female

femme nf woman *la femme* womankind
féminin, e adj [having qualities seen as female. A term with positive connotations] feminine
féminité nf femininity

femelle *adj* [in biology] female
femelle *nf* **1** [in biology] female **2** [pejorative and insulting] BrE (piece of) crumpet

35.8 *Groupes de gens* Many people together

groupe *nm* [general word, used of people and things] group *Ils s'étaient mis en groupe pour la photo.* They were standing together as a group for the photograph. *Les trois statues forment un groupe.* The three statues together form a group.
de groupe (used as an adjective) [done in a group] group *thérapie de groupe* group therapy *photographie de groupe* group photograph *réduction de groupe* group discount
foule *nf* [large, static or in motion] crowd *Il y a foule sur la place.* There's a crowd in the square. *La foule s'est précipitée pour voir passer la voiture de la star.* The crowd rushed to see the star's limousine go past.
affluence *nf* [like **foule**, but mainly used in contexts of shopping and public transport] crowd *L'affluence commence bien avant l'ouverture du magasin.* The crowd starts building up long before the shop opens. *aux heures d'affluence* in the rush hour
cohue *nf* [pejorative. People jostling, often in order to reach a place first] crush *J'ai failli perdre les jumeaux dans la cohue autour des vitrines de Noël.* I nearly lost the twins in the crush around the Christmas window displays.
bande *nf* **1** [pejorative. People coming together for a negative purpose] gang *une bande de voyous* BrE a gang of yobs AmE a gang of delinquents **2** [pejorative. People sharing an undesirable characteristic] bunch *une bande d'imbéciles* a bunch of idiots
rassemblement *nm* [sometimes pejorative. Small group assembled usu in the street for a political purpose] gathering *Un rassemblement s'était constitué devant l'ambassade.* A gathering had formed in front of the embassy.
attroupement *nm* [small group, in the street, assembling out of curiosity] group *Un attroupement s'est formé autour du blessé.* A group formed around the injured man.
le (gros du) troupeau [very pejorative] the crowd *Elle n'a jamais de position sur quoi que ce soit et suit le gros du troupeau.* She has no firm opinion about anything and just follows the crowd.
assemblée *nf* **1** [non-random group, usu seated in a room, to debate a political or other topic] assembly *l'Assemblée (nationale)* the (French) National Assembly **2** [people in a room] audience *Quand vous ouvrirez le colloque, n'oubliez pas que vous vous adressez à une assemblée en majorité anglophone.* When you open the conference, don't forget that you're addressing a mainly English-speaking audience.

équipe *nf* **1** [people working together] team **2** [people working in shifts] shift *L'équipe de 20 heures vient d'arriver.* The 8 o'clock shift has just arrived.

35.9 *Former un groupe* To form a group

grouper {6} *vt* [general term] to group (together)
se grouper *v refl* to form a group *Les ministres du nouveau gouvernement se sont groupés devant les photographes.* The new cabinet ministers stood in a group in front of the press cameras.
rassembler {6} *vt* [same meaning as **grouper**, but stresses the selection process] to put together *Nous souhaitons rassembler une équipe hors pair.* We would like to put together a high-quality team.
se rassembler *v refl* [subj: e.g. group, party] to gather *Les instituteurs ont demandé aux enfants de se rassembler dans le hall.* The teachers asked the children to gather in the hall.
s'assembler {6} *v refl* [come together as a group, with a common purpose] to congregate

s'attrouper {6} *v refl* [slightly pejorative. Come and stand together to stare at a scene] to gather *Les voyageurs s'attroupaient devant les panneaux annonçant la grève-surprise.* Passengers were gathering in front of the notices announcing the lightning strike.

35.10 *Les gens seuls* People who are alone

ermite *n* [suggests a liking for meditation] hermit
misanthrope *n* [someone, usu a man, who hates mankind] misanthrope
vieux garçon *nm* [pejorative. Implies ingrained habits] bachelor
vieille fille *nf* [very pejorative. Implies narrow-mindedness] old maid
enfant *n* **unique** only child
fils *nm* **unique** only son
fille *nf* **unique** only daughter
célibataire *n* **1** [neutral term] unmarried person *rester célibataire* to remain unmarried **2** [a more pejorative term when used of a woman than a man] *C'est une célibataire.* She's a spinster. *C'est un célibataire.* He's a bachelor.

Locution Idiom
faire bande à part [used of a pair or a group, sometimes used of one person] to go one's own way
C'est un ours. [usu refers to men] He's a grumpy old sod.

35.11 *Solitude* Loneliness

seul, e *adj* **1** (after noun) [stresses absence of company, by choice or not] lonely *Elle a toujours été une femme seule.* She was always a lonely woman. *Nous sommes seuls maintenant que notre fille est mariée.* We're on our own now that our daughter has got married. *être tout(e) seul(e)* to be all alone *Je préfère en parler seul(e) à seul avec lui.* I'd rather talk about it with him privately.

solitaire *adj* and *n* [stresses a liking for being alone] solitary *C'est un solitaire.* He's a loner.

solitude *nf* loneliness *La solitude ne me fait pas peur.* I'm not afraid of being alone.

isolé, e *adj* **1** [in physical isolation. Describes: e.g. person, village] cut off **2** [psychologically] isolated

indépendant, e *adj* [a positive description, stressing a person's capacity for taking initiatives] independent

abandonné, e *adj* **1** [describes: e.g. child] abandoned **2** [describes: e.g. lover] forsaken

abandonné à lui-même *adj m*, **abandonnée à elle-même** *adj f* left to his/her own devices

36 Politics, society and community

36.1 *Société* Society and community

see also **35.3 Gens vivant ensemble**

société *nf* **1** [people among whom we live, their culture and habits] society *une société d'économie mixte* a mixed-economy society *Considérons les conséquences sur la société de notre politique écologique.* Let us consider the social consequences of our ecological policy. **2** [people in general] society *Notre société n'accepte pas l'inceste.* Our society does not tolerate incest.

en société [sometimes used ironically] in (polite) company *On ne met pas ses coudes sur la table en société.* You don't put your elbows on the table in polite company.

social, e *adj*, *mpl* **sociaux 1** [concerning the relationships between sections of the population. Describes: e.g. problem, development] social *Est-ce que les rapports sociaux se dégradent dans les grandes villes?* Is the social fabric disintegrating in the larger towns? **2** [relating to the welfare state] social *un travailleur social* a social worker *la sécurité sociale* social security *les charges sociales* employers' overheads *des logements sociaux* BrE council dwellings AmE subsidized housing

social *nm* [everything that is connected with the welfare state] social welfare *Le gouvernement prétend investir dans le social.* The government claims to invest in social welfare.

False friend **social** meaning sociable
Although *social* can be used to refer to relationships between friends or acquaintances, this meaning tends to be restricted to scientific descriptions, e.g. *L'enfant acquiert un comportement social en imitant ses proches.* Children learn to behave sociably by imitating their immediate family. *L'abeille est un insecte social.* Bees are social insects.

commune *nf* [basic French administrative division] municipality

communal, e *adj* municipal

intercommunal, e *adj* shared between several districts *un projet intercommunal de ramassage des ordures* a rubbish collection scheme organized by several districts

collectivité locale
The name *collectivité locale* refers to public associations or groups set up at the level of the town or district, of several towns or districts, or of the department.
For example, *Nos collectivités locales sont très actives en matière de recyclage des déchets.* Our local organizations take an active part in the recycling of waste.

36.2 *Classes sociales* Social classes

classe *nf* **sociale** social class

classe ouvrière working class

bourgeoisie *nf* middle class *petite bourgeoise* lower middle class *grande bourgeoisie* upper (middle) class

prolétariat *nm* proletariat

sous-classe *nf*, *pl* **sous-classes** underclass

36.3 *Politique* Politics

politique *nf* **1** [political life] politics *J'aurais voulu faire de la politique mais maintenant c'est trop tard.* I would have liked to go into politics but now it's too late. *Je ne fais pas de politique.* I'm not political. **2** [type of political ideas] policy *Ils font une politique de droite/gauche.* They follow right-wing/left-wing policies.

politique *adj* political *Quelle est sa ligne politique?* What are her politics? *demander l'asile politique* to ask for political asylum

politique *nm*, ALSO **homme politique** (male) politician

femme *nf* **politique** (female) politician

politiquement *adv* politically *Politiquement, il se situe où?* Where does he stand, politically speaking?

gouvernement *nm* [the members of the cabinet] government *entrer au gouvernement* to join the government

The French political system
The head of state and the nation's leader is the president, *le Président de la République*, elected for seven years by universal suffrage. Political power is exercised by the president, with his appointed prime minister, *le Premier Ministre* and the cabinet, *le gouvernement*. The elected representatives of the people are the deputies, *les députés*, who form the National Assembly, *l'Assemblée Nationale*, also called *le Parlement*. In the parliament building, *la Chambre des députés*, their seats are ranged in a semicircle, hence one of the names which the newspapers use for the *Chambre*, *l'hémicycle*. The descriptions 'right-wing' and 'left-wing', in English, and their equivalents, *de droite* and *de gauche*, come from the parties' seating arrangements, to the right and the left of the semicircle as you look towards the front. Each *député* represents a constituency, *une circonscription*. The other house is the Senate, *le Sénat*, whose members, *les sénateurs*, are elected by the deputies and other officials. Before becoming law, a bill must be approved by both houses, which may mean it has to shuttle between the *Assemblée* and the *Sénat*. In case of disagreement, the *Assemblée* has the final say. The basis for the constitution of the French Republic resides in the *Déclaration des Droits de l'Homme et du Citoyen*, written in 1789. It has been continuously added to and modified by statute law since.

France first became a republic, *une république*, in 1792. The first republic lasted until 1804. Three different republics followed, 1848–52, 1870–1940, and 1944–58. The constitution for the current (fifth) republic, *la Cinquième République*, was approved in referenda in 1958 and 1962. When used in the context of France, the adjective *républicain, e* does not usually refer to a particular party, but to the egalitarian principles of the state, e.g. *les institutions républicaines*, the institutions of the (French) republic. However, the term is sometimes used in the context of political parties, in which case it means 'of the Parti républicain' (France) or 'of the Republican party' (e.g. the United States).

Main ministerial titles and their closest British and American equivalents
Premier ministre Prime Minister
Ministre de l'Intérieur BrE Home Secretary AmE Secretary of the Interior
Ministre des Finances BrE Chancellor of the Exchequer AmE Treasury Secretary
Garde des Sceaux BrE Lord Chancellor AmE Attorney General
Ministre des Affaires Étrangères BrE Foreign Secretary AmE Secretary of State

---

Names for places of central government
(le Palais de) l'Élysée the Elysee Palace (where the president works and may reside)
Matignon the prime minister's office
Bercy the Ministry for Finance
le Quai d'Orsay the Foreign Office

Local politics
Except in the case of very large cities, the basic local government unit in France is *la commune*. Each *commune* has a town hall, *la mairie*, which is headed by a mayor, *le maire*, and a council *le conseil municipal*, which administers the area within its jurisdiction, *la municipalité*. Large cities, like Paris or Lyons, are divided into smaller sections called *arrondissements*, each of which functions like a *commune* and has a *mairie*. There is also a *mairie* for the whole city, e.g. *la Mairie de Paris*.

Women
Women mayors vary in their preferences as to what title they wish to be given. A recent tendency is to change the masculine noun *maire* into a feminine, *la maire*. This is surprising to many, who favour *Madame le maire*, or simply *le maire*. The word *la mairesse* is used, but may sound disrespectful. Similarly, women members of parliament may prefer to be referred to as *le député, la députée*, or *Madame le député*.

36.4 *Les élections* Elections

élection(s) *nf (pl)* election(s)
électeur, -trice *n* voter
présidentielles *nf pl* elections to elect the president (of the republic)
législatives *nf pl* elections to elect the members of parliament
candidat, e *n* candidate *candidat sortant* outgoing candidate
parlementaire *adj* parliamentary
partielles *nf pl* BrE by-elections AmE special election
référendum *nm* referendum
scrutin *nm* **1** [election] poll *Le dernier scrutin a vu la*

victoire de la droite. The right won the last election.
2 [mode of electing] ballot *au scrutin secret* by secret ballot
vote *nm* **1** [one person's suffrage] vote **2** [fact of electing] voting *Elles n'avaient pas le droit de vote.* They weren't entitled to vote.
voter {6} *vt* and *vi* to vote *Je ne voterai pas pour eux.* I won't vote for them.
se présenter (à une élection) BrE to stand for election AmE to run for election

36.5 *Les partis et les idéologies* Parties and ideologies

parti *nm* **(politique)** (political) party
centrisme *nm* centrist politics
socialisme *nm* socialism
anarchisme *nm* anarchism
communisme *nm* communism
impérialisme *nm* imperialism
fascisme *nm* fascism
Gaullisme *nm* Gaullism
libéralisme *nm* [economic doctrine] free enterprise
démocratie *nf* democracy
démocratique *adj* démocratic
dictature *nf* dictatorship
propagande *nf* propaganda

36.6 *Termes péjoratifs désignant les appartenances politiques* Pejorative terms for political orientations

rouge *adj* and *nm* [informal] red
coco *adj* and *nm* [informal] commie
facho *adj* and *nm* [informal] fascist

36.7 *Les luttes* Struggles

revendication *nf* [by a union] demand
gréviste *n* striker
grève *nf* strike *se mettre en grève*, ALSO *faire grève* to strike
manifestation *nf* demonstration
manif *nf* BrE demo
manifestant, e *n* demonstrator
rébellion *nf* [implies suddenness] rebellion
révolte *nf* [more deep-seated than **rébellion**] revolt
coup *nm* **d'État** coup *Il y a eu un coup d'État contre Gorbatchev.* There was a coup against Gorbachev.

36.8 *La révolution* Revolution

The French Revolution
When French people talk about *la Révolution*, they usually mean the Revolution of 1789, the most significant event in France's history, which destroyed the old order, *l'Ancien Régime*, and changed the country from a monarchy into a republic. The beginning of the period is symbolized by the taking of the Bastille prison, celebrated to this day as the national holiday, *la fête nationale*, on 14th July. The other symbolic event of the Revolution took place in 1793, when the king, Louis XVIth, was guillotined.

36.9 *Les ambassades* Embassies

ambassade *nf* embassy
ambassadeur *nm* **1** [post-holding diplomat] ambassador
  Son Excellence l'Ambassadeur du Japon His Excellency the
  Japanese Ambassador **2** [person on a mission] envoy
ambassadrice *nf* **1** [post-holder] ambassador *Son
  Excellence l'Ambassadrice des États-Unis* Her Excellency
  the American Ambassador **2** [spouse] ambassador's wife
consulat *nm* consulate
consulaire *adj* consular
consul *nm* consul

36.10 *Monarchie* Monarchy

monarchie *nf* monarchy
monarque *nm* [male only] monarch
royauté *nf* [refers to the system but focuses on the fact
  that there is a king or queen] monarchy
royal, e *adj, mpl* **royaux** [describes: e.g. palace, family,
  prerogative] royal
régicide *adj* and *n* regicide
Majesté *nf* [in titles] Majesty *Sa Majesté le roi* His Majesty
  the king *Leurs Majestés se promenaient dans le parc.* Their
  Majesties walked in the park.
règne *nm* reign
régner {10} *vi* to reign *régner sur un pays/peuple* to reign
  over a country/a people
interrègne *nm* interregnum
cour *nf* court *à la cour* at court
couronnement *nm* coronation
couronne *nf* crown
trône *nm* throne

36.11 *Titres royaux et titres de noblesse* Royal and noble titles

Male	Female
roi *nm* king	**reine** *nf* queen
prince *nm* prince	**princesse** *nf* princess
dauphin *nm* the king's eldest son	**dauphine** *nf* wife of the dauphin
empereur *nm* emperor	**impératrice** *nf* empress
duc *nm* duke	**duchesse** *nf* duchess
comte *nm* BrE earl AmE Count	**comtesse** *nf* countess
vicomte *nm* viscount	**vicomtesse** *nf* viscountess
baron *nm* baron	**baronne** *nf* baroness
marquis *nm* marquess	**marquise** *nf* marchioness

36.12 *Noblesse* Nobility

noblesse *nf* **1** [collective term for nobles] nobility **2** [high-
  mindedness] nobility (of mind)
noble *adj* [describes: e.g. family, ancestor, gait, mien]
  noble
noble *n* nobleman, noblewoman *Il a épousé une noble.* He
  married a noblewoman.
aristocratie *nf* aristocracy
aristocrate *n* aristocrat
aristocratique *adj* [of the aristocracy; also befitting an
  aristocrat] aristocratic
crime *nm* **de lèse-majesté** crime against the monarch's
  authority
roitelet *nm* petty king

Locutions Idioms
heureux comme un roi as happy as a king
Le roi n'est pas son cousin. [informal. Refers to someone
  so conceited that they consider themselves closer even to
  the king than a cousin] He's far too full of himself.

Citation Quotation
Je meurs innocent, je pardonne à tous mes ennemis.
[Allegedly Louis XVIth's last words before being guillotined]
I die an inocent man, I forgive all my enemies.
Ils n'ont rien appris, ni rien oublié. [The comment by
the French diplomat Talleyrand about the nobles who fled
from France during the revolution and returned after the
fall of Napoleon] They've learned nothing and forgotten
nothing.

37 Control, authority and the law

37.1 *Contrôle* Control

contrôle *nm* **1** [making sure that a machine, document, etc
  is in good order] check(ing), inspecting **2** [mastery over
  one's behaviour, a vehicle, an animal] control *le contrôle
  de soi* self-control *Il a perdu le contrôle de son véhicule.*
  He lost control of his vehicle.
contrôler {6} *vt* **1** [have power to check what sb does] to
  check *Mon travail consiste à contrôler les magasiniers.* My
  job is to check the (work of the) warehousemen. **2** [be
  influential over] to control *Elle contrôle le budget mais n'a
  aucun pouvoir de décision sur l'équipe de créatifs.* She
  controls the budget but has no decision-making power
  over the creative team.
pouvoir *nm* **1** [in general] power **2** [in politics] political
  power *Elle a toujours visé le pouvoir.* She has aimed at
  political power all her life.
diriger {8} *vt* **1** [lead and exert overall control over. Obj:
  e.g. company, team] to manage **2** [give instructions] to
  direct *C'est elle qui a dirigé les opérations de sauvetage.*
  She directed the rescue operations.
gérer {6} *vt* **1** [be in charge of an organization on behalf of
  the owner] to run *Elle gère une petite surface à Hyères.*
  She runs a small supermarket in Hyères. **2** [to be in overall
  charge of. Stresses the financial, rather than the strategic
  aspects of management. Obj: e.g. company, organization]
  to manage. *Elle gérait le pays comme elle aurait géré une
  épicerie.* She managed the country as she would have
  managed a grocer's store. **3** [have financial and
  administrative responsibility. Obj: e.g. budget, accounts,
  stock] to manage.
commander {6} *vt* [in the army. Obj: e.g. regiment] to be
  in charge of *Ça n'est pas toi qui commandes ici!* You're
  not the boss around here!
coordonner {6} *vt* to coordinate
discipliner {6} *vt* **1** [impose a sanction on. Obj: rebel,
  disruptive pupil] to punish **2** [teach some self-control to.
  Obj: child, soldiers] to bring into line
dominer {6} *vt* [psychologically] to dominate
administrer {6} *vt* [obj: e.g. organization, project] to
  administer
influencer {7} *vt* [obj: e.g. person, events] to influence
influer {6} *vi* [same meaning as **influencer** but does not
  have people at its object] *influer sur* to influence
mener {9} *vt* **1** [pejorative. Obj: gang] to lead **2** [in battle,
  election, match] to lead *mener des troupes à la victoire* to
  lead troops to victory
régenter {6} *vt* [literary] to control *La favorite avait fini par
  tout régenter à la cour.* The king's mistress was eventually
  in control of everything and everyone at court

37.2 *Ceux et celles qui contrôlent* People who exercise authority

see also **84.6 Les sociétés**
administrateur, -trice *n* administrator
chef *nm* (male) boss
chèfe *nf* [informal. Sometimes used humorously] (female) boss
patron, -tronne *n* [informal, used in all professions] boss
contremaître, -tresse *n* foreman, forewoman
contrôleur, -leuse *n* [in trains, on buses] ticket collector
directeur, -trice *n* [head of a department in e.g. business organizations] director
dirigeant, e *n* [in politics] leader
leader *nm* [synonym for **dirigeant**] leader
responsable *n* [this term applies to people in charge in all sorts of organizations and at many levels in the hierarchy] person in charge *Appelez-moi le responsable.* I want to speak to the person in charge.
gérant *nm* [employee in charge of a shop, a hotel, a bank] manager
gérante *nf* [as above] manageress

Asking to see the manager
If you want someone to 'fetch the manager' you should say something like *'je voudrais parler au directeur/à la directrice s'il vous plaît'* or *je voudrais parler au responsable/à la responsable'*. The terms *gérant* and *gérante* tend to be used mainly to denote status as employee.

---

gouverneur *nm* [historical. In colonies] governor
garde-chiourme *nm, pl* **gardes-chiourmes** [pejorative and informal. Can refer to a real prison officer or to someone who behaves like one] jailer
maître *nm* **1** [painter, head of household with servants] master **2** [in music] maestro **3** [at primary school] (male) teacher
maîtresse *nf* **1** [in a household with servants] mistress **2** [at primary school] (female) teacher
puissant, e *adj* and *n* [wielding power] powerful *les puissants* the powerful

Locutions Idioms
tirer les ficelles to pull (all) the strings
avoir droit de regard sur qqch to be entitled to a say about sthg

37.3 *Organisation sociale* Organization of society

organisation *nf* **1** [group] organization *une organisation humanitaire* a humanitarian organization **2** [process] organizing
établissement *nm* **1** [general term for schools and colleges] school *Maquillage et bijoux sont interdits dans de nombreux établissements scolaires.* In many schools, it is forbidden to wear make-up or jewellery. **2** [slightly old-fashioned term referring to small or middle-sized companies, including their buildings] company *Les établissements Desruelle ont dû fermer à cause de la crise.* Desruelle and Co have had to close because of the recession.
institution *nf* **1** [religious college] (denominational) school *Elle a été mise en pension à l'institution Sainte-Catherine.* She was sent to Saint-Catherine's College as a boarder. **2** [long-established organization or tradition. Sometimes used humorously] institution *La plupart de nos institutions nationales ont été créées pendant la Révolution.* Most of

our national institutions have their origins in the French Revolution. *Le steak-frites est une véritable institution.* Steak and chips is a national institution.
institut *nm* **1** [learned organization] institute **2** [for buying cosmetics and having beauty treatment] beauty parlour

37.4 *Faire marcher une organisation* To run an organisation

siège *nm* **(social)** (company) head office *La maison a son siège à Rotterdam.* The company's head office is in Rotterdam.
président *nm* chair(man) (person)
présidente *nf* chair(woman)
présider {6} *vi* and *vt* to chair
secrétaire *nm* [to a committee] secretary *sécretaire général* General Secretary
membre *nm* member *Brigitte est un des plus anciens membres de l'association de consommateurs de sa région.* Brigitte is one of the longest-serving members of her local consumer association.
comité *nm* committee *être au comité* to be on the committee *Il y a réunion du comité à 14 heures demain.* There is a meeting of the committee tomorrow at 2 p.m.

37.5 *Lois et règlements* Laws and regulations

loi *nf* **1** [act passed by a government] law, act *C'est interdit par la loi de 1932.* It's forbidden under the 1932 Act. *qui fait force de loi* legally binding **2** [that which is legal] the law *La loi est dure mais c'est la loi.* The law may be hard but it is the law. **3** [in scientific usage] law *une des lois de la nature* one of the laws of nature
légal, e *adj, mpl* **-gaux** legal *la limite légale de paiement de l'impôt* the legal limit for payment of tax owed
légalement *adv* lawfully
illégal, e *adj, mpl* **-gaux** illegal
légiférer {6} *vi* to legislate

Locutions Idioms
Nul n'est censé ignorer la loi. Ignorance of the law is no excuse.
C'est la loi du talion. It's an eye for an eye and a tooth for a tooth.
règle *nf* [decision made by a group or a person] rule
en règle (used as an adjective) [conforming to the law] legal, in order *Il a des papiers en règle.* His papers are in order. *Je suis en règle avec le fisc.* My tax affairs are sorted out.
règlement *nm* [set of decisions made a group] regulations *Pour lui, le règlement c'est le règlement.* He's stickler for regulations.
réglementaire *adj* regulation *papier aux dimensions réglementaires* regulation-sized paper
réguler {6} *vt* [administrative term] to regulate
contrat *nm* contract *Je suis sous contrat.* I'm under contract.

37.6 *Judiciaire* The Judiciary

In this area of vocabulary it is very difficult to provide accurate translations, since the judicial systems in France, Britain and the US are so different. In topics 37.7 to 37.11 below you will find a few translations, but mostly descriptions, of the various divisions of the French judicial system and rough equivalents where it is possible to give them.

le droit pénal criminal law
le droit civil civil law

37.7 *Crimes et délits* Offences

infraction *nf* In everyday language, a minor offence. In legal language, any offence, serious or minor.
crime *nm* In everyday language, a murder. In legal language, a serious breach of the law.
contravention *nf* In everyday language, a motoring fine. Also, a breach of traffic regulations. In legal language a minor breach of the law.
délit *nm* In everyday language, an offence not involving death or bodily harm. In legal language a breach less serious than *un crime* but more serious than *une contravention*.

The phrases *an offence* and *une offense* can be a source of confusion, not only because of their spelling but also their meaning. The French word is literary and means an affront: e.g. *Tu as mis en doute l'honneur de ma mère: une telle offense se lave dans le sang!* You have questioned my mother's honour: only blood can wash away such an insult!

37.8 *Les policiers et leurs actions* Police officers and their duties

policier *nm* policeman
femme *nf* **policier** policewoman
gardien *nm* **de la paix**, ALSO **agent** *nm* **(de police)** [in charge of general policing esp in towns] policeman
gendarme *nm* [member of a military unit specializing in policing, mainly traffic duty] policeman
CRS *nm* [member of the *Compagnies Républicaines de Sécurité*, a special police force used by the state for crowd control, for dealing with major incidents, or on state occasions] special policeman
flic *nm* [slang] cop
barbouze *nm* secret police agent
suspect, e *n* suspect
soupçonner {6} *vt* (often + *de*) to suspect *La police le soupçonne d'avoir recruté un tueur à gages.* The police suspect him of having hired a professional killer.
soupçon *nm* suspicion *avoid des soupçons* to be suspicious
suspecter {6} *vt* (often + *de*) [more pejorative than **soupçonner**] to suspect *Il est suspecté d'avoir détourné des fonds.* He's under suspicion of embezzlement.
arrestation *nf* arrest
arrêter {6} *vt* to arrest
garde *nf* **à vue** (police) custody *mis*, ALSO *placé en garde à vue* placed in (police) custody
descente *nf* **de police** police raid
fouille *nf* **corporelle** body search

37.9 *Prison* Prison

prison *nf* prison
maison *nf* **d'arrêt** [official term] prison
(maison) centrale [official term] large prison
taule *nf* [slang] BrE nick AmE slammer *S'il continue comme ça, il va se retrouver en taule.* If he carries on like this, he'll end up in the nick.
prisonnier, -nière *n* prisoner
détenu, e *n* [slightly informal] prisoner

37.10 *Juristes* Lawyers

le parquet the legal profession
le barreau the bar
juriste *n* lawyer, attorney
avocat, e *n* A lawyer whose work includes advocacy on behalf of a client in a court of law, similar to an English barrister, or in some circumstances a solicitor.
notaire *nm* A practising solicitor whose work does not involve advocacy.

37.11 *Au tribunal* In court

cour *nf* court
juge *nm* judge
témoin *nm* witness
le banc des témoins the witness box
les jurés the jurors
l'accusé the defendant
le banc des accusés BrE the dock
avocat, e *n* BrE barrister
accusation *nf* **1** charge *mettre qqn en accusation* to charge sb **2** [team of lawyers] *l'accusation* the prosecution
accuser {6} *vt* (often + *de*) [subj: police] to charge *Il est accusé de détournement de mineur.* He's been charged with corrupting a minor. *De quoi suis-je accusé?* What am I charged with?
défense *nf* **1** [procedure for defending oneself] defence *Sa seule défense consiste à nier.* His only defence is that he denies the facts. **2** [defendant's lawyers] *la défense* the defence
défenseur *nm* **1** [in criminal law] counsel (for the defence) **2** [in civil law] defendant's counsel
plaignant, e *n* plaintiff
caution *nf* bail *verser une caution de 100.000 francs* to stand bail for 100, 000 francs *sous caution* on bail
être jugé, e 1 [during trial] to stand trial *être jugé pour vol à main armée* to stand trial for armed robbery **2** [as a result of a trial] to be sentenced *Il sera jugé demain.* He'll be sentenced tomorrow.
tribunal *nm, pl* **-naux 1** [building] court(house) **2** [scene of trials] court *comparaître devant un tribunal* to appear before a court *tribunal de commerce* commercial court *tribunal pour enfants* juvenile court

Other types of tribunal
The *tribunal de grande instance* is a higher court with jurisdiction over civil and criminal cases. The *tribunal correctionnel* is part of this higher court, and deals with serious breaches of the law and claims for damages. The *tribunal d'instance* deals with less serious cases.

plaider {6} **1** *vi plaider coupable* to plead guilty *plaider non coupable* to plead not guilty **2** *vt plaider la légitime défense* to plead self-defence

procès nm trial intenter un procès à qqn to sue sb instruire un procès to prepare a (criminal) case. Ils ont contesté l'héritage et ils ont fait un procès. They contested the will and instituted proceedings.

poursuivre qqn en justice, ALSO **engager des poursuites (judiciaires) contre qqn** to prosecute sb Toute personne voyageant sans billet s'expose à des poursuites judiciaires. Persons travelling without a valid ticket will be prosecuted.

preuve nf (piece of) evidence preuve recevable/non recevable admissible/inadmissible evidence preuve indirecte circumstantial evidence

verdict nm verdict Les jurés ont rendu leur verdict. The jury has returned its verdict.

peine nf sentence une peine de prison a prison sentence une lourde peine a harsh sentence une peine légère a light sentence condamné à la peine de mort sentenced to death commuer une peine to commute a sentence

condamner {6} vt (often + à) to sentence condamner qqn à des travaux d'intérêt général to sentence sb to community service

---

Citation Quotation

J'accuse! [title of Émile Zola's famous open letter defending Dreyfus, published in 1898 in the newspaper L'Aurore] I accuse!

37.12 *Liberté* Freedom

libre adj **1** [not in prison] free Vous êtes libre. You are free (to go). **2** [not occupied. Describes: e.g. space, time] free Je ne serai pas libre avant huit heures. I won't be free until eight o'clock.

liberté nf **1** [as opposed to imprisonment] freedom **2** [state of being unrestrained] (often + de) freedom liberté de pensée freedom of thought liberté du culte freedom of religion

libérer {1} vt **1** [obj: e.g. prisoner, country] to free **2** (often + de) [remove constraints from] to free Un assistant vous libérerait des tâches les plus immédiates. An assistant would relieve you of the most pressing tasks.

libération nf [in historical or political contexts] liberation la Libération de Paris en août 44 the liberation of Paris, in August 1944.

relâcher {6} vt [obj: e.g. prisoner, captive animal] to release

---

The verbs **échapper à** and **s'échapper de**
The reflexive verb **s'échapper** {6}, used with de, refers to a physical escape from a place: Hier, un dangereux criminel s'est échappé de la prison des Guiermes. Yesterday, a dangerous criminal escaped from the prison at Guiermes. By contrast, **échapper à** implies avoiding a situation, responsibility, etc: e.g. Il a simulé des troubles psychiques pour échapper au service militaire. He pretended to be mentally ill in order to escape military service.

Locutions Idioms

faire le mur [informal. Escape from prison, boarding school or mental hospital] to go over the wall

libre comme l'air [without any constraints. Implies joyous and adventurous] footloose and fancy-free

libre à toi/vous de le faire It's up to you if you want to do it.

Citation Quotation

Liberté, égalité, fraternité [The motto of the French Republic, adopted in 1793 and reproduced in townhalls all over France.] Liberty, equality, fraternity

37.13 *Autorisation* Allowed

see also **110.1 (Gambits)**

permettre {56} vt ([tolerate] to allow J'ai permis à Julien de sortir hier soir. I allowed Julian to go out last night. Tu me permets une remarque? Would you allow me one observation?

se permettre v refl **1** [pejorative] to allow oneself Il s'est permis une remarque désobligeante sur mes compétences. He allowed himself to speak disparagingly about my abilities. **2** [when requesting something politely. Frequently, this is not translated, as English is more direct] to take the liberty of Je me permets de vous écrire pour vous demander un conseil. I am writing to ask you for advice.

permission nf permission Il faut demander à l'éditeur la permission de reproduire les illustrations. Permission to reproduce the drawings must be sought from the publisher. avoir la permission de minuit to be allowed to stay out until midnight.

autorisation nf [more official than **permission**] authorization

---

Autorisation de sortie du territoire français
A minor may leave French territory only if he or she is carrying not only a passport or identity card, but also a document called an autorisation de sortie du territoire (français). This has to be signed by one of the young person's parents.

---

avoir le droit de to be allowed to À huit ans, il n'a pas encore le droit de traverser la rue tout seul. At eight, he's not allowed to cross the road on his own.

avoir droit à to be entitled to Vous avez droit à des allocations chômage. You're entitled to unemployment benefit(s).

---

usage

Using **permettre** in mock courtesy
You can pretend to seek permission while really imposing your will, using phrases like: e.g. Vous permettez que je fasse une remarque? Will you allow me to make a comment? More forcefully: e.g. Permettez! J'étais là avant vous! Do you mind! I was here before you!

Locution Idiom

Il/Elle se croit tout permis. He thinks he/She thinks she can get away with anything.

37.14 *Interdit* Forbidden

interdire {78} vt to forbid Le règlement interdit tout contact avec l'extérieur. All contact with the outside world is forbidden under the regulations. Le médecin lui a interdit le sucre. The doctor has told him to stay off sugar. Je t'interdis de sortir avec ce garçon. I won't allow you go out with that boy. Et alors, je ronfle, c'est pas interdit! So, I snore, there's no law against it, is there?

interdit, e adj forbidden rue interdite road with no access la Cité Interdite the Forbidden City Il est interdit de séjour en France. He's not allowed on French territory.

interdiction nf [very strong] prohibition Les enfants ont interdiction de traverser la rue tout seuls. The children are strictly forbidden to cross the road on their own.

Il/Elle n'a pas le droit de faire . . . He's/She's is not allowed to do . . . On n'a pas le droit de cumuler les deux allocations. You're not allowed to receive both kinds of allowance.

Signs and notices prohibiting certain things:
Interdit aux chiens No dogs
Colportage interdit No hawkers
Il est interdit de se pencher au dehors. Do not lean out.
Interdiction de fumer. Smoking prohibited

prohiber {6} *vt* [forbidden by law] to outlaw *Le port d'armes est prohibé sur tout le territoire.* Carrying weapons is illegal throughout the country.
censure *nf* censorship
censurer {6} *vt* to censor
tabou *nm* taboo

Citation Quotation
Il est interdit d'interdire. [a slogan popular at the time of May 1968, reflecting people's frustration with authoritarian prohibitions] It's forbidden to forbid.

37.15 *Culpabilité* Guilt

coupable *adj* 1 [recognized as responsible after a trial] guilty *coupable de meurtre* guilty of murder 2 [assumed to be responsible for a bad situation] guilty *Je me sens coupable.* I feel guilty. *De quoi suis-je coupable à tes yeux?* What am I guilty of in your eyes?
culpabilité *nf* 1 [in law] guilt 2 [blameworthiness] guilt *porter la culpabilité de qqch* to be guilty of sthg
blâme *nm* 1 [formal. Severe judgment on someone's actions] disapproval 2 [in school] formal warning *Après trois blâmes, l'élève peut être exclu du lycée.* A student may be expelled after having been given three formal warnings.
blâmer {6} *vt* (often + *de*) [fairly formal. Express disapproval of] to condemn, to blame *Qui pourrait blâmer une mère d'avoir voulu protéger son enfant?* Who could blame a mother for having tried to protect her child?
responsable *adj* (often + *de*) responsible *Je ne suis pas responsable de tout ce qui va mal dans cette maison!* I'm not reponsible for everything that goes wrong in this house!
responsabilité *nf* (often + *de*) responsibility *La responsabilité de l'accident lui incombe.* He bears responsibility for the accident.
tort *nm* [respect in which one is wrong] mistake *Son tort, c'est de n'avoir pas communiqué ses soupçons à ses supérieurs.* Where she went wrong was in not letting her superiors know about her suspicions.

Locutions Idioms
C'est la faute à qui? ALSO **À qui la faute?** Who's to blame?
Il/Elle est dans son tort. He's/She's in the wrong.

37.16 *Mauvais* Wicked

mauvais, e *adj* (after the noun) [moralistic and slightly dated word. Used of people only] wicked *Aucun enfant n'est naturellement mauvais.* No child is naturally wicked.
méchant, e *adj* (before the noun) [who habitually hurts others] bad *Ce n'est pas un méchant homme, mais quand il a bu il ne se contrôle plus.* He's not a bad man, but he can't control himself when he's drunk.
vilain, e *adj* [used of or to children] naughty
immoral, e *adj* [respecting no moral rules, esp as far as sex or money are concerned] immoral **immoralité** *nf* immorality
vicieux, -cieuse *adj* [excessively interested in sex] depraved

vice *nm* 1 [sexual depravity] *le vice* vice 2 [socially unacceptable habit or character trait] weakness *Lui, son vice, c'est l'alcool.* His great weakness is alcohol. *Il a tous les vices.* He's bad through and through. 3 [disposition towards evil] sinfulness
péché *nm* [in religious contexts] sin *le péché originel* original sin

37.17 *Soumission et passivité* Enduring and being passive

see also **43.2 Qui se conforme à ce que l'on demande**
supporter {6} *vt* to put up with, to endure *Le malheureux a supporté la maladie et la misère jusqu'à sa mort en 1887.* The wretched man endured ill-health and poverty until his death in 1887. *Je supporterai tout, sauf l'infidélité.* I'll put up with anything, but not infidelity. *Quand il a une migraine, il ne supporte pas la lumière du jour.* When he has a migraine, he can't bear daylight.
soumission *nf* being submissive *En tant que représentant syndical, je vous en conjure, n'optez pas pour la soumission!* As union representative, I beg of you, don't act like sheep!
se soumettre {56} *v refl* (often+ *à*) to submit *Il s'est soumis de bonne grâce à une fouille corporelle.* He submitted with good grace to a body search.
soumis, e *adj* 1 [as a character trait] submissive 2 [temporarily] cowed
lèche-bottes *nm inv* toady, sycophant

Citation Quotation
Il faudra se soumettre ou se démettre. [Words addressed by the Republican orator Gambetta to the Conservative President of the French Republic, MacMahon, warning him that he must heed the will of the people expressed through universal suffrage] You must give in (to the will of the people) or resign.

37.18 *Victimes* Victims

victime *nf* victim *C'est lui la victime dans cette affaire.* He was the victim in this matter.
bouc *nm* **émissaire** [person who is punished for others] scapegoat
souffre-douleur *nm inv* [victim of bullying] scapegoat
esclave *n* slave
lavette *nf* [used as an insult] wimp

Locutions Idioms
obéir au doigt et à l'oeil to do as you're told *Il obéissait au doigt et à l'œil à son père* He toed the line with his father.
se laisser mener par le bout du nez to be led by the nose
courber la tête ALSO **l'échine devant qqn** [slightly literary] to grovel before sb
s'aplatir devant qqn 1 [always] to be sb's doormat 2 [on a particular occasion] to cave in to sb

38 Rituals and beliefs

38.1 *Coutumes* Customs

coutume *nf* [ritualized behaviour going back many generations] custom *C'est la coutume chez nous de donner un cadeau aux enfants le jour de leur fête.* It's our custom to give children a present on their saint's day. *A Pâques, on cache des chocolats dans le jardin, c'est la coutume qui veut ça.* At Easter, chocolates are hidden in the garden, it's a custom.

tradition *nf* [wider than **coutume**. Can refer to whole ways of thinking or behaving] tradition *Nous vivons selon des traditions judéo-chrétiennes.* We live according to Judeo-Christian traditions.

culture *nf* [set of traditions of a group of people] way of life *pays de culture musulmane* a country with an Islamic cultural tradition

38.2 *Fêtes* Celebrations

fêter {6} *vt* 1 [rejoice and have a party in honour of] to celebrate *Elle fête ses cinquante ans demain.* She'll celebrate her fiftieth birthday tomorrow. *Fêtons Noël ensemble.* Let's celebrate Christmas together. *On a fêté le 14 juillet avec un bal de rue et un feu d'artifice.* We celebrated Bastille day with a street party and a fireworks display. 2 [in the Christian tradition] to celebrate the saint's day of *Demain, on fête les Étienne.* Tomorrow is the saint's day of people called Étienne.

fête *nf* 1 [organized public activity] day (of celebration) *la fête nationale* Bastille day *la fête du travail* Labour day *la fête des mères* Mothers' day 2 [in the Christian tradition] saint's day *C'est quand ta fête?* When is your saint's day? *offrir une montre à un enfant pour sa fête* to give a child a watch on his saint's day 3 [private function] party *Nous faisons une fête samedi soir, vous viendrez?* We're having a party on Saturday evening, will you come?

Les Fêtes
The phrase *Les Fêtes* refers to the period around Christmas and up to New Year's Day. At that time, people wish each other *Bonnes* ALSO *Joyeuses Fêtes*, meaning 'Have a good time at Christmas and the New Year'

---

anniversaire *nm* 1 [day of a person's birth] birthday *Joyeux anniversaire!* Happy birthday! 2 [commemoration of an event] anniversary *anniversaire de mariage* wedding anniversary *l'anniversaire du référendum sur l'indépendance de l'Algérie* the anniversary of the referendum on Algerian independence

anniversaire *adj* anniversary *le jour anniversaire de sa mort* the anniversary of her death *le jour anniversaire de la prise de la Bastille* the anniversary of the fall of the Bastille

38.3 *Cérémonies religieuses* Religious ceremonies

baptême *nm* christening *robe de baptême* christening robe *nom de baptême* Christian name
parrain *nm* godfather
marraine *nf* godmother
filleul *nm* godson
filleule *nf* goddaughter
bar mitsva *nm* Bar Mitzvah

38.4 *La cérémonie du mariage* The wedding ceremony

fiançailles *nf pl* 1 [set of customs] engagement *bague de fiançailles* engagement ring 2 [party] engagement party *Pour leurs fiançailles, ils ont loué un bateau-mouche sur la Seine.* For their engagement party, they hired a pleasure cruiser on the Seine. *repas de fiançailles* engagement party

se fiancer {7} *v refl* to get engaged *Ils se sont fiancés en mai dernier.* They got engaged last May. *Elle s'est fiancée à un Italien.* She got engaged to an Italian.

se marier {15} *v refl* to get married *Ils se sont mariés dans l'intimité.* They had a simple wedding ceremony.

mariage *nm* 1 [set of customs, civil status] marriage *Le mariage doit être public selon la loi française.* According to French law the marriage vows must be taken in public. 2 [ceremony, party] wedding *un grand mariage* a lavish wedding

acte *nm* **de mariage** marriage certificate
contrat *nm* **de mariage** marriage contract
mariée *nf* bride
marié *nm* groom
témoin *nm* witness *Ma sœur sera mon témoin.* My sister will be my witness (at my wedding).

Witnessing the civil ceremony
In France a civil wedding ceremony must take place for the marriage to be legally valid. Couples who also want their marriage to be celebrated in church will therefore go through two separate marriage ceremonies, often on the same day. It is a legal obligation for the bride and groom to each have a witness present at the civil ceremony. The presence of a best man or a bridesmaid is a matter of tradition and personal choice.

---

garçon *nm* **d'honneur** best man
demoiselle *nf* **d'honneur** bridesmaid
alliance *nf* wedding ring
robe *nf* **de mariage** ALSO **de mariée** wedding dress
voile *nm* **(de mariée)** wedding veil
bouquet *nm* **de la mariée** wedding bouquet
réception *nf* (wedding) reception
lune *nf* **de miel** honeymoon *Nous avons passé notre lune de miel au Colorado.* We honeymooned in Colorado.
séparation *nf* separation *séparation de corps* legal separation
se séparer {6} *v refl* to separate *Elle et son mari se sont séparés.* She and her husband have separated. *Mireille s'est séparée de Guillaume.* Mireille has separated from Guillaume.
divorce *nm* divorce
divorcer {6} *v refl* to get divorced *Ils vont divorcer.* They're going to get divorced.
divorcer {6} *vi* (always + de) to divorce *Elle a divorcé d'avec son premier mari en 1995.* She divorced her first husband in 1995.

38.5 *Enterrement* Funeral

enterrement *nm* 1 [ceremony and procession] funeral *à l'enterrement de mon oncle* at my uncle's funeral 2 [putting in the grave] burial
enterrer {6} *vt* to bury *On enterre Adeline demain.* Adeline is being buried tomorrow.
cimetière *nm* cemetery *quand je serai au cimetière* when I'm dead (and buried)
tombe *nf* grave *mettre des fleurs sur la tombe de qqn* to put flowers on sb's grave
pierre *nf* **tombale** gravestone
cercueil *nm* coffin
couronne *nf* **(mortuaire)** wreath *Ni fleurs ni couronnes.* No flowers.

porteur *nm* **de cercueil** pallbearer
croque-mort *nm, pl* **croque-morts** [informal] undertaker ('s assistant)
employé, e *n* **des pompes funèbres** undertaker
fourgon *nm* **mortuaire** hearse
veillée *nf* **mortuaire** wake
veiller {6} *vt* [while the dead person is laid out, before they are placed in the coffin] to keep vigil over *Elle a veillé son père toute la nuit.* She stayed up all night by the side of her dead father.
incinérer {10} *vt* to cremate *Après ma mort, je veux me faire incinérer.* When I die I want to be cremated.
incinération *nf* cremation
deuil *nm* **1** [event] bereavement *Un deuil a frappé leur famille.* Their family suffered a bereavement. **2** [feelings] mourning *Je ne sortirai jamais de ce deuil.* I will never stop mourning. **3** [clothes] *(vêtements de) deuil* mourning clothes *Les femmes quittaient le deuil,* ALSO *cessaient de porter le deuil dix ans après la mort de leur mari.* Women could stop wearing mourning (clothes) ten years after their husband's death.
être en deuil 1 [feelings] to mourn *Le pays tout entier est en deuil.* The whole country is in mourning. **2** [in black clothes] to be in mourning (clothes)
prendre le deuil (de qqn) [wear black] to go into mourning (for sb)
nécrologie *nf* ALSO **notice** *nf* **nécrologique** obituary
testament *nm* will

38.6 *Croyance* Believing

croire {68} *vt* [think probable] to believe *Je n'arrive pas à croire qu'il a cinquante ans!* I can scarcely believe that he's fifty! *Tu l'as cru quand il t'a dit qu'il avait perdu son chéquier?* Did you believe him when he told you he'd lost his chequebook?
croire *vi* **1** [have faith] to be a believer *Ça fait longtemps que je ne crois plus.* I ceased to be a believer a long time ago. **2** [think something is real] *croire en Dieu* to believe in God *croire au père Noël* to believe in Father Christmas/Santa Claus **3** [in conversation] *Tu crois?* Do you think so?
croyance *nf* [element within a system of beliefs] belief *Elle a étudié les croyances de ces peuplades insulaires.* She studied the beliefs of these islanders.
croyant, e *adj* [having faith] religious *Il est très croyant.* He's very religious.
croyant, e *n* believer *une famille de croyants* a religious family
foi *nf* [belief which is not amenable to reasoning] faith *avoir la foi* to believe in God *avoir foi en quelqu'un* to trust sb
conviction *nf* [strong belief, arrived at through intuition or reasoning] conviction *J'ai la conviction qu'on est venu ici en mon absence.* I'm convinced that somebody was here while I was out. *Elle a été élue pour ses convictions européennes.* She was elected because she believes in Europe.

38.7 *La force de ce que l'on croit* The strength of one's beliefs

aveugle *adj* [pejorative. Describes faith] blind
inébranlable *adj* [describes: e.g. faith, conviction, certainty] unshakeable
ferme *adj* [describes conviction] firm **ferme,** ALSO **fermement** *adv Les leçons de l'expérience, j'y crois ferme* ALSO *fermement.* I'm a firm believer in learning from experience.

38.8 *Croire trop facilement* To believe too easily

gogo *nm* [slang] sucker
avaler {6} *vt* [informal. Believe without questioning] to swallow *J'ai inventé une histoire de rendez-vous tardif; heureusement, il a tout avalé.* I made up some story about a late appointment; fortunately he swallowed it. *On te ferait avaler n'importe quoi.* You'd believe anything anybody told you.
gober {6} *vt* [more slang and more pejorative than **avaler**] to swallow (whole)
crédule *adj* [believes things without questioning them] gullible

Locutions Idioms
avoir la foi du charbonnier [refers to a legendary stubborn coal merchant] to have a blind faith
Il n'y a que la foi qui sauve! [used ironically] Hope springs eternal!
prendre quelque chose pour argent comptant to take something at face value
parole d'évangile [words which you can believe in] gospel truth *Tout ce qu'elle raconte, pour lui c'est parole d'évangile.* To him everything she says is (the) gospel truth. *Ils ont promis le remboursement mais ne prends pas ça pour parole d'évangile.* They've promised to pay the money back but don't assume they'll keep their word.
croire dur comme fer à/en [informal] to believe in sthg implicitly
faire avaler des couleuvres à qqn to feed sb lies
C'est à peine croyable! [it's a cause for wonder] It's unbelievable!
C'est à ne pas croire! [as above, the sense of wonder is even greater] Who'd believe it!

38.9 *Religion* Religion

religion *nf* religion *Quelle est votre religion?* What religion are you?
religieux, -gieuse *adj* [describes: e.g. conviction, education] religious
religieux, gieuse *n* member of a religious order
foi *nf* faith *J'ai perdu la foi.* I have lost my faith. *Elle a été élevée dans la foi catholique.* She was brought up in the Catholic faith.

38.10 *Les religions dans le monde* World religions

chrétienté *nf* Christianity **Chrétien, -tienne** *n* Christian
chrétien, -tienne *adj* Christian
bouddhisme Buddhism **Bouddhiste** *n* Buddhist **bouddhiste** *adj* Buddhist
hindouisme *nm* Hinduism **Hindou, e** *n* Hindu **hindou, e** *adj* Hindu
judaïsme *nm* Judaism **Juif** *nm* Jew, **Juive** *nf* Jewess **juif, -ve** *adj* Jewish
islam *nm* Islam
Musulman, e *n* Muslim **musulman, e** *adj* Muslim

38.11 *Religions chrétiennes* Christian denominations

catholique *n* and *adj* Catholic
protestant, e *n* and *adj* Protestant
orthodoxe *adj* (Greek or Russian) Orthodox
copte *n* Copt **copte** *adj* Coptic

38.12 *Divinités* Divine beings

Dieu *nm* (the Christian) God
dieu *nm* god
déesse *nf* goddess
Allah *nm* Allah
Bouddha *nm* Buddha
Mohammed *nm* Mohammed
Jéhovah *nm* Jehovah
Jésus (Christ) *nm* Jesus (Christ)
le Christ Christ
le Saint-Esprit the Holy Spirit
la Vierge Marie the Virgin Mary
Satan *nm* Satan
ange *nm* angel *ange gardien* guardian angel
diable *nm* devil
saint, e *adj* saint *Saint Paul* Saint Paul *Sainte Anne* Saint
   Anne
prophète *nm* prophet **prophétique** *adj* prophetic
prophétie *nf* prophecy

Locutions Idioms
Nul n'est prophète en son pays. [proverb] No one is a
   prophet in his own country.
par l'opération du Saint-Esprit [ironic] miraculously
   *Allez, remue-toi, tes devoirs ne vont pas se faire par
   l'opération du Saint-Esprit!* Come on, get a move on, your
   homework isn't going to get done by a miracle!

38.13 *Le clergé* The clergy

curé *nm* [in charge of a Catholic parish] priest
vicaire *nm* [priest's assistant in a Catholic parish] curate
prêtre *nm* priest
prêtrise *nf* priesthood
pasteur *nm* [in the French Protestant Church] minister
ministre *nm* **(du culte)** [formal for **pasteur**] minister
rabbin *nm* rabbi
mollah *nm* mullah
imam *nm* imam
pope *nm* [Greek orthodox] pope
Pape *nm* pope *le Pape Jean-Paul II* Pope John Paul II
moine ALSO **religieux** *nm* monk
religieuse *nf* nun
sœur *nf* [informal] nun *Elle a été élevée chez les sœurs.* She
   went to a convent school.
monastère *nm* monastery
couvent *nm* convent

portail *nm* portal
porche *nm* porch
clocher *nm* steeple
contrefort *nm* buttress

banc *nm* **(d'église)** pew
nef *nf* (central) aisle
bas-côté *nm, pl* **bas-côtés** (side) aisle
fonts *nm pl* **baptismaux** font
bénitier *nm* stoup
chaire *nf* pulpit
autel *nm* altar

église *nf* church *Ils ne vont pas à l'église.* They're not
   churchgoers. *l'Église catholique* the Catholic Church
   l'Église anglicane the Church of England
temple *nm* **1** [in the French Protestant Church] church **2**
   [Buddhist, Hindu] temple
synagogue *nf* synagogue
mosquée *nf* mosque

38.14 *Le culte* Worship

culte *nm* **1** [in any religion, act of venerating] worship **2** [in
   the French Protestant Church] (church) service
adorer {6} *vt* to worship
office *nm* **(religieux)** [formal] (religious) service
messe *nf* mass *aller à la messe* to attend mass *dire la messe*
   to say mass *Je l'ai remarquée à la sortie de la messe.* I
   noticed her as people were coming out of mass.
prier {15} **1** *vi* to pray *Prions.* Let us pray. *Priez pour nous.*
   Pray for us. **2** *vt* [obj: e.g. God, Mary] to pray to
prière *nf* prayer *dire,* ALSO *réciter ses prières* to say one's
   prayers
pater *nm* [informal. Prayer] Our Father
ave *nm* [informal. Prayer] Ave Maria
missel *nm* prayer book
chapelet *nm* rosary *égrener son chapelet* BrE to tell one's
   beads AmE to say the rosary
cantique *nm* canticle *livre de cantiques* hymnal *le Cantique
   des Cantiques* the Song of Songs
psaume *nm* psalm
prêcher {6} *vi* and *vt* to preach
prédicateur *nm* preacher
sermon *nm* sermon
confession *nf* confession *entendre qqn en confession* to
   hear sb's confession **confessional** *nm* confessional
se confesser {6} *v refl* **1** [speak confidentially to a priest] to
   confess (one's sins) **2** [as a practice] to go to confession *Je
   me confessais toutes les semaines.* I used to go to
   confession every week.
bénédiction *nf* blessing *donner sa bénédiction à qqn* to
   bless sb
bénir {19} *vt* to bless
béni, e *adj* blessed *Votre union est bénie.* Your marriage
   has been blessed.
eau *nf* **bénite** holy water
fidèle *n* churchgoer *les fidèles* the faithful *l'assemblée des
   fidèles* the congregation
croyant, e *adj* religious

38.15 *Textes sacrés* Sacred writings

la Bible the Bible
l'Ancien Testament the Old Testament
le Nouveau Testament the New Testament
l'Évangile the Gospel
l'Évangile selon Saint Jean/Matthieu the Gospel
   according to St John/Matthew
le Coran the Koran

38.16 *Saint* Holy

saint, e *adj* **1** (before the noun) [in phrases describing
   religious symbols] holy *les saintes huiles* the holy oils *la
   Sainte Famille* the Holy Family *le Saint-Esprit* the Holy
   Spirit *le saint sacrement* the Sacrament of Holy
   Communion **2** (before the noun) [embodying holiness.
   Used of people only] holy *un saint homme* a holy man *une
   sainte femme* a holy woman **3** (after the noun) [with a
   sacred meaning] holy *un lieu saint* a holy place *un livre
   saint* a sacred book *une guerre sainte* a holy war
sacré, e *adj* [similar to **saint 3**] holy *la colline sacrée* the
   Holy Mount
divin, e *adj* [coming from a deity] divine *le divin enfant* the
   Holy Child
pieux, pieuse *adj* [a slightly old-fashioned term, not
   pejorative] pious *Le livre raconte l'histoire d'une jeune
   femme très pieuse.* The book tells the story of a very
   devout young woman.

dévot, e *adj* devout
bigot, e *adj* [pejorative. Implies sanctimoniousness and frequent visits to church] excessively devout

38.17 *L'au-delà* Life after death

âme *nf* **1**[spiritual dimension to a person] soul **2** [literary. Person] soul *un village de cinq cents âmes* a village of 500 souls
spirituel, -tuelle *adj* [concerning the soul] spiritual
paradis *nm* Heaven
enfer *nm* Hell
purgatoire *nm* Purgatory

38.18 *La non-croyance* Non-belief

athéisme *nm* atheism
athée *n* atheist
agnostique *n* agnostic
laïc, laïque *adj* **1** [not linked to a religion] secular **2** [performing a religious function but not in holy orders] lay
laïc, laïque *n* [not a member of the clergy] lay person
laïcité *nf* [the principle of *laïcité* underlies the whole of French state education, in which there are no collective acts of worship and no religious teaching] secularism

38.19 *Astrologie* Astrology

astrologie *nf* astrology
astrologue *n* astrologer
horoscope *nm* horoscope *lire son horoscope* to read one's horoscope
signe *nm* (star) sign *mon signe du Zodiaque* my sign of the Zodiac *Tu es né sous quel signe?* What sign were you born under?
zodiaque *nm* zodiac

Les signes du zodiaque Signs of the zodiac
le Verseau Aquarius
les Poissons Pisces
le Bélier Aries
le Taureau Taurus
les Gémeaux Gemini
le Cancer Cancer
le Lion Leo
la Vierge Virgo
la Balance Libra
le Scorpion Scorpio
le Sagittaire Sagittarius
le Capricorne Capricorn

39 Dangers, risks and conflicts

39.1 *Guerre* War

guerre *nf* war *guerre civile* civil war *guerre nucléaire* nuclear war *la première/deuxième guerre mondiale* the First/Second World War
soldat *nm* soldier
troufion *nm* [slang] BrE squaddy AmE soldier
militaire *adj* military **militaire** *nm* soldier
guerrier, -rrière *adj* [literary] warlike **guerrier** *nm* warrior

martial, e *adj, mpl* **-tiaux** [literary] martial
officier *nm* officer *officier d'active/de réserve* regular/reserve officer *officier de liaison* liaison officer
gradé *nm* officer
sous-officier *nm, pl* **sous-officiers** non-commissioned officer
adjudant *nm* warrant officer

39.2 *L'armée de terre* The army

maréchal *nm, pl* **-chaux** field marshal
général *nm, pl* **-raux** general
colonel *nm* colonel
lieutenant-colonel *nm, pl* **lieutenants-colonels** lieutenant colonel
chef *nm* **de bataillon** major
capitaine *nm* captain
lieutenant *nm* lieutenant
sergent-chef *nm, pl* **sergents-chefs** staff-sergeant, colour sergeant
sergent *nm* sergeant
caporal-chef *nm, pl* **caporaux-chefs** BrE corporal AmE corporal
caporal *nm, pl* **-raux** (lance) corporal
(simple) soldat *nm* private
homme *nm* **de troupe** private
infanterie *nf* infantry

The term *général* may be used to refer to three ranks: *général de corps d'armée* lieutenant general, *général de division* major general, and *général de brigade* brigadier.

39.3 *L'armée de l'air* The air force

maréchal *nm, pl* **-chaux** [the French word denotes rank, while its British equivalent is a title] Marshal of the RAF
général *nm* **de l'armée de l'air** (*pl* **généraux**) air marshall
général *nm* **de brigade aérienne** (*pl* **généraux**) air vice-marshal
colonel *nm* **de l'armée de l'air** air commodore
colonel *nm* **(de l'armée de l'air)** group captain
lieutenant-colonel *nm, pl* **lieutenants-colonels** wing commander
commandant *nm* squadron leader
capitaine *nm* **(de l'armée de l'air)** flight lieutenant
lieutenant *nm* **(de l'armée de l'air)** flying officer
sous-lieutenant *nm* pilot officer
sergent-chef *nm, pl* **sergent-chefs** flight sergeant
caporal *nm, pl* **caporaux** senior aircraftman
soldat *nm* **(de l'armée de l'air)** airman

39.4 *La marine* The navy

amiral *nm, pl* **-raux** **(de France)** admiral of the fleet
vice-amiral *nm, pl* **vice-amiraux (d'escadre)** vice-admiral
contre-amiral *nm, pl* **-raux** rear-admiral
contre-amiral *nm, pl* **-raux** commodore
capitaine *nm* captain
capitaine de frégate commander
capitaine de corvette lieutenant commander
enseigne *nm* **de vaisseau première classe** lieutenant
enseigne de vaisseau deuxième classe sublieutenant
maître *nm* chief petty officer *second maître* petty officer
matelot *nm* **(breveté)** able seaman
matelot ordinary seaman
homme *nm* **d'équipage** hand

39.5 *Les armes* Weapons

arme *nf* weapon *arme conventionnelle/nucléaire* conventional/nuclear weapon *armes chimiques* chemical weapons
armement *nm* armament
munitions *nf pl* ammunition
armer {6} *vt* to arm *être armé de* to be armed with
armure *nf* armour
balle *nf* bullet
poudre *nf* powder
mitrailleuse *nf* machine gun
mortier *nm* mortar
obus *nm* shell
char, ALSO **tank** *nm* tank
blindé *nm* armoured car
division *nf* **blindée** armoured division

39.6 *Se battre* To fight

se battre {55} *v refl* to fight *Ils se sont battus contre les Allemands.* They fought the Germans.
se rendre {53} *vi* to surrender
conquérir {24} *vt* to conquer
envahir {19} *vt* to invade
défendre {53} *vt* to defend
victoire *nf* victory
défaite *nf* defeat
siège *nm* siege *faire le siège d'une ville* to besiege a town
position *nf* **avancée** advanced position
tir *nm* **1** [action] shooting **2** [noise] gunfire
tirer {6} *vt* to shoot
tireur *nm* rifleman *tireur embusqué* sniper

Locutions Idioms
À la guerre comme à la guerre! In an emergency you just have to make do!
C'est de bonne guerre. All's fair in love and war.
faire la guerre à [obj: bad habit, absenteeism, disease] to wage war on

39.7 *Se battre ailleurs qu'à la guerre* To fight other than in war

se battre {55} *v refl* [exchange blows] to fight
se bagarrer {6} *v refl* [informal for **se battre**. Subj: e.g. drunkards, rivals] to fight *Les enfants, arrêtez de vous bagarrer!* Children, stop fighting!
bagarre *nf* [informal. Often without weapons] fight *Attention ça va être la bagarre!* Careful, there's going to be a fight!
bagarreur, -rreuse *adj* [inclined to fight] *Il est bagarreur.* He's always getting into fights.
échauffourée *nf* [brief fight between two or more men] scrap
rixe *nf* [usu between several men who have been drinking] brawl
baroudeur *nm* [man who is attracted by the idea of fighting, in the street or in wars] (street) fighter

39.8 *Opposition et hostilité* Opposition and hostility

adversaire *nf* [in war, sport, debate] opponent
opposant, e *nf* [in politics, in a debate] opponent
ennemi, e *adj* enemy *frères ennemis* warring brothers

ennemi, e *n* enemy *ennemi public (numéro un)* public enemy (number one) *On ne lui connaissait pas d'ennemis.* She had no known enemies.
inimitié *nf* [slightly formal]] enmity
inamical, e, mpl -caux *adj* [slightly formal] unfriendly
hostilité *nf* **1** [feeling] hostile feeling *Elle me traite avec hostilité.* She's hostile towards me. **2** [in war] *hostilités* fighting *faire cesser les hostilités* to stop the fighting
hostile *adj* [describes: e.g. person, country, army, reefs, weather] hostile

39.9 *Verbes d'opposition* Verbs of opposition

repousser {6} *vt* to reject *Elle n'a jamais aimé ce quatrième fils, et elle l'a toujours repoussé.* She never loved her fourth son and she has always rejected him. *repousser les avances de qqn* to rebuff sb
brouiller {6} *vt brouiller deux amis* to drive a wedge between two friends *être brouillé avec qqn* to have fallen out with sb
se disputer {6} *v refl* to argue
se chamailler {6} *v refl* [more petty than **se disputer**] to bicker
se brouiller {6} *v refl* to fall out *Il s'est brouillé avec son frère.* ALSO *Son frère et lui se sont brouillés.* He has fallen out wih this brother.

39.10 *Rancune* Grudges

rancune *nf* [long-lasting] grudge *garder rancune à qqn de qqch* to bear sb a grudge for sthg *Sans rancune!* No hard feelings!
en vouloir à qqn to hold it against sb *Je lui en ai toujours voulu d'avoir détruit mes illusions.* I've always held it against her that she destroyed my illusions.
reprocher {6} *vt reprocher qqn à* to hold sthg against *Qu'est-ce que vous lui reprochez, à votre frère?* What have you got against your brother? *Qu'est-ce que tu lui reproches, à cette omelette?* What don't you like about this omlette?
reproche *nm* criticism *Je ne te fais pas de reproches, mais . . .* I don't want to criticize you, but . . . *Le reproche qu'on peut leur faire c'est la qualité de la nourriture.* The thing one could criticize about them is the quality of the catering.

39.11 *Risque* Risk

risque *nm* risk *prendre un risque* to take a risk *courir le risque de rencontrer qqn/de perdre son investissement* to run the risk of meeting sb/of losing one's investment *C'est un risque à courir.* It's a risk we'll have to take.
risquer {6} *vt* to risk *risquer sa vie/sa santé* to risk one's life/one's health *Si tu ne signes pas le contrat, tu risques de rater une très belle occasion.* If you don't sign the contract, there's a risk that you may miss a splendid opportunity.
risqué, e *adj* [containing the possibility of danger or failure. Describes : e.g. initiative, investment] risky *C'est trop risqué.* It's too risky.
s'aventurer {6} *v refl* (often + à + infinitive) to venture *Je ne m'aventurerais pas à prédire nos performances sur le marché européen l'année prochaine.* I wouldn't venture to predict our performance in the European market next year.
aventureux, -reuse *adj* [pejorative synonym for **risqué**] adventurous

aventure nf **(à risque)** risky undertaking se lancer dans l'aventure to run a (big) risk
hasardeux, -deuse adj [less strong than **risqué**] chancy
péril nm [literary] hasard Ignorant des périls qui l'attendaient, notre héros partit pour l'Afrique. Unaware of the hasards awaiting him, our hero left for Africa.
cellule nf **de crise** emergency committee
capitaux nm pl **à risques** venture capital
risque-tout n inv [slightly stilted or humorous] daredevil

Locutions Idioms
jouer avec le feu to play with fire
l'avoir échappé belle to have had a narrow escape On l'a échappé belle, les Bonnard viennent demain mais heureusement on sera partis! We've had a narrow escape, the Bonnards are coming tomorrow but thankfully we'll be gone!
crier au loup to cry wolf
Le jeu n'en vaut pas la chandelle. It's not worth the risk.
Qui ne risque rien n'a rien [proverb] Nothing ventured nothing gained.
au péril de sa vie at the risk of his/her life
C'est à tes/vos risques et périls. On your head be it.
Attention! Careful!

39.12 *Assuré* Made safe

assurance nf **1** [commercial] insurance policy assurance au tiers third-party insurance assurance tous risques comprehensive insurance **2** [pledge] assurance donner à qqn l'assurance que . . . to assure sb that . . .
assurer {6} vt **1** [by means of a contract] to insure **2** [make sure that something is safe, or available] to ensure Le guide avait pris toutes les précautions nécessaires pour assurer sa cordée. The guide had taken all necessary precautions to ensure the safety of the climbers. Il nous faut nos deux salaires pour assurer l'ordinaire et le superflu. We need both salaries to cover basic needs and a few extras. être assuré (contre le vol/le dégât des eaux) to be insured (against theft/flood damage)
s'assurer v refl to take out insurance
assuré, e n [legal term. Having paid an insurance premium] policyholder les assurés sociaux BrE those entitled to National Insurance benefits AmE those qualified for public assistance (including Social Security, unemployment benefits and welfare)
rassurer {6} vt [psychological] to reassure Rassurez-vous, l'inspecteur ne viendra que le mois prochain. Don't worry, the inspector isn't coming until next month.
compagnie nf **d'assurances** insurance company
courtier nm **en assurances** insurance broker
police nf ALSO **contrat** nm **d'assurance** insurance policy
prime nf **d'assurance** insurance premium
demande nf **d'indemnité** insurance claim
assurance-vie nf, pl **assurances-vies** life assurance/insurance
sécurité nf [being safe from worry or from physical dangers] safety sécurité routière road safety consignes de sécurité safety instructions
en sécurité [away from physical danger or material risk] somewhere safe J'ai mis les bijoux en sécurité. I've put the jewels away somewhere safe.
de sécurité [describes: e.g. device, mechanism] safety
en lieu sûr [similar to **en sécurité**] somewhere safe Voici ton argent, va le mettre en lieu sûr. Here's your money, put it away in a safe place.
sûreté nf [being safe from physical dangers, esp those arising from war, civil unrest, acts of terrorism, etc] safety la sûreté de l'État the security of the state mettre qqch en sûreté to make sure sthg is safe

sauveteur nm [after an accident] rescuer
sauveur nm [religious] saviour
sauvegarde nf [of historic buildings or endangered species] preservation
sauvegarder {6} vt [obj: historic buildings, endangered species, rare manuscripts] to preserve
paix nf [absence of war, of disturbance, or of noise] peace Le pays est en paix. The country is at peace.

Locution Idiom
Deux précautions valent mieux qu'une. [proverb] It's better to make doubly sure.

39.13 *Protection* Protection

protection nf **1** [fact of protecting] protection Ils étaient sans protection contre la maladie. They had no protection against disease. **2** [device] guard Le casque intégral est une bonne protection. Wraparound helmets provide good protection.
protéger {14} vt to protect Un sac de couchage le protégeait du froid. A sleeping bag gave him protection against the cold. Seigneur protégez-nous! Lord protect us!
protecteur, -trice n protector
protectorat nm protectorate territoire sous protectorat français French protectorate
abriter {6} vt [implies a roof or physical protection] to shelter
abri nm [building with a roof, vegetation forming a roof, etc] shelter abri d'autobus bus shelter à l'abri under shelter se mettre à l'abri sous un arbre to shelter under a tree
asile nm [political and religious contexts] asylum La France, terre d'asile France, a traditional asylum for the persecuted
refuge nm **1** [against enemies] safe haven **2** [in the mountains] refuge
se réfugier {15} v refl to take refuge
réfugié, e n refugee camp de réfugiés refugee camp
Sauve qui peut! [in cartoons or adventure stories] Run for it!

39.14 *Objets protecteurs* Objects that protect

protège-cahier nm, pl **protège-cahiers** cover (for an exercise book)
protège-dents nm inv BrE gum shield AmE mouth protector
protège-oreilles nm inv (set of) ear-muffs
protège-tibia nm, pl **protège-tibias** shin pad

Locution Idiom
sous son aile protectrice under his/her wing

39.15 *Héroïsme et courage* Heroism and courage

courageux, -geuse adj brave
courage nm bravery du courage! be brave!
audacieux, -cieuse adj daring
audace nf **1** [willingness to take risks] daring **2** [pejorative. Nerve] audacity
hardi, e adj **1** [same meaning as **audacieux**] daring **2** [not easily intimidated] undaunted
hardiesse nf boldness

s'enhardir {19} *v refl* to become bolder *s'enhardir (jusqu')à*
. . . to become bold enough to . . . *Le petit a lâché la main
de sa mère et s'est enhardi jusqu'à venir vers moi.* The
toddler let go of his mother's hand and was bold enough
to come up to me.
téméraire *adj* foolhardy
témérité *nf* foolhardiness
brave *adj* [willing to face physical danger] brave
bravoure *nf* [in the face of physical danger] bravery
intrépide *adj* fearless
impavide *adj* [literary] impassive (in the face of danger)
vaillant, e *adj* **1** [able to face danger] brave **2** [able to face
hard work] hardworking
héroïque *adj* heroic
héroïsme *nm* heroism
héros *nm* hero
héroïne *nf* heroine

Locutions Idioms
prendre son courage à deux mains [to overcome fear
and find courage] to pluck up courage
Il/Elle n'a pas froid aux yeux. [informal] He's/She's pretty
fearless.
La fortune sourit aux audacieux. [proverb] Fortune
favours the brave.
À cœur vaillant rien d'impossible. [proverb] There's no
such word as 'can't'.
Du cran! [informal] Buck up!
Il est courageux mais pas téméraire. [ironic] He's no
hero. *Je ne prends pas ma bicyclette dans Paris, je suis
courageuse mais pas téméraire!* I don't ride my bicycle in
Paris. I may be brave but I'm not foolhardy.

40 Disputes and negotiations

40.1 *Désaccord* Disagreement

see also **128. 2 (Gambits)**

> ### usage
>
> *Describing disagreement*
> The word **désaccord** *nm*, meaning disagreement, is
> slightly formal and implies some degree of
> reasonableness in a conflict e.g.: *Le désaccord qui les
> sépare porte sur la façon d'élever leur fils.* The
> disagreement between them is about the (best) way to
> bring up their son. Because of its moderateness, it is not
> the best word to use when one needs to express
> disagreement with some force. For this, **n'être pas
> d'accord**, to disagree, is more useful, e.g.: *Moi je pense
> que le moment est venu de vendre la maison mais mon
> mari n'est pas d'accord.* I think this is the right time to
> sell the house but my husband disagrees.

désapprouver {6} *vt* [implies strong moral judgment] to
condemn *L'Histoire a désapprouvé le comportement du
Maréchal Pétain.* History has condemned the conduct of
Marshal Pétain.
discorde *nf* [disharmony] discord
ne pas s'accorder [subj: e.g. stories, testimonies] to
conflict
controverse *nf* controversy
controversé, e *adj* controversial

40.2 *Conflits entre personnes* Personal disagreements

see also **39.10 Rancune**
dispute *nf* quarrel, argument
querelle *nf* [more durable and serious than **dispute**]
(lasting) quarrel
crêpage *nm* **de chignon** [between women only] squabble
scène *nf* **de ménage** (marital) row
mésentente *nf* [not getting on together. Often within a
family or with close associates] friction
incompatibilté *nf* **d'humeur** incompatibility

Locutions Idioms
avoir l'esprit de contradiction to be argumentative
semer la zizanie [set people against one another] to cause
trouble
la pomme de discorde [phrase often used humorously]
the apple of discord

40.3 *Inflexible* Inflexible

inflexible *adj* **1** [describes a person who will not be
influenced] unbending *Ils viendront vous supplier mais il
faut rester inflexible.* They'll beg you but you mustn't
change your mind. **2** [describes a person who keeps to
routines] rigid **3** [describes: e.g. regulations, policy]
inflexible
impitoyable *adj* [emotionally unbending] pitiless
intransigeant, e *adj* [intellectually rigid] uncompromising

Locutions Idioms
n'avoir pas de cœur, ALSO **être sans cœur** to be hard-
hearted
On ne le fera pas changer d'avis. You'll never get him to
change his mind.
faire la sourde oreille to refuse to listen *J'ai essayé
plusieurs fois de lui parler d'argent, mais elle fait la sourde
oreille.* I've tried several times to mention money to her
but she refuses to listen.

40.4 *Refus* Refusal

refuser {6} *vt* (often + *de* + infinitive) to refuse *S'il me
demande de venir, je refuserai.* If he asks me to come I'll
refuse. *Il a refusé de participer au pot d'adieu de la
secrétaire.* He refused to make a contribution to the
farewell drinks party for the secretary.
refus *nm* refusal *opposer son refus à une proposition* to
refuse a proposal *un refus catégorique* a flat refusal
mettre son veto à qqch to veto sthg
faire un signe de dénégation 1 [with one's hand] to
signal one's refusal **2** [with one's head] to shake one's
head in refusal

Locutions Idioms
Il/Elle se ferait hacher menu plutôt que de . . .
He'd/She'd die rather than . . .

40.5 *Accord* Agreement

see also **40.1 Désaccord, 128 (Gambits)**
accord *nm* agreement *Il y a eu un accord entre les deux
pays sur la non-prolifération d'armes nucléaires.* An
agreement was reached between the two countries on
halting the spread of nuclear weapons. **d'accord** in
agreement *D'accord?* OK?

être d'accord (avec qqn) to agree (with sb) *Vos parents sont d'accord?* Do your parents agree? *Ils sont tombés d'accord sur la nécessité d'ajourner les travaux.* They (finally) agreed on the need to postpone the work.

être en accord avec qqch to agree with sth

s' accorder {6} *v refl* to concur *Les congressistes s'accordent sur ce point.* The members of the conference concur on this point. *Le frère et la sœur ne parviennent pas à s'accorder.* The brother and sister can't reach an agreement.

rapprocher {6} *vt* to bring together *Ce drame les a rapprochés.* This tragedy brought them together.

entente *nf* [between persons] relationship *vivre en bonne entente* to live harmoniously together

concorder {6} *vi* to concur *Les témoignages concordent.* The testimonies concur.

n'est-ce pas? [phrase used to ask for agreement] isn't it? isn't that so?

bien sûr [phrase used to state agreement] of course

Locutions Idioms
Qui ne dit mot consent. [proverb] Silence is taken to be agreement.

être de connivence avec to be in league with

s'entendre comme larrons en foire to get on like a house on fire

40.6 *Persuasion* Persuasion

see also **126 (Gambits)**

convaincre {60} *vt* [implies use of rational proof] to convince

persuader {6} *vt* [similar to **convaincre**, but implies that eloquence is used] to persuade

persuasion nf persuasion

influencer {7} *vt* to influence

influer {6} *vi* influer sur to influence

argument *nm* **convaincant** convincing argument

40.7 *Acceptation* Acceptance

accepter {6} *vt* to agree to *Elle accepte toutes vos conditions.* She agrees to all your conditions. *Je n'accepterai jamais le divorce.* I'll never agree to a divorce.

acceptation *nf* acceptance *Il exigeait de moi une acceptation totale de son style de vie.* He demanded from me total acceptance of his lifestyle.

admettre {56} *vt* [agree that something is a fact] to accept *Il n'a jamais admis mon point de vue.* He never accepted my point of view. *J'admets que je n'avais pas mesuré les conséquences de ma décision.* I admit I hadn't thought through the consequences of my decision.

avouer {6} *vt* **1** [recognize that one did something wrong] to own up to *Elle a avoué son larcin.* She owned up to the theft. **2** [concede] to admit *J'avoue que je n'y connais rien en électricité.* I admit I don't know anything about electricity.

avouer *vi* to confess *Vers 3 heures du matin, il a finalement avoué.* About 3 o'clock in the morning he finally confessed.

reconnaître {64} *vt* [obj: e.g. truth, error] to admit

s'incliner {6} *v refl* (often + *devant*) [used humorously] to give way, to bow (to) *Je m'incline devant ton savoir-faire.* I bow to your (superior) know-how. *Si c'est ton prof qui t'a dit ça, alors je m'incline.* If your teacher's the one who told you this, I'll bow to his superior knowledge.

concéder{10} *vt* [in a debate, a joust. Obj: e.g. advantage, victory, point] to concede

Locutions Idioms
se rendre à l'évidence to accept the obvious
baisser les bras to give in

40.8 *Suggestion* Suggestion

see also **127 (Gambits)**

suggestion *nf* [idea given to someone, rather tentatively] suggestion

suggérer {10} *vt* and *vi* to suggest

conseil *nm* [more resolute than **suggestion**] piece of advice *donner un conseil à qqn* to give sb a piece of advice *donner des conseils à qqn* to give sb advice

conseiller, -llère *n* adviser *conseiller d'orientation* careers adviser

-conseil [suffix used after names of professions to denote consultant] *avocat-conseil* legal consultant **ingénieur-conseil** consultant engineer

conseiller *vt* **1** [encourage someone to behave in a particular way] to recommend, to advise *conseiller qqch à qqn* to recommend sthg to sb *Je te conseille le boudin aux pommes.* I'd recommend (you try) the black pudding with apples. *conseiller à qqn de faire* to advise sb to do *Le médecin m'a conseillé de ralentir mes activités.* The doctor advised me to slow down a bit. **2** [give advice to] to advise *C'est lui qui me conseille quand j'achète une voiture.* He advises me whenever I buy a car. *bien/mal conseiller qqn* to give sb good/bad advice **3** (in the impersonal form) *il est conseillé de* it is advisable to *il n'est pas conseillé de* it is inadvisable to

proposition *nf* [more formal suggestion, worked out in some detail] proposal

proposer {6} *vt* (often + *de* } [offer as an idea] to suggest *Pour terminer, je vous propose le dessert du chef.* To finish your meal, I suggest the chef's dessert. *Il m'a proposé de monter une affaire avec lui.* He suggested we started a business together. *Je lui ai proposé de l'emmener dîner.* I offered to take him out to dinner.

recommandation *nf* recommendation

recommander {8} *vt* (often + *de* + infinitive) [similar to **conseiller 1**] to recommend *Je vous recommande la visite du château* ALSO *de visiter le château.* I recommend you visit the château. *Recommandez-leur la prudence* ALSO *d'être prudents.* Tell them to be careful.

Locution Idiom
Les conseilleurs ne sont pas toujours les payeurs. [the noun **conseilleur** is not used much other than in this phrase] Advice comes cheap when you don't have to foot the bill.

40.9 *Promettre* To promise

see also **118 (Gambits)**

promesse *nf* promise *faire une promesse* to make a promise *tenir une promesse* to keep a promise *promesse électorale* election pledge

promettre {56} *vt* to promise *Je lui ai promis de venir la voir demain* ALSO *que je viendrai la voir demain.* I promised her I'd visit her tomorrow.

donner sa parole d'honneur (que) to promise solemnly (that)

parole d'honneur! [used to guarantee the truth of what one is saying] I swear (it)!

engagement *nm* commitment *prendre un engagement* to take on a commitment *prendre l'engagement de faire qqch* to commit oneself to doing sthg *remplir ses engagements* to honour one's commitments

Locutions Idioms

Chose promise chose dûe. [used to assure someone that a promise will be kept] A promise is a promise. *Je te donne tes cinquante francs, chose promise chose dûe.* Here's your 50 francs, a promise is a promise.

une promesse d'ivrogne [a promise made by someone who is likely to forget what was promised] an empty promise

Croix de bois, croix de fer, si je mens, je vais en enfer! [literally 'Wooden cross, iron cross, let me go to hell if there is a word of a lie in what I'm saying'] Cross my heart and hope to die!

40.10 *S'interposer* To intervene

s'interposer {6} *v refl* [act decisively to change the course of an action. Not pejorative. Subj: person] to intervene *La police voulait fermer le collège mais heureusement la mairie s'est interposée.* The police wanted to close the college but fortunately the council intervened.

intervenir {23} *vi* **1** [similar to **s'interposer**, but less decisive] to intervene **2** [take part in a conversation, usu when one has not been invited to do so] to speak *Puis-je intervenir?* May I speak? *Personne ne vous a demandé d'intervenir.* Nobody asked you to speak. **3** [take part in a conference] to speak *Notre collègue italien interviendra tout à l'heure pour vous résumer l'état des recherches en la matière.* Our Italian colleague will shortly be speaking to you in order to summarize the state of research in this area.

interférer {10} *vi* [may be slightly pejorative. Subj: factor, influence] to interfere *Son élection ne s'explique pas uniquement par ses idées politiques, d'autres éléments ont interféré.* Her success in the election can't be explained by her political ideas alone, other factors played a part.

Locutions Idioms

se mêler de qqch [pejorative] to interfere in sthg *De quoi te mêles-tu?* What business is it of yours?

mettre, ALSO **fourrer son nez dans qqch** [pejorative. Investigate] to stick one's nose into sthg

mettre son grain de sel (dans qqch) [pejorative. Give one's unsolicited opinion] to stick one's oar in.

41 Showing, giving and owning

41.1 *Montrer* To show

montrer {6} *vt* [general term] to show *J'ai dû montrer ma carte de presse pour entrer.* I had to show my press card before I was allowed in. *montrer qqn/qqch du doigt* to point at sb/sthg (with one's finger)

désigner {6} *vt* **1** [with a finger] to point at **2** [with a nod] to nod in the direction of **3** [select] to single out *Personne ne se proposant pour la vaisselle, il m'a fallu désigner quelqu'un.* As nobody volunteered, I had to single out someone to do the dishes.

signaler {6} *vt* [indicate something which others have not noticed] to point out *Le petit Marc ne voit pas bien le tableau, il faut que je le signale à ses parents.* Little Marc can't see the blackboard properly, I'll have to point this out to his parents. *Le tournant dangereux n'est pas*

signalé. There's no sign warning you of the dangerous curve in the road.

prouver {6} *vt* [show scientifically, logically or mathematically] to prove

41.2 *Montrer pour se faire admirer* To show in order to be admired

faire étalage de, ALSO **étaler** {6} *vt* [pejorative. Obj: knowledge, erudition] to show off

afficher {6} *vt* [pejorative. Obj: e.g. knowledge, sorrow, wealth] to flaunt

s'afficher *v refl* to show off, to flaunt oneself *Il a les moyens de s'afficher dans tous les endroits élégants.* He can afford to show off in all the chic places.

41.3 *Montrer le chemin* To show the way

see also **4.3 Visites**; **6.2 Voyages et déplacements**

indication(s) *nf (pl)* [printed on a map or handwritten] directions *Suis l'indication que je t'ai donnée* ALSO *les indications que je t'ai données.* Follow the directions I gave you.

indiquer {6} *vt* [show something so that others will notice or understand] to show *Quelqu'un m'a indiqué la direction.* Somebody showed me the way.

guide *nm* [book] guide book

guide *n* [person] guide *Elle est guide de montagne depuis 1993.* She's been a mountain guide since 1993.

visite *nf* **guidée** guided tour

guider {6} *vt* **1** [show the way] to guide *Je recule avec la remorque, tu peux te mettre sur le trottoir et me guider?* I'll back up with the trailer, could you stand on the pavement and guide me? **2** [help with a task] to advise *Je ne connais pas bien ce travail, j'ai besoin qu'on me guide.* I don't know this type of work very well, I need advice.

41.4 *Endroits où l'on montre des objets* Places where things are displayed

musée *nm* museum

vitrine *nf* showcase

maison-témoin *nf, pl* **maisons-témoins** BrE show-house AmE model house

appartement-témoin *nm, pl* **appartements-témoins** BrE show-flat AmE model apartment

salon *nm*, ALSO **foire-exposition** *nf, pl* **foires-expositions** show *le salon de la plaisance/de l'automobile* the boat/car show

salle *nf* **d'exposition 1** [in a museum] gallery **2** [at a fair] showroom

exposer {6} *vt* [in a museum] to exhibit

mettre en évidence to display (prominently) *Placez votre ticket de stationnement en évidence sur votre pare-brise.* Display your parking ticket on your windscreen.

41.5 *Choses montrées* Things displayed

pièce *nf* **1** [in art exhibition] exhibit **2** [in court of law] *pièce (à conviction)* exhibit

échantillon *nm* [of material, carpet] sample

spécimen *nm* [text] sample page

41.6 *Évident* Obvious

évident, e *adj* [plain to see] obvious *À la lecture des faits, la gêne de l'accusé était évidente.* When the facts were read, the defendant's unease was obvious (to all).
de toute évidence obviously *De toute évidence, il avait bu.* He had obviously been drinking.
évidemment *adv* **1** [as anyone can see] obviously *On ne peut évidemment pas sortir sous cette pluie.* Obviously we can't go out in this rain. **2** [predictably enough] no wonder *Marine a renversé son lait! – Évidemment, elle ne fait jamais attention!* Marine spilled her milk! – No wonder, she never watches what she's doing!
clair, e *adj* [easily worked out] clear *Si elle me réclame une pension alimentaire, je ne pourrai pas payer, c'est clair!* If she asks me for alimony, clearly I won't be able to pay! *clair et net* crystal clear **clairement** *adv* clearly

Locution Idiom
C'est pas évident! [informal cliché] It's not easy.*Trouver des fringues pas chères mais de qualité, c'est pas évident!* Finding good cheap clothes isn't easy!

41.7 *Donner et transmettre* General terms for giving

donner {6} *vt* (often followed by *à* + name or description of the person receiving) **1** [general term] to give *je lui ai donné une serviette propre.* I gave her a clean towel. *J'ai donné un peu d'argent aux enfants.* I gave the children a little money. *On nous a donné un formulaire à remplir.* We were given a form to complete. *J'ai déjà donné.* I have already made a contribution. **2** [stresses the fact that things are given for free] to donate *Donnez-nous vos vieux vêtements, nous les recyclerons.* Donate your unwanted clothes, we'll recycle them.
passer {6} *vt* (often followed by *à* + name or description of the person receiving) [give quickly, usu by hand] *Passe-moi le tournevis.* Hand me the screwdriver. *Pouvez-vous me passer le sel?* Could you pass the salt? *On m'a passé un papier.* I was handed a piece of paper.
remettre {56} *vt* (often followed by *à* + name or description of the person receiving) [implies transferring ownership] to hand over *Les propriétaires nous remettront les clés demain.* The owners will hand over the keys to us tomorrow.
céder {10} *vt* (often followed by *à* + name or description of the person receiving) [give for a lower price than anticipated] to let (it) go for *Ils ont finalement cédé la maison et le terrain pour trois cent mille francs* They finally let the house and the land go for 300,000 francs.
laisser {6} *vt* (often followed by *à* + name or description of the person receiving) [as inheritance] to bequeath

41.8 *Donner généreusement* To give away

offrir {27} *vt* (often followed by *à* + name or description of the person receiving) [obj: e.g. gift, chocolates, jewel] to give (as a present) *Je pense lui offrir un bracelet en argent pour son anniversaire.* I'm thinking of giving her a silver bracelet for her birthday. *On va partager les frais, voici cinquante francs. – Non, non, c'est moi qui offre.* Let's split the cost, here's 50 francs. – Certainly not, it's my treat. **2** [give free as part of advertising drive] to give (away) *Pendant le mois de février, nous offrons un stylo à tout acheteur de montre.* During February we are giving (away) a pen to anyone purchasing a watch.

cadeau *nm, pl* **-x** gift, present *un cadeau d'anniversaire* a birthday present *faire cadeau de qqch à qqn* to give sb sthg as a present *Ses collègues lui ont fait cadeau d'un vase de cristal.* Her colleagues gave her a crystal vase as a present.
pourboire *nm* tip *donner un pourboire au garçon* to tip the waiter. *Elle m'a donné cinquante francs de pourboire.* She tipped me 50 francs.
offre *nf* **1** [suggestion] proposition *Je t'avais dit que je pouvais t'aider, et mon offre tient toujours.* I told you I could help you, and my offer still stands. **2** [by shop or commercial outfit] (special) offer
charité *nf* charity *faire la charité à qqn* to give to sb out of charity *Ils ne veulent pas qu'on leur fasse la charité.* They don't want handouts.
charitable *adj* [describes: e.g. person, attitude, act] charitable
caritatif, -tive *adj* [describes: e.g. organization, association] charitable
donation *nf* donation
donneur, -nneuse *n* donor *donneur de sang* blood donor *donneur d'organe* organ donor

41.9 *Faire en sorte que des choses soient données* To ensure that things are given

fournir {19} *vt* (often followed by *à* + name or description of the person receiving) [give so that someone may have all the things they need, or all the things they have ordered] to provide *Le traiteur fournira tout y compris les couverts.* The caterer will provide everything including knives and forks.
munir {19} *vt* (always followed by name or description of receiver, + *de* + thing received) [give so that someone may have the thing they need for survival or protection] to provide *Munissez votre enfant d'un bonnet de laine pour les jours d'excursion par temps froid.* For cold-weather outings, make sure you provide your child with a hat.
délivrer {6} *vt* (often followed by *à* + name or description of the person receiving) [in administrative contexts] to issue

41.10 *Donner à plusieurs personnes ou se donner l'un l'autre* To give to several people or to each other

partager {8} *vt* **1** [split something and give a piece to each of a number of people] to share *Les enfants, il faut partager les bonbons.* Children, you have to share the sweets. **2** [give up part of something in order to use jointly] to share *Il m'a proposé de partager le taxi avec lui.* He offered to share his taxi with me.
distribuer {6} *vt* [similar to **partager 1**, but implies that the recipients are entitled to the things received] to give out *Notre organisation distribue des couvertures aux réfugiés.* Our organization gives out blankets to the refugees.
échanger {8} *vt* **1** [give to each other. Obj: e.g. news, advice] to swap **2** [in shops, when goods are unsatisfactory] to exchange
troquer {6} *vt* [acquire goods or services by exchange, doing away with the need for money] to swap

Locutions Idioms
Donner c'est donner, reprendre c'est voler. [children's saying] Once you've given something away you can't change your mind and take it back.

La façon de donner vaut mieux que ce qu'on donne. [Corneille's line in *Le Menteur*, 1635] It's not what you give, it's the way you give it that matters.

Un 'tiens' vaut mieux que deux 'tu l'auras'. A bird in the hand is worth two in the bush.

La plus belle fille du monde ne peut donner que ce qu'elle a. [proverb] You can't give what you haven't got.

41.11 *Tenir et garder* To hold and to keep

tenir {23} *vt* **1** [in one's grip] to hold, to clasp *L'enfant tenait la balle serrée dans sa main.* The child clasped the ball in his/her hand. *Je l'ai tenue dans mes bras longtemps ce soir-là.* I held her in my arms for a long time that night. *Tiens le verre à deux mains.* Hold the glass with both hands. **2** [under one's influence] to hold *Elle avait trouvé l'argument qu'il fallait et elle tenait son auditoire.* She'd found the right argument and she held her audience. *Les nationalistes tiennent la ville.* The nationalists are holding the town.

tenir *vi* [remain in position] to hold *Le clou est trop court, le tableau ne tiendra pas.* The nail's too short, the picture won't hold. *Tu peux monter, l'échelle tient.* You can go up, the ladder's safe.

se tenir *v refl* to steady oneself *Tiens-toi bien, le bus démarre!* Hold on tight, the bus is about to start! *se tenir à un mur/une grille* to cling to a wall/a railing

serrer {6} *vt* to hold tight(ly) *Il serrait la pièce dans sa main.* He held the coin tightly in his hand. *Serre-moi dans tes bras.* Hold me tight (in your arms).

maintenir {23} *vt* [fix] to hold *Un petit peigne doré maintenait ses cheveux (en place).* A small golden comb held her hair (in place) *Des baguettes maintiennent la photo en place.* Strips of wood keep the photograph in place.

détenir {23} *vt* **1** [have something which others might want. Obj: e.g. record, information] to hold *Le notaire détient son testament.* The lawyer holds her will. **2** [obj: e.g. suspect, criminal] to detain

retenir {23} *vt* [prevent from falling] to hold *Des embrasses retenaient les épais rideaux de velours.* The thick velvet curtains were held in position with ties.

conserver {6} *vt* **1** [maintain in a good state. Obj: e.g. food, materials, archives, data] to keep *Nos olives sont conservées dans de la saumure.* Our olives are kept in brine. **2** [hold on to] to keep *Je souhaite conserver mon travail.* I want to keep my job.

garder {6} *vt* **1** [retain for oneself] to keep, to hold on to *Gardez la monnaie.* Keep the change. *garder le pouvoir* to hold on to power **2** [keep for sb else] to save *Il faut garder des cerises pour maman quand elle rentrera.* We must save some cherries for when mother gets home.

recueillir {28} *vt* [take something precious often from nature or through a careful process. Obj: e.g. sap, honey] to collect *Mettez le lait dans des pots et le lendemain recueillez la crème.* Pour the milk into pots and collect the cream on the following day. *Nous avons déjà recueilli 300 signatures.* We've already collected 300 signatures.

Locution Idiom
Qui trop embrasse mal étreint. [proverb warning against excessive ambition] By trying to grasp too many different things, you may end up losing everything.

41.12 *Prendre* To take

prendre {54} *vt* [so as to have something] to take *J'ai pris l'argent et je lui ai donné un reçu.* I took the money and gave her a receipt.

reprendre {54} *vt* [after lending or showing something to someone] to take back *Je peux reprendre mon stylo?* May I have my pen back?

passer prendre to collect *Vous pouvez passer prendre votre voiture demain.* You can come and collect your car tomorrow.

enlever {9} *vt* **1** [so as to prevent harm] to remove *enlever qqch à qqn* to take sthg from sb *Enlève-lui ce couteau.* Take that knife from him. **2** [detach] to take off *J'enlève le prix?* Shall I take the price label off?

41.13 *Prendre vite* To grab and to catch

saisir {19} *vt* [implies agility or speed] to grab *Il saisit la lettre et déchira l'enveloppe.* He seized the letter and tore it open.

s'emparer de {6} *v refl* [similar to **saisir**, with more firmness and even some brutality] to grab (hold of) *Un individu s'est emparé de son sac.* A man grabbed (hold of) her bag.

attraper {6} *vt* [when something is moving fast] to catch *Essaie d'attraper la balle d'une seule main.* Try catching the ball with one hand.

rattraper {6} *vt* [when something or someone is falling] to catch *Je l'ai rattrapée juste à temps pour empêcher sa tête de heurter le sol.* I caught her just before her head hit the floor.

41.14 *Acquérir* To acquire

acquérir {24} *vt* [get for permanent use. Implies the the thing obtained is large, expensive or important] to acquire *Ma famille a acquis ces terres pendant les années cinquante.* My family acquired this land in the fifties.

se procurer {6} *v refl* [implies that some effort is expended in obtaining e.g.: special ingredient, special issue of magazine etc] to get *Où est-ce qu'on peut se procurer du gingembre frais?* Where can one get fresh ginger?

obtenir {23} *vt* [have a required object given to one. Implies effort, but ultimate success is within the control of the giver] to get *J'ai fini par obtenir deux billets au premier rang.* In the end I managed to get two front-row tickets.

trouver {6} *vt* [informal synonym for **se procurer**] to get *Je trouve tout ce que je veux chez l'épicier d'à côté.* I can get anything I need at the local grocer's.

prendre {54} *vt* [obtain on a regular basis. Obj: e.g. newspaper, bread, milk] to get *C'est chez lui que je prends mon pain depuis vingt ans.* I've been getting my bread from his shop for 20 years.

avoir {1} *vt* [informal synonym for all the verbs listed above] to get *Où est-ce que tu as eu ton canapé?* Where did you get your sofa from?

Locutions Idioms
mettre la main sur to lay one's hand(s) on
Bien mal acquis ne profite jamais. [proverb seeking to encourage honesty] Ill-gotten gains seldom prosper.

41.15 *Posséder* To own

posséder {10} *vt* to own *Tout est à ma femme, je ne possède rien en propre.* Everything belongs to my wife, I don't have anything in my own name. *Qui, dans notre société, possède les moyens de production?* Who, in our society, owns the means of production?

propriétaire *n* [general term] owner *Qui est le propriétaire de la Ford bleue garée devant la porte?* Who is the owner of the blue Ford parked outside the door?

propriété *nf* **1** [fact of owning] ownership *titre de propriété* proof of ownership *accession à la propriété* home ownership **2** [house, or house with land around it] property *L'entrée de la propriété est à gauche après l'église.* The drive leading to the house is on the left after the church.

affaires *nf pl* (personal) belongings *N'oublie pas tes affaires dans la classe.* Don't leave your belongings in the classroom.

appartenir {23} *vi appartenir à* to belong to *Ce livre appartient à . . .* This book belongs to . . .

avoir *nm* [legal term] *leur/mon avoir* their/my assets

Citation Quotation
La propriété, c'est le vol. This partial quotation from Proudhon's 1840 essay *Qu'est-ce que la propriété?* is often rendered in English as 'Property is theft', corresponding to sense 2 of **propriété** above. However, a better translation would correspond to sense 1 above: 'Property ownership is theft'.

42 Temperament and emotion

42.1 *Tempérament et comportement* Temperament and behaviour

caractère *nm* [long-term psychological traits] character *avoir mauvais caractère* to be bad-tempered *avoir bon caractère* to be good-tempered *avoir du caractère* to be a strong character *n'avoir aucun caractère* to be a weak character *troubles du caractère* personality disorders
personnalité *nf* [attitudes and behaviour. Can be used in psychological contexts] personality *troubles de la personnalité* personality disorders *Elle a une forte personnalité.* She has a strong personality.
tempérament *nm* [attitudes and emotions typical of someone] nature *Il est de tempérament indulgent.* He has a forgiving nature.
comportement *nm* [what a person or an animal does, in general or on a particular occasion] behaviour
se comporter {6} *v refl* [habitually or in a given situation] to behave *Tu t'es bien comporté hier.* You behaved well yesterday. *Elle s'est mal comportée dans sa jeunesse.* She behaved badly in her youth.
se conduire {82} *v refl* [like **se comporter**, but with moral overtones] to behave *Devant la tentation de la corruption, certains savent se conduire dignement.* Faced with the temptation of corruption, there are those who know how to behave with dignity.

42.2 *Humeurs qui passent* Short-lived moods

humeur *nf* **1** [good or bad frame of mind] mood *De quelle humeur est-elle ce matin?* What (sort of) mood is she in this morning? *de bonne humeur* in a good mood *de mauvaise humeur* in a bad mood **2** [pejorative] bad mood *Excusez-moi pour ce matin, j'ai eu un mouvement d'humeur.* I apologise for sounding off this morning. *Il ne sait pas cacher ses humeurs.* He doesn't know how to conceal his moods.
disposition *nf* [particular feelings at a given time] frame of mind *Vous allez le trouver dans une excellente disposition.* You'll find him in a positive frame of mind.
manières *nf pl* [used pejoratively in connection with old-fashioned standards of polite behaviour] behaviour *faire des manières* to put on airs

42.3 *Émotion* Emotion

émotion *nf* **1** [strong mood affecting one] emotion *L'émotion lui nouait la gorge.* He could hardly speak for emotion. **2** [particular feeling]] feeling *À la vue des enfants, je sens une douce émotion m'envahir.* Watching the children, I am filled with a feeling of tenderness. *Cette fin de match, que d'émotion!* What a thrilling end to the match! *donner une émotion à qqn* to give sb a shock
émotif, -tive *adj* **1** [feeling and showing emotions readily] sensitive **2** [pejorative. Unable to control one's emotions] excitable

affectif, -tive *adj* [describes: e.g. reaction, state, behaviour] emotional *Notre vie affective est influencée par les expériences vécues dans notre enfance.* Our emotional life is influenced by things which happened to us when we were young children.

affectif, émotionnel and **émotif**
All three adjectives mean emotional, but *affectif* is a psychological term and speakers use it when they want to sound objective. *Émotionnel* and *émotif*, on the other hand, describe an impressionable person or a reaction of an extremely emotive type.

ému, e *adj* [describes a person under the influence of an emotion] moved *La présidente, visiblement émue, a souhaité bonne chance à son successeur.* Showing considerable emotion, the president wished her successor good luck.
sentiment *nm* [any emotion, good or bad] feeling
sentimental, e *adj, mpl* **-taux** [usu pejorative] sentimental
sensible *adj* sensitive
sensibilité *nf* sensitivity
sensiblerie *nf* [pejorative] mawkishness

42.4 *Verbes d'émotion* Verbs expressing emotion

émouvoir {44} *vt* to move *Cette scène a ému les télé-spectateurs du monde entier.* Viewers all over the world were moved by this scene.
sentir {25} *vt* [be aware of a feeling, sometimes a subtle one] to feel *Je sens une grande tristesse m'envahir.* I feel a great sadness sweeping over me. *Amour ou amitié, il n'est pas toujours facile de sentir ces nuances.* Love or friendship, it's not always easy to feel the difference.
ressentir {25} *vt* [slightly more formal than **sentir**. Be under the influence of a lasting emotion] to feel *Ce que je ressens pour lui n'est pas de l'amour.* What I feel for him is not love. *ressentir une grande émotion* to feel a powerful emotion
éprouver {6} *vt* [to be under the influence of] to feel *éprouver de la jalousie* to feel jealous *éprouver un sentiment* to have a feeling

Locutions Idioms
Son sang n'a fait qu'un tour. His/Her blood ran cold.
tourner les sangs à qqn BrE to give sb a turn AmE to cause a strong emotion in sb

43 Observing and failing to observe rules of behaviour

43.1 *Moralité et vertu* Morality and virtue

See also **43.15 Gentillesse et générosité**

bon, bonne *adj* (after noun) [an old-fashioned term. Disposed towards helping fellow-beings] good *Il a toujours été bon envers nous.* He was always good to us. *Sa mère était une femme bonne, qui s'occupait beaucoup des pauvres.* His mother was a good woman who did a lot for the poor.

bonté *nf* goodness

bien *nm* [philosophical or religious term] good *le bien et le mal* good and evil

innocent, e *adj* **1** [not guilty] innocent *innocent de ce dont on l'accuse* innocent of what he is being accused of **2** [not wicked, nor to do with sex] innocent *À leur âge, leurs jeux sont encore innocents.* At that age, their games are still innocent.

innocence *nf* innocence *en toute innocence* in all innocence *clamer,* ALSO *crier son innocence* to protest one's innocence

pur, e *adj* [describes: e.g. motivation, thought] pure **pureté** *nf* purity

moral, e *adj, mpl* **-raux 1** [ethical. Describes : e.g. question, judgment, principle] moral **2** [of good character. Describes: e.g. person, life] moral, decent

moralement *adv* morally *moralement parlant* morally speaking

morale *nf* **1** [edifying message] moral *et la morale de l'histoire, c'est . . .* and the moral of the story is . . . **2** [rules of conduct] moral principles *La morale n'est plus enseignée à l'école.* They don't teach schoolchildren moral principles any more. *Je suis assez grand pour savoir ce que j'ai à faire, ne me fais pas la morale,* ALSO *épargne-moi tes leçons de morale.* I'm old enough to know what I have to do, don't lecture me.

usage

La morale and **le moral**
Beware of the masculine noun *le moral*, which has nothing to do with morals, but refers to one's inner perception of how one is faring in life, e.g. *Il a le moral.* He's feeling good about things. See also **48.1 Robuste**.

moralité *nf* **1** [set of moral rules] morality *Sa moralité ne me regarde pas.* His moral standards are no concern of mine. *la moralité publique* public morality **2** [informal. To conclude] consequence *Tu n'avais pas prévenu que tu serais en retard, moralité on t'a cherché partout.* You didn't say you were going to be late: the consequence was that we were looking for you everywhere.

conscience *nf* [awareness of good and evil] moral sense

avoir bonne conscience to have a clear conscience

pour se donner bonne conscience (purely) to salvage one's conscience

avoir mauvaise conscience to have something on one's conscience

devoir *nm* duty *faire son devoir* to do one's duty

vertu *nf* [literary] virtue

vertueux, -tueuse *adj* [literary] virtuous

Locutions Idioms

C'est une bonne pâte. ALSO **Il est bon/Elle est bonne comme le bon pain.** He's/She's got a heart of gold.

C'est une pâte d'homme [similar to above, but applies only to males] He's full of the milk of human kindness.

C'est une sainte-nitouche. [used of women, implies outward show of virtue, belied by slyness] Butter wouldn't melt in her mouth.

43.2 *Qui se conforme à ce que l'on demande* Well-behaved

see also **37.17 Soumission et passivité, 66.13 Raison**

sage *adj,* ALSO **gentil, -tille** *adj* [used of or to children. Obedient] being well-behaved *Sois gentille avec Grand-mère pendant que je suis partie.* Behave yourself with Grandma while I'm out.

obéissant, e *adj* obedient

obéir {19} *vi* (often + *à*) to obey *obéir à qqn* to obey sb *obéir à un ordre* to obey an order *Tais-toi et obéis!* Be quiet and do as you're told! *Obéissant à un pressentiment, il revint chez lui, juste à temps pour sauver sa famille de l'incendie.* Prompted by feelings of foreboding he came home just in time to save his family from the fire.

obéissance *nf* obedience *Ils devaient obéissance à leur seigneur.* They owed obedience to their liege lord.

Locution Idiom

sage comme une image [used mainly of children] as good as gold

43.3 *Égoïsme* Selfishness

égoïste *adj* selfish

égoïsme *nm* selfishness

égocentrique *adj* self-centred

égocentrisme *nm* self-centredness

Locutions Idioms

On n'est jamais si bien servi que par soi-même. If you want a job done properly, do it yourself.

Il/Elle se prend pour le nombril du monde. He thinks he is/She thinks she is the centre of the universe.

Il n'y en a que pour lui/elle. [informal] With him/her, it's always 'me, me me'

Citation Quotation

Après nous le déluge. [allegedly uttered by Madame de Pompadour to comfort Louis the XVth after a military defeat. Reflects the cynicism and selfishness attributed to the royal entourage] Who cares what happens after we've gone.

43.4 *Cérémonieux* Formal

cérémonieux, -nieuse *adj* [describes: e.g. person, welcome, dinner] very formal

cérémonie *nf* **1** [formal event] ceremony *C'était émouvant, j'ai pleuré pendant la cérémonie.* It was moving, I cried during the ceremony. **2** [fact of acting formally] ceremony *Les déplacements du président s'entourent de beaucoup de cérémonie.* Much ceremony surrounds the presidential trips.

digne *adj* dignified *Il est resté digne sous les huées du public.* He remained dignified when faced with the booing of the audience.

dignité *nf* dignified attitude *On a sa dignité!* You have to remain dignified!

pompeux, -peuse *adj* [pejorative] pompous

Locutions Idioms
en grande cérémonie, ALSO **pompe** with great ceremony
mettre les petits plats dans les grands to lay on a feast
être (très) collet monté [old-fashioned and insisting on
proper behaviour] to belong to the old school

43.5 *Simple* Informal

simple adj 1 [without pretentiousness, by implication,
sincere. Describes: e.g. family, welcome, meal] unassuming
Ce sont des gens simples, malgré leur notoriété. They are
unassuming people in spite of their fame. 2 [without
complexity] plain *expliquer quelque chose dans un
langage simple* to explain something in plain language
simplement adv [with no unnecessary fuss or frills]
informally
à la bonne franquette [always applies to meals, simple
and friendly] *Venez dîner demain soir, ce sera à la bonne
franquette*. Come for dinner tomorrow night, you'll have
to take pot luck.
relax adj inv [in common informal usage] cool *Elle est
relax, ta mère, elle te laisse sortir quand tu veux*. Your
mother's cool, she lets you go out whenever you want.
intime adj [describes: e.g. reunion, engagement party,
wedding ceremony] involving close friends and relatives
only

43.6 *Courtoisie* Politeness

politesse nf [general term. Refers to conventional
standards of behaviour] politeness *formule de politesse*
letter ending
poli, e adj polite *un sourire poli* a polite smile *Ce n'est pas
poli d'interrompre les gens*. Butting in to people's
conversation is rude. *Le serveur a été à peine poli*. The
waiter was almost rude. *Dites donc, vous, soyez poli!* Hey,
you, don't be so rude!
bien élevé, e adj [describes: child. Refers to conventional
standards of upbringing] polite *Eux, ils ont dit merci, voilà
des enfants bien élevés!* They said thank you, now that's
what I call polite children.
courtoisie nf [implies more of a deep-seated politeness]
courteousness. *Par pure courtoisie, il n'a jamais évoqué le
passé de son amie*. He refrained from ever mentioning his
girlfriend's past out of sheer courteousness.

Locution Idiom
L'exactitude est la politesse des rois. [attributed to
Louis XVIII] Punctuality is the politeness of kings.

43.7 *Grossièreté* Rudeness

grossier, -ssière adj 1 [offending against conventional
standards of behaviour] (very) rude *Sa tenue à table a été
considérée comme grossière par toute la famille*. His table
manners were considered (very) rude by the whole family
2 [offending against decency] vulgar *Il a eu un geste
grossier*. He made a vulgar gesture.
grossièreté nf rudeness
mal élevé, e adj [describes: child. Refers to conventional
standards of upbringing] rude *Veux-tu arrêter de tirer la
langue, en voilà un petit garçon mal élevé!* Will you stop
sticking your tongue out at people, what a rude little boy
you are!
malpoli, e adj [more informal than **mal élevé**, applying to
persons of any age] rude *Je ne vais plus chez ce
poissonnier, il est malpoli*. I don't go to that fishmonger's
any more; he's rude.
vulgaire adj [failing to achieve conventional standards of
good taste] vulgar *Leur fille parle de façon vulgaire*. Their
daughter uses vulgar language.
de mauvais goût *des cartes d'anniversaire de mauvais
goût* birthday cards in bad taste
goujat, ALSO **butor** nm lout

Monsieur et Madame Roger Liégeois
Monsieur et Madame Jean Priault
Madame Claude Gérard

sont heureux de vous faire part du mariage
de leurs enfants et petits-enfants

Emmanuel et Marie-Blanche

à Rivaux-la-Vieille

le samedi 13 février 1999

Le mariage sera célébré dans l'intimité en l'église Saint-Sébastien

2, avenue Mozart
89190 Le Plessis

M and Mrs Robin Prior
M and Mrs Paul Victor
Mrs Gerard Tomlinson

are happy to announce the marriage of

Emmanuel and Catherine

which will take place at the
church of Saint Nicholas
Church Lane
Dibney, Hants
on Saturday 13th February 1999

2, Barleycroft Avenue
Heddesdon HD6 6RY

43.8 *Traiter quelqu'un grossièrement* To treat somebody rudely

injure *nf* insult
injurier {6} *vt* to insult
insulte *nf* [stronger than **injure**] insult
insulter {6} *vt* [stronger than **injurier**] to insult
invective *nf* [powerful insult or curse] abuse
gros mot *nm* [children's language] swearword *dire des gros mots* to use bad language
grossièreté *nf* very rude remark
les cinq lettres [euphemism for **merde**] a four-letter word *Je te dis les cinq lettres!* F . . . you!

43.9 *Effronterie* Cheekiness

effronté, e *adj* [not without charm] cheeky **effronterie** *nf* [in common usage] cheek
impudent, e *adj* [pejorative and more formal than **effronté**. Implies a superior attitude to others] arrogant **impudence** *nf* arrogance
impertinent, e *adj* [lacking respect and interfering] disrespectful
impertinence *nf* **1** [character trait] disrespect **2** [remark] disrespectful remark
insolent, e *adj* [more disrespectul than **impertinent**] insolent
insolence *nf* **1** [character trait] insolence **2** [remark] insolent remark

All the terms above can describe attitude, expression, remarks. When they refer to persons, the implication is usually that the person is young. **Culotté** below, on the other hand, can describe people of any age.

culotté, e *adj* [informal] having a lot of nerve
culot *nm* [informal] nerve *T'as du culot!* You've got a nerve!

43.10 *Vantardise* Boastfulness

vantard, e *adj* boastful
vantardise *nf* **1** [character trait] boastfulness **2** [remark] boast
vanter {6} *vt* [to speak positively of, usu in order to sell] to sing the praises of *une publicité qui vante les mérites d'une marque de voiture* an advert singing the praises of a brand of car.
se vanter *v refl* (often + *de* + infinitive*)* **1** [say out loud in order to be admired] to boast *Il se vante d'avoir des amis en haut lieu.* He boasts of having friends in high places. **2** [in negative phrases, as a euphemism for keeping things secret] *Il n'y a pas de quoi se vanter!* It's nothing to be proud of! *À ta place je ne m'en vanterais pas.* I wouldn't shout it from the rooftops, if I were you. *Il a volé l'idée à son collègue mais il ne s'en est pas vanté.* He stole the idea from his colleague but he kept it quiet.
frime *nf* [informal. Behaviour adopted in order to attract sympathy or respect] pretence *Sa migraine, c'est de la frime.* Her migraine attack is just a pretence. *Il dépense beaucoup pour la frime.* He spends a lot of money on things designed solely to impress.
frimer {6} *vi* [informal. Boast or parade one's possessions in order to impress] to show off *Regarde-le avec son téléphone portatif, il frime!* Just watch him showing off with his mobile phone!
bluff *nm* bluffing *Ne l'écoutez pas, c'est du bluff!* Don't listen to her, she's bluffing you!

bluffer {6} **1** *vi* [informal] BrE to try it on AmE to bluff *Ils ont menacé de licencier tout le monde, mais ils bluffent.* They threatened to sack everybody, but they're just trying it on. **2** *vt* [obj: person] BrE to have on AmE to put on *Il te bluffe, en fait il n'est jamais allé en Afrique.* He's having you on, in fact he's never been to Africa.

43.11 *Modestie* Modesty

modestie *nf* [absence of boastful tendencies in someone's character] modesty *fausse modestie* false modesty
modeste *adj* [not boastful] modest *Il a eu le triomphe modeste.* He was modest about his success.
humble *adj* **1** [not ostentatious. Describes: e.g. meal, home] simple **2** [religious overtones. Not proud] meek
humilité *nf* [religious overtones. Harbouring no pride] humility

usage

humble
Before a noun, *humble* means simple, not sophisticated, or not large. Beware of the difference between, e.g. *une humble demeure* 'a simple dwelling' and *des paroles humbles* 'words full of humility'.

43.12 *Fierté et vanité* Pride and vanity

fier, fière *adj* **1** [satisfied with one's achievements, with good reason] proud **2** [pejorative] vain
fierté *nf* **1** [justified feeling] pride **2** [excessive self-regard] vanity
orgueil *nm* **1** [pejorative] arrogance *Il ne s'excusera jamais, il a trop d'orgueil.* He'll never apologize, he is too arrogant. **2** [value which one places on one's actions] pride *Par orgueil, elle n'a jamais demandé un centime à sa famille.* Through sheer pride, she never asked her family for even a penny.
s'enorgueillir de {19} *v refl* [to be justifiably self-congratulatory about] to take pride in *Je m'enorgueillis d'avoir eu un père objecteur de conscience.* I take pride in the fact that my father was a conscientious objector.
amour-propre *nm* **1** [pejorative] self-satisfaction **2** [value which one attaches to one's actions] pride *des satisfactions d'amour-propre* reasons to feel proud
vaniteux, -teuse *adj* **1** [excessively self-regarding] self-satisfied **2** [excessively proud of one's looks] vain
vanité *nf* **1** [excessive self-regard] self-importance **2** [excessive pride in one's looks] vanity

Locutions Idioms
se croire sorti de la cuisse de Jupiter [pejorative] to think one is God's gift to mankind
fier comme un coq ALSO **paon** [pejorative] proud as a peacock
fier comme Artaban [used as an affectionate comment on, for example, a small child achieving a difficult feat] pleased as Punch
vaniteux comme un paon [pejorative] vain as a peacock

43.13 *Injustice* Unfairness

injuste adj (often + *envers*) unfair *Ne sois pas injuste (envers lui), il a beaucoup travaillé.* Don't be unfair (to him) he's worked hard. **injustement** adv [formal] unjustly
injustice nf **1** [unfairness] injustice *Il est révolté par l'injustice.* He cannot bear injustice. **2** [unfair action] act of injustice *être victime d'une injustice* to be the victim of an act of injustice
préjugé nm prejudice *plein de préjugés* prejudiced
partial, e adj, mpl **-tiaux** [fairly formal contexts only. Describes: e.g. judge, press article, opinion] biased

---

false friend **partial**
Beware : the French adjective *partial* has only one meaning, i.e. 'biased', unlike its English equivalent 'partial'

---

racisme nm racism **raciste** adj and n racist
sexisme nm sexism **sexiste** adj and n sexist

Locution Idiom
Il n'y a pas de justice. There's no justice in this world.

43.14 *Équité* Fairness

juste adj fair *Il a eu plus de dessert que moi, c'est pas juste!* He's had more dessert than me, it's not fair! *Je dois me montrer juste envers tous.* I must be fair to all.
justice nf **1** [impartiality] justice *agir selon la justice* to act in a just manner **2** [institution] law *respecter la justice* to respect the law *témoigner en justice* to be a witness in court
à juste titre [slightly formal] rightly (so)
équitable adj [more formal than **juste** but less formal than English 'equitable'. Describes: e.g. share, character] fair
équité nf [more formal than **justice** but not as formal as English 'equity'] justice *En toute équité, nous devons leur donner leur chance.* To be absolutely fair, we have to give them a chance.

Locutions Idioms
Ce n'est que justice. It's only fair.
se faire justice (à soi-même) to do away with oneself (rather than be judged in court)
Bien fait pour toi!, ALSO **Tu ne l'as pas volé!** [in informal speech] Serves you right!

43.15 *Gentillesse et générosité* Kindness and generosity

see also **43.1 Moralité et vertu**
gentil, -tille adj [used both sincerely and for thanking politely] kind *C'est un homme très gentil.* He's a very kind man. *Voulez-vous que je vous rapporte quelque chose du marché? – Non, merci, vous êtes gentille.* Would you like me to bring you something from the market? – No thanks, but it's kind of you to offer.
gentillesse nf kindness
aimable adj [always ready to welcome or help. Can be a purely conventional attitude] friendly *Ils sont toujours très aimables, dans ce magasin.* The people in this shop are always very friendly. *Je te propose un café, tu pourrais au moins être aimable!* I'm offering you a coffee, couldn't you at least be nice about it!
amabilité nf friendliness
délicat, e adj tactful **délicatesse** nf tactfulness
généreux, -reuse adj generous

générosité nf generosity
sympathique adj **1** [describes a person whom others tend to like, often on first acquaintance] nice. *Il est très sympathique, le nouveau maire.* The new mayor's a really nice man. **2** [generous. Describes e.g. action, thought] kind. *Elle m'a proposé de garder les enfants pour que je me repose, c'est sympathique.* She's kindly offered to look after the children so I can get some rest.
sympa adj [informal. Similar to both senses of **sympathique**] nice, kind *Elle m'a proposé de m'aider, c'est sympa, non?* She offered to help me. Kind of her, wasn't it?

Locutions Idioms
être plein d'attentions pour qqn to be very attentive towards sb
être aux petits soins pour qqn [informal] to lavish attention upon sb

43.16 *Compassion* Compassion

pitié nf [this term expresses a form of sympathy which is sometimes felt to be patronizing] pity *avoir pitié de qqn* to pity sb *Les petits mendiants leur faisaient pitié.* Their hearts went out to the child beggars. *Ce n'est pas de la pitié que demandent les handicapés, ce sont des actes.* The disabled aren't after pity, they want action. *Donne-moi un de tes sacs, tu me fais pitié.* I'll take pity on you and carry one of your bags.
compassion nf [slightly formal. Deep sympathy] compassion
compatir {19} vi to sympathize *Nous compatissons à leur malheur, mais la vie doit reprendre ses droits.* We feel for them in their loss, but life must go on.
plaindre {59} vt to feel sorry for *Encore deux jours à passer en sa compagnie, je te plains!* Another two days to put up with him, I feel sorry for you! *Il/elle n'est pas à plaindre.* There's no reason to feel sorry for him/her.
partager la peine de qqn to share in sb's grief
être de tout cœur avec qqn, ALSO **être avec qqn en pensée** [suitable for sad or happy occasions] to be with sb in one's thoughts

43.17 *Clémence* Clemency

see also **122 (Gambits)**
clémence nf [literary. Generous forgiveness, often on the part of high-ranking persons] clemency
indulgence nf **1** [overlooking faults] leniency **2** [slightly pejorative. Forgiveness exercised in a slightly lax way, esp by parents] indulgence
indulgent, e adj lenient *Soyez indulgents, il n'a que quatorze ans.* Don't be too harsh, he's only fourteen.
grâce nf (official) pardon *accorder sa grâce à qqn* to pardon sb *Ses avocats ont sollicité la grâce présidentielle.* His lawyers sought an official pardon from the president.
recours nm **en grâce** [official term for **grâce**] pardon *Le recours en grâce a été accordé.* The pardon was granted.
amnistie nf amnesty
pitié nf [feeling sorry and relenting] *avoir pitié de qqn* to be sorry for sb *Le professeur a eu pitié de nous, il nous a autorisé l'usage du dictionnaire pendant le test.* The teacher was sorry for us, he allowed us to take a dictionary into the test.
sans pitié pitilessly
sans merci [archaic literary phrase] mercilessly

43.18 *Exercer sa clémence* To show clemency

épargner {6} *vt* **1** [against expectations] to spare *Son grand âge lui a épargné la prison.* Because of his great age he was spared a prison sentence. **2** [at the last minute] to reprieve *La crue a baissé et les maisons du faubourg ont été épargnées.* The river level went down and the houses on the edge of town were saved.
pardonner {6} *vt* **1** [religious or moral] to forgive *pardonner qqch à qqn* to forgive sb sthg **2** [official] to pardon
excuser {6} *vt* **1** [forgive esp for minor fault] to provide an excuse for *Excusez-la, elle n'a pas eu le temps de finir tout le travail que vous lui aviez donné.* Please excuse her, she didn't have time to complete all the work which you had given her. *Lui, on peut l'excuser, puisqu'il n'avait pas été mis au courant.* He has an excuse: he was not informed.*Tu l'excuses toujours parce que c'est ta sœur!* You're always finding excuses for her, just because she's your sister! **2** [allow to escape punishment] to let off *Allez, pour cette fois-ci, je t'excuse.* All right, I'll let you off this once.
gracier {15} *vt* to grant a(n official) pardon to
amnistier {15} *vt* to grant an amnesty to

Locutions Idioms
Faute avouée est à moitié pardonnée. [proverb used to exhort esp children to own up to a misdeed] A sin confessed is a sin half pardoned.
passer l'éponge to overlook misdeeds *Bon, on va passer l'éponge.* Alright, Let's pretend it never happened.

43.19 *Honte* Shame

honte *nf* **1** [emotion] shame *avoir honte* to be ashamed (of oneself) *Prendre de l'argent à un enfant, tu n'as pas honte!* Taking money from a child? You should be ashamed of yourself! *J'aurais dû apporter des fleurs, j'ai honte!* I should have brought flowers, I'm really ashamed of myself! *faire honte à qqn* to make sb ashamed **2** [person. Often humorous] black sheep *Tu es la honte de la famille!* You're a disgrace to the family!
honteux, -teuse *adj* **1** [feeling shame] ashamed **2** [looking ashamed] sheepish **3** [causing shame. Describes e.g. behaviour, event] shameful
scandale *nm* [public shame] scandal *C'est un scandale!* It's outrageous! *Un sein nu et les gens crient au scandale!* A glimpse of bare breast and people are outraged!
repentir *nm* [formal] remorse *avoir du repentir* to feel remorse
se repentir {25} *v refl* **1** [formal] to repent **2** (often + *de*) [in everyday speech] to regret *Je ne lui ai pas réclamé l'argent mais je m'en suis repenti après.* I didn't ask for the money but I regretted it later.

Locutions Idioms
J'aurais voulu rentrer sous terre ALSO **me fourrer dans un trou de souris.** I wanted the earth to swallow me up.
être rouge comme une tomate OR **pivoine** to be bright red with embarrassment
avoir le rouge (de la honte) au front [literary or for comic effect] BrE to blush with embarrassment AmE to get red as a beet
tête basse *Il est rentré tête basse.* He came home with his head hung low.
la queue entre les jambes ALSO **la queue basse** with his tail between his legs
sans fausse honte quite naturally *Il parlait sans fausse honte du passé fasciste de son père.* He spoke in a straightforward manner about his father's fascist activities in the past.

43.20 *Honnêteté* Honesty

honnête *adj* **1** [not crooked. Refers to permanent character trait or behaviour on a particular occasion] honest *un marchand honnête* an honest shopkeeper *Elle m'a remboursé immédiatement, c'était honnête, non?* She paid me back immediately, wasn't it an honest thing to do? **2** [just] fair *Il faut être honnête, l'erreur ne venait pas de lui.* To be fair, he wasn't to blame for the mistake. **3** [old-fashioned or used humorously. Not immoral] *une femme honnête* an honest woman
honnêtement *adv* **1** [without cheating or thieving] honestly **2** [without pretending] honestly *Honnêtement, je ne vois pas comment tu aurais pu refuser leur invitation.* Honestly, I don't see how you could have refused their invitation.
honnêteté *nf* honesty
intègre *adj* [slightly literary. Used of someone who will not compromise his or her honesty] principled *Vous ne pouvez pas la soupçonner, elle est parfaitement intègre.* You really cannot suspect her, she's a woman of great integrity.
intégrité *nf* integrity
transparence *nf* [made fashionable in political and journalistic language by 'glasnost', for which this term is a translation] open government
probe *adj* [literary synonym for **honnête 1**] honest
probité *nf* [literary] honesty

43.21 *Malhonnêteté* Dishonesty

malhonnête *adj* [cheating or thieving] dishonest
malhonnêteté *nf* **1** [character trait] dishonesty **2** [instance] dishonest action *Ce serait une malhonnêteté de ta part de lui donner le chèque, le compte étant à découvert.* It would be dishonest on your part if you gave him the cheque while knowing it would bounce.
malhonnêteté *nf* **1** [character trait] dishonesty **2** [action or thought] piece of dishonesty

43.22 *Types de malhonnêtetés* Dishonest actions

escroquerie *nf* swindle
arnaque *nf* [slang] rip-off *Les entrées à 35 francs! C'est de l'arnaque!* 35 francs to get in, it's a rip-off!
malversation *nf* [while in an official capacity] embezzlement
détournement *nm* **de fonds** misappropriation of funds
abus *nm* **de confiance** breach of trust
tromperie *nf* cheating *L'auteur n'a pas cité ses sources, et j'estime qu'il y a eu tentative de tromperie de sa part.* The author failed to quote his sources, and I think that was an attempt at cheating, on his part. *tromperie sur la marchandise* BrE breach of the trades description act
escroquer {6} *vt* to swindle
arnaquer {6} *vt* [slang synonym for **escroquer**] to rip off
tricher {6} *vi* [used of small-scale swindlers] to cheat
tromper {6} *vt* [used of small or large swindlers] to cheat *Il a trompé ses clients pendant trois ans avant d'être arrêté.* He cheated his customers for three years before he was arrested.

43.23 *Escrocs* Crooks

escroc *nm* crook
arnaqueur, -queuse *n* [slang synonym for **escroc**] crook
tricheur, -cheuse *n* [particularly at cards] cheat
filou *nm* **1** [small-time crook, a slightly old-fashioned term] rogue **2** [used as a term of endearment] rogue *Petit filou, va!* You little rogue!
aigrefin *nm* [literary or humorous synonym for **escroc**] crook
véreux, -reuse *adj* [used esp of people in positions of trust] crooked *avocat/banquier véreux* crooked banker/lawyer

43.24 *Brigands et vols* Robbers and thefts

vol *nm* theft
voler {6} *vi* and *vt* to steal *voler qqch à qqn* to steal sthg from sb
voleur, -leuse *n* thief

Différents vols Types of theft
vol à la tire pickpocketing
vol à l'étalage shoplifting
vol à main armée armed robbery
vol à l'arraché BrE bag-snatching AmE purse-snatching
vol à la roulotte stealing from cars

43.25 *Verbes synonymes de voler* Other verbs for 'to steal'

dérober {6} *vt* [more formal word than **voler**. Suggests more discretion] to steal *le ruban dérobé par Chérubin* the ribbon which Cherubino had stolen
piquer {6} *vt* [slang synonym for **voler**] BrE to nick AmE to rip off
chaparder {6} *vi* and *vt* [small-scale opportunistic thefts] to pinch *Étant enfants nous chapardions des fruits dans les vergers.* As children, we used to steal apples from the orchards.

43.26 *Autres méthodes de vol* Other ways of stealing

cambrioler {6} *vt* to burgle
cambrioleur, -leuse *n* burglar
piller {6} *vt* to loot
pillage *nm* **(de magasins) 1** [on foot] looting **2** [with a car] *pillage avec bris de vitrine* BrE ram-raiding
grivèlerie *nf* not paying for one's drinks or meal in a restaurant
larcin *nm* [language of newspaper reports] (petty) theft *Elle avait commis deux ou trois larcins quand elle était adolescente.* She'd done a little petty thieving when she was an adolescent.
agression *nf* **(de rue)** mugging
kidnapping *nm* kidnapping
kidnapper {6} *vt* to kidnap
rançon *nf* ransom
ravisseur, -sseuse *n* kidnapper
chantage *nm* blackmail
chanter {6} *vi* to talk (when subjected to blackmail) *faire chanter qqn* to blackmail sb

44 Doing things well and doing them badly

44.1 *Fiabilité* Reliability

fiable *adj* reliable
fiabilité *nf* **1** [of testimony, of promise] reliability **2** [of person] trustworthiness
confiance *nf* trust *faire confiance à qqn* to trust sb *avoir toute confiance en qqn* to trust sb implicitly *gagner la confiance de qqn* to gain sb's trust *trahir la confiance de qqn* to betray sb's trust
compter {6} *vt* (always + *sur*) to rely on *Je compte sur toi pour le convaincre.* I'm relying on you to persuade him. *Demain soir à neuf heures, je compte sur vous, hein?* Tomorrow night at nine, be there, won't you? *Est-ce qu'on peut compter sur lui?* Is he dependable?
sûr, sûre *adj* [describes: e.g. person, information, machine] reliable *Nous savons de source sûre que . . .* We know from reliable sources that . . .

Locution Idiom
donner carte blanche à qqn to give sb a free hand

44.2 *Consciencieux* Conscientious

consciencieux, -cieuse *adj* thorough
conscience *nf* **professionnelle** conscientiousness
attention *nf* care (and attention) *faire attention à ses affaires* to look after one's things
attentif, -tive *adj* [attending carefully to what is being explained] attentive *Il est toujours très attentif en cours.* He always applies himself in class.
attentivement *adv* assiduously
appliqué, e *adj* [giving all one's attention to the task in hand] conscientious
application *nf* care *faire qqch avec application* to do sthg carefully
soin *nm* care *prendre soin de qqn/qqch* to take care of sb/sthg *Prenez soin de ne pas laisser paraître votre mécontentement.* Be careful not to let your dissatisfaction show. *avec soin* carefully
soigneux, -gneuse *adj* [stresses neatness of result] neat (and careful) **soigneusement** *adv* neatly (and carefully)
prudence *nf* [anticipation of what might go wrong] care, caution *conduire avec prudence* to drive cautiously
prudent, e *adj* [anticipating what might go wrong] careful, cautious

44.3 *Paresseux* Lazy

paresseux, -sseuse *adj* lazy **paresseux, -sseuse** *n* lazybones
paresse *nf* laziness
paresser {6} *vi* to laze around
fainéant, e *adj* [informal] idle **fainéant, e** *n* BrE idler, AmE slacker
flemmard, e *adj* [informal] BrE bone idle
flemmarder {6} *vi* [informal] to loaf around doing nothing *On a flemmardé au lit toute la journée.* We lounged around in bed all day.
indolent, e *adj* [showing no energy. Can imply negligence of one's duty] indolent

Locutions Idioms
avoir un poil dans la main [informal. Permanent character trait] to be lazy *Il a un poil dans la main*. He never does a thing.
Il a/J'ai la flemme. [informal] He can't/I can't be bothered. *Elle a la flemme de se lever pour fermer la fenêtre.* She can't be bothered to get up and shut the window.

44.4 *Négligence* Sloppiness

négligent, e *adj* [in one's work or duties] careless
négligé, e *adj* **1** [describes: e.g. handwriting, exercise book] sloppy **2** [describes: e.g. person, clothes] scruffy
négligence *nf* **1** [lack of care] sloppiness **2** [specific instance] careless mistake
torchon *nm* [describes a messy exercise book, letter, document, etc] (complete) mess *Va me recopier ce torchon!* Take this mess away and copy it all out neatly again!
imprudence *nf* **1** [tendency to fail to anticipate what might go wrong] carelessness **2** [specific instance] careless action *commettre une imprudence* to do something careless. *Attention, en montagne, pas d'imprudences!* Beware, when in the mountains, you must exercise caution.
imprudent, e *adj* careless *L'accident a été causé par un automobiliste imprudent.* The accident was caused by a driver who wasn't exercising caution.

44.5 *Faire les choses sans soin* To do things carelessly

All expressions below are pejorative in the senses shown.
expédier {15} *vt* [fast and badly] to dash off (carelessly) *Il a expédié ses devoirs pour courir rejoindre ses copains.* He dashed off his homework so he could go and meet his pals.
bâcler {6} *vt* to bungle
faire qqch par-dessous la jambe to do sthg in a slipshod way
faire qqch à la va-comme-je-te-pousse [informal] to do sthg any old way

44.6 *Agilité* Agility

agilité *nf* [physical] agility *avec agilité* nimbly *Il a grimpé avec agilité sur le rebord de la fenêtre.* He climbed nimbly up on (to) the window sill.
agile *adj* nimble
adresse *nf* [involves coordination of hand and eye] skill *avec adresse* skilfully *Elle a envoyé avec adresse la boulette de papier dans la cheminée.* She skilfully threw the crumpled ball of paper into the fire.
adroit, e *adj* skilfull
souple *adj* **1** [describes: e.g. body, movement] flexible **2** [fit and slim] lithe **souplesse** *nf* litheness

44.7 *Maladresse* Clumsiness

maladresse *nf* **1** [lack of coordination] clumsiness *avec maladresse* clumsily **2** [result of clumsiness] *Encore une maladresse de Robert!* Robert's been clumsy again!
maladroit, e *adj* clumsy
gauche *adj* [physical and psychological] awkward
gaucherie *nf* awkwardness

Locutions Idioms
avoir la main lourde [put too much of an ingredient in a dish] to be heavy-handed *C'est un peu trop pimenté, j'ai eu la main lourde.* It's too hot, I went too heavy on the spices.
Faites chauffer la colle! [called out with humorous intent when someone has just dropped an object on the floor and broken it or spilled its contents] Whoops, butterfingers!

45 Positive and negative feelings

45.1 *Confortable* Comfortable

confortable *adj* comfortable *un fauteuil confortable* a comfortable armchair *une position confortable* a comfortable position **confortablement** *adv* comfortably
confort *nm* [physical or material well-being] comfort *Chez nous c'est petit mais il y a tout le confort.* Our home is small but very comfortable. *un appartement tout confort* a flat/apartment with all modern conveniences *une salle de bains sans aucun confort* a Spartan bathroom
bien assis, e *adj* sitting comfortably *On est bien assis dans cette chaise à bascule.* This rocking chair is very comfortable.
luxueux, -xueuse *adj* luxurious *de luxueux tapis d'Orient* luxurious Oriental rugs
douillet, -llette *adj* snug *J'adore lire le soir dans un bon lit douillet.* I love reading at night snug in my bed.
à l'aise [feeling right about one's clothes, surroundings, companions, etc] comfortable *Je me sens à l'aise dans mon vieux pull noir.* I feel comfortable wearing my old black sweater. *Il se sentait à l'aise chez nous.* He felt comfortable in our house.

45.2 *Mal à l'aise* Uncomfortable

see also **45.1 Confortable**
mal à l'aise [this phrase is used as an invariable adjective] uncomfortable *On est mal à l'aise sur ce canapé.* The sofa's uncomfortable. *Nous nous sommes sentis mal à l'aise lorsqu'il a fait son discours.* We felt uncomfortable during his speech.
mal ALSO **pas bien dans sa peau** [same usage as *mal à l'aise*. Implies profound and long-lasting inner sense of unease] worried *Depuis que son mari l'a quittée, elle est mal* ALSO *elle n'est pas bien dans sa peau.* She's not been at all well in herself since her husband left her.
gêner {6} *vt* [physically or psychologically] to make uncomfortable *Mes nouvelles bottes me gênent aux talons.* My new boots are uncomfortable at the heels. *Ça ne t'a pas gêné quand il s'est mis à chanter tes louanges devant tout le monde?* Didn't you feel uncomfortable when he started singing your praises in front of everyone?
coincer {7} *vt* **1** [place in a tight position] to get stuck *Ils ont coincé le piano dans l'escalier.* They got the piano stuck on the stairs. **2** [informal. To put in an uncomfortable situation] to corner *Il m'a vaguement promis de m'aider mais je vais lui téléphoner puis je vais le coincer.* He made a vague promise to help me but I'm going to ring him up and corner him.
coincé, e *adj* **1** [physically] stuck *une fermeture à glissière coincée* a stuck BrE zip AmE zipper **2** [slightly humorous word describing a psychological trait] repressed

45.3 *Affection* Affection

see also **50.3 Les séducteurs**

aimer {6} *vt* **1** (sometimes + *bien*) [feel pleasure or affection for] to like *J'aime (bien) son style.* I like his style. *J'aime (bien) le fromage.* I like cheese. *Aimez-vous le blues?* Do you like the blues? **2** [be in agreement with] to approve *Je n'aime pas beaucoup leur façon de travailler.* I don't approve of their way of working. **3** (in the conditional, and followed by *bien*) [have a yearning for] to love *J'aimerais bien aller en Amérique.* I'd love to go to America. *J'aimerais bien quelque chose à boire.* I'd love something to drink.

adorer {6} *vt* [be extremely fond of: applies to anything from food to great passions] to love *Les écureuils adorent les noisettes.* Squirrels love hazelnuts. *J'adore ta grand-mère.* I think your grandmother's wonderful. *Il adorait la jeune femme.* He was passionately in love with the young woman.

adoration *nf* [used only for being besotted, usu with someone] worship *Il a une adoration pour Mozart/sa fille.* He worships Mozart/his daughter.

affection *nf* [implies long-term feeling, sometimes of tenderness] fondness *J'ai beaucoup d'affection pour elle.* I have a great fondness for her.

avoir une propension à faire qqch [habitual behaviour] to have a liking for doing sthg *Il a une propension à passer des heures au téléphone.* He likes to spend hours on the phone.

avoir un penchant pour qqch [habitual behaviour] to have a liking for sthg *Son penchant pour la bouteille lui a valu bien des mésaventures.* His fondness for the bottle has caused him a lot of problems.

avoir un faible pour [liking for pleasures of the flesh] to be partial to *Elle a toujours eu un faible pour les blonds.* She's always been partial to blond men.

45.4 *Les gens qui aiment quelque chose ou quelqu'un* Fans and enthusiasts

fan *nm* [of rock group] fan
supporter *nm* [of football] supporter
mordu, e *n* [informal] fan *des mordus de l'informatique* computer fanatics *un mordu de la musique* a music lover
amateur *nm* [person who is keen on something] enthusiast *un amateur de mots croisés* a crossword enthusiast *Elle est grand amateur de chats persans.* She's a great lover of Persian cats.
partisan, e *n* [person who is in favour of an idea, a policy] supporter *les partisans de la peine de mort* supporters of capital punishment *une méthode d'éducation qui n'a plus beaucoup de partisans* an educational method with very few supporters left

45.5 *Être aimé* To be liked

aimé, e *adj* (often + *de*) (well-)loved *sa fille tant aimée* the daughter he loved so much *les athlètes aimés du grand public* athletes much loved by the general public
bien vu, e *adj* (often + *de*) [held in high regard socially] approved of *J'étais bien vue au lycée parce que j'étais très disciplinée.* I was well thought of at school because I always did as I was told. *Faire du cheval, c'est bien vu dans certains milieux.* Horseriding is the done thing among some social groups.
couru, e *adj* [describes: e.g. film, play] popular
fréquenté, e *adj* [describes: e.g. bar, cinema, church] popular

populaire *adj* [loved by the greatest number of people] popular *un chanteur populaire en Égypte* a singer much appreciated in Egypt *être populaire auprès de* to be popular with
prendre {54} *vi* to catch on *Le style femme d'affaires prend bien chez les 25-30 ans.* Power-dressing is catching on among 25- to 30-year-old women.

Locutions Idioms
à mon goût to my liking
une femme/un homme comme je les aime a man/woman after my own heart
avoir les faveurs de qqn to be (well) in with sb
être dans les petits papiers de qqn [informal] BrE to be in sb's good books AmE to be in sb's good graces

45.6 *Amour* Love

see also **45.3 Affection**
aimer {6} *vt* to love *Je t'aime.* I love you.
amour *nm* **1** (in this sense, this word is feminine in the plural) [feeling] love **2** [as a term of endearment, to address lovers or children] love *Viens m'embrasser, mon amour.* Come and give me a kiss, my love.
aimant, e *adj* loving *une famille aimante* a loving family
histoire *nf* **d'amour 1** [real life events] love story *Entre tes parents, ça a été une grande histoire d'amour.* Your parents' life was a storybook romance. **2** [in fiction] love story
amoureux, -reuse *adj* in love *Ne cherche pas à lui faire entendre raison, il est amoureux.* Don't try to make him see sense, he's in love.
amoureux, -reuse *n* [person in love] boyfriend, girlfriend *Allons, les amoureux, un peu de tenue!* Come on, we know you two are in love, but behave yourselves!

45.7 *L'amour hors mariage* Love outside marriage

The phrases below all sound a little old-fashioned now that extramarital relationships are much more socially acceptable.

liaison *nf*, ALSO **aventure** *nf* affair *Ils ont eu une liaison.* They had an affair. *Elle a une liaison avec son assistant.* She's having an affair with her assistant.
amant *nm* **1** [male] lover *partagée entre son mari et son amant* torn between her husband and her lover **2** [person having an extramarital relationship, or a relationship while not married] lover *Qu'ils soient amants ou non ne te regarde pas.* It is none of your business whether they are lovers or not.
maîtresse *nf* mistress
extraconjugal, e *adj*, *mpl* **-gaux** extra-marital *des rapports extraconjugaux* an extra-marital relationship
petit ami *nm* boyfriend
petite amie *nf* girlfriend
copain *nm* [informal. Man with whom a woman lives] partner
copine *nf* [informal. Woman with whom a man lives] partner
compagnon *nm* [slightly formal. Man with whom a woman lives] partner
compagne *nf* [slightly formal. Woman with whom a man lives] partner
concubin, e *n* [used in legal contexts. When used in everyday language the term is pejorative] cohabitee
draguer {6} *vt* [slang] to (try to) pick up *Il m'a draguée au cours d'une soirée.* He tried to pick me up at a party.
baratiner {6} *vt* [informal] to chat up

béguin *nm* infatuation *avoir le béguin pour qqn* to be infatuated with sb
sortir {25} *vi* (often + *with*) [suggests enjoying the company of the other sex, esp in public places of entertainment] to go out (with) *Il sort avec elle depuis un mois.* He's been going out with her for a month. *Ils sortent ensemble.* They're going out together.
fréquenter {6} *vt* [suggests a regular relationship. Obj: e.g. boy, girl] to see *Je ne veux pas que tu fréquentes ce garçon.* I don't want you to see this boy. *On s'est fréquentés un peu, étant jeunes.* We saw a bit of each other when we were younger.

Locutions Idioms
avoir qqn dans la peau [suggests strong desire] to be besotted with sb
faire la cour à qqn [suggests slightly old-fashioned, romantic courtship] to woo sb
conter fleurette à qqn [suggests old-fashioned, innocent style of courtship] to pay court to sb

45.8 *Noms affectueux* Terms of endearment

The following terms can be used in addressing boys or girls, men or women, regardless of whether the term of endearment is masculine or feminine. The exception is *ma chérie*, which may only be used to girls or women.
mon (petit) trésor my little treasure
mon chéri my darling
ma chérie my darling
mon amour my love
mon (petit) canard my little ducky
mon (petit) chaton my little lamb
ma (petite) puce my little pet
mon (petit) chou my darling

45.9 *Amitié* Friendship

ami, e *n* friend *une amie d'enfance* a childhood friend *Les Lucet sont des amis à nous.* The Lucets are friends of ours. *se faire des amis* to make friends *rester amis* to stay friends
amitié *nf* friendship *Une vieille amitié nous unit.* We've been friends a very long time. *se prendre d'amitié pour qqn* to become friends with sb *On prend le verre de l'amitié?* Shall we have a drink for friendship's sake?
copain *nm* [informal, used by all except the older generations. Male, although in the plural it may refer to a group containing both males and females] friend, pal *Tous mes copains ont le droit de sortir le soir.* All my pals are allowed to go out in the evening.
copine *nf* [informal. Female] (girl)friend
camarade *n* [in school, in the army, among people who work together] friend, mate, pal
rapports *nm pl* relationship *rapports d'amitié* friendly relationship *rapports de voisinage* neighbourly relationship *entretenir de bons rapports avec qqn* to be friendly with sb
connaissance *nf* acquaintance *Une de mes connaissances m'a dit qu'il avait travaillé avec vous.* One of my acquaintances told me he'd worked with you.
proche *n*, ALSO **intime** *n* close friend *Il compte la fille du Président parmi ses proches.* The President's daughter is a close friend of his.

45.10 *Autres types d'amitiés* Other kinds of friendships

solidarité *nf* solidarity
solidaire *adj* on the same side *Nous sommes tous solidaires.* We're all united. *Nous agissons par solidarité avec les opprimés.* We are taking action to show our sympathy with the oppressed.
compagnon *nm* [implies shared past journey or experiences] companion *Il a été mon compagnon de la première heure, nous avons monté l'entreprise ensemble.* He was my companion from the very early days, we set up the company together.
copinage *nm* [pejorative. Unfair practice in recruitment, etc] giving preference to one's friends

45.11 *Comportement amical* Friendly behaviour

amical, e *adj*, *mpl* **-caux** [taking place between friends] friendly *un match amical* a friendly match *une conversation amicale* a friendly chat
gentil, -tille *adj* [encouraging good relations] friendly *Les nouveaux voisins sont gentils.* The new neighbours are friendly. **gentiment** *adv* in a friendly way
chaleureux, -reuse *adj* [hospitable] warm **chaleureusement** *adv* warmly
ouvert, e *adj* **1** [accessible] open *Tu peux lui parler de tes problèmes d'argent, il est très ouvert, il comprendra.* Do talk to him about your money worries, he's very approachable, he'll understand. **2** [without prejudice] broad-minded
fidèle *adj* [with long-lasting loyalty] loyal *C'est un ami fidèle, sur lequel on peut compter même dans l'adversité.* He's a loyal friend, who can be relied upon even in hard times.
fidélité *nf* loyalty *Votre fidélité lors de mon procès m'a beaucoup touché.* I was very moved by your loyalty to me during my trial.
s'entendre (bien) avec {53} *v refl* to get on (well) with *Je m'entends bien avec mes frères.* I get on well with my brothers.

Locutions Idioms
rompre, ALSO **briser la glace** to break the ice
Les petits cadeaux entretiennent l'amitié. The occasional present helps to keep a friendship going.
s'entendre comme larrons en foire [implies friendly complicity, sometimes mischievous] BrE to get on like a house on fire
être comme cul et chemise (avec) [informal and pejorative] to work in cahoots (with)

45.12 *Salutations* Greetings

saluer {6} *vt* [obj: person] to greet *Il m'a salué d'un signe de tête.* He greeted me with a nod.
salutation *nf* **1** [formal and conventional gestures and words] greeting *Après les salutations d'usage, chacun a pris place et s'est tu pour écouter l'orateur.* After the usual greetings, everyone sat down and prepared to listen to the speaker in silence. **2** [at the start of a friendly letter or postcard] opening formula **3** [at the end of a friendly letter or postcard] closing formula
serrer {6} *vt* to grip *serrer la main de qqn* to shake sb's hand *Je ne vous serre pas la main, je fais un gâteau et j'ai de la farine partout!* Sorry, I can't shake hands with you, I'm making a cake and I'm covered in flour!

se serrer la main to shake hands
poignée *nf* **de main** handshake
faire un signe de tête à qqn to nod to sb
faire un signe de la main à qqn to wave to sb
embrasser {6} *vt* **1** [with one's mouth] to kiss *Embrasse ton cousin.* Give your cousin a kiss. **2** [formal, e.g. when a politician welcomes an official visitor in front of television cameras] to embrace
baiser *nm* kiss *baiser sur la joue /les lèvres* kiss on the cheek/lips
bise *nf* [informal. Used with children, or with adult relatives and close friends] kiss *faire la bise à qqn* to give sb a kiss (on the cheek)
bisou *nm* [baby language, used among older children and adults in family contexts] kiss *Viens me donner un (gros) bisou!* Come and give me a (big) kiss!
donner l'accolade à [formal hug] to embrace *Le président a embrassé son homologue russe.* The president embraced his Russian opposite number.
présenter {6} *vt* (often + à) to introduce *présenter son futur mari à sa famille* to introduce one's future husband to one's family *Je vous présente Roger Fermault.* Let me introduce Roger Fermault.
présentations *nf pl* introduction *Je fais les présentations: Lionel, Aline.* Let me make the introductions: Lionel, this is Aline, Aline, this is Lionel.
accueillir {28} *vt* to welcome *Ils nous ont accueillis avec beaucoup de chaleur.* They gave us a very warm welcome. *Ils nous ont très mal accueillis.* They gave us a very poor welcome.
accueil *nm* welcome *faire bon accueil à qqn* to welcome sb *faire mauvais accueil à qqn* to give sb a poor welcome *Je vous conseille l'auberge du village, l'accueil y est formidable.* I recommend the village inn, they really know how to make you welcome there.

45.13 *Enthousiasme* Enthusiasm

enthousiasme *nm* keenness *avec enthousiasme* enthusiastically
enthousiaste *adj* keen
enthousiaste *n* keen amateur *un enthousiaste de la randonnée pédestre* a keen hiker
passionné, e *adj* [stronger than **enthousiaste**] (very) keen *Elle est passionnée de photo.* She's very keen on photography.
passionné, e *n* fan *un passionné de blues* a blues fan *une passionnée d'opéra* an opera fan

Locutions Idioms
sauter sur l'occasion (de faire) to jump at the chance (to do)
Il/Elle en veut. [informal] He's/She's really keen.
Il/Elle est folle de . . . He's/She's mad about . . .

45.14 *Manque d'enthousiasme* Indifference

manque *nm* **d'enthousiasme** ALSO **d'intérêt** indifference *Ils ont accueilli ce projet avec leur manque d'enthousiasme habituel.* The greeted the project with their usual lack of enthusiasm.
indifférence *nf* indifference
indifférent, e *adj* indifferent
tiède *adj* lukewarm

Locutions Idioms
Ça m'est égal. I don't care.
Ça m'indiffère, ALSO **Ça me laisse indifférent.** I have no particular opinion (about it) one way or the other.
Il n'est pas chaud/Elle n'est pas chaude pour faire . . . [informal] He's/She's not too keen on doing . . .
faire la sourde oreille (à qqch) to remain unmoved (by sthg)
Laisse tomber! [informal] Forget it!

45.15 *Applaudir et louer* To applaud and to praise

see also **135 (Gambits)**
applaudissements *nm pl* applause
applaudir {19} *vi* to clap *Les gens applaudissaient à tout rompre.* People were clapping for all they were worth.
ovationner {6} *vt* to give an ovation to
louer {6} *vt* to praise
louanges *nf pl* [literary] praise *adresser des louanges à qqn* to direct praise at sb
flatteur, -tteuse *adj* complimentary *J'ai lu une critique flatteuse de ta pièce.* I read a very complimentary review of your play.
digne *adj* **d'éloges** [describes: e.g. person, attitude, behaviour] praiseworthy
louable *adj* [can be used slightly patronizingly, unlike the two entries above and below. Describes: e.g. effort, attitude, behaviour] praiseworthy
méritoire *adj* commendable
féliciter {6} *vt* to congratulate *Je vous félicite d'avoir pensé à tout.* I congratulate you for having thought of everything.
félicitations *nf pl* congratulations *Vous êtes reçu avec les félicitations du jury.* You have passed with distinction.
compliment *nm* **1** [true or untrue statement of praise] compliment *faire un compliment à qqn* to compliment sb **2** [in honour of sb, for a particular occasion] short speech *L'institutrice leur a appris un petit compliment à réciter pour la fête des Mères.* The teacher taught them a short speech to recite on Mother's Day.

Locutions Idioms
Je ne te/vous fais pas mes compliments. I can't say I'm impressed with what you've done.
chanter les louanges de qqn [unlike **louanges** by itself, this is an everyday phrase] to sing the praises of sb

45.16 *Admiration* Admiration

admiration *nf* [feeling of wonder] admiration *Je suis plein d'admiration devant cette prouesse.* I am lost in admiration of this feat.
admirable *adj* remarkable *Vous avez eu un courage admirable.* You showed remarkable bravery.
admirer {6} *vt* to admire *Les passants admiraient la vitrine richement décorée pour Noël.* Passers-by were admiring the shop window which had been luxuriously decorated for Christmas. *Quatre enfants et une carrière de médecin, je t'admire!* Four children and a career as a doctor, I admire you. *Admirez le travail!* [can be ironic] Just look at this, isn't it wonderful?
respect *nm* [feeling of wonder and recognition of someone's moral worth] respect *avoir du respect pour qqn* to have respect for sb
respecter {6} *vt* to have respect for *Il faut respecter les convictions de chacun.* We must respect each other's beliefs. *Si tu ne me respectes pas, respecte au moins mon*

travail. If you can't respect me, at least show some respect for my work.

estime *nf* estimation *baisser/monter dans l'estime de qqn* to go down/up in sb's estimation *Ah, tu remontes dans mon estime!* Ah, you're going up in my estimation again! *avoir beaucoup d'estime pour qqn* to hold sb in high esteem

45.17 *Cruauté* Cruelty

see also **48.5 Brutal** and **45.20 Horreur et effroi**
cruel, cruelle *adj* cruel
cruauté *nf* cruelty
barbare *adj* barbaric
barbarie *nf* barbarity
sadique *adj* sadistic
sadisme *nm* sadism
atrocité *nf* atrocity *les atrocités commises pendant la guerre* the atrocities committed during the war

45.18 *Personnes cruelles* Cruel people

tortionnaire *n* torturer
bourreau *nm, pl* **-x 1** [Nazi criminal, psychopath] torturer **2** [historically] executioner
monstre *nm* **(de cruauté)** monster

45.19 *Haine* Hatred

haine *nf* hatred *Je n'éprouve pas de haine envers mon agresseur.* I feel no hatred towards my attacker.
haineux, -neuse *adj* [showing aversion] full of hatred *Elle suivait ses mouvements d'un regard haineux.* She followed his movements with hatred in her eyes.
haineusement *adv* with hatred *regarder qqn haineusement* to watch sb with hatred in one's eyes *parler haineusement* to speak with hatred in one's voice
haïssable *adj* **1** [deserving of intense dislike] hateful *Il avait l'habitude haïssable de laisser des mégots partout.* He had the detestable habit of leaving cigarette ends lying about everywhere. *La guerre est haïssable, où qu'elle se trouve.* War is hateful, wherever it is. **2** [deserving of hatred] hateful *l'homme haïssable auquel ses parents l'avaient mariée* the hateful man to whom her parents had married her
haïr {20} *vt* [feel emotional aversion towards] to hate
détester {6} *vt* [less intense than **haïr**. Can apply to things or to people] to hate *Je déteste le chou.* I hate cabbage. *Elle déteste son père.* She hates her father.
détestable *adj* [less intense than **haïssable**] awful *Je trouve sa façon de toujours se mettre en avant détestable.* I find it awful the way he always tries to hog the limelight.

Locutions Idioms
prendre qqn en grippe [sudden or gradual feeling. Not used to refer to really deep feelings such as one has for close relatives] to dislike *Peu à peu, j'ai pris mon voisin en grippe.* I've gradually got to really dislike my neighbour.
Il/Elle ne peut pas sentir, ALSO **souffrir . . .** He/She can't stand . . . [applies to people or things] *Je n'ai jamais pu sentir les maths/mon frère.* I never could stand mathematics/my brother.
avoir une dent contre qqn to have a grudge against sb
s'entendre comme chien et chat to fight like cat and dog
être à couteaux tirés avec qqn to be sworn enemies with sb *Ces deux-là sont à couteaux tirés.* Those two are sworn enemies.
être la bête noire de qqn to be sb's pet hate

Citation Quotation
Va, je ne te hais point. [In Corneille's *El Cid*, the heroine Chimène, thus reveals her love for Rodrigue. Often quoted as a perfect example of understatement, or litotes] Go, I do not hate you.

45.20 *Horreur et effroi* Horror and fright

horreur *nf* horror *Toute l'horreur de son acte criminel lui apparut enfin.* At last he understood the whole horror of his crime.

> *usage*
>
> Adjectives expressing frightfulness
> The six adjectives below each have an emphatic meaning, implying great evil, and a much milder one, implying unpleasantness. The milder meaning is very common. It has been listed as sense 1 in each of the following entries.

affreux, -ffreuse *adj* **1** [unpleasant] awful, frightful *Écoute-la, c'est affreux, elle chante faux!* Listen to her, it's frightful, she can't sing in tune! **2** [causing great emotion and pity] ghastly *Ils n'ont pas supporté l'affreux spectacle qui les attendait derrière les portes du camp d'internement.* They couldn't bear the awful scenes which they found when they went inside the gate of the internment camp.
horrible *adj* **1** [unpleasant] awful, frightful *Il est horrible, son pull!* His sweater is awful! **2** [causing horror] horrible *Un rictus horrible déformait le visage du mort.* A horrible grimace disfigured the dead man's face.
terrible *adj* **1** [unpleasant] terrible *Ta mère a oublié de te donner un casse-croûte, mais c'est terrible, ça!* Your mother forgot to give you a snack, how terrible! **2** [causing terror] terrible, awesome *'Je me vengerai!' cria-t-il d'une voix terrible.* 'I'll have my revenge!', he yelled in an awesome voice.
épouvantable *adj* **1** [unpleasant] awful, atrocious *Il fait un temps épouvantable.* The weather's atrocious. **2** [causing horror] terrible *l'épouvantable accident qui vient d'endeuiller notre ville* the dreadful accident which has just plunged our town into mourning.
atroce *adj* **1** [unpleasant] awful, appalling *Ils nous ont servi des petits pois avec de la confiture, atroce!* They served peas with jam, how appalling! **2** [causing great emotion and pity] awful *Regarder ces enfants affamés qui tendent la main, c'est atroce.* It's awful to watch these hungry children holding out their hands. **3** [very strong] dreadful *le spectacle atroce des villageois massacrés* the dreadful sight of the slaughtered villagers.
effroyable *adj* **1** [causing disapproval] awful *C'est effroyable la quantité de viande que je suis obligé d'acheter chaque semaine pour nourrir toute cette famille.* I have to buy an awful lot of meat each week to feed this family. **2** [causing horror] terrible *Je suis arrivé juste après l'accident, il y avait du sang partout, c'était effroyable.* I arrived immediately after the accident, there was blood everywhere, it was terrible.

45.21 *Horreur et dégoût* Horror and disgust

repoussant, e *adj* [physically] repulsive *Il est d'une saleté repoussante.* He's repulsively dirty.
répugnant, e *adj* [usu physically] disgusting *Les toilettes ont débordé, c'est répugnant.* The toilet's overflowed, it's disgusting. *Dans ce conflit, les nations soi-disant civilisées*

ont commis des actes répugnants. In this war so-called civilized nations have committed revolting acts.

répulsion *nf* [usu physical] repulsion

dégoûtant, e *adj* [usu physical. Can refer to intense feelings or be more light-hearted] disgusting *Va te laver les mains, elles sont dégoûtantes.* Go and wash your hands, they're disgusting. *Ils ne lui ont même pas fait de cadeau d'adieu, c'est vraiment dégoûtant!* They didn't even give her a leaving present, how disgusting!

dégoût *nm* [usu physical] disgust

dégoûter {6} *vt* **1** [distasteful, morally or physically] to disgust. *Tu me dégoûtes avec ton imperméable graisseux.* You disgust me, wearing that greasy raincoat. *La vie me dégoûte.* Life makes me sick. **2** [in food contexts] *Je ne mange jamais de cervelle, ça me dégoûte.* I never eat brain, I find it disgusting. *Ma mère me forçait à boire du lait, ça m'a dégoûté des laitages pour toujours.* My mother used to force me to drink milk; it put me off dairy products for life.

écœurant, e *adj* **1** [morally or physically repulsive] nauseating **2** [mildly nauseating] cloying *Avec toute cette crème, je trouve leurs gâteaux un peu écœurants.* There's too much cream on their cakes; I find them rather cloying.

écœurement *nm* **1** [moral or physical repulsion] disgust, abhorrence *L'écœurement nous saisit lorsque nous regardons ces photos des camps de concentration.* A feeling of abhorrence takes over when we see those photos of concentration camps. **2** [when eating] nausea. *Elle mange des chocolats jusqu'à l'écœurement.* She eats chocolates till she feels nauseous.

écœurer {6} *vt* **1** [be strongly repellent morally or physically] to sicken *Quand on voit les agissements des hommes politiques, il y a de quoi vous écœurer.* When you see what the politicians are up to it's enough to make you sick. **2** [be nauseating. In food contexts] to make nauseous. *Le café froid, ça m'écœure.* Cold coffee makes me nauseous.

nausée *nf* nausea *avoir la nausée* to feel nauseous

haut-le-cœur *nm inv* wave of nausea *avoir un haut-le-cœur* to feel a sudden wave of nausea

dégueulasse *adj* [informal and very common way of expressing physical or moral disapproval] disgusting *Il est dégueulasse, ton café.* Your coffee's foul. *Ils ont refusé d'accorder 2% aux infirmières, c'est dégueulasse.* They've refused to give the nurses a two per cent pay rise, how disgusting!

Locutions Idioms

J'étais/Il était glacé d'horreur My/His blood ran cold.

Ça fait froid dans le dos. [refers to physical or moral causes for feeling of horror] It gives you the shivers.

Ça le/la rend malade. [implies great moral distress] It makes him/her ill.

Voir des enfants dans cet état-là, ça me rend malade. When I see children in that state, it makes me (feel) ill.

45.22 *Peur* Fear

peur *nf* fear *avoir peur de qqn/qqch* to be afraid of sb/sthg *faire peur à qqn* to frighten sb

peureux, -reuse *adj* [habitual trait] fearful

apeuré, e *adj* [slightly formal. Temporary state, caused by a particular sight, thought, etc] frightened

effrayer {16} *vt* to frighten

frayeur *nf* fright *faire une grosse frayeur à qqn* to give sb a big fright

lâche *adj* cowardly **lâche** *n* coward

poltron, -ronne *n* [literary synonym for **lâche**] coward

45.23 *Fortes peurs* Strong fears

effroi *nm* [strong fear] fright *Elle fixait avec effroi l'homme qui brandissait le couteau.* She stared aghast at the man with the knife.

épouvante *nf* [caused by, for example, uncontrollable or supernatural things] horror, terror *saisi d'épouvante en entendant venir les vagues de bombardiers* filled with terror at the sound of the approaching bombers *film d'épouvante* horror film

épouvanter {6} *vt* to terrify

hantise *nf* [obsessive fear of something that might happen] fear *Elle a la hantise de mourir avant lui.* She is obsessed by the fear that she might die before him.

panique *nf* panic *pris de panique* panic-stricken *Pas de panique!* Calm down!

paniquer {6} *vi* to panic

terreur *nf* terror *une terreur folle* blind terror

terrifier {15} *vt* to terrify

45.24 *Peurs moins fortes* Lesser fears

craindre {59} *vt* **1** [general term, slightly more formal than *avoir peur*. Applies to physical or mental fears] to fear *Ne crains rien!* Don't you worry! *Je crains qu'il (ne) pleuve.* I'm afraid it might rain. **2** [expresses nervousness or reluctance] to be afraid of *Elle craignait qu'on (ne) s'aperçoive de ce qu'elle avait fait.* She was afraid that someone would realize what she had done. *Il ne faut pas craindre de les arroser.* Water them generously. *Je crains les chatouilles.* I hate being tickled.

crainte *nf* fear *Sois sans crainte.* Never fear. *Ils ont fermé les frontières par crainte d'un exode de la population.* Fearing a mass exodus of the population, they closed the borders.

effaroucher {6} *vt* [cause to hide or flee in fear. Obj: e.g. child, deer] to frighten away

alarmer {6} *vt* [worry someone about a possible danger] to worry *Je ne voudrais pas vous alarmer mais on a vu quelqu'un qui rôdait autour de chez vous.* I don't want to worry you but someone was seen loitering near your house.

alerter {6} *vt* [warn of something worrying or untoward] to alert *La police a été alertée.* The police were alerted.

appréhender {6} *vt* [have an uneasy feeling prior to doing something] to fear, to dread *appréhender d'aller chez le dentiste* to dread going to the dentist

appréhension *nf* [unease prior to an event] fear, dread

redouter {6} *vt* [slightly stronger than **appréhender**] to dread. *Nous redoutions tous les visites de la tante Roberta.* We all used to dread Aunt Roberta's visits.

45.25 *Manifestations de la peur* Describing fear

être blanc, blanche, ALSO **blême** to be white with fear

être mort, e de peur to be scared to death

être cloué, e au sol (de peur) to be transfixed with fear

glacer les sangs à qqn to make sb's blood run cold

avoir des sueurs froides to break out in a cold sweat

trembler comme une feuille to shake like a leaf

46 Help and encouragement

46.1 *Aide* Help

serviable *adj* [ready to offer assistance] helpful
obligeant, e *adj* [same meaning as **serviable**, but implies more generosity] obliging
obligeance *nf* helpfulness *avec obligeance* helpfully
assistant, e *n* assistant
auxiliaire *n* [temporary helper] assistant
adjoint, e *n* [in a post] assistant
allié, e *n* [in a war, in negotiations] ally
s'allier avec {6} *v refl* to ally oneself with
aide *nf* **1** [general term] help *avec l'aide de qqn* with sb's help *à l'aide d'un marteau* by using a hammer *venir en aide à qqn* to come to sb's help **2** [humanitarian] aid

46.2 *Sortes d'aides* Kinds of help

assistance *nf* [implies that the helper is skilled and that the process lasts a while] assistance *Il a fallu l'assistance de plusieurs corps de pompiers pour maîtriser l'incendie.* The assistance of several firefighting units was needed in order to deal with the blaze.
porter, ALSO **prêter assistance à qqn** to come to sb's assistance
collaboration *nf* [at work, or when participating in a project] collaboration
concours *nm* [term used in official language. May imply sponsoring] help *Le festival a été organisé avec le concours de la commune.* The festival was organized with the help of the district council. *fournir son concours à qqn* to assist sb
secours *nm* [urgently needed, usu financial or medical] help *secours catholique* Catholic aid organization **2** [medical] help *aller chercher du secours* to go and get help *les (premiers) secours* first aid
service *nm* [usu involves personal help, in kind rather than in terms of money] favour *rendre un service à qqn* to do sb a favour *rendre service à qqn* to be of service to sb
entr'aide *nf* **1** [between two individuals or groups of equal status] mutual help **2** [dispensed to a group in need] aid *Une association d'entr'aide distribue des tickets-repas gratuits aux enfants les plus défavorisés.* A charitable organization hands out free meal tokens to the poorest children.
dépannage *nm* **1** [when a vehicle or machine has broken down] (breakdown) repair **2** [in general] temporary help *Tu peux me prêter 1.000 francs, juste pour un dépannage?* Could you lend me 1,000 francs just to tide me over?

46.3 *Verbes exprimant l'aide* Verbs for helping

aider {6} *vt* and *vi* [general term] to help
secourir {33} *vt* **1** [general term. Implies emergency] to help **2** [subj: e.g. fire service, motorway patrol, mountain rescue team] to rescue
s'entr'aider {6} *v refl* to help one another
contribuer {6} *vi* [be part of a positive or negative process] to contribute *contribuer à qqch* to contribute to sth *un système d'amortisseurs qui contribue à la stabilité du véhicule* a shock-absorber system which contributes to the stability of the vehicle *contribuer à faire qqch* to help (to) do sth *Le chômage contribue à marginaliser certains*

jeunes. Unemployment is a contributory factor in the alienation of some young people.
favoriser {6} *vt* [be a positive or negative factor in] to help *Le lait favorise la croissance des enfants.* Milk helps a child's growth. *La chaleur favorise la multiplication des bactéries.* Heat helps bacteria to multiply.
dépanner {6} *vt* **1** [when a vehicle or machine has broken down] to repair **2** [general term] to help out (temporarily) *Je n'avais plus de farine, mon voisin m'a dépanné.* I ran out of flour, my neighbour helped me out.

46.4 *Appeler à l'aide* To call for help

appel *nm* **de détresse** distress call
signal *nm* **de détresse** distress signal
appeler au secours to shout for help
au secours! ALSO **à l'aide!** help!

S.O.S
S.O.S. is the abbreviation used as cry for help, e.g.: S.O.S! Mayday! In addition, this acronym is often used in the names of various help or aid organizations, notably in the anti-racist movement 'S.O.S. Racisme', and the medical aid organization 'S.O.S. Médecins'.

Locutions Idioms
Qu'est-ce que je peux faire pour vous? How can I help you?
Aide-toi et le ciel t'aidera. [proverb] God helps those who help themselves.
donner un coup de main à qqn [informal] to give sb a hand
prêter main-forte à qqn [slightly formal] to lend sb a (helping) hand
C'est le bras droit de . . . [implies that a lot of help is given often unobtrusively] *Lumet, c'est le bras droit du patron.* Lumet is the boss's right-hand man.

46.5 *Encouragement* Encouragement

encouragement *nm* **1** [urging on] encouragement *La foule poussait des cris d'encouragement.* The crowd was shouting encouragement.
encourageant, e *adj* encouraging *Il fait des progrès encourageants.* He's making encouraging progress.

46.6 *Verbes exprimant l'encouragement* Verbs expressing encouragement

encourager {8} *vt* to encourage *Ce sont eux qui l'ont encouragée à composer sa première œuvre.* They encouraged her to compose her first piece.
pousser {6} *vt* [help by coercing] to push *Elle ne s'intéressera jamais à la musique si tu ne la pousses pas.* She'll never develop an interest in music unless you push her. *pousser qqn à faire qqch* to encourage sb to do sth
entraîner {6} *vt* **1** [help by providing an example, for good or ill] to encourage *C'est lui qui les entraîne à sécher les cours.* He's the one who's leading them into truancy. **2** [in sport] to coach
s'entraîner *v refl* **1** [in music, at a hobby] to practise **2** [in sport] to train
engager {8} *vt* [help by persuading] *engager qqn à faire* to encourage sb to do *Nous avons engagé nos collègues à publier les résultats de leurs travaux.* We encouraged our colleagues to publish the results of their work.

inviter {6} *vt* [same meaning as **engager**, but stresses courtesy] to invite *inviter qqn à faire* to invite sb to do *Ensuite le président l'invitera à témoigner.* Then the chairperson will invite her to testify.

soutenir {23} *vt* [obj: e.g. ally, friend, partner] to support *Mon mari me soutient dans mes projets.* My husband supports me in my plans.

47 Alertness and degrees of contentment

47.1 *Tension* Tenseness

tension *nf* [state of nerves] tension *tension nerveuse* tenseness *Je suis continuellement sous tension.* I'm under pressure all the time.

nervosité *nf* jumpiness

tendu, e *adj* [describes: e.g. person, situation, conversation] tense

nerveux, -veuse *adj* 1 [permanently] nervous 2 [temporarily] jumpy

crispé, e *adj* [describes: e.g. smile, hand, reply] tense

se crisper {6} *v refl* to become tense

crispant, e *adj* annoying

Locutions Idioms

C'est un paquet de nerfs. ALSO **Il/Elle a les nerfs en pelote.** He's/She's a bundle of nerves.

être sur les nerfs to be extremely tense *être constamment sur les nerfs* to live on one's nerves

Il/Elle ne tient plus en place. [stresses uncontrollable movement e.g. up and down a room, to the window and back, etc] He/She can't sit still.

47.2 *Exaltation* Excitement

Translating 'exciting'
The adjective **excitant, e** often has a pejorative connotation, because of associations with stimulants or sex, which makes it difficult to use as a translation of 'exciting' in most cases. Depending on context, the English word is rendered as follows. When it implies an intense feeling, it can be translated as *exaltant* or *passionnant*: e.g. *Mon métier est passionnant.* I have a really exciting job. *Comme c'est exaltant, d'arriver au sommet et d'embrasser toute la vallée d'un regard!* How exciting to reach the summit and survey the whole of the valley below! The word *émotion* can also be used, e.g. *Ils ont vu leur fille gagner la finale, quelle émotion!* They watched their daughter winning the final, how exciting! When it is used routinely to imply enthusiasm or merely interest in something, 'exciting' can be translated as *drôlement bien* (neutral), *très chouette* (informal), *super* (informal), etc: *On est allés faire du patin à glace cet après-midi. – Ça devait être drôlement bien!* We went skating this afternoon. – How exciting!

excitant, e *adj* 1 [pejorative. Describes the action of coffee, stimulants] overexciting 2 [sexually] arousing

excitation *nf* [slightly pejorative. Nervous agitation] excitement *Pas d'excitation, les enfants, il va bientôt être l'heure d'aller au lit.* No excitement, children, please, it'll be bedtime soon.

surexcitation *nf* [pejorative] overexcitement

sensations *nf pl* **fortes** 1 [triggered by dramatic events] (high) excitement 2 [triggered by e.g. fairground rides] thrills

effervescence *nf* [collective feeling] atmosphere of excitement *Toute la rue était en effervescence.* Everyone in the street was highly excited.

exaltation *nf* [noble excitement] elation

énervé, e *adj* [pejorative. Describes: children] (over)excited

chauffé, e au rouge/à blanc beside oneself with excitement

déchaîné, e *adj* out of control (with excitement)

excité, e *adj* [slightly pejorative] (over)excited

hystérique *adj* [strongly pejorative. Implies screaming, etc. Describes women] hysterical

survolté, e *adj* [describes: e.g. crowd, audience] at fever pitch

47.3 *Sérénité* Serenity

tranquille *adj* 1 [undisturbed. Describes: e.g. village, holiday] peaceful 2 [person] quiet *avoir l'esprit tranquille* to have peace of mind *avoir la conscience tranquille* to have a clear conscience

tranquillité *nf* peace (and quiet)

tranquillement *adv* 1 [in silence] quietly 2 [without worry] calmly, evenly *Il a replié son journal, puis il est tranquillement sorti du bar.* He folded his paper, then walked calmly out of the bar.

paisible *adj* [describes: e.g. person] quiet **paisiblement** *adv* peacefully *Elle dort paisiblement.* She's sleeping peacefully.

paix *nf* 1 [absence of worry] peace *paix intérieure* inner peace 2 [absence of war] peace

serein, e *adj* [literary] serene

sérénité *nf* [literary] serenity

nirvana *nm* nirvana *atteindre le nirvana* to reach a state of nirvana

Locutions Idioms

à tête reposée when one's mind is fresh *C'est compliqué, attendons demain pour voir ça à tête reposée.* It's a bit complicated, let's wait until tomorrow and deal with it when our minds are fresh.

Fiche-moi/Fiche-lui la paix. Leave me/him in peace.

47.4 *Curiosité* Curiosity

curieux, -rieuse *adj* 1 [pejorative. Wanting to know things which others want to keep secret] nosy 2 [wanting to know. No idea of secrecy] (always + *de* + infinitive) interested *Je serais curieux de savoir comment tu vas t'y prendre.* I'd be interested to see how you tackle it. 3 [ready to broaden one's knowledge] (sometimes + *de*) keen to learn *Dès son plus jeune âge il s'est montré curieux de tout.* From his earliest childhood he was keen to learn about everything.

curiosité *nf* 1 [pejorative. Interference in other people's business] nosiness 2 [healthy interest in the world] enquiring turn of mind

indiscret, -rète *adj* 1 [failing to respect other people's privacy] nosy 2 [repeating things which have been told to one in confidence] indiscreet

fouiner {6} *vi* [look in other people's cupboards, papers, etc. Pejorative] to poke around *Tu es encore venu fouiner dans ma chambre!* You've been poking around in my bedroom again!

Locutions Idioms

Il est curieux/Elle est curieuse comme une fouine BrE
He's/She's a real nosy parker. AmE He's/She's too nosy for his/her own good.

mettre, ALSO **fourrer** [informal] **son nez dans** to poke one's nose into

Mêle-toi de ce qui te regarde!/Mêlez-vous de ce qui vous regarde! Mind your own business!

De quoi je me mêle? [informal. Only used with *je*] What business is it of yours!

La curiosité est un vilain défaut. [expression used to rebuke childen for being nosy] Curiosity killed the cat

Les murs ont des oreilles. Walls have ears.

47.5 *Surprise* Surprise

surprise *nf* [reaction; also thing or event causing the reaction] surprise *faire une surprise à qqn* to surprise sb

surprendre {54} *vt* to take by surprise

surprenant, e *adj* surprising

étonnant, e *adj* [slightly stronger than **surprenant**] astonishing

saisissant, e *adj* [causing one to stop still with surprise] amazing

ahurissant, e *adj* [surprising and unbelievable] staggering

inattendu, e *adj* [not part of predictable events] unexpected

insolite *adj* [literary. Surprising because never met before] unusual

coup *nm* **de théâtre** [unexpected] dramatic turn of events

47.6 *Surprise désagréable* Unpleasant surprise

prendre qqn sur le fait to catch sb in the act

prendre qqn la main dans le sac to catch sb with their fingers in the till

en flagrant délit 1 [legal] in flagrante (delicto)
2 [figurative] in the act *Je l'ai pris en flagrant délit de mensonge.* I caught him telling a bare-faced lie.

faire un choc à qqn to give sb a shock

Elle a fait une remarque qui est arrivée ALSO **venue comme un cheveu sur la soupe** [unexpected and unwanted] She made a remark which was totally out of place.

un coup de tonnerre dans un ciel serein a bolt out of the blue

47.7 *Réactions de surprise* Surprised reactions

étonné, e *adj* [slight reaction] surprised

stupéfait, e, *adj* [strong reaction] astounded

déconcerté, e *adj* [unsure what to do] disconcerted *tout déconcerté par ce bruit au milieu de son discours* put off his stride by this noise in the middle of his speech

ébahi, e *adj*, ALSO **ahuri, e** *adj* [suggests open-mouthed astonishment] dumbfounded

saisi, e *adj* [as if petrified] amazed

bouche bée open-mouthed *En entendant ça, il est resté bouche bée.* When he heard this, his jaw dropped.

en être comme deux ronds de flan [informal] to be flabbergasted

Il n'en revient pas. He can't get over it.

Les bras lui en sont tombés. [phrase with comic effect] His jaw dropped.

à la stupéfaction générale to everybody's amazement

une fois l'effet de surprise passé, je . . . once I'd recovered from my surprise, I . . .

47.8 *Heureux* Happiness

heureux, -reuse *adj* [experiencing happiness] happy *Je me sens heureux.* I feel happy. *rendre son mari heureux/sa femme heureuse* to make one's husband/wife happy

bonheur *nm* **1** [lasting state] happiness *Enfin, à l'âge de cinquante ans, je connais le bonheur.* At fifty, I now know what happiness is. **2** [something good that happens] happy event *Son retour a été pour moi un grand bonheur.* I was so happy when she came back.

content, e *adj* [experiencing satisfaction] (really) pleased *Je suis content, cette année j'ai mon samedi libre.* I'm really pleased that I have Saturday off this year. *Le client a rapporté la tondeuse hier, il n'avait pas l'air très content.* The customer returned the lawnmower yesterday, he didn't look too pleased.

joyeux, -yeuse *adj* [in extremely good humour] happy *Vous êtes tous très joyeux aujourd'hui, c'est l'anniversaire de quelqu'un?* You all look pretty happy today, is it someone's birthday?

joie *nf* [intense and short-lived state, sometimes caused by aesthetic or mystical experiences] joy *Devant la mer enfin retrouvée, la joie lui emplit le coeur.* When at last she found herself looking at the sea again, her heart was filled with joy.

gai, e *adj* [similar to *joyeux*, but can also be a permanent trait of character] *C'est quelqu'un qui est toujours gai.* He is a happy person.

gaieté *nf* **1** [permanent] happiness *Il apportait à notre petit groupe une gaieté contagieuse.* He made everyone in our little group feel happy. **2** [temporary] cheeriness *Allons, un peu plus de gaieté!* Come on, don't be so glum!

enjoué, e *adj* [temporary state, expressed in cheery words or tone of voice] good-humoured

bonne humeur *nf* good mood *Les préparatifs se faisaient dans la bonne humeur générale.* The preparations were made in an atmosphere of general good humour. *être de bonne humeur* to be in a good mood

ravi, e *adj* delighted *Il a été reçu à son audition, il est ravi.* He got the part, he's delighted.

Locutions Idioms

être au septième ciel to be in (the) seventh heaven

être aux anges BrE to be over the moon AmE to be thrilled to death

47.9 *Rire* Laughter

rire *nm* laughter *un petit rire* a chuckle *un gros rire* a guffaw *le rire clair des enfants* the tinkling laughter of little children *J'entendais des hurlements de rire venant de la pièce à côté.* I could hear gales of laughter coming from next door. *Le public hurlait de rire.* The audience was howling with laughter. *Quand je lui ai dit ça, elle a éclaté de rire.* When I told her this, she burst out laughing.

fou rire *nm* fit of the giggles *Pris d'un fou rire au micro, il a été obligé de passer de la musique.* He got a fit of the giggles at the microphone and had to put some music on.

rire {79} *vi* to laugh *rire sous cape* to laugh up one's sleeve *rire jaune* to force a laugh *rire aux larmes* to laugh until one cries *rire à gorge déployée* to howl with laughter *rire au nez de qqn* to laugh in sb's face *pour rire* (just) for a joke

éclat *nm* **de rire** hoot of laughter

rigoler {6} *vi* **1** [common informal synonym for **rire**] to laugh *Je ne pouvais plus m'arrêter de rigoler.* I couldn't stop laughing. *On a bien rigolé l'autre soir.* We had great fun the other night. **2** [informal. In phrases expressing incredulity] *Tu rigoles?* You must be kidding! *900 francs la nuit? Ils veulent rigoler ou quoi?* 900 francs for the night? They can't be serious!

ricaner {6} *vi* [stupidly or nastily] to sneer

hilare *adj* [with expression of intense hilarity on face, broad grin, etc] beaming

47.10 *Expressions décrivants les effets du rire* Describing laughter

plié, e en deux (de rire) doubled up (with laughter)

être mort, e de rire ALSO **se tordre de rire** to laugh fit to burst

Il/Elle se tenait les côtes (de rire). He/She was in stitches (with laughter).

J' étais écroulé, e (de rire). I was rolling about (with laughter).

Je n'en pouvais plus (de rire). I was killing myself laughing.

Locution Idiom
Rira bien qui rira le dernier. [proverb] He who laughs last laughs longest.

47.11 *Sourire* Smile

sourire *nm* smile *Fais-moi un sourire.* Give me a smile. *un sourire entendu* ALSO *en coin* a knowing smile *un joli sourire* a lovely smile *Elle a son sourire commercial.* She's wearing her professional smile. *Elle supporte tout avec le sourire.* She puts up with a lot but still keeps smiling.

sourire {79} *vi* to smile *Je prends la photo! Souriez!* I'm ready to take the shot! Say cheese! *sourire de toutes ses dents* to give a toothy grin

47.12 *Amusant* Funny

amusant, e *adj* [mildly entertaining] funny *Tiens, on a le même nom, c'est amusant.* Hey, we've got identical names, that's funny.

amuser {6} *vt* to amuse *Pendant la conférence il y aura une garderie avec des jeux pour amuser les enfants.* During the conference there will be a creche with games to keep the children amused.

s'amuser *v refl* **1** [enjoy oneself] to have fun *Laisse-les s'amuser, ils auront le temps de travailler quand ils seront grands.* Let them have (their) fun, there'll plenty of time for them to work when they're grown up. **2** [subj: e.g. child] to play *Où est la petite? – Elle s'amuse dehors.* Where's the little girl? – She's outside, playing.

drôle *adj* [stronger than **amusant**] funny *Tu as entendu Devos? Il est très drôle.* Have you heard Devos? He's very funny. *Il était enfermé dehors en pyjama, et il ne trouvait pas ça drôle du tout!* He was locked out in his pyjamas and he didn't think it was at all funny!

humour *nm* humour *l'humour anglais* English humour

humoristique *adj* humorous

hilarant, e *adj* hilarious

47.13 *Choses amusantes* Amusing things

plaisanterie *nf* joke

blague *nf* [informal synonym for **plaisanterie**] joke

gag *nm* [in show business, on television] gag

farce *nf* practical joke

mot *nm* **d'esprit** witticism

bon mot *nm* witty remark

calembour *nm* pun

canular *nm* hoax *canular téléphonique* telephone hoax

47.14 *Moquerie* Mockery

moquerie *nf* [remark, usu hurtful] remark designed to poke fun (at someone)

se moquer de {6} *v refl* **1** [have fun at someone's expense] to make fun of *Ne vous moquez pas de ceux qui sont moins privilégiés que vous.* Do not make fun of those less fortunate than yourselves. **2** [defy] to ignore *La pluie? je m'en moque!* I don't care if it's raining!

taquinerie *nf* **1** [words] teasing remark **2** [deed] something done to tease *Je n'aime pas les taquineries.* I don't like to be teased.

taquiner {6} *vt* to tease

dérision *nf* [strong, implies contempt] derision *tourner qqch en dérision* to deride sthg

sarcasme *nm* sarcastic remark

ironie *nf* irony

Locutions Idioms

faire des gorges chaudes de qqch to make a huge joke out of sthg

se payer la tête de qqn [informal] to poke fun at sb

se payer la gueule de qqn [very informal] BrE to take the mickey out of sb AmE to put someone on

se foutre de la gueule de qqn [very strong phrase, which may offend] BrE to take the piss out of sb AmE to put someone on

47.15 *Plaisir* Pleasure

plaisir *nm* [temporary satisfaction brought about by an event, a meal, an aesthetic or sexual experience] pleasure *faire plaisir à qqn* to please sb

How to express enjoyment of something
The French verb *plaire* is the most useful one for saying how you enjoyed something, but it is an impersonal verb constructed as follows:

Ça me plaît. I enjoy it
Ça t'a plu? Did you enjoy it?
Ça vous a plu, Messieurs-Dames? [waiter to diners] Did you enjoy your meal?
Moi, j'ai bien aimé le film, mais il n'a pas plu à mon mari. I rather liked the film, but my husband didn't enjoy it.

Enjoyment can also be expressed using **aimer**, e.g.: *J'aime beaucoup le ski.* I really enjoy skiing. *Tu aimes le jazz?* Do you enjoy jazz?

apprécier {15} *vt* [like, in a refined way, intellectually or aesthetically] to enjoy *J'ai beaucoup apprécié votre conférence.* I enjoyed your talk a lot.

47.16 *Satisfaction* Satisfaction

see also **47.8 Heureux**

satisfaire {62} *vt* **1** [provide the right amount of enjoyment for] to satisfy *Nous avons prévu toutes sortes de jeux, de quoi satisfaire le public le plus exigeant.* We've got all sorts of games planned, enough to satisfy the most demanding audience. *J'espère que tu es satisfait!* I hope you're satisfied! **2** [respond to] to fulfil *Notre magasin ne peut satisfaire la demande de produits biologiques.* Our shop can't satisfy the demand for organic produce.

satisfaction *nf* **1** [feeling of being pleased] satisfaction *Le travail étant prêt à temps, sa satisfaction était évidente.* He was obviously pleased with the fact that the work was ready on time. **2** [reason for being pleased] satisfaction *Votre crème à épiler vous donnera toute satisfaction pourvu que vous observiez les précautions d'emploi.* You will be completely satisfied with your depilatory cream providing you follow the instructions for use. *Elle donne beaucoup de satisfactions à ses professeurs.* She gives her teachers much cause for satisfaction. *Démissionner pour que vous preniez ma place? Je ne vous donnerai pas cette satisfaction!* Resign so you can take my place? I wouldn't give you the satisfaction!

combler {6} *vt* [provide maximum pleasure or joy] to gratify *combler qqn* to make sb delighted *Mon fils est revenu, et ma fille vient d'avoir un bébé, je suis comblée.* My son has returned and my daughter has just had a baby, I'm delighted.

épanouissement *nm* [happy development of all one's emotional and other potential] fulfilment

épanoui, e *adj* fulfilled *Maintenant qu'elle pratique un métier qui lui plaît, elle est enfin épanouie.* She's fulfilled at last, now that she has a job that she likes.

s'épanouir {19} *v refl* to develop (to) one's full potential

Locution Idiom
Satisfait ou remboursé [sign in shops, or on adverts] Your money back if you're not completely satisfied with our product

47.17 *Tristesse* Sadness

tristesse *nf* sadness *C'est avec tristesse que je vous quitte, mes amis.* I am sad at leaving you, my friends.

triste *adj* [describes: e.g. person, situation, landscape] sad *Ça me rend triste.* It makes me sad.

attrister {6} *vt* to sadden

s'attrister *v refl* to become sad

malheureux, -reuse *adj* [longer-lasting than **triste**. Describes: e.g. person, life, marriage] unhappy *Toute sa vie, elle a été malheureuse.* She was unhappy during her whole life. *rendre qqn malheureux* to make sb unhappy

47.18 *Degrés de tristesse* Degrees of sadness

chagrin *nm* **1** [great] sorrow *Le chagrin la submergeait.* She was overcome by sorrow. **2** [small] disappointment *un chagrin d'enfant* a child's disappointment

chagriné, e *adj* [small sorrow only] disappointed *J'ai été chagriné de ne plus trouver chez l'antiquaire les 'Mémoires de guerre', qui pourtant y étaient encore la semaine dernière.* I was disappointed not to find the *War Memoirs* at the antiquarian bookshop, because they were still there last week.

contrariété *nf* annoyance *les petites contrariétés de la vie* life's little annoyances

contrarié, e *adj* annoyed *J'ai été très contrarié quand il m'a annoncé qu'il ne viendrait pas.* I was rather annoyed when he said he wouldn't come.

serrement *nm* **de coeur** pang of sadness

47.19 *Grande tristesse* Extreme sadness

désespoir *nm* despair *être au désespoir* to be in despair

désespéré, e *adj* despairing **désespéré, e** *n* [someone about to commit suicide or some other desperate act] desperate person

désespérer {10} **1** *vi* (sometimes + *de*) to despair *Ne désespérons pas.* Let us not despair. *Je désespérais de la revoir jamais lorsqu'un jour elle frappa à ma porte.* I despaired of ever seeing her again when one day she came knocking at my door. **2** *vt* to drive to despair *Ses infidélités me désespéraient.* His infidelities drove me despair.

se désespérer *v refl* to despair

détresse *nf* [very grave emotional state] distress *Depuis la mort de sa femme, il est dans une grande détresse.* He's been in a very distressed state since his wife died.

abattement *nm* prostration

abattu, e *adj* prostrate

47.20 *Manifestations de la tristesse* Showing sadness

pleurer {6} *vt* and *vi* to cry *pleurer à chaudes larmes* to weep

sangloter {6} *vi* to sob

larme *nf* tear *en larmes* in tears

sanglot *nm* sob *entre deux sanglots* between (two) sobs

avoir les yeux rougis to be red-eyed

Locutions Idioms
avoir des idées noires to have a fit of the blues
en avoir gros sur le cœur ALSO **sur la patate** [informal] to be (very) upset
avoir le cœur gros to have a heavy heart
avoir le cœur serré [temporary feeling of poignancy] to feel a pang (of sadness)
avoir le cœur brisé to be broken-hearted
pleurer toutes les larmes de son corps to cry one's eyes out
pleurer comme une Madeleine [indicates floods of tears, and sometimes also the speaker's scepticism about the sincerity of the crying] to cry like a baby
des larmes de crocodile crocodile tears
Ne fais/faites pas cette tête-là! [informal] Don't look so unhappy!

47.21 *Déception* Disappointment

déception *nf* disappointment

décevoir {38} *vt* to disappoint *être déçu* to be disappointed. *Je ne veux pas décevoir mes parents.* I don't want to disappoint my parents.

désabuser {6} *vt* to take away the illusions of *Si ton mari te croit heureuse, le temps est venu de le désabuser.* If your husband thinks you're happy, the time has come to disabuse him.

Locutions Idioms
Ça a été une douche pour lui/elle. [informal. Implies sudden disappointment with a calming effect] It came as a great shock to him/her.

Il ne va pas être déçu! [ironic and informal. The subject is unaware of the importance of what is to be revealed] Have we got news for him!

47.22 *Colère* Anger

colère *nf* anger *être en colère (contre qqn)* to be angry (with sb) *se mettre en colère (contre qqn)* to get angry (with sb) *passer sa colère sur qqn* to take out one's anger on sb *faire une colère* to have a tantrum
coléreux, -euse ALSO **colérique** *adj* bad-tempered.
fureur *nf* fury *entrer en fureur* to get into a rage
furieux, -euse *adj* furious *furieux (de ce) que je l'aie critiqué* furious that I criticized him *furieux contre qqn* furious with sb
furie *nf* **1** [rage] fury *en furie* enraged **2** [woman] fury, harpy *entrer/sortir comme une furie* to storm in/out (in a rage)
rage *nf* rage *des manifestants en rage* enraged demonstrators
enrager {8} *vi* to be infuriated [but *faire enrager qqn* to tease sb mercilessly]
irritation *nf* irritation, annoyance
exaspération *nf* exasperation **exaspéré, e** *adj* exasperated, infuriated.
agacement *nm* [due to minor causes] (slight) annoyance
agacé, e *adj* (slightly) annoyed, irritated
courroux *nm* [literary. Often in religious contexts] ire, wrath
courroucé, e *adj* [less formal] irate, wrathful
fâcher {6} *vt* to make cross
se fâcher *v refl* to get cross *Il s'est fâché*. He got cross. *Il s'est fâché tout rouge* [humorous]. He got very cross (indeed).
Ils se sont fâchés. 1 [plural of **Il s'est fâché**]. They got angry. **2.** [reciprocal] They had a falling out.
fâché, e *adj Ils sont fâchés* [reflexive] They are cross/angry. [reciprocal] They are not on speaking terms.

47.23 *Colère brève* Short-lived anger

s'emporter {6} *v refl* to fly into a temper *Elle s'emporte facilement.* She's very short-tempered.
emportement *nm* burst of temper
emporté, e *adj* short-tempered
accès *nm* **de colère** fit/burst of anger
éclat *nm* (de colère) angry outburst
éclater, exploser {6} *vi* [let out repressed anger] to explode *Il a éclaté en reproches.* His resentment came pouring out.
hors de soi adjectival phrase [often justifiable anger] beside oneself (with anger), incensed *Il était hors de lui/elle était hors d'elle.* He/she was incensed. *Sa réponse m'a mis hors de moi.* His answer infuriated me.

47.24 *Colère durable* Lasting anger

hargne *nf* [combines tenacity with vindictiveness] spite
hargneux, -euse *adj* spiteful
grogne *nf* [informal. A patronizing way of describing social discontent] *la grogne des enseignants* grumblings among the teaching profession
grognon *adj* [informal. Used affectionately, of males and females] grumpy **grogner** *vi* to grumble

Citation Quotation
la hargne, la grogne et la rogne Groaning, grumbling and moaning [De Gaulle, referring to unrest in sections of the French population in 1968]

décolérer {10} *vi* [always negative, often with duration specified, implies a cause for the anger] *Il ne décolère pas depuis hier.* He's been in a rage since yesterday. *Ils l'ont remplacée, et elle ne décolère plus.* They replaced her and she's been livid (about it) ever since.
fulminer {6} *vi* [literary or humorous. Anger expressed verbally against a person or thing which may be present or absent] to rant (and rave), to bluster *Elle fulminait contre nous.* She was cursing us.

Locutions Idioms
(sentir que) la moutarde vous monte au nez (to feel that) one is about to lose one's temper *La moutarde commençait à me monter au nez.* I was beginning to lose my temper.
La colére est mauvaise conseillère. Anger is a bad counsellor.
être soupe au lait [humorous, slightly patronising] to be permanently on a short fuse
voir rouge to see red
sortir de ses gonds [sudden indignation, causing the person to behave untypically] *Il est sorti de ses gonds.* He blew his top.
échauffer les oreilles à qqn [informal. Often with commencer] *Tu commences à m'échauffer les oreilles!* You're getting on my nerves!

48 Strength and weakness

48.1 *Robuste* Strong

robuste *adj* [having muscular strength and good health. Describes: e.g. person, tree, plant] robust, strong
fort, e *adj* [general term] strong *Il était petit mais fort.* He was short but strong.
costaud *e adj* **1** [informal synonym for **robuste**. Describes: e.g. person] strong **2** [humorous and informal. Describes: e.g. door, drink] pretty strong
vigoureux, -reuse *adj* [growing strongly or moving things energetically] sturdy, vigorous *de beaux enfants bien vigoureux* fine-looking, sturdy children *Il a repoussé l'armoire contre le mur d'un coup d'épaule vigoureux.* With a powerful heave of his shoulder he pushed the wardrobe back against the wall.
énergique *adj* **1** [forceful and dynamic] energetic **2** [strong and fast] brisk
solide *adj* [able to resist illness or psychological ordeals] strong
puissant, e *adj* [muscular] powerful
en pleine forme to be completely fit
avoir le moral to be in good spirits

48.2 *Renforcer* To make stronger

renforcer {7} *vt* [used literally or metaphorically] to strengthen *J'ai renforcé l'enveloppe avec de l'adhésif.* I strengthened the envelope with sticky tape. *Nous avons partagé des épreuves qui ont renforcé notre amitié.* We've been through ordeals which strengthened our friendship.
fortifier {6} *vt* **1** [give someone the means to resist a psychological ordeal] to strengthen *Ces critiques n'ont fait que la fortifier dans sa résolution* These criticisms merely strengthened her resolve. **2** [old-fashioned. Subj: e.g. medicine, beverage] to fortify

ragaillardir {19} *vt* [give new vigour to. Subj: esp breath of bracing air, glass of whisky, pep talk] to cheer up

Locutions Idioms
C'est un roc. He's/She's a tower of strength.
fort, e comme un boeuf strong as an ox
avoir de la poigne to have enormous strength in one's hands
faire un/le bras de fer avec qqn to do some arm-wrestling with sb
du poil de la bête [new vigour. Used only in the following phrases] *reprendre du poil de la bête* to get going again *Voilà qui va lui redonner du poil de la bête!* This'll get him going again!

48.3 *Faible* Weak

faiblesse *nf* **1** [physical or mental state] weakness *Par faiblesse, j'ai accepté tout ce qu'il a voulu.* Out of weakness, I let him do anything he liked. **2** [instance] weakness *Le deuxième chapitre a quelques faiblesses.* There are some weaknesses in the second chapter. *la faiblesse de son argumentation* the weakness of his argument
affaiblir {19} *vt* [obj: e.g. patient, position, building] to weaken *Ne fais rien qui puisse affaiblir ton autorité.* Do nothing that could weaken your authority. *L'érosion a affaibli les fondations.* The foundations were weakened by erosion.
s'affaiblir *v refl* to become weaker *Le malade s'affaiblit d'heure en heure.* The patient is getting weaker with every passing hour.
faible *adj* [lacking physical strength or moral fibre] weak *Elle est trop faible pour aller à Paris en train.* She's too weak to go to Paris on the train. **faible** *n* [someone with a lack of moral fibre] weak person *d'énormes sommes qui peuvent attirer les faibles* enormous amounts of money liable to attract weak-willed individuals.
piètre *adj* (before noun) [pejorative. Insufficient] feeble *de piètres résultats* feeble results
malingre *adj* [pejorative. Small and weak] puny *Étant enfant, il était d'apparence malingre.* He looked puny as a child.
fragile *adj* **1** [weakened by illness or age] frail *Vers la fin, grand-mère était devenue très fragile.* Grandmother had become very frail towards the end. **2** [psychologically] fragile *C'était un jeune homme fragile, souvent suicidaire.* He was a fragile young man with suicidal tendencies. **3** [thin. Describes: e.g. paper, veil, structure] flimsy
frêle *adj* [looking fragile due to paleness or thinness. Describes: e.g. boat, flower, woman, shoulder] frail
vulnérable *adj* [unable to repel illness or other hazards] vulnerable
impuissant, e *adj* [unable to achieve something] powerless *Les autorités sont impuissantes face à l'épidémie.* The authorities are powerless to stop the epidemic.
sans défense [unable to defend oneself] helpless *Les réfugiés sont sans défense face au choléra.* The refugees are helpless faced with the threat of cholera.
mauviette *nf* [pejorative] weakling, wimp

Locutions Idioms
avoir du sang de navet (dans les veines) [be without energy, enthusiasm or warmth] to be lily-livered
Il/Elle ne tient pas debout. He's/She's too weak to stand.
Il/Elle n'a pas le moral. He's/She's feeling down.

48.4 *Doux* Gentle

see also **43.15 Gentillesse et générosité**
doux, douce *adj* [implies soft movements and calm. Describes humans as well as animals] gentle **douceur** *nf* gentleness
doucement *adv* **1** [with kindness] gently **2** [with care] carefully
doucereux, -reuse *adj* [pejorative. Describes humans only, their looks or remarks] BrE sugary, smooth AmE slick
tendre *adj* [more loving than **doux**. Describes: e.g. lover, look, scene] tender
tendresse *nf* tenderness **tendrement** *adv* tenderly
caressant, -e *adj* [wanting to stroke or to be cuddled. Describes: e.g. dog, child] (physically) affectionate *un enfant très caressant* a very affectionate child
câlin, -line *adj* [more playful than **caressant**] cuddly *un enfant très câlin* a child who loves cuddles **câlin** *nm* cuddle
apprivoisé, -e *adj* **1** [stresses the human skill. Describes dangerous animals] tame *montrer des lionceaux apprivoisés* to show tame lion-cubs **2** [less stress on skill. Describes unusual pets] pet (as adj) *Il a une pie apprivoisée.* He has a pet magpie.
dressé, -e *adj* **1** [describes dangerous animals] tamed **2** [describes: e.g. dogs, monkeys] trained
inoffensif, -sive *adj* [naturally unable to cause harm or disabled by humans] harmless *un chien inoffensif* a harmless dog *rendre une panthère inoffensive par une piqûre* to knock out a panther with an injection

Locution Idiom
doux comme un agneau ALSO **mouton** [can be slightly pejorative] meek as a lamb

48.5 *Sauvage* Wild

see also **45.17 Cruauté**
sauvage *adj* **1** [living in the wild] wild *des oies sauvages* wild geese **2** [untameable] shy *Les biches sont très sauvages.* Deer are very shy animals. **3** [describes humans who avoid company] timid **4** [pejorative.Behaving like a wild animal] savage **sauvage** *n* **1** [person who shuns others. A judgmental but not always pejorative use] loner **2** [member of a primitive society. Pejorative use, now regarded as offensive] savage
sauvagerie *nf* [of humans only] savagery **sauvagement** *adv* savagely
violent, -e *adj* [implies lack of control rather than wilfulness] violent **violence** *nf* violence **violemment** *adv* violently
farouche *adj* [scared of humans. Describes mammals, birds or people] shy
féroce *adj* **1** [violent by nature. Describes animals] fierce **2** [stronger than **sauvage**. Describes humans, their actions or expressions] ferocious
férocement *adv* ferociously
sanguinaire *adj* **1** [literary or used for emphatic effect. Describes: e.g. tyrant, warrior] bloodthirsty **2** [literary. Describes carnivorous animals] savage
brute *nf* **1** [literary. Animal considered as a lower form of life] beast **2** [pejorative or used for comic effect. Person showing no refinement] lout
brutal, -e *adj*, *mpl* **-taux** brutal **brutal** *n* [who solves conflict by force] bully **brutalement** *adv* brutally
fauve *nm* [lion, tiger] big cat **fauve** *adj* [in set phrase] *bête fauve* big cat
agressif, -ssive *adj* **1** [attempting to dominate. Describes social animals including humans] threatening *le comportement agressif du chef de meute* the threatening

behaviour of the pack leader **2** [ready to quarrel. Describes humans] aggressive **agressivité** nf aggressiveness

Locutions Idioms
Il est prêt à mordre. [enraged to the point of losing control] He's just about to blow his top.
On n'est pas des sauvages! [phrase used e.g. to reassure someone that unacceptable behaviour will not be indulged in] We do know how to behave (in public)!
un enfant sauvage [who has grown up without humans] a wild child
le mythe du bon sauvage [belief in the natural goodness of non-civilized people, most often associated with the 18th-century philosopher Jean-Jacques Rousseau] the myth of the noble savage

49 Aesthetic feelings

49.1 *Beauté* Beauty

beau, belle adj, mpl **beaux**, fpl **belles 1** [aesthetically pleasing. Describes: e.g. work of art, landscape] beautiful **2** [good-looking. Describes esp persons] attractive **3** [morally pleasing] handsome *beau geste* noble gesture
beauté nf **1** [quality] beauty **2** [woman] beauty *Sa sœur est une beauté.* His sister is a beauty. **3** [place] beauty spot *les beautés de la Corse* the beauty spots of Corsica

> ### usage
>
> **beau**
> When **beau** comes before a noun starting with a vowel or a silent *h*, it changes to **bel**: e.g. *un bel homme* a handsome man *un bel ornement* a beautiful ornament

joli, e adj [suggests grace and charm, with a lighter impact on the viewer than **beau**. Not used of men, unless a slur is intended] pretty *de jolis enfants* pretty children
esthétique adj [everyday use] beautiful *Enlève cette vieille nappe, ell n'est pas très esthétique.* Take that old tablecloth off the table; it isn't very beautiful.
gracieux, -cieuse adj [describes: e.g. woman, child] graceful
grâce nf gracefulness
élégant, e adj [noble and graceful in looks, or dress style] elegant *Il était toujours élégant.* He was always elegantly dressed. **élégance** nf elegance
magnifique adj [beautiful in an impressive way. Describes: e.g. costume, landscape, person's body] magnificent
mignon, -gnonne adj [describes esp small things or children] cute

49.2 *Rendre plus beau* To make more beautiful

embellir {19} **1** vt [obj: e.g. room, city] to make more beautiful *Des jardinières de géraniums embellissent les maisons.* Window boxes full of geraniums make the houses look more beautiful. **2** vi [subj: woman] to look more beautiful *Elle a embelli depuis le début de sa maternité.* She has grown more attractive since the beginning of her pregnancy.
décorer {6} vt [add decorations to] to decorate *décorer une mousse de saumon avec de fines tranches de concombre* to decorate a salmon mousse with thin slices of cucumber

orner {6} vt **1** [subj: person] to decorate *La mode était d'orner les jardins de statues.* It was fashionable to decorate gardens with statues. **2** [literary. Be a beautiful feature of] to embellish *Un blason ornait la grande cheminée.* The great fireplace was embellished with a coat of arms.
parer {6} vt [literary. To dress with finery] to adorn *Ses servantes mettaient longtemps à la parer.* Her maids took a long time dressing her in all her finery. *parer qqn pour une cérémonie* to help sb put on ceremonial dress

Locutions Idioms
beau (belle) comme un astre ALSO **comme le jour** [of persons only] stunningly beautiful
beau comme un dieu (grec) [of men only] incredibly handsome
joli [of women and children only] **comme un ange** ALSO **coeur** as pretty as a picture
agréable à regarder [of persons. Euphemism] easy on the eye

49.3 *Laideur* Ugliness

laid, e adj ugly
laideur nf ugliness
enlaidir {19} vt to make uglier
laideron nm ugly girl
affreux, -reuse adj [informal, commonly used for any unpleasing sight or sound] horrible
horrible adj [stronger than **affreux** but can be used informally, in exaggeration] hideous *les horribles images de guerre que nous voyons à la télévision* the hideous images of war which we see on television *Il est horrible, son pull!* His jumper is hideous.
moche adj [informal. Describes people or things] ugly

Locutions Idioms
être laid ALSO **moche comme un pou** [people only] BrE to have a face like the back of a bus AmE to have a face that would stop a clock
épouvantail à moineaux [man or woman] hideous person
Il/elle est à faire peur [temporary state] He/she looks a fright.

50 Wanting to have, seeking and finding

50.1 *Désir et passion* Desire and passion

see also **45.3 Affection**

désir *nm* **1** [longing for a specified thing] longing *mon désir de verdure/paix* my desire for greenery/peace **2** [used on its own, refers to carnal longing] desire

désirer {6} *vt* **1** [want carnal relations with. Obj: e.g. man, woman] to desire **2** [in shops, restaurants, etc] would like *Je désire une bière, s'il vous plaît.* I would like a beer, please.

passion *nf* [great love of anything, from food to persons] passion *avoir une passion pour qqch* to have a passion for sthg *Elle a une passion pour l'électronique.* She's mad about electronics. *Elle a une passion pour le copain de son frère.* She's besotted with her brother's friend.

se passionner {6} *v refl* [obj: e.g. hobby, art, writings] to feel passionately about things *se passionner pour qqch* to be passionately interested in sthg

passionner {6} *vt* [interest, usually associated with a desire to deepen one's knowledge of a subject or activity] to fascinate *La politique le passionne.* He's fascinated by politics. *Elle est passionnée de foot/de culture chinoise.* She's totally wrapped up in football/Chinese culture.

se passionner *v refl* (often + *pour*) [be intensely interested in, and want to learn more about] to become involved *Les enfants se passionnent pour les jeux vidéo.* Children get very involved in video games.

envie *nf* [sudden need for something, often physical] longing *une envie de femme enceinte* a pregnant woman's craving

avoir envie de 1 [feel a temporary but intense need for] to want *J'ai envie d'un manteau en cuir.* I want a leather coat. *J'ai envie de tout casser.* I felt like smashing everything up. **2** [want carnal relations, possibly fleeting, with. Obj: man, woman] to want *J'ai envie de toi.* I want you.

caprice *nm* [short-lived longing, considered as frivolous] whim *passer un caprice à qqn* to give into sb's whim

usage

manquer à
This expresses the idea of missing somebody or something, and the phrase is created by putting the longed-for person or thing first (as the subject of *manquer*), followed by the indirect object pronoun that shows who does the longing: e.g. *Il me manque.* I miss him. *La mer lui manque.* He misses the sea.

Locutions Idioms
Le roi dit 'nous voulons'. [phrase used to remind children not to ask too rudely for something e.g. by saying 'je veux . . .'] Only the king can say 'I want'.
Vos désirs sont des ordres. [used in humorous courtesy or ironically] Your wish is my command.

50.2 *Séduction* Seductiveness

séduisant, e *adj* **1** [describes: e.g. person, dress style, perfume] attractive **2** [describes: e.g. idea, philosophy] seductive **3** [describes: e.g. plan, course of action] tempting

séduction *nf* seductiveness

séduire {82} *vt* **1** [charm, in a general way] to attract *La nouvelle attachée de presse a séduit tout le monde.* Everyone found the new press attaché absolutely charming. *C'est d'abord l'affiche du film qui m'a séduit.* I was first attracted by the poster for the film. **2** [persuade into a sexual relationship] to seduce *Je l'ai poursuivi de mes assiduités pendant trois mois avant de parvenir à le séduire.* I laid siege to him for three months before I managed to seduce him.

charmant, e *adj* [light and pleasing, as well as possibly amusing. Describes: e.g. scene, person, book, reply] delightful

charme *nm* attraction *être sous le charme (de)* to be bewitched (by)

50.3 *Les séducteurs* Seductive people

séducteur *nm* **1** [with positive connotation] Lothario **2** [in 19th-century novels. A man who seduces a defenceless young woman] seducer

idole *nm* [star, usu of the cinema] heart-throb

femme *nf* **fatale** femme fatale

homme *nm* **à femmes** womanizer

Prince *nm* **Charmant** Prince Charming

50.4 *Envie* Envy

envie *nf* [wanting the same as someone else] envy

envier {15} *vt* to envy *Je t'envie!* I envy you. *envier qqch à qqn* to envy sb sthg *Elle m'envie ma liberté.* She's envious of my freedom.

envieux, -vieuse *adj* envious **envieux, -vieuse** *n* envious person

jaloux, -louse *adj* **1** [sexually] jealous **2** [wanting what someone else has] envious

jaloux, -louse *n* **1** [sexually] jealous man, jealous woman **2** [wanting what someone else has] envious person *Ta nouvelle maison va faire des jaloux.* People will envy you your new house.

jalousie *nf* **1** [sexual] jealousy **2** [desire for what someone else has] envy

jalouser {6} *vt* [not sexual] to be envious of

convoiter {6} *vt* [want to take away from someone] to covet

convoitise *nf* covetousness

cupide *adj* [literary. Wanting money] acquisitive

cupidité *nf* [literary. Desire for money] greed

50.5 *Chercher* To search

chercher {6} *vt* and *vi* [physically or mentally] to look for *Je cherche mes lunettes.* I'm looking for my glasses. *chercher une solution* to look for a solution

recherche *nf* **1** [in science, to advance knowledge] research *de l'argent pour la recherche contre le cancer* money for cancer research **2** [in medicine, to help diagnosis] test *faire une recherche en reconnaissance de paternité* to do a paternity test **3** [in plural. Police investigation] *recherches* search *Les recherches continueront demain.* The search will start again tomorrow.

rechercher {6} *vt* [obj: criminal, missing person] to look for

avis *nm* **de recherche 1** [on police poster] wanted notice **2** [in radio bulletin] missing persons announcement

fouiller {6} *vt* **1** [looking for something lost or deliberately hidden. Obj: e.g. wardrobe, area] to search *La police a fouillé la maison.* The police searched the house. **2** (+ *dans*) [pejorative. Search messily or nosily] to rummage around in

fouille *nf* **1** [patting clothes and going through pockets] search **2** [checking body orifices] body search **3** [in plural. At archaeological site] *fouilles* excavations *Les fouilles ont commencé en 1903.* The site was first excavated in 1903.

fureter {12} *vi* [pejorative. Look around trying not to be seen] to snoop (around) *Je le vois souvent fureter dans les bureaux et je n'aime pas ça.* I often see him snooping around in the offices and I don't like it.

perquisition *nf* [with warrant] search

perquisitionner {6} *vi* [subj: police] to search *Ils ont perquisitionné chez elle/à son bureau.* They searched her house/office.

50.6 *Espionnage* Spying

espion, -pionne *n* spy

espionnage *nm* spying *roman d'espionnage* spy thriller

avion-espion *nm, pl* **avions-espions** spy plane

espionner {6} *vt* to spy on

Locutions Idioms

passer au peigne fin to search with a fine tooth comb

Quand on cherche, on trouve! If you look proprely, you'll find it!

C'est comme si on cherchait une aiguille dans un tas de ALSO **une botte de foin.** It's like looking for a needle in a haystack.

50.7 *Trouver* To find

trouver {6} *vt* [obj: e.g. key, solution] to find *Je ne trouve pas son adresse dans mon carnet.* I can't find her address in my notebook. *On a trouvé un très bon restaurant pas loin de chez nous.* We've found a very good restaurant near where we live.

trouvaille *nf* [something unexpected which is just what was wanted] find *J'ai fait une trouvaille aux Puces, la théière qui manquait à mon service Meissen.* I made a great find at the flea market, the teapot to complete my Meissen set.

découvrir {27} *vt* **1** [find what was hidden or not known] to discover *Il a découvert l'Amérique.* He discovered America. *tant que les scientifiques n'auront pas découvert un vaccin* as long as scientists haven't discovered a vaccine

tomber sur [informal. Implies surprise or accidental find] to stumble across, to happen to find *Dans une vente aux enchères, je suis tombé sur une gravure originale de Daumier.* In an auction, I came across an original engraving by Daumier.

50.8 *Inventer* To invent

inventer {6} *vt* [create something which didn't exist] to invent *Alfred Nobel a inventé la dynamite.* Alfred Nobel invented dynamite. *Tu n'as qu'à inventer une excuse.* Just invent some excuse.

invention *nf* **1** [creating] inventiveness *L'invention n'est pas mon fort.* Inventiveness is not my strong point. **2** [gadget or scheme] invention *faire breveter une invention* to patent an invention **3** [pejorative. Lie] fabrication *Son rendez-vous chez le dentiste, c'est une invention.* His appointment at the dentist's is a pure fabrication.

inventeur, -teuse *n* inventor

concocter {6} *vt* [pejorative. Invent unconvincingly] to make up *Ils ont dû concocter cette histoire ensemble.* They must have made up this cock-and-bull story together.

50.9 *Perdre* To lose

perdre {53} *vt* [temporary or permanent. Obj: e.g. key, document, dog] to lose *Elle perd toutes ses affaires.* She always loses her things.

perte *nf* loss *la perte de cheveux chez les hommes de plus de vingt ans* hair loss among men over twenty

semer {9} *vt* **1** [informal. Lose things habitually] to mislay *Il sème tout le temps ses clés.* He's always losing his keys everywhere **2** [in a chase on foot or in a car] to shake off *Ça y est, on les a semés!* There, we've shaken them off!

Locutions Idioms

Un(e) de perdu, dix de retrouvé(e)s. [informal. To console someone who has lost a boyfriend, a girlfriend, etc] There are lots more fish in the sea.

Ce n'est pas une grosse perte! [similar to **Un de perdu . . . .** used of people] It's no great loss!

la salle des pas perdus [in large railway stations, area where one can find oneself walking round and round as if lost] station concourse

51 Wanting to happen, effort and difficulty

51.1 *Vouloir* To want

vouloir {48} *vt* **1** [have as one's aim] to want *Elle veut réussir.* She wants to succeed. *Je ne voulais pas la vexer.* I didn't mean to hurt her feelings. **2** [have as a hope] to want *Ma femme voulait un garçon.* My wife wanted a boy. **3** [expresses an order] to want *Je veux un reçu.* I want a receipt.

compter {6} *vi* (+ infinitive) **1** [implies definite plan] to intend to *Nous comptons rentrer en passant par Dijon.* We're intending to go through Dijon on our way back. **2** [implies hope] to hope to *Tu comptes pouvoir me le dire quand?* When do you hope to be in a position to tell me?

avoir l'intention de [implies definite plan] to intend to *J'ai l'intention de lui téléphoner dès que possible* I intend to ring her as soon as possible.

se proposer de (+ infinitive) [more formal and more definite than *avoir l'intention de*] to propose to

51.2 *Ce qui est voulu* Things intended

volonté *nf* [determinate idea] wish *Les événements de la soirée ont été organisés selon leur volonté.* The evening's events were arranged according to their wishes. *ses dernières volontés* his last wishes

intention *nf* [often implicit] intention *Moi aussi, j'ai apporté un gâteau, je ne pouvais pas deviner tes intentions.* I brought a cake, too. I couldn't guess what you were intending to do. *avoir l'intention de* to propose to *Nous nous proposions d'inviter les Brunaut, qu'en pensez-vous?* We were proposing to invite the Brunauts, what do you think about it?

plan *nm* 1 [in stories, cunning idea thought out in some detail] scheme *Heureusement, notre héroïne avait son plan.* Fortunately, our heroine had a plan. 2 [administrative term] plan *plan quinquennal* five-year plan

projet *nm* [often involving a team] project *Il y a un projet d'assainissement des berges du lac.* A project has been set up to drain the land around the lake.

dessein *nm* [literary. Often ambitious and long-term] intention *Ils avaient le dessein de réviser la constitution.* Their intention was to revise the constitution.

velléité *nf* [pejorative. Thing wanted by someone who will not apply themselves seriously to bringing it about] whim

51.3 *Adjectifs décrivant la volonté* Determination

décidé, e *adj* [showing determination on a specific occasion] determined *Cette fois-ci, il est décidé, il ira jusqu'au procès s'il le faut.* This time, he's determined, he'll go to court if necessary.

volontaire *adj* [permanent character trait] determined *Elle a toujours été très volontaire.* She's always been a very determined person.

volontariste *adj* [showing active involvement. Describes policies, government plans] enterprising

têtu, e *adj* [pejorative] stubborn

velléitaire *adj* [pejorative] impulsive

51.4 *Essayer* To try

essayer {16} *vt* 1 [attempt an action] to try *Ça ne répond pas, à son bureau, essaie chez elle.* There's no answer at her office number, try her house. 2 [obj: e.g. food, dish, wine] to sample 3 [obj: e.g. shoe, garment, model] to try on 4 [obj: e.g. new car, new plane, new weapon] to try out

s'essayer à *v refl* [try for the first time] to have a go at *Cet été, je vais m'essayer au tricot.* This summer, I'll have a go at knitting.

tâcher {6} *vt* [suggests more effort than **essayer**] to endeavour *tâcher de faire* to try and do *Tâche de finir avant le déjeuner.* Try to finish before lunch.

essai *nm* [test] trial *à titre d'essai* on a trial basis *vol d'essai* test flight *à l'essai* on trial *mettre une machine à l'essai* to try out a machine *prendre qqn à l'essai* to take sb on on trial

tenter {6} *vt* [used when the undertaking is risky] to attempt *Ils vont tenter de descendre les rapides.* They'll attempt the rapids.

tentative *nf* [used when the undertaking is risky] attempt *Ils ont fait une tentative de réorganisation des horaires de travail, qui a échoué.* They made an attempt at reorganizing work schedules which failed.

tâtonner {6} *vi* [implies that success has not yet been achieved] to go through a trial and error process *On*

tâtonne encore pour trouver un remède. They're looking for a remedy but it's still trial and error.

expérience *nf* [scientific] experiment *faire une expérience* to carry out an experiment *faire des expériences* to experiment

expérimenter {6} *vt* [use in a test or tests] to test (out) *On a expérimenté le nouveau système de freinage, qui donne de bons résultats.* The new breaking system was tried out, and found to produce satisfactory results.

51.5 *Difficile* Difficult

difficile *adj* difficult **difficulté** *nf* difficulty

compliqué, e *adj* complicated

délicat, e *adj* [requiring tact] tricky *Je n'ose pas le lui dire que je ne veux pas d'elle dans mon équipe, c'est délicat.* I daren't tell her that I don't want her on my team, it's tricky.

pénible *adj* [disagreeable and difficult. The translation of this depends on context] unpleasant *Marcher, c'est pénible par cette chaleur.* Walking in this heat is really unpleasant. *Il faut repasser par chez eux, que c'est pénible!* We have to go back via their place, what a drag! *Les enfants ont été pénibles, cet après-midi.* The children were hard work this afternoon.

51.6 *Situations difficiles* Difficult situations

problème *nm* [general term] problem

ennui *nm* [something which affects you] problem *J'ai un gros/petit ennui.* I have a big/small problem.

imbroglio *nm*, ALSO **micmac** *nm* [informal. Situation with many confusing aspects] mix-up

casse-tête *nm inv* **chinois** [problem which you cannot think your way through] (complete) conundrum

dédale *nm* [bureaucratic complications] maze *dans le dédale de la procédure judiciaire* in the legal maze

dilemme *nm* dilemma *se trouver devant un dilemme* to be in a dilemma

pétrin *nm* [informal. Literally baker's kneading trough] terrible mess *N'attends pas que je te sorte de ce pétrin.* Don't expect me to get you out of this mess. *On s'est retrouvés dans le pétrin.* We found ourselves between a rock and a hard place.

Locutions Idioms

Il serait plus facile de passer par le trou d'une aiguille. It's as difficult as going through the eye of a needle.

On est dans de beaux draps! Now what do we do?

51.7 *Effort* Effort

effort *nm* effort *un gros effort* a big effort *Encore un petit effort!* Just one more go! *faire un effort* ALSO *des efforts* to make an effort *sans effort* effortlessly

ardu, e *adj* [demanding. Describes: e.g. theory, book, film] abstruse

malaisé, e *adj* [presenting complications. Describes: e.g. negotiations, conversation] awkward

51.8 *Verbes signifiant l'effort* Verbs of effort

s'efforcer de {7} *v refl* (+ infinitive) to try one's best to

s'évertuer à {6} *v refl* (+ infinitive) [implies that one encounters a lot of difficulty] to do one's utmost to

s'escrimer à {6} *v refl* (+ infinitive) [implies a harder task than **s'évertuer à**] to struggle to
se démener {9} *v refl* [stresses energy expended] to put oneself out *Je me suis démené pour lui obtenir un visa.* I had to go to great lengths to get him a visa. *Il a fallu qu'elle se démène pour nous obtenir l'appartement.* She really had to put herself out to get us the flat.

Locutions Idioms
à la sueur de son front by the sweat of his/her brow
faire des pieds et des mains pour que . . . to move heaven and earth in order to . . .
pâlir sur qqch *pâlir sur un problème de maths/un livre* to make oneself ill trying to solve a maths problem/to get the hang of a book
se casser la tête (sur qqch) [often used in the negative] to make an effort (to try to do sthg) *C'est tout ce que tu a mis sur ta carte postale? Tu ne t'es pas cassé la tête!* Is that all you wrote on your postcard? You didn't make much of an effort, did you?
suer sang et eau pour . . . [slightly informal] to sweat blood in order to . . . *On a sué sang et eau pour obtenir cette subvention.* We sweated blood to get this subsidy.
un coup de collier [slightly informal] a big effort *Il va falloir donner un coup de collier si tu veux réussir à ton examen.* You're going to have to make an effort if you want to pass your exam.
mettre les bouchées doubles to redouble one's efforts

51.9 *Obstacles* Obstacles

obstacle *nm* **1** [object in the way] obstacle *J'ai buté sur un obstacle dans le noir.* I walked into an obstacle in the dark. **2** [thing preventing success] hurdle, barrrier *Il abandonne toujours au premier obstacle.* He tends to give up at the first hurdle. *Si seulement il n'y avait pas l'obstacle des langues.* If only the language barrier didn't exist.
barrière *nf* **1** [around land] fence **2** [which opens] gate **3** [obstacle] barrier *Il y a encore bien des barrières entre nos communautés.* There are still many barriers to understanding between our communities. **4** [sign indicating dangerous road during a period of thaw] *barrière de dégel* road closed
barrage *nm* **1** [in geography] dam **2** [on road] roadblock
chicane *nf* **1** [in car racing] chicane **2** [in motorcycle racing] zigzag
pierre *nf* **d'achoppement** stumbling block *Nous avons un produit de qualité mais la pierre d'achoppement c'est notre retard en matière de structures commerciales.* We have a quality product but our weakness in terms of marketing is the stumbling block.
hic *nm* [informal] snag *Seulement elle n'a pas l'âge, c'est le hic!* But she's not old enough: that's the snag!
écueil *nm* **1** [in sea] reef **2** [dangerous obstacle] pitfall *Quand on monte son entreprise, on rencontre les plus grands écueils au cours des deux premières années.* When you set up in business, you're exposed to the worst pitfalls in the first two years.
obstruction *nf* [on road, in artery, in sewer] blockage

51.10 *Échouer devant l'obstacle* To fall before an obstacle

achopper {6} *vi* [slightly formal] to be halted in one's progress *J'avais bien maîtrisé la prononciation de l'arabe mais j'ai achoppé devant l'alphabet.* I was getting on well with spoken Arabic, but the alphabet proved a real stumbling block.

se casser le nez [informal] to come a cropper *Leur entreprise avait bien démarré mais il y a eu une crise et ils se sont cassé le nez.* Their business had got off to a good start but there was a recession and they came a cropper.

51.11 *Franchir l'obstacle* To overcome an obstacle

franchir l'obstacle, ALSO **passer le cap** to overcome the obstacle
contourner l'obstacle to get round the problem
passer outre to forge ahead

51.12 *Bloquer* To block

empêcher {6} *vt* [general term] to stop *La mairie a essayé d'empêcher les manifestations.* The local authorities tried to stop the demonstrations. *Tu m'empêches de m'amuser.* You're stopping me having fun. *Il faut empêcher que le scandale n'éclabousse des innocents.* We have to stop innocent people being implicated in the scandal.
bloquer {6} *vt* [immobilize] *bloquer un ballon* to block a ball *La direction était prête à céder mais c'est le gouvernement qui bloque.* The management was ready to give way but the government blocked the negotiations.
blocus *nm* [by army, fishing fleet, etc] blockade *faire le blocus autour d'une ville* to blockade a city
blocage *nm* [on rents, prices, wages] freeze *C'est le deuxième blocage des salaires depuis 1990.* It's the second wage freeze since 1990.

Locutions Idioms
faire opposition à to oppose *faire opposition à un chèque* [subj: account holder] to stop a cheque
soulever des difficultés pour faire qqch to kick up a fuss about doing sthg
mettre un frein à qqch to slow sthg down *Je voudrais bien mettre un frein à sa consommation d'alcool.* I'd really like to slow his drinking down.
mettre, ALSO **opposer son veto à qqch** to veto sthg
y mettre le holà to put a stop to it *Il y a trop d'absentéisme en ce moment, mettez-y le holà.* There's too much absenteeism at the moment. Put a stop to it.

51.13 *Facile* Easy

facile *adj* [general term] easy *lecture facile* easy reading *Critiquer les autres, c'est trop facile.* It's too easy just to criticize. *C'est quelqu'un d'assez facile.* She's fairly easy-going.
facilité *nf* ease *faire qqch avec beaucoup de facilité* to do sthg with the greatest of ease *la solution de facilité* the easy way out
aisé, e *adj* [literary] easy *Il a un style aisé.* He has an effortless style.

Locutions Idioms
C'est la simplicité même, ALSO **C'est simple comme bonjour.** It's a piece of cake.
C'est un jeu d'enfant. It's child's play. *Ce serait un jeu d'enfant de crocheter cette serrure.* A child could pick that lock.
C'est à la portée de tout le monde. Anybody could do it.
Je fais ça ALSO **Je pourrais faire ça les doigts dans le nez.** [informal] I could do that with my hands tied behind my back.

Ça ne va pas te tomber tout cuit (dans le bec).
[informal] It won't just land in your lap, you know.
gagner dans un fauteuil [usu in sports contexts] to win
hands down

52 Wanting to achieve, success and failure

52.1 *Réputation* Fame

réputation *nf* [way in which a person or thing is known,
good or bad] reputation *Nous avons acquis une
réputation internationale dans le domaine des
microprocesseurs.* We have built up an international
reputation in the field of microprocessors. *La clinique a
bonne réputation.* The clinic has a good reputation. *Je
n'enverrai pas mes enfants dans un collège qui a mauvaise
réputation.* I will not send my children to a school with a
bad reputation. *Vous avez du courage de les inviter à
déjeuner, ils ont une réputation de fins gastronomes.* It's
brave of you to invite them to lunch; they have a
reputation for being very discriminating when it comes to
food.
réputé, e *adj* [famous for some exclusive quality. Describes:
e.g. cheese, wine, surgeon, furniture-maker] of repute

> *usage*
>
> **Notoriété** *nf* and **notoire** *adj*
> **Notoriété** means fame, and **notoire** means famous.
> These words do not necessarily have negative
> connotations in French, but derive their sense from the
> context: e.g. *Il y avait au village une dentellière dont la
> notoriété s'étendait à des kilomètres à la ronde.* In the
> village there was a lacemaker who was famous for miles
> around. *un ivrogne notoire* a notorious drunkard *un
> botaniste notoire* a noted botanist

célèbre *adj* [known to many, possibly world-wide] famous
connu, e *adj* [known to many. Could be local fame, or
much wider] well-known
fameux, -meuse *adj* [old-fashioned synonym for **connu**]
well-known
illustre *adj* [literary. Describes: e.g. author, soldier,
ancestor] illustrious
les gens célèbres ALSO **connus** celebrities

52.2 *Glorieux* Glorious

gloire *nf* [great reputation, esp one acquired on the battle-
field] glory
glorieux, -rieuse *adj* [describes: e.g. king, reign, battle]
glorious
grandeur *nf* [used mainly of historical characters and their
palaces, theatres, etc] greatness *avoir la folie des
grandeurs* to suffer from delusions of grandeur
gloriole *nf* [pejorative] vainglory

Citation Quotation
À vaincre sans péril on triomphe sans gloire. [line
from Pierre Corneille's play *Le Cid*, 1636] Victories gained
without danger do not reflect glory on the victor.

52.3 *Inconnu* Unknown

inconnu, e *adj* **1** [not part of one's knowledge] not known
*Cette coutume est inconnue de tous les gens que j'ai
consultés.* None of the people I consulted knew of this custom. **2** [not famous] obscure *Le concours a été remporté
par un chanteur inconnu.* The competition was won by an
unknown singer.
obscur, e *adj* [before the noun. More pejorative than
inconnu 2] unknown *Celui qui a remporté la descente est
un obscur employé de banque norvégien.* The man who
won the downhill is a completely unknown Norwegian
bank clerk.
ignorer {6} *vt* **1** [have no knowledge about] not to know
*J'ignore ce qu'elle a pu lui dire, mais maintenant il est
monté contre moi.* I don't know what she told him but
he's dead set against me now. **2** [refuse to notice. Obj: e.g.
criticism, frown, interruption, visitor] to ignore **3** [have
been spared the experience of] *une société qui ignore le
divorce* a society where divorce is unknown
jamais entendu parler de never heard of *À dix-huit ans,
je n'avais jamais entendu parler de préservatifs.* At
eighteen, I'd never heard of condoms. *Mais si, tu te
rappelles, Michaud . . . ? Jamais entendu parler!* – Yes,
Michaud, you remember . . . ? Never heard of him!

52.4 *Occupé* Busy

occupé, e *adj* **1** (often + *à* followed by infinitive)
[describes: e.g. person] busy *Elle est occupée à réparer sa
voiture.* She's busy fixing her car. **2** [on toilet door]
occupied **3** [on the telephone] busy *La ligne est occupée,
Monsieur, vous patientez?* The line's busy, will you hold?
Ça sonne occupé, je rappellerai. BrE I'm getting the
engaged tone, I'll call again. AmE I'm getting the busy
signal, I'll call again.
pris, e *adj* [unable to commit oneself to an appointment]
busy *Malheureusement je suis pris lundi matin.*
Unfortunately I'm busy Monday morning.
chargé, e *adj* [describes: e.g. day, week, timetable] busy
actif, -tive *adj* [enjoying being busy] active, busy *Ma
grand-mère, c'est quelqu'un de très actif.* My
grandmother has always been a very active person.

52.5 *Agir* To take action

acte *nm* act [general term] act *Son premier acte en tant
que président a été de décréter une amnistie générale.* His
first act as president was to declare a general amnesty.
action *nf* **1** [similar to **acte**. Initiative] act *une action
humanitaire* a humanitarian act **2** [events] *l'action* activity
Il ne se plaît que dans l'action. He thrives on activity. *au
coeur de l'action* where the action is
activité *nf* [undertaking] activity *avoir de nombreuses
activités* to do a lot
actif, -tive *adj* **1** [doing a lot] active *Elle est très active dans
les associations de consommateurs.* She's very active in the
field of consumer associations. **2** [taking initiatives]
proactive
agir {19} *vi* to act *Il faut agir avec énergie contre
l'épidémie.* We must take firm action against the
epidemic. *Laissez le temps au médicament d'agir.* Allow
time for the drug to take effect.
mesure *nf* measure *prendre*, ALSO *adopter des mesures en
faveur de* to act in favour of *Les mesures prises pour
empêcher la progression du sida s'avèrent insuffisantes.*
Measures taken to halt the progress of the AIDS virus are
proving inadequate.

exécuter {6} *vt* [obj: e.g. decision, measure, project] to carry out

entreprendre {54} *vt* [implies great energy, and sometimes a pioneering spirit] to undertake *Il a entrepris de repaver la cour tout seul.* He undertook to redo the paving in the yard on his own. *entreprendre le recensement de la population* to take a census of the population

Locutions Idioms

mettre le pied à l'étrier [begin a demanding project] to make a start

prendre le taureau par les cornes [be energetic] to grab the bull by the horns [face up to difficulties] BrE to grasp the nettle

se jeter à l'eau [begin a risky undertaking] to take the plunge

aller au charbon [take action in the face of a daunting task] to get stuck in *J'ai préparé mon sujet, classé mes notes, fait mon plan au brouillon: maintenant je n'ai plus qu'à aller au charbon.* I've researched my topic, sorted my notes, drafted a general synopsis: all that remains now is for me to get stuck in.

52.6 *Inaction* Doing nothing

inaction *nf* doing nothing, failure to act

inactif, -tive *adj* passive *On ne peut pas rester inactif devant une telle souffrance.* Faced with such suffering one just has to do something.

non-interventionnisme *nm* [in economics and politics] non-interventionism

attentisme *nm* [in politics] wait-and-see attitude

Locutions Idioms

se tourner les pouces [implies failure to help] to twiddle one's thumbs

Dans le doute abstiens-toi. [proverb] When in doubt, do nothing.

Il/Elle n'a pas levé le petit doigt. [implies failure to help] He/She didn't lift a finger (to help).

52.7 *Succès* Success

succès *nm* **1** [refers to achieving something in general] success *avoir du succès* to be successful *Son premier compact a eu beaucoup de succès.* His first CD was very successful. *Je vois que mes petits pâtés ont du succès.* My little pies are popular, I see. *avec succès* successfully *sans succès* unsuccessfully **2** [circumstances] success *Après son succès de l'année dernière, il est parti écrire, seul, sur une île grecque.* After his success last year, he went off to write alone on a Greek island. **3** [in sexual relationships] *Il/Elle a du succès.* He/She is popular with the opposite sex.

réussite *nf* **1** [successful outcome] success *N'ouvrez pas la porte du four pendant la cuisson: la réussite de votre soufflé en dépend.* Don't open the oven door during the cooking: the success of your soufflé depends on this. **2** [in social, professional and financial contexts] success (in life)

réussir *vi* **1** [be a professional or financial success] to succeed. *Ce n'est pas en traînant dans les cafés que tu vas réussir dans la vie.* Hanging about in bars isn't going to help you make a success of your life. *les gens qui ont réussi* successful people **2** *réussir à* [successfully bring something about, good or bad] to manage, to succeed *Tu as réussi à l'avoir au téléphone?* Did you manage to get her on the telephone? *Il n'a réussi qu'à faire soupçonner sa soeur.* All he managed to do was get his sister suspected.

réussir {19} *vt* to get . . . right *J'ai réussi ma confiture de fraises.* I've got my strawberry jam right.

réussi, e *adj* [which somebody has got right, according to particular standards. Can be linked to money and conventional measures of success, but not necessarily] good, rewarding *Je pense avoir eu une vie réussie.* I think I've had a good life. *une carrière réussie* a successful career

arriver {6} *vi* **1** (followed by *à* + infinitive) to manage to *Il est arrivé à attacher ses lacets tout seul.* He managed to tie his shoelaces by himself. *Aide-moi à finir ma lettre, je n'y arrive pas.* Help me finish my letter, I can't manage. **2** (followed by *à* + noun) to reach *arriver à un résultat* to reach a result *arriver à une réconciliation* to arrive at a reconciliation *arriver à ses fins* to get one's way

victoire *nf* [implies that there has been a contest, literally or figuratively] victory *sa victoire sur le cancer* his victory in his fight against cancer *victoire à la Pyrrhus* Pyrrhic victory

victorieux, -rieuse *adj* victorious

triomphe *nm* [stronger than **victoire**. Implies public acclaim] triumph

triomphal, e *adj*, *mpl* **-phaux** triumphant

fructueux, -tueuse *adj* [slightly formal. Bearing fruit as a result of hard work. Describes: e.g. negotiation, discussion] fruitful

couronné, e *adj* **de succès** [describes: e.g. attempt, initiative] successful *Quand je débutais dans la carrière, mes efforts n'étaient pas toujours couronnés de succès.* In the early days of my career, my efforts didn't always meet with success.

battre {55} *vt* and *vi* [stresses aggression in competition] to beat

gagner {6} **1** *vt* [be the winner in a contest. Obj: e.g. war, game, prize] to win **2** *vi* (often followed by *à*) [stresses final outcome of competition] to win *On a gagné!* We won! *gagner au loto/aux courses* to win at bingo/at the races

l'emporter (sur) [more formal than **battre**] to have the upper hand (over) *À un tour de l'arrivée, impossible de dire qui va l'emporter.* One lap away from the finish, it is impossible to predict the winner. *Nantes l'a emporté sur Bordeaux par un but à zéro.* BrE Nantes beat Bordeaux one-nil. AmE Nantes beat Bordeaux one to nothing.

s'en sortir [stresses the difficult situation which preceded the success] to manage *L'examen était difficile mais elle s'en est sortie brillamment.* The exam was very difficult, but she managed brilliantly.

marcher {6} *vi* [informal] to go, to work (out) *Ça a marché, ton entrevue?* How did your interview go? *Ça marche ton nouveau boulot?* How did your new job work out? *Pour conserver plus longtemps du persil coupé, mets-le dans un verre d'eau avec un plastique par-dessus, tu verras, ça marche.* To make cut parsley last longer, put it in a glass of water, covered with a plastic bag, you'll see, it works.

52.8 *Les gens qui ont du succès* Successful people

champion, -pionne *n* [usu in sport] champion

vainqueur *nm* [in politics, in sports, in a battle] winner

débrouillard, e *adj* [informal. Succeeds by cunning and sometimes improvisation] (a) resourceful (person) *Il est débrouillard.* There are no flies on him.

Expressions used to congratulate someone on being successful
Bravo! well done!
bien joué! [when success is the result of manoeuvring, in games, politics, etc] well done!
beau résultat! [sometimes used ironically] Oh, that's just great!

52.9 *Échec* Failure

échec *nm* failure *quand on a eu un échec professionnel* when you've had a failure in your work *Elle n'a jamais connu d'échec sentimental.* She's never experienced failure in her love life.

52.10 *Types d'échec* Types of failure

fiasco *nm* [failure of a scheme, often in politics] fiasco
four *nm* [in the performing arts] flop
bide *nm* [slang synonym for **four**] flop
coup *nm* **dur** [informal] hard knock *J'ai eu des coups durs dans ma vie.* I have taken a lot of hard knocks in my time.
déculottée *nf* [humiliation] thrashing *Ils ont pris une déculottée contre le club de Lille.* They took a beating in the match against the Lille club.

52.11 *Avoir un échec* To fail

échouer {6} *vi* to fail *échouer à un examen* to fail an exam *échouer dans ses projets* to fail to carry out one's plans *Le négociateur a échoué dans sa mission.* The negotiator failed in his mission.
rater {6} **1** *vt* to fail, to mess up *Ne rate pas ta vie comme j'ai raté la mienne.* Don't mess up your life as I did mine. *rater une occasion* to miss an opportunity **2** *vi* to fail *L'attentat a raté.* The assassination attempt failed.
louper {6} *vt* [more informal than **rater**] to mess up *J'ai loupé mon créneau quand j'ai passé mon permis pour la première fois.* I messed up on backing into a parking space the first time I took my test.

Locutions Idioms
manquer son coup [informal] to mess things up *Ils voulaient monter une entreprise mais ils ont manqué leur coup.* They wanted to start their own company but they messed things up.
tourner en eau de boudin [used of projects, ideas or relationships that fail after a promising start] to come to a sticky end
faire chou blanc [esp failure to find someone or something] to draw a blank
faire la culbute [informal] **1** [subj: firm] to crash **2** [subj: politician] to take a tumble
subir un revers de fortune [slightly formal] to go down in the world

52.12 *Récompenses* Rewards

récompense *nf* [money or honorific prize, given to a child or to an adult] reward
récompenser {6} *vt* [at school, after a military feat, for productivity, etc] to reward *Le prix Goncourt est enfin venu la récompenser.* She finally achieved recognition with the award of the Prix Goncourt. *pour récompenser vos efforts* in order to reward you for your effort

décoration *nf* [military or civilian. Refers to the honour and to the ribbon or medal] decoration
décorer {6} *vt* [obj: e.g. soldier, brave civilian] to award a decoration to
prix *nm* [esp for literary, artistic or scholastic achievement] prize *décerner un prix à qqn* to award sb a prize
bon point *nm* **1** [at school] star **2** [used to mock effort at virtuous behaviour] brownie point *J'ai nettoyé toutes les vitres de la maison, ça vaut bien un bon point, non?* Do I get brownie points for having cleaned all the windows in the house?
médaille *nf* medal
trophée *nm* trophy
hochet *nm* [pejorative] bauble

Knowledge and thought processes

53 Ways of knowing and finding out

53.1 *Savoir et connaître* To know

usage

The difference between **savoir** and **connaître**
Both *savoir* {41} and *connaître* {64} are usually translated by 'to know', but the table below shows when to use one in preference to the other:

Choose connaître when:
The verb 'to know' has a direct object, and
• the knowledge referred to is practical:
E.g. You probably already know how a CD ROM works. *Vous connaissez déjà sûrement le fonctionnement du CD ROM.*
• it is relational knowledge:
E.g Do you know my sister? *Tu connais ma soeur?*
• it is experiential or academic knowledge of a more complex kind than is indicated in the column opposite:
E.g. for those who know Paris *pour ceux qui connaissent Paris*
She introduced me to Plato. *Elle m'a fait connaître Platon.*

Choose savoir when:
The verb 'to know' has a direct object, and
• the knowledge referred to is school-type, memory-based knowledge, such as lists of capitals, multiplication tables, etc.
E.g. I know all my lessons for tomorrow. *Je sais toutes mes leçons pour demain.*

• the verb 'to know' is followed by an adverb or a conjunction e.g.
E.g. Did you know that we were not insured?*Vous saviez que nous n'étions pas assurés?* Do you know whether she's home?*Sais-tu si elle est rentrée?*
• there is nothing following the verb 'to know'
E.g. No sugar for me. Yes, I know. *Pas de sucre pour moi! Oui, je sais.* You can throw that old watch away, you know, it never worked. *Tu sais, tu peux la jeter, cette vieille montre, elle n'a jamais marché.*

Finally, use savoir when:
• the context is competence in something, often expressed by 'be able to' or 'can':
E.g. If you can ski, you can skate. *Quand on sait skier, on sait patiner.*

Idioms with **savoir** and **connaître**
par cœur by heart *Il sait par cœur tous les verbes irréguliers.* He knows all the irregular verbs by heart.*On connaît par cœur tous tes alibis.* We know all your excuses by heart.
comme sa poche [used when discussing places] *Il connaît Marseille comme sa poche.* He knows Marseilles like the back of his hand.
sur le bout du doigt [used when discussing academic knowledge] *Elle connaît le cours sur le bout du doigt.* She knows the coursework backwards.
connaître quelqu'un comme si on l'avait fait(e) [humorous. Used when discussing people] *Je te dis qu'il sera en retard, je le connais comme si je l'avais fait!* I'm telling you, he won't be on time, I know him so well!
en savoir long sur [pejorative. Have inside knowledge about] to know quite a bit about
s'y connaître [to be an expert in a subject, practical or theoretical] *Il s'y connaît en cuisine.* He's an excellent cook. *Je m'y connais assez bien en Égyptologie.* I'm a bit of an expert on Egyptology.
connaître les ficelles du métier to know the tricks of the trade
connaître la musique to know the ropes

Locutions Idioms
avoir conscience de to be aware of *As-tu conscience du mal que tu lui as fait?* Are you aware of the harm you have done her?
avoir conscience (du fait) que to be aware that *J'ai conscience du fait qu'il est tard et que vous souhaitez rentrer chez vous.* I'm aware that it's late and that you want to go home.
avoir la science infuse [humorous or ironic] to know it all. *Pourquoi n'as-tu pas enregistré l'émission d'hier? – Il aurait fallu m'expliquer comment faire, je n'ai pas la science infuse, moi!* Why didn't you record the programme yesterday? – How was I supposed to know how to do it?
un puits de science [ironic. Used of someone with wide-ranging knowledge] fount of knowledge *Demande à la bibliothécaire, c'est un puits de science, cette femme.* Ask the librarian, that woman's a real fount of knowledge.

53.2 *Comprendre* To understand

comprendre {54} vt [find a process, a text, a phenomenon, a person's behaviour, etc intelligible] to understand *Ça y est, j'ai tout compris!* Now I understand everything! *Tu comprends l'arabe?* Do you understand Arabic? *Mes parents ne comprendraient pas que je demande le* *divorce.* My parents wouldn't understand my getting a divorce.

pénétrer {10} *vt* [more formal than **comprendre**. Understand the deep meaning of] to discover *La science nous a permis de pénétrer les secrets de la matière.* Science has allowed us to discover the secrets of the material world.

se rendre compte de [understand suddenly, or understand after having been in the dark] to realize *Il avait rayé ma carrosserie en se garant, mais je ne m'en suis pas rendu compte sur le moment.* He'd scratched my car as he parked but I didn't realize it at the time. *Il est déjà onze heures, tu te rends compte?* Do you realize it's eleven already?

réaliser {6} *vt* **1** [more informal than **se rendre compte de**] to realize. *Plus tard, j'ai réalisé qu'elle m'avait menti.* Later, I realized that she had lied to me. **2** [informal. Be aware of] to realize *Tu réalises ce que ça va nous coûter?* Do you realize how much this is going to cost us?

piger {8} *vt* **1** [slang synonym for **comprendre**] to get (it) *Je veux plus te voir tourner autour de ma soeur, t'as pigé?* I don't want to see you hanging around my sister again, got it? **2** [slang synonym for **réaliser**] to catch on *Une fois que t'as pigé, c'est facile.* It's easy once you've caught on.

saisir {19} *vt* **1** [literary. Understand through intuition] to feel *saisir la beauté d'une musique* to feel the beauty of a piece of music **2** [understand words in a short time] to catch *Tu as saisi l'allusion désobligeante?* Did you catch the nasty little innuendo? *Il parlait trop vite, j'ai à peine saisi quelques mots.* He spoke too fast, I only caught a few words.

53.3 *Hypothèses* Guesses

supposer {6} *vt* [judge on the basis of rational thinking] to assume *Le téléphone a cessé de sonner au moment où j'ai décroché, je suppose que Paul a tenté de me joindre.* The phone stopped ringing when I picked it up, so I assume Paul tried to contact me. *On peut supposer qu'il y a, disons, 5.000 sans-abri parmi la population.* Let's say there are, at a guess, 5,000 homeless people among the population.

Introducing a supposition in conversation
Mettons (literally: 'let's put [it] ') and **disons** ('let's say') can be used at the beginning or in the middle of a statement, e.g.: *Mettons que tu fasses le travail en deux semaines, tu serais libre en février pour venir en vacances avec nous.* Let's say you do the job in two weeks, then you'd be free in February to come on holiday with us. *J'en ai pour, disons, deux heures et demie.* It'll take me, let's say, two and a half hours.
supposition *nf* speculation *les suppositions les plus folles* the wildest speculations
deviner {6} *vt* **1** [judge without information] to guess *À son regard, on devine qu'il a beaucoup souffert dans sa vie.* Looking at his eyes, you can guess that he has had a lot of suffering in his life. *Devine combien j'ai dépensé cette semaine?* Guess how much I spent this week? **2** [estimate correctly] to work out *J'ai deviné que tu devais avoir besoin d'aide.* I worked out that you must be in need of help.

Devinettes
A **devinette** *nf* is a guessing game. A very common kind of *devinette*, also called *une charade*, typically goes
Mon premier est un chiffre
Mon second est l'opposé de la mort
Mon troisième est propre
Mon tout est un mystère

Réponse: deux - vie - net: DEVINETTE!

When playing devinettes or other guessing games, children will ask the person guessing: *Tu donnes ta langue au chat?* Give up?

hypothèse *nf* **1** [guess supported by rational thinking] assumption *La première hypothèse, c'est qu'il a envoyé le chèque en oubliant de le signer.* First, let's assume that he sent the cheque but forgot to sign it. *Ce ne sont que des hypothèses!* It's only guesswork. **2** [guess supported by scientific evidence] hypothesis
thèse *nf* [like **hypothèse 1**] theory
envisager {8} *vt* [explain the unexplained in a tentative way] to contemplate *Sa famille refuse d'envisager qu'elle se soit suicidée* Her family refuses to contemplate the possibility that she committed suicide.
estimer {6} *vt* [guess on the basis of a calculation] to estimate *On estime à 250.000 le nombre des patients atteints de cette maladie chaque année.* The number of patients diagnosed as having this disease every year is estimated to be 250,000.
estimation *nf* **1** [guess on the basis of a calculation] prediction **2** [prediction in an opinion survey] estimation *Les estimations les plus récentes donnent 25% au candidat de la droite.* The most recent estimates give 25% to the right-wing candidate.

53.4 *Intéresser* To interest

intéresser {6} *vt* to interest *L'entomologie l'intéresse.* Entomology interests her. *Tes problèmes ne m'intéressent pas!* I'm not interested in your problems!
s'intéresser à *v refl* to be interested in *L'enfant commence très tôt à s'intéresser au monde qui l'entoure.* The child begins to show interest in the world around her at a very early stage.
intérêt *nm* interest *avoir de l'intérêt pour*, ALSO *porter de l'intérêt à* to show an interest in *Je suis allé voir le film, il est sans intérêt.* I went to see the film but it wasn't worth it.
intéressant, e *adj* interesting
intéressé, e *adj* **1** [showing an interest] interested **2** [when talking about money matters] (financially) involved interested **3** [having a stake in the matter under discussion] motivated by self-interest
captivant, e *adj*, ALSO **passionnant, e** *adj* [stronger than **intéressant**. **Captivant** can imply obsession] fascinating
fascinant, e *adj* [stronger than **captivant**] mesmerizing
animé, e *adj* [full of events and people. Describes: e.g. street life, entertainment, evening] lively
vivant, e *adj* [similar to **animé**. Describes street life] lively **2** [bringing to life things which might have been dull] alive *Ses cours d'anthropologie sont très vivants.* Her anthropology lectures bring the subject to life.
mettre de l'ambiance [positive or ironic] to liven up things up.

54 Thinking

54.1 *Penser* To think

penser {6} *vi* **1** (often + à) [be aware of] to think *Pense aux autres.* Think of others. *J'ai pensé à acheter du café hier, puis j'ai oublié.* I thought about buying coffee yesterday, then I forgot. *Il faut penser que les conséquences peuvent être graves.* You have to bear in mind that the consequences may be serious. **2** [have such and such an idea, belief] to think *Tu penses qu'elle a déjà pris sa décision?* Do you think she's already made her mind up?

pensée *nf* **1** [idea, particularly a caring one, or a concern] thought *Je suis avec toi par la pensée.* My thoughts are with you. *À la pensée d'avoir à tout recommencer, je suis découragé d'avance.* At the thought of having to begin everything all over again, my courage has already failed me. **2** [opinion] thinking. *exprimer sa pensée sur un sujet* to say what one thinks about a topic **3** [way of thinking of a group, social class, country, at a particular time] thinking *un courant de pensée* a school of thought

penseur, -seuse *n* [person who has made a career or reputation out of thinking] thinker *les grands penseurs du XVIIIème siècle* the great 18th-century thinkers

tenir compte de, ALSO **prendre en compte** to take into account *Avez-vous tenu compte des agios ?* ALSO *Avez-vous pris les agios en compte*? Did you take the bank charges into account?

bien-pensant, e *adj* [agreeing with the way of thinking of the majority, esp as far as the Catholic religion is concerned] conformist

mal-pensant, e *adj* [departing from established ways of thinking, esp as far as the Catholic religion is concerned] dissident

54.2 *Réfléchir* To think carefully

réfléchir {19} *vi* [explore the pros and cons] to think *Je te ferai part de ma décision demain, il faut que je réfléchisse.* I'll give you my decision tomorrow, I've got to think about it.

raisonner {6} *vi* [follow a logical line of thinking] to think logically *Les nouveaux logiciels apprennent aux enfants à raisonner.* The new software helps children to learn to think logically. *Tu raisonnes mal.* You're not thinking straight.

songer {8} *vi* (often + à) [literary or old-fashioned synonym for **penser 1**] to think *Il faut maintenant songer à l'avenir.* We must now think about the future.

cogiter {6} *vi* [usu humorous] to think *Il est dans son bureau, laisse-le, il cogite.* He's in his study, leave him alone, he's doing some thinking.

54.3 *Absorbé dans ses pensées* Absorbed in thought

pensif, -sive *adj* [appearing preoccupied] pondering *Elle regardait son bloc-notes, pensive.* She was pondering over the contents of her notepad.

rêveur, -veuse *adj* **1** [tending to daydream] *un enfant/mari rêveur* a child/husband who's always daydreaming **2** [as if dreaming] dreamy *demain, peut-être . . . dit-elle d'un air rêveur* tomorrow, maybe . . . she said with a dreamy look on her face *Ça laisse rêveur.* It makes you think.

rêveur, -veuse *n* daydreamer

songeur, -geuse *adj* [slightly old-fashioned equivalent of **rêveur** adj 2] absorbed *Vous avez l'air songeur, il y a quelque chose qui vous préoccupe?* You seem absorbed, do you have something on your mind?

ruminer {6} *vi* [have negative and esp repetitive thoughts] to brood

broyer du noir [stronger than **ruminer**] to be despondent *Depuis la mort de son mari, elle reste à sa fenêtre et broie du noir.* Since her husband died, she's been at her window, despondent.

Citations Quotations

Je pense donc je suis. [Descartes' aphorism in his *Discours de la Méthode*, 1637] I think therefore I am.

L'homme n'est qu'un roseau, le plus faible de la nature; mais c'est un roseau pensant. [image from Pascal's *Pensées*, 1670, which contrasts the physical weakness of mankind, with its intellectual superiority over the rest of the universe] Man is only a reed, the weakest made by nature, but he is a thinking reed.

Ce que l'on conçoit bien s'énonce clairement Et les mots pour le dire arrivent aisément. [in his *Art poétique*, 1674, Boileau lays down the basic condition for a sound writing style. His words have been used to teach essay writing to many generations of French schoolchildren] That which is clearly thought out can be clearly expressed And the words to express it can easily be found.

54.4 *Sérieux* Serious

see also **53.1 Nécessité et obligation**; opposite **57.11 Négligeable**

important, e *adj* [needing to be given prime consideration. Describes: e.g. ideas, people] important *J'ai quelque chose d'important à vous annoncer.* I have important news for you. *des visiteurs importants* important visitors

sérieux, -rieuse *adj* **1** [not joking] serious *Écoute ce que je te dis, c'est sérieux!* Listen to what I have to say, I'm being serious! **2** [showing professionalism] responsible *Les enquêteurs n'ont même pas fouillé les bureaux du journal, ce n'est pas sérieux!* The investigators didn't even search the offices of the newspaper, it's not a responsible way to go about things! **3** (before noun) [extreme] drastic *un sérieux changement de politique* a drastic policy change

grave *adj* [implies potentially painful or even fatal consequences] serious *dans un état grave* seriously hurt *Elle a menti au juge, c'est grave.* She lied to the judge, it's a serious matter. **gravement** *adv* seriously

prendre en compte to take into account

donner la primeur à [journalistic phrase] to give pride of place to

Locutions Idioms

sérieux comme un pape [not inclined to levity] solemn as a judge

C'est une question de vie ou de mort It's a matter of life or death.

54.5 *Bonne idée* Good idea

idée *nf* [thought which is likely to help solve a problem] idea *J'ai une idée! D'un seul coup, il m'est venu une idée.* BrE I had a sudden brainwave. AmE I had a sudden brainstorm. *Ça, c'est une idée!* Now, that's an idea!

inspiration *nf* [creative power and the thing created] inspiration *Tu cherches l'inspiration?* Are you looking for inspiration?

trouvaille *nf* [unexpected or cunning idea. Can be ironic] inspiration *La veste à carreaux avec le pantalon rayé, ça c'est ce que j'appelle une trouvaille!* The check jacket worn with the striped trousers, that's what I call a stroke of inspiration!

Ça a fait tilt! [informal. Alludes to the noise made by a slot machine] BrE The penny's dropped! AmE The fog lifted.

55 Differentiating and identifying

55.1 *Objets* Types of objects

chose *nf* [this is the most general term] thing *C'est une chose, un animal ou une plante?* Is it a thing, an animal or a plant?

objet *nm* [refers to a manufactured thing] object *On a retrouvé des objets décoratifs dans les sarcophages.* They found decorative objects in the sarcophagi. *des objets de consommation courante* everyday consumer goods

article *nm* [refers to things for sale] article *Nous n'avons plus cet article.* We no longer sell this article.

truc *nm*, ALSO **machin** *nm* [very common informal synonym for **chose**] thingummy, whatsit

dispositif *nm* [stresses mechanical or functional features of the object] device

gadget *nm* [describing something with this term implies that you think it is ingenious but of limited value] gadget

bidule *nm* [very common informal synonym for **dispositif** or **gadget**] thingumabob

55.2 *Différencier les objets et les êtres* Describing categories

genre *nm* **1** [sort] kind *C'est quel genre de chauffage, chez toi?* What kind of heating do you have? **2** [scientific usage] genus *le genre humain* humankind

sorte *nf* [same as **genre**] kind *Les bonbons, tu les veux de quelle sorte?* What kind of sweets would you like?

race *nf* [refers to humans and animals] race

variété *nf* [refers to plants] variety *variété cultivée* cultivated variety

catégorie *nf* [used particularly when discussing ideas, quantities, etc, rather than things] category *champion toutes catégories* overall champion

type *nm* [sort. Used in classifications] type *On distingue plusieurs types de virus.* There are several types of virus to be distinguished. *C'est quel type de voiture, berline ou break?* BrE What kind of car is it, saloon or estate? AmE What kind of car is it, sedan or station wagon?

marque *nf* [commercial] brand *Il a quelle marque de voiture, ton père, une Citroën ou une Peugeot?* What brand of car has your father got, a Citroën or a Peugeot?

style *nm* [used when discussing the aesthetic qualities of things or the way things are done] style *Quel style de fauteuil cherchez-vous?* Which style of armchair are you looking for? *C'est un style d'argumentation qui me déplaît.* I dislike this way of arguing. *un style de direction autoritaire* an authoritarian management style

espèce *nf* **1** [sort. Used when the speaker is not sure what the object is] kind *Sur l'avant-bras, j'avais une espèce de bouton.* I had a kind of pimple on my forearm. **2** [scientific usage. Refers to animals and plants] species **3** (+ *de*) [as an insult] *Espèce d'imbécile!* You idiot! *Espèce de voyou!* you lout!

usage

une espèce de
'A kind of' is translated by *une espèce de*: *une espèce de pierre rose* a kind of pink stone *une espèce d'obsession* a kind of obsession. Many French people use the phrase in the masculine when a masculine noun follows: *un espèce de mur en briques* a kind of brick wall, *un espèce de micro* a kind of microphone. This is not generally accepted as correct, and the forms *une espèce de mur en briques*, *une espèce de micro* tend to be preferred.

55.3 *Comparer* To compare

see also **55.7 Contraster, 89.4 Copier**

comparer {6} *vt* to compare *comparer qqch à* ALSO *avec* to compare sthg to ALSO with

comparaison *nf* comparison. *Entre les deux, il n'y a pas de comparaison.* There's just no comparison between them.

usage

pareil, -reille *adj*
Pareil à is literary: *Tu es pareille à la rose.* Thou art as a rose. Informal when used without *à*, **pareil** is frequent in speech: *les deux frères sont pareils, ils adorent le sport.* The two brothers are the same, they both love sport. *Tu lui as dit en face ou tu lui as laissé un mot, parce que c'est pas pareil!* Did you tell her to her face or did you leave her a note, because it's not at all the same thing! A frequently heard very informal construction is: *pareil que*: *Il est pareil que moi.* He's just like me.

55.4 *Égal* Equal

égal, e *adj*, *mpl* **égaux** [describes esp measurable things] equal *à superficie égale, le domaine des Lambert est plus rentable.* Although equal in area, the Lamberts' land is more profitable.

égal, e *n*, *mpl* **égaux**, *fpl* **égales** [refers to personal or social status] equal *Elle ne fréquente pas des gens qui sont ses égaux.* She doesn't socialize with her equals. *Les hommes sont-ils les égaux des femmes?* Are men equal to women?

égalité *nf* equality *Les deux équipes sont à égalité.* The two teams are equal.

équivalent, e *adj* [equal in value] equal *une somme équivalente à celle que tu m'as donnée* a sum of money equal to that which you gave me

pair *nm* peer, equal *Il sera soumis au jugement de ses pairs.* He will have to submit to the judgment of his peers.

identique *adj* identical

55.5 *Être similaire* To be alike

ressembler {6} *vt* (always + *à*) *ressembler à qqn* to look like sb

se ressembler *v refl* to be alike

tenir {23} *vt* (always + *de*) [Used of likeness between an ancestor and a descendant] *tenir de qqn* to look like sb *Elle tient de son père.* She looks like her father.

s'apparenter {6} *vt* (always + *à*) [Slightly formal term, indicating general similarity of type] to be of the same order as *Son style s'apparente à celui du Caravage.* Her style resembles that of Caravaggio.

évoquer {6} *vt* to be reminiscent of *Ce goût évoque celui de la goyave.* This taste is reminiscent of guava. *Chypre m'évoque la Grèce.* Cyprus reminds me of Greece.

55.6 *Gens semblables* Similar people

see also **33.1 Bébés**
clone *nm* clone
sosie *nm* [originally the name of a character from the play *Amphytrion* by Molière, the term is now part of everyday language] double *On dirait ton sosie.* He looks just like you.

Locutions Idioms
se ressembler comme deux gouttes d'eau to be alike as two peas
être le portrait craché de qqn to be the spitting image of sb
C'est bonnet blanc et blanc bonnet. It comes to exactly the same thing.
Les deux font la paire. [of two people with similar attitudes] They're two of a kind.
Qui se ressemble s'assemble. Birds of a feather flock together.
Les grands esprits se rencontrent. [often ironical] Great minds think alike.

55.7 *Contraster* To contrast

différent, e *adj* **1** (often + *de*) [dissimilar] different *Le frère et la sœur sont très différents l'un de l'autre.* The brother and sister are very different from each other. **2** [varied] various *Dans un aquarium, on voyait évoluer différents poissons.* A variety of fish could be seen swimming in an aquarium.
contraire *adj* opposite *Le café et les somnifères produisent des effets contraires.* Coffee and sleeping pills produce opposite results.
autre *adj* **1** [used before the noun. Alternative] another *Donnez-moi une autre fourchette, celle-ci est tordue.* Give me another fork, this one is bent. **2** [used after the noun. Literary] other *Quand j'étais jeune, mes ambitions étaient autres.* When I was young, I had other (kinds of) ambitions.
autre *pron* other (one), another (one) *Demande aux autres.* Ask the others.
autrui *pron* [fairly formal term used in philosophical or biblical contexts] the other person, others
autrement *adv* differently *Réécris-le autrement.* Write it again differently. *J'ai été obligée de signer, comment faire autrement?* I had to sign, what else could I do?

Locution Idiom
Si tu n'aimes pas ça, n'en dégoûte pas les autres! If you don't like it, that doesn't mean you have to put other people off it!

55.8 *Types de différences* Kinds of differences

see also **55.7 Contraster**
différence *nf* difference *C'est le même travail, à cette différence près que vous pouvez le faire à la maison.* It's the same work, the only difference being that you can do it at home. **différemment** *adv* differently
contraste *nm* [in artistic contexts] contrast

distinction *nf* [a sharp, but not easily noticeable difference] difference *faire une distinction entre* to differentiate clearly between
nuance *nf* [small difference. Often used ironically to refer to a big difference] difference *J'ai dit responsable, je n'ai pas dit coupable, nuance!* I said responsible, I didn't say guilty, there is a difference!

> ### usage
> **différemment** *adv* and **autrement** *adv*
> Note the two separate constructions: *Il a réagi différemment de moi.* but *Il a réagi autrement que moi.* Both mean: He responded differently from the way I did.

55.9 *Voir ou créer la différence* Differentiating

différencier {15} *vt* (often + *entre*) to differentiate
se différencier *v refl* (+ *de*) to be seen as different *Le chameau se différencie du dromadaire par le nombre des bosses.* You can tell the difference between camels and dromedaries by the number of humps.
distinguer {6} *vt* to tell apart. *On les distingue uniquement à* ALSO *par la couleur de leurs yeux.* You can tell them apart only by the colour of their eyes. *Distinguons la vraie psychose de la simple névrose.* Let's distinguish between real psychosis and mere neurosis.

> ### usage
> **différend** *nm* and **différent** *adj m*
> Beware of the potential confusion with the noun **différend**, which means disagreement: *Un différend les a opposés quand ils avaient vingt ans et depuis ils ne se parlent plus.* They had a disagreement when they were twenty and they haven't spoken since.

Locutions Idioms
ça n'a rien à voir avec . . . it's as got nothing to do with . . .
C'est le jour et la nuit. It's as different as chalk and cheese.

55.10 *Spécifique* Specific

see also **96.13 Expliquer**
spécifique *adj* [slightly formal] specific **spécifiquement** *adv* specifically
particulier, -lière *adj* [general term] special *Si l'élève suit un régime particulier, l'établissement doit en être averti par écrit.* If the child has a special diet, the school must be notified in writing. **particulièrement** *adv* particularly
en particulier specifically
précision *nf* **1** [quality of a description] precision **2** [instance] detail *Il me manque quelques précisions pour bien comprendre ce qui s'est passé.* I'm not clear what happened because I'm missing some of the details.
préciser {6} *vt* to make clear *Je précise bien que mon client n'avait pas connaissance des faits à l'époque.* I must make it clear that my client was unaware of the facts at the time. *N'oubliez pas de préciser votre profession et celle de votre conjoint.* Please give details of your profession and that of your spouse. *Précisez votre pensée.* Be more specific about what you mean.

spécifier {6} *vt* [more formal or technical than **préciser**] to specify

55.11 *Généraliser* To generalize

général, e *adj, mpl* **-raux 1** [not restricted] general *grève générale* general strike *médecine générale* general medicine *de l'avis général* according to the general consensus **2** [in names of academic disciplines] general *linguistique générale* general linguistics

généralement *adv* generally

en général in general

du général au particulier from the general to the particular

généraliser {6} *vt* [often pejorative] to generalize *Tous les hommes ne sont pas égoïstes, ne généralise pas!* Not all men are selfish; don't generalize!

généralisation *nf* [often pejorative] generalization *Évitez les généralisations dans votre dissertation.* Avoid generalizations when writing your essay.

généralités *nf pl* **1** [can be used neutrally or pejoratively] general points. *Je commencerai mon exposé par quelques généralités.* I'll begin my talk with a few general points. *se perdre dans des généralités* to spout generalities

générique *adj* [scientific usage] generic

commun, e *adj* [applicable to all] common *lieux communs* clichés

dans l'ensemble on the whole

55.12 *Désignation* Names and naming

désignation *nf* [way of referring to people or things] name *En français la désignation 'chaussure' est préférée à celle de 'soulier'.* In French we use the word 'chaussure' in preference to 'soulier'.

appellation *nf* [used for wines or foodstuffs whose exclusive right to their name is officially regulated] *C'est une appellation 'Bourgogne Contrôlée'* This Burgundy wine is officially classified under the 'appellation contrôlée' system. *Les pruneaux d'Agen ont maintenant leur appellation d'origine.* Agen prunes now have their own official trademark.

55.13 *Nommer* To give names to

appeler {11} *vt* [refers to all names and titles] to call *Comment dois-je vous appeler, oncle ou Franck?* What shall I call you, uncle or Franck? *Chez lui, on l'appelle 'Titou'.* At home they call him 'Titou'.

s'appeler *v refl* to be called *Je m'appelle Roblet.* My name is Roblet.

nommer {6} *vt* [less common than **appeler**, except when it has the special meaning 'to give as a nickname'] to call *On le nommait le 'Roi-Soleil'.* They called him the 'Sun-King'.

se nommer *v refl* to be called.

prénommer {6} *vt* [give as a first name] to call *Son nom de famille était Kennedy, et ils l'ont prénommé John.* His last name was Kennedy and they called him John.

baptiser {6} *vt* [in Christian church service] to christen *Ils l'ont baptisé Julien.* They christened him Julien.

surnommer {6} *vt* to nickname

intituler {6} *vt* [obj: e.g. works of art, newspaper article] to entitle *Comment vas-tu l'intituler?* What title are you going to give it?

s'intituler *v refl* [subj: e.g. film, book] to be called

55.14 *Sortes de noms* Types of names

nom *nm* name *Mon nom est Frédéric.* My name is Frédéric. *apposer son nom au bas d'un document* to sign one's name at the bottom of a document *nom de famille* last name *nom de jeune fille* maiden name

prénom *nm* first name *deuxième prénom* middle name *Nous nous appelons par nos prénoms.* We're on first name terms. *Vous permettez que je vous appelle par votre prénom?* [e.g., to someone called Bill Jones] May I call you Bill?

titre *nm* [name of work, or rank of person] title *Faut-il vous donner le titre de maire ou de président?* What title should one give you, Mayor or President?

un nom à coucher dehors [informal, pejorative and humorous. A name that is difficult to say] quite a mouthful

surnom *nm* nickname

pseudonyme *nm* pen-name

anonyme *adj* anonymous **anonymement** *adv* anonymously

incognito *adv* incognito *rester incognito* to remain incognito

sans nom [pejorative] unrecognizable *Ils nous ont servi une mixture sans nom.* They served us some unrecognizable mish-mash.

état-civil *nm* civil status *décliner son état-civil* to give one's surname, first name and middle name.

étiquette *nf* [always pejorative in this context] label *Je n'aime pas qu'on me colle une étiquette.* I don't like being labelled.

L'état-civil

In France new babies must be registered at the *mairie* of their birthplace. First names used to be strictly limited to saints' names, but today parents are free to choose what they like, within reason. The official registering the child may still object to what appears to be an unacceptable name. Most parents give only two names, the first one of which is often a compound one. Compound first names, or *prénoms composés* can be a juxtaposition of any two names, although many hyphenated names of boys are formed with Jean- and of girls with Marie-.

---

56 Selecting and ordering

56.1 *Classifier* To put in order

see also **27.2 Séparation**

classer {6} *vt* **1** [group into classes. Obj: e.g. words, numbers, documents] to put in order **2** [in an office] to file

classifier {6} *vt* [slot into a classification] to classify *Linné a classifié de nombreuses espèces végétales.* Linnaeus classified a great many plant species.

classification *nf* **1** [action of grouping] classifying **2** [in sport] ranking *obtenir une bonne classification aux épreuves préliminaires* to get a good position in the heats

classement *nm* rank ordering *premier au classement* ranked first

trier {6} *vt* [unlike **classer**, this verb applies to physical objects only. Obj: e.g. letters, clothes, fruit] to sort *une machine à trier le courrier* a letter-sorting machine

tri *nm* sorting (out) *J'ai fait le tri de mes vieux vêtements pour le vide-grenier.* I sorted out my old clothes for the jumble sale.

ordonner {6} *vt* [arrange so as to obtain orderly results] to structure *Votre style est bon mais vous devez apprendre à ordonner vos arguments.* Your style is good, but you have to learn to organize your reasoning processes.

ordre *nm* order *mettre de l'ordre dans une chambre* to tidy up a bedroom *mettre de l'ordre dans ses comptes* to straighten out one's accounts

en ordre 1 [used as an adjective] in order *Avant de mourir, je veux que mes affaires soient en ordre.* Before I die, I want my affairs to be put in order. **2** [used as an adverb] in order *mettre des fiches en ordre* to put index cards in order **3** [specified by an adjective] *en ordre ascendant/descendant* in ascending/descending order

par ordre de in order of *personnages par ordre d'entrée en scène* characters in order of appearance *des chiffres énumérés par ordre de grandeur* figures listed in numerical sequence

cataloguer {6} *vt* [in libraries] to catalogue

répartir {19} *vt* [share out amongst several people] to divide up *Tu seras chargé de répartir les tâches selon les disponibilités de chacun.* You'll be in charge of dividing up the work according to each person's availability.

répartition *nf* sharing out *Cette année nous exigeons une répartition plus équitable des fonds disponibles.* This year we're insisting on a fairer share-out of available funds.

Locutions Idioms

affaire classée! [in law, in investigative journalism. Also used figuratively] case closed! *Pour moi, mon problème de relations avec ma soeur, c'est une affaire classée.* My relationship problem with my sister is over as far as I'm concerned.

en rang d'oignon [in a neat line. Sometimes this also means lined up in order of height] *Toute la famille attendait en rang d'oignon devant la maison.* The whole family was lined up outside the house just waiting.

56.2 *Systèmes* Systems

moyen *nm* way *Il y a (un) moyen de la contacter.* There's a way to get hold of her. *Il n'y a pas moyen de verrouiller ce garage.* There is no way to lock up this garage. *par tous les moyens* by every available means

procédé *nm* [technique] procedure *Ils ont mis au point un procédé pour traiter la rouille.* They developed a method for dealing with rust.

procédure *nf* [series of steps to be taken in order to achieve a result] procedure *Quelle est la procédure pour obtenir un passeport?* What's the procedure for getting a passport ?

processus *nm* [series of changes taking place on the way to a result] process *Le fromage prend un goût salé au cours du processus de maturation.* The cheese becomes saltier as it matures.

façon, *nf* ALSO **manière** *nf* way *Ce n'est pas la bonne* ALSO *manière façon de procéder.* It's not the right way to go about it. *Il le fait à sa façon.* He does it his way. *des pommes de terre à ma façon* potatoes done (in) my special way *d'une façon* ALSO *manière ou d'une autre* somehow or other

méthode *nf* method

technique *nf* technique

système *nm* system *le système D* an improvised way of doing things *Lui, c'est le champion du système D!* He's a great one for improvising!

Locution Idiom

Qui veut la fin veut les moyens. ALSO **La fin justifie les moyens.** [proverb] The end justifies the means.

56.3 *Sélection* Choosing

choisir {19} *vt* [obj: e.g. solution, item of food, course of studies] to choose

adopter {6} *vt* [select and keep as one's own] to choose *adopter un style vestimentaire* to choose a way of dressing *adopter une méthode* to choose a method

choix *nm* choice *faire son choix* to choose *Dans le paquet, je peux vous mettre des caramels ou des truffes, au choix.* I can put toffees or truffles in the packet, whichever you prefer.

sélectionner {6} *vt* [implies methodical comparison between several alternatives] to select *Les meilleures pouliches ont été sélectionnées pour la course.* The best fillies were selected for the race. **sélection** *nf* selection

aimer mieux [contrasts what has been chosen with what has been rejected] to prefer *Je ne regarde pas beaucoup la télévision, j'aime mieux la radio.* I don't watch much television, I prefer the radio.

plutôt *adv* rather *L'agence propose des voyages en Chine mais j'irais plutôt au Népal.* The travel agents offer tours of China but I'd rather go to Nepal.

plutôt . . . que rather . . . than *Nous faisons plutôt du badminton que du tennis.* We play badminton rather than tennis.

soit . . . soit *conj* [introduces past, present or future alternatives] either . . . or *Soit j'irai en Espagne, soit j'irai en France.* Either I'll go to Spain, or I'll go to France.

tantôt . . . tantôt *adv* [introduces past or present alternatives] either . . . or *Tantôt il a trop de travail, tantôt il n'en a pas assez.* He's either got too much work or not enough.

56.4 *Choisir au hasard* Choosing at random

tirer qqch au sort to draw lots for sthg *Le nom du gagnant sera tiré au sort à la fin de la kermesse.* The winner's name will be drawn from a hat at the end of the fete.

tirer qqch à la courte paille to draw lots for something

Locutions Idioms

On n'a que l'embarras du choix. BrE We're spoilt for choice AmE The only problem is choosing.

comme bon vous/me semble as you/I think fit. *Il fera comme bon lui semblera.* He'll do as he thinks fit.

mettre deux choses dans la balance to weigh the pros and cons up

Il a mis dans la balance la liberté que cela va lui procurer et l'argent que cela va lui coûter. He had to choose between the freedom it will give him against the money it will cost him.

trié, e sur le volet [implies selection of only the best or the top people] hand-picked *une anthologie qui ne comprend que des auteurs triés sur le volet* an anthology comprising a selection of handpicked authors

Comme on fait son lit, on se couche. [proverb] As you have made your bed, so you must lie in it.

57 Evaluating and judging

57.1 *Mauvaise opinion que l'on a des autres* Low opinion of others

mépris nm [considering others as morally inferior] contempt
méprisant, e adj contemptuous
mépriser {6} vt to despise
dédain nm [considering others as not worthy of one's note] disdain
dédaigneux, -gneuse adj disdainful

57.2 *Absurdité* Absurdity

absurde adj **1** [as a value judgment] ridiculous **2** [in the theatre, etc] absurd
absurdité nf **1** [feature of story, behaviour, thought process] absurdity **2** [something said or done] (piece of) nonsense *Ne dis pas d'absurdités.* Don't talk nonsense.
balivernes nf pl [often used humorously] BrE tommyrot AmE balderdash
loufoque adj [absurd and funny] zany
grotesque adj [pejorative. Offending against reason and good taste] grotesque *500 francs de dédommagements pour les victimes de la pollution, c'est grotesque.* 500 francs' compensation for the pollution victims, it's ludicrous.
ridicule adj ridiculous **ridicule** nm ridicule *se couvrir de ridicule* to be totally ridiculous *Ne publie pas cette lettre, tu vas te couvrir de ridicule.* Don't publish this letter, you'll be made to look totally ridiculous. *Le ridicule ne tue pas* ALSO *n'a jamais tué personne.* Being made to look silly won't kill you.
risible, ALSO **dérisoire** adj [ridiculous and inadequate. Describes: e.g. efforts, ambitions, resources] laughable
être la risée du village/du quartier to be the laughing stock of the village/neighbourhood
se ridiculiser {6} v refl [slightly more formal than **se couvrir de ridicule**] to incur derision

Locutions Idioms
Ça n'a aucun sens. It's nonsense.
Ça ne tient pas debout (cette histoire). That's a cock-and-bull story.
une histoire sans queue ni tête ALSO **une histoire à dormir debout** a cock-and-bull story
Il/Elle n'a aucune suite dans les idées. He's/she's completely illogical.
passer du coq à l'âne, ALSO **faire un coq-à-l'âne** to jump to a completely unconnected topic
en faire des gorges chaudes to have a good laugh about it *Tout le bureau en a fait des gorges chaudes.* It was the office joke.

57.3 *Perfection* Perfection

see also **Gambits 36** and **37**
perfection nf perfection *à la perfection* to perfection
parfait, e adj perfect *Tout le monde ne peut pas être parfait.* Nobody's perfect. **parfaitement** adv perfectly
bon, bonne adj **1** (before noun) (compar **meilleur, e,** superl **le meilleur, la meilleure**) [of quality] good *une très bonne idée* a very good idea *un bon livre* a good book *une bonne joueuse de tennis* a good tennis player *Le*

temps est meilleur qu'hier. The weather's better than yesterday. **2** (after noun) [having moral virtues] good *Ton père était un homme bon.* Your father was a good man.
bien adv (compar **mieux,** superl **le mieux**) **1** [in a very satisfactory way] well *Ils ont très bien joué.* They played very well. *bien habillé* well-dressed *bien élevé* well-brought-up *Agissez pour le mieux.* Act for the best. **2** (used as an adj) [very satisfactory] good *Elle est bien, la nouvelle patronne, elle a mis tout le monde en confiance.* The new boss is good, she's got everybody to trust her. **3** [socially acceptable] respectable *une famille bien* a respectable family

57.4 *Bon mais sans plus* Reasonably good

pas mal not bad *La maison n'est pas mal, mais il y a une route très passante juste devant.* The house isn't bad, but there's a very busy road right outside.
agréable adj pleasant *L'endroit est agréable, nous y retournerons peut-être.* The place is (quite) nice, maybe we'll go back there.
faisable adj [informal] bearable *Pas trop dur, le voyage en train jusqu'à Oran? – Non, c'était faisable.* Was it tough, travelling by train to Oran? – No, it was OK.
convenable adj [of no more than passable quality] decent *L'hôtel était convenable.* The hotel was of a decent standard.
passable adj [on the borderline between acceptable and unacceptable] so-so *Il est comment, ce gigot? – Passable.* What's the leg of lamb like? – So-so.

57.5 *Très bon* Very good

excellent, e adj [general term] excellent
remarquable adj [better than comparable things] outstanding *On a bu un vin remarquable.* We drank an outstanding wine.

Words expressing great enthusiasm
All the adjectives below are used in the same way: to express great enthusiasm for something. The only difference is in the age-group which typically favours the use of one rather than the other, although there are no well-defined rules about this.

merveilleux, -lleuse adj marvellous
fantastique adj fantastic
fabuleux, -leuse adj fabulous
formidable adj terrific
super adj [informal. Much used by younger people] great
génial, e adj, mpl **-niaux** [similar usage to **super**, but stronger] fantastic
épatant, e adj [slightly old-fashioned] fabulous

57.6 *Choses parfaites* Perfect things

chef d'œuvre nm masterpiece
merveille nf marvel *Ils viennent de sortir un appareil-photo qui est une petite merveille.* They've just brought out an absolutely marvellous little camera.
coup ALSO **éclair** nm **de génie** stroke of genius

57.7 *Progrès* Progress

see also **89.3 Amélioration**
progrès nm [greater well-being brought about by science and technology] progress

perfectionnement *nm* [in the technical efficiency of something, the level of knowledge of someone] improvement *Je vais prendre des cours de perfectionnement en langues/informatique.* I'm going to take a course to improve my language/computer skills.

perfectionner {6} *vt* [take a skill from a good to a high standard] to refine *Je pars un mois à Padoue pour perfectionner mon italien.* I'm going to Padua for a month to refine my Italian.

se perfectionner *v refl* (often + *en*) [go from good to excellent in a skill] to improve and reach a high standard

57.8 *Supérieur* Superior

supérieur, e *adj* 1 (often + à) [in a scale of values] better, higher *avoir des résultats supérieurs à la moyenne* to get higher-than-average results 2 [in advertising] top-quality *laine de qualité supérieure* top-quality wool 3 [in academic contexts] advanced *mathématiques supérieures* advanced mathematics 4 [pejorative. Describes: e.g. tone, look] superior

supérieur, e *n* superior

supériorité *nf* [pejorative] *avec supériorité* in a superior manner

prééminence *nf* [formal term] (pre)eminence *Sa prééminence internationale en mécanique quantique lui a valu un prix Nobel.* His international reputation in quantum physics earned him a Nobel prize.

dominer {6} 1 *vi* to be in a leading position *La France domine en matière de télécommunications.* France is in a leading position in telecommunications technology. 2 *vt* to lead *À la fin du premier set, Markova dominait nettement la jeune Américaine.* By the end of the first set, Markova had a commanding lead over the young American. *Ce sont les chaînes privées qui dominent le marché.* Private TV channels have a leading share of the market.

être en avance [at school] to be ahead

57.9 *Convenable* Suitable

see also **57.3 Perfection**

adéquat, e *adj* [slightly formal term. Describes: e.g. word, procedure, policy, punishment] appropriate *Trouvez pour chacun des verbes du texte une définition adéquate.* Find an appropriate definition for each of the verbs in the text.

approprié, e *adj* [right for the circumstances] suitable *Les jours de plein air, envoyez votre enfant à l'école dans une tenue appropriée.* On days when there are outdoor activities, please send your child to school wearing suitable clothing.

correct, e *adj* [suited to the technical specifications] right *Je voudrais brancher mon rasoir, mais il me faudrait une prise correcte.* I'd like to plug in my shaver but I need the right plug.

convenable *adj* 1 [fulfilling the social or psychological requirements] suitable *Nous les rééduquons en leur apprenant des comportements convenables.* We rehabilitate them by teaching them to develop acceptable behaviour 2 [not liable to offend] decent *Une robe à manches courtes, ce n'est pas une tenue convenable pour entrer dans une mosquée.* You can't go into a mosque wearing a short-sleeved dress. It's not considered decent.

convenir {23} *vi* (often + à) 1 [be suited to practical requirements] to suit *Je rapporte la veste que j'ai achetée hier, elle ne convient pas.* I'm returning the jacket I bought yesterday, it's not right. *Le médecin lui a prescrit le traitement qui convient.* The doctor prescribed the appropriate treatment. 2 [be pleasing to someone] to suit *Rendez-vous demain soir à huit heures, ça vous convient?* Let's meet tomorrow at 8 p.m. Does that suit you?

opportun, e *adj* [coming at the right time] timely *L'arrivée opportune d'un livreur m'a permis de couper court à cette pénible discussion.* The timely arrival of a delivery person enabled me to put an end to this difficult conversation.

pertinent, e *adj* 1 [sharp-witted. Describes: e.g. remark, description, criticism] accurate 2 [slightly formal term. Related to the point under discussion] relevant *Cette objection est-elle pertinente?* Is this objection relevant?

propre *adj propre à* likely to *des moyens propres à empêcher le triomphe de la droite* measures likely to stop the right from sweeping to power

à propos *adv* [a rather formal term] appropriate *Je trouve tout à fait à propos de lui rappeler ses responsabilités.* I think it's quite appropriate to remind him of his responsibilities.

s' appliquer {6} *v refl* (often + à) [be relevant] to apply *Dès le passage de la douane, les règlements en vigueur sur le territoire turc s'appliquent.* On the other side of the customs post, regulations in force on Turkish territory apply. *Ce que je viens de dire ne s'applique pas à toi.* What I've said doesn't apply to you.

57.10 *Méchant et mauvais* Bad and nasty

méchant, e *adj* 1 [character trait] bad *On la croyait méchante, en fait elle était malheureuse.* They thought she was bad, in fact she was unhappy. 2 [misbehaving. Term used of, by or to children] naughty 3 [informal. Paltry] pathetic *Je n'avais qu'un méchant bout de fromage à leur offrir.* I only had this pathetic bit of cheese to offer them.

mauvais, e *adj* (before noun) 1 [inclined to do harm] bad, nasty *de mauvaise humeur* in a bad mood *Arrête d'embêter ton petit frère, que tu es mauvais, des fois!* Stop annoying your little brother, you're so nasty sometimes! 2 [physically unpleasant] bad *les mauvaises odeurs* bad smells *le mauvais temps* bad weather *une mauvaise grippe* a bad dose of flu *Il a fait une mauvaise chute.* He had a bad fall. 3 [unfavourable] poor, bad *J'ai une mauvaise opinion de ces gens-là.* I have a poor opinion of these people. *Il a mauvaise réputation.* He has a bad reputation. 4 (often + en) [incompetent] bad *J'ai toujours été mauvais en géographie.* I was always bad at geography.

sale *adj* [informal. Stronger synonym for **mauvais 2**] nasty, appalling *Il fait un sale temps.* It's very nasty weather. *Elle a un sale caractère.* She has an appalling temper. *C'est un sale coup pour son entreprise.* It's a bad blow for her business.

néfaste *adj* [related to or predicting bad things] bad, harmful *les effets néfastes du tabac* the harmful effects of smoking

odieux, -dieuse *adj* [behaving in a way designed to make others hate one] obnoxious *Elle était jalouse de sa sœur et s'est montrée odieuse.* She was jealous of her sister and behaved obnoxiously. *La compagnie, qui est responsable de l'accident, refuse toute compensation aux familles des victimes, c'est odieux.* The company, which is responsible for the accident, is refusing to compensate the families of the victims, it's scandalous.

déplaisant, e *adj* [mild term] unpleasant *Il critique constamment son père, c'est déplaisant.* It's unpleasant the way he's always criticizing his father.

mal *adv* bad *Ça va mal finir.* It'll turn out badly. *aller de mal en pis* to go from bad to worse *tomber mal* ALSO *mal tomber* to come at the wrong moment *Les affaires vont* *mal.* Business is not going well. *Ma tante va mal.* My aunt's not well.

mal *nm, pl* **maux** harm, ill *Elle va organiser une réunion d'information. Ce ne sera pas un mal!* She's going to set up a meeting for disseminating information, which will be no bad thing!

pire *adv* worse *Au moins tu es sorti indemne de l'accident, ç'aurait pu être pire.* At least you came away unscathed from the accident, things could have been worse.

nuisible *adj* [liable to cause great harm. When referring to humans implies likelihood of inflicting serious bodily harm or death] harmful

nuire {82} *vi* (often + *à*) [cause harm] to be harmful *mettre qqn hors d'état de nuire* to neutralize sb so that they can no longer cause harm *les pesticides qui nuisent à l'environnement* pesticides harmful to the environment

Les gens méchants Bad people
salaud *nm* [very strong and liable to cause offence. Devoid of any moral compunction] bastard
traître *nm* traitor **traîtresse** *nf* (woman) traitor
poison *nm* [refers esp to women] evil bitch
ordure *nf* [very strong. Shows extreme contempt] (piece of) filth

57.11 *Négligeable* Unimportant

see also **54.4 Sérieux**
négligeable *adj* [which can be ignored] unimportant *être pris pour quantité négligeable* to be considered unimportant
bénin *adj m*, **bénigne** *adj f* [without grave consequences] minor *une maladie bénigne* a minor illness *une tumeur bénigne* a non-malignant tumour
mineur, e *adj* [low in order of importance. Describes: consideration, problem] minor

Locutions Idioms
C'est sans importance ALSO **ça n'a pas d'importance.** It's unimportant.
Cela ne prête ALSO **ne tire pas à conséquence.** It's of no consequence.
Peu importe! [slightly formal] No matter!
Qu'importe? [slightly formal] What does it matter?
Il s'en moque comme de sa première chemise! He couldn't give a damn about it!
Ce n'est pas la mer à boire! [exhorts someone to make less fuss about some task] It's not that difficult!

Citation Quotation
Qu'importe le flacon pourvu qu'on ait l'ivresse. [The early 19th-century poet Alfred de Musset thus extolled the virtues of loving for the sake of loving, regardless of whom one loves. The line is still quoted, with this more general meaning] The means are unimportant, only the ends matter.

57.12 *Inférieur* Inferior

inférieur, e *adj* (sometimes + *à*) [in quality or status] inferior *des marchandises de qualité inférieure à celles que nous envoie habituellement notre fournisseur* goods inferior in quality to those our supplier normally sends us
infériorité *nf* inferiority *complexe d'infériorité* inferiority complex

Les inférieurs People in a position of inferiority
inférieur, e *n* [in a hierarchy] inferior

subalterne *n* [in a hierarchy. No pejorative connotation] inferior *Il faut que vous appreniez à déléguer le travail à vos subalternes.* You must learn to delegate to your inferiors.
subordonné, e *n* [same usage as **subalterne**] junior
vassal *nm, pl* **vassaux** [historical] vassal
sous-fifre *nm, pl* **sous-fifres** [pejorative and humorous] minion

57.13 *Évaluer* To judge

évaluer {6} *vt* to assess
évaluation *nf* **1** [in general] assessment **2** [yearly interview, in a job] appraisal
juger {8} *vi* and *vt* to make a judgment *À vous de juger!* It's up to you to make your own judgment!
jugement *nm* [statement, often considered definitive by its author] judgment *Il est trop hâtif dans ses jugements.* He's too hasty in his judgments.
point *nm* **de vue** [opinion on personal or general topics] point of view
appréciation *nf* [a manager's judgment of an employee's performance, or a critic's judgment of an artist] estimation *porter une appréciation sur qqn* to make a judgment about sb

58 Quantifying and measuring

58.1 *Grand* Big

see also **58.13 Dimensions**
grand, e *adj* **1** [in height] tall, big *Les grands, asseyez-vous derrière pour que les petits puissent voir.* If you're tall, sit at the back so the little ones can see. **2** [capacious] large, big *une grande valise* a large suitcase *un grand manteau* a large coat **3** [larger than other similar things] big, great *la grande pyramide de Chéops* the great pyramid at Cheops
grand, e *n* [children's talk. A child older than other children, or a grown-up] older one *Les grands auront le droit de se coucher plus tard.* The older ones can go to bed later.
grandeur *nf* **1** [vertical dimension] height *deux immeubles de la même grandeur* two buildings of equal height **2** [all dimensions] size *La malle, vous la voulez de quelle grandeur?* What size trunk do you want?
vaste *adj* [spacious, sometimes implies excessively so] very large *un vaste jardin* a very large garden *La maison est devenue trop vaste pour elle.* The house has become too big for her.
ample *adj* [spacious and flowing. Describes esp: clothes, curtains] wide *une jupe ample* a wide skirt
énorme *adj* [larger than expected or imagined] huge *Pour déplacer l'engin il faut un énorme camion.* A huge truck is needed to pull the machine.
immense *adj* [stretching out or up further than the eye can see] huge *d'immenses champs de maïs* huge fields of corn *une grue immense* a huge crane
considérable *adj* [large and impressive] extensive *Elle a une cave considérable.* Her wine cellar is extensive.
géant, e *adj* [word used in fun, or in advertising] giant *On dirait une pomme de terre géante.* It looks like a giant potato. *lessive en paquet géant* jumbo packet of washing powder

58.2 *Devenir plus grand* To get bigger

agrandir {19} *vt* [obj: e.g. company, estate] to make bigger
s'agrandir *v refl* **1** [subj: e.g. hole, river bed] to get bigger
2 [move into a larger place] *Depuis la naissance des jumeaux, ils cherchent à s'agrandir.* Since the birth of the twins, they've been looking for a larger place to live.
grandir {19} *vi* **1** [taller] to grow (taller) **2** [older] to grow up
s'étendre {53}*v refl* [increase its surface] to spread *La ville s'est étendue.* The town has spread.

Locution Idiom
Petit poisson deviendra grand. [proverb] From little acorns great oak trees grow.

58.3 *Grande quantité* Large quantity

see also **91.1 Entier, 91.2 Suffisant, 58.1 Grand, 29.4 Groupes d'objets; opposite 58.7 Petite quantité**
beaucoup de a lot of *beaucoup de pain* a lot of bread *beaucoup de chaises* a lot of chairs *beaucoup de courage* a lot of courage
quantité de ALSO **une grande quantité de** ALSO **une quantité de** plenty of *Il y avait (une) quantité de fruits frais sur le marché.* There was plenty of fresh fruit on the market.
abondance *nf* [great quantity. Can imply excess] abondance *Dans les villes de la côte vous trouverez une abondance de fruits de mer.* In the coastal cities, you will find an abundance of seafood. *sociétés d'abondance* affluent societies
majorité *nf* **1** [large quantity] majority *une majorité de gens pensent que . . .* a majority of people think that . . . **2** [largest quantity] majority *Parmi nos ayant-droit, les familles monoparentales sont en majorité* There is a majority of single-parent families among our claimants.
maximum *adj* [see usage for feminine and plural forms] maximum *Le nombre maximum de participants est de 12.* The maximum number of participants is 12.
maximum *nm* **1** [largest number or amount] maximum *Cet ascenseur ne peut contenir qu'un maximum de dix personnes* BrE This lift takes a maximum of ten people. AmE This elevator takes a maximum of ten people. **2** [a great deal of] much, many *Il nous faut un maximum de preuves.* We need as much proof as possible.

usage

maximums and **maxima**
Both are used when the adjective is feminine (singular and plural), or masculine plural. For example, *On atteint des prix maximums* ALSO *maxima au-delà desquels le client ne veut pas payer.* We are reaching maximum prices, above which customers refuse to pay. *aller à des vitesses maximums* ALSO *maxima de 120 à 130 km/h* to do maximum speeds of 120 to 130 km/h. It is customary for, e.g., weather forecasters to use **maxima:** *températures maxima pour demain: 25 à Biarritz et 20 à Arcachon* maximum temperatures tomorrow: 25 degrees in Biarritz and 20 degrees in Arcachon

Mots familiers désignant les grandes quantités Informal words for large quantities
un ALSO **des tas de** [informal] loads of *Elle leur donne toujours un tas de bonbons.* She always gives them loads of sweets.

des masses de [informal] masses of *Il y avait des masses de caravanes sur la route.* They were masses of caravans on the road.
à revendre [more than is needed] *Tiens, prends quelques pots de confiture, j'en ai à revendre.* Here, have a few pots of jam, I have loads more than I need.

58.4 *Petit* Small

petit, e *adj* **1** [in size] small *une petite maison* a small house **2** [in quantity] little *un petit peu de* a little bit of
petit, e *n* [child. An emotive word] little one *Elle a emmené le petit chez le médecin.* She took the little one to the doctor's.
petit *nm* [animal] young *la louve et ses petits* the she-wolf and her young

usage

petit
Petit has many overtones. It can be used to minimize a negative point: *Je vais vous faire faire une petite prise de sang.* I'll arrange for you to have a quick blood test. It can indicate contempt for small-mindedness: *Ne dérangeons pas ses petites habitudes !* We mustn't upset his little routine! It can stress the pleasantness of an event: *Que dirais-tu d'un petit souper aux chandelles ?* What would you say to a nice little candlelit dinner?

58.5 *Très petit* Very small

minuscule *adj* tiny *un jardin minuscule* a tiny garden
miniature *adj* [always after the noun] miniature
miniature *nf* **1** [in the arts] miniature **2** [reproduction] model

usage

Diminutive suffixes
The meaning of many nouns can be made to stress smallness if suffixes like -et or -ette are added: *un jardinet* a small garden, *une maisonnette* a small house, *un garçonnet* a little boy, *une fillette* a little girl, *une kitchenette* a mini-kitchen, *une piécette* a small amount of money.

58.6 *Devenir plus petit* To become smaller

rétrécir {19} *vi* **1** [subj : e.g. garment] to shrink **2** [subj: e.g. country lane] to become narrower
rapetisser {6} *vi* [subj: e.g. aging person] to shrink, grow shorter

Locutions Idioms
grand comme un mouchoir de poche [describes: e.g. garden, room] tiny
haut comme trois pommes [informal] knee-high to a grasshopper

Citation Quotation
On a toujours besoin d'un plus petit que soi. [In his fable *Le Lion et Le Rat*, La Fontaine stresses the interdependence of the powerful and the humble] You always need someone smaller than yourself.

58.7 *Petite quantité* Small quantity

see also **58.4 Petit**, **91.3 Incomplet**; opposite **58.3 Grande quantité**

un peu de a bit of, a little *un peu de pain* a bit of bread *un peu de curiosité* a little curiosity

un brin de [used with positive or pleasant things] *faire un brin de toilette* to freshen up (a little) *Il a un brin de fantaisie.* He has a whimsical streak to him.

un atome de [humorous. Refers to personal qualities] an iota of *si tu avais un atome de bon sens . . .* if you had an ounce of common sense . . .

un grain de 1 [similar to **atome**] a grain of *Elle n'a pas un grain de talent.* She hasn't a grain of talent. **2** [in set phrase] *un grain de folie* a touch of madness

une pointe de [used esp of things giving some spice to food, or to life in general] *une pointe d'ail* just a little bit of garlic *une pointe d'humour* a little bit of humour *une pointe de jalousie* a hint of jealousy

une poignée de 1 [in cooking] a handful of *Faites infuser une poignée de tilleul dans de l'eau.* Steep a handful of dried lime in boiling water. **2** [indicates poor turnout] a handful *Il n'y avait qu'une poignée de gens dans le hall.* There was only a handful of people in the hall.

minimum *adj* [see usage for feminine and plural forms] minimum *Il a fait un effort minimum.* He made a minimum amount of effort.

minimum *nm* **1** [smallest amount] minimum **2** [a very small amount] *Comme je partais en avion, j'ai emmené le minimum.* As I was flying, I packed a minimum of things.

> ## usage
>
> **minimums** and **minima**
> Both are used when the adjective is feminine (singular and plural), or masculine plural. E.g. *On atteint des prix minimums* ALSO *minima en-deçà desquels le producteur fait faillite.* We are reaching minimum prices, below which producers go bankrupt. *Respectez les quantités minimums* ALSO *minima de médicament à prendre.* Be sure to take the minimum dosage prescribed. It is customary for, e.g., weather forecasters to use **minima**: *températures minima pour demain: 18 à Biarritz et 16 à Arcachon* minimum temperature tomorrow: 18 degrees in Biarritz and 16 degrees in Arcachon

58.8 *Petites quantités de liquides* Small quantities of liquids

un doigt de [used esp of wine, spirits] a drop of *un doigt de rhum dans mon café* a drop of rum in my coffee

un soupçon, ALSO **un nuage de** [esp with milk] a drop of *un soupçon de lait dans mon thé* a drop of milk in my tea *Vous prenez du lait? – Un nuage!* Do you take milk? – Just a drop!

une larme ALSO **une goutte de** [with spirits or milk] a drop of *une larme de cognac dans la pâte à crêpes* a drop of brandy in the pancake batter

Locutions Idioms

Il y avait deux pelés et trois tondus ALSO **trois pelés et quatre tondus.** [humorous. Indicates a poor turnout.] There was hardly anyone there.

il (n') y en a pas lourd! [more informal without the *n'* negation] there isn't all that much! *Dis donc, la sauce, il y en a pas lourd!* Hey, there's hardly any gravy!

58.9 *Augmenter* To increase and to multiply

see also **1.7 Changements de forme**, **58.1 Grand**, **61.1 Gros**

augmentation *nf* **1** [change from smaller to bigger] increase **2** [in money] BrE rise AmE raise

augmenter {6} *vt* **1** [make bigger] to increase **2** [obj: e.g. employee] to give a rise to

hausse *nf* [in statistics] increase *la hausse des prix* price increases *la hausse du taux de chômage* the increase in the rate of unemployment

croissance *nf* **1** [in economics] growth **2** [of a child] growing *être en pleine croissance* to be growing fast

croître {67} *vi* **1** [in economics] to increase *Nos chiffres de vente ne cessent de croître.* Our sales figures are increasing. **2** [literary or botanical] to grow *Les papyrus croissent le long du Nil.* Papyrus grows along the Nile.

étendre {53} *vt* [obj: e.g. power, influence] to increase

Expressions d' augmentation tirées du langage mathématique Terms for increasing taken from the language of mathematics

addition *nf* addition *sans addition de sucre* without added sugar

additionner {6} *vt* to add *du vin additionné d'eau* wine with water added

s'additionner *v refl* to add up *Les fautes finissent par s'additionner et on est renvoyé.* Mistakes eventually add up and you get sacked.

multiplication *nf* (manifold) increase *Il y a une multiplication des agences immobilières dans mon quartier.* There are more and more (real) estate agents in my area.

multiplier {6} *vt* to do something repeatedly *J'ai multiplié les coups de téléphone, sans résultat.* I rang and rang, to no avail. *Tu multiplies vraiment les âneries!* You just go on doing stupid things, don't you?

se multiplier *v refl* to increase *Les risques d'empoisonnement se multiplient dès lors qu'il n'y a plus de contrôles sanitaires.* There is an ever-increasing risk of food-poisoning, as soon as health checks are withdrawn.

double *nm* twice as much *Mettez-moi le double de bifteck.* Give me twice as much steak. **double** *adj* double

doubler {6} *vt* to double *Il s'est mis au régime fiscal des artistes mais ça lui a doublé ses impôts.* He went on the artists' tax schedule but his tax bill doubled.

triple *nm* three times as much. *Il me faut le triple de peinture laquée.* I need three times as much gloss paint.

triple *adj* triple *J'ai un triple rôle de formatrice, gérante et vendeuse.* I have a triple role as trainer, manager and salesperson.

tripler {6} *vt* to increase threefold *Ils ont triplé mes horaires sans me payer plus.* They've trebled the number of hours I work without any extra pay.

se sentir des forces décuplées to feel ten times stronger

au centuple many times over *Il la déteste et elle le lui rend au centuple.* He hates her and she pays him back in kind many times over.

Multiples Multiples

double *nm* double *J'en veux le double.* I want double the quantity.

triple *nm* three times as much

quadruple *nm* four times as much

quintuple *nm* five times as much

sextuple *nm* six times as much

centuple *nm* a hundred times as much

Other multiples
The word *fois*, 'times' is used to express other multiples:
e.g. *sept fois plus* seven times as many, *trente-deux fois plus* thirty-two times as many, etc.

58.10 *Augmenter dans une dimension particulière* To increase in a specific dimension

approfondir {19} *vt* to dig . . . deeper *Ils ont approfondi le trou pour faire la piscine.* They dug the hole deeper to make the swimming pool.
s'approfondir *v refl* to become deeper
s'allonger {8} *v refl* **1** [subj: roll of pastry, elastic band] to stretch further **2** [when talking about a growing child] *Il s'allonge!* He's growing taller!
élargir {19} *vt* [obj: e.g. road, circle] to widen
s'élargir *v refl* to become wider
s'étaler {6} *v refl* [subj: e.g. batter, cream, oil] to spread (out)
se répandre {53} *v refl* [slightly pejorative] to spill over *Des constructions nouvelles se sont répandues dans la campagne environnante.* New buildings have spilled over into the surrounding countryside.

Locution Idiom
se répandre comme une traînée de poudre [refers to things that become shared very quickly, like fashions, ideas or epidemics] to spread like wildfire

58.11 *Expressions figurées désignant l'augmentation* Expressions used metaphorically to describe an increase

faire tache d'huile [spread rapidly. Often slightly pejorative] to mushroom *Les industries ont fait tache d'huile dans le quartier* Factories have mushroomed in the area.
faire boule de neige [increase rapidly in size] to snowball *Les ventes d'appareils multimédia ont fait boule de neige.* Sales of multimedia equipment have snowballed.

58.12 *Diminuer* To decrease

see also **58.4 Petit**
diminution *nf* **1** [change from bigger to smaller] decrease **2** [in knitting] *faire des diminutions* to decrease
diminuer {6} *vi* **1** [make smaller] to decrease **2** [slightly literary. Make seem less prestigious] to diminish *Cette remarque l'a diminué à mes yeux.* That remark lessened him in my eyes.
baisse *nf* [in statistics] drop *la baisse des taux d'intérêt* the drop in interest rates
abaisser, ALSO **baisser** {6} *vt* [obj: e.g. interest rate, exchange rate] to lower
baisser {6} *vi* [subj esp levels, rates] to drop
réduction *nf* **1** [lessening of volume] cut *une réduction des heures de travail* a cut in working hours *des réductions de personnel* cuts in staff **2** [similar to **baisse**] drop *la réduction du taux de mortalité infantile* the drop in infant mortality rates
réduire {82} *vt* [obj: esp levels, rates, numbers] to reduce
couper en deux to halve
couper en trois/quatre to cut into three/four (pieces)

décimer {6} *vt* [pejorative] to decimate *L'électronique a décimé les industries traditionnelles de la région.* The growth in electronics has decimated the traditional industries in the area.
tomber {6} *vi* [informal synonym for **baisser**] *vi* to drop *Sa fièvre est tombée.* His temperature has dropped.
fondre {53} *vi* **1** [subj: e.g. savings, obstacles] to vanish **2** [slightly informal. Subj esp overweight person] to slim drastically *Tu as fondu!* There's nothing left of you!

Locution Idiom
fondre come neige au soleil [refers to things that should have been preserved but have not, such as savings or good intentions] to dwindle to nothing

58.13 *Dimensions* Dimensions

see also **58.1 Grand, 61.1 Gros**
profondeur *nf* depth
profond, e *adj* deep
longueur *nf* length
long, longue *adj* long
largeur *nf* width
large *adj* wide
hauteur *nf* height
haut, haute *adj* high
peu profond, e *adj* shallow
étroit, e *adj* narrow

usage

Large
When **large** is used after *être* or after a noun, it denotes a measurement, e.g. : *La voiture est trop large pour passer là.* The car is too wide to get through there. *Il a les épaules larges.* He is broad-shouldered. **Large** can come before a noun. In this case it is used to convey an impression of spaciousness, e.g.: *de belles et larges avenues* beautiful wide avenues **Aussi large que haut** is a mocking way of describing a short fat person.

usage

Thick
Dense refers to groups of people or objects crowded together into a small space, e.g. *une forêt dense* a deep dark forest. **Épais** implies that the object referred to is almost solid, and may lack in refinement, e.g. *un tissu épais* bulky material. **Consistant** is used of thick, liquid foods and implies good nutritional value, e.g. *une soupe consistante* a thick soup.
une foule dense/compacte a dense crowd
une soupe épaisse/consistante thick soup
une fumée dense/épaisse thick smoke

58.14 *Mensurations* Measurements

mesurer {6} **1** *vt* [to take the dimensions of] to measure **2** *vi* [to have as its dimension] *La pièce mesure combien?* How big is the room?
mesure *nf* measurement *prendre les mesures d'un objet* to measure an object
échelle *nf* scale *carte à l'échelle* map drawn to scale
superficie *nf* [of land, estate or room] (surface) area
taille *nf* [dimension of objects, particularly tall ones. Also used to describe dimensions of objects which fit other objects, for instance, in ironmongery and clothing] size *Vous en avez dans ma taille?* Do you have it in my size?

pointure *nf* [for footwear, socks and gloves only] size *Vous faites quelle pointure?* What size do you take?
mensurations *nf pl* [related to clothes sizes] measurements
tour *nm* **de cou** [for men only] collar size *Quel est votre tour de cou?* What collar size do you take?

---

usage

Asking or being asked about size
If you are asked *Quelle est votre taille?* in a shop it means What size do you take? The same question asked by the person who issues your passport means *How tall are you?*

58.15 *Parler de ses mensurations* Describing one's size

Je fais 1 mètre 61. I'm 1 metre 61
Je fais du 12. I take a size 12.
Je fais du 39. I take a size 7 ALSO a continental size 39 (in shoes)
à sa taille in his/her size *Je n'ai pas trouvé de vêtements à sa taille.* I didn't find any clothes in his size.

Locution Idiom
trouver chaussure à son pied to meet the person of one's dreams

58.16 *Mathématiques* Mathematics

mathématiques *nf pl* mathematics
maths *nf pl* [informal] maths *Elle est bonne en maths.* She's good at maths.
arithmétique *nf* arithmetic
géométrie *nf* geometry
algèbre *nf* algebra
calcul *nm* **1** [operation] calculation *Vingt divisé par deux, le calcul est vite fait.* Twenty divided by two, it's easy to work out. **2** [primary school activity] BrE sums AmE arithmetic *faire du calcul* to do sums *faire du calcul mental* to do mental arithmetic
calculer {6} *vt* and *vi* to calculate *J'essaie de calculer la somme qu'il va nous falloir.* I'm trying to calculate how much money we'll need.
somme *nf* **1** [result of an addition] sum **2** [amount] sum (of money)

58.17 *Les opérations arithmétiques* Arithmetical operations

addition *nf* BrE sum AmE addition *faire une addition* to do a sum
additionner {6} *vt* and *vi* to add up
2 plus 3 font, ALSO **égale cinq** 2 plus 3 is 5
soustraction *nf* subtraction *faire une soustraction* to do (a) subtraction
soustraire {61} **1** *vi* to do (a) subtraction **2** *vt* to subtract *soustraire 23 de 43* to subtract 23 from 43
retrancher, ALSO **ôter** {6} *vt* to take away
5 moins 3 font, ALSO **égale 2** 5 minus 3 is 2
multiplication *nf* multiplication *faire une multiplication* to do (a) multiplication *les tables de multiplications* the multiplication tables
multiplier {15} *vt* and *vi* to multiply
32 multiplié par 2 égale 64 32 times 2 is 64
division *nf* division *faire une division* to do (a) division

diviser {6} *vt* and *vi* to divide
30 divisé par 2 égale 15 30 divided by 2 is 15
je pose 3 et je retiens 1 I put down 3 and carry 1
retenue *nf faire une retenue* to carry a figure over
total *nm* total (figure) *Qu'est-ce que tu trouves comme total?* What's your total figure?

58.18 *Fractions* Fractions

moitié *nf* half
tiers *nm* third
quart *nm* quarter

58.19 *Instruments* Instruments

règle *nf* **à calcul** slide rule
compas *nm* compass
rapporteur *nm* protractor
calculette *nf* ALSO **calculatrice** *nf* calculator

58.20 *Nombres* Numbers

chiffre *nm* **1** [arithmetic symbol] figure *écrire une date en chiffres* to write out a date using figures **2** [mathematical entity] number
nombre *nm* [mathematical entity] number
pair, e *adj* even *les nombres pairs* even numbers
impair, e *adj* odd *les nombres impairs* odd numbers
compter {6} *vt* and *vi* to count
moyenne *nf* [in statistics] average *La moyenne des sondés ne sait pas quel rôle jouent les forêts dans l'écologie de la planète.* On average, those taking part in the survey don't know what role forests play in the ecology of the planet. *La moyenne d'âge de nos lecteurs est de vingt-cinq ans.* The average age of our readers is 25. *au-dessus/au dessous de la moyenne* above/below average *en moyenne* on average

58.21 *Les chiffres cardinaux* Cardinal numbers

0 zéro
1 un
2 deux
3 trois
4 quatre
5 cinq
6 six
7 sept
8 huit
9 neuf
10 dix
11 onze
12 douze
13 treize
14 quatorze
15 quinze
16 seize
17 dix-sept
18 dix-huit
19 dix-neuf
20 vingt
21 (see panel overleaf)

21, 22, 23, etc

Multiples of 10 (except 70 and 90, see below) all follow the same pattern; thus, for the 20 series: 21 *vingt-et-un*, 22 *vingt-deux*, 23 *vingt-trois*, 24 *vingt-quatre*, 25 *vingt-cinq*, 26 *vingt-six*, 27 *vingt-sept*, 28 *vingt-huit*, 29 *vingt-neuf*. When 1 is added to the multiple of 10, gender agreement operates, e.g.: *vingt-et-un garçons et vingt-et-une filles* twenty-one boys and twenty-one girls

30 trente
40 quarante
50 cinquante
60 soixante
70 (see second panel below)
80 (see first panel below)
90 (see second panel below)
100 cent (see third panel below for number agreement)
1,000 mille (invariable)
10,000 dix mille
100,000 cent mille
1,000,000 un million

80

This number is expressed as **quatre-vingt** if followed by another numeral as in *quatre-vingt dix*. Otherwise it is spelt **quatre-vingts**.

70 and 90

In the French language as it is spoken in France these two numbers are *soixante-dix* and *quatre-vingt-dix* respectively. In Belgium and Switzerland, as well as some parts of eastern France, they are *septante* and *nonante* respectively. This is how to add units to them:

In the French which is spoken in France:
70 soixante-dix
71 soixante-et-onze
72 soixante-douze
73 soixante-treize
74 soixante-quatorze
75 soixante-quinze
76 soixante-seize
77 soixante-dix-sept
78 soixante-dix-huit
79 soixante-dix-neuf
90 quatre-vingt-dix
91 quatre-vingt-onze
92 quatre-vingt-douze, etc as for the 70 series

In Belgium, Switzerland and parts of eastern France:
70 septante
71 septante-et-un, etc as for the 20 series
90 nonante
91 nonante-et-un, etc as for the 20 series

100

Cent, one hundred, is invariable when not multiplied: *cent pommes* one hundred apples; also *cent trois francs* one hundred and three francs. When multiplied, it is spelt *cents*: e.g. *trois cents personnes* three hundred people. However, it remains invariable when multiplied but followed by another number, as in *trois cent deux dossiers* three hundred and two files.

58.22 *Les chiffres ordinaux* Ordinal numbers

Abbreviations for ordinal numbers

The abbreviation for second, 2ième, is the model for all ordinal number abbreviations except first, as shown below.

1st premier, -mière [abbreviation, 1er, 1ère]
2nd deuxième [abbreviation, 2ième]
3rd troisième
4th quatrième
5th cinquième
6th sixième
7th septième
8th huitième
9th neuvième
10th dixième
11th onzième
12th douzième
13th treizième
14th quatorzième
15th quinzième
16th seizième
17th dix-septième
18th dix-huitième
19th dix-neuvième
20th vingtième
21st (see panel below)
30th trentième
40th quarantième
50th cinquantième
60th soixantième
70th soixante-dixième, ALSO septantième [in Belgium and Switzerland]
80th quatre-vingtième
90th quatre-vingt-dixième, ALSO nonantième [in Belgium and Switzerland]
100th centième
1,000th millième
10,000th dix millième
100,000th cent millième
1,000,000th millionnième

21st, 22nd, 23rd, etc

Ordinal numbers adding one unit to each multiple of ten go as follows:
21st vingt-et-unième
22nd vingt-deuxième
23rd vingt-troisième, etc
The exceptions to this, as for cardinal numbers, are the 70 and 90 series which go like this:
71st soixante-et-onzième
72nd soixante-douzième
73rd soixante-treizième
74th soixante-quatorzième
75th soixante-quinzième
76th soixante-seizième
77th soixante-dix-septième
78th soixante-dix-huitième
79th soixante-dix-neuvième
91st quatre-vingt-onzième
92nd quatre-vingt-douzième, etc as above

58.23 *Quantités approximatives* Approximate quantities

demi-douzaine *nf* half a dozen *une demi-douzaine d'œufs* half a dozen eggs

dizaine *nf* about ten *une dizaine d'enveloppes* about ten envelopes

douzaine *nf* dozen *une douzaine d'œufs* a dozen eggs

quinzaine *nf* about fifteen *une quinzaine de personnes* about fifteen people

vingtaine *nf* **1** [quantity] about twenty *une vingtaine de vaches* about twenty cows **2** [age] *avoir une vingtaine d'années* to be twentyish

trentaine *nf* **1** [quantity] about thirty *une trentaine de billes* about thirty marbles **2** [age] *avoir la trentaine* to be thirtyish

quarantaine *nf* **1** [quantity] about forty *une quarantaine de spectateurs* about forty spectators **2** [age] *avoir la quarantaine* to be fortyish

cinquantaine *nf* **1** [quantity] about fifty *une cinquantaine de bouteilles* about fifty bottles **2** [age] *avoir la cinquantaine* to be fiftyish

soixantaine *nf* **1** [quantity] about sixty *une soixantaine de croissants* about sixty croissants **2** [age] *avoir la soixantaine* to be sixtyish

centaine *nf* about a hundred *une centaine de voitures* about a hundred cars

millier *nm* **1** [1,000] a thousand *un millier de francs* a thousand francs **2** [approximate quantity] about a thousand *un millier de signatures* about a thousand signatures

milliard *nm* **1** [1,000 million] billion **2** [approximate quantity] huge numbers of *des milliards d'étoiles* huge numbers of stars

près de *adv* approximately *Il y a près de deux ans que je ne l'ai pas vue.* I haven't seen her for about two years. *D'ici à Paris, ça fait près de cent kilomètres.* It's approximately a hundred kilometres from here to Paris.

grosso modo, ALSO **en gros** roughly (speaking) *Tu me dois en gros 120 francs.* Roughly (speaking) you owe me 120 francs. *On a grosso modo deux mois pour le faire.* We have two months to do it (roughly speaking).

58.24 *Poids et peser* Weights and weighing

poids *nm* weight *vendre qqch au poids* to sell sthg by weight *Le poids du colis est de 300 grammes.* The parcel weighs 300 grams. *poids brut/net* gross/net weight

charge *nf* load *charge utile* payload

peser {9} *vi* and *vt* to weigh *Je vais peser les pêches et les abricots séparément.* I'll weigh out the peaches and the apricots separately. *La lettre pèse 100 grammes.* The letter weighs 100 grams. *La valise pèse lourd.* The suitcase is heavy.

unité *nf* unit

étalon *nm* standard

lourd, e *adj* heavy

léger, -gère *adj* light

58.25 *Poids* Units of weight

kilogramme *nm* [abbreviation: *kg*] kilogram

kilo *nm* [abbreviation: *kg*] kilo

milligramme *nm* [abbreviation: *mg*] milligram

centigramme *nm* [abbreviation: *cg*] centigram

décigramme *nm* [abbreviation: *dg*] decigram

hectogramme *nm* [abbreviation: *hg*] hectogram

livre *nf* [used when weighing foodstuffs] pound

quintal *nm*, *pl* **quintaux** [abbreviation: *q*] (metric) quintal

tonne *nf* [abbreviation: *t*] (metric) ton, tonne

58.26 *Machines à peser* Weighing machines

balance *nf* (pair of) scales *balance de ménage* kitchen scales

bascule *nf* weighing machine

pèse-personne *nm*, *pl* **pèse-personnes** [domestic] bathroom scales

pèse-bébé *nm*, *pl* **pèse-bébés** scales for weighing babies

58.27 *Volumes* Volumes

volume *nm* volume

capacité *nf* capacity *Quelle est la capacité de cette carafe?* How much does this jug hold?

cube *nm* [abbreviation: ^{3}] cube *un mètre cube*, ALSO *1 m³* one cubic metre *un centimètre cube*, ALSO *1cm³* one cubic centimetre

cubique *adj* cubic

litre *nm* [abbreviation: *l*] BrE litre AmE liter

millilitre *nm* [abbreviation: *ml*] BrE millilitre AmE milliliter

centilitre *nm* [abbreviation: *cl*] BrE centilitre AmE centiliter

décilitre [abbreviation: *dl*] BrE decilitre AmE deciliter

hectolitre *nm* [abbreviation: *hl*] BrE hectolitre AmE hectoliter

stère *nf* [for wood] BrE cubic metre AmE cubic meter

59 Education, learning and teaching

59.1 *Enseignement* Education

enseigner {6} *vt* and *vi* [general term] to teach *J'enseigne les mathématiques aux classes terminales.* I teach mathematics to the senior glasses. *C'est ma grand-mère qui m'a enseigné la lecture.* My grandmother taught me to read.

enseignement *nm* **1** [system] educational system *l'enseignement public* state education **2** [profession] teaching *Il se destine à l'enseignement.* He wants to go into teaching.

éduquer {6} *vt* [wider than **enseigner.** Includes developing the personality and teaching social skills] to educate

éducation *nf* **1** [sum of knowledge] education(al background) **2** [institution] education *le Ministère de l'éducation nationale* the (French) Ministry of Education

culture *nf* [knowledge] education *Elle a une bonne culture générale.* She's well educated. *culture littéraire* knowledge of the arts *culture scientifique* knowledge of science

primaire *adj* primary **primaire** *nm* primary sector

secondaire *adj* secondary **secondaire** *nm* secondary sector

supérieur *nm* higher education

supérieur, e *adj* higher

School
The word *école* is used as a translation for 'school' only in the context of infant and primary schools and in the names of higher or further education colleges, e.g. *J'ai fait une École de Journalisme.* I went to a School of Journalism. The term *école* is not normally used when referring to secondary schools.

scolaire *adj* **1** [belonging to the school environment] school *des livres scolaires* schoolbooks *l'année scolaire* the school year **2** [pejorative. Parroting and simple-minded] simplistic *Le catalogue qu'il a rédigé pour l'exposition est très complet mais un peu scolaire.* The catalogue he compiled for the exhibition is very exhaustive but a bit simplistic.

apprendre {54} *vt* and *vi* to learn

apprenant, e *n* learner

leçon *nf* [at primary or secondary school] lesson

cours *nm* [at secondary school or university] lesson, class

exercice *nm* exercise

Preschool education
Children as young as two are accepted for state-funded preschool education at *la maternelle*, and may stay there until they are six. Provision for preschool education varies: it is usually available in large urban centres and sparser in rural areas. Methods used at the *maternelle* with the younger children are akin to those used in many British playgroups, but gradually teachers start preparing children for the reading and writing which they will be doing once they start their primary education.

Primary education
Compulsory schooling starts at the age of six. At primary school, *l'école primaire*, all children follow the French national curriculum

Secondary education
Children start secondary education at the age of eleven. At the lower school, *le collège d'enseignement général* or *C.E.S.*, they spend four years, during the first two of which they all follow the same curriculum. From the third year onwards, students may choose different options, and at the end of the fourth year, all students take a national exam, *le brevet des collèges*. They may then choose to leave school or to go on to *le lycée*. Those who elect to carry on will spend three years at the *lycée*, at the end of which they will take the end of secondary school exam, *le baccalauréat*. Students who pass the *baccalauréat* gain automatic access to a university education.

écolier, -lière *n* [in pre-primary or primary school] schoolchild

élève *n* [in pre-primary, primary or secondary school] pupil

collégien, -gienne *n* secondary school student (at a *collège*)

lycéen, -céenne *n* secondary school student (at a *lycée*)

Higher education
University students may follow a 'long' or a 'short' course of study. The short course, *le cycle court*, is open to holders of the baccalauréat, *les bacheliers*, and leads to the *D.E.U.G* (*Diplôme d'Études Universitaires Générales*) for humanities students. This is sometimes known as *bac + 2* because it is obtained two years after the *baccalauréat*. The science and technology equivalent is the *D.E.U.S.T* (*Diplôme d'Études Universitaires Scientifiques et Techniques*). The second course, *le deuxième cycle*, leads to a degree, *la licence*, three years after the *baccalauréat* (and thus also known as *bac + 3*), or to a master's degree, *la maîtrise* (*bac + 4*). The more advanced course, *le troisième cycle*, leads to the D.E.S.S. (*Diplôme d'Études Supérieures Spécialisées*). or to a doctorate, *le doctorat*.
Another way of studying within the higher education system is to prepare for the selective-entry higher education establishments, *les grandes écoles*, which admit students on the basis of very competitive exams,

and traditionally produce the elite of the nation. There are many different *grandes écoles*, producing engineers, higher civil servants, leaders of industry and commerce, and university teachers as well as the most qualified and best-paid teachers in the secondary sector.

université *nf* university

I.U.T. *nm* [Institut Universitaire de Technologie] university technological institute [similar to the former poytechnics in Britain]

faculté *nf* faculty *la faculté des lettres et sciences humaines* the faculty of arts and social sciences

fac *nf* [informal] **1** [department of a university] school *la fac des lettres* the humanities school **2** [as a whole] university

Age levels
At primary school, classes are known by the following names
le cours préparatoire or *CP* (6–7 year-olds)
le cours élémentaire 1 or *CE1* or *la dixième* (7–8 year-olds)
le cours élémentaire 2 or *CE2* or *la neuvième* (8–9 year-olds)
le cours moyen 1 or *CM1* or *la huitième* (9–10 year-olds)
le cours moyen 2 or *CM2* or *la septième* (10–11 year-olds)
In the secondary sector, the first class that pupils enter when they start secondary school is called *la sixième*. (11–12 year-olds) From then on, the names given to the successive years are as follows:
la cinquième (12–13 year-olds)
la quatrième (13–14 year-olds)
la troisième (14–15 year-olds)
la seconde (15–16 year-olds)
la première (16–17 year-olds)
la terminale (17–18 year-olds)

Academic periods
trimestre *nm* term
semestre *nm* semester

Going back after the summer break
The word *la rentrée*, literally 'going back', refers to the period of the year when schoolchildren, university students, teachers, parents and even television and radio broadcasters and M.P.s all go back to work after the summer break. It also refers to the marketing opportunities for books, stationery and schoolclothes which start in the second half of August and last until approximately the beginning of November. Large signs saying *La rentrée* appear in the windows of shops selling these goods. Even novel-writing is subject to this yearly rhythm, in that bookshops will display new books under headings such as *la rentrée littéraire*, 'new novels', or *les actualités de la rentrée*, 'new current affairs', and usually sell larger numbers at that time.

59.2 *Compétence* Competence

adroit, *adj* **1** [general] skilful **2** [in one's movements, with one's hands] agile **adresse** *nf* skill

dextérité *nf* [with hands or fingers] skill *Il faut de la dextérité pour lever les filets d'une sole.* Filleting a sole requires deft fingers.

apte à able to

aptitude *nf* ability

brio *nm* talent

compétence *nf* competence *avoir compétence pour faire qqch* to be competent to do sthg

compétent, e *adj* [can be used to damn with faint praise when not preceded by an intensifier like *très*] competent
habile *adj* [same meanings as **adroit** but may also imply cunning] skilful, agile *habile de ses mains* clever with one's hands *Elle a été très habile et elle les a convaincus de signer.* She was very skilful (about it) and persuaded them to sign.
habileté *nf* [applies to all kinds of activities. May imply cunning] skill *Son habileté au clavier m'a toujours étonné.* His skill at the keyboard has always amazed me. *Il manipulait les conférences de presse avec beaucoup d'habileté.* He handled press conferences with great skill and cunning.
habilité à empowered to *Je ne suis que l'assistant de Monsieur le Consul, et je ne suis pas habilité à vous répondre.* I'm only the Consul's assistant and I'm not empowered to answer your questions.
maestria *nf* [implies brilliant execution] brilliance *Elle s'est garée avec maestria entre les deux motos.* She made a brilliant job of parking between the two motorbikes.

59.3 *Personnes compétentes* Competent people

professionnel, -nelle *n* [non-amateur; also expert in some area] pro(fessional)
spécialiste *n* expert
virtuose *n* **1** [in music] virtuoso **2** [figurative use] brilliant person *un virtuose du volant/de la pêche à la ligne* a brilliant driver/angler.
expert, e *n* [in a scientific, technical or practical subject] expert

Locutions Idioms
Il/Elle a le coup pour faire . . . [informal] He's/she's got the knack of doing . . .
prendre le coup pour faire . . . [informal] to learn the trick of doing . . .
faire quelque chose en deux temps trois mouvements [informal] to do something as quick as a flash
avoir de la ressource to be resourceful
avoir plusieurs cordes ALSO **plus d'une corde à son arc** to have more than one string to one's bow
avoir des doigts de fée [of women only] to be an accomplished seamstress

59.4 *Bêtise* Stupidity

bête *adj* stupid
bêtise *nf* **1** [character trait] stupidity *Elle a eu la bêtise de lui avouer sa liaison.* She was stupid enough to own up to him about her affair. **2** [instance of stupidity] stupid thing to do *C'est une bêtise, d'avoir peint la grille avant de poser la serrure!* How stupid to have painted the railing before fitting the lock! *En l'épousant, j'ai fait une bêtise.* I made a stupid mistake when I married him. *Les enfants ont fait des bêtises.* The children have been naughty.
bébête *adj* [informal. Stupid and pusillanimous] foolishly sentimental
abêtir {19} *vt* to make stupid *Ne leur donne pas à lire des romans qui les abêtissent.* Don't make them read novels that stultify their minds
idiot, e *adj* [same meaning as **bête**] stupid **idiot, e** *n* idiot
idiotie *nf* [same meanings as **bêtise**] stupidity, stupid thing to do
sot, sotte *adj* stupid [old-fashioned or literary term. Same meaning as **bête**] stupid
imbécile *adj* [stronger than **bête**. Implies the ability to do

harm through stupidity] idiotic **imbécillité** *nf* crass stupidity
abrutir {19} *vt* [stronger than **abêtir**] *abrutir qqn* to stupefy sb *L'alcool les a complètement abrutis.* Alcohol has turned them into complete zombies.
s'abrutir *v refl* [become dulled] to wear oneself out *Je m'abrutis à rester toute la journée à mon clavier d'ordinateur.* I'm driving myself silly, spending all day at my computer keyboard. **2** [become stupid] to turn into a moron *Cet après-midi, faites autre chose que de vous abrutir devant la télévision.* This afternoon, don't just stay glued to the television like morons: do something.
abruti, e *adj* [made stupid by, for example, a repetitive noise, a steady intake of alcohol] dazed
hébété, e *adj* [made stupid by a blow, a shock, a drug] dazed
bonnet *nm* **d'âne** dunce's cap

59.5 *Insults* Insults

âne (bâté) *nm* ass
oie *nf*, ALSO **bécasse** *nf* [used of women only] silly goose
(gros) bêta *nm*, **(grosse) bêtasse** *nf* [used affectionately] big silly *Ne pleure pas, gros bêta, elle va revenir, maman.* Don't cry you big silly, your mother will be back.
crétin, e *n* [used aggressively] cretin
nigaud, e *n* [used contemptuously or affectionately] dumbo

Locutions Idioms
Il/Elle est bête comme ses pieds ALSO **bête à manger du foin** ALSO **bête comme une oie** BrE He's/She's as thick as two short planks. AmE He's/She's as dumb as they come.
C'est un/une simple d'esprit. [euphemism] He's/She's a bit simple.
faire l'âne pour avoir du son to pretend to be stupid in order to gain something
Ce n'est pas un aigle. [humorous] He/She isn't exactly a genius.
Il/Elle n'a pas inventé le fil à couper le beurre ALSO **pas inventé la poudre.** [humorous] He'll/She'll never set the world on fire.

59.6 *Incompétence* Incompetence

All the phrases below are pejorative.
nul, nulle *adj* [informal. Describes: e.g. person, film, excursion, gadget] useless *J'étais nul à l'école.* I was useless at school. *Il est nul, ton raisonnement!* That's a ridiculous way of thinking! *Elle est nulle, ta sauce!* Your sauce is rubbish!
incompétent, e *adj* [more formal than **nul**. Lacking a particular skill] incompetent **incompétence** *nf* incompetence
inepte *adj* [more pejorative than **incompétent**. Describes: e.g. person, behaviour] inept
incapable *adj* [lacking ability] incompetent **incapable** *n* good for nothing. *Ses fils sont tous des incapables.* His sons are all good for nothing.
en dilettante, ALSO **en amateur** amateurishly

Locution Idiom
Il/Elle ne sait rien faire de ses dix doigts [cannot do manual jobs, through clumsiness or lack of interest] He's/She's got two left thumbs.
C'est un bon à rien. [used mostly in the masculine although **bonne à rien** is also possible. Implies that the person will never amount to much] He's a total waster.

59.7 *En classe* In the classroom

classe *nf* classroom
récréation *nf* break(time)
récré *nf* [children's slang] break
faire l'appel BrE to take the register (of the pupils in a class) AmE to take roll
devoir *nm* piece of homework. *Tu as des devoirs à faire?* Have you got any homework to do?
bulletin *nm* BrE school report AmE (school) report card
fournitures *nf pl* (**scolaires**) school materials
classe *nf* classroom
bureau *nm* desk
tableau *nm, pl* **-x** *nm* blackboard
trousse *nf* pencil case
manuel *nm* textbook
cahier *nm* exercise book *cahier de brouillon* rough book

59.8 *Les matières* Subjects

see also **58.16 Mathématiques**
français *nm* [language, literature] French
lettres *nf pl* (**françaises**) French literature
latin *nm* Latin
grec *nm* (Ancient) Greek
physique *nf* physics
chimie *nf* chemistry
science(s) *nf (pl)* science(s) *sciences naturelles* biology
sciences nat *nf pl* [in secondary school. Informal] biology
biologie *nf* [at university] biology
histoire *nf* history
géographie *nf* geography
géo *nf* [informal] geography

59.9 *Les enseignants* The teaching profession

instituteur, -trice *n* (primary) schoolteacher
maître, maîtresse *n* [word used by children. Primary only] teacher
professeur *n* **1** [at school] (secondary) schoolteacher **2** [at university] lecturer **3** [at university, chair-holder] professor
universitaire *n* university teacher

59.10 *Les contrôles* Assessment

contrôle *nm* class test
interrogation *nf* test *interrogation orale* test (by oral question and answer) *interrogation écrite* written test
examen *nm* examination *examen blanc* mock exam
concours *nm* competitive examination
oral *nm* **1** [in modern languages] oral exam **2** [as a complement to a written examination] BrE viva AmE oral exam

59.11 *Enseignement professionnel* Vocational schooling and training

stage *nm* (vocational) course
stagiaire *n* **1** [on a course] member **2** [at work] person obtaining work experience
L.E.P. *nm* [*Lycée d'Enseignement Professionnel*] vocationally oriented (secondary) school
apprenti, e *n* apprentice
apprentissage *nm* [in a trade] apprenticeship

59.12 *Intelligence* Intelligence

intelligent, e *adj* [describes: e.g. person, scheme, comment] intelligent
intelligence *nf* intelligence
doué, e *adj* [able to perform exceptionally well in general, or with a specific skill] gifted
surdoué, e *adj* [stronger than *doué*] extremely gifted
calé, e *adj* [informal. In an academic subject] *Elle est calée en maths.* She has a head for maths.
savant, e *adj* [a slightly old-fashioned term of praise] learned

59.13 *Formes d'intelligence* Kinds of intelligence

rusé, e *adj* cunning
astucieux, -cieuse *adj* [able to work out unexpected ways of extricating oneself from difficult situations] astute
malin, maligne *adj* [same meaning as **astucieux**] crafty
finaud, e *adj* [able to see through people and their manoeuvres] shrewd
roublard, e *adj* [clever, cunning and knowing. Used in grudging admiration, or pejoratively] fly
futé, e *adj* [combines the meanings of **astucieux** and **roublard**. Not pejorative] sharp, clever

Bison Futé
Literally 'clever Bison'. In humorous imitation of native American names, *Bison Futé* is a traffic information bureau, which broadcasts on national radio and television networks and recommends alternative routes at times of heavy congestion on the roads, such as national holidays and festivals.

Locutions Idioms
la fuite des cerveaux the brain drain
un remue-méninges [humorous] a brainstorming session
C'est un cerveau! [informal. Refers to abstract intelligence] He's/she's pretty brainy.
Fais travailler tes méninges! [informal] Think!
Il est malin comme un singe. [mostly in the masculine. Said, e.g., of children] He's so sharp he'll cut himself one of these days.
C'est une fine mouche. [applies to men and women] There's not much you can put past him/her.
Il n'est pas né/Elle n'est pas née de la dernière pluie. He/she wasn't born yesterday.
Il y en a là-dedans! [informal saying, accompanied by a gesture with index finger tapping temple] He/she's got a lot up here!
À malin, malin et demi . . . [no matter how clever a person thought they were being, someone is about to outdo them] Two can play at that game.

59.14 *Livres et lecture* Books and reading

livre *nm* book *C'est mon livre de chevet.* It's the book I keep on my bedside table. *Mon livre de chevet, cet été, c'est une biographie de Léon Blum.* This summer I'm reading a biography of Léon Blum.
bouquin *nm* [very common informal synonym for **livre**] book
bouquiner {6} *vt* and *vi* [informal] to read *Elle passe son temps à bouquiner.* She's always got her nose stuck in a book.
ouvrage *nm* [formal term. Refers to a book as a physical object and as a work of the mind] work *J'ai ici un très bel*

ouvrage sur l'histoire de la colonisation. I have here an excellent work on the history of colonization.

œuvre *nf* **1** [book or piece of art. Stresses literary or artistic qualities] work *l'œuvre à laquelle Proust/Giacometti a consacré sa vie* the work to which Proust/Giacometti dedicated his life **2** [the life's work of an author or artist] *les œuvres de Balzac/Villon* the works of Balzac/Villon
titre *nm* title
lettre *nf* **(de l'alphabet)** letter (of the alphabet) *en lettres majuscules/minuscules* in capitals/in lower case
page *nf* page
au verso overleaf
T.S.V.P. P.T.O.

59.15 *Livres de fiction* Story books

roman *nm* novel, story *un roman d'amour/d'aventures* a love/an adventure story *un roman policier* a thriller
histoire *nf* [simpler, less literary than roman] story *Raconte-moi une histoire.* Tell me a story.
conte *nm* [involves legendary or supernatural beings] story *conte de fées* fairy tale *un très beau livre de contes du Limousin* a beautiful collection of legends from the Limousin region.
fiction *nf* fiction *La réalité dépasse la fiction.* Truth is stranger than fiction.
personnage *nm* character
intrigue *nf* plot
aventure *nf* adventure *roman d'aventures* adventure novel

59.16 *Livres relatant la vie de personnes existantes* Biographies

biographie *nf* biography *une biographie officielle* an authorized biography
biographique *adj* biographical
biographe *n* biographer
autobiographie *nf* autobiography
journal *nm* **(intime)**, *pl* **-naux (intimes)** diary

59.17 *Livres de référence et autres* Reference books

dictionnaire *nm* dictionary *dictionnaire analogique* thesaurus
encyclopédie *nf* encyclopedia
album *nm* **1** [for one's own photographs and of an artist's published photographs] album **2** [collection] book of cartoons **3** [book containing a story] cartoon strip book *J'ai trois des albums de Tintin.* I have three of the Tintin books.

59.18 *La littérature* Literature

littérature *nf* literature
littéraire *adj* literary *faire de la critique littéraire* to write literary criticism
prose *nf* prose
écriture *nf* [one's way of expressing oneself in a text] prose style *J'aime son écriture un peu poétique.* I like her rather poetic style of writing.
poésie *nf* **1** [genre] poetry **2** [text] poem *Apprenez par cœur une courte poésie de votre choix.* Learn one of your favourite short poems by heart.
poétique *adj* poetic

vers *nm* line (of a poem)
strophe *nf* stanza
paroles *nf pl* [of a song] lyrics, words *J'ai oublié les paroles.* I've forgotten the words.

59.19 *Production des livres* Book production

éditeur, -trice *n* publisher
maison *nf* **d'édition** publishing house
auteur *nm* [male or female] author *Elle est l'auteur de plusieurs ouvrages scientifiques.* She's the author of several scientific books.
avance *nf* [for an author] advance (payment)
droits *nm pl* **d'auteur** copyright
éditer {6} *vt* and *vi* to publish
lecteur, -trice *n* publisher's editor
corriger {8} *vt* [obj: e.g. text, manuscript, paragraph] to edit
publication *nf* **1** [making public] publication *date de publication* publication date **2** [book or magazine] publication *une publication sur la viticulture* a book on winegrowing
imprimeur *nm* printer
imprimerie *nf* printer's *Le dernier volume est à l'imprimerie.* The last volume is at the printer's.

59.20 *L'utilisation des livres* Using books

lecture *nf* **1** [process and pastime] reading *faire la lecture à qqn* to read aloud to sb *Prends de la lecture, tu vas sûrement attendre chez le médecin.* Take something with you to read, you'll probably have to wait at the doctor's. **2** [way one reads] reading *Une lecture attentive du contrat aurait dû vous alerter sur les risques encourus.* If you'd read the contract carefully, you'd have been alerted to the attendant risks.
niveau *nm*, *pl* **-x de lecture** BrE reading age AmE reading level *Il a le niveau de lecture d'un enfant de huit ans.* He has a reading age of eight.
lire {77} *vt* and *vi* to read *lire un conte à un enfant* to read a story to a child *lire un journal/roman* to read a newspaper/novel
lecteur, -trice *n* reader *Notre magazine est destiné à des lecteurs jeunes.* Our magazine is aimed at a young readership.
libraire *n* bookseller
librairie *nf* bookshop
bibliothèque *nf* library
bibliothécaire *n* librarian

The prix Goncourt
A famous literary prize awarded each November to a fiction writer, the prix Goncourt was endowed in 1870 by Edmond de Goncourt, one of two novelist brothers. The actual monetary value of the award is nominal, but the prestige, the press and media coverage, and resulting book sales make it one of the most important and profitable events of the French literary year.

59.21 *Papeterie* Stationery

see also **77.1 Bureau**
carnet *nm* notebook *carnet à spirale* spiral-bound notebook
bloc-note *nm*, *pl* **blocs-notes** notepad
crayon *nm* (lead) pencil

stylo *nm* (ballpoint) pen
règle *nf* ruler *règle à calcul* slide rule
équerre *nf* set square
gomme *nf* eraser
gommer {6} *vt* to rub out (with an eraser)
effacer {7} *vt* **1** [with an eraser] to rub out **2** [on screen] to delete

---

Stationery for school
At the beginning of an academic year students in French schools are expected to come equipped with a set of stationery and other equipment (set square, pair of compasses, sheets of plastic for covering schoolbooks, etc), known as **fournitures** *nf pl* **scolaires** i.e. stationery for school. At primary school each year group is issued by its teacher with a list of the relevant *fournitures* for that year's study.

---

60 Correct and wrong

60.1 *Erreur* Making a mistake

faute *nf* **1** [at school, when doing a piece of work] mistake *Tu as fait deux fautes dans ta dictée.* You made two mistakes in your dictation. *faute d'orthographe* spelling mistake *faute de frappe* typing error *faute d'impression* typographical error **2** [in tennis] fault *double faute* double fault
fautif, -tive *adj* **1** [describes: e.g. use, choice] wrong **2** [describes: person] at fault *C'est lui qui est fautif.* He's the one who's at fault.
erreur *nf* [something wrong in a piece of work, an argument. This term is more general than **faute**] error, mistake *Une erreur s'est glissée dans notre éditorial de la semaine dernière.* An error crept into last week's editorial. *Ils croient renflouer l'économie par les privatisations, c'est une erreur.* They think they're helping the economy by privatizing but they're wrong. *Il y a erreur.* There's a mistake. *Tu dis qu'il a les cheveux bruns, il doit y avoir erreur sur la personne.* You're saying he's got brown hair, we're obviously not talking about the same person. *faire erreur* to be mistaken
erroné, e *adj* [formal. Describes: e.g. reasoning, calculation, spelling] erroneous
coquille *nf* misprint
erratum *nm, pl* **errata**, erratum
erreur judiciaire miscarriage of justice
faute *nf* [in school] mistake *une faute d'orthographe* a spelling mistake *une faute d'étourderie* a careless mistake *une faute de frappe* a typing error
gaffe *nf* [error which is liable to offend] blunder
malentendu *nm* misunderstanding
se tromper {6} *v refl* **1** [be under an illusion] to be mistaken *Je me trompais en croyant que tu me soutiendrais.* I was mistaken in thinking you'd support me. *De Gaulle ne se trompait pas sur l'Europe.* De Gaulle was right about Europe. **2** [fail to apply the rules correctly in spelling, maths, etc] to get it wrong *Tu te trompes, il faut rajouter deux zéros.* You've got it wrong, you have to add two zeros. **3** [judge somebody or something to be better or worse than is the case] to be mistaken *Je me suis trompé sur elle, elle n'est pas capable de gérer un budget.* I was mistaken about her, she can't manage a budget. *Tu t'es trompé sur elle, elle est tout à fait de taille à diriger une équipe.* You underestimated her, she's well up to leading a team. *Nous nous sommes trompés sur*

l'évaluation de nos charges. We misjudged the size of our overheads.
à tort mistakenly *On croit, à tort, que les poux ne viennent que sur les cheveux sales.* People believe, mistakenly, that lice infest only dirty hair.
par mégarde [due to confusion or lack of concentration] by mistake
par inadvertance [through lack of concentration] inadvertently
On s'est mal compris. We misunderstood each other.

Locution Idiom
L'erreur est humaine . . . To err is human . . .

60.2 *Exact* Exact

exact, e *adj* exact *Tu as l'heure exacte?* Do you have the correct time? **exactement** *adv* exactly
exactitude *nf* precision *Décrivez avec le plus d'exactitude possible la disposition des lieux.* Please describe the layout of the place as precisely as possible.
juste, ALSO **correct, e** *adj* correct *345, la réponse est juste* 345, it's the correct answer *si mes suppositions là-dessus sont correctes* if I'm not mistaken in supposing this
justement *adv* correctly *comme elle le remarque très justement* as she very correctly points out
justesse *nf* accuracy *Elle voit les choses avec justesse.* She sees things very clearly.
précis, e *adj* exact *l'endroit précis où se trouve notre maison* the exact location of our house *à l'heure précise où le contrat était signé* at the exact moment when the contract was signed
précisément *adv* exactly
bon, bonne *adj* [describes: calculation, sum, result] correct
pile *adv* [informal. Used with timings] dead *on deux heures pile* BrE dead on two AmE exactly two o'clock

60.3 *Inexact* Incorrect

faux, fausse *adj* (before or after the noun) [accidentally incorrect. Describes: e.g. calculation, result] wrong *Le dessin est faux car il omet de représenter la porte d'entrée.* The drawing is wrong because it fails to show the front door. *une fausse note* a wrong note *un faux numéro* a wrong number
incorrect, e *adj* [describes: e.g. spelling, information] wrong
incorrectement *adv* wrongly *Ils ont épelé mon nom incorrectement.* They've spelt my name wrongly.

The wrong address, number, date, etc
One of the most common ways of indicating that something is wrong, is to use *bon, bonne,* in a negative construction, e.g.:
Ce n'est pas la bonne adresse. It's the wrong address.
Ce n'est pas le bon jour. It's the wrong day.
Ce n'est pas la bonne taille. That's the wrong size.
Ce n'est pas le bon numéro. It's the wrong number.
(except when it's a wrong number on the telephone. In this case it is more natural to say *C'est un faux numéro*).

Locutions Idioms
Il/Elle a tout faux. [from the language of the classroom. Used when someone has totally misunderstood a situation] BrE He's/She's got completely the wrong end of the stick.

se mettre le doigt dans l'œil (jusqu'à l'os) [very informal. Implies wrong assessment of a situation, and inappropriate way of acting on it] to be barking up the wrong tree

avoir la langue qui a fourché ALSO **avoir la fourche qui a langué** [humorous] to have made a slip of the tongue

faire un sans faute [informal. By analogy with a school assignment containing no errors] to perform faultlessly

61 Cause and effect

61.1 *Cause* Cause

cause *nf* cause *C'est l'humidité qui est la cause de cette décoloration du mur.* Damp is the cause of the discoloration on the wall.

à cause de because of

pour cause de [on notices, for example in shop windows] due to *fermé pour cause de vacances annuelles* annual closure

raison *nf* reason *La vraie raison de sa colère c'est qu'il se sent coupable.* The real reason for his anger is his feeling of guilt.

en raison de [slightly more formal than **à cause de**] because of *En raison de son grand âge, il n'a pu assister à la remise des prix.* Because of his great old age, he couldn't attend the award ceremony.

61.2 *Verbes exprimant la cause* Verbs of cause

entraîner {6} *vt* [be the start of an inevitable process] to bring about *L'infection entraîne un affaiblissement de toutes les fonctions vitales.* The infection brings about a weakening of all the vital functions

déclencher {6} *vt* [be the starting point of. Usu fast or instantaneous action] to trigger *déclencher une opération militaire* to trigger a military operation *déclencher un tollé général* to provoke a wave of protests

provoquer {6} *vt* [have as a result, often negative] to cause *C'est ce qui a provoqué l'incendie.* That's what caused the fire

amener {9} *vt* [implies a long period of time between cause and effect] to bring in its wake *un front froid qui nous amène la pluie* a cold front bringing rain in its wake

un lien de cause à effet a cause and effect relationship *Il y a un lien de cause à effet entre ces deux choses.* There's a cause-and-effect relationship between these two things.

Expressing 'because of'
Be careful to distinguish between because of (a good thing), expressed with *grâce à*, and because of (a bad thing), expressed with *à cause de*. For example, *C'est grâce à l'imagerie médicale qu'on peut localiser très précisément les tumeurs.* Thanks to medical imaging, it is possible to know the exact location of a tumour. Contrast this with: *À cause des orages, les récoltes n'ont pas donné le rendement prévu.* The crops did not yield as much as expected because of storm damage.

61.3 *Résultat* Result

résultat *nm* result *obtenir un résultat* to achieve a result *comme résultat de mes efforts* as a result of my efforts *Elle ne m'avait pas prévenu, résultat, le plombier est venu*

alors que j'étais absent. She didn't warn me, consequently the plumber came when I wasn't in.

résulter {6} *vi résulter de* to result from *les bénéfices qui résultent de cette vente* the profit resulting from this sale *Il résulte de la réunion d'hier que nous allons prendre le projet en sous-traitance.* As a consequence of yesterday's meeting it was decided that we will work as contractors on the project.

conséquence *nf* consequence *Il risque d'y avoir des conséquences graves.* There's a risk of serious consequences. *Cela ne porte pas à conséquence.* It's of no importance. *sans s'occuper des conséquences éventuelles* without any regard for the possible consequences

en conséquence therefore

par conséquent therefore

consécutivement à [formal] as a consequence of

suite *nf* [of an affair, of a project, of a disease] sequel *une proposition qui n'a pas eu de suites* a proposal which was not taken up *à la suite de* as a consequence of *à la suite de quoi* as a result of which

par suite as a result

du coup [informal] as a result *Il s'est disputé avec mon mari et du coup, il ne vient plus nous voir.* He quarrelled with my husband and as a result he no longer visits us.

aboutir {19} *vi* **1** [have a final result, usu good] to come to a conclusion *Les négociations ont abouti.* The negotiations came to a (positive) conclusion. **2** *aboutir à qqch* to end finally in *Leur politique aboutit à la paupérisation des masses.* The ultimate consequence of their policy is the impoverishment of the masses. *Même si tu te plains au maire, tu vas aboutir à quoi?* Even if you take a complaint to the mayor, what do you think the result will be, in the end?

se solder par {6} *v refl* [have as a final result, usu negative] to end up with *Elle a toujours négligé de surveiller les coups de téléphone de sa fille et ça se solde par une facture de 2.000 francs* She never bothered to check on her daughter's telephone calls and she ends up with a phone bill for 2,000 francs.

62 Describing the human body

62.1 *Gros* Fat

gros, grosse *adj* **1** [stresses obesity. Before or after noun] fat *un homme gros* ALSO *un gros homme* a fat man **2** [stresses volume] big *un gros arbre* a tree with a big trunk
gras, grasse *adj* [with surplus fat, but not necessarily as big as **gros**] fat *une petite femme grasse* a chubby little woman
épais, -paisse *adj* [lacking grace. Describes e.g. nose, waist] thick
grosseur *nf* **1** [neutral term] size *une tumeur de la grosseur d'une orange* a tumour as big as an orange **2** [pejorative] fatness
corpulent, e *adj* [both tall and fat] portly
obèse *adj* [excessively fat] obese **obèse** *n* very overweight person

62.2 *Parties du corps grosses* Parts of the body which are fat

corpulence *nf* **1** [neutral, medical or police term] body weight *de corpulence moyenne* of medium build **2** [pejorative] excess weight *Sa corpulence le gêne pour monter les escaliers.* He has trouble going upstairs because he is overweight.
embonpoint *nm* [similar to **corpulence 2**, but describes the overall shape] overweight *Elle prend de l'embonpoint.* She's putting on weight.
bourrelet *nm* roll of fat
culotte *nf* **de cheval** [shape typical of cellulitis at the top of the thighs] saddlebags
brioche *nf* [rather affectionate term] pot-belly

62.3 *Adjectifs affectueux désignant la grosseur* Terms for fatness: affectionate

joufflu, e *adj* chubby-cheeked.
potelé, e *adj* [describes esp babies] chubby
rondouillard, e *adj* [humorous. Describes adults and implies small stature] tubby

62.4 *Termes péjoratifs et insultes désignant la grosseur* Terms for fatness: unflattering

gros lard! ALSO **gros-plein-de-soupe!** fat slob!
mastodonte *nm* [man or woman. Tall, large and ugly] great hulk
patapouf *nm* [male or female child. Clumsy and fat] fatty

62.5 *Devenir gros* To become fat

grossir {19} *vi* to put on weight
engraisser {6} *vi* [used pejoratively of humans and neutrally of animals] to put on weight
prendre des kilos [informal] to put on weight *Tu as pris combien de kilos?* How much (weight) have you put on?
prendre du ventre [informal] to acquire a middle-age spread

62.6 *Maigreur* Thin

maigre *adj* **1** [not bulky or curvy] thin *un gamin maigre* a skinny kid *quelques maigres arbustes* a few scrawny shrubs **2** [not generously served. Describes : e.g. meal] skimpy **3** [watery. Describes: e.g. broth] meagre **4** [containing very little or no fat] fat-free
maigreur *nf* [of person only] thinness

Beware of the false friend *maigre* and 'meagre': *un régime maigre* is not 'a meagre diet' but 'a fat-free diet'.

62.7 *Minceur* Terms for thinness: attractive

mince *adj* slim **minceur** *nf* slimness
mincir {19} *vi* to become slimmer
svelte *adj* slender (and graceful) **sveltesse** *nf* slenderness
fuselé, e *adj* [describes: e.g. fingers, limbs] slim and shapely
élancé, e *adj* [stresses grace, lightness and height] tall and slim
avoir des attaches fines to have a graceful neck, a well-turned ankle and a slender wrist

62.8 *Termes négatifs indiquant la maigreur* Terms for thinness: unflattering

squelettique *adj* skeleton-like
émacié,e *adj* emaciated
efflanqué, e *adj* [showing the ribcage. Describes: e.g. person, horse, cat] scrawny
famélique *adj* [thin and hungry-looking] half-starved
cadavre *nm* **ambulant** walking skeleton
grande perche *nf* ALSO **grand échalas** *nm* beanpole
Elle a le bassin étroit. [always used as a criticism] She doesn't have child-bearing hips.

62.9 *Maigrir* To lose weight

maigrir {19} *vi* to lose weight
régime *nm* **1** [food taken for medical reasons or in order to slim] diet *faire un régime* to be on a diet *se mettre au régime* to go on a diet **2** [eating habits] diet *avoir un régime équilibré* to eat a balanced diet
anorexie *nf* anorexia (nervosa) *faire de l'anorexie* to be anorexic
anorexique *adj* anorexic

Locutions Idioms

n'avoir que la peau et les os ALSO **n'avoir que la peau sur les os** to be all skin and bone

plate comme une planche à pain ALSO **à repasser** [of a woman or a woman's chest] flat as a board

62.10 *Postures* Body positions

position *nf* [way the body and limbs are placed] position

attitude *nf* [position expressing one's feelings] bearing *Elle se tenait devant la tombe, dans une attitude d'accablement.* She stood by the grave, her grief reflected in her bearing.

62.11 *Être ou se mettre debout* Standing up and straightening up

debout *adv* standing *Mets-toi debout.* Stand up. *J'étais debout derrière elle.* I was standing behind her.

se lever {9} *v refl* **1** [from a lying position] to get up **2** [from a sitting or kneeling position] to stand up

se redresser {6} *v refl* **1** [from a reclining to a semi-upright position] to sit up *Il a du mal à se redresser dans son fauteuil à cause de son lumbago.* He has trouble sitting up in his chair because of his lumbago **2** [sit correctly] to sit up straight *Redresse-toi, et ne mets pas tes coudes sur la table.* Sit up straight, and take your elbows off the table. **3** [stand correctly] to straighten up

62.12 *Postures de repos* Resting positions

assis, e *adj* sitting (down) *parmi les personnes assises au premier rang* amongst the people sitting in the front row *Quand l'hymne a retenti, les gens sont restés assis.* When the anthem sounded, people remained seated. *Non, je vous en prie, restez assis!* Please don't get up!

place *nf* **assise 1** [in a vehicle] seat *30 places assises* seating capacity 30 **2** [in an auditorium] seat *Il n'y a plus de places assises.* There is standing room only.

s'asseoir {49} *v refl* **1** [from a standing position] to sit down *Je vous en prie, entrez et asseyez-vous.* Please come in and sit down **2** [from lying down] to sit up *Elle a du mal à s'asseoir toute seule.* She can't really sit up without help.

en tailleur sitting cross-legged

allongé, e *adj* **1** [horizontal] lying down *Commencez le mouvement allongé sur le sol et les genoux repliés.* Start the exercise lying down on the floor with your knees up. **2** [in bed] lying down *Pendant la sieste, les enfants ne dorment pas toujours, mais ils doivent rester allongés.* During their afternoon nap, the children don't always go to sleep but they must be lying down. *Vers la fin de sa maladie, elle passait le plus clair de son temps allongée.* Towards the end of her illness, she spent most of her time lying in bed.

s'allonger {8} *v refl* to lie down *Je vais m'allonger un peu cet après-midi.* I'll go and lie down for a while this afternoon.

> ### usage
>
> *Other positions*
> **sur le dos** on one's back
> **sur le ventre** on one's stomach
> **sur le côté** ALSO **flanc** on one's side
> In French, unlike in English, these phrases do not include a variable personal pronoun: e.g. *Allongez-vous tous sur le dos.* Lie on your backs.

62.13 *Proche du sol* Close to the ground

accroupi, e *adj* squatting

s'accroupir {19} *v refl* to squat (down) *Il s'est accroupi pour parler à l'enfant.* He squatted down to talk to the child.

se tapir {19} *v refl* [used of animals only] to crouch *Le chat se tapit, prêt à bondir.* The cat crouched, ready to pounce.

à genoux [general phrase] on one's knees *se mettre à genoux* to get down on one's knees

agenouillé, e *adj* [in prayer or supplication] kneeling

s'agenouiller {6} *v refl* [in prayer or supplication] to kneel

à quatre pattes on all fours *Tout le monde était à quatre pattes sur le tapis pour l'aider à retrouver son verre de contact.* Everybody was on all fours on the carpet to help him look for his contact lens.

62.14 *Postures inclinées* Bending positions

pencher {6} *vt* **1** [in order to take a better look at, or to listen] to bend *pencher le front* to bow one's head **2** [with whole body] to lean *se pencher par la fenêtre* to lean out of the window *Mettez vos skis à plat et penchez-vous en avant.* Make sure your skis are flat on the ground, and lean forward.

incliner {6} *vt* **1** [as when talking to someone lower in height] *incliner le buste* to lean over **2** *incliner la tête* to bow one's head

s'incliner *v refl* [to pick up an object, to talk to a child, in greeting, acceptance] to bow

voûté, e *adj* **1** [careless posture] slouching *Ne te tiens pas voûté, ce n'est pas bon pour ta colonne.* Don't slouch, it's bad for your spine. **2** [through age or illness] stooping *Il marche un peu voûté depuis qu'il a quatre vingts ans.* He stoops a bit now that he's eighty.

faire une révérence [before royalty, the pope] to curtsey

saluer {6} *vi* [at the end of a show] to bow

faire des courbettes [pejorative] to bow and scrape

62.15 *Anatomie – interne* Human body – internal

os *nm inv* bone *un fragment d'os* a splinter of bone *avoir les os fragiles* to have weak bones

osseux, -sseuse *adj* **1** [of the nature of bone] *les parties osseuses du corps* the bony parts of the body **2** [skinny] skinny *un grand gaillard osseux* a tall skinny fellow

articulation *nf* joint *J'ai mal dans les articulations.* My joints are giving me trouble.

muscle *nm* muscle *les muscles des bras* the arm muscles *avoir des muscles* ALSO *du muscle* to have strong muscles

musculaire *adj* [scientific term] muscle (used as adj) *tissu musculaire* muscle tissue

musculeux, -leuse *adj* [not pejorative. Describes: e.g. person, body] muscular

organe *nm* organ *une greffe d'organe* an organ transplant *organes reproducteurs* reproductive organs

sang *nm* blood *Tu as une égratignure mais il n'y a pas de sang.* You've grazed the skin but it's not bleeding. *donneur de sang* blood donor

veine *nf* vein *On voyait les veines du dos de sa main.* The veins stood out on the back of her hand.

artère *nf* artery *avoir les artères encrassées* to have hardened arteries

nerf *nm* nerve *Le dentiste a touché un nerf.* The dentist touched a nerve.

nerveux, -veuse *adj* nervous, nerve (used as adj) *système nerveux* nervous system *terminaison nerveuse* nerve ending

ADN *nm* [short for *acide désoxyribonucléique*] DNA
noyau *nm* **cellulaire** nucleus
cellule *nf* cell
gène *nm* gene
chromosome *nm* chromosome

62.16 *Le squelette* The skeleton

bassin *nm* pelvis
cage *nf* **thoracique** [in common usage] rib cage
clavicule *nf* [in common usage] collarbone
colonne *nf* **vertébrale** [in common usage] spine
côte *nf* rib
crâne *nm* skull
omoplate *nf* shoulder blade
rotule *nf* kneecap
squelette *nm* skeleton

62.17 *Organes internes* Internal organs

cerveau *nm* brain
cœur *nm* heart
diaphragme *nm* diaphragm
estomac *nm* stomach
foie *nm* liver
pancréas *nm* pancreas
poumon *nm* lung
rate *nf* spleen
rectum *nm* rectum
rein *nm* kidney
trachée(-artère) *nf* [in common usage] trachea
vessie *nf* bladder

---

rein and **rognon** *nm*
A kidney has a different name, depending on whether it is an organ of the human body (*rein*) or the corresponding organ in certain animals used as food (*rognon*).

---

amygdale *nf* tonsil
appendice *nm* appendix
intestin *nm* intestine *intestin grêle* small intestine *gros intestin* large intestine *les intestins* the bowels

62.18 *Le système reproducteur* The reproductive system

see also **38.2 Avoir un bébé** and **64.15 Sexe**
ovaire *nm* ovary
trompe *nf* **de Fallope** Fallopian tube
vagin *nm* vagina
œuf *nm* egg
sperme *nm* [fluid] sperm
spermatozoïde *nm* [term in common use. Cell] sperm

62.19 *Le corps et l'esprit* Mind and body

mental, e *adj*, *mpl* **mentaux** mental *santé mentale* mental health
mentalement *adv* mentally
physique *adj* physical *exercice physique* physical exercise
physiquement *adv* physically *Physiquement il est très en forme.* He's very fit, physically speaking.
corps *nm* body *J'ai des frissons dans tout le corps.* I feel shivery all over.
esprit *nm* mind, head *Il faut que je garde l'esprit clair.* I must remain clear-headed.

Citation Quotation
un esprit sain dans un corps sain [expresses the ideal of physical and mental fitness. A traditional educational precept, sometimes quoted in Latin as: *mens sana in corpore sano*] a healthy mind in a healthy body

62.20 *Couleur des cheveux* Hair colour

noir, e *adj* black
roux, rousse *adj* red-haired
brun, e *adj* brown
châtain *adj inv* light brown, auburn
blond, e *adj* blond *un enfant blond filasse* a flaxen-haired child
poivre et sel *adj inv* [usu of beards] BrE salt and pepper AmE salt and pepper gray
cuivré, e *adj* [describes: e.g. locks, tint, sheen] auburn

62.21 *Geste* Gesture

see also **62.23 Mouvements du corps**
geste *nm* **1** [expressing a feeling or conveying a meaning] gesture *De loin, il fit un geste que je ne compris pas.* From a distance he waved at me but I couldn't understand. *D'un geste de la main, il les a fait taire.* He silenced them with a movement of his hands. *Elle n'a pas eu un geste pour me retenir.* She made no attempt to stop me from going. **2** [movement] move *D'un geste malencontreux, il a envoyé la cruche se briser sur le sol de la cuisine.* In one clumsy move, he sent the jug crashing to the kitchen floor. *Un seul geste et je te descends!* One move and you're dead! *Pas un geste!* Nobody move!
gesticuler {6} *vi* **1** [to attract attention] to wave one's arms about **2** [because one is agitated] to gesticulate

62.22 *Quelques gestes courants* Some common gestures

secouer la tête 1 [for yes] to nod **2** [for no] to shake one's head
montrer qqn du doigt to point at sb
faire un bras d'honneur à qqn [very offensive gesture, involving a clenched fist and the whole of the forearm. The English phrases that follow have an equivalent meaning, but are not an exact translation] BrE to show two fingers to sb AmE to give sb the finger
agiter la main [implies greeting or saying goodbye] to wave
agiter les bras [implies urgent message] to wave one's arms about

62.23 *Mouvements du corps* Movements of the body

see also **63.21 Geste**
bouger {8} *vi* **1** [general term] to move *J'ai vu quelqu'un bouger derrière les buissons.* I saw someone move behind the bushes. *Que personne ne bouge!* Nobody move! **2** [pejorative. Move when one should be still] to fidget *Arrête de bouger sur ta chaise.* Stop fidgeting on your chair.
se mouvoir {44} *v refl* [slightly formal. Stresses relationship of human movement to the space within which it takes place] to move *Les acteurs apprennent à se mouvoir sur scène.* Actors learn to move (about) on stage.

évoluer {6} *vi* [stresses gracefulness of movement] to move around *Les nageurs évoluent ensemble à la surface de l'eau.* The swimmers move (around) together on the surface of the water.
remuer {6} *vi* [move feebly] to move *Le blessé ne remuait plus.* The wounded man had stopped moving.
mouvement *nm* move *faire un mouvement* to move

63 The senses

63.1 *Regarder et voir* To look and to see

see also **66.3 Handicaps**
regarder {6} *vt* and *vi* **1** [purposeful action] to look (at), to watch *Maman, regarde! Regarde les couleurs de l'automne, comme elles sont belles!* Look at the autumn colours, how beautiful they are! *Hier on a regardé une vidéo.* Yesterday we watched a video. **2** [turn one's eyes towards. Not necessarily seeing] to look at *Pendant que j'étais à son chevet, elle me regardait sans me voir.* While I was at her bedside, she was looking at me without really seeing me.

Different ways of looking
English verbs for different ways of looking are often best rendered by *regarder* followed by the appropriate adverb: e.g. to stare *regarder fixement*, to peep *regarder furtivement*, to gawp at sb *regarder qqn bouche bée*.

---

voir {39} *vt* and *vi* to see *Venez voir le château de sable que j'ai fait!* Come and see the sandcastle I built! *Sans le vouloir, je les ai vus s'embrasser.* I accidentally spotted them kissing. *Je ne vois plus sans mes lunettes.* I can't see without my glasses now.
vue *nf* eyesight *avoir une bonne vue* to have good eyesight *Ma vue baisse.* My eyesight's failing.
vision *nf* [scientific term] eyesight *J'ai des troubles de la vision.* I'm having trouble with my eyesight.
œil *nm, pl* **yeux** eye *regarder qqn dans le blanc des yeux* to look someone straight in the eye

63.2 *Regarder ou voir vite* To glance, to scan

---

un coup d'oeil
A quick look or glance is *un coup d'œil*. Different verbs can be used with this phrase, but the meaning is the same, e.g., *J'ai jeté un coup d'œil dans la pièce avant de partir.* I had a quick look around the room before I left. *Donne un coup d'œil à la soupe pour voir si elle bout.* Have a quick look at the soup to see if it's boiling. *Elle a jeté un coup d'œil dans ma direction.* She glanced at me.

---

parcourir {33} *vt* **1** [obj: e.g. page, newspaper] to look through **2** [obj: e.g. contract, draft] to run one's eye over
feuilleter {11} *vt* [obj: e.g. book, notebook, magazine] to leaf through
scruter {6} *vt* [obj: horizon, battlefield] to scan
balayer {16} *vi* **1** [subj: computer, eye] to scan **2** [subj: person] to scrutinize *balayer une pièce/un jardin du regard* to scan a room/garden

63.3 *Regarder soigneusement* To look carefully

examiner {6} *vt* [at length, in detail, often for scientific purposes] to examine
examen *nm* [long and detailed look] examination *À l'examen, on voit des traces de sang sur les vêtements de la victime.* On closer examination, you can find traces of blood on the victim's clothes.
inspecter {6} *vt* [suggests systematic look at an object, usu by a person in authority] to check. *Fais voir tes mains, que j'inspecte tes ongles.* Let me see your hands so I can check your nails. *Ils ont inspecté mes papiers.* They checked my papers (one by one).
vérifier {6} *vt* [look for proof that things are done correctly. Can be quicker than **inspecter**] to check *Vous avez vérifié votre niveau d'huile?* Did you check your oil level?
contrôler {6} *vt* [similar to **vérifier**. Can be detailed or brief] to check
observer {6} *vt* [long and carefully, usu for scientific reasons, through admiration or curiosity] to observe

63.4 *Regarder de façon déplaisante* To look unpleasantly

lorgner {6} *vt* [with sexual desire or greed] to ogle
reluquer {6} *vt* [as **lorgner**, but informal] to leer at
toiser {6} *vt* [from head to toe, in a superior manner] to eye up and down

63.5 *Voir ce qui n'est pas facile à voir* Noticing, glimpsing

découvrir {27} *vt* [be the first to see] to discover *Viens voir le nid d'hirondelles que j'ai découvert sous le toit.* Come and see the swallows' nest which I've discovered under the eaves.
remarquer {6} *vt* [see a telltale sign, something which is amiss or something which others want to hide] to notice *Tu as remarqué comme il a maigri?* Did you notice how thin he's grown?
distinguer {6} *vt* [manage to see things which do not stand out] to pick out *Et avec ces verres-ci, distinguez-vous les lettres de la première ligne?* And with these glasses on, can you pick out the letters in the first line?
apercevoir {38} *vt* [see part of, or see from a distance, or see for a short while] to catch a glimpse of *J'ai aperçu Martin hier, mais je n'ai pas eu le temps de lui parler.* I caught a glimpse of Martin yesterday but I didn't have time to speak to him.
entr'apercevoir {38} *vt* [like **apercevoir**, but suggests greater distance, shorter time] to catch a (very quick) glimpse of *Il y avait tant de monde à l'exposition que j'ai à peine entr'aperçu 'Les Nymphéas'.* The exhibition was so crowded that I barely managed to catch a glimpse of 'Les Nymphéas'.

63.6 *Mouvements des paupières* Blinking and winking

cligner des yeux, ALSO **avoir les yeux qui clignent** [involuntary] to blink
faire un clin d'oeil [deliberate] to wink

63.7 *Vigilance et surveillance* Watching and supervising

Périodes de surveillance Periods during which one keeps watch

garde *nf* **1** [by a soldier] (tour of) guard duty **2** [by a sailor] watch **3** [in medicine] duty *le médecin/pharmacien de garde* the doctor/chemist on duty **4** [after a divorce] custody *avoir la garde des enfants* to have custody of the children

surveillance *nf* **1** [watching so that nothing goes wrong] looking after *Qui assure la surveillance des enfants à partir de 16 heures?* Who looks after the children from 4 p.m. onwards? **2** [at examinations] BrE invigilating AmE monitoring **3** [by police, detectives] surveillance

usage

garde *nmf* and **garde** *nf*
Do not confuse the masculine/feminine term referring to people and the feminine-only word which means a period spent keeping watch.

63.8 *Verbes exprimant différents types de vigilance* Verbs for different kinds of watching

faire attention à [general term] to be on the lookout for *En relisant, faites attention à l'orthographe.* When you read through again, watch out for spelling mistakes.

s'occuper {6} *v refl* (often + *de*) [fulfill the needs of, on a daily basis] to look after *C'est moi qui m'occupe des enfants/plantes/comptes.* I'm the one who looks after the children/plants/accounts.

surveiller {6} *vt* **1** [general term. Implies that remedial or punitive action is expected if things go wrong] to keep an eye on **2** [at examinations] BrE to invigilate AmE to monitor

veiller {6} *vt* (followed by *à* or *sur*). [Implies a desire to protect] to keep an eye on *L'oncle veillait aux intérêts de ses nièces.* The uncle kept an eye on his nieces' interests. *Promets que tu veilleras bien sur notre petite fille pendant mon absence.* Promise that you'll look after our little girl while I'm away.

garder {6} *vt* **1** [ensure that no harm happens to a property] to look after *Pendant leur absence, le jardinier garde la maison.* The gardener looks after the house when they're away. **2** [contrive to retain] to keep *Une fois cette somme versée, ils pourront garder la maison.* Once they've paid that money, they'll be able to keep the house. **3** [retain, voluntarily or not] to keep *Il a gardé tous ses cheveux.* He's kept a full head of hair.

épier {15} *vt* [watch inconspicuously. Pejorative] to spy on

Locution Idiom
Chacun son métier et les vaches seront bien gardées. [popular saying encouraging individualistic behaviour] Each to his own and all will be well.

63.9 *Les gens qui surveillent* People who keep watch

garde *n* [protecting a palace] guard *garde du corps* bodyguard

garde-malade *n, pl* **gardes-malades** [looks after the long-term sick in the patient's home] home nurse

gardien, -dienne *n* **1** [in prison] warden **2** [in park] keeper

surveillant, e *n* **1** [in French schools, someone who keeps order in corridors, at mealtimes and during private study sessions] BrE supervisor AmE monitor **2** [in prison] warder **3** [in industry] overseer

veilleur *nm* **de nuit** night watchman

63.10 *Instruments pour regarder* Things with which to look

lunettes *nf pl* glasses *lunettes de soleil* sunglasses *lunettes à double foyer* bifocals *Elle porte des lunettes.* She wears glasses.

verres *nm pl*, ALSO **lentilles** *nf pl* **de contact** contact lenses

jumelles *nf pl* binoculars

loupe *nf* magnifying glass

63.11 *Ce qu'on voit ou ne voit pas* Vision, visible

spectacle *nm* [anything to see] sight

vue *nf* [landscape, things forming a picture, usu in the distance] view *De ma fenêtre, j'ai vue sur les montagnes.* From my window, I can enjoy a view of the mountains.

vision *nf* [something wonderful, terrible or prophetic to see, usu in the mind's eye] vision *Une ombre qui rôde dans le jardin? Tu as des visions!* A shadow lurking in the garden? You must be seeing things!

visible *adj* obvious *avec une gêne visible* with obvious embarrassment **visiblement** *adv* visibly

invisible *adj* invisible **invisiblement** *adv* invisibly

visibilité *nf* [in a car] visibility *La visibilité est mauvaise, soyez prudents.* Visibility is poor, be careful.

à vue d'œil 1 [measuring with one's eyes, and not with an instrument] approximately *Il y avait à vue d'œil cinq mètres entre la voiture et le passage piéton.* There was a distance of approximately five metres between the car and the pedestrian crossing. **2** [as one looks at it] before one's very eyes *À cette saison, les pois de senteur grandissent à vue d'oeil.* At this season, sweet peas grow before your very eyes.

Locutions Idioms
avoir un œil de lynx [see physical objects clearly] to have eyes like a hawk

Il/Elle n'a pas les yeux dans sa poche. [has good powers of observation. Often implies that one should beware of the person] You can't put anything past him/her.

Il/Elle a l'œil sur . . . [keeps checking in order to make sure nothing goes wrong] He/she's keeping an eye on . . .

Ça saute aux, ALSO **crève les yeux.** [describes someone's jealousy, ambition, etc] It's plain for all to see.

Tu n'as pas les yeux en face des trous! [informal] You can't see what's in front of your face!

63.12 *Couleurs* Colours

rouge *adj* and *nm* red *rouge sang* blood red

jaune *adj* and *nm* yellow *jaune d'or* buttercup yellow

bleu, e *adj* blue *bleu ciel* sky blue *bleu roi* royal blue *bleu marine* navy blue **bleu** *nm* blue

vert, e *adj* green *vert pomme* bright green *vert bouteille* bottle green **vert** *nm* green

rose *adj* and *nm* pink *rose bonbon* chocolate-box pink *rose fluo* fluorescent pink

orange *adj* and *nm* orange

violet, -lette *adj* [this colour is more blue than red] purple
  violet *nm* purple
mauve *adj* and *nm* mauve
beige *adj* and *nm* beige
fauve *adj* tawny
noir, e *adj* black **noir** *nm* black
blanc, blanche *adj* white **blanc** *nm* white
gris, e *adj* grey **gris** *nm* grey
marron *adj inv* brown
orangé, e *adj* orangey-brown

Brown
The most commonly used adjective for referring to the
colour brown is *marron*. The adjective *brun, e* is mostly
used for describing hair, and much more rarely for other
things. So a brown cow is *une vache marron* and brown
eyes are *des yeux marrons*. The nouns are used with the
same restrictions, thus: *Pour peindre les branches, prends
du marron*. To paint the branches, use brown, and *Le
brun que tu as remarqué hier, c'était mon frère*. The
dark-haired man you noticed yesterday was my brother.

63.13 *Décrire les couleurs* To describe colours

criard, e *adj* [pejorative. Too bright or contrasted for
  conventional good taste] gaudy
pâle *adj* [lacking strength of colour] pale
clair, e *adj* [used when a contrast with its opposite, dark, is
  suggested] light
foncé, e *adj* [used when a contrast with its opposite, light,
  is suggested] dark
sombre *adj* [implies gloominess] dark
profond, e *adj* [rich and intense] deep

usage

When an adjective like *pâle*, *clair*, *foncé*, *sombre* or
profond modifies an adjective of colour, the two
adjectives together do not agree with the noun which
they describe. E.g. *des chemises bleu pâle* pale blue
shirts *des yeux vert clair* light green eyes

Locutions Idioms
noir comme de l'encre/du charbon as black as ink/coal
blanc comme neige [stresses purity and light] as white as
snow
blanc comme un linge [stresses pallor of face] as white as
a sheet
blanc comme un cachet d'aspirine [humorous. Not
suntanned] white-skinned

usage

When an adjective of colour is made more specific by
the addition of the name of a coloured object, e.g. *vert
bouteille*, bottle green, they are invariable: e.g. *des
chapeaux vert bouteille* bottle green hats.

When you use the names of various things or animals to
express the colour which they typically are, e.g. *des gants
beurre frais* gloves the colour of fresh butter *des écharpes
pivoine* peony-red scarves *des volets sang-de-boeuf* blood-
red shutters, as happens frequently in fashion contexts, the
colour noun (*beurre*, *pivoine*, *sang*) does not agree.

Modifying and combining colours
When an adjective of colour has the suffix *-âtre*, it
implies a slightly unpleasant shade of the colour
mentioned, for example, *des traces bleuâtres sur la peau*
bluish marks on the skin *un teint jaunâtre* a sallow
complexion
Colour adjectives can be combined, using a hyphen.
These combinations do not agree with the nouns which
they describe, e.g. *des yeux bleu-vert* blue-green eyes *des
robes bleu-gris* blue-grey dresses.

63.14 *Entendre* To hear

see also **66.3 Handicaps**
entendre {53} *vt* and *vi* to hear *être entendu* to be heard
  *On a du mal à se faire entendre quand tous les enfants
  sont dans la pièce*. It's difficult to make oneself heard
  when all the children are in the room.
écouter {6} *vt* [obj: e.g. music, voices, recommendations] to
  listen to *écouter aux portes* to listen at keyholes

---

entendre and **écouter**
The verb **écouter** always implies an intention to catch
the words or sounds, whereas **entendre** can be
accidental: e.g. *Je ne voulais pas vous écouter tous les
deux, mais je vous ai quand même entendus*. I didn't
intentionally listen to you two, but I nevertheless heard
what you said.

---

auditeur, -trice *n* listener
auditoire *nm* audience
ouïe *nf* hearing *Il a l'ouïe très fine*. He has an acute sense
  of hearing.
oreille *nf* **1** [in music] good ear for music *Je n'ai jamais su
  chanter car je n'ai pas d'oreille*. I never could sing because
  I haven't got a good ear for music. **2** [when learning
  foreign languages] good ear for languages *Il a appris
  l'arabe en le parlant, ça prouve qu'il a une bonne oreille*.
  He learned Arabic by speaking it, which proves he has a
  good ear for languages.
à l'oreille in the ear *Viens me le dire à l'oreille*. Come and
  whisper it in my ear.
dresser l'oreille to prick up one's ears

Locutions Idioms
Ce qu'il faut pas entendre! [in very informal speech
only] The things you hear!
Il vaut mieux entendre ça que d'être sourd! [informal
and always ironic. Implies that the thing which has just
been said is absurd] Well, I couldn't have lived without
that piece of information!
ouvrir toutes grandes ses oreilles to listen very carefully
Ça entre par une oreille et ça ressort par l'autre.
[informal] It goes in one ear and out the other.
mettre la puce à l'oreille à qqn [give sb a hint that
something is going on which others are trying to keep
secret] to enable sb to catch on *Ce qui m'a mis la puce à
l'oreille, c'est quand il a commencé à m'éviter dans la rue*.
I began to think something must be going on when he
started avoiding me in the street.

63.15 *Les choses que l'on entend* Things you hear

bruit *nm* [neutral to unpleasant. Usu unpleasant when used with *le* or *du*] noise *La nuit, on entend des bruits dans la maison.* At night you can hear strange sounds in the house. *une maison où il y a du bruit* a noisy house
son *nm* [in general usage, also scientific and musical. Usu neither pleasant nor unpleasant] sound
ton *nm* **1** [feelings carried by the voice. Usu unpleasant] tone (of voice). *Ne me parle pas sur ce ton!* Don't use that tone (of voice) with me! **2** [in music] tone *demi-ton* semitone
vacarme *nm* [pejorative. Usu caused by people or animals in large numbers] racket
tapage *nm* [pejorative. Caused by people] racket *tapage nocturne* disturbing the peace at night

63.16 *Bruit* Noise

see also **14.7 Bruits d' animaux**
bruyant, e *adj* [describes: e.g. child, airport, engine] noisy
bruyamment *adv* noisily
assourdissant, e *adj* deafening
audible *adj* [describes: e.g. sigh, clock ticking, distant sound] audible *à peine audible* ALSO *tout juste audible* barely perceptible

63.17 *Bruits et choses bruyantes* Ways of making noises

cloche *nf* bell
corne *nf* **de brume** fog horn
sirène *nf* **1** [in factory, for fire-drill] alarm bell **2** [on police car] siren
boum *nm* bang *Il a allumé l'allumette et ça a fait boum!* He lit the match and it went bang!
patatras *nm* crash *Et patatras! la pile de livres est tombée.* The whole pile of books went down with a crash.
sifflet *nm* whistle *siffler dans un sifflet* to blow a whistle
siffler {6} *vt* and *vi* to whistle
sonner {6} *vt* and *vi* to ring
sonnerie *nf* **1** [noise caused by: e.g. alarm bell, telephone] ring(ing) **2** [of door] doorbell **3** [in school] bell

63.18 *Amplifier les bruits* To make noises louder

haut-parleur *nm, pl* **haut-parleurs 1** [for listening to music] (loud)speaker **2** [used: e.g. by police] BrE loudhailer AmE megaphone
baffle *nm* [in stereophonic equipment] (loud)speaker
micro *nm* [informal] mike
ampli *nm* ALSO **amplificateur** *nm* amplifier
amplifier {6} *vt* to amplify

63.19 *Utiliser la voix* Ways of using the voice

élever la voix [for practical reasons or in anger, or rebuke] to raise one's voice
hausser le ton [in anger] to raise one's voice (in anger)
à portée de voix within earshot
à voix haute ALSO **à haute voix** [not in one's head or whispering] aloud *lire un poème à voix haute* to read a poem aloud

tout haut [not in secret] aloud *dire tout haut ce que les autres pensent tout bas* to say out loud what others merely think
à haute et intelligible voix [often slightly humorous] loud and clear
voix de crécelle high-pitched voice
voix de stentor booming voice

Locutions Idioms
On ne s'entend pas ici! You can't hear yourself think around here!
casser la tête ALSO **les oreilles à qqn** to give sb a headache *Tu me casses les oreilles!* You're giving me a headache
crever les tympans à qqn to deafen sb

63.20 *Silence* Silence

silence *nm* **1** [fact of there being no noise] silence *le silence de la tombe* the silence of the grave **2** [interval between noises] silence *Il y a eu un silence, puis il a répondu.* There was a silence, then he answered.
silencieux, -cieuse *adj* **1** [where there is no noise] quiet *Au petit matin, les rues sont enfin silencieuses.* In the early hours, the streets are quiet at last. **2** [not using the voice] silent *la majorité silencieuse* the silent majority *rester silencieux* to remain silent
silencieusement *adv* silently
en silence 1 [with no noise] silently *Le groupe marchait derrière le corbillard en silence.* The group walked behind the hearse in silence. **2** [with little noise] quietly *Entrez deux par deux et en silence!* Go in two by two and quietly!
muet, muette *adj* **1** [unable to speak] dumb **2** [refusing to or refraining from speaking] silent **3** [describes: cinema, film] silent
inaudible *adj* inaudible
calme *adj* [describes: e.g. street, village, child,] quiet
calme *nm* peace and quiet *manifester dans le calme* to carry out a peaceful demonstration
paix *nf* [absence of noise and agitation] peace (and quiet) *Une fois Tante Clara partie, la paix revint dans la maison.* With Aunt Clara gone, peace and quiet returned to the house. *Hé, vous là-bas, la paix!* Hey, you over there, shut up! *Il ferait n'importe quoi pour avoir la paix.* He'd do anything for a quiet life. *Maintenant, la paix!* Quiet now!
se taire {63} *v refl* **1** [refrain from talking] to be silent *Tais-toi!* Be quiet! **2** [refrain from making revelations] to keep quiet (about something)

Utiliser la voix sans bruit Ways of using the voice quietly
tout bas [deliberate, through discretion or secretiveness] very quietly
entre ses dents [to stop people hearing what you say while making it plain that you're criticizing] under one's breath

Locutions Idioms
Il/Elle n'a pas desserré les dents. He/she never uttered a word.
On aurait entendu une mouche voler. You could have heard a pin drop.
à pas de loup (treading) softly
faire des messes basses [pejorative. Whisper conspiratorially] *Dites donc, vous deux, qu'est-ce que c'est que ces messes basses?* What are you two muttering about?
Tu as a avalé ta langue? Cat got your tongue?
Motus et bouche cousue! [informal and humorous] Mum's the word!

63.21 *Rendre les choses ou les gens silencieux* Silencing people

faire taire qqn 1 [stop a person talking] to make sb be quiet **2** [stop a person making revelations] to shut sb up
bâillonner {6} *vt* [obj: e.g. press, media, newspaper] to gag
étouffer {6} *vt* to muffle *On entendait des conversations étouffées.* You could hear the sound of muffled conversations.
chut *interj* hush

Citation Quotation
Le silence éternel de ces espaces infinis m'effraie. [Pascal expressing his awe in the face of the unknown universe, in his *Pensées*, first published in 1670] The eternal silence of these infinite spaces terrifies me.

63.22 *Toucher* To touch

toucher {6} *vt* **1** [receive a sensation] to feel *Touche son front, tu ne penses pas qu'il a de la fièvre?* Feel his forehead, don't you think he's got a temperature? **2** [deliberate or not. Make contact] to touch *Le philodendron va finir par toucher le plafond.* The philodendron will soon be touching the ceiling.
au toucher to the touch *Laisser reposer la pâte jusqu'à ce qu'elle soit ferme au toucher.* Allow the pastry to rest until it's firm to the touch.
tâter {6} *vt* [deliberate, to determine what the object touched is, or what state it is in] to feel *Quand j'achète des poires j'aime les tâter pour voir si elles ne sont pas trop mûres.* When I buy pears I like to feel them to make sure they're not overripe.
à tâtons [touching things to find one's way] by feel *Les pompiers avançaient à tâtons, tant la fumée était épaisse.* The firefighters had to feel their way forward, so thick was the smoke.
palper {6} *vt* [same meaning as **tâter**, but used in medical contexts] to palpate
effleurer {6} *vt* [lightly touch the surface of] to touch lightly upon *effleurer une page avec un pinceau* to touch a page lightly with a paintbrush
manier {6} *vt* [hold and use. Obj esp hand-held mechanical object or tool] to handle *un aspirateur facile à manier* an easy-to-handle vacuum cleaner
manipuler {6} *vt* [use all the moving parts of. Obj: complex mechanical object] to handle *Je n'arrive pas à manipuler cette poussette.* I can't steer this pushchair.

Toucher affectueusement To touch with affection
caresser {6} *vt* [gentle, loving. Obj: e.g. child, lover, animal] to fondle
flatter {6} *vt* [used with animals only, except for idiom below] to stroke
tripoter {6} *vt* [pejorative. Implies unwelcome sexual touch] to paw *Arrêtez de me tripoter!* Stop pawing me!
chatouiller {6} *vt* to tickle

Locution Idiom
flatter qqn dans le sens du poil [informal] to butter sb up

Toucher avec vigueur To touch with some force
appuyer {17} *vi* (+ *sur*) [apply pressure, usu to trigger a mechanism] *appuyer sur* to press *appuyer sur l'interphone* to press the intercom button *appuyer sur une pédale de piano* to press down a piano pedal
masser {6} *vt* [obj: e.g. person, thigh, neck] to massage
pétrir {19} *vt* [obj: e.g. putty, dough] to knead

63.23 *Mou* Soft

doux, douce *adj* **1** [pleasant to touch] soft *Le mohair est doux au toucher.* Mohair is soft to the touch. **2** [even to the touch] smooth *doux comme une peau de bébé* smooth as a baby's skin
mou, molle *adj* **1** [lacking firmness] soft *Les carottes sont toutes molles.* The carrots have gone soft. *un matelas mou* a soft mattress **2** [lacking firmness and unpleasant] limp *une poignée de main molle* a limp handshake

ramolli, e *adj* [more pejorative than **mou**. No longer fresh] stale and limp *une baguette ramollie* a stale and limp baguette
tendre *adj* [which can be bitten into easily] tender *du boeuf tendre* tender beef *des petites pousses tendres* tender little shoots
adoucisseur *nm* **(d'eau)** water softener

63.24 *Pliable* Easily bent

flexible *adj* [describes hard materials with some give in them] flexible *un rétroviseur sur tige flexible* a side-view mirror on a flexible mount
souple *adj* [describes: e.g. leather, wrist] supple

pliable and **pliant, e**
Pliable describes the quality of a substance such as plastic, whereas *pliant, e* refers to objects which are collapsible and may be folded, such as a stool or a baby buggy.

63.25 *Rigide* Hard

dur, e *adj* **1** [solid. Used appreciatively or pejoratively] hard *Le beurre est trop dur pour faire des tartines.* The butter is to hard to spread on the bread. *un muscle bien dur* a nice hard muscle **2** [pejorative. Describes: e.g. meat, bread] tough
ferme *adj* [said appreciatively of an object which doesn't have too much give] firm *des seins fermes* firm breasts

Locution Idiom
dur comme du bois ALSO **comme la pierre** as hard as a rock

63.26 *Qui ne plie pas* Unbending

rigide *adj* [which cannot bend. Often describes character trait] fixed *miroir monté sur tige rigide* mirror mounted on a fixed stem *un esprit rigide* an unbending cast of mind
raide *adj* [with no movement in the joints] stiff *Après l'accident, j'ai longtemps gardé le genou raide.* For a long time after the accident my knee stayed stiff.

Citation Quotation
Je plie mais ne romps pas. [in the fable by La Fontaine entitled *Le chêne et le roseau*, 'The Oak and the Reed', this is the reed's proud claim to being a survivor, owing to its talent for adapting to situations, whereas the oak is unbending and is blown down in a gale] I bend but I don't break.

63.27 *Rugueux* Rough to the touch

rugueux, -gueuse *adj* [with wrinkles on its surface] rough to the touch *L'écorce du vieil arbre est rugueuse.* The bark of the old tree is rough to the touch.

râpeux, -peuse *adj* [less uneven than **rugueux**] slightly rough to the touch *La langue du chat est râpeuse.* The cat's tongue is slightly rough to the touch.

grossier, -ssière *adj* [lacking refinement] coarse *une étoffe grossière* a coarse weave

irrégulier, -lière *adj* [which does not have a straight surface or edge] uneven *Attention, le sol est irrégulier!* Watch out, the ground is uneven!

grumeleux, -leuse *adj* [describes: e.g.: sauce] lumpy

bosselé, e *adj* [describes: e.g. pillow, hat] lumpy

cranté, e *adj* [describes: e.g. blade, edge] serrated

63.28 *Lisse* Smooth

lisse *adj* [pleasant to the touch or the eye. Describes esp skin, leather, water surface] smooth

uni, e *adj* [describes esp liquid surfaces] smooth

plat, e *adj* [in geometry, also common usage] flat

plan, e *adj* [in geometry only] flat

63.29 *Lisser* To make smooth

lisser {6} *vt* to smooth out

aplatir {19} *vt* [by pressing down. Obj: esp creased or rough-surfaced objects] to flatten out

aplanir {19} *vt* **1** [obj: e.g. rough plank] to plane . . . flat **2** [obj: e.g. uneven ground] to level out

63.30 *Odeurs* Smells

odeur *nf* [general term] smell *une odeur de caramel* a smell of caramel *une bonne odeur* a nice smell *une mauvaise odeur* a bad smell

odorat *nm* sense of smell *J'ai un bon odorat.* I have a good sense of smell.

sentir {25} **1** *vt* to smell *Je sens une odeur de brûlé.* I smell something burning. *La pièce sent le renfermé.* The room smells musty. **2** *vi* [pejorative and informal] to smell *Ça sent, dans le panier du chat!* The cat's basket smells.

puer {6} **1** *vt* [informal] to stink *Ça pue les chaussettes sales.* It stinks of dirty socks. **2** *vi* [informal] to stink

puanteur *nf* stink

avoir du nez 1 [subj: person] to have a good sense of smell **2** [subj: wine] to have a good nose

flairer {6} *vt* [smell by putting one's nose close to the object. Subj: esp dogs] to sniff

humer {6} *vt* [smell with relish or professional interest] to sniff *Un connaisseur hume le vin longuement dans le verre avant de le goûter.* Connoisseurs spend a long time sniffing the wine in their glass before they taste it.

renifler {6} *vt* and *vi* [noisily, because of crying, or in order to detect a smell] to sniff

63.31 *Types d'odeurs* Types of smell

parfum *nm* [sold in bottles or coming off a flower] perfume

arôme *nm* [pleasant smell of flower, cheese, wine, casserole] smell

effluve *nf* [good or bad smell coming from a place slightly distant] smell *Les effluves des jasmins du jardin*

parvenaient jusque dans nos chambres. The smell of the jasmines wafted up from the garden into our bedrooms.

miasme *nm* [bad smell, usu of decomposing matter] stench

Locutions Idioms

Ça ne sent pas la rose ALSO **violette!** [euphemism for a bad smell] It smells a bit strong!

L'argent n'a pas d'odeur. [money acquired disreputably is as good as any] Money is money, no matter where it comes from.

64 Anatomy and physiology

64.1 *Anatomie – externe* Anatomy – external

aile *nf* **du nez** nostril
aisselle *nf* armpit
barbe *nf* beard
bouche *nf* mouth
bras *nm* arm
cheveu *nm, pl* **-x** hair *mes cheveux* my hair
cheville *nf* ankle
cil *nm* eyelash
cou *nm* neck
cou-de-pied *nm, pl* **cous-de-pied** instep
coude *nm* elbow
cuisse *nf* thigh
doigt *nm* finger
dos *nm* back
épaule *nf* shoulder
fesse *nf* buttock
front *nm* forehead
genou *nm, pl* **-x** knee
globe *nm* **oculaire** eyeball
hanche *nf* hip
jambe *nf* leg
joue *nf* cheek
lèvre *nf* lip
lobe *nm* **(de l'oreille)** earlobe
mâchoire *nf* jaw
main *nf* hand
mamelon *nm* nipple
menton *nm* chin
moustache *nf* moustache
nez *nm* nose
nombril *nm* navel
nuque *nf* back of the neck
œil *nm, pl* **yeux** eye
ongle *nm* fingernail
ongle *nm* **de pied** toenail
oreille *nf* ear
orteil *nm* toe
parties *nf pl* **génitales** genitals
paume *nf* **(de la main)** palm
paupière *nf* eyelid
pénis *nm* penis
pied *nm* foot
plante *nf* **du pied** sole
poignet *nm* wrist
poil *nm pl* **(pubien)** (pubic) hair
poing *nm* fist
poitrine *nf* chest
pouce *nm* thumb
pupille *nf* pupil
sein *nm* breast

sourcil *nm* eyebrow
taille *nf* waist
talon *nm* heel
testicule *nm* testicle
tête *nf* head
tibia *nm* shin
ventre *nm* stomach
visage *nm* face
vulve *nf* vulva

sihouette *nf* [shape of body, esp in terms of attractiveness] figure *Retrouvez la silhouette de vos vingt ans.* Get back the figure you had at twenty.
carrure *nf* [body in terms of size and strength and breadth of shoulders, esp man's] build
gabarit *nm* [body size and bulk. Not pejorative] build *Son frère, c'est un grand gabarit.* His brother is of a large build.
membre *nm* limb
traits *nm pl* features *de traits fins* delicate features

---

sourcil *nm* and **arcade** *nf* **sourcilière**
Whilst *sourcil* refers specifically to the eyebrow hairs, and the eyebrows themselves, the phrase *arcade sourcilière* is used in everyday language to refer to the flesh and bone behind the eyebrow, the arch on which the eyebrow hairs grow. Thus if someone is injured on that part of the face it could be said, e.g. *Il s'est ouvert l'arcade sourcilière.* He's cut his eyebrow.

64.2 *À l'intérieur de la bouche* Inside the mouth

see also **65.4 Dentiste**
langue *nf* tongue
gencive *nf* gum
salive *nf* saliva

64.3 *La peau* Skin

peau *nf, pl* **-x** skin
teint *nm* complexion
grain *nm* **de beauté** beauty spot
tache *nf* **de vin** strawberry birthmark
pore *nm* pore
sueur *nf*, ALSO **transpiration** *nf* sweat *être en sueur* to be sweating
suer {6} *vi* to sweat
bouton *nm* pimple
point *nm* **noir** blackhead
bleu *nm* bruise

64.4 *Respiration* Breathing

respiration *nf* breathing *reprendre sa respiration* to catch one's breath *retenir sa respiration* ALSO *son souffle* to hold one's breath
respirer {6} *vt and vi* 1 [physiological process] to breathe (in and out) *Une fois sorti de la ville, enfin, on respire!* Once you get out of the city, you can breathe freely at last! 2 [sign of relief] to breathe again *Le locataire est enfin parti, on respire!* The tenant has moved out at last, phew, what a relief!
inspirer {6} *vt* and *vi* to breathe in *Inspirez . . . , expirez!* Breathe in . . . and out!
expirer {6} **1** *vt* and *vi.* [in sport] to breathe out **2** *vi* [When dying] to expire

aspirer {6} *vt* [when smoking] to inhale
haleine *nf* breath

Respiration forte ou difficile Breathing forcefully or with effort
haleter {12} *vi* [short shallow breaths, caused by, e.g. heat] to pant
siffler {6} *vi* to wheeze
souffler {6} *vi* [breathe noisily, because of, e.g. illness, effort] to pant *souffler comme un phoque* to pant heavily
être à bout de souffle [breathless and exhausted] to be out of breath
avoir le souffle court ALSO **l'haleine courte** [audibly breathless. Could be due to illness] to be short of breath
irrespirable *adj* **1** [polluted. Describes: esp city air, air in heatwave] unbreathable **2** [unpleasant. Describes: esp ambience] oppressive *Je suis arrivée en pleine scène de ménage, l'air était irrespirable.* I arrived just as they were in the middle of a domestic row, you could have cut the atmosphere with a knife.

64.5 *Bonne mémoire* Good memory

see also **64.6 Mauvaise mémoire**
mémoire *nf* [capacity for remembering] memory *avoir bonne mémoire* to have a good memory *Quelle est la capacité de mémoire de ton nouvel ordinateur?* What size memory does your new computer have?
se souvenir {23} *v refl* (+ *de*) to remember *Je me souviens de leur mariage.* I remember their marriage. *se souvenir de qqch comme si c'était hier* to remember something as if it was yesterday
souvenir *nm* **1** [thought about a past experience] memory *J'ai un souvenir de mon père, jeune, au volant de notre toute première voiture.* I have a memory of my father as a young man at the wheel of our very first car. **2** [object] souvenir *acheter des souvenirs en vacances* to buy souvenirs while on holiday
rappeler {11} *vt* **1** (+ *à*) [jog the the memory of] to remind *Peux-tu me rappeler l'adresse de Julia?* Could you remind me of Julia's address? *Je lui ai rappelé la date de notre rendez-vous.* I reminded her of the date of our appointment. *Rappelle à Lisa qu'elle doit payer sa cotisation.* Remind Lisa that she has to pay her subscription. **2** [bring to mind] to be evocative of *un paysage qui rappelle la Toscane* a landscape that is reminiscent of Tuscany. *Elle me rappelle sa mère.* She reminds me of her mother.
se rappeler *v refl* to remember *Tu te rappelles la semaine que nous avons passée à Vérone?* Do you remember the week we spent in Verona?

u s a g e

The difference between **se souvenir** and **se rappeler**
The meaning of these two verbs is the same, but the difference is in the construction. *Se souvenir* is followed by *de* whereas *se rappeler* is followed by a direct object.
Using **se rappeler**
When reminding someone of a fact, it is possible to use either *rappeler à quelqu'un* and direct object, as in the examples above, or rappeler à qqn que, e.g., *La veille de la réunion, téléphonez à ma secrétaire et rappelez-lui que vous serez présent.* Ring my secretary the day before the meeting and remind her that you'll be attending. When reminding someone of something they have to do, the French structure is something like, e.g., *Je te rappelle que tu dois réserver les billets pour demain.* May I remind you that you have to book the tickets for tomorrow? *Rappelle-moi qu'il faut que je vérifie le niveau d'huile.* Remind me to check the oil.

Ça me revient. It's coming back to me.
se remémorer {6} *v refl* [formal. Obj: esp event from the distant past, historical fact] to remember

Locution Idiom
Il/elle a une mémoire d'éléphant. He/she never forgets a thing.

64.6 *Mauvaise mémoire* Poor memory

see also **64.5 Bonne mémoire**
avoir mauvaise mémoire to have a poor memory
oublier {15} *vt* **1** [obj: e.g. fact, idea, date, lover] to forget *Je ne t'oublierai jamais.* I'll never forget you. **2** [obj: e.g. book, gloves, key] to leave (behind) *N'oublie pas tes affaires.* Don't forget to pick up your things.
oubli *nm* **1** [fact of not remembering] forgetfulness *un auteur tombé dans l'oubli* a now forgotten author **2** [instance of forgetfulness] omission *Je n'avais pas l'intention de le snober, si son nom n'est pas sur la liste c'est un simple oubli.* I didn't mean to snub him, it was only through an omission that his name was left off the list.
oublieux, -lieuse *adj* [rather formal] forgetful
distrait, e *adj* absent-minded
amnésique *adj* amnesic **amnésique** *n* person who suffers from amnesia
oubliettes *nf pl* [an underground or secret prison in a castle, etc] dungeon *Finalement, le projet est tombé aux oubliettes.* In the end, the project was buried.

Locutions Idioms
Ça m'est sorti de l'esprit. It just went out of my mind.
avoir la tête comme une passoire to have a mind like a sieve
être tête en l'air [affectionate criticism] to be a scatterbrain
loin des yeux, loin du cœur out of sight, out of mind
être dans la lune to be in a dream (world)
avoir un mot sur le bout de la langue to have a word on the tip of one's tongue

64.7 *Sommeil* Sleep

sommeil *nm* **1** [state of not being awake] sleep *J'ai le sommeil lourd/léger.* I'm a heavy/light sleeper. **2** [feeling of drowsiness] sleepiness *avoir sommeil* to feel sleepy
dormir {32} *vi* to sleep *J'ai bien dormi.* I slept soundly. *Il a mal dormi la nuit dernière.* He didn't sleep well last night. *avoir envie de dormir* to feel sleepy
dodo *nm* [baby language] bye-byes *Fais dodo.* Go to bye-byes.

64.8 *S'endormir* To fall asleep

endormir {32} *vt* [cause to become drowsy] to send to sleep *endormir un enfant en le berçant* to rock a child to sleep. *Faire mes comptes, ça m'endort.* I fall asleep when I do my accounts.
s'endormir *v refl* to fall asleep *Elle s'est endormie.* She fell asleep.
endormi, e *adj* asleep

Locutions Idioms
dormir comme un loir [*loir*, a dormouse is commonly thought of as a very sleepy animal] to sleep like a top
dormir comme un sonneur [The comparison with a *sonneur*, a bell-ringer, is based on the belief that bell-

ringers' hearing was damaged and therefore that nothing could wake them when they slept] to sleep like a top
Le marchand de sable est passé. [to children] The sandman's coming.
faire la grasse matinée to sleep in
Il/Elle ne tient plus debout. He/She is fit to drop.

64.9 *Manifestations du sommeil* Behaviour associated with sleep

ronfler {6} *vi* to snore
rêver {6} *vi* (often + *de*) to dream *J'ai rêvé de toi.* I dreamt about you. *J'ai rêvé que je volais.* I dreamt I was flying.
rêve *nm* dream *faire un rêve* to dream
bâiller {6} *vi* to yawn
être à moitié endormi to be half asleep
s'étirer {6} *v refl* to stretch
sieste *nf* afternoon nap *faire la sieste* to have an afternoon nap

64.10 *Fatigue* Tiredness

fatigue *nf* tiredness *La fatigue le gagne.* He's getting tired.
fatigué, e *adj* tired
fatigant, e *adj* tiring
fatiguer {6} *vt* to tire *Ne fatigue pas ta grand-mère, elle n'est pas bien.* Don't tire your grandmother, she's not well.
se fatiguer *v refl* to get tired *Je me fatigue vite depuis ma grippe.* Since I had the flu, I get tired quickly.
épuisement *nm* [being drained of physical or mental resources] exhaustion
épuisé, e *adj* exhausted
épuisant, e *adj* exhausting
épuiser {6} *vt* to exhaust
s'épuiser *v refl* to become exhausted
claqué, e *adj* [informal. Physically very tired] shattered
crevé, e *adj* [very informal. Often used as an exaggeration for tired] BrE knackered AmE bushed

64.11 *Sommeil troublé* Disturbed sleep

cauchemar *nm* nightmare *faire un cauchemar* to have a nightmare
somnambulisme *nm* sleepwalking
insomnie *nf* insomnia
nuit *nf* **blanche** sleepless night *passer une nuit blanche* to have a sleepless night

64.12 *Après le sommeil* After sleep

réveiller {6} *vt* to wake *Ne réveille pas le bébé.* Don't wake the baby. *être bien réveillé* to be wide awake **être mal réveillé (e)** to be half awake
se réveiller *v refl* to wake up *À quelle heure est-ce que tu te réveilles d'habitude?* What time do you normally wake up?
s'éveiller {6} *v refl* [more literary than **se réveiller**] to wake up *La reine venait de s'éveiller lorsque des gardes firent irruption dans sa chambre.* The queen had just woken up when guards burst into her bedroom.

Locutions Idioms
Il ne faut pas réveiller le chat qui dort. Let sleeping dogs lie.
faire un bruit à réveiller les morts to make a noise loud enough to wake the dead

64.13 *Repos et détente* Rest and relaxation

see also 81.1 Loisirs

repos *nm* [lack or lessening of activities] rest *Le chirurgien a un weekend de repos sur trois.* The surgeon has one weekend off in three.

relaxation *nf* **1** [any activity which one doesn't associate with worries. More physical than **détente**] relaxing activity *Tricoter me sert de relaxation.* I find knitting relaxing. **2** [technique for relaxing] relaxation *Elle fait du tai chi pour apprendre la relaxation.* She does tai chi to learn relaxation.

se relaxer {6} *v refl* to relax

se reposer {6} *v refl* [more physical than **se détendre**] to rest *se reposer un peu* to have a little rest *Je me suis bien reposé.* I had a proper rest.

détente *nf* [physical and mental state] relaxing *Il a besoin de détente.* He needs to relax.

se détendre {53} *v refl* [physical and mental] to relax *Le soir j'aime bien me détendre en regardant la télévision.* In the evening I like to relax in front of the television.

décompresser {6} *vi* [get rid of pressure] to unwind *Quand je vais à la campagne, je décompresse.* When I go to the countryside, I unwind.

64.14 *Moment de repos* Time for resting

pause *nf* [short, between two daytime activities] break *faire une pause* to (have a) break *On fait une pause pour le déjeuner?* Shall we break for lunch?

pause-café *nf, pl* **pauses-café** coffee break

halte *nf* [stopping, usu in the middle of shopping or on a trip] break *faire une halte* to (have a) break *Nous avons fait une halte au salon de thé de la rue principale.* We stopped for a break at the tea-rooms in the main street.

halte-garderie *nf, pl* **haltes-garderies** [where parents can drop children off for usu a maximum of two hours while they go shopping] BrE crèche

récréation *nf* [at school] break *Les enfants ont deux récréations chaque jour, une le matin et une l'après-midi.* The children have a morning break and an afternoon break every day.

distraction *nf* **1** [something to do which allows one to forget a worry for the time being] break *Laisse tes révisions et va m'acheter du pain, ça te fera une distraction.* Put your revision work on one side and go and buy some bread for me, that'll be a break for you. **2** [permanent] pastime *La lecture est sa plus grande distraction.* Her main pastime is reading.

congé *nm* [rest from work] time off *Le médecin m'a donné un congé (de maladie) de trois jours.* The doctor said I must take three days off work. *Pour Pâques, on a deux jours de congé.* We have two days off work for Easter. *congé sabbatique* sabbatical leave

arrêter {6} *vt* [informal. Subj: e.g. doctor] to give time off work to *Le docteur m'a arrêtée pendant une semaine.* The doctor gave me a week off work.

Vacances Holidays

vacances *nf pl* holiday(s) *être en vacances* BrE to be on holiday AmE to be on vacation *partir en vacances* to go on holiday *Où as-tu passé tes vacances?* Where did you spend your holidays? *Vous avez passé de bonnes vacances?* Did you have a good holiday?

congés *nm pl* [holiday entitlement] (paid) holidays *Tu as combien de congés dans ton nouveau poste?* How much holiday do you get in your new job?

vacancier, -cière *n* BrE holidaymaker AmE vacationer

64.15 *Sexe* Sex

sexe *nm* **1** [gender] sex *Les patients des deux sexes attendent dans la même salle d'attente.* Both sexes use the same waiting room. **2** [organ] sex **3** [sexual activity in general] sex *À cet âge-là, ils commencent à s'intéresser au sexe.* At that age they start getting interested in sex.

sexuel, -xuelle *adj* **1** [to do with gender] sexual *la différentiation sexuelle chez les oiseaux* sexual differentiation in birds **2** [to do with sex life] sexual *le harcèlement sexuel* sexual harassment **sexuellement** *adv* sexually

64.16 *Sexy* Sexy

sexy *adj inv* [Describes: e.g. clothes, smile, person] sexy

érotique *adj* [sexually arousing but respectable. Describes: e.g. pose, literature, painting] erotic

pornographique *adj* [pejorative] pornographic

porno *adj* and *nm* [slang. Same meaning as **pornographique**] porn

cochon, -chonne *adj* [informal. Pejorative and sometimes humorous. Describes: e.g. language, picture, scene] smutty

64.17 *Rapports sexuels* Sexual intercourse

rapports *nm pl* (**sexuels** ALSO **intimes**) [slightly formal. Used in e.g. doctor-patient dialogue] sexual intercourse *Quand avez-vous eu des rapports pour la dernière fois?* When did you last have sexual intercourse?

acte *nm* **sexuel** [same usage and meaning as **rapports**, but more restricted to penetration] sexual act

vierge *adj* [applies to both sexes] virgin *Il/Elle était encore vierge.* He/She was still a virgin. **vierge** *nf* [female only] virgin

pucelle *nf* [old-fashioned term for female virgin] virgin

puceau *nm, pl* **-x** [old-fashioned term for male virgin] virgin

virginité *nf* [neutral term] virginity

Common euphemisms which retain some power to shock
faire l'amour to make love *faire l'amour avec qqn* to make love with sb *faire l'amour à qqn* to make love to sb

coucher {6} *vi* to sleep *coucher avec qqn* to sleep with sb *Ils ont couché ensemble.* They have slept together.

baiser {6} *vi* [slang but very commonly used] to screw

sauter {6} *vt* [slang. Implies that the man takes the initiative. Disrespectful to women] to lay

copuler {6} *vi* ALSO **s'accoupler** {6} *v refl* [often used of animals. Very pejorative when referring to people] to copulate

forniquer {6} *vi* [religious overtones. Very pejorative] to fornicate

se reproduire {82} *v refl* [biological term. Subj: humans, animals] to breed

procréer {6} *vt* [slightly formal term, used in sociological contexts] to procreate *L'humanité est animée par le désir de procréer.* Mankind is motivated by the desire to procreate.

64.18 *Pendant l'acte sexuel* During the sexual act

prélude *nm*, ALSO **préliminaires** *nm pl* foreplay
éjaculer {6} *vt* to ejaculate
orgasme *nm* orgasm *avoir un orgasme* to have an orgasm *jusqu'à l'orgasme* to orgasm
jouir {19} *vi* [in erotic or pornographic contexts] to come
érection *nf* [neutral term, used e.g. in doctor-patient dialogue] erection
bander {6} *vi* [slang. Have an erection] to have a hard-on

64.19 *Crimes de sexe* Crimes involving sex

viol *nm* rape **violer** {6} *vt* to rape
abus *nm* **sexuel** sexual abuse *victime d'abus sexuel* victim of sexual abuse
abuser de qqn to abuse sb sexually
inceste *nm* incest *commettre un incest* to commit incest
incestueux, -tueuse *adj* incestuous

64.20 *Prostitution* Prostitution

prostituée *nf* (female) prostitute
prostitué *nm* (male) prostitute
putain *nf*, ALSO **pute** *nf* [very common slang. Also used as term of abuse] whore
bordel *nm* brothel *le quartier des bordels* ALSO *des prostituées* the red-light district
faire le trottoir [commonly used slang] BrE to be on the game AmE to walk the streets
passe *nf* [slang] trick *Elle fait 20 passes en une heure.* She can turn 20 tricks in an hour.

64.21 *Contraception et mesures anti-infectieuses* Contraception

contraceptif, -tive *adj* [describes: e.g. device, method, drug] contraceptive **contraceptif** *nm* contraceptive device
moyen *nm* **anti-conceptionnel** contraceptive method
contraception *nf* **1** [techniques in general] contraception *La contraception s'est mieux développée dans certains pays que dans d'autres.* Contraception proved more successful in some countries than in others. **2** [an individual's method. Used in doctor-patient dialogue] contraceptive method *Quelle méthode de contraception pratiquez-vous?* Which method of contraception do you use?
contrôle *nm* **des naissances** [sociological term] birth control
diaphragme *nm* diaphragm
pilule *nf* **(contraceptive)** (contraceptive) pill *prendre la pilule* to be on the pill *commencer à prendre la pilule* to go on the pill
préservatif *nm* condom *mettre un préservatif* to wear a condom

64.22 *Préférences sexuelles* Sexual orientation

The first three terms listed below are neutral and can be used without giving offence
hétérosexuel, -xuelle *adj* and *n* heterosexual
bisexuel, -xuelle *adj* and *n* bisexual

homosexuel, -xuelle *adj* and *n* homosexual *les homosexuels masculins* male homosexuals *une homosexuelle* a female homosexual

These terms have shortened forms which mean the same as their respective longer counterparts, but belong to a much more relaxed register of (mainly) spoken French. They are: *hétéro* and *homo*. *Homo* is often used pejoratively.

Pejorative terms for sexual orientation
pédéraste *nm* [same as **homosexuel**, with no implication of using children as sex objects] (male) homosexual
pédé *nm* [slang. Often used pejoratively] homo
lesbienne *nf* [often used pejoratively] lesbian

65 Health professions

65.1 *Médecin généraliste* General practitioner

see also **68.1 Traitements et médicaments, 66.1 Maladies et blessures**
médecin *nm* doctor *médecin généraliste* ALSO *médecin de médecine générale* general practitioner
docteur *nm* doctor
doctoresse *nf* (woman) doctor
généraliste *n* [slightly informal] GP
médecine *nf* **générale** general practice

usage

docteur, médecin, doctoresse
1 Refer to the doctor as *le médecin* but address him or her as '*docteur*'. For example: *Le médecin est venu, et elle a ordonné des antibiotiques.* The doctor came and she prescribed antibiotics. *Vous allez lui faire une piqûre, docteur?* Will you give him an injection, doctor?
2 When using the doctor's full title and name, always add the definite article: *Je suis allé voir le docteur Hirsch.* I went to see Dr Hirsch.
3 The term *doctoresse* is often felt to diminish the prestige of the person referred to. It is safer to use *le médecin*, even for women, as in the example above. If you need to stress the fact that she is a woman, say e.g.: *Au village, nous avons une femme médecin.* In the village we have a woman doctor.

examen *nm* **1** [done by the doctor] (medical) examination **2** [involving a lab] test *faire faire des examens complémentaires* to have further tests done
cabinet *nm* **(médical)** (doctor's) BrE surgery AmE office *cabinet collectif* group practice
médical, e *adj*, *mpl* **-caux** medical
consultation *nf* visit (to the doctor) *heures de consultation* surgery hours
consulter {6} *vt* [obj: e.g. doctor, specialist. Slightly formal] to consult *Êtes-vous allé consulter?* Did you consult a doctor?
analyse *nf* (pathology) test *une analyse de sang/d'urine* a blood/urine test
ordonnance *nf* prescription *Je vais vous faire une ordonnance.* I'll write you a prescription. *Ces médicaments ne sont délivrés que sur ordonnance.* You can only get these drugs on prescription.

In the French National Health Service, the patient may decide to go straight to a specialist without being referred by the GP. Whether consulting a generalist or a specialist the patient has to pay a fee to the doctor, after which the patient may reclaim part of the sum by filling in the appropriate form, or **feuille de soins,** handed out by the doctor. A medical practitioner who works within the National Health system is **un médecin conventionné,** i.e. he/she has signed a *convention* (agreement) with the French state, which regulates the fees that can be charged.

65.2 *Hôpital* Hospital

hôpital *nm, pl* **-taux** hospital
clinique *nf* [smaller than **hôpital,** usu private] clinic
maternité *nf* maternity hospital

> **usage**
>
> **maternité** and **hôpital**
> Although the maternity wards may be located inside a hospital, the term **maternité** is always used, not **hôpital,** which tends to be associated with illness: e.g. *quand je suis allée à la maternité pour avoir mon fils* when I went to hospital to have my son.

centre *nm* **hospitalier** [suggests large, modern] hospital *centre hospitalier universitaire* teaching hospital *centre hospitalier spécialisé* psychiatric hospital
service *nm* department *dans le service du Dr Mériel* in Dr Mériel's department **le service des Urgences** BrE the Casualty department AmE emergency room
salle *nf* ward
ambulance *nf* ambulance
ambulancier, -cière *n* paramedic
infirmière *nf* nurse
infirmier *nm* (male) nurse
spécialiste *n* **1** [doctor with medical specialization] specialist **2** [senior doctor] consultant

65.3 *Chirurgie* Surgery

chirurgien, -gienne *n* surgeon
chirurgie *nf* surgery *chirurgie esthétique* plastic surgery
opérer {10} *vt* [obj: e.g. patient, growth, limb] to operate on
opération *nf* operation *faire une opération* to operate
intervention *nf* [slightly more formal than **opération**] operation *Vous allez avoir besoin d'une petite intervention.* You are going to need a minor operation.
bloc *nm* **opératoire** BrE operating theatre AmE operating room
sous le bistouri [informal] under the (surgeon's) knife
sur le billard [informal] on the (operating) table
anesthésie *nf* anaesthetic *sous anesthésie locale/générale* under local/general anaesthetic

65.4 *Dentiste* Dentist

chirurgien-dentiste *nm, pl* **chirurgiens-dentistes** dental surgeon
dent *nf* tooth *dent de lait* baby tooth *dent de sagesse* wisdom tooth *J'ai mal aux dents.* I have toothache.
dentier *nm* set of false teeth
dentaire *adj* dental
soins *nm pl* **dentaires** dental hygiene

plaque *nf* **(dentaire)** plaque
couronne *nf* crown
roulette *nf* drill
plombage *nm* filling
appareil *nm* brace *Elle a un appareil.* She wears braces.

66 Being well and being ill

66.1 *Maladies et blessures* Diseases and injuries

maladie *nf* **1** [medical condition] disease *petite maladie* minor complaint *maladie sexuellement transmissible* sexually transmitted disease **2** [period in which one is ill] illness *pendant sa maladie* during her illness
malade *n* sick person *mon malade* my patient *(une) malade imaginaire* a hypochondriac **malade** *adj* [describes: person animal] ill
être malade 1 [general] to be ill **2** [euphemism for to vomit] to be sick
blessure *nf* **1** [being hurt] injury *Il n'a eu que des blessures.* He was only injured. **2** [place on the body where damage has occurred] wound *une blessure à la tête* a head wound
blesser {6} *vt* to hurt *Sa chaussure la blesse au pied.* Her shoe hurts her foot.
allergie *nf* allergy *avoir une allergie au lait de vache* to be allergic to cow's milk
allergique *adj* **1** [medical usage] allergic *allergique au pollen* allergic to pollen **2** [informal metaphor] allergic *Je suis allergique aux jeux télévisés.* I'm allergic to television games.
épidémie *nf* epidemic *une épidémie de choléra* a cholera epidemic
crise *nf* attack *crise cardiaque* heart attack *crise d'asthme* attack of asthma *Il a eu une crise de nerfs.* He had a fit of hysterics. *Tu vas avoir une crise de foie.* You'll upset your digestion.
attaque *nf* **1** [cerebral] stroke *Elle a eu une attaque.* She had a stroke. **2** (often + *de*). Slightly less commonly used than **crise**] fit *une attaque d'épilepsie* an epileptic fit

66.2 *Quelques problèmes de santé* Some ailments

rhume *nm* cold *avoir un rhume* to have a cold
grippe *nf* flu *avoir la grippe* to have the flu
angine *nf* throat infection
migraine *nf* migraine
brûlures *nf pl* **d'estomac** heartburn
être, ALSO **se sentir barbouillé** to feel sick
ampoule *nf,* ALSO **cloque** *nf* blister
verrue *nf* wart
panaris *nm,* ALSO **mal** *nm* **blanc** whitlow
toux *nf* cough
tousser {6} *vi* to cough
vomir {2} *vt* and *vi* to vomit
rendre {53} *vi* [more informal than **vomir**] to be sick

66.3 *Handicaps* Disabilities

handicap *nm* disability
handicapé, e *n* person with a disability **handicapé, e** *adj* disabled

infirme *n* [more old-fashioned and pejorative than
  handicapé] handicapped person **infirmité** *nf* (physical)
  handicap
boiteux, -teuse *adj* lame **boiteux** *nm*, **-teuse** *nf* person
  with a limp
muet, muette *adj* mute, dumb **muet** *nm*, **muette** *nf* mute
  (person)
sourd, e *adj* deaf **sourd, e** *n* deaf person
malentendant, e *n* person with impaired hearing
sourd-muet *nm*, **sourde-muette** *nf*, *mpl* **sourds-muets**
  BrE deaf and dumb person AmE deaf-mute
surdi-mutité *nf* deaf-and-dumbness
aveugle *adj* and *n* blind (person)
borgne *n* one-eyed person **borgne** *adj* blind in one eye
mal-voyant, e *n*, *mpl* **mal-voyants** person with visual
  impairment

Locutions Idioms
malade comme un chien sick as a dog
sourd(e) comme un pot deaf as a post
**Il n'est de pire sourd que celui qui ne veut pas
  entendre.** There are none so deaf as those who will not
  hear.
Au pays des aveugles, les borgnes sont rois. In the
  country of the blind, the one-eyed man is king.

66.4 *Symptômes* Symptoms

usage

mal *nm*, *pl* **maux**
The most common way of talking about pain is by using
mal, meaning pain or ache, in one of two ways.
1. Always with **avoir** and the preposition **à**, e.g.: *avoir
  mal à la tête* to have a headache, *avoir mal aux pieds*
  to have sore feet, *avoir mal au ventre* to have stomach
  ache, *avoir mal aux dents* to have toothache, *avoir mal
  au dos* to have backache.
2. With the article, e.g.: *Le mal de dos coûte beaucoup
  de journées de travail au pays.* Backache costs the
  country many days of lost work. *traiter le mal de dents
  par l'aspirine* to treat toothache with aspirin. *Après ça,
  je n'ai plus jamais eu de maux de tête.* I never had any
  headaches again after that.

66.5 *Douleur* Pain

symptôme *nm* symptom
douleur *nf* **1** [general, physical] pain *J'ai une douleur dans
  le côté.* I have a pain in my side. **2** [of pregnant woman]
  labour pain **3** [psychological] pain *la douleur de perdre un
  être cher* the pain of losing a loved one
douloureux, -reuse *adj* [describes: e.g. illness, injury, part
  of the body, physiological process] painful *N'ayez pas
  peur, c'est un test qui n'est pas douloureux.* Don't worry,
  this test won't be painful. *règles douloureuses* painful
  menstrual periods
endolori, e *adj* [temporary] sore *J'ai le bras endolori à
  cause du vaccin.* The vaccination left me with a sore arm.
gêner {6} *vt* to make uncomfortable *Le cathéter le gêne.*
  The catheter makes him uncomfortable.
souffrir {27} *vi* to feel pain *Il souffre beaucoup.* He's in a
  lot of pain.
souffrance *nf* [when expressing physical pain, much less
  commonly used than **douleur** or **mal**] suffering *les
  souffrances d'un père séparé de ses enfants* the suffering
  of a father separated from his children

crampe *nf* cramp *avoir une crampe* to have cramp
avoir un chat dans la gorge to have a frog in one's
  throat
avoir des fourmis dans les jambes/bras to have pins
  and needles in one's legs/arms
être ankylosé(e) [after staying in the same position too
  long] to be stiff
courbature *nf* [feeling of pain and stiffness] ache *avoir des
  courbatures* [after sudden or excessive exercise] to feel
  stiff *J'ai des courbatures dans les bras.* My arms are aching.
courbatu, e *adj* [literary] ALSO **courbaturé, e** *adj* **1** [after
  sudden or excessive exercise] to be stiff **2** [because of
  fever] to be aching (all over)
avoir de la fièvre, ALSO **température** to have a
  temperature
saigner {6} *vi* to bleed *saigner du nez* to have a nosebleed
  Elle saigne de la jambe. Her leg is bleeding.
s'évanouir {19}*v refl* to faint
tomber dans les pommes, ALSO **tourner de l'œil**
  [informal] to pass out
se tordre de douleur to be doubled up with pain

66.6 *Décrire sa douleur* Describing pain

Ça fait mal! That hurts!
Ça pique! That stings!
Ça brûle! That burns!
Ça (me/le) lance! It's a throbbing pain!
Ça tire! [when a stitch is being removed] It's pulling my
  skin!
Ça me démange! I've got an itch (there)!
C'est comme si on m'enfonçait des aiguilles. It feels as
  if needles were being pushed into me.
aïe! ouch!

66.7 *Bonne santé* Good health

bien *adv* well *se porter bien* to be well *Il ne se porte pas
  bien.* He's unwell *se sentir bien* to feel well *se sentir bien
  (dans sa peau)* to feel great (mentally and physically)
sain, e *adj* **1** [describes: e.g. person, animal, lifestyle,
  nutrition] healthy **2** [not rotten. Describes: e.g. apple,
  grain] sound
forme *nf* [physical state] shape *en bonne* ALSO *pleine
  forme* in the best of health *garder la forme* to stay fit
bien portant, e *adj* in good health

Locutions Idioms
avoir une santé de fer to have the constitution of an ox
avoir un estomac d'autruche to have a cast-iron stomach
avoir une forte constitution to be in very good health

66.8 *Mauvaise santé* Poor health

mal *adv* unwell *se sentir mal* [generally] to feel unwell [at
  one point] to feel faint *Il se sent mal dans sa peau.* He
  doesn't feel well (physically or mentally).
malade *adj* [describes: person, animal] ill
délicat, e *adj* delicate
patraque *adj* [informal] BrE off-colour AmE peaked
chétif, -tive *adj* puny
malingre *adj* [skinny and often ill] sickly
indisposée *adj* [euphemism. Describes a woman who feels
  unwell when menstruating] under the weather,
  indisposed

Locutions Idioms
C'est une petite nature [pejorative. Said of men or women] He's/she's a wimp.
avoir une fièvre de cheval to have very high temperature
être au plus mal to be dying

66.9 *Folie* Madness

see also **66.10 Termes généraux,
66.11 Termes médicaux, 66.12 Insultes**
In French as in English, terms relating to problems of the mind are often used very loosely. When these words are used with humorous intent or in exaggeration they can become offensive.

66.10 *Termes généraux* General terms

psychologique *adj* [relating to the psyche. Also used disparagingly of symptoms, to contrast with physical ones] psychological
psychologue *n* psychologist
psy *n* [informal. Any practitioner in mental health or related fields] specialist (in mental illness)
folie *nf* madness *C'est de la folie furieuse!* It's complete madness! *la folie des grandeurs* megalomania *aimer qqn à la folie* to love sb to distraction
fou *nm* madman **folle** *nf* madwoman
fou, folle *adj* mad *devenir fou* to go mad *fou à lier* stark staring mad
malade *n* **mental, e** [until recently, a neutral term. Now can be felt to be offensive] mentally ill person
lunatique *adj* [behaving unpredictably] temperamental
n'avoir plus toute sa tête [euphemism. Said esp of victim of senility] to be confused
perdre l'esprit/la tête BrE to go off one's head AmE to go out of one's head *Non, mais tu perds la tête?* BrE Have you gone off your head? AmE Have you gone out of your mind?

66.11 *Termes médicaux* Medical terms

névrose *nf* neurosis **névrosé, e** *adj* neurotic
psychose *nf* psychosis **psychotique** *adj* psychotique
paranoïa *nf* paranoia
paranoïaque *n* paranoid patient
parano *adj* [informal. Behaving persecuted] (completely) paranoid *Personne n'a touché à sa voiture, complètement parano, ce mec!* Nobody touched his car, he's totally paranoid!
délire *nm* **1** [a fit, during which one talks incoherently] delirium **2** [any state in which one is unreasonable] abandonment *L'amour est un délire à deux* Love is a shared abandonment. *délire collectif* collective madness *120 francs la pièce, c'est du délire!* 120 francs each, it's crazy!
délirer {1} *vt* **1** [suffering from delirium] to be delirious **2** [be unreasonable] to be out of one's mind *Construire une piscine dans le jardin? tu délires!* Build a pool in the garden? you're out of your mind!
phobie *nf* phobia
schizophrénie *nf* schizophrenia
schizophrène *n* and *adj* schizophrenic

66.12 *Insultes* Insulting terms and phrases

dingue *adj*, ALSO **cinglé, e** *adj*, ALSO **toqué, e** *adj* [very informal] nuts *T'es pas un peu cinglé?* Are you nuts?

gâteux, -teuse *adj* senile
gaga *adj* [informal] gaga
débile *adj* [formerly referring to mental debility, this term now expresses only contempt] brainless
débile *n* moron *Ce sont des pubs pour débiles.* These advertisements are for morons.

Locutions Idioms
avoir une araignée au plafond to have a screw loose
Il est tombé sur la tête [implies madness] BrE He's gone off his head. AmE He's out of his mind
Ça va pas la tête? [very informal] BrE have you gone off your head? AmE Have you gone out of your mind?
pas folle, la guêpe! [informal. Implies that the speaker or the person spoken about is much shrewder than others had credited them with being] He's/She's no fool. *Je lui ai fait signer un reçu, pas folle la guêpe!* I made her sign a receipt, I'm no fool!

Citation Quotation
Qui vit sans folie n'est pas si sage qu'il croit. [maxim by the 17th-century moralist La Rochefoucauld, praising the wisdom of taking leave of one's senses from time to time] He who lives without madness is not as wise as he thinks.

66.13 *Raison* Sanity

see also **43.2 Qui se conforme à ce que l'on demande**
sagesse *nf* **1** [of sages and philosophers] wisdom **2** [of children] good behaviour *Il a été un modèle de sagesse cet après-midi.* He was beautifully behaved this afternoon.
sage *adj* **1** [describes: e.g. philosopher, decision, attitude] wise **2** [describes: e.g. child] well-behaved
logique *adj* **1** [conforming to the laws of logic] logical **2** [informal. Which follows on from something as an inevitable consequence] natural *Quand un animal a peur, il attaque, c'est logique.* When an animal is frightened, it goes on the attack, it's only natural.
raison *nf* **1** [faculty of the mind] reason **2** [argument] reason *Il n'y a aucune raison de lui faire confiance.* There is no reason to trust her. *sans raison* gratuitously
raisonner {6} **1** *vt* [persuade sb to adopt what is from the point of view of the persuader a more reasonable attitude] to prevail upon *Elle ne voulait pas quitter ses enfants et personne n'a pu la raisonner.* She refused to leave her children and nobody could prevail upon her (to do so). **2** *vi* [think] to reason *Essayons de raisonner calmement.* Let's try and think calmly.
se raisonner *v refl* [to control one's emotions through one's reason] to control oneself *J'avais envie de le gifler mais je me suis raisonné.* I felt like slapping his face, but I kept myself in check.
raisonnable *adj* [describes: e.g. person, decision, opinion] sensible
raisonneur, -nneuse *adj* [pejorative. Describes: esp child] argumentative
âge *nm* **de raison** [the period around his seventh year when a child can be expected to act more rationally] age of reason
bon sens *nm* common sense *une attitude pleine de bon sens* a common-sense attitude

Locutions Idioms
avoir la tête sur les épaules to be level-headed
avoir les pieds sur terre to have both feet (firmly planted) on the ground
Ça va lui mettre du plomb dans la cervelle [implies that the person spoken of is irresponsible] That'll teach him a thing or two.

Citation Quotation
Le cœur a ses raisons que la raison ne connaît point.
[This line from Blaise Pascal, the 17th-century philosopher, is often quoted. It is due as much to its meaning, excusing irrational behaviour as long as it stems from the heart, as to its poetic form] The heart has its reasons that reason does not recognize.

67 Hurting, killing and dying

67.1 *Violence et heurts* Hitting, beating

frapper {6} *vt* [hit intentionally, with part of body or instrument] to strike
taper {6} *vt* [with the flat of the hand or a flat object] to hit
coup *nm* **1** [general term. Intentional or not] blow **2** [with a body part] *un coup de poing* a punch *un coup de pied* a kick *un petit coup de coude* a nudge *un violent coup de coude* a hard poke (with the elbow) *un coup de bec* a peck **3** [with an instrument] *un coup de couteau* a stab *un coup de bâton* a blow with a stick
maltraitance *nf* [sociological term] battery *Les enfants victimes de la maltraitance ont besoin de l'aide de la société.* Battered children need help from society.

Donner des coups agressivement To hit aggressively
cogner {6} *vi* and *vt* [hit hard, usu with fist] to hit
gifler {6} *vt* [hit the cheek with the flat of the hand] to slap
coups *mpl* **et blessures** *fpl* grievous bodily harm

Donner plusieurs coups agressivement To hit aggressively and repeatedly
battre {55} *vt* **1** [hit intentionally, with any part of the body or instrument] to beat **2** [in parent-child or man and woman relationships] to batter *enfant battu* battered child
fouetter {6} *vt* to whip
marteler {12} *vt* [using the fist as if it were a hammer] to pound *L'enfant martelait la porte de ses petits poings.* The child pounded on the door with its little fists.

Heurter légèrement To hit lightly
tapoter {6} *vt* to tap (lightly)
pichenette *nf*, ALSO **chiquenaude** *nf* flick (of the finger)

Types de coups Types of blows
tape *nf* [anywhere on the body, with the flat of the hand] smack
gifle *nf* [always on the cheek] slap
fessée *nf* spanking
passage *nm* **à tabac** [maltreating of sb by police] beating-up

Locutions Idioms
Ils/Elles en sont venu(e)s aux mains. They came to blows.
taper à bras raccourcis sur qqch/qqn [hard and repeatedly, as if one were never going to stop] to set upon sthg/sb
rouer qqn de coups [the verb **rouer** {6} is used only in this phrase] to beat sb black and blue
secouer qqn comme un prunier to shake the living daylights out of sb
sans coup férir [from the obsolete verb **férir**, which is used only in this phrase] without a single blow

67.2 *Collision* Collision

heurter {6} *vt* [when falling or moving] to hit *Ma tête a heurté le mur.* I knocked my head against the wall.
heurt *nm* [blow received when falling or moving] knock
percuter {6} *vt* [subj: esp. vehicle] to hit *Sa voiture a percuté un arbre.* Her car hit a tree.
collision *nf* collision *entrer en collision avec* to collide with
de plein fouet [used of vehicles hitting other vehicles or pedestrians] BrE full on AmE head on *Elle a été heurtée de plein fouet par la voiture.* She was hit full on by the car.
donner dans [informal. Being propelled into a hard object. Often with *aller*] *Il est allé donner dans le mur.* He went crashing into the wall.

67.3 *Mourir* To die

mourir {34} *vi* (often + *de*) [general word] to die *Elle est morte du sida.* She died of AIDS. *Ne crie pas si fort, tu ne vas pas en mourir!* Don't make such a noise, it won't kill you!
décéder {10} *vi* [official overtones] to die *Nous avons le regret de vous annoncer que votre mère est décédée cette nuit.* We regret to inform you that your mother died last night.
partir {25} *vi* [euphemism] to pass away *Je ne croyais pas qu'il partirait si vite.* I didn't think he'd pass away so quickly.
disparaître {64} *vi* [used esp when talking about well-known people] to die *Fellini a disparu en 1993.* Fellini died in 1993.
périr {19} *vi* [used esp when talking about deaths at sea, or from natural calamities] to perish *La Marie-Joseph a coulé et tout l'équipage a péri.* The 'Marie-Joseph' sank and the whole crew perished.
crever {9} *vi* **1** [slangy, pejorative and aggressive way of referring to a person's death] to cash in one's chips *Ils peuvent bien crever, je m'en fous.* They can snuff it, I don't care. **2** [an acceptable way of referring to an animal's death, although not used when referring to a pet] to die

67.4 *Mort* Dead

mort, e *adj* **1** [describes human beings and animals] dead **2** [informal. Describes: e.g. machine, battery] kaput, dead
mort *nm* dead man *les morts* the dead
à mort [indicates the extreme form of whatever action is being described. Informal] *accélérer à mort* [when driving a car] to put one's foot right through the floor
morte *nf* dead woman
mort *nf* death *trouver la mort* to meet one's end
feu, e *adj* [used formally or humorously] the late *feu Albert Reynard* the late Albert Reynard *feue sa tante* his late aunt
cadavre *nm* corpse
pourrir {19} *vi* [can be used of humans, animals and plants] to rot
se décomposer {6} *v refl* [more scientific than **pourrir**] to decompose

Locutions Idioms
raide mort [emphasizes suddenness of death and shock of discovery] stone dead
mort, e et bien mort [describes people or customs] dead and gone
mort, e et enterré, e [describes people or customs] dead and buried
sur son lit de mort on his/her deathbed

67.5 *Tuer* To kill

tuer {6} *vt* [general term. Accidental or voluntary] to kill *Je ne lui pardonnerai jamais d'avoir tué sa mère en conduisant trop vite.* I'll never forgive her for killing her mother by driving too fast.
suicide *nm* suicide
se suicider {6} *v refl* to commit suicide
euthanasie *nf* euthanasia

67.6 *Tuer avec intention de tuer* To kill with intent

meurtre *nm* murder
meurtrier *nm* murderer
meurtrière *nf* murderess
tueur, tueuse *n* killer *tueur à gages* hired killer
assassin *nm* **1** [general term] murderer **2** [who kills for political reasons] assassin
abattre {55} *vt* [with gun, suggests cold-bloodedness] to shoot down
exécuter {6} *vt* [in retribution, legal or not] to execute
assassiner {6} *vt* **1** [general term] to murder *La jeune fille a été assassinée dans un bois.* The girl was murdered in a wood. **2** [for political reasons] to assassinate
massacrer {6} *vt* [suggests mutilations before death] to slaughter
supprimer {6} *vt* [for political or financial motives. Implies that the victim is an obstacle to an individual's or a group's plans] to get rid of
achever {9} *vt* [give the final blow, dose, of poison etc to sb] *achever qqn* to finish sb off

67.7 *Méthodes pour mourir ou tuer* Ways of dying, killing

empoisonner {6} *vt* to poison
s'empoisonner *v refl* to take poison
noyer {6} *vt* to drown oneself
se noyer *v refl* **1** [accidentally] to drown **2** [on purpose] to drown oneself
pendre {53} *vt* to hang
se pendre *v refl* to hang oneself
asphyxier {6} *vt* to gas
s'asphyxier *v refl* to gas oneself
étrangler {6} *vt* to strangle
s'étrangler *v refl* to strangle oneself

67.8 *La peine de mort* The death penalty

la peine capitale ALSO **de mort** the death penalty
condamnation *nf* **à mort** death sentence
guillotine *nf* guillotine
guillotiner {6} *vt* to guillotine
chaise *nf* **électrique** electric chair
chambre *nf* **à gaz** gas chamber

67.9 *Tuer les animaux* Killing animals

piquer {6} *vt* [kill humanely, with an injection. Obj: e.g. cat, dog] BrE to put down AmE to put to sleep
assommer {6} *vt* [obj: e.g. bullock, sheep] to stun
abattoir *nm* slaughterhouse

67.10 *Mortel* Lethal

mortel, -telle *adj* **1** [likely to cause death. Describes: e.g. dose, poison] lethal **2** [likely to be followed by death. Describes : e.g. illness, wound] mortal **3** [informal. Boring] deadly boring *Son dernier roman est mortel!* Her latest novel is deadly boring!
fatal, e *adj*, *mpl* **fatals** [literary. Describes: e.g. blow, weapon, decision] fatal

68 Treatments and substances affecting the body

68.1 *Traitements et médicaments* Treatments and medicines

see also **65.1 Médecin généraliste, 66.1 Maladies et blessures**
traitement *nm* treatment
soins *nm pl* treatment

Treatment
Traitement refers to the more medical aspects of patient care, while *soins* (rarely used in the singular in this sense) includes medical and general looking after; e.g. *Pour mon asthme, le médecin veut essayer un nouveau traitement.* The doctor wants to try a new treatment for my asthma. *Les visiteurs ne seront pas admis à l'heure des soins.* No visitors admitted during routine nursing care.

traiter {6} *vt* to treat *Cela ne se traite pas.* There's no cure for it.
soulager {8} *vt* [make better temporarily] to help *Bois, ça va te soulager.* Drink it, it'll make you feel better. *On a maintenant de bons médicaments pour soulager l'asthme.* There are now some effective drugs available to help asthma sufferers.
médicament *nm* medicine *Il prend des médicaments pour son diabète.* He's taking medication for his diabetes.
remède *nm* [slightly old-fashioned term] medicine *remèdes homéopathiques* homoeopathic remedies
thérapie *nf* **1** [term used by doctors] treatment *suivre une thérapie homéopathique* to follow a homeopathic treatment **2** [psychology] therapy *thérapie de groupe* group therapy
guérir {2} **1** *vt* to cure *Elle m'a guéri de mes allergies.* She cured my allergies. **2** *vi* [subj: e.g. person, wound, boil] to get better *Sa blessure a mis longtemps à guérir.* It took a long time for her wound to heal.
guérison *nf* being cured *Continuez le traitement jusqu'à la guérison complète.* Continue the treatment until you are completely cured.
se rétablir {2} *v refl* to get well again
récupérer {6} *vi* [stage after **se rétablir**, when the person is regaining strength] to recuperate
convalescence *nf* convalescence *être en convalescence* to convalesce
cure *nf* [treatment based on special diet or taking the waters at a spa] course of treatment *Tous les ans je fais une cure à Vichy.* Each year I take the waters at Vichy. *faire une cure de carotte* to follow a special diet based on carrots.

usage

médical, e adj, mpl **-caux** and **médicinal, e** adj, mpl
-naux
Médical describes any treatment or procedure which
may be prescribed by a doctor. **Médicinal** refers to
plant-based treatments: *L'ortie a des propriétés
médicinales.* Nettles have curative properties

68.2 *Chez le pharmacien* At the pharmacy

pharmacie nf BrE chemist's shop AmE pharmacy
pharmacien, -cienne n BrE chemist AmE pharmacy
cachet, ALSO **comprimé** nm tablet
pastille nf (medicinal) lozenge
pommade, ALSO **crème** nf ointment
ampoule nf ampoule
gélule nf capsule
collyre nm eye lotion
suppositoire nm suppository *mettre un suppositoire à un
enfant* to give a child a suppository
sirop nm mixture *sirop contre la toux* cough mixture
goutte nf [informal. Dispensed from a dropper] drop
compte-gouttes nm inv a dropper

Si vous êtes malade en France If you're ill in France
The procedure for getting free or partly free medicines
under the French health system is as follows: go to the
pharmacy with your prescription and a form given to you
by the doctor called a **feuille** nf **de soins**. The
pharmacist sells you the relevant medicines, each of
which bears a tear-off stamp or **vignette** nf showing
what proportion of the price will be refunded, or
remboursé, e adj. The vignette has to be transferred
from the package to the *feuille de soins*, and the
pharmacist may help you to do this correctly. You then
have to send the completed *feuille de soins* to your local
refunds office, the **Caisse d'Assurance Maladie,** which
will eventually reimburse your costs.

68.3 *Secourisme* First aid

les premiers soins ALSO **secours** first aid
secouriste n first-aid worker
dégager les voies respiratoires to clear the airways
en position latérale de sécurité in the recovery position
étendre {53} vt [obj: e.g. patient, casualty] to stretch out,
to lay down

68.4 *Autres soins et accessoires* Other treatments and accessories

piqûre nf injection *faire une piqûre de morphine à qqn* to
give sb a morphine injection
seringue nf (hypodermic) needle
thermomètre nm **(médical)** thermometer *thermomètre
frontal* BrE fever strip
prendre le pouls de qqn to take sb's pulse
prendre la tension de qqn to take sb's blood pressure
prendre la température de qqn to take sb's temperature
fauteuil nm **roulant,** ALSO **petite voiture** nf [informal]
wheelchair
bouche à bouche nm mouth-to-mouth resuscitation *faire
du bouche à bouche à qqn* to give sb mouth to mouth
resuscitation

Dans la boîte à pharmacie First Aid
coton nm **(hydrophile)** cotton wool
pansement, ALSO **sparadrap®** nm BrE plaster AmE
bandage
alcool nm **à 90** surgical spirit
sérum nm **anti-venin** anti-venom serum
compresse nf compress

68.5 *Tabac* Tobacco

fumer {6} vt and vi to smoke *s'arrêter de fumer* to stop
smoking
tabagisme nm [seen as an addiction] smoking
campagne nf **anti-tabac** anti-smoking campaign
cendrier nm ashtray
cigarette nf cigarette
fume-cigarette nm, pl **fume-cigarettes** cigarette holder
pipe nf pipe *fumer la pipe* to smoke a pipe
briquet nm lighter
cigare nm cigar
mégot nm [informal] BrE fag-end AmE cigarette butt
sèche nf [smoker's slang] BrE ciggie AmE cig

68.6 *Drogues* Drugs and drug abuse

drogue nf drug
se droguer {6} v refl to take drugs

Les drogues douces Soft drugs
herbe nf grass
shit nm [slang. Pronounced a little like the English word
'sheet'] pot
joint nm joint

Les drogues dures Hard drugs
héroïne nf heroin
héro nf [slang. Short for **héroïne**] horse
crack nm crack
stupéfiant nm narcotic (drug)
stup nm [slang] narcotic (drug)
se shooter {6} v refl [slang] **1** [as a habit] to inject
2 [describes one action] to shoot up

Effets des drogues Effects of drugs
planer {6} vi to be on a trip
trip nm trip
être en manque to feel withdrawal symptoms

Le monde des drogués The world of drug addicts
drogué, e n [general term. Pejorative] drug addict
toxicomane n [more medical and neutral than **drogué**]
drug addict
toxico n [slang] junkie
revendeur nm dealer
dealer nm [slang] dealer
dealer {6} vi [slang] to deal
avoir une dépendance à la drogue to have a drug habit
être accro à [slang] to be hooked on
la brigade des stups [slang] the Drug Squad

69 Caring for the body

69.1 *Hygiène du corps* Personal hygiene

se laver {6} *v refl* to wash
prendre un bain/une douche to have a shower/bath
faire sa toilette BrE to have a wash AmE to get washed up
se débarbouiller {6} *v refl* BrE to have a quick wash (of one's face) AmE to get washed up quickly *Lave-toi comme il faut, tu t'es juste débarbouillé.* You need a proper wash. That was just a lick and a promise

69.2 *Articles pour la toilette* Toiletries

savon *nm* soap
savonnette *nf* bar of soap
bain *nm* **moussant** bubble bath
gel *nm* **pour la douche** shower gel
déodorant *nm* deodorant
talc *nm* talcum powder
gant *nm* **de toilette** [pocket-shaped] BrE flannel AmE wash cloth
éponge *nf* (bath) sponge
serviette *nf* **(de bain)** (bath) towel

69.3 *Soins des cheveux* Hair care

brosse *nf* **à cheveux** hairbrush
peigne *nm* comb
shampooing *nm* shampoo *se faire un shampooing* to wash one's hair
baume *nm* **démêlant** conditioner
laque *nf* hairspray
sèche-cheveux *nm, pl* **sèche-cheveux,** ALSO **séchoir** *nm* **à cheveux** hair dryer
coiffeur, -ffeuse *n* hairdresser *aller chez le coiffeur* to go to the hairdresser's
coupe *nf* **de cheveux** [styled] haircut *se faire faire une coupe* to have one's hair cut (and styled)
couper {6} *vt* [obj: e.g. hair, beard] to cut *se faire couper les cheveux* to have a haircut
pince *nf* **à épiler** (pair of) tweezers

69.4 *Hygiène dentaire* Dental care

brosse *nf* **à dents** toothbrush
se brosser les dents to clean one's teeth
dentifrice *nm* toothpaste *un tube de dentifrice* a tube of toothpaste
fil *nm* **dentaire** dental floss
rince-bouche *nm, pl* **rince-bouches** mouthwash

69.5 *Rasage* Shaving

rasoir *nm* **(électrique)** shaver *rasoir mécanique* razor
lame *nf* **de rasoir** razor blade
crème *nf* **à raser** shaving cream
blaireau *nm, pl* **-x** shaving brush
produit *nm* **après-rasage,** ALSO **aftershave** *nm* aftershave

69.6 *Manucure* Nail care

manucure *nf* manicure *se faire faire une manucure* to have one's nails manicured
brosse *nf* **à ongles** nailbrush
lime *nf* **à ongles** nail file
ciseaux *nm pl* **à ongles** nail scissors
coupe-ongles *nm* (nail) clippers

69.7 *Hygiène féminine* Feminine hygiene

tampon *nm* **(périodique)** tampon
serviette *nf* **(périodique)** BrE sanitary towel AmE sanitary napkin
protège-slip *nm, pl* **protège-slips** panty-liner

70 Fruit and vegetables

70.1 *Fruits* Fruit

fruit *nm* piece of fruit *des fruits* fruit
fruité, e *adj* fruity

70.2 *Fruits courants* Common fruit

pomme *nf* apple *une pomme à couteau* an eating apple
 une pomme à cuire a cooking apple
poire *nf* pear
banane *nf* banana *un régime de bananes* a bunch of
 bananas
raisin *nm* grape *des raisins* grapes *une grappe de raisins* a
 bunch of grapes
pêche *nf* peach
nectarine *nf*, ALSO **brugnon** *nm* nectarine
abricot *nm* apricot
prune *nf* plum
melon *nm* melon
pastèque *nf* watermelon

70.3 *Agrumes* Citrus fruit

orange *nf* orange
citron *nm* lemon
citron *nm* **vert** lime
pamplemousse *nm* grapefruit
mandarine *nf* mandarin
clémentine *nf* clementine

70.4 *Fruits rouges et baies* Red fruit and soft fruit

cerise *nf* cherry
fraise *nf* strawberry
framboise *nf* raspberry
mûre *nf* blackberry
cassis *nm* blackcurrant *un grain de cassis* a blackcurrant
groseille *nf* redcurrant
groseille *nf*, *pl* **-s à maquereau** gooseberry
myrtille *nf* blueberry

70.5 *Fruits exotiques* Exotic fruit

ananas *nm* pineapple
mangue *nf* mango
kiwi *nm* kiwi fruit
fruit *nm* **de la passion** passion fruit
litchi *nf* lychee

70.6 *Fruits souvent consommés secs* Dried fruit

raisin *nm* **sec** raisin
raisin *nm* **de Corinthe** currant
raisin *nm* **de Smyrne** sultana
pruneau *nm*, *pl* **-x** prune
datte *nf* date
figue *nf* fig

70.7 *Parties des fruits* Parts of fruit

peau *nf*, *pl* **-x** [general term] skin
écorce *nf* [citrus fruit and melon] rind
zest *nm* [usable skin of citrus fruit, grated or peeled.
 Excludes pith] rind
partie *nf* **blanche**, ALSO **peau** *nf* [in citrus fruit] pith
quartier *nm* [of citrus fruit] segment
pépin *nm* [small, in apples, citrus fruit, grapes,
 strawberries, etc] pip
noyau *nm*, *pl* **-x** [big, in peach, mango, date] stone
trognon *nm* [of apple, pear] core

70.8 *Fraîcheur des aliments* Condition of foodstuffs

frais, fraîche *adj* **1** [not dried or preserved] fresh *des fruits
 frais* fresh fruit **2** [not stale or off] fresh *du lait frais* fresh
 milk *du pain frais* fresh(ly-baked) bread *des oeufs frais*
 fresh or new-laid eggs
fraîcheur *nf* freshness *Pour vérifier la fraîcheur d'un
 poisson, regardez l'œil et la couleur des ouïes.* To check
 how fresh a fish is, look at the eyes and at the colour of
 the gills.
mûr, e *adj* ripe *bien mûr* (nice and) ripe *trop mûr* overripe
vert, e *adj* [not ripe enough] unripe *des raisins trop verts*
 grapes that aren't ripe
pourri, e *adj* [describes: e.g. meat, fish, vegetables, fruit]
 rotten
mûrir {19} *vi* to ripen *des raisins qui mûrissent au soleil*
 grapes ripening in the sun *faire mûrir des tomates sur un
 balcon* to ripen tomatoes on a balcony
blet, blette *adj* [brown and going rotten. Describes: pears]
 overripe
talé, e *adj* [marked with brown patches after having been
 dropped or handled roughly] bruised
date *nf* **de péremption** [on packaging] BrE sell-by date
 AmE freshness date *qui a dépassé sa date de péremption*
 past its sell-by date
s'abîmer {6} *v refl* [subj: e.g. fruit, vegetables] to go bad

70.9 *Famille des noix* Nuts

casse-noisette, ALSO **casse-noix** *nm* nutcrackers
coquille *nf* **(de noix)** (nut)shell
cerneau *nm*, *pl* **-x (de noix)** kernel
amande *nf* almond
noix *nf* walnut
noix *nf* **du Brésil** Brazil nut
noix *nf* **de cajou** cashew
noix *nf* **de coco** coconut

noix *nf* **de pecan** pecan nut
cacahuète *nf* peanut
pistache *nf* pistachio
châtaigne *nf* sweet chestnut
châtaigne *nf* **d'eau** water chestnut
marron *nm* chestnut *marrons grillés* roasted chestnuts
noisette *nf* hazelnut

70.10 *Légumes* Vegetables

légume *nm* [everyday term] vegetable
légumineuse *nf* [botanical term] leguminous plant

70.11 *Légumes verts* Green vegetables

chou *nm, pl* -**x** cabbage
choux *nm* **de Bruxelles** Brussel sprout
chou-fleur *nm, pl* **choux-fleurs** cauliflower
petit pois *nm* pea
haricot *nm* bean
haricot *nm* **vert** green bean
haricot *nm* **blanc** haricot bean
haricot *nm* **frais** fresh haricot bean
fève *nf* broad bean
broccoli *nm* broccoli
épinards *nm pl* spinach *épinards en branche* leaf spinach
asperge *nf* asparagus *pointe d'asperge* asparagus tip

70.12 *Tubercules* Root vegetables

pomme *nf* **de terre** potato
carotte *nf* carrot
panais *nm* parsnip
navet *nm* turnip
patate *nf* **1** [informal. Potato] spud **2** [root vegetable]
   patate (douce) sweet potato

70.13 *Autres légumes courants* Other common vegetables

champignon *nm* mushroom
poivron *nm* pepper *poivron vert/rouge* green/red pepper
piment *nm* pepper *piment doux* capsicum *piment rouge*
   chilli
aubergine *nf* BrE aubergine AmE eggplant
oignon *nm* onion
échalotte *nf* shallot
poireau *nm, pl* -**x** leek
ail *nm, pl* **aulx** garlic
courgette *nf* BrE courgette AmE zucchini
avocat *nm* avocado
courge *nf* BrE marrow AmE squash
maïs *nm* sweetcorn *maïs en épi* corn on the cob
artichaut *nm* (globe) artichoke
topinambour *nm* Jerusalem artichoke
potiron *nm* pumpkin
lentille *nf* lentil

70.14 *Légumes à faire en salade* Salad vegetables

salade *nf* **1** [dish] salad *salade composée* mixed salad **2**
   [vegetable] lettuce *Achète une salade.* Buy some lettuce.
laitue *nf* lettuce
tomate *nf* tomato

radis *nm* radish
oignon *nm* **vert** BrE spring onion AmE scallion
concombre *nm* cucumber
céleri *nm* celery *branche nf de céleri* stick of celery
betterave *nf* BrE beetroot AmE beets
cresson *nm* watercress

---

endive *nf* and **chicorée** *nf*
Beware of the following: while **endive** in French refers
to chicory, **chicorée** is the name for the salad vegetable
called endive in English: e.g. *chicorée frisée* curly endive.

---

71 Bread, biscuits and cake

71.1 *Pain* Bread

la croûte *nf* crust
la mie *nf* **(de pain)** dough
une miette *nf* crumb
un morceau de pain a piece of bread
un bout de pain (informal) a bit of bread
farine *nf* flour
levure *nf* **(de boulanger)** baker's yeast
levure *nf* **chimique** baking powder

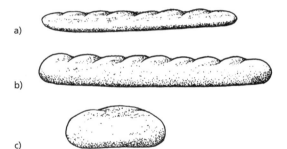

a)

b)

c)

a) une baguette (a French stick)
b) un pain (a French loaf)
c) un pain (de campagne), also une miche de pain (a round
loaf)

71.2 *Biscuits* Biscuits

> ### *usage*
>
> **biscuit** *nm* and **petit gâteau** *nm*
> These terms are used interchangeably when referring to
> cracker-type biscuits: e.g. *des biscuits* ALSO *petits
> gâteaux salés pour l'apéritif* salty biscuits to have with
> drinks before the meal. With sweet biscuits or cookies,
> use either *biscuit* or *petit gâteau*: e.g. *Veux-tu un petit
> gâteau pour tremper dans ton lait chaud?* Would you
> like a biscuit to dip in your hot milk? The only types of
> biscuit which cannot be referred to as *petit gâteau* are
> *biscuit à la cuillère*, light sponge finger, and *biscuit de
> Savoie*, light sponge cake.

gâteau *nm* **sec** [sold in packets] (sweet) biscuit
sablé *nm* shortbread biscuit

71.3 *Autres denrées à base de pâte* Other dough-based foods

pâte *nf* **(à tarte)** [for pies and tarts] dough *pâte sablée* short pastry *pâte feuilletée* flaky pastry *pâte à choux* puff pastry

gâteau *nm, pl* **-x 1** [with a cream or fresh fruit filling] gâteau, cake *un gâteau d'anniversaire* a birthday cake **2** [sponge-type or with dried fruit filling] cake *Je ne mange jamais de gâteaux.* I never eat cakes

cake *nm* fruit cake

brioche *nf* [milk-based dough. Comes in individual sizes, or as a large loaf] sweet bun

pâtisserie *nf* **1** [with a cream or custard filling] pastry **2** [flan case with fresh fruit or a filling] tart *La maison Verdier fait de très bonnes pâtisseries.* Maison Verdier's cakes and tarts are very good.

pièce *nf* **montée** [for weddings, first communions and baptisms] cake for a special occasion

tourte *nf* **1** [covered. With meat, fish, onion, etc filling] pie *tourte à la viande* meat pie **2** [uncovered. With savoury filling containing milk and eggs] flan *tourte au fromage* cheese flan

tarte *nf* tart *tarte aux prunes* plum tart *tarte à l'oignon* onion tart

une piece montée, (a wedding cake)

une grosse brioche et trois petites brioches, (a large sweet bun and three small ones)

pâtes *nf pl* [usu Italian] pasta

nouille *nf* [informal word for pasta, but neutral word for Chinese noodle] noodle *des nouilles* noodles

Citation Quotation
S'ils n'ont pas de pain, qu'ils mangent de la brioche! [famous remark attributed, perhaps wrongly, to Marie-Antoinette in 1789. Symbolizes the cynicism of the ruling classes, their indifference to the people's suffering and their ignorance insofar as shortage of bread would surely entail shortage of brioche as well. Regardless of what a brioche actually is, the usual translation is as follows] If they have no bread, let them eat cake!

72 Food derived from animals

72.1 *Produits laitiers et crémerie* Dairy products

crémerie *nf* (cheese shop and) dairy
crémier, -mière *n* dairy shop owner

It used to be possible to buy dairy products at local *crémeries* in any high street. Nowadays this kind of shopping is done mostly in supermarkets or small grocers' shops. However, good shopping arcades and flourishing high streets sometimes still boast a *crémerie* piled high with cheeses. Street markets all have one or more cheese stalls, commonly referred to as *la crémerie* or, more informally, as *le marchand* (or *la marchande*) *de fromages*. In practice, *crémerie* and *fromagerie* are used interchangeably.

fromagerie *nf* cheese shop
fromager, -gère *n* cheese seller

72.2 *Produits animaux* Animal products

lait *nm* milk *lait entier/semi-écrémé/écrémé* BrE full-fat/semi-skimmed/skimmed milk AmE whole/one per cent or two per cent/skimmed milk **laitier, -tière** *adj* [related to or derived from milk] milk (as adj) **laiteux, -teuse** *adj* [of the consistency of milk] milky

beurre *nm* butter *beurre doux* unsalted butter *beurre demi-sel* slightly salted butter *beurre à la motte* ALSO *en vrac* loose butter, butter in slabs

beurrer {6} *vt* to butter

au beurre 1 [describes: e.g. pancake, potatoes] served with butter **2** [describes: e.g. biscuit, pastry] made with butter

fromage *nm* cheese
French cheeses divide into *fromages à pâte cuite*, cheeses that have been heated (such as mountain cheeses) and *fromages à pâtes fermentées*, cheeses that have been left to mature by fermentation (like *camembert*, *brie*, etc). Processed cheeses are usually referred to as *fromages à tartiner*, or spreads. What British supermarkets call 'fromage frais' is called *fromage blanc* in France, while *du fromage frais* is the generic phrase for all non-fermented and uncooked cheeses, which are liquid and often sold in pots, or ladled loose into special plastic bags. The closest generic phrase is cottage cheese, although typically 'curdy' cottage cheese cannot be obtained in France.

If you buy *fromage à la coupe*, or 'loose' cheese from a specialist shop or market stall, a reputable seller will ask you which day you intend to serve it, and will take care to choose and wrap it in such a way that it is at its best for your table.

yaourt, ALSO **yoghourt** *nm* yoghurt *yaourt maigre* low-fat yoghurt

crème *nf* **(fraîche)** (fresh) cream
French cream tastes naturally slightly sour. *Crème épaisse* is thicker, *crème liquide* is thinner, but there is no real equivalent for double, single, whipping or clotted cream.

œuf *nm*, *pl* **œufs** egg *œuf (à la) coque* soft-boiled egg *œuf dur* hard-boiled egg

72.3 *Huiles et graisses* Fats and oils

see also **72.2 Produits animaux**
margarine *nf* margarine

matières *nf pl* **grasses**
The fat content of foodstuffs is expressed on their labels in terms of percentages, e.g. *40% de matières grasses* 40% fat content

huile *nf* oil *huile pour assaisonnement* salad oil *huile à friture* frying oil

Locutions Idioms
mettre du beurre dans les épinards [bring home a bit of extra money, so as to make life pleasanter] to add some creature comforts
Ça compte pour du beurre. [Informal. From the language of playground games] That doesn't count. *Et moi, je compte pour du beurre?* Don't I count, too?
On ne peut pas avoir le beurre et l'argent du beurre. You can't have your cake and eat it.
entre la poire et le fromage 1 [refers to casual comments made towards the end of a meal] over coffee. **2** [remarks made in a relaxed way, although their impact may be great] casually

72.4 *Boucherie* Meat products

see also **14.1 Animaux de la ferme, 79.1 Agriculture**
viande *nf* meat
boucherie *nf* **1** [trade] butcher's trade **2** [products] meat, poultry and offal *Je prends toute ma boucherie chez Desseaux.* I buy all my meat from Desseaux.

72.5 *Viande rouge et viande blanche* Red and white meat

bœuf *nm* beef
rosbif *nm* **1** [before it is cooked] BrE joint (of beef) AmE piece of beef **2** [cooked] roast beef
veau *nm* veal
agneau *nm* lamb
mouton *nm* mutton
porc *nm* pork

72.6 *Découpe de la viande* Cuts of meat

morceau *nm*, *pl* **-x** cut *les bons morceaux* prime cuts *les bas morceaux* the cheap(er) cuts
rôti *nm* **de boeuf** roast beef

u s a g e

rôti
Although the word *rôti* implies that the meat has been roasted, and its translation is 'roast', it is also used when referring to the cut of raw meat sold by the butcher for roasting. E.g.: *Je vous coupe un petit rôti de veau?* Shall I cut you a nice little piece of veal? As some butchers also sell ready-roasted beef or pork by the slice, *acheter un rôti de porc* could mean to buy pork for roasting or to buy some cooked pork, depending on circumstances.

côte *nf* **1** [of beef] rib **2** [of pork, veal] chop
côtelette *nf* **1** [of pork] chop **2** [of lamb, veal] cutlet
steak *nm* (slice of beef) steak
gigot *nm* **1** [of lamb] leg of lamb **2** [of mutton] leg of mutton
épaule *nf* shoulder
gras, grasse *adj* fatty **gras** *nm* piece of fat
maigre *adj* lean **maigre** *nm* lean part (of the meat)

72.7 *Abats* Offal

see also **62.17 Organes internes**
foie *nm* liver
rognon *nm* kidney
abats *nm pl* **de volaille** giblets

72.8 *Charcuterie* Pork products

saucisson *nm* [dried and matured, sometimes smoked, to be eaten raw or cooked] sausage
saucisse *nf* [to be cooked] sausage
boudin *nm* **noir** BrE black pudding AmE blood pudding
jambon *nm* (cooked) ham *jambon de pays* (raw) ham
saindoux *nm* lard

Lard and bacon
Don't be misled: the French word *lard*, ALSO *lard de poitrine* refers to bacon, and if you want a rasher of bacon, you will need to ask for *une tranche de lard*. It will be sliced much thicker than British and American bacon is, so as to be cut into thick cubes for browning and for using in recipes. What the French call *du bacon* is smoked loin or gammon.

72.9 *Volaille et gibier* Poultry and game

volaille *nf* **1** [collective noun] poultry **2** [single animal] chicken
pintade *nf* guinea fowl
chevreuil *nm* venison *cuissot de chevreuil* haunch of venison
gibier *nm* game
venaison *nf* game meat

72.10 *Magasins vendant de la viande* Shops selling meat

boucherie *nf* butcher's (shop) *boucherie chevaline* butcher's specializing in horse meat

Types of butchers
In France butchers sell all kinds of meat, except for horse-meat (which is only sold in *boucheries chevalines*). But the most varied choice of pork products is to be had from *charcuteries*. Shops combining a wide choice of pork with the sale of all other meats are called *boucheries-charcuteries*. A shop specializing in offal is *une triperie*. A trader selling mainly poultry and rabbits is *un volailler*.

72.11 *Pêche et poissonnerie* Fishing and fish products

see also **17 Poissons et animaux marins**
pêche *nf* fishing
pêcher {6} *vt* to fish *la pêche en rivière* freshwater fishing *la pêche en mer* sea fishing
pêcheur, -cheuse *n* **1** [in rivers] angler **2** [in the sea] fisherman, fisherwoman
filet *nm* net
morue *nf* cod *morue fraîche* (fresh) cod *morue salée* salt cod
cabillaud *nm* [another name for **morue fraîche**] (fresh) cod
saumon *nm* salmon
hareng *nm* herring
thon *nm* tuna
anguille *nf* eel
sardine *nf* sardine *sardines à l'huile* sardines in oil
darne *nf* [slice cut across a fish] (fish) steak
arête *nf* (fish)bone
raie *nf* skate

72.12 *Fruits de mer* Sea-food

coquillage *nm* shellfish
palourde *nf* clam
bulot *nm* whelk

usage

Crustacés and **mollusques**
The terms **crustacé** *nm* and **mollusque** *nm* are used in scientific language. They are also everyday terms used when discussing recipes and menus involving these animals. *Crustacés* are shellfish including more particularly lobster and crayfish. *Mollusques* are shellfish such as mussels and oysters (also including snails). For example, *J'ai envie de manger des crustacés ce soir.* I fancy something like lobster or crayfish tonight.
Une crevette is either a prawn or a shrimp. Sometimes *crevette rose* is specified for prawn and *crevette grise* for shrimp.

crabe *nm*, ALSO **tourteau** *nm, pl* **-x** (edible) crab
langouste *nf* crayfish
écrevisse *nf* (freshwater) crayfish
homard *nm* lobster
huître *nf* oyster *huître perlière* pearl oyster *une bourriche d'huîtres* a bushel of oysters

In large French cities, oysters are sold from the fronts of cafés throughout the Christmas season

Oysters used to be considered unsafe for consumption out of their season, which consisted of those months with a letter 'R' in their name. Hence, the still surviving advice to eat oysters only *pendant les mois en R*, slightly irrelevant with today's methods for farming and distribution.

Locutions Idioms
du menu fretin [immature fish. Also insignificant people] small fry
marcher en crabe ALSO **en écrevisse** to walk crabwise
serré(e)s comme des sardines ALSO **harengs** packed together like sardines

73 Flavours and seasonings

73.1 *Saveurs* Flavours

saveur *nf* **1** [kind of flavour] taste *Quelle est cette saveur?* What flavour is this? **2** [used to express a positive evaluation] (food) taste *La viande de Charolais a beaucoup de saveur.* Charolais beef has a lot of flavour.
savoureux, -reuse, *adj* tasty
goûteux, -teuse *adj* [more formal than *savoureux*] tasty
goût *nm* [flavourfulness] taste *une viande qui a du goût* a tasty piece of meat *Le goût de la vanille domine.* The taste of vanilla is predominant.

73.2 *Les sensations gustatives de base* Basic sensations of taste

sucré, e *adj* sweet
salé, e *adj* **1** [sensation on tastebuds] salty **2** [describes: e.g. dish, recipe, course in a meal] savoury
aigre *adj* sour
aigrelet, -lette *adj* slightly sour
acide *adj* acid, sharp
amer *adj* bitter
douceâtre *adj* sweetish

73.3 *Ingrédients et aromates* Ingredients and flavourings

sel *nm* salt
poivre *nm* pepper
vinaigre *nm* vinegar
gingembre *nm* ginger
muscade *nf*, ALSO **noix** *nf* **muscade** nutmeg
persil *nm* parsley
ciboulette *nf* chives
thym *nm* thyme
menthe *nf* mint
fenouil *nm* fennel
cerfeuil *nm* cervil
basilic *nm* basil
(fines) herbes *nf pl* mixed herbs

73.4 *Compliments sur le goût* Judging flavours

délicieux, -cieuse *adj* delicious
exquis, e *adj* exquisite
fin, e *adj* subtle *un dessert fin* a subtle dessert *un repas fin* a gourmet meal
appétissant, e *adj* tempting *C'est appétissant, ce que tu prépares!* What you're preparing looks really tempting!

Locution Idiom
Ça me fait venir ALSO **me met l'eau à la bouche.** It makes my mouth water.

Critiques sur le goût Critical judgments on taste
insipide *adj* tasteless
fade *adj* bland
farineux, -neuse *adj* [describes: e.g. pear, apple] tasteless
fort, e *adj* [describes: e.g. cheese, cabbage] (too) strong

73.5 *Sauces* Sauces

sauce *nf* **1** [general term] sauce **2** [made with meat juices] gravy **3** [on salads] dressing

73.6 *Préparations salées* Savoury foods

au vinaigre pickled *cornichons au vinaigre* pickled gherkins
vinaigrette *nf* oil and vinegar dressing
épice *nf* spice **épicé, e** *adj* hot
saumure *nf* brine
moutarde *nf* mustard *moutarde forte* hot (Dijon) mustard
bouillon-cube *nm*, *pl* **bouillons-cubes** BrE stock cube AmE bouillon cube
gelée *nf* BrE (meat) jelly AmE gelatin
assaisonner {6} *vt* to season
assaisonnement *nm* seasoning

> ## *usage*
>
> **conserve** *nf* and **conserver** {6} *vt*
> **Conserver** is the general verb for keeping food (*Conservez le beurre au froid.* Keep butter chilled.) as well as the general term for preserving food. A **conserve** is food that has been preserved by bottling (*en bocal*), canning (*en boîte*), or sealing in fat (*confit*). So *faire des haricots/pêches en conserve* is to bottle beans/peaches. Commonly however, *conserve* and *en conserve* refer to tinned goods: *Pendant la semaine on ne mange que des conserves.* We eat nothing but tinned food during the week. *J'ai acheté du céleri en boîte.* I bought some tinned celery.

73.7 *Préparations sucrées* Sweet foods

sirop *nm* syrup
miel *nm* honey
compote *nf* stewed fruit puree
confiture *nf* jam *faire de la confiture* ALSO *des confitures* to make jam
gelée *nf* [clear jam] jelly
glace *nf* icecream *glace à la fraise* strawberry icecream
sorbet *nm* sorbet *sorbet au cassis* blackcurrant sorbet

73.8 *Friandises* Sweets

sucrer {6} *vt* **1** [obj: preparation] to sweeten **2** [obj: e.g. coffee] to put sugar in
sucre *nm* **1** [substance] sugar *du sucre cristallisé* crystallised sugar *du sucre semoule* caster sugar *du sucre glace* BrE icing sugar AmE confectioners' sugar **2** [lump] *un paquet de sucre en morceaux* a packet of cube sugar *un morceau de sucre* a lump of sugar
sucre *nm* **d'orge**, *pl* **sucres d'orge** barley sugar
chocolat *nm* chocolate
bonbon *nm* BrE sweet AmE candy
caramel *nm* **1** [sweet] toffee **2** [cooked sugar] caramel
sucette *nf* lollipop

Locutions Idioms
Il n'est pas en sucre! [implies that sb is being overprotected] He can look after himself!
Il est tout sucre et tout miel. [deceptively unctuous] He looks as if butter wouldn't melt in his mouth.
casser du sucre sur le dos de qqn to criticize sb behind his/her back

74 Cooking and eating

74.1 *Faire la cuisine* To cook

cuisinier, -nière *n* cook
être en cuisine to be busy cooking
cuisiner {6} *vt* [to cook, including preparation before heat is applied] to (prepare and) cook *Comment est-ce que vous cuisinez le sanglier?* How do you prepare and cook wild boar?
cuisson *nf* cooking *La sauce doit réduire à la cuisson.* The sauce must reduce during the cooking. *Pour le porc il faut un assez long temps de cuisson.* Pork needs a fairly long cooking time.
cuit, e *adj* cooked
crue, e *adj* raw

La cuisson à la chaleur Cooking with heat

All the cooking verbs below can be used transitively, e.g. *v + n*, or preceded by *faire + v + n*. E.g.: *dorer des oignons* or *faire dorer des oignons*. Both mean: to brown onions. The cooking verbs can also be used intransitively: *pendant que les oignons dorent* while the onions are browning

cuire {82} *vt* and *vi* **1** [obj: all foods except dough-based] to cook *cuire à la vapeur* to steam *cuire au bain-marie* to cook in a double-boiler **2** [obj: dough-based foods] to bake
dorer {6} *vt* and *vi* to cook until golden brown
griller {6} *vt* and *vi* to grill
rôtir {19} *vt* and *vi* to roast
roussir {19} *vt* and *vi* [usu applies to potatoes] to fry until golden brown
rissoler {6} *vt* and *vi* [has the same meaning as **roussir** but applies to a variety of foods] to fry until golden brown
bouillir {31} *vt* and *vi* to boil *bouillir à gros bouillons* to boil fast *bouillir à petits bouillons* to simmer slowly

The verbs below can be used transitively with *faire + v + n*. E.g.: *faire frémir le bouillon* to let the stock simmer. They can also be used intransitively, with a subject only: *Le bouillon frémit.* The stock is simmering.

mijoter {6} *vi* to simmer
frémir {19} *vi* to simmer very gently
frire {81} *vt and vi* to fry
faire revenir to brown
gratiner {6} *vt* to brown the top of
flamber {6} *vt* to flambé
pocher {6} *vt* to poach

74.2 *Couper les aliments* To cut up food

débiter {6} *vt* **1** [obj: chicken] to cut up **2** [obj: salami] to slice
éplucher {6} *vt* to peel
peler {12} *vt* [like **éplucher**, but applies to fruit] to peel
écosser {6} *vt* to shell
râper {6} *vt* to grate
émincer {7} *vt* to cut into thin slices

74.3 *Plats à emporter* Food to take away

crêpe *nf* pancake *crêpe salée* pancake with savoury filling *crêpe sucrée* pancake with sweet filling
croque-monsieur *nm inv* ham and cheese on toast
croque-madame *nm inv* ham and cheese on toast with fried egg
hamburger *nm* hamburger
hot dog *nm* hot dog
fast-food *nm* fast-food restaurant

usage

French sandwiches
The word **sandwich** *nm* is widely used, and refers to a piece of *baguette* with a filling, or to a more recent import, the triangular sliced bread sandwich. In the language of cafés, a ham sandwich is *un jambon-beurre*, and its gherkin variant is *un jambon-beurre-cornichons*.

74.4 *Repas* Meals

petit déjeuner *nm* breakfast
p'tit déj *nm* [informal, humorous] breakfast
déjeuner *nm* lunch
dîner *nm* [evening meal] dinner
souper *nm* **1** [late meal, after e.g. the theatre] supper **2** [in some country areas, synonym for **dîner**] dinner
thé *nm* [British-style late afternoon meal with tea and cakes] tea

usage

Meals at various times of the day
When asking about the various meals of the day, times of the day are often substituted. Thus: *Qu'est-ce que tu manges d'habitude à midi?* means What do you normally have for lunch? and *Qu'est-ce que je vais leur faire ce soir?* is the equivalent of What shall I give them for dinner? *Le matin je prends du fromage* means that you eat cheese at breakfast, not mid-morning or at lunchtime.

74.5 *La nourriture* Food

Because the word **nourriture** *nf* has scientific overtones, it is often avoided when the speaker wishes to refer to day-to-day eating. E.g.: *des plats chinois* Chinese food *un régime végétarien* vegetarian food *Tu as acheté à manger pour ce soir?* Did you get food for tonight?

bouffe *nf* [slang] grub
en-cas *nm* snack
portion *nf* [helping cut out of a cheese or cake] portion
se servir {35} *v refl* (often + *de*) to help oneself *Servez-vous de la salade.* Help yourself to some salad.

74.6 *Éléments du repas* Courses

entrée *nf* starter
hors-d'œuvre *nm pl* (cold) starter
plat *nm* **de poisson** fish course
plat *nm* **principal** main course
fromage *nm* cheese course *J'ai attendu le fromage pour sortir mon Châteauneuf-du-Pape* I waited until the cheese course before I served my Châteauneuf-du-Pape
dessert *nm* **1** [last part of the meal] BrE pudding AmE dessert *Qu'est-ce qu'on a comme dessert?* What have we got for pudding? **2** [confection] dessert *Elle sait très bien faire les desserts.* She's very good at desserts.

74.7 *Repas spéciaux* Special meals

banquet *nm* [meal commemorating or celebrating something] banquet
lunch *nm pl* **lunch(e)s** [mainly at weddings] reception
collation *nf* refreshments *Une légère collation sera servie à l'entr'acte.* Light refreshments will be served during the intermission.
pique-nique *nm* picnic
pique-niquer {6} *vi* to have a picnic
méchoui *nm* whole roast mutton barbecue
barbecue *nm* barbecue

Le réveillon
Two special meals are known as **le réveillon**. *Le réveillon de Noël* is Christmas eve supper, for which families tend to come together. It is usually taken late in the evening of the 24th of December, and consists of festive food such as oysters, foie gras, roast turkey or goose with chestnuts, and a Yule log. The second *réveillon* usually takes place late on New Year's Eve, and includes some of the foods mentioned above, perhaps with venison or wild boar instead of roast fowl. The *réveillon du Jour de l'An* is less of a family occasion than a festival to be celebrated with friends, sometimes in a restaurant or a night club.

74.8 *Restaurants et cafés* Eating and drinking places

restaurant *nm* restaurant
resto *nm* [informal, short for restaurant] restaurant
café *nm* [serves various beverages including alcohol, and often sandwiches and snacks] café
brasserie *nf* [serves the same things as a café, but has more elaborate meals available at lunchtime] (large) café
auberge *nf* [usu situated in the countryside or in a village. May have rooms to rent] inn

menu *nm* menu *le menu à 240 f* the menu at 240 francs *Vous allez prendre à la carte ou au menu?* Will you order à la carte or have the set menu?

74.9 *Personnel* Catering staff

serveur *nm* waiter
serveuse *nf* **1** [serving at table] waitress **2** [behind the bar] barmaid

When calling a waiter to your table, you can call out *garçon!*, but modern usage inclines towards saying *monsieur!* instead. With the waitress, use *mademoiselle!* or *madame!*, always adding *s'il vous plaît* for politeness' sake.

chef *nm* **(de cuisine)** chef
cuisinier, -nière *nf* [in an institution or community] cook
barman *nm, pl* **barmans** ALSO **barmen** barman

74.10 *Manger* To eat

manger {8} *vt* and *vi* **1** [refers to feeding in general and to consuming a particular food] to eat *Elle n'a pas le droit de manger des féculents.* She's not allowed to eat starchy foods. *Je viens de manger une banane.* I've just eaten a banana. **2** [to have a meal] to eat *Vous avez mangé?* Have you eaten? *Viens manger dimanche midi.* Come over for Sunday lunch.
donner à manger à [commonly used phrase] to feed *Tu as donné à manger aux enfants?* Did you feed the children? *Qu'est-ce qu'on donne à manger à un poisson rouge?* What do you feed a goldfish on?
nourrir {19} *vt* [more formal than **donner à manger**. Scientific language] to feed *Un enfant de moins de trois mois doit de préférence être nourri au lait maternel.* A child less than three months old should preferably be fed on his mother's milk. *J'ai à peine assez d'argent pour nourrir ma famille.* I have barely enough money to feed my family.
goûter (à) {6} *vt* and *vi* (often + à) [to try for the first time, or to see if something is cooked] to taste *J'ai remis du sel, tu veux goûter?* I added some salt, do you want to taste? *Goûte aux cailles, elles sont délicieuses.* Taste the quails, they're delicious.
consommer {6} *vt* [term with economic overtones] to eat *Les Français consomment beaucoup d'huîtres à Noël.* The French eat a lot of oysters around Christmas time.

74.11 *Façons de manger* Ways of eating

manger comme un cochon to eat messily
manger comme un chancre to eat enormous amounts
dévorer {6} *vt* and *vi* to devour
avaler {6} *vt* to swallow
ronger {8} *vt* to gnaw
mâcher {6} *vt* and *vi* to chew
bouffer {6} *vt* and *vi* [slang] to eat *Qu'est-ce qu'on bouffe?* What is there to eat? *À quelle heure on bouffe?* What are we eating?
déguster {6} *vt* **1** [when referring to wines, brandy, etc] to taste *Quand on déguste des vins, il faut utiliser son nez au moins autant que sa bouche.* When tasting wines, you must use your nose as much as your mouth. **2** [to eat or drink, paying great attention to the taste] to enjoy *Nous avons dégusté une excellente cuisse de chevreuil.* We enjoyed a wonderful haunch of venison.

sucer {7} *vt* **1** [obj: e.g. sweet] to suck **2** [obj: e.g. bone] to gnaw
savourer {6} *vt* to relish
grignoter {6} **1** *vt* [take tiny pieces with one's teeth] to nibble at **2** *vi* [eat insufficiently] to eat like a bird
s'empiffrer {6} *v refl* [informal] to stuff oneself

When you come upon people eating, or when you leave a group of people who are eating, it is polite to say *bon appétit!* (literally, 'have a good appetite') have a nice meal. Whereupon, if they assume that you, too are, going to eat, they will answer *Merci, vous aussi* 'Thank you, same to you'

74.12 *Gens qui mangent* Describing eaters

gourmand, e *adj* [pejorative] greedy
gourmand, e *n* [pejorative] greedy person
gourmet *adj m* and *nm* gourmet
convive *nm* [at table] fellow-guest
gros mangeur *nm*, **grosse mangeuse** *nf* hearty eater

Locutions Idioms
Qui dort dîne. [If you haven't had enough to eat, find relief in sleep] He who sleeps eats.
avoir un appétit d'oiseau to eat like a bird
avoir un bon coup de fourchette [sometimes used ironically to mean being greedy] to have a healthy appetite

74.13 *Faim* Hunger

faim *nf* **1** [need for food between normal meals] hunger *avoir faim* to be hungry *un bébé qui a faim* a hungry baby *Je n'ai pas faim.* I'm not hungry. *J'ai une faim de loup.* I could eat a horse. **2** [famine] hunger *des pays où les gens meurent de faim* countries where people are dying of hunger
affamé, e *adj* [suffering in a famine. Sometimes describes hunger, without real suffering involved] hungry *les populations affamées du Sahel* the hungry people of the Sahel *Les enfants revenaient toujours affamés de ces longues promenades en montagne.* The children always returned (starving) hungry from those long mountain treks.
carence *nf* [absence of a necessary nutrient from a diet] deficiency *des carences en vitamine B* vitamin B deficiencies
famine *nf* famine
malnutrition *nf* [sociological term] malnutrition *des enfants qui souffrent de malnutrition* undernourished children

Locutions Idioms
Tu as/Il a les yeux plus grands que le ventre. [phrase used esp to children] Your eyes are bigger than your tummy/his eyes are bigger than his tummy.
avoir l'estomac dans les talons to be starving hungry
Il/Elle a la reconnaissance du ventre It's (only) cupboard love.

Citation Quotation
Ventre affamé n'a point d'oreilles. [From La Fontaine's fable *Le milan et le rossignol*, 1694] Someone who is hungry will not listen to reason.

75 Drinks and drinking

75.1 *Boissons* Drinks

boisson *nf* [term mainly used by drinks manufacturers and in catering and advertising] drink
boire {69} *vt* to drink *Qu'est-ce que vous buvez?* What will you have (to drink)? *Le chien a soif, donne-lui à boire.* The dog's thirsty, give him something to drink.
soif *nf* thirst *avoir soif* to be thirsty **mourir de soif** to die of thirst

---

In social drinking, references to 'a drink' are usually made without the word *boisson*, but with the verb *boire* instead. For example, *Viens boire quelque chose.* Come and have a drink.*Tu n'as pas oublié d'acheter à boire?* Did you remember to buy the drinks?

75.2 *Boissons alcoolisées courantes* Common alcoholic drinks

alcool *nm* alcohol *bière sans alcool* non-alcoholic beer *bière à faible taux d'alcool* low-alcohol beer
alcoolisé, e *adj* [containing alcohol] *une boisson légèrement alcoolisée* a drink with low alcohol content *une boisson alcoolisée* an alcoholic drink
vin *nm* wine
bière *nf* beer *bière blonde* lager *bière brune* stout
demi *nm* half a pint (of beer) *demi pression* half a pint of draught beer
cidre *nm* cider
panaché *nm* shandy
12/14 degrés d'alcool 12/14 per cent volume

Drinking before and after a meal
L'apéritif *nm*
It is customary to spend a little time before lunch and before dinner having one or more drinks, sometimes while nibbling peanuts, olives etc. This occasion is called *l'apéritif*. It is not impolite to invite someone you know really well for *l'apéritif*, but not for the meal that follows, although the host would be expected to have made this clear beforehand. For example, *Viens juste pour l'apéritif demain.* Come tomorrow, just for drinks before the meal. The drinks normally taken on this occasion are also called *un apéritif*: e.g. *Qu'est-ce que tu veux comme apéritif, un porto?* What will you have before we eat, a port?
Le digestif *nm* and **le pousse-café** *nm*
At the end of a large meal, you may be offered *un digestif*: This is a glass of anything alcoholic purporting to aid digestion: i.e. spirits or a liqueur. A more informal phrase is *un pousse-café*, meaning a glass of spirits taken with or after coffee.

75.3 *Boissons non alcoolisées* Soft drinks

eau *nf, pl* **-x** water *eau minérale* mineral water *eau gazeuse* sparkling water *eau non-gazeuse* still water *eau du robinet* tap water
jus *nm* juice *jus de fruit* fruit juice *jus d'orange* orange juice
limonade *nf* lemonade
diabolo *nm* [fruit syrup with still water] BrE cordial AmE fruit syrop *diabolo-menthe* mint-flavoured cordial *diabolo-fraise* strawberry-flavoured cordial

75.4 *Boissons chaudes* Hot drinks

café *nm* coffee *café décaféiné* decaffeinated coffee *café en grains* coffee beans *café moulu* ground coffee *café instantané* instant coffee
déca *nm* [informal] decaf
thé *nm* tea *thé en sachet* teabags *thé en feuilles* loose tea
sachet *nm* **de thé** teabag
feuilles *fpl* **de thé** tea leaves
chocolat *nm* (**chaud**) (hot) chocolate

Ordering coffee and tea
If you simply order *'un café, s'il vous plaît'*, you may well be asked for more information about the desired size: *'un grand?'* or *'un double?'* (a large one?), or *'un petit?'* (which refers to an espresso-sized coffee). But it will be assumed that you want it black. If you don't, make sure you specify *'un café au lait'*, or *'un crème'*. The latter will come with milk, not cream.
When ordering tea, the request for *'un thé, s'il vous plaît'* will usually result in questions such as *'nature?'* (with nothing in), *'citron?'* (with a slice of lemon). If you want it with milk, make sure you ask for *'un thé au lait, s'il vous plaît'*.

Being invited for coffee
You may be invited for coffee after a meal. *Venez prendre le café* may not mean 'Come and have coffee' (i.e., at around 11 a.m. as in Britain), but 'Come for coffee after the meal' (e.g., at about 1.30 p.m.). A variant on this type of invitation is *Venez prendre le café et le dessert*. In this case you are being invited to join the last part of the meal.

75.5 *Spiritueux* Spirits

eau-de-vie *nf, pl* **eaux-de-vie** fruit brandy
spiritueux *nm* [term used in the trade and in advertising] spirits *commerce de spiritueux* wines and spirits trade
armagnac *nm* brandy (from the Armagnac region)
cognac *nm* brandy (from the Cognac region)
calvados *nm* apple brandy (from Normandy)
scotch, ALSO **whisky** *nm* (Scotch) whisky
rhum *nm* rum
vodka *nf* vodka

75.6 *Accessoires* Drinking accessories

bouchon *nm* cork *Ce vin sent le bouchon.* This wine is corked.
tire-bouchon *nm*, **tire-bouchons** corkscrew
capsule *nf* [on bottle of lemonade, etc] (metallic) top
décapsuleur *nm* bottle opener
seau *nm, pl* **-x à glace** wine bucket
boîte *nf* can *une boîte de Coca* a can of Coke
canette *nf* [for beer] small bottle

75.7 *Boire* To drink

boire {69} *vt* to drink *boire à petits coups* ALSO *petites gorgées* to sip *boire à grands traits* to gulp down
tremper ses lèvres dans to take a sip of
lapper {6} *vt* to lap up
assoiffé, e *adj* [slightly formal] thirsty

75.8 *Alcoolisme* Alcoholism

boire {69} *vi* [abuse alcohol] to drink (too much) *Je ne bois pas.* I don't drink (alcohol).

saoûl, e *adj* drunk

ivre *adj* [more formal than **saoûl**] drunk

ivrogne *nm,* **ivrognesse** *nf* [pejorative and slightly informal] drunkard

alcoolique *n* [more formal] alcoholic

gueule *nf* **de bois** hangover *avoir la gueule de bois* to have a hangover

cure *nf* **de désintoxication** treatment for alcoholism *Il a fait plusieurs cures de désintoxication.* He went in several times to be treated for alcoholism.

sobre *adj* [describes permanent non-drinkers, also person with no alcohol in their system at a particular time] sober, abstemious, teetotal

sobriété *nf* sobriety

Locutions Idioms

être (un petit peu) pompette to be (a little bit) tipsy

avoir un verre dans le nez to have had a drop too much

être rond(e) comme une queue de pelle, ALSO **être saoûl(e) comme une barrique**, ALSO **être plein(e) comme un œuf** BrE to be plastered AmE to be drunk as a skunk

76 Work and working conditions

76.1 *Emploi* Employment

emploi *nm* **1** [occupation] job *être sans emploi* to be jobless *perdre son emploi* to lose one's job *retrouver un emploi* to get a new job (after being unemployed) *trouver un nouvel emploi* to get a new job (as a change from the previous one)
employer {17} *vt* to employ *employer qqn comme secrétaire* to employ sb as a secretary *Chez Luminex, ils emploient 400 personnes.* They have 400 people on the payroll at Luminex.
employé, e *n* employee
employeur, -yeuse *n* employer
petit boulot *nm* [informal. Unqualified occupation taken typically by students] (temporary) job
personnel *nm* staff *direction du personnel* personnel department
main-d'œuvre *nf, pl* **mains-d'œuvre** labour force

Locution Idiom
Qu'est-ce que vous faites/tu fais dans la vie? What do you do for a living?

76.2 *Chômage et recherche d'emploi* Unemployment and looking for a job

chômage *nm* unemployment *le taux de chômage* the unemployment rate *être au chômage* to be unemployed *pointer au chômage* BrE to be on the dole AmE to be collecting public assistance [especially unemployment benefits] *le chômage longue durée* long-term unemployment
chômeur, -meuse *n* unemployed person
demandeur, -deuse *n* **d'emploi** [actively looking for a job] unemployed person
chômer {6} *vi* [due to unemployment, or other causes] to be without work *Elle a chômé deux ans avant de trouver du travail.* She was unemployed for two years before she found a job. *Avec tout ce linge à repasser, je ne vais pas chômer cet après-midi!* What with all the ironing to do, I'm not going to be idle this afternoon!
Agence *nf* **Nationale Pour l'Emploi** ALSO **A.N.P.E.** BrE job centre AmE National Agency for Employment
entretien *nm* **professionnel** ALSO **d'embauche** job interview
postulant, e ALSO **candidat, e** *n* candidate (for a job)
Assedic *nm pl* [short for **Association pour l'Emploi dans l'Industrie et le Commerce**] unemployment benefit(s) *toucher les Assedic* to get unemployment benefit(s)
engager {8}, ALSO **embaucher** {6} *vt* BrE to take on AmE to hire
licencier {6} *vt* and *vi* to lay off
licenciement *nm* lay-off
embauche *nf* hiring, taking-on *La situation de l'embauche n'est pas bonne en ce moment.* Employers aren't taking people on at the moment.

76.3 *Conditions de l'emploi* Conditions of employment

charges *nf pl* **patronales** (employer's) overhead(s)
cotisation *nf* contribution to benefits, paid out of earnings *cotisation ouvrière* employee's contribution *cotisation patronale* employer's contribution
travail *nm* **au noir** [as part of the black economy] working on the side
travailler {6} *vi* to work *travailler à son compte* to be self-employed *travailler au noir* to work on the side *Leur nounou travaille au noir, ils ne la déclarent pas.* Their nanny is working on the side, they're not paying any contributions for her.
pension *nf* **d'invalidité** disability pension
congé-maladie *nm, pl* **congés-maladies** ALSO **congé** *nm* **de maladie** sick leave
congé-maternité *nm, pl* **congés-maternités** ALSO **congé** *nm* **de maternité** maternity leave
allocation *nf* BrE benefit AmE subsidy *allocations familiales* BrE child benefit AmE subsidies for (dependent) children
prud'hommes *nm pl*, industrial tribunal *aller aux prud'hommes* to go to an industrial tribunal

76.4 *Le temps du travail* Time at work

travailler à temps plein to work full time
travailler à temps partiel to work part-time
travailler à mi-temps to work half-time
avoir des horaires flexibles BrE to work flexitime AmE to have flexible working hours
faire des heures supplémentaires to work overtime
faire les trois-huit to work an eight-hour shift
pointer {6} *vi* to clock on

76.5 *Syndicats et patronat* Unions and management

syndicat *nm* (trade) union
syndical, e *adj, mpl* **-caux** (trade-)union
syndicaliste *n* union member
se syndiquer {6} *v refl* to join a union
partenaires *nm pl* **sociaux** [in negociations] management and unions
patronat *nm* management

76.6 *Travail* Work

travail *nm* **1** [task] work *Trouvez un travail à donner à l'intérimaire.* Find some work for the temp to do **2** [paid employment] work *une journée de travail* a day's work *J'ai de la chance de faire un travail qui me passionne.* I'm lucky enough to have a job which I love. **3** [load] work *Il y a beaucoup de travail à terminer avant le week-end.* There's a lot of work to finish before the weekend.
travaux *nm pl* [achievements expected or realized in the course of a project] work *Les travaux du comité seront publiés avant la fin du mois.* The committee's work will be published before the end of the month.

travailler {6} *vi* to work *mère qui travaille* working mother *Je travaille comme laborantin.* I work as a lab assistant. *Elle ne travaille plus.* She no longer works.
travailleur, -lleuse *n* [any person who works] worker
ouvrier, -rière *n* [in industry or in the trades] worker
charge *nf* **de travail** workload
boulot *nm* [informal synonym for **travail**, all senses] work
bosser {6} *vi* [informal synonym for **travailler**] to work
boîte *nf* [slang. One's place of work] *On a beaucoup de boulot en ce moment à la boîte.* We've got a lot on at work at the moment.

76.7 *Effort au travail* Effort at work

besogne *nf* [implies hard, difficult] task
dur, e *adj* **à la tâche** willing to work till one drops
surmenage *nm* overwork
se surmener {9} *v refl* to overwork
bourreau *nm, pl,* **-x de travail** workaoholic

Locutions Idioms
avoir du pain sur la planche to have a great deal of work to do
travailler comme un fou ALSO **un malade** to work like a slave
aller vite en besogne 1 [used as a compliment] to be a fast worker **2** [pejorative] to jump ahead

77 Office work

77.1 *Bureau* Office

bureau *nm, pl* **-x 1** [room where one works] office *Je passe au bureau chercher mes dossiers.* I'll drop in at the office and pick up my files. **2** [building] **bureaux** offices *La société a ses bureaux Boulevard de la Loire.* The company's offices are in Boulevard de la Loire.

77.2 *Équipement* Equipment

see also **98.1 Informatique**
bureautique *nf* [registered trademark used as a common name] electronic office equipment
ordinateur *nm* computer
clavier *nm* keyboard
écran *nm* screen
souris *nf* mouse
traitement *nm* **de texte** [software] word processor
tableur *nm* spreadsheet
base *nf* **de données** database
imprimante *nf* printer *imprimante laser* laser printer
scanner *nm* scanner
modem *nm* modem
photocopieuse *nf* photocopier
photocopie *nf* photocopy
serveur *nm* (computer) server
disquette *nf* floppy disk
moniteur *nm* monitor
disque *nm* **dur** hard disk drive
lecteur *nm* **de CD Rom** CD Rom drive
curseur *nm* cursor
multimédia *adj inv* multimedia
PC *nm* PC, personal computer *un PC multimédia* a multimedia PC

77.3 *Fournitures de bureau* Office stationery

agenda *nm* diary
chemise *nf* **(cartonnée)** folder
classeur *nm* **1** [book] binder *classeur à anneaux* ringbinder **2** [cabinet] filing cabinet
intercalaire *nm* [for ringbinder] divider
dossier *nm* file

77.4 *Personnel* Staff

employé, e *n* **de bureau** office worker
secrétaire *n* secretary *sécretaire de direction* personal assistant
dactylo *n* typist
réceptionniste *n* receptionist
intérimaire *n* temp
standardiste *n* switchboard operator

78 Shopping

78.1 *Magasins* Shops/Stores

see also **108 (Gambits)**
magasin *nm,* ALSO **commerce** *nm* BrE shop AmE store *Tous les commerces se trouvent Rue Abélard.* All the shops are in Rue Abélard.
faire les commissions ALSO **courses** [refers to everyday shopping for food, etc] to shop *Va faire les courses pour ta mère, s'il te plaît.* Could you go and buy a few things for your mother please?
liste *nf* **de commissions** ALSO **de courses** shopping list

78.2 *Commerces d'alimentation* Food shops/stores

see also **72.1 Produits laitiers et crémerie**
boulangerie *nf* BrE baker's (shop) AmE bakery
pâtisserie *nf* cake shop
charcuterie *nf* pork butcher's and delicatessen
boucherie *nf* BrE butcher's (shop) AmE butcher shop
triperie *nf* butcher's (specializing in offal)
épicerie *nf* BrE grocer's (shop) AmE grocery store
alimentation *nf,* ALSO **magasin** *nm* **d'alimentation** BrE grocer's (shop) AmE grocery store
primeurs *nm pl* BrE greengrocer's (shop) AmE fruit and vegetable store
poissonnerie *nf* BrE fish shop AmE fish store
commerce *nm* **de vins** BrE off-licence AmE wine store

Traiteur
The word **traiteur** *nm* refers to high-class catering, e.g. for private parties, often with delivery to the home. Whenever you see the word *traiteur* on a shop front, as in *charcutier traiteur, poissonnier traiteur*, expect a choice of prepared dishes to take away. A shop bearing the name *traiteur* tends to supply more refined foods than an ordinary shop, and to charge accordingly.

78.3 *Autres commerces* Other shops/stores

mercerie *nf* BrE haberdasher's AmE fabric store
bureau *nm* **de tabac** [licensed to sell tobacco and stamps] cigarette shop
Maison *nf* **de la Presse** [registered trade name of a large chain of stores selling newspapers, books, tobacco, stamps] BrE newsagent's AmE news dealer
pharmacie *nf* BrE chemist's (shop) AmE pharmacy
quincaillerie *nf* ironmonger's
boutique *nf* **1** [any small shop] shop **2** [selling clothes] boutique
fonds *nm* **de commerce** [legal term] shop *céder son fonds de commerce* to sell one's shop

78.4 *Grandes surfaces* Large shops/stores

supermarché *nm* supermarket
hypermarché *nm* hypermarket
supérette *nf* (small) supermarket
libre-service *nm, pl* **libres-services** self-service shop
grand *nm* **magasin** department store

> **usage**
>
> The phrases *grande surface, petite surface* and, less frequently, *moyenne surface*, are used commonly to refer to a large supermarket, a small supermarket and a middle-sized supermarket respectively. *Nous n'avons pas ça, Madame, vous ne le trouverez qu'en grande surface.* We don't stock this item, madam, you'll only find it in a supermarket. Note that the word *surface* is not used on its own in this context.

78.5 *Dans le magasin* In the shop/store

comptoir *nm* counter
caisse *nf* **1** [in a small shop] *caisse (enregistreuse)* BrE till AmE register *Tenez, madame, voici votre paquet, vous pouvez passer à la caisse.* Here you are, here's your purchase, please go to the till. **2** [in supermarket] cash desk *On fait la queue à toutes les caisses.* There's a queue at each cash desk.
Caddie *nm* [registered trademark], ALSO **chariot** *nm* BrE (supermarket) trolley AmE shopping cart
vitrine *nf* shopwindow
étalage *nm* window display
rayon *nm* [in a department store] department *Où est le rayon des gants, s'il vous plaît?* Where's the glove department, please?

78.6 *Les commerçants* Shopkeepers/storeowners

see also **72.1 Produits laitiers et crémerie**
Below, we have assumed that each listed shopkeeper is an owner. While this may not always be the case in reality, this is often the way we refer to them. Another possible translation, avoiding the ownership issue, is 'the man/woman in the bookshop', 'the man/woman in the dairy', etc.
boulanger, -gère *n* baker
pâtissier, -ssière *n* cake shop owner
charcutier, -tière *n* pork butcher
boucher, -chère *n* butcher
tripier, -pière *n* butcher (specializing in offal)

épicier, -cière *n* grocer
poissonnier, -nnière *n* BrE fishmonger AmE fish dealer
marchand, e de fruits et légumes ALSO **marchand, e** *n* **de primeurs** greengrocer
marchand, e *n* **de vins** BrE wine merchant AmE wine shop owner
mercier, -cière *n* BrE haberdasher AmE fabric store owner
buraliste *n* [licensed to sell tobacco and stamps] tobacconist
pharmacien, -cienne *n* BrE chemist AmE pharmacist
quincaillier, -llière *nf* BrE ironmonger AmE hardware store owner

78.7 *Magasins où l'on nettoie les vêtements* Laundries

teinturerie *nf*, ALSO **blanchisserie** (dry-)cleaners' *J'ai porté ton pantalon à la teinturerie* ALSO *blanchisserie*. I've taken your trousers to the cleaners.
laverie *nf* (**automatique**) launderette

79 Farming

79.1 *Agriculture* Farming

agriculture *nf* farming *méthodes d'agriculture* farming methods
agricole *adj* **1** [in economics] agricultural *politique agricole commune* common agricultural policy **2** [of a farm or farms] farm (as adj) *exploitation agricole* farm *ouvrier agricole* farm labourer
monoculture *nf* single-crop farming
ferme *nf* **1** [business] farm *ferme d'élevage* cattle (breeding) farm *animaux de la ferme* farm animals **2** [building] farmhouse *cour de ferme* farmyard
fermier *nm* farmer
fermière *nf* **1** [in her own right] woman farmer **2** [spouse] farmer's wife
cultiver {6} *vt* to farm *Ils cultivent deux cents hectares en Beauce.* They farm two hundred hectares in the Beauce. *Je ne cultive plus que du colza.* My only crop now is rapeseed.
cultivateur *nm*, ALSO **agriculteur** *nm* **1** [owner or tenant of a farm] farmer **2** [general term] farm worker
cultivatrice *nf* ALSO **agricultrice** *nf* [owner or tenant of farm] woman farmer
culture *nf* **1** [process] farming *la culture du pavot* poppy farming **2** [land] sown field *Ne passe pas à travers les cultures.* Don't walk across the sown fields.
paysan, -sanne *n* [not pejorative] **1** [person who owns and works a small plot of land] small farmer **2** [labourer] farm worker
ouvrier, -rière agricole [synonym for **paysan 2**] farm worker
métayer, -yère *n* share-cropper
labourer {6} *vi* and *vt* [by hand or with a machine] BrE to plough AmE to plow

79.2 *La terre* Farmland

champ *nm* field *champ de pommes de terre* potato field
prairie *nf* meadow
verger *nm* orchard
terres *nf pl* **maraîchères** market gardens
vignoble *nm* vineyard
pré *nm*, ALSO **pâturage** *nm* pasture (for grazing)

haie *nf* hedge
fossé *nm* ditch
bocage *nm* [mainly in western France] farmland with
  hedgerows

79.3 *Bâtiments à usage* agricole Farm buildings

grange *nf* barn
étable *nf* cowshed
porcherie *nf* pigsty
laiterie *nf* dairy
silo *nm* silo
les dépendances de la ferme the farm outbuildings

79.4 *Machines agricoles* Farm machinery

charrue *nf* BrE plough AmE plow
tracteur *nm* tractor
remorque *nf* trailer
moissonneuse-batteuse *nf* combine harvester

79.5 *Cultures* Arable farming

récolte *nf* 1 [what is harvested] crop *une grosse récolte de
  tomates* a heavy crop of tomatoes 2 [process] harvesting
  au moment de la récolte at the time of harvesting
récolter {6} *vt* 1 [have by way of crop] to grow 2 [collect.
  Obj: e.g. tomato, potato] to harvest
moisson *nf* (wheat) harvest
moissonner {6} *vi* and *vt* to harvest
vendanges *nf pl* [in wine-making] grape-picking
vendanger {8} *vi* [in wine-making] to pick the grapes
cueillette *nf* [of fruit, nuts and flowers. By hand] picking
fenaison *nf* hay-making

79.6 *Cultures céréalières* Cereal crops

céréale *nf* cereal crop
blé *nm* wheat
maïs *nm* [for animal feed] corn
orge *nf* barley
avoine *nf* oats
seigle *nm* rye
foin *nm* hay
meule *nf* (**de foin**) haystack
botte *nf* **de foin** bale of hay
paille *nf* straw
chaumes *nm pl* [after harvesting] stubble *faire brûler les
  chaumes* to burn the stubble

79.7 *Productivité agricole* Farm productivity

terre *nf* land *bonne terre* fertile land *terre maigre* ALSO
  pauvre poor land
engrais *nm* fertilizer *mettre de l'engrais (sur un champ)* to
  manure (a field)
engraisser {6} *vt* 1 [obj: e.g. land] to fertilize 2 [obj: e.g.
  cattle] to fatten
purin *nm* [made by animals] liquid manure
fumier *nm* (animal) dung *tas de fumier* dung heap

79.8 *Élevage de bestiaux* Sheep and cattle farming

berger *nm* shepherd **bergère** *nf* shepherdess
troupeau *nm*, *pl* **-x** herd
bestiaux *nmpl* [commonly used term. Large animals reared
  for meat] livestock
ovins *mpl* [scientific and farming term] sheep
bovins *mpl* [scientific and farming term] dairy and meat
  cattle
tondre {53} *vt* to shear
traire {61} *vt* to milk *machine à traire* milking machine

80 Gardening

80.1 *Jardin et activités du jardinier* Garden and gardener's activities

jardiner {6} *vi* to do gardening
jardinier, -nière *n* gardener
jardinage *nm* gardening *faire du jardinage* to garden
creuser {6} *vt* and *vi* [obj: e.g. earth, hole] to dig
tondre {53} *vt* to mow
désherber {6} *vt* and *vi* to weed
mauvaise herbe *nf* weed *enlever les mauvaises herbes* to
  remove the weeds.
semer {9} *vt* and *vi* to sow
planter {6} *vt* to plant
tailler {6} *vt* 1 [obj: e.g. tree] to prune 2 [obj: e.g. hedge] to
  trim
élaguer {6} *vt* [obj: e.g. branch] to prune
éclaircir {19} *vt* [obj: e.g. seedlings] to thin (out)
jardin *nm* garden
pelouse *nf* lawn
herbe *nf* grass
plate-bande *nf*, *pl* **plates-bandes** flowerbed
serre *nf* greenhouse
tuteur *nm* (supporting) cane
compost *nm*, ALSO **terreau** *nm* compost heap
tondeuse *nf* lawnmower

80.2 *Ustensiles de jardinier* Gardener's tools

bêche *nf* spade
fourche *nf* fork
plantoir *nm* trowel
pioche *nf* pick
cisaille *nf* (pair of) shears
sécateur *nm* (pair of) secateurs
binette *nf* hoe
rateau *nm*, *pl* **-x** rake
rouleau *nm*, *pl* **-x** roller
brouette *nf* wheelbarrow

80.3 *Le sol* The soil

sol *nm* 1 [emphasizes chemical make-up] soil *un sol acide*
  acid soil 2 [refers to surface or area] ground *Le sol était
  durci par le gel.* Frost had hardened the ground.
terre *nf* 1 [standard term] earth *La bêche retourne la terre.*
  The spade turns the earth over. 2 [like **sol** 1] soil *une
  bonne terre* a rich soil
terrain *nm* [estate] land *La maison est vendue sans le
  terrain.* The house is for sale without the land.

Locution Idiom

avoir la main verte, ALSO **les doigts verts** BrE to have green fingers AmE to have a green thumb

81 Relaxing, playing and sport

81.1 *Loisirs* Leisure

see also **64.13 Repos et détente**, **81.4 Jeux**, **81.9 Sport**

loisirs nm pl [pursuits, time devoted to these] leisure *Quelles sont vos activités de loisirs?* What do you do with your leisure time? *pendant mes loisirs* in my free time

à mes/tes/ses heures perdues in my/your/his/her spare time

passe-temps nm inv pastime

violon nm **d'Ingres** [implies unusual] hobby

81.2 *Loisirs de plein air* Outdoor hobbies

pêche nf **à la ligne** angling

canne nf **à pêche** (fishing) rod

hameçon nm hook

appât nm (piece of) bait

pêcher {6} vt and vi to fish

camping nm **1** [activity] camping *faire du camping sauvage* to camp in the wild **2** [site] camp(ing) site

tente nf tent

sac nm **de couchage** sleeping bag

camper {6} vi to camp

campeur, -peuse n camper

bivouaquer {6} vi [overnight or for a short while, usu in a group, outside of designated camp(ing) sites] to camp

filet nm **à papillons** butterfly net

attraper {6} vt [obj: e.g. fish, butterfly] to catch

81.3 *Aires de jeu et fêtes foraines* Parks and funfairs

jardin nm **public** park

aire nf **de jeu** play area

fête nf **foraine** funfair

marchand, e n **de glaces** ice cream seller

barbe nf **à papa** BrE candy floss AmE cotton candy

manège nm merry-go-round

attraction nf [in funfair] ride

diseuse nf **de bonne aventure** fortune teller

balançoire nf swing

balançoire nf **à bascule** seesaw

toboggan nm slide

bac nm **à sable** sandpit

cage nf **à poules** climbing frame

banc nm (public) park bench

tourniquet nm carousel

81.4 *Jeux* Games

jouer {6} vt and vi to play *jouer à la balle* to play ball *jouer à la marchande* to play shops *jouer au docteur* to play doctor(s) *jouer aux échecs* to play chess

jeu nm, pl **-x 1** [activity] game *une famille passionnée de jeux de cartes* a family that loves card games **2** [object or objects] *un jeu de dominos* a set of dominoes *un jeu de sept familles* [card game] a game of happy families

joueur, joueuse n player

partie nf game, match *une partie de poker* a game of poker *une partie d'échecs* a chess match

jeu nm, pl **-x informatique** computer game

console nm **de jeux** video game (machine)

81.5 *Jeux d'enfants* Children's games

jouet nm toy *une cuisine en jouet* a toy kitchen *un petit ramoneur en jouet* a toy chimney sweep

joujou nm [child's word] toy

poupée nf doll

maison nf **de poupée** doll's house

bille nf marble

train nm **électrique** train set

81.6 *Jeux de cartes* Card games

carte nf card *jouer aux cartes* to play cards *donner les cartes* to deal *un jeu de cartes complet* a complete pack of cards

couleur nf (card) suit

donne nf [set of cards dealt] hand (of cards) *une nouvelle donne* a redeal

pli nm trick *faire un pli* to take a trick

battre les cartes to shuffle the cards

les sept familles happy families *jouer (au jeu des) sept familles* to play happy families

---

Les couleurs

The suits below are used in the singular form when referring to suits in the plural: e.g. *Tu as du trèfle?* Have you got any clubs?

pique nm spades

cœur nm hearts

trèfle nm clubs

carreau nm diamonds

---

valet nm **de pique** jack of spades

reine nf **de cœur** queen of hearts

roi nm **de carreau** king of diamonds

as nm **de trèfle** ace of clubs

joker nm joker

81.7 *Jeux de société* Board games

jeu nm **de société** board game

échiquier nm chessboard

damier nm BrE draughtboard AmE checkerboard

échecs nm pl chess *Échec et mat!* Checkmate!

tour nm move *À toi le tour!* It's your move!

pion nm pawn

tour nf castle

cavalier nm knight

roi nm king

reine nf queen

fou nm bishop

81.8 *Jeux d'argent et de hasard* Gambling and games of chance

jouer {6} vi to gamble

joueur, joueuse n gambler

parier {6} vi to bet *parier sur un cheval* to bet on a horse

casino nm casino

loterie nf lottery *loterie nationale* national lottery

81.9 *Sport* Sport

see also **25.1 Habillement**

sport *nm* [any activity involving the development of the body] sport *faire du sport* to go in for sport

gymnastique *nf* **1** [movements for muscle-building and endurance training. Can be a competitive sport] gymnastics **2** [informal. Movements aimed at keeping fit] exercise

81.10 *Faire du sport* To go in for sport

jouer {6} *vt* and *vi* to play *Je joue au tennis.* I play tennis. *Tu joues au football?* Do you play football?

pratiquer {6} *vt* [more formal than **jouer**. Sometimes translated by an English verb indicating the particular sport being discussed] to play, to do *Je pratique le rugby.* I play rugby. *Ils pratiquent la musculation.* They do weight training. *Tu pratiques l'aviron?* Do you row? *J'ai un peu pratiqué le ski, quand j'étais jeune.* I did a little skiing when I was young.

faire {62} *vt* [informal for **pratiquer**] to play, to do *Je fais du badminton.* I play badminton. *Nous faisons de la natation ensemble le mardi.* We go swimming together on Tuesdays.

marquer {6} *vi* and *vt* to score *marquer un but* to score a goal

score *nm* score

faute *nf* foul *Il y a faute.* It's a foul.

tacler {6} *vi* to tackle

tacle *nm* tackle *faire un tacle* to tackle

but *nm* goal

corner *nm* corner

surface *nf* **de réparation** penalty area

81.11 *Les sportifs* Sports people

sportif, -tive *n* **1** [competitive athlete] sportsman, sportswoman **2** [person who likes sport] sports enthusiast

concurrent, e *n* competitor

équipe *nf* team

équipier, -pière *n* team member

arbitre *n* **1** [in football] referee **2** [in tennis] umpire

juge *n* **de ligne** [in tennis] linesman

juge *n* **de touche** [in rugby, football] linesman

81.12 *La compétition* Competition

compétition *nf* **1** [general word for playing to win] competition, competitiveness *avoir l'esprit de compétition* to be competitive **2** [event] contest

disputer {6} *vt* disputer un match to play in a match *disputer une compétition* to take part in a competition

tournoi *nm* [in tennis] tournament

match *nm*, *pl* **matchs** ALSO **matches** match *un match de rugby* a rugby match

partie *nf* [friendly match] game *une partie de tennis* a game of tennis

81.13 *Endroits où l'on fait du sport* Places where sports are played

stade *nm* stadium

piste *nf* track

couloir *nm* [on a track or in a swimming pool] lane

terrain *nm* BrE pitch AmE field *terrain de football* BrE football pitch AmE soccer field

court *nm* [in tennis, badminton] court

81.14 *Jeux de ballon et de volant* Racket and ball games

tennis *nm* tennis

badminton *nm* badminton

ping-pong *nm* table tennis

football *nm* BrE football AmE soccer

rugby *nm* rugby

basket *nm* basketball

volley(ball) *nm* volleyball

81.15 *Athlétisme* Athletics

athlétisme *nm* athletics *épreuves d'athlétisme* athletics events

athlétique *adj* athletic

athlète *n* athlete

course *nf* (running) track race

courir {33} *vi* and *vt* to run *courir le cent mètres* to run the hundred metres

coureur, -reuse *n* runner

marathon *nm* marathon

haie *nf* hurdle *le cent mètres haies* the hundred metres hurdle

sprinter *nm* sprinter

footing *nm* jogging *Je vais faire un petit footing.* I'll go for a little jog.

tour *nm* lap *tour d'honneur* lap of honour

saut *nm* jump *saut en longueur* long jump *saut en hauteur* high jump *saut à la perche* pole vault

javelot *nm* javelin

disque *nm* discus

poids *nm* shot

marteau *nm* hammer

lancer *nm* throw *le lancer du javelot* throwing the javelin *le lancer du poids* shot putting

81.16 *Sports nautiques* Water sports

natation *nf* swimming *faire de la natation* to swim

nager {8} *vi* and *vt* to swim

brasse *nf* breast stroke

crawl *nm* crawl

dos *nm* **crawlé** back stroke

nage *nf* stroke *nage indienne* side stroke *nage papillon* butterfly stroke

plongeon *nm* dive

plonger {8} *vi* to dive

plongeoir *nm* diving board

flotter {6} *vi* to float

faire la planche to float

81.17 *Quelques sports de gymnase* Some gymnasium sports

musculation *nf* weight training

aérobic *nm* aerobics

yoga *nm* yoga

81.18 *Arts martiaux* Martial arts

boxe *nf* boxing

boxeur *nm* boxer

ring *nm* ring

gant *nm* **de boxe** boxing glove

catch *nm* (professional) wrestling

sumo *nm* sumo wrestling

judo *nm* judo
karaté *nm* karate
escrime *nm* fencing

81.19 *Quelques sports de plein air* Some outdoor sports

cycliste *n* cyclist
cyclisme *nm* cycling
planche *nf* **à roulettes** skateboard *faire de la planche à roulettes* to do skateboarding
patin *nm* **à roulettes** roller-skate *faire du patin à roulettes* to roller-skate
patin *nm* **en ligne** roller-blade

81.20 *Randonnées et escalade* Walking and climbing

see also **6.2 Voyages et déplacements**
randonnée *nf* [similar to **excursion** but involves walking, or the use of a bicycle, canoe or horse] trip *faire une randonnée pédestre* to go rambling *faire une randonnée équestre* ALSO *à cheval* BrE to go for a hack AmE to go horseback riding *faire une randonnée à (dos de) poney* to go for a pony ride *faire une randonnée cycliste* to go for a bicycle tour
randonnée *nf* **(pédestre)** walking
randonneur, -nneuse *n* walker
escalade *nf* [general term] climbing
escalader {6} *vt* [general term] to climb
grimpeur, -peuse *n* [general term] climber
varappe *nf* [on cliff faces] rock-climbing *faire de la varappe* to go rock-climbing
varappeur, -ppeuse *n* [on cliff faces] rock-climber
alpinisme *nm* [on high mountains] mountaineering
alpiniste *n* [on high mountains] mountaineer
descente *nf* **en rappel** BrE abseiling AmE rappelling
chaussure *nf* **de marche** walking shoe

81.21 *Sports d'hiver* Winter sports

ski *nm* **1** [activity] skiing *le ski de fond* cross-country skiing *le ski alpin* downhill skiing **2** [piece of equipment] ski
bâton *n* **de ski** ski stick
chaussure *nf* **de ski** ski boot
patinage *nm* skating
patin *nm* **à glace** ice skate
patineur, -neuse *n* ice skater
patinoire *nf* ice rink
luge *nf* **1** [as competitive sport] toboggan *piste de luge* toboggan run **2** [for children] sledge *faire de la luge* to go sledging
bob ALSO **bobsleigh** *nm* bobsleigh

81.22 *Sports aériens* Aerial sports

parachute *nm* parachute *faire du parachute* to go parachuting *un saut en parachute* a parachute jump
parachutiste *n* parachutist
aile *nf* **libre**, ALSO **deltaplane** *nm* hang-glider *faire du deltaplane* to go hang-gliding
libériste *n* hang-glider
ULM ALSO **ultra-léger** *nm* **motorisé** microlight
montgolfière *nf* hot air balloon *faire de la montgolfière* to go ballooning

81.23 *Sports de tir* Target sports

tir *nm* shooting
exercices *nm pl* **de tir** target practice
arc *nm* bow
flèche *nf* arrow
cible *nf* target
archer, -chère *n* archer
fléchettes *nf pl* darts
fléchette *nf* dart
cible *nf* **(pour fléchettes)** dartboard
centre *nm* **de la cible** bull's eye
tir *nm* **(au fusil)** (rifle) shooting
tirer {6} *vi* and *vt* to shoot
cible *nf* target

81.24 *Boules et billard* Bowls and billiards

boules *nf pl* BrE bowls AmE lawn bowling
tirer {6} *vi* and *vt* to bowl
cochonnet *nm* jack
billard *nm* billiards
queue *nf* **de billard** billiard cue
table *nf* **de billard** billiard table

81.25 *Sports équestres* Equestrian sports

équitation *nf* [refers to the hobby aspect of the sport] BrE horse riding AmE horseback riding *faire de l'équitation* to go horse riding
monter {6} *vi* and *vt* [refers to the technical aspect of the sport] to ride *Tu sais monter (à cheval)?* Can you ride (a horse)? *Ce matin, vous allez monter Jocrisse.* You'll be riding Jocrisse this morning. *monter à cru* to ride bareback *monter en amazone* to ride sidesaddle
cavalier, -lière *n* rider
à cheval on horseback
cheval *nm*, *pl* **-vaux** horse
selle *nf* saddle
étrier *nm* stirrup
bride *nf* bridle
rêne *nm* rein
culotte *nf* **de cheval**, ALSO **jodhpurs** *nm pl* BrE jodhpurs AmE riding breeches
jockey *nm* jockey

Horses at different speeds
allure [of a horse, like trotting, cantering, etc] speed
aller au pas to walk
trotter to trot
aller au petit trot to canter
galoper to gallop

81.26 *Événements équestres* Equestrian events

saut *nm* **d'obstacles** showjumping
obstacle *nm* obstacle *franchir un obstacle* to clear a jump
dressage *nm* dressage
gymkhana *nm* gymkhana
turf *nm* horseracing
turfiste *n* racegoer
course *nf* **(de chevaux)** race *frequenter les courses* to go to the races regularly

82 The media and the performing arts

82.1 *Journalisme* Journalism

presse *nf* **1** [newspaper] the press *lire la presse* to read the press *la presse écrite* the newspapers *la presse parlée* the radio **2** [journalists] the press *La presse ne nous laisse pas un instant de répit.* The press won't leave us alone.
média(s) *nm pl* the media
médiatique *adj* geared to the media *une campagne électorale médiatique* an electoral campaign fought in the media
journal *nm, pl* **-naux** newspaper *journal télévisé* television news *journal d'opinion* [giving analysis as well as news] quality newspaper
quotidien *nm* daily (newspaper)
hebdomadaire *nm* weekly (magazine)
journaliste *n* journalist
article *nm* article *article de fond* in-depth article
éditorial *nm* editorial
magazine *nm* [general interest or specialized] magazine
revue *nf* **1** [usu special interest, and sold through subscription] magazine **2** [academic] journal
colonne *nf* **1** [on the page] column **2** [symbolizes the newspaper itself] *dans nos colonnes* within these pages
titre *nm* **1** [phrase printed above an article] headline *gros titre* main headline *très gros titre* banner headline **2** [journalist's term, referring to a newspaper] newspaper *Ce soir tous les titres ont une photo des sextuplés en première page.* Tonight all the newspapers have a picture of the sextuplets on the front page.
être à la une [on page one] to be headline news
canard *nm* [slang, often used affectionately] paper *Passe-moi le canard.* Pass the paper, please.
feuille *nf* **de chou** [pejorative. Worthless paper] rag

82.2 *Théâtre et cinéma* Theatre and cinema

jouer {6} *vt* and *vi* [as an actor, a musician, an entertainer] to play *jouer la comédie* to be an actor
spectacle *nm* [any type] show
donner un spectacle [used of a troupe or a person performing in a one-man-show] to put on a show
music hall *nm* variety entertainment *un spectacle de music hall* a variety show
variétés *nf pl* easy-listening music *un chanteur de variétés* a singer of popular songs
public *nm* [in general, people being entertained. Also, people in a particular auditorium] audience
studio *nm* [for making a film, a television or a radio programme] studio
metteur *nm* **en scène** director *Elle est metteur en scène depuis cinq ans.* She's been a director for five years.
programme *nm* programme *Demandez le programme!* Programme, Sir?/Madam?
art *nm* **dramatique** [form of expression] drama *établissement d'enseignement d'art dramatique* drama school
auteur *nm* **dramatique** playwright
tragédie *nf* tragedy **tragique** *adj* tragic
comédie *nf* **1** [theatre play] comic play **3** [in the cinema] comic film **2** [genre] comedy
comique *adj* comic
théâtre *nm* theatre **1** [form of entertainment] *le théâtre* the theatre **2** [place] theatre, playhouse

pièce *nf* **(de théâtre)** play
scène *nf* **1** [place] stage *entrer en scène* to come on (stage) **2** [part of play or film] scene
cinéma *nm* **1** [form of entertainment] *le cinéma* the cinema **2** [place] cinema
ciné *nm* [informal synonym for **cinéma 1** and **2**] cinema *Si on allait au ciné?* Do you want to go and see a film?
film *nm* film
écran *nm* screen *Elle passe bien à l'écran.* She looks good on screen. *sur grand écran* on the big screen
plan *nm* shot
premier plan *nm* foreground
première *nf* first night *J'ai toujours le trac les soirs de première.* I always suffer from stage fright on first nights.

Locutions Idioms
jouer la comédie 1 [in the theatre] to play **2** pejorative. Pretend] to put on an act
faire son cinéma [informal] **1** [pretend] to put on an act **2** [be fussy] to make a great scene about it

82.3 *Télévision et radio* Television and radio

télévision *nf* **1** [broadcasting system] television *Qu'est-ce qu'il y a à la télévision ce soir?* What's on television tonight? **2** [channel] (television) station *Toutes les télévisions ont diffusé ces images.* These pictures were shown on all the channels. **3** [receiver] television (set) *Dans le coin, une télévision braillait.* In the corner a television was blaring.
télé *nf* [informal] TV
chaîne *nf* channel
rembobiner {6} *vt* to rewind
avance *nf* **rapide** fast-forward *Appuie sur avance rapide.* Fast-forward it.
arrêt *nm* **sur image** BrE freeze frame AmE pause
radio *nf* **1** [broadcasting system] radio *Je l'ai entendu à la radio.* I heard it on the radio. **2** [channel] (radio) station *une radio de quartier* a local radio station **3** [receiver] radio
poste *nm* set *poste de télévision* television set *poste de radio* radio set
transistor *nm* (transistor) radio
chiffre(s) *nm (pl)* **d'écoute** ratings
émission *nf* programme *émission télévisée* television programme *émission de radio* radio programme
émettre {56} *vt* to broadcast *Nous émettons sur 657m ondes moyennes.* We broadcast on 657m medium wave.
série *nf* **télévisée** television series

82.4 *Acteurs* Actors

acteur, -trice *n* actor, actress
comédien, -dienne *n* [more prestigious than **acteur**. Can be theatre or cinema, but implies a solid theatrical background] actor, actress
comique *n* [usu telling gags to cabaret or studio audiences] comedian
rôle *nm* part *Dans 'Le Cid', il joue le rôle principal.* He plays the title role in 'Le Cid'.
doublure *nf* understudy
trac *nm* stage fright *avoir le trac* to suffer from stage fright
les méchants et les gentils [used humorously] the bad guys and the good guys

82.5 *Danse* Dance

see also **25.1 Habillement**

danse *nf* dance *faire de la danse classique* to do ballet dancing *les danses de salon* ballroom dancing

danser {6} *vt* and *vi* to dance *Elle a dansé dans 'Coppélia'.* She danced in 'Coppelia'. *Je sais encore danser le tango.* I can still dance the tango.

danseur, -seuse *n* dancer *une danseuse étoile* a prima ballerina

claquettes *nf pl* tap-dancing *faire des claquettes* to tap-dance

bal *nm* [indoors or outdoors] dance *Quand j'étais jeune, j'allais au bal le samedi soir.* When I was young, I used to go out dancing on Saturday nights.

discothèque *nf* disco

boîte *nf* [slang] *On sort en boîte ce soir.* We're going to a disco tonight.

82.6 *Musique* Music

musique *nf* music *faire de la musique* to play music

musical, e *adj, mpl* **-caux** musical

musicien, -cienne *n* musician

jouer {6} *vt* and *vi* (often followed by *de* + name of instrument) to play *jouer de la guitare* to play the guitar *De quel instrument joues-tu?* Which instrument do you play?

compositeur, -trice *n* composer

composer {6} *vt* and *vi* to compose

composition *nf* composition

82.7 Sortes de musique Types of music

la musique classique ALSO **le classique** classical music

la musique de chambre chamber music

le jazz jazz

le rock [1950s and 1960s music] rock 'n' roll *danser le rock* to jive

le reggae reggae (music)

la musique pop pop music

la musique folk ALSO **le folk** folk music

le blues the blues

82.8 *Caractéristiques de la musique* Aspects of music

mélodie *nf* [implies popular music] tune

mélodique *adj* **1** [as an appreciation] tuneful **2** [technical term] melodic *la ligne mélodique* the melodic line

air *nm* **1** [melody] tune **2** [in opera] aria

rythme *nm* [technical and general term] rhythm

cadence *nf* [general term] rhythm *Frappez dans vos mains en cadence.* Clap your hands in rhythm.

rythmique *adj* rhythmic

mesure *nf* **1** [between two bar lines] bar *les premières mesures sont fortissimo.* The opening bars are fortissimo. **2** [shown by conductor's baton] beat *Recommencez, en mesure.* Start again, following the beat. *battre la mesure* to mark the beat **3** [unit of time] *Dans le premier mouvement les mesures sont à trois temps.* There are three beats to the bar in the first movement.

harmonie *nf* harmony

discordance *nf* clash

82.9 *Ensembles musicaux* Musical ensembles

orchestre *nm* orchestra *orchestre symphonique* symphony orchestra *orchestre de chambre* chamber orchestra

chef *nm* **d'orchestre** conductor *Elle est chef d'orchestre depuis quatre ans.* She's been a conductor for four years.

baguette *nf* **(du chef d'orchestre)** (conductor's) baton

groupe *nm* [usu modern music] group *groupe de rock* rock group

fanfare *nf* [brass, usu associated with a town or a regiment] band

accompagner {6} *vt* to accompany

accompagnement *nm* accompaniment

solo *nm* solo *un solo de batterie* a drum solo

soliste *n* soloist

duo *nm* duet

trio *nm* [a work, also players] trio

quartette *nm* [players, mainly jazz] quartet

quatuor *nm* [a work, also players] quartet *quatuor à cordes* string quartet

82.10 *Instruments de musique* Musical instruments

instrument *nm* **(de musique)** (musical) instrument

instrument à cordes stringed instrument

instrument à vent woodwind instrument

les cordes the strings

les instruments à vent the woodwind section

les cuivres the brass section

les percussions the percussion section

soliste *n* soloist

Instruments à cordes Stringed instruments

violon *nm* violin **violoniste** *n* violinist

alto *nm* viola **altiste** *n* viola player

violoncelle *nm* cello **violoncelliste** *n* cellist

contrebasse *nf* double bass **contrebassiste** *n* double bass player

guitare *nf* guitar **guitariste** *n* guitarist

harpe *nf* harp **harpiste** *n* harpist

archet *nm* bow

corde *nf* string

Instruments à vent Woodwind instruments

hautbois *nm* oboe **hautboïste** *n* oboist

clarinette *nf* clarinet **clarinettiste** *n* clarinettist

flûte *nf* flute **flûtiste** *n* flautist

basson *nm* bassoon **joueur** *nm* **de basson** bassoonist

saxophone *nm* saxophone **saxophoniste** *n* saxophonist

Cuivres Brass instruments

trompette *nf* trumpet **trompettiste** *n* trumpeter

trombone *nm* trombone **tromboniste** *n* trombone player

cor *nm* French horn **joueur** *nm*, **joueuse** *nf* **de cor** French horn player

tuba *nm* tuba **joueur** *nm*, **joueuse** *nf* **de tuba** tuba player

Percussions Percussion instruments

percussionniste *n* percussionist

timbales *nf pl* timpani **timbalier, -lière** *n* timpanist

tambour *nm* drum

cymbale *nf* cymbal **cymbalier, -lière**, ALSO **cymbaliste** *n* cymbalist

xylophone *nm* xylophone **xylophoniste** *n* xylophonist

Instruments à clavier Keyboard instruments

piano *nm* piano **piano à queue** grand piano **pianiste** *n* pianist

orgue *nm* organ **organiste** *n* organist
touche *nf* key
clavier *nm* keyboard
pédale *nf* pedal

82.11 *Musique vocale* Vocal music

chanter {6} *vt* and *vi* to sing *Nous avons chanté le Requiem de Mozart.* We sang Mozart's Requiem.
chant *nm* **1** [activity] singing **2** [piece of music] song
chanteur, -teuse *n* singer
chorale *nf* choir **choral, e** *adj* choral *le chant choral* choral singing
choriste *n* chorister
soprano *nf* [female singer] soprano **soprano** *nm* [boy voice, score, instrument] soprano
contralto *nf*, ALSO **alto** *nf* [female singer] alto **alto** *nm* [female voice, instrument] alto
ténor *nm* [singer, voice, instrument] tenor
baryton *nm* [singer, voice] baritone
basse *nf* [singer, voice, score, instrument] bass
haute-contre *nm*, *pl* **hautes-contre** countertenor *voix de haute-contre* countertenor voice
opéra *nm* opera *chanteur nm d'opéra* opera singer *air nm d'opéra* operatic aria

82.12 *Événements musicaux* Musical events

concert *nm* concert *concert de rock* rock concert
comédie *nf* **musicale** musical
récital *nm* recital

82.13 *Œuvres musicales* Musical works

symphonie *nf* symphony
concerto *nm*, *pl* **concertos** ALSO **concerti** concerto *un concerto pour violon* a violin concerto
ouverture *nf* overture
chanson *nf* song
morceau *nm*, *pl* **-x** piece (of music)

82.14 *Solfège* Music theory

solfège *nm* **1** [subject of study] music theory **2** [book] music theory book
note *nf* note
portée *nf* stave
gamme *nf* scale *la gamme de do majeur* the scale of C major
la *nm* A
si *nm* B
do *nm* C
ré *nm* D
mi *nm* E
fa *nm* F
sol *nm* G

clef *nf* **de sol** treble clef
clef *nf* **de fa** bass clef
armature *nf* key signature
accord *nm* chord
octave *nm* octave
dièse *nm* sharp
bémol *nm* flat

82.15 *Musique enregistrée* Recorded music

enregistrement *nm* recording *L'enregistrement réalisé en 1994 par Paul Muneau* Paul Muneau's recording of 1994
disque *nm* record
compact *nm*, ALSO **disque** *nm* **compact** compact disc
CD *nm* CD
cassette *nf* cassette
album *nm* [usu implies popular music] album
coffret *nm* boxed set
stéréo *nf* stereo *Je préfère écouter le concert en stéréo.* I prefer listening to the concert in stereo.
hifi *nf* **1** [reproduction] stereo system quality sound **2** [goods] stereo system equipment
magnétophone *nm* tape recorder
minicassette *nm* [registered trademark] cassette recorder
tourne-disque *nm*, *pl* **tourne-disques** record player
gramophone *nm* gramophone
chaîne *nf* **(hifi)** hi-fi system
platine *nf* turntable
casque *nm* (set of) headphones
lecteur *nm* **de cassettes** cassette player
lecteur *nm* **de compacts** CD player
mini-chaîne *nf* small stereo system

83 The visual arts, arts and crafts

83.1 *Peinture et dessin* Painting and drawing

artiste(-peintre) *n*, *pl* **artistes-peintres** artist
artistique *adj* artistic **artistiquement** *adv* artistically
peintre *n* painter
peindre {57} *vt* and *vi* to paint
illustrateur, -trice *n* illustrator
illustrer {6} *vt* to illustrate
tableau *nm*, *pl* **-x** [work] painting

Travaux artistiques et manuels Arts and crafts
see also **26.1 Textiles**

beaux-arts *nm pl* [refers mainly to painting, drawing and sculpture, sometimes includes architecture] art
poser {6} *vi* [subj: e.g. painter's model, sculptor's model, photographer's model] to pose
pose *nf* pose *prendre une pose* to strike a pose

83.2 *Fournitures pour artistes* Artists' materials

peinture *nf* paint *peinture acrylique* acrylic paint *peinture à l'huile* oil paint
pinceau *nm*, *pl* **-x** paintbrush
couleur *nf* colour *couleurs pour aquarelle* watercolours
palette *nf* palette
toile *nf* [material] canvas
chevalet *nm* easel
fusain *nm* charcoal crayon
pastel *nm* pastel crayon

83.3 *Oeuvres artistiques* An artist's work

peinture *nf* painting
toile *nf* [more formal term than **peinture**] painting
fusain *nm* charcoal drawing
pastel *nm* pastel drawing
portrait *nm* portrait
dessin *nm* [picture, also activity] drawing
croquis *nm* sketch
caricature *nf* (caricaturist's) cartoon
illustration *nf* **1** [picture] illustration **2** [activity] illustrating
premier plan *nm* foreground
arrière-plan *nm* background
perspective *nf* perspective
œuvre *nf* work (of art)

83.4 *Photographie* Photography

photo *nf* photo *prendre une photo de qqch* ALSO *prendre qqch en photo* to photograph sthg
photographique *adj* photographic
photogénique *adj* photogenic
photographe *n* photographer
photographie *nf* **1** [activity] photography **2** [image] photograph
photographier {6} *vt* to photograph
appareil-photo *nm*, *pl* **appareils-photos** [for still pictures only] camera
objectif *nm* lens *objectif grand-angle* wide-angle lens
téléobjectif *nm* telephoto lens
pellicule *nf* (roll of) film
négatif *nm* negative
diapositive *nf* slide
chambre *nf* **noire** darkroom
labo *nm* **photo** [informal] photographic lab
développer {6} *vt* [obj: e.g. film, picture] to develop
agrandir {19} *vt* to enlarge
agrandissement *nm* enlargement

83.5 *Sculpture* Sculpture

sculpture *nf* **1** [object] sculpture **2** [activity] sculpting
sculpteur *nm* sculptor *une femme sculpteur* a woman sculptor
sculpter {6} *vt* and *vi* to sculpt
statue *nf* statue
potier, -tière *n* potter
tour *nm* **(de potier)** potter's wheel
poterie *nf* **1** [activity] pottery **2** [object] pot
terre *nf* **glaise** (potter's) clay

83.6 *Travaux d'aiguille* Needlework

coudre {73} *vt* and *vi* to sew
couture *nf* **1** [activity] sewing *J'ai horreur de faire de la couture.* I hate sewing. *Elle fait de la couture à domicile.* She takes in sewing. **2** [two pieces of cloth together] seam **3** [work] needlework *Apporte-moi ma couture, elle est dans le panier.* Bring me my sewing, it's in the basket.
patron *nm* pattern
coton *nm*, ALSO **fil** *nm* **(à coudre)** BrE cotton AmE thread
laine *nf* wool
enfiler {6} *vt* to thread
point *nm* stitch *point avant* front stitch *point arrière* back stitch *point de feston* blanket stitch
crochet *nm* **(d'art)** crochet *faire du crochet* to crochet
crocheter {12} *vt* to crochet

tricot *nm* **1** [activity, also work in progress] knitting *As-tu fini ton tricot?* Have you finished your knitting? **2** [garment] jumper
tricoter {6} *vt* and *vi* to knit
maille *nf* *maille à l'endroit* knit stitch *maille à l'envers* purl stitch
brin *nm* **de laine** length of yarn
machine *nf* **à coudre** sewing machine
aiguille *nf* needle
bobine *nf* **de fil** BrE reel of cotton AmE spool of thread
pelote *nf* **à épingles** pincushion
broderie nf embroidery
tambour *nm* **à broder** embroidery frame
crochet *nm* crochet hook
aiguille *nf* **à tricoter** knitting needle
pelote *nf* **(de laine)** ball of wool
bouton *nm* button

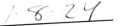

...usiness

84.3 *Prêts et emprunts* Lending and borrowing: nouns

dette *nf* debt *avoir une dette/des dettes* to be in debt *régler une dette* to pay a debt
endettement *nm* falling into debt
échéance *nf* [when in debt] date of repayment
remboursement *nm* **1** [sum] repayment *effectuer un remboursement de 1.000 francs* to repay 1,000 francs **2** [process] repaying *J'ai la possibilité d'étaler le remboursement de la dette sur dix ans.* I can repay the debt over a period of ten years.
compte-crédit *nm*, *pl* **comptes-crédits** [in a large store] store account
créancier, -cière *n* creditor
saisie *nf* [of a house, a yacht, etc] repossession
huissier *nm* bailiff
rééchelonner {6} *vt* [obj: e.g. debt] to reschedule

... *opérations bancaires*
Banks and banking

banque *nf* bank *avoir de l'argent en banque* ALSO *à la banque* to have money in the bank *Quelle est votre banque?* Who do you bank with?
compte *nm* account *compte en banque* ALSO *compte bancaire* bank account *compte courant* current account *compte de dépôt* deposit account *avoir un compte créditeur/débiteur* to have an account in credit/debit
employé, e *n* **de banque** bank clerk
banquier, -quière *n* banker
bancaire *adj* bank *références bancaires* banker's references
agence *nf* (*bancaire*) branch (of the bank)
guichetier, -tière *n* BrE (bank) cashier AmE teller
guichet, ALSO **distributeur** *nm* **automatique** cash dispenser, cash point

84.4 *Verbes exprimant les prêts et emprunts* Verbs of lending and borrowing

emprunter {6} *vt* to borrow *Je voudrais t'emprunter ta voiture.* I'd like to borrow your car. *Il m'a emprunté beaucoup d'argent.* He borrowed a lot of money from me.
prêter [{6} *vt* to lend *Peux-tu me prêter ton dictionnaire?* Could you lend me your dictionary? *Il a prêté cent francs à Robert.* He lent Robert 100 francs.
devoir {42} *vt* to owe *devoir de l'argent à qqn* to owe sb money
rembourser {6} *vt* **1** [obj: creditor] to pay back *Je te prête 1.000 francs mais tu me rembourses avant le week-end.* I'll lend you 1,000 francs as long as you pay me back before the weekend. **2** [obj: debt, money, sum] to repay *Je ne peux lui rembourser que 500 francs par semaine.* I can only (afford to) repay her 500 francs a week.
hypothéquer {10} *vt* to mortgage
s'endetter {6} *v refl* to fall into debt

84.2 *Documents et transactions* Documents and transactions

carnet *nm* **de chèques**, ALSO **chéquier** *nm* cheque book
chèque *nm* cheque *Il m'a fait un chèque sans provision.* He wrote me a cheque that bounced.
talon *nm* **de chèque** cheque stub
agio *nm* bank charge
traite *nf* **bancaire** bank draft
prélèvement *nm* **automatique** banker's order
virement *nm* transfer *faire un virement de 5.000 francs sur un compte* to transfer 5,000 francs to an account
position *nf* [state of one's account at a given time] balance *Quelle est ma position?* What is my current balance?
solde *nm* **(bancaire)** [amount on account after debit and credit have been computed. Term used in statements] (bank) balance
découvert *nm* overdraft *avoir un découvert (de 5.000 francs)* to be overdrawn (by 5,000 francs)
économies *nf pl* savings *faire des économies* to save
économiser {6} *vi* to save
relevé *nm* **de compte** bank statement

84.5 *Faire des affaires* To do business

commerce *nm* [buying and selling goods] trade, trading *le commerce des vins/de l'agro-alimentaire* the wine/food trade *Ils font le commerce des peaux.* They trade in animal hides.
affaires *nf pl* [trade] business *Les affaires vont bien/mal* Business is good/bad. *faire des affaires* to do (good) business *Elle est dans les affaires.* She's in business. *rendez-vous/réunion d'affaires* business appointment/meeting *homme d'affaires* businessman *femme d'affaires* businesswoman
concurrent, e *n* competitor
concurrence *nf* **1** [rivalry] competition **2** [rivals] competitors
s'associer avec {6} *v refl* **1** [referring to two people] to set up in association with **2** [referring to one person] to take on as an associate
partenariat *nm* partnership
association *nf* **professionnelle** trade association
exposition *nf* **commerciale** trade fair
exporter {6} *vt* and *vi* to export

Bank cards
The most widespread Switch-type card, debiting money directly from a current account, is called *la carte bleue*. It can be used at a cash dispenser, or to pay for a purchase in a shop. You give it to the salesperson, and he or she asks you to punch your PIN into a mini-keyboard. They turn away from you as you do so, to make sure they do not see the keys which you are punching. International credit cards and shopping scheme cards issued by some chain stores are called *cartes de crédit*. When paying by cheque in France you are not usually asked to produce a card to guarantee your cheque.

importer {6} *vi* and *vt* to import
import-export *nm* international trading *être dans l'import-export* to be in the import-export business
exportateur, -trice *n* exporter
importateur, -trice *n* importer
marque *nf* trademark *Il commercialise son miel sous la marque 'Avidor'.* He sells his honey under the trademark 'Avidor'. *marque déposée* registered trademark
nom *nm* **commercial** registered trademark

84.6 *Les sociétés* Companies

see also **37.2 Ceux et celles qui contrôlent**
entreprise *nf* company *monter une entreprise* to set up a company
société *nf* [same meaning as **entreprise**] company *société à responsabilité limitée* ALSO SARL limited liability company *Reverdex SARL* Reverdex Ltd
chef *nm* **d'entreprise**, ALSO **entrepreneur** *nm* company director
directeur *nm* **commercial**, **directrice** *nf* **commerciale** business manager
école *nf* **de commerce** business school
raison *nf* **sociale** company name

84.7 *Le commerce* Commerce

commerce *nm* **1** [place] BrE shop AmE store *J'ai mon commerce dans la rue Remouvier.* My shop is in Remouvier Street. **2** [trading] trade *Il a un commerce de maroquinerie.* He has a leather goods shop.
commerçant, e *n* **1** [owner] shopkeeper *Les commerçants de la ville s'opposent à l'ouverture de la nouvelle grande surface.* The town's shopkeepers are opposed to the opening of a new supermarket. **2** [person in a shop] shopkeeper *J'ai demandé à un commerçant de me dire où était l'hôpital.* I asked a shopkeeper to tell me where the hospital was.
marchand, e *n* **1** [in a market. Old-fashioned word] stall holder *jouer à la marchande* to play shops **2** [in a larger concern] trader *Ils sont marchands de vins de père en fils.* They've been in the wine trade for generations.
négociant, e *n* [like **marchand**] trader *gros négociant en fourrures* fur trader with a large company
représentant *nm* **(de commerce)** [selling door to door] sales rep, salesman *un représentant en aspirateurs* a vacuum cleaner salesman
concessionnaire *n* [with a franchise] dealer *votre concessionnaire Peugeot/Moulinex* your Peugeot/Moulinex dealer
promotion *nf* **1** [article] special offer *poires en promotion* pears on special offer **2** [action] offering as a special deal *faire une promotion sur les articles de sport* to do a special offer on sports goods
stocker {6} *vt* to stock
stock *nm* stock *Désolé, je n'ai pas cet article en stock.* This article is not in stock, I'm afraid.
entrepôt *nm* warehouse
entreposer {6} *vt* to warehouse
bail *nm*, *pl* **baux** [usu three years in duration] lease *bail à céder* lease for sale

84.8 *L'argent et les placements* Money and investment

chiffre *nm* **d'affaires**, ALSO **C.A.** turnover
exercice *nm* **courant** current trading year

perte *nf* loss *de grosses pertes* heavy losses *pertes et profits* profits and loss account *faire passer qqch par pertes et profits* to write sthg off
frais *nm pl* expenses *avoir beaucoup de frais* to have a lot of expense *frais généraux* overhead(s) *remplir une note de frais* to fill in an expenses claim
bénéfices *nm pl* profit *faire des bénéfices* to make a profit
bénéficiaire *adj* [describes: e.g. operation, company] profitable *marge bénéficiaire* profit margin
budget *nm* budget *inscrire qqch au budget* to budget for sthg
action *nf* share **actionnaire** *n* shareholder
placement *nm* [investing money or shares] investment *un bon placement* a sound investment
capital *nm* capital
intérêt *nm* interest *taux d'intérêt* interest rate *acheter qqch par traites à un taux d'intérêt de 10%* to buy sthg at an credit interest rate of ten per cent
analyste *n* **en placements** investment analyst
investissement *nm* **1** [spending money on buildings, equipment etc] investment **2** [as placement] investment *un investissement rentable* an investment with a good return
investir {19} *vt* and *vi* to invest
courtier *nm* broker *un courtier en assurances* an insurance broker
inventaire *nm* BrE stocklist AmE inventory *faire l'inventaire* BrE to stocktake AmE to take inventory
ristourne *nf*, ALSO **remise** *nf*, ALSO **rabais** *nm* discount
bilan *nm* balance sheet

84.9 *Acheter et vendre* Buying and selling

acheter {12} *vt* and *vi* **1** [general term] to buy *J'ai acheté un poulet pour ce soir.* I bought a chicken for tonight. *Ils ont acheté des actions Eurotunnel.* They bought some shares in Eurotunnel.
s'acheter *v refl* to be available from *Certains produits diététiques s'achètent uniquement en pharmacie.* Some health products can be bought only at the pharmacy.

Acheter quelque chose à quelqu'un
Beware of the two meanings of this construction, i.e. buying something for someone, or from someone. For example, *J'ai acheté un jouet à ma fille.* I bought a toy for my daughter. *J'ai acheté du poisson au marchand qui est sous la halle.* I bought fish from the fishmonger in the covered market.

---

achat *nm* purchase *payer un achat en liquide* to pay cash for a purchase *aller faire des achats* to go shopping
acheteur, -teuse *n* [private or professional] buyer
pouvoir *nm* **d'achat** purchasing power
prix *nm* **d'achat** purchase price
racheter {12} *vt* **1** [to repurchase an object which one had had previously sold] to buy back *Je vais lui racheter sa voiture.* I'll buy his car back from him. **2** [when the original purchase is inadequate, lost or broken, or when a further purchase is needed] to buy another *Il a grandi, il faut que je lui rachète des chaussures.* He's grown, I'll have to buy him another pair of shoes. *Il faut que tu ailles racheter du pain et du lait.* You must go and buy some more bread and milk. **3** [remove someone's financial interest in something] to buy out *Je te rachète ta part de l'héritage.* I'll buy you out of your share of the inheritance.
rachat *nm* [in company dealings] buyout
client, e *n* customer
compte *nm* **client** store account
clientèle *nf* customers
vendre {53} *vt* and *vi* to sell *vendre son affaire* BrE to sell up AmE to sell out

se vendre v refl to sell *Les crèmes solaires se vendent bien en ce moment.* Suntan lotions are selling well at the moment. *L'immobilier se vend mal.* Property sales are sluggish.

vente nf sale *vente aux enchères* auction (sale)

prix nm **de vente** selling price

vendeur, -deuse n **1** [of house, company] seller **2** [in shop] salesperson

prix n **de vente** selling price

solder {6} vt [in shops, for clearance; also in company dealings] to sell at a sale price

marchander {6} vt to bargain

marchandage nm bargaining

payer {16} vt and vi to pay

paiement nm payment

versement nm [partial] payment, instalment

verser {6} vt [in instalments, or as fee, gift, etc] to pay, to donate *J'ai versé 1.000 francs à Amnesty International.* I donated 1,000 francs to Amnesty International.

régler {10} vt and vi [refers to choice of cash, cheque or credit card] to pay *Vous réglez comment?* How are you going to pay for this?

règlement nm paying *faire un règlement par chèque/par carte* to pay by cheque/with a credit card *en règlement de votre facture* in payment of your invoice

mauvais payeur nm bad debtor

84.10 À la *Bourse* On the Stock Exchange

marché nm market *marché des titres* stock market *marché demandeur* buyer's market *marché vendeur* seller's market

marchand, e n **de titres** BrE dealer AmE broker

cours nm **du marché** market price

valeur nf **en Bourse** market value

acheter et vendre des actions to deal in shares

84.11 *Coûts et preuves d'achat* Expenditure and receipts

coût nm cost

coûter {6} vt to cost *Le manteau bleu coûte 1.500 francs.* The blue coat costs 1,500 francs. *coûter une fortune* to cost a fortune

dépenses nf pl expenditure *faire des dépenses* to spend money *faire des dépenses inconsidérées* to spend money like water

dépenser {6} vi and vt to spend

tarif(s) nm (pl) price, price list *Je n'ai pas augmenté mes tarifs depuis l'an dernier.* I haven't increased my prices since last year.

ticket nm **de caisse** (till) receipt

reçu nm receipt

facture nf invoice *établir une facture* to make out an invoice

facturer {6} vt to invoice *Je ne vous ai pas encore facturé les rideaux.* I haven't invoiced you for the curtains yet.

gratuit, e adj free **gratuitement** adv for free

liquide nm, ALSO **espèces** nf pl cash *payer qqch en liquide* ALSO *espèces* to pay cash for sthg *Tu as du liquide sur toi?* Do you have any cash (on you)?

Locutions Idioms

avoir du mal à boucler ses fins de mois ALSO **avoir des fins de mois difficiles** to have trouble making ends meet

Ça se vend comme des petits pains. It's selling like hot cakes.

acheter quelque chose chat en poche to buy a pig in a poke

Les conseilleurs ne sont pas les payeurs. [proverb] It's all very well to give advice when you don't have to pay.

84.12 *Argent* Money

argent nm money *Je n'ai plus d'argent.* I have no money left. *argent liquide* cash *argent de poche* pocket money *l'argent du contribuable* the taxpayer's money

monnaie nf change *de la petite monnaie* small change *faire de la monnaie* to change a note (into small change) *Vous pouvez me faire de la monnaie s'il vous plaît?* Could you change this note, please? *Vous m'avez rendu ma monnaie?* Did you give me my change?

fric nm [informal] dough *Rends-moi mon fric!* Let's have my dough back!

masse nf **monétaire** money supply

deniers nm pl **publics** taxpayers' money

numismatique nf **1** [hobby] coin and medal collecting **2** [area of expertise] numismatics

84.13 *Les devises* Currencies

franc nm franc *franc belge* Belgian franc *franc suisse* Swiss franc

centime nm (French) centime

livre nf pound sterling

lire nf (Italian) lira

mark nm mark

peseta nf peseta

drachme nm drachma

florin nm guilder

dollar nm (American) dollar

changer {8} vt to change *changer de l'argent* to change money *Pouvez-vous me changer 1.000 francs?* Could you change 1,000 francs for me?

cambiste n **1** [place] bureau de change **2** [person] money changer

euro nm euro

84.14 *Les objets associés à l'argent* Money and containers

billet nm bank note *le billet vert* the American dollar

coupure nf [usu with large denomination] banknote

pièce nf coin

piécette nf [small in value] coin *Donne-lui quelques piécettes.* Give him a few pennies.

porte-monnaie nm inv BrE purse AmE change purse

porte-feuille nm inv wallet

tirelire nf BrE money box AmE piggy bank

cochon-tirelire nm, pl **cochons-tirelires** piggy bank

sac nm **banane** BrE bum bag AmE fanny pack

84.15 *Comptabilité* Accounting

comptabilité nf **1** [figures] accounts *Montrez-moi votre comptabilité.* Show me your accounts books. **2** [area of expertise] accounting

comptable n accountant

expert-comptable nm, pl **experts-comptables** BrE chartered accountant AmE Certified Public Accountant *une femme expert-comptable* a chartered accountant

comptes nm pl accounts *faire,* ALSO *tenir ses comptes* to do one's accounts

livre nm **de comptes** (accounts) ledger

Locutions Idioms
On en a pour son argent! You get your money's worth!
aux frais de la princesse [in a bar] on the house [in other situations] at someone else's expense
Un sou est un sou. Money is money.
faire des comptes d'apothicaire [pejorative and humorous] to count every penny
rendre la monnaie de sa pièce à qqn to pay sb back (in kind)

84.16 *Peu cher* Cheap

bon marché 1 (used as an adjective, invariable) cheap *Les jupes étaient bon marché.* The skirts were cheap. **2** (used as an adverb) cheap(ly) *acheter qqch bon marché* to buy sthg cheap
peu cher (used as an adj) cheap *des produits d'entretien peu chers* cheap cleaning products
pas cher 1 (used as an adjective) [slightly informal] cheap *des vêtements pas chers* cheap clothes **2** (used as an adverb) *Tu l'as eue pour combien, ta voiture? – Je l'ai eue pour pas cher.* How much did you pay for your car? – I got it cheap.
camelote *nf* something cheap and of poor quality *C'est de la camelote, ton fer à repasser, il est tout neuf et déjà en panne.* Your iron is a piece of junk, it's brand new and it's already broken.

Locutions Idioms
C'est une occasion! It's a bargain!
C'est donné! [informal] It's dirt cheap!
de pacotille (used as an adjective) cheap and of poor quality

84.17 *Cher* Expensive

cher, chère *adj* [always follows the noun] expensive *des fruits chers* expensive fruit
cher *adv* *payer qqch cher* to pay a lot of money for sthg *Ils le vendent trop cher.* They're asking too much (money) for it.
coûteux, -teuse *adj* costly
cherté *nf* dearness *la cherté de la vie* the high cost of living
dispendieux, -dieuse *adj* [formal. Describes: e.g. habit, lifestyle] extravagant
onéreux, -reuse *adj* [formal] expensive
exorbitant, e *adj* [describes: e.g. price, cost] astronomical

Locutions Idioms
Ça vaut de l'or. It's worth a lot of money.
coûter la peau des fesses [informal] to cost an arm and a leg
C'est de l'arnaque. [slang] It's a rip-off.

84.18 *Riche* Rich

riche *adj* wealthy *un riche héritier* a rich heir **riche** *n* rich person
richesse *nf* wealth *La reine possédait des richesses inimaginables.* The queen possessed unimaginable riches.
enrichir {19} *vt* to make rich *Il est mort dans la misère mais ses droits d'auteur ont enrichi ses descendants.* He died destitute but his royalties made his descendants rich.
s'enrichir *v refl* to get rich

Nouveau riche
In French, there are two way of referring to newly made fortunes: **nouveau** *nm* **riche** (*pl* **nouveaux riches**) implies recently acquired wealth, but does not say whether it has been earned or inherited, whereas **parvenu, e** *adj* and *n*, is a word expressing contempt, and refers to wealth acquired in possibly illegal or at least unscrupulous ways.

fortune *nf* fortune *faire fortune* to make a fortune
fortuné, e *adj* [owning a fortune] wealthy
impôt *nm* **sur les grandes fortunes** wealth tax
coureur *nm* **de dot** fortune hunter
moyens *nm pl* (financial) means *avoir de gros moyens* to be well off

Locutions Idioms
avoir le portefeuille bien garni to be well off
être riche à millions/riche comme Crésus [informal] to be rolling in it
être plein aux as [slang] to be filthy rich
s'en mettre plein les poches [informal] to line one's pockets

84.19 *Pauvre* Poor

pauvre *adj* (after the noun) [describes: e.g. person, country, company] poor *parent pauvre* poor relation
pauvre *n* poor person *les pauvres* the poor *nouveau pauvre* new poor *tronc des pauvres* poor box
pauvresse *nf* [old fashioned term] poor woman
indigent, e *adj* [very poor] destitute
nécessiteux, -teuse *adj* and *n* [slightly old-fashioned] needy
misérable *adj* poverty-stricken
pauvreté *nf* poverty *en-dessous du seuil de pauvreté* below the poverty line
ruiner {6} *vt* [cause someone to lose his/her livelihood] to ruin
se ruiner *v refl* **1** [lose all one's money] to be ruined **2** [repeatedly overspend] to spend all one's money on *Elle s'est ruinée en appareils électroménagers.* She spent a fortune on domestic gadgets.

Locutions Idioms
pauvre comme Job poor as a church mouse
être sur la paille to be penniless
mettre qqn sur la paille to ruin sb
être sans le sou to be penniless
être dans le besoin to be in need *des familles dans le besoin* families in need
tirer le diable par la queue to struggle to make ends meet

85 Worth

85.1 *Valeur* Value

valoir {47} *vt* to be worth *La bague vaut 300 francs.* The ring is worth 300 francs. *Le boîtier est beau mais le mécanisme ne vaut rien.* The case is beautiful but the mechanical parts are worth nothing. *Les aquarelles de Jean Blot valent cher.* Jean Blot's watercolours are worth a lot. *D'après moi ton idée ne vaut rien.* I don't think much of your idea.
précieux, -cieuse *adj* precious

prix *nm* **1** [money] price **2** [value] worth
de prix, ALSO **de valeur** valuable *de grand prix*, ALSO *de grande valeur* very valuable
valeur *nf* value *un bijou d'une valeur marchande de 10.000 francs* a jewel worth 10,000 francs on the open market *C'est un objet qui a une grande valeur sentimentale pour moi.* This object has considerable sentimental value for me. *prendre/perdre de la valeur* to go up/down in value *sans valeur* worthless
rapport *nm* **qualité-prix** value for money *C'est d'un bon rapport qualité-prix.* It's good value for money.
appréciation *nf* increase in value
dépréciation *nf* depreciation
évaluer {6} *vt* to value *Le bijoutier a évalué mon émeraude à 40.000 francs.* The jeweller valued my emerald at 40,000 francs.
s'élever à {9} *v refl* [subj: e.g. fortune, damage] to be worth *Ses biens personnels s'élèvent à 3 millions.* Her personal possessions are worth three million.
trésor *nm* **1** [precious objects] treasure *Les archéologues ont ouvert la tombe et découvert un trésor.* The archaeologists opened the tomb and discovered a treasure. **2** [administrative and journalistic term] *le Trésor* the Treasury

Locutions Idioms
J'y tiens comme à la prunelle de mes yeux. It's worth more than my life to me.
Ça (en) vaut la peine. It's worth it. *Ne te mets pas en colère pour un petit oubli, ça n'en vaut pas la peine.* Don't get in such a state about a little oversight, it's not worth it.

85.2 *Gaspiller* To waste

see also **32.5 Ordures**, **91.6 Défaire et casser**
gaspiller {6} *vt* [obj: e.g. natural resources, materials, money] to waste *N'appuie pas si fort sur le tube, tu gaspilles la colle!* Don't squeeze the tube so hard, you're wasting glue!
gaspillage *nm* (often + de) waste *lutter contre le gaspillage des ressources de notre planète* to fight the waste of our planet's resources *Ils ont tout laissé dans leur assiette, c'est du gaspillage!* They left all their food on their plates, what a waste!
gâcher {6} *vt* [similar to **gaspiller,** but applies to resources and materials lost, not to money] to waste
gâchis *nm* [applies to natural resources, materials, money] waste

85.3 *Gaspiller l'argent* To waste money

dépensier, sière *adj* [who spends their money] extravagant **2** [who spends huge sums] big-spending
jeter l'argent par les fenêtres to throw money out the window
dépenser sans compter [spend without a thought for the consequences] to throw one's money around

Locution Idiom
C'est un panier percé. Money burns a hole in his/her pocket.

86 Economy

86.1 *L'économie* The economy

économie *nf* **1** [of a country] economy *L'économie va mal.* The economy is in poor shape. *une économie mixte* a mixed economy **2** [study, subject area] economics
économique *adj* **1** [belonging to economics] economic *selon tous les indicateurs économiques* according to all economic indicators **2** [cheap] economical *C'est plus économique d'acheter en gros.* It's more economical to buy wholesale.
économiste *n* economist
économe *adj* [usu in the context of someone's housekeeping qualities] thrifty
rendement *nm* **1** [extent of productiveness] productivity **2** [volume of production] output
rentable *adj* **1** [describes: e.g. land, factory] profitable

86.2 *La taxation* The system of taxation

impôt *nm* tax *impôt sur le revenu* income tax
taxe *nf* tax

Tax
While the term *impôt* covers all forms of tax, including income tax, *taxe* refers particularly to money levied on goods and services.

fisc *nm* BrE inland revenue AmE Internal Revenue (Service)
fiscal, e *adj*, *mpl* **-caux** fiscal, tax (as *adj*)
contributions *nf pl* [slightly more technical term] tax *contributions directes/indirectes* direct/indirect taxes
imposition *nf* level of taxation *tranche d'imposition* tax bracket
imposable *adj* taxable
déclaration *nf* **d'impôts** tax form
abattement *nm* tax allowance
redressement *nm* **fiscal** tax adjustment
dégrèvement *nm* **d'impôts** tax deduction
percepteur *nm* tax collector
fraude *nf* **fiscale** tax evasion
contribuable *n* taxpayer

Le tiers provisionnel
In France, a taxpayer has to pay tax each year, based on an estimate of his/her earnings the previous year. The sum is divided into three equal parts or *tiers*. Thus, one pays *le premier tiers provisionnel*, then *le second tiers provisionnel*, etc. Dates are set nationally by which these sums must be paid, with reminders to the public, broadcast on the media. The sum is adjusted the following year to take account of possible increases or decreases in one's level of income.

86.3 *La crise* The recession

crise *nf* **1** [slump] recession *C'est la crise!* There's a recession on! **2** [difficult situation] (economic) crisis *Le taux d'inflation actuel risque de provoquer une crise.* The current rate of inflation could cause an economic crisis.
inflation *nf* inflation *inflation galopante* galloping inflation
relance *nf* (**économique**) reflation

87 Existence, presence and absence

87.1 *Être et exister* To be and to exist

éternel, -nelle *adj* **1** [religious] everlasting **2** [pejorative] endless *Popeye et ses éternels épinards!* Popeye and his endless spinach!

infini, e *adj* **1**[philosophical] infinite **2** [great] boundless *avec une tendresse infinie* with boundless love

devenir {23} *vi* **1** [talking about the fate of people] to become *Qu'est-ce que tu deviens?* How are things with you? *Il est devenu coiffeur.* He became a hairdresser. **2** [subj: esp colours, moods] to turn *Il est devenu tout rouge.* He turned bright red.

existence *nf* **1** [philosophical] (the fact of) existing **2** [in common usage] life *Dans l'existence, on ne fait pas toujours ce que l'on veut.* You can't always do what you want in life.

identité *nf* identity *carte d'identité* identity card

vie *nf* life *à vie* for life *sans vie* dead

vivre {76} *vi* **1** [biological sense] to live **2** [to experience events] to live *Elle a beaucoup vécu.* She has lived an eventful life.

vivre *vt* to go through *Je viens de vivre des moments difficiles.* I've just been through a difficult time.

présence *nf* **1** [attendance] (fact of) being there *la présence de jeunes dans l'auditoire ce soir* the fact that there are young people in the audience tonight **2** [personal impact] presence *Elle a beaucoup de présence.* She has a great presence.

présent, e *adj* **1** [in attendance] here *Le coupable est présent parmi nous.* The culprit is here in our midst. *Verdier? – présent!* Verdier? – here! **2** [having impact] influential *Elle est très présente aux réunions.* She's rather influential at meetings.

87.2 *Se produire* To happen

arriver {6} *vi* **1** [with *il* or *ça, cela*. Subj: esp infrequent or unpredicted things] to happen *Il arrive que nous ne soyons pas d'accord.* We sometimes happen to disagree. **2** [subj: period, season, esp something that has been eagerly awaited or dreaded] to come *quand les vacances arrivent* come the holidays *Le jour de l'examen est arrivé.* The day of the exam came.

se passer {6} *v refl* [happen over time, move towards completion] to go. *Sa première journée d'école s'est bien passée.* Her first day at school went well. *Son mal de gorge ne se passait pas.* His sore throat wouldn't go away.

avoir lieu [esp when a particular place or time is envisaged] to take place *Le mariage aura lieu en l'église Saint-Joseph à onze heures* The marriage ceremony will take place at Saint-Joseph's church at 11 a.m.

se trouver {6} *v refl* [subj: esp chance happenings] to happen *Nous nous sommes trouvés ensemble dans la salle d'attente.* We happened to meet in the waiting room. *Il s'est trouvé qu'elle habitait la même rue que moi.* She happened to live in the same street as me.

tomber {6} *vi* [informal. Stresses the coincidence of the event with a date or other event] to fall *Cette année Noël tombe un lundi.* This year Christmas falls on a Monday.

87.3 *Ce qui se produit* Events and circumstances

événement *nm* [general term for anything that happens, simple or complex, happy or not] event

circonstance *nf* [one of the particulars of an event] detail *On n'a pas élucidé toutes les circonstances de l'accident.* The full details of the accident are not known.

cas *nm* [event typical of some trend or general rule] case *On a relevé des cas de typhoïde dans la région.* There have been cases of typhoid in the area.

occasion *nf* [good thing that happens, to be grasped and made the most of] opportunity. *C'est l'occasion de montrer ce que tu sais faire.* It's your opportunity to show what you're capable of. *J'ai saisi l'occasion.* I grabbed the chance (while I could).

incident *nm* [less grave than accident, never used of fatalities] incident

acte *nm* [involves a human cause] action *être responsable de ses actes* to be responsible for one's actions

87.4 *Comment sont les choses* The way things are

état *nm* **1** [durable way of being] state *un pays en état de guerre* a country in a state of war **2** [of a patient] state of health *Son état s'améliore depuis hier.* She's been better since yesterday. *dans un état grave* seriously ill

situation *nf* **1** [set of circumstances] situation *Tenez-moi au courant de la situation.* Let me know how the situation develops. **2** [personal circumstances, esp one's job] position *avoir une bonne situation* to have a good position *Sa situation est difficile depuis qu'il est à son compte.* He's been in a difficult (financial) situation since he's been self-employed.

Locutions Idioms

les choses étant ce qu'elles sont . . . , ALSO **dans l'état des choses . . .** [cliché implying powerlessness in the face of things] things being what they are . . .

Ce sont des choses qui arrivent. These things happen.

Un malheur ALSO **un accident est si vite arrivé!** [remark made when trying to prevent a dangerous situation from developing] It's so easy to have an accident!

en tout état de cause in any case

87.5 *Absence* Absence

absence *nf* **1** [non-availability] absence *en l'absence de preuve* in the absence of any proof **2** [in common usage. Defaulting on a commitment] being away *Il y a combien d'absences ce matin?* How many people are away this morning?

absent, e *adj* **1** [in common usage. Not in attendance] away *Il était absent de l'école hier.* He was away from school yesterday. **2** [not concentrating. In this sense the adjective can be qualified] distracted *Elle est très absente en ce moment.* She's often a bit distracted these days.

absent, e *n* [absent person] *Il y a un absent?* Is somebody missing? *Il y a combien d'absents?* How many people are missing?

absentéisme *nm* **1** [neutral term] absenteeism **2** [absence from work for spurious health reasons] malingering

manque *nm* lack *Nous sommes confrontés à un manque de personnel qualifié.* We are faced with a lack of qualified staff.

pas là [informal, spoken] not around *Je (ne) serai pas là ce soir.* BrE I shan't be around tonight. AmE I won't be there tonight.

ailleurs *adv* elsewhere *Elle a l'esprit ailleurs.* Her mind is elsewhere.

Locutions Idioms

Les absents ont toujours tort. [saying by which one justifies criticizing or contradicting people in their absence] Those who weren't there can't have a say.

briller par son absence [humorous] *Le repas était copieux mais les bons vins brillaient par leur absence.* There was plenty of food but fine wines were conspicuous by their absence.

Il est aux abonnés absents. [humorous reference to the telephone list of subscribers temporarily not in residence] You can never get hold of him.

Elle m'a fait faux bond. [to let sb down, e.g. by not turning up] She left me in the lurch.

Il m'a posé un lapin. [Informal. To fail to turn up for an appointment, usu in a love affair] He stood me up.

88 Truth, reality and illusion

88.1 *Qui dit la vérité* Truthful

sincère *adj* [voicing inner feelings and thoughts truthfully] sincere

sincérité *nf* sincerity

franc, franche *adj* [permanent character trait or behaviour on a particular occasion. Speaking out, even in adverse circumstances] frank

franchise *nf* truthfulness

candide *adj* [slightly pejorative. Truthful through inexperience] naive

candeur *nf* [slightly pejorative] naivety

Locutions Idioms

Il/Elle a son franc-parler, ALSO **Il/Elle ne mâche pas ses mots** He/she calls a spade a spade.

Il/elle joue franc-jeu, ALSO **Il/elle joue cartes sur tables** He/she plays fair.

Il est franc/Elle est franche comme l'or. He/she is always straight with you.

88.2 *Vérité* The truth

see also **88.7 Réel**

vrai, e *adj* **1** [describes: e.g. statement, story] true *C'est vrai que tu te maries?* It it true that you're getting married? **2** (often before the noun) [describes: e.g. nature, intentions] real *On n'a jamais connu les vraies raisons de son départ.* We never knew the real reasons why he left.

vraiment *adv* truly

vérité *nf* **1** [true facts] *la vérité* the truth *dire la vérité* to tell the truth **2** [remark encapsulating the truth] truth *C'est une vérité qui va lui faire de la peine.* He'll be hurt by it but it's the truth

avéré, e *adj* [formal. Which has been shown to be true] proven *Sa culpabilité est maintenant avérée.* It's now been proven that he's guilty.

véridique *adj* [describes words, speeches, stories] true

authentique *adj* **1** [not altered since it was made] authentic *un authentique fauteuil XVIIIème* a genuine 18th-century armchair *Les cuisines du château ont été modernisées, mais les robinets sont authentiques.* The kitchens of the château have been modernized, but the taps are genuine originals. **2** [in commerce and advertising. Describes: e.g. leather, cashmere] genuine **3** [representing truthfully one's inner feelings] authentic *Le film représente les émotions des survivants du massacre de façon authentique.* The film portrays the emotions of the survivors in an authentic way. **4** [not a lie] true *une histoire authentique* a true story

fait *nm* fact

Locutions Idioms

C'est trop beau pour être vrai. It's too good to be true.

Jurez de dire la vérité, rien que la vérité, (et) toute la vérité. Swear to tell the truth, the whole truth and nothing but the truth.

Toutes les vérités ne sont pas bonnes à dire. There are things which (although true) are better left unsaid.

La vérité sort de la bouche des enfants. [often used ironically when an adult has blurted out a truth] Out of the mouths of babes and sucklings . . .

dire ses quatre vérités à qqn to tell somebody exactly what one thinks of them.

C'est la vérité vraie! [informal. To emphasize one's sincerity] It really is true.

88.3 *Mensonges* Lies

faux, fausse *adj* (before the noun) [not true] untrue *C'est faux, je n'étais pas chez moi le soir du crime!* It's not true, I wasn't at home on the night of the murder! *faire une fausse déclaration* to make a false statement

faussement *adv* falsely *faussement accusé de viol* wrongly accused of rape

mensonge *nm* lie *dire un mensonge* to tell a lie *mensonge pieux* white lie

mentir {25} *vi* to lie *Ne me mens pas!* Don't lie to me!

menteur, -teuse *n* and *adj* liar *C'est une menteuse.* She's a liar. *Il est menteur.* He's a liar.

mensonger, -gère *adj* [describes : e.g. statement, advertisement] misleading

bobard *nm* [slang synonym for **mensonge**] fib *raconter des bobards* to tell fibs

contre-vérité *nf* [euphemism for **mensonge**] lie *proférer des contre-vérités* to be economical with the truth

Locutions Idioms

C'est vrai, ce mensonge? [jocularly said to children to encourage them to admit to a small lie, or to confirm a truth] So, was it true, what you said?

Elle ment comme elle respire. [is a habitual liar] She'll swear that black is white.

Il ment comme un arracheur de dents. He's a consummate liar.

parler la langue de bois [typically, politicians evading embarrassing questions] to use weasel words

88.4 *Cacher* To hide

see also **33.1 Couvert**

cacher {6} *vt* [general term. Intentional or accidental] to hide *L'animal creuse des galeries pour y cacher ses provisions d'hiver.* The animal digs underground burrows where it hides its winter food supply.

se cacher v refl to hide Le petit Paul s'était caché sous le lit. Little Paul was hiding under the bed.

dissimuler {6} vt [mostly implies intention to deceive] to hide J'essayais de leur dissimuler ma fatigue. I was trying to hide from them how tired I was.

camoufler {6} vt [similar to **dissimuler** but implies a cover or a cover-up] to hide Il portait des cols montants pour camoufler les cicatrices qu'il avait au cou. He wore high collars to hide the scars on his neck. camoufler un crime en suicide to disguise a murder to look like suicide

masquer {6} vt [involves a screen or something screening what you want to see] to conceal Je vais poser une tenture pour masquer la porte qui mène au garage. I'll put up a curtain to conceal the door to the garage.

voiler {6} vt [literary. Evokes a thin veil or gauze] to veil Une brume dorée voilait les bosquets. A golden mist hung like a veil over the shrubbery.

se voiler v refl [literary] se voiler une vérité to hide a truth from oneself

occulter {6} vt [put something disturbing out of sight or out of mind] to blank out J'avais occulté tout son passé troublant. I had mentally blanked out his dubious past.

planquer {6} vt [slang synonym for **cacher**. Often implies illegality] to hide

se planquer v refl [slang. Subj: e.g. criminal, refugee] to be in hiding

en cachette de without the knowledge of Elle sort la nuit en cachette de ses parents. She goes out at night without her parents' knowledge.

cachette nf hiding-place

cache nf [for dirty money, illegal drugs, weapons] cache

planque nf [slang] hiding-place

cache-cache nm inv hide and seek On fait une partie de ALSO on joue à cache-cache? Shall we play hide-and-seek?

88.5 Choses cachées Secrets

mystère nm mystery

secret nm secret C'est un secret de Polichinelle. It's an open secret.

arrière-pensée nf, pl **arrière-pensées** [hidden reason] ulterior motive C'est sans arrière-pensée que je lui avais offert de l'emmener en voiture jusqu'à Nice. I had no ulterior motive for offering to give her a lift to Nice.

88.6 Choses qui cachent d'autre choses Hiding things

paravent nm (folding) screen

cache nm 1 [for artists, designers, photographers] mask 2 [to cover part of a text] mask(ing) card

cache-sexe nm inv G-string

cache-prise nm inv socket protector

cache-pot nm inv potted plant holder

code nm (secret) secret code un message en code a coded message

Citations Quotes

Pour vivre heureux, vivons cachés. [from 17th-century fabulist Florian. Used ironically to stigmatize the cowardliness of those who fear political or social commitment] It's always better to avoid sticking one's neck out.

Attention, un train peut en cacher un autre. Take care, one train may hide another. [sign found at old-fashioned railway crossings. Now used humorously to indicate the need to be doubly cautious in some circumstances]

Cachez ce sein que je ne saurais voir! [Molière's famous line, spoken by Tartuffe in the play of that name to symbolize his hypocrisy as he leers at Elmire's cleavage] Cover this breast which I must not see!

88.7 Réel Real

see also **88.2 Vérité**

réalité nf [the world as it is, often implicitly compared to what we expect or would like it to be] reality Oui, mais la réalité c'est qu'il ne viendra pas. Yes, but the fact is, he's not coming. En réalité, c'est elle qui décide In fact, she's the one who makes the decisions.

réel, réelle adj real 1 [not imaginary] real Elle a un réel talent. She has real talent. 2 [not inadequate] considerable Pour réussir, il faut une réelle expérience du métier. You need considerable job experience in order to succeed.

vraisemblable adj 1 [appearing possible] convincing Invente une excuse, mais il faut qu'elle soit vraisemblable. Make up some excuse, but be sure it's convincing. 2 [probably true] likely Il est vraisemblable qu'il nous a dit la vérité. It is very likely that he told us the truth.

concret, -crète adj [not vague. Describes e.g.: plan, idea] tangible, positive On parle de divorce, mais il n'y a encore rien de concret. There's talk of a divorce, but nothing positive yet.

concrètement adv in actual fact Concrètement, qu'avez-vous à proposer? What do you suggest, in (actual) fact?

en fait adv [contrasts what has just been said with what is about to be said] in fact Elle avait dit vingt minutes mais en fait elle est arrivée deux heures plus tard. She'd said twenty minutes but in fact she arrived two hours later.

usage

réellement adv and **effectivement** adv

Réellement stresses that something is not imaginary, e.g.: J'ai réellement mal à la tête. I really do have a headache. **Effectivement** confirms a previously mentioned fact, or a fact which others may have at first doubted, e.g.: Il se plaignait de la tête et effectivement, on lui a découvert une tumeur. He complained of headaches and indeed they found he had a tumour.

Locutions Idioms

Ne prends pas tes désirs pour des réalités. Don't indulge in wishful thinking. [the set phrase is in the negative, but it was subverted by students in May 1968 and became a rallying cry for the libertarian movement: Prenez vos désirs pour des réalités! Act out your fantasies!]

La réalité dépasse la fiction. [a comment made when 'real life' events are felt to border on the fantastic] Truth is stranger than fiction.

88.8 Irréel Unreal

see also **88.9 Apparance**

faire semblant (often + de + infinitive) to pretend Ne fais pas semblant! Don't pretend! faire semblant de dormir to pretend to be asleep

imaginer {6} vt and vi to imagine

imagination nf imagination

imaginaire adj imagined

irréel, -réelle adj [evokes the supernatural. Describes e.g.: light, landscape] unreal

chimérique adj [colourful and unrealizable. Describes e.g.: plan, ambition] fanciful

illusion nf illusion. *Je n'ai* ALSO *ne me fais aucune illusion là-dessus.* I have no illusions about this.
illusoire adj [unrealisable though convincing] illusory *La véritable démocratie est illusoire.* True democracy is an illusion.
fantoche nm and adj [political contexts] puppet *un gouvernement fantoche* a puppet government

Locutions Idioms
C'est une vue de l'esprit. [expresses polite scepticism] All that is rather theoretical.
Il plane complètement. [very informal] He's in a world of his own.
Elle se fait des idées ALSO **illusions.** It's all in her mind.
Des châteaux en Espagne *Il bâtit des châteaux en Espagne.* He builds castles in the air. *Tout ça, ce sont des châteaux en Espagne.* All that's just (his) imagination.
Il/elle prend des vessies pour des lanternes. [imagines that things are much better than they really are] He/she can't recognize things for what they are.

88.9 *Apparence* Appearance

see also **88.8 Irréal**

apparence nf **1** [pejorative. Implies intention to deceive] show *Il t'a bien accueilli mais ce n'est qu'une apparence.* He gave you a fine welcome but it's all put on. *Les apparences sont trompeuses.* Things aren't always what they seem. *pour sauver les apparences* to keep up appearances **2** [outward features, not necessarily deceptive] look *À son âge, il conserve encore une belle apparence.* He still looks good for his age.
aspect nm **1** [general visible features] look *Le vieux voilier a un bel aspect.* The old yacht looks impressive. *L'insecticide se présente sous l'aspect d'un comprimé.* The insecticide comes in tablet form. **2** [suggests deceptiveness. Not necessarily pejorative] angle *Tout dépend de l'aspect sous lequel tu présentes la chose.* It all depends on the way you present the idea. *sous un aspect flatteur* in a flattering light
apparent, e adj **1** [noticeable. In this sense, the adjective can be qualified] obvious *Son mécontentement est (très) apparent.* He is (very) obviously angry. **2** [obvious but deceptive] apparent *Son mépris apparent de l'argent cache un tempérament calculateur.* Her apparent contempt for money conceals her calculating character.
air nm [less formal than **apparence.** Often refers to the face] look *un air malheureux* a look of misery *Ne prends pas cet air!* Don't look like that! (+ adj m) *Elle a l'air déçu.* She looks disappointed. (+ de + n) *Tu as l'air d'un clown.* You look like a clown. (+ de + infinitive) *Il a l'air de se fatiguer.* He looks as though he's getting tired.
façade nf [pejorative] outward show *Sous sa façade d'homme du monde, c'est un goujat.* Despite his outward show of urbanity, he's a lout. *de façade* superficial
semblant nm [pejorative. Feeble attempt at deceiving] semblance *un semblant de courage* a semblance of bravery *un semblant d'espoir* a glimmer of hope
faux-semblant nm [very pejorative. Calculated to deceive] pretence
impression nf [personal perception of things. Not necessarily mistaken] feeling *Elle donne l'impression d'avoir beaucoup souffert par le passé.* She gives the impression of someone who has suffered a lot in the past. *La maison donne une impression de vide.* The house feels empty.
figure nf [the way people or things present themselves to observers] *faire bonne figure* to create a good impression *faire triste* ALSO *piètre figure* to cut a sorry figure *faire belle figure* to cut an attractive figure *faire figure de qqch*

to appear to be sthg *Elle fait figure de victime mais c'est elle qui a tout manigancé.* She appears to be the victim but it was she who set up the whole thing.
jeter {11} vt, ALSO **lancer** {7} vt **de la poudre aux yeux** [impressing with brilliance, fame, etc] *Avec ses relations dans le spectacle elle nous jetait de la poudre aux yeux.* She used her show business connections to impress us.
paraître {64}, ALSO **sembler** {6} vi to seem
paraître vi [pejorative. Implies snobbery] to be seen to be doing well *Ils s'attachent beaucoup à paraître.* It matters a lot to them how they appear to the outside world.
apparaître {64} vi [formal. Expresses a judgment. No idea of deceptive appearances] to appear *L'idée apparaît (comme) excellente.* This idea does appear to be an excellent one.

> **u s a g e**
>
> **apparaître, paraître** and **sembler**
> **Paraître** and **sembler** are less formal than **apparaître** but have the same meaning. *L'idée semble,* ALSO *paraît excellente.* It seems to be an excellent idea.[Both imply that the impression received is mistaken, particularly when the verb is in a past tense] *La soirée semblait,* ALSO *paraissait finie.* To all appearances, the evening was at an end.
> Because **sembler** and **paraître** express a personal impression, use them when toning down a statement, e.g.:*Tu sembles,* ALSO *parais (être) contrarié.* You seem (to be) upset. For a more informal synonym, use **avoir l'air,** e.g.: *Tu as l'air (d'être) contrarié.* You look (as though you are) upset.

88.10 *Magie* Magic

magie nf [phenomenon, technique] magic *par magie* magically *comme par magie* as if by magic *magie noire* black magic *un tour de magie* a magic trick
magique adj **1** [describes: e.g. powers, formula] magic **2** [in names of products] *encre magique* invisible ink
magicien, -cienne n [entertainer or in fairy tale] magician
baguette nf **magique** (magic) wand *d'un coup de baguette magique* by waving a wand
sort nm spell *jeter un sort sur qqch* to cast a spell on sthg *jeter un sort sur qqn* to cast a spell on sb
truc nm (magic) trick

88.11 *Êtres magiques* Magic beings

fée nf fairy *conte de fées* fairy tale *au royaume des fées* in fairyland
gnome nm gnome
lutin nm elf
sorcier, -cière n wizard, witch *la méchante sorcière* the wicked witch

88.12 *Le surnaturel* The supernatural

esprit nm spirit
fantôme nm ghost *On dirait que tu viens de voir un fantôme.* You look as if you've just seen a ghost.
revenant, e n ghost (of a dead person)
hanter {6} vt to haunt
occultisme nm occult practices
occulte adj occult

89 Transformation and imitation

89.1 *Substituer* To substitute

remplacer {7} *vt* **1** [put or use instead of] to substitute *Remplacez le sucre par du miel.* Substitute honey for sugar **2** [subj: e.g. person] to substitute for *C'est vous qui me remplacerez pendant Noël.* You will stand in for me during the Christmas break. **3** [obj: esp things needing renewing] to replace *Je vais devoir remplacer les essuie-glaces.* BrE I'll have to replace the windscreen wipers. AmE I'll have to replace the windshield wipers.
se remplacer *v refl* to substitute for each other
prendre la place de [similar meaning to **remplacer 1**] to take the place of
substituer {6} *vt* [slightly more formal than **remplacer 1**. Always + *à*] *substituer quelquechose à autre chose* to substitute something for something else *Pour peindre les mobiliers d'enfants substituez les laques sans plomb aux laques traditionnelles.* When painting children's furniture, replace traditional glosses with lead-free ones.
de substitution alternative *des énergies de substitution* alternative forms of energy

usage

People replacing one another in their jobs
The person who deputizes for the public prosecutor is **le substitut du procureur.** A mayor's replacement is **le maire-adjoint.** Both phrases are masculine even when referring to a woman. When directly addressing a woman holder of such posts say *Madame le substitut (du procureur), Madame le maire-adjoint.* A person sent to represent a group is a **délégué, e** *n*: e.g. *Le syndicat a envoyé cinq déléguées.* The union sent five women delegates. A **représentant, e** *n* stands in for a political, administrative or commercial group: e.g. *Les représentants des principaux groupes automobiles étaient là.* Representatives of the main car manufacturers were in attendance. A male or female secretary standing in for another is **un** or **une intérimaire,** a temp. A male or female actor substituting for another is **une doublure,** an understudy.

89.2 *Transformer* To transform

changer {8} *vi* **1** to change *Les temps changent.* Times are changing. *Tu as changé!* [looks] You look very different! [personality] You've changed!
changer *vt* **1** [vary] to alter. *Changez la disposition des tables selon l'activité pratiquée par la classe.* Alter the arrangement of the tables to suit what the children are doing in class. **2** [replace with a new or different one. Obj: e.g. spark plug] to change **3** (always + *en*). [in magic] *changer qqn/qqch en* to change sb/sthg into
changement *nm* change *Un changement d'air me fera du bien.* I'll benefit from a change of environment. *Il y a eu beaucoup de changements dans ma société.* There have been a lot of changes in my company.
transformer {6} *vt* [may indicate greater changes then **changer**] to transform *L'informatique a transformé notre vie.* Computers have transformed our lives.
transformation *nf* transformation

adapter {6} *vt* (often + *à*) to adapt *Nous devons adapter nos modes de pensée à la nouvelle situation.* We must adapt our ways of thinking to the new situation.
s'adapter *v refl* (often + *à*) to adjust *Ils ont eu des triplés et il a fallu que toute la famille s'adapte.* They had triplets and the whole family had to adjust.
modifier {6} *vt* [change only slightly] to modify
modification *nf* modification
réformer {6} *vt* [obj: e.g. law, policy, religion] to reform
réforme *nf* reform
varier {6} **1** *vi* to vary *Son emploi du temps quotidien ne varie jamais.* His daily schedule never varies. **2** *vt* [change in different ways, usu for pleasure] to vary *J'essaie de varier les menus.* I try to vary the menus.
se métamorphoser {6} *v refl* **1** (often + *en*) to undergo a change *La grenouille s'est métamorphosée en prince.* The frog changed into a prince. **2** [positive or negative changes to looks or personality] to change drastically *Après la naissance de son fils il s'est métamorphosé.* He changed drastically after the birth of his son.
métamorphose *nf* drastic change.

Locution Idiom
retourner qqn comme une crêpe to force sb to make a complete U-turn

89.3 *Amélioration* Improvement

see also **57.7 Progrès**
améliorer {6} *vt* to improve *améliorer les rendements* to improve productivity **amélioration** *nf* improvement *Aucune amélioration n'est à prévoir pour la fin de la semaine.* No improvement is forecast for the weekend.
s'améliorer *v refl* to improve *Son travail en classe s'est amélioré.* His school work has improved.
progrès *nm* improvement *Tu en es à la page 345, il y a du progrès!* You're up to page 345, that's better! *faire des progrès* to improve *Tu as fait des progrès en musique.* You've improved in music.
Il y a du mieux. [informal. Often when discussing sb's health] Things are a bit better.

89.4 *Copier* To copy

copier {15} *vt* **1** [neutral term] to copy **2** [at school. Pejorative] to crib
copie *nf* [neutral term] copy
imiter {6} *vt* [neutral term. Suggests more skill than **copier**] to imitate
imitation *nf* **1** [neutral term] imitation **2** [commercial. Not pejorative] imitation *Le manteau n'est pas en lapin, c'est une imitation.* The coat is not made of rabbit fur, it's imitation. **3** [pejorative] forgery *Méfiez-vous des imitations.* Beware of forgeries.
faux *nm* [pejorative] forgery
faux, fausse *adj* (before noun) forged *faux passeport* forged passport *un faux nom* an alias
faussaire *n* **1** [making money] forger **2** [imitating branded goods] pirate
reproduction *nf* **1** [of painting] reproduction **2** [of statue, temple, cave paintings] replica
reproduire {82} *vt* to reproduce
fabriqué, e *adj* [describes: e.g. document, coin, bill] forged
contrefait, e *adj* [describes: e.g. signature] forged
postiche *adj* [describes: e.g. hair, beard] false
postiche *nm* **1** [hair] wig **2** [beard] false beard
plagiat *nm* [in art, especially literature] plagiarism
plagiaire *n* plagiarist
pastiche *nm* [implies art and skill in the imitation of a style. Usu for comic effect] pastiche *un pastiche de Kafka* a pastiche of Kafka

89.5 *Copier les gens et leurs comportement* Copying people and their behaviour

imitateur, -trice *n* impersonator
mouton *nm* **(de Panurge)** [pejorative] sheep *Les gens sont des moutons (de Panurge).* People behave like sheep.
se faire passer pour qqn to pretend to be sb

90 Full and empty

90.1 *Plein* Full

plein, e *adj* (often *de* + noun) full *Son verre est plein.* Her glass is full. *une cuvette pleine à ras bord* a basin full to the brim *un cartable plein de livres* a schoolbag full of books *à moitié plein* half full *Ne parle pas la bouche pleine.* Don't talk with your mouth full.
remplir {19} *vt* [obj: e.g. suitcase, cupboard] to fill
se remplir *v refl* [subj: e.g. bottle, bath] to fill up
combler {6} *vt* [fill until there is no room left. Obj: hole] to fill in
comble *adj* [so full that it feels crowded. Describes: e.g. room, hotel] full
complet, -plète *adj* [with no spare capacity. Often found on signs in hotel windows] full (up)

90.2 *Remplir une cavité* To fill a hole

boucher {6} *vt* [fill a hole that should not be there. Obj: hole] to fill (in)
plomber {6} *vt* [in dentistry] to fill
mastiquer {6} *vt* **1** [obj: e.g. window, glass pane] to seal with putty **2** [obj: e.g. join, gap] to fill (with filler).
rembourrer {6} *vt* [obj: e.g. quilt, pillow] to stuff

90.3 *Trop plein* Overfull

bondé, e *adj* [describes: e.g. room, station, train, bus] completely full
bourré, e *adj* (often *de* + noun) [describes: e.g. bag, drawer] completely full (with), stuffed full with *un placard bourré de médicaments* a drawer completely full with medicines
bourrer {6} *vt* **1** [pejorative] to overfill **2** [obj: pipe] to fill
se bourrer de *v refl* [pejorative] to stuff oneself with *Tu vas grossir si tu te bourres de chocolats.* You'll put on weight if you stuff yourself with chocolates.

usage

Having your petrol tank filled
Because self-service petrol stations are less numerous in rural areas of France than in the UK, you will often have to ask for petrol when travelling. Here's how to do it:
Le plein s'il vous plaît! Fill her up please!
Le plein de super, s'il vous plaît! Fill her up with four-star please!

Locution Idiom
On a fait salle comble. 1 [at a party, a show or a function] The place was full to bursting. **2** [in the theatre] It was a full house.

90.4 *Vide* Empty

vide *adj* [describes: e.g. bottle, room, drawer] empty *à moitié vide* half empty *C'est triste de rentrer le soir dans une maison vide.* It's sad to come home to an empty house at night. *La pièce était vide, les cambrioleurs avaient tout emporté.* The room was bare, the burglars had taken everything away.
vider {6} *vt* **1** [obj: e.g. cupboard, pocket, vehicle] to empty (out) **2** [in order to dispose of it. Obj: water, liquid] to pour out *Vide ton verre dans l'évier.* Empty your glass into the sink. **3** [drink] *vider son verre* to drain one's glass.
se vider *v refl* **1** [lose its contents. Subj: e.g. tube, bottle] to empty *La citerne se vide dans le tuyau.* The cistern empties into the pipe. **2** [become depopulated. Subj: e.g. office, street, village] to empty, to become deserted *La pièce s'est vidée.* The room emptied.
désert, e *adj* ALSO **déserté, e** *adj* [lacking a human presence. Describes e.g. office, town, village] deserted
décharger {8} *vt* [obj: vehicle] to unload
creux, creuse *adj* [with a dip or a cavity] hollow *des assiettes creuses* soup plates
creux *nm* hollow *J'ai un creux.* I'm hungry.
vierge *adj* [not yet filled. Describes: page, cassette, film] blank

Choses creuses ou vides Things that are hollow or empty
cadavre *nm* **(de bouteille)** empty *Les cadavres s'accumulent dans les poubelles après une fête.* The empties pile up in the waste bins after a party.
carie *nf* [in a tooth] hole
double fond *nm* [in a suitcase] false bottom
double paroi *nf* [in a wall, for insulation] cavity
double vitrage *nm* BrE double glazing AmE storm windows

Locution Idiom
La nature a horreur du vide. Nature abhors a vacuum.

91 Whole and fragmented

91.1 *Entier* Whole

entier, -tière *adj* **1** [not broken, divided or adulterated] whole *Tu boiras un verre entier de jus de fruits?* Will you drink a whole glass of fruit juice? *Es-tu sûr de manger ce gâteau entier?* Are you sure you'll eat this whole cake? *Il a avalé un abricot tout entier.* He swallowed an apricot whole. *faire entière confiance à qqn* to trust sb wholly **2** [in mathematics] *un nombre entier* a whole number
entièrement *adv* wholly
complet, -plète *adj* [comprising all the parts required] complete *la collection complète des oeuvres de Balzac* the complete works of Balzac **complètement** *adv* completely
plein, e *adj* [containing as much as it is possible to contain] full *une carafe pleine* a full carafe *à temps plein* full time *la pleine lune* the full moon
plénier, -nière *adj* [describes: meeting] plenary
intégral, e *adj*, *mpl* **-aux** [describes esp record collections] complete *la collection intégrale des enregistrements de Pavarotti* the complete collection of Pavarotti recordings
intact, e *adj* [which has not been broken or broached. Describes: e.g. vase, car after an accident] intact
indemne *adj* [describes esp person after an accident] unharmed

total, e *adj, mpl* **-aux** [affecting the whole of something]
total *avec une concentration totale* with total
concentration **totalement** *adv* totally
en tout (all) in all *Ça fait combien en tout?* How much is it
in all?

91.2 *Suffisant* Sufficient

suffisant, e *adj* **1** [when referring to quantities] enough
Deux citrons ne sont pas suffisants. Two lemons aren't
enough. **2** [in logic] sufficient *une condition nécessaire et
suffisante* a necessary and sufficient condition
suffire {81} *vi* (often preceded by *me, te, lui*, etc) to be
enough *Un coup de téléphone suffira.* A phone call will be
enough. *ça suffit!* that's enough! *Deux sacs en plastique,
ça te suffit?* Will two plastic bags be enough for you?
il suffit de 1 (+ infinitive) *Il suffit d'envoyer une enveloppe
timbrée.* Just send a stamped envelope. **2** (+ noun) *Il suffit
parfois d'un moment d'inattention pour changer une vie.*
Sometimes you let your mind wander for a moment and
it's enough to change your life.
suffisamment *adv* enough *On t'a suffisamment prévenu.*
You've had enough warning.
limiter {6} *vt* (often + *à*) to limit *limiter les naissances* to
limit the number of births (in a population)
se limiter à *v refl* to be limited *Entre nos deux familles, les
échanges se limitent à des cartes de Nouvel An.* Contact
between our two families is limited to exchanging New
Year's cards.

Locutions Idioms
à chaque jour suffit sa peine sufficient unto the day . . .
J'en ai assez! I've had enough!
J'en ai ras-le-bol! [informal] I'm sick to death of it.
Il se suffit à lui-même. [psychologically] He doesn't need
other people.

91.3 *Incomplet* Incomplete

partie *nf* [neutral. Also scientific term] part
morceau *nm, pl* **-x** piece
bout *nm* [informal. Can be pejorative] bit *un bout de
ficelle* a bit of string *un vieux bout de fromage* an old
piece of cheese
section *nf* [of things that have been cut neatly] section
quartier *nm* [of the moon] quarter
tronçon *nm* section *un nouveau tronçon d'autoroute* a
new section of motorway
complément *nm* extra bit *un complément d'information*
some extra information
parcelle *nf* (small) piece *une parcelle de terrain* a small
plot of land *une parcelle de minerai* a fragment of ore
inachevé, e *adj* unfinished *La symphonie inachevée* the
Unfinished Symphony
à peine ébauché 1 [drawing] only sketched out **2** [project]
embryonic
morcelé, e *adj* [describes esp land] divided up
manquer {6} *vi* **1** to be missing *Un bouton manquait.* A
button was missing. *Il manque un nez à ton bonhomme
de neige.* Your snowman is missing a nose. **2** *vt* (+ *de*) to
lack *Ton explication manque de précisions.* Your
explanation lacks precise details.

Locutions Idioms
Il ne fait pas les choses à moitié. BrE He doesn't do
things by halves. AmE He doesn't go halfway.
des morceaux choisis an anthology
finir en queue de poisson [to end without going
through the expected final stages] *La pièce finit en queue
de poisson.* The play doesn't have a proper ending.

91.4 *Inclusion* Inclusion

inclure {71} *vt* [a formal or scientific word] to include *Les
vertébrés incluent les reptiles.* Vertebrates include reptiles.
inclus, e *adj* included *Les piles ne sont pas incluses.*
Batteries are not included.
ci-inclus, e *adj* enclosed *Le bon de commande ci-inclus
vous permettra de faire votre achat sans attendre.* The
enclosed order form will enable you to complete your
purchase without delay.
ci-joint, e *adj* **1** [with a stapler or a clip] attached **2** [in
same letter] enclosed
comprendre {54} *vt* [a more neutral synonym for **inclure**]
to include *La maison comprend quatre chambres et deux
salles de bain.* The house includes four bedrooms and two
bathrooms.
compris, e *adj* [describes: e.g. prices, rates, fees] included
*Nous sommes tous allés faire une promenade en
montagne, enfants et chiens compris.* We all went off for
a walk in the mountains, children and dogs included.
y compris included *Ils ont licencié tout le personnel, y
compris la direction.* They sacked the entire staff,
including the management.
comporter {6} *vt* to comprise *Les mathématiques
comportent plusieurs branches, dont l'algèbre et la
géométrie.* Mathematics comprises several branches
including algebra and geometry.
dont *rel pron* of which, included within which *J'ai quatre
enfants dont deux sont installés à l'étranger.* I have four
children, including two who have settled abroad.
constituer {6} *vt* to constitute *L'abolition de la monarchie
a constitué un élément essentiel de la pensée politique
française moderne.* The abolition of the monarchy
constituted one of the founding principles of modern
French political thought.
être constitué, e de to be made up of *L'eau est constituée
d'oxgène et d'hydrogène.* Water is made up of oxygen
and hydrogen.
faire partie de to belong to *Je fais partie d'un groupe de
défense des consommateurs.* I belong to a consumer
protection group.
être, ALSO **faire partie intégrante de** to be part and
parcel of *Ce sont des responsabilités qui sont partie
intégrante de votre charge.* These responsibilities are an
integral part of your job.

91.5 *Exclusion* Exclusion

sauf *adv* except
excepté, e *adj* (before or after noun. Agrees with the noun
if placed after) [slightly more formal than **sauf**] except
*Rangez tous les livres par ordre alphabétique, excepté les
dictionnaires* ALSO *les dictionnaires exceptés.* Place all the
books in alphabetical order except for the dictionaries.
omettre {56} *vt* [slightly formal term] to omit *Dans la liste,
quelqu'un a omis leurs noms.* Someone omitted their
names from the list. *Elle a omis de me prévenir.* She
omitted to let me know.

*Expressions servant à désigner l'exclusion d'une personne
par une autre* Phrases for expressing social exclusion
ne pas faire attention à qqn [often when sb is attention
seeking] to ignore sb
faire semblant de ne pas voir qqn to pretend not to see
sb
faire comme si qqn n'était pas là to ignore sb's
presence
mettre qqn en quarantaine [as punishment, for example,
social misbehaviour] to send sb to Coventry, to ostracize sb

91.6 *Défaire et casser* To undo and to break

see also **91.11 Couper**

casser {6} *vt* **1** [cause to be no longer functioning. Obj: e.g. clock, machine] to break **2** [cause to be no longer whole. Obj: e.g. glass, stick] to break **3** [remove from its main part. Obj: e.g. lid, branch] to break off

briser {6} *vt* [same meanings as **casser**. This term is used less, except in some parts of France] to break

abîmer {6} *vt* [to impair the condition of sthg, often through carelessness] to damage *Des shampooings trop fréquents abîment les cheveux.* Washing your hair too frequently damages it.

s'abîmer {6} *v refl* [deteriorate over a period of time] to get damaged

endommager {8} *vt* [more formal than **abîmer**. Can be wilful, and stresses the loss of value of the affected object] to damage *Des vandales ont endommagé la statue.* Vandals damaged the statue.

défaire {62} *vt* [take apart. Can be reversed] to undo *Les coutures n'étaient pas au bon endroit, j'ai tout défait.* The seams were not in the right place, I undid them all.

démonter {6} *vt* [as **défaire**, but with obj: esp mechanism, construction] to dismantle *Pour faire passer le piano, il vous faudra démonter la porte.* You'll have to take down the door to get the piano through.

dégats *nm pl* damage *Les dégats se montent à trois millions.* Three millions' worth of damage has been caused.

91.7 *Détruire complètement ou presque* To destroy

détruire {82} *vt* [general term. Implies irreversible damage] to destroy *L'hélicoptère a été entièrement détruit.* The helicopter was completely destroyed.

démolir {19} *vt* **1** [for a reason, good or bad] to destroy *Ils voulaient démolir la vieille ville.* They wanted to destroy the old part of the city. **2** [for no good reason] to wreck *Il démolit tous ses jouets.* He wrecks all his toys.

démolition *nf* [used of buildings or ships only] demolition

destruction *nf* destruction *assister à la destruction de son pays* to watch one's country being destroyed

ravager {8} *vt* [wreak havoc on, ravage. Obj: esp country, features, crops] to devastate

anéantir {19} *vt* [reduce to nothing. Obj: e.g. fortified place, hopes] to annihilate, wreck

pulvériser {6} *vt* [reduce to powder through an enormous shock. Obj: e.g. window, meteorite] to smash to smithereens

effondrer {6} *vt* [make flat] to cause to collapse *Il était trop lourd et il a effondré le transat.* He was too heavy and the deckchair collapsed under him.

91.8 *Abîmer la surface* To damage surfaces

érafler {6} *vt* [very slight damage] to scratch slightly

écailler {6} *vt* [cause to come off in layers] to flake (off)

griffer {6} *vt* [with nails or claws] to scratch

rayer {16} *vt* [cause grooves or lines to appear of the surface of] to scratch

accroc *nm* **1** [in a garment] hole **2** [in tights] BrE ladder AmE run

dégrader {6} *vt* [obj: e.g. monument] to deface

91.9 *Abîmer en appuyant* To crush

étouffer {6} *vt* [stop from breathing] to smother

écraser {6} *vt* **1** [press down vertically on] to crush **2** [with a vehicle] to run over

cabosser {6} *vt* [obj: car body] to dent

91.10 *Abîmer exprès* To damage deliberately

saboter {6} *vt* **1** [damage for malicious reasons] to sabotage **2** [do badly and too fast] to bungle

vandaliser {6} *vt* [damage gratuitously] to vandalize

gâcher {6} *vt* [cause something to be less good than it could have been] to waste *Ne gâche pas les plus belles années de ta vie.* Don't waste the best years of your life.

gâter {6} *vt* [cause natural things like fruit, vegetables, a person's beauty, to be destroyed] to ruin *Les pluies ont gâté les récoltes.* Rain has ruined the crops.

Locutions Idioms

étouffer qqch dans l'oeuf to nip sthg in the bud

aller de mal en pis to go from bad to worse

tomber de Charybde en Scylla [a common phrase, in spite of its learned appearance] to jump out of the frying pan into the fire

91.11 *Couper* To cut

couper {6} *vt* **1** [divide] to cut (up) *Je coupe mes vieux tabliers pour en faire des chiffons.* I cut up my old aprons to make rags. **2** [make shorter] to cut *couper les ongles/cheveux d'un enfant* to cut a child's nails/hair **3** [remove] to cut (off) *couper un fil qui pend* to cut off a dangling thread

91.12 *Coupures sur le corps* Cuts to the body

coupure *nf* [always accidental] cut

égratignure *nf* [superficial] graze

amputer {6} *vt* [surgical only] to amputate

sectionner {6} *vt* [surgical, or by accident. Implies clean cut, with no possibility of repair] to cut (through) *Le fragment de verre lui a sectionné le doigt.* The glass shard cut through her finger.

poignarder {6} *vt* [with knife or dagger. The object of the verb is always a person, never a part of the body] to stab *Ils avaient poignardé le gardien de nuit.* They had stabbed the night watchman.

décapiter {6} *vt* [as punishment, or in accident] to decapitate

trancher {6} *vt* [savage cut, which separates at one blow] to slash. *On lui avait tranché la gorge.* He'd had his throat slashed.

avec un instrument contondant [in descriptions of murders or assault] with a blunt instrument

91.13 *Couper de la nourriture* To cut food

découper {6} *vt* **1** [in preparation, by butcher or cook Implies skill. Obj: e.g. chicken, piece of raw meat] to cut up **2** [at table] to carve

hacher {6} *vt* [into shreds. Obj: e.g. meat, onions] to mince

entamer {6} *vt* [remove the first slice from a loaf, a portion of cheese, etc] to start on *On entame le pain de seigle?* Shall we start on the rye bread?

91.14 *Couper des matériaux durs* To cut hard objects

fendre {53} *vt* [cut through the thickness of an object, usu into two pieces, with great force] to split *fendre des bûches pour le feu* to split logs for the fire
percer {7} *vt* **1** [make a hole or holes in] to pierce *Ne pas percer l'aérosol.* Do not pierce the aerosol can. *Percer le couvercle de la boîte en deux endroits.* Pierce two holes in the lid of the can. **2** [obj: tunnel] to bore
scier {15} *vt* [subj: esp person with saw, also rodent with teeth] to saw (off)
cisailler {6} *vt* [with scissors, usu implies a botched result. Obj: e.g. cable, metal sheet] to hack (at)
tronçonner {6} *vt* [cut a long object into several chunks] to cut up

Locutions Idioms
couper les cheveux en quatre to split hairs
Il/elle se ferait couper en rondelles pour moi. He/she'd do anything for me.
se mettre en quatre pour quelqu'un to go to great trouble for sb
à couper au couteau [very thick. The phrase is used in these two contexts] *brouillard à couper au couteau* thick fog *accent à couper au couteau* very strong accent/an accent you could cut with a knife
Je donnerais ma tête à couper que . . . I'd bet my life that . . .

91.15 *Détérioration* Deterioration

see also **57.10 Méchant et mauvais**
détérioration *nf* **1** [worsening] decline *Il y a eu une détérioration des rapports de confiance qui s'étaient établis entre nos deux nations.* There's been a decline in trust between our two nations. **2** [implies a loss of something that was once good] damage *Les détériorations dûes à la tempête n'ont pas encore été chiffrées.* Storm damage has not yet been evaluated yet.
détériorer {6} *vt* [make worse by impairing the qualities or effectiveness of. Intentional or accidental] to damage *La lumière du soleil a fini par détériorer les tranches des livres.* Sunlight eventually damaged the spines of the books.
se détériorer {6} *v refl* to decline
aggravation *nf* [going from bad to worse] worsening *Nous craignons l'aggravation du conflit.* We fear the conflict will get worse.
aggraver {6} *vt* to make worse *N'aggravez pas votre cas en mentant.* Don't make things worse for yourself by lying.
s'aggraver *v refl* [subj: e.g. situation, illness] to get worse, to worsen
empirer {6} *vi* [synonym for *s'aggraver*] to worsen *Son état n'a fait qu'empirer depuis ma dernière visite.* His condition has become steadily worse since I last visited him.

Locutions Idioms
aller de mal en pis to go from bad to worse
Ça pourrait être pire. It could be worse.
J'ai connu pire! [informal] I've known worse!

Être détruit petit à petit To be gradually destroyed
user {6} *vt* [through age or use] to wear out
s'user *v refl* to wear out *La pile s'use.* The battery is wearing out.
usure *nf* wear and tear
érosion *nf* [scientific term] erosion
s'éroder {6} *v refl* [scientific term] to erode
péricliter {6} *vi* [lose one's power. Subj: e.g. society, system] to decline
dépérir {19} *vi* [lose one's vitality. Subj: living beings] to fade away

92 Certainty, probability and possibility

92.1 *Possible* Possible

see also **92.4 Probable, 37.13 Autorisation**; opposite **92.3 Impossible, 92.5 Improbable, 37.14 Interdiction**
pouvoir {43} *vt* to be able to *Je ne peux pas vous accorder cette autorisation* I am not able to grant you permission in this instance.
possible *adj* **1** [which can be done] possible *si possible* if possible *autant que possible* as far as possible *Elle nous a opposé tous les arguments possibles et imaginables.* She listed every possible reason why not. **2** [which potentially exists] possible *dans le meilleur des mondes possibles* in the best of all possible worlds **3** [in the following informal phrases, to express surprise] *C'est pas possible!* It can't be! *C'est pas Dieu possible!* It simply can't be true! **possibilité** *nf* possibility
faisable *adj* [slightly informal] feasible *Paris–Nantes en trois heures, c'est faisable par le TGV.* Paris to Nantes in three hours is feasible if you use the TGV.
viable *adj* [likely to endure despite adverse conditions. Describes: e.g. project, financial operation] viable
réalisable *adj* [constituting a practical possibility] achievable
permettre {56} *vt* [cause to become possible] to allow *On fera un pique-nique si le temps le permet* We'll have a picnic, weather permitting. *Mon salaire ne me permet pas des vacances tous les ans.* My income doesn't allow me to take a holiday every year.
peut-être *adv* possibly *'Vous viendrez?' 'Peut-être, je ne suis pas sûr.'* 'Will you come?' 'Possibly, I'm not sure'

u s a g e

on peut
The simplest way to express a general possibility is to use *pouvoir* in the indeterminate *on* form: e.g. *On peut faire tenir 120 voitures sur le pont du ferry.* It is possible to fit 120 cars on the ferry deck. *On ne peut pas prévoir l'avenir.* It's not possible to predict the future. The same applies to practical possibilities: e.g. *On ne peut pas copier une disquette protégée.* You can't copy a protected disk.

Locutions Idioms
Qui veut la fin veut les moyens. [proverb. If your desire to achieve a particular outcome is great enough, you'll have to use whatever means are necessary] He who wills the end wills the means.
Il n'est pas donné à tout le monde de ALSO **à n'importe qui de** . . . (+ infinitive). Not everybody can . . . (+ infinitive)

92.2 *Le possible* Things which are possible

Ce n'est pas/C'est du domaine du possible It's not within/It's within the bounds of possibility
venir à bout de qqch to manage (to finish) sthg *C'est un gros roman mais j'en suis quand même venu à bout.* It's a long novel but I still managed to finish it.
être en mesure de faire qqch ALSO **être à même de faire qqch** to be in a position to do sthg

Locution Idiom
Ce n'est pas la mer à boire. It's not asking the impossible.

92.3 *Impossible* Impossible

see also **92.5 Improbable**, **37.14 Interdiction**; opposite **92.1 Possible**, **92.4 Probable**, **37.13 Autorisation**
impossible *adj* [describes: e.g. event, deal, project] impossible *Pour moi, mai est impossible, je suis en vacances.* I can't possibly make it in May, I'm on holiday. *'Il est jaloux.' 'Ça n'est pas impossible.'* 'He's jealous.' 'Could well be.' *si par impossible il vous contactait* if against all likelihood he were to contact you
impossibilité *nf* impossibility *Je suis dans l'impossibilité de vous recevoir demain.* It will not be possible for me to see you tomorrow.

Locutions Idioms
C'est exclu! ALSO **C'est hors de question!** It's out of the question!
À l'impossible nul n'est tenu. [proverb] Nobody can be expected to work miracles.
Impossible n'est pas français. There's no such thing as 'can't'.
Quand les poules auront des dents [postpones the realization of whatever is being discussed to a future time that will never come] *Ton argent, tu le reverras quand les poules auront des dents.* Get your money back? You'll get it back when pigs can fly!

92.4 *Probable* Probable

see also **92.1 Possible**; opposite **92.3 Impossible**, **92.5 Improbable**
probable *adj* probable **probablement** *adv* probably
concevable *adj* conceivable *Il a peut-être déshérité ses enfants. – C'est à peine concevable!* He may have disinherited his children. – It's barely conceivable!
sûrement, ALSO **certainement** *adv* [implies a small element of doubt] (very) probably *Il sera sûrement d'accord.* He's almost certain to agree.
à la rigueur if I/you/we, etc, have to *Tu peux lui demander de s'occuper des enfants une matinée, à la rigueur, mais un dimanche entier, non.* You could ask her to look after the children for a morning if you have to, but certainly not for the whole of Sunday.
être prêt(e) à parier que to be ready to bet that
risquer {6} *vt* (+ de) *Il risque de pleuvoir.* It's likely that it will rain. *Tu risques de ne trouver personne au bureau.* It's likely that you'll find that there's no one in the office.
Il y a toutes les chances que (+ subj) There's every possibility that

92.5 *Improbable* Improbable

see also **92.3 Impossible**; opposite **92.1 Possible**, **92.4 Probable**
improbable *adj* [slightly formal] improbable
inconcevable *adj* unthinkable
douteux, -teuse *adj* unlikely. *Il est douteux qu'elle puisse participer aux frais comme elle l'a promis.* It's unlikely that she will be able to contribute to the expenses as she promised.
risquer {6} *vt* (+ de) *Il ne risque pas de pleuvoir.* There's no chance of rain. *Si tu téléphones avant 22 heures, tu ne risques pas de nous déranger.* If you phone before 10 p.m., it's unlikely you'll disturb us.
Il y a peu de chances que (+ subj) There's little chance that

92.6 *Certitude* Certainty

see also **41.6 Évident**
certain, e *adj* **1** (always after noun) [which will happen] certain *promis à une mort certaine* facing certain death **2** [having no doubt about sthg] certain *Je suis certaine que c'est son frère.* I'm certain it's her brother. *Tu es certain d'avoir fermé à clé?* Are you certain that you locked up?
certitude *nf* **1** [quality of things which are not in doubt] assurance *se prononcer avec certitude* to say something with assurance **2** [belief] certainty *Il n'y a pas de certitudes en ce monde.* There are no certainties in this world.
sûr, e *adj* **1** [same meaning as **certain 2**, but less categorical] sure *Je suis sûr que c'est vrai.* I'm sure it's true. **2** [feeling able to rely on] *sûr de qqn* sure of sb *Un journaliste doit être sûr de ses sources.* A journalist must be able to rely on his sources.
garantie *nf* **1** [promise] guarantee **2** [given by manufacturer, shop] warranty
garanti, e *adj* **1** [informal. Which can be stated as certain] *Tu auras fini demain?' 'C'est pas garanti.'* 'Will you have finished by tomorrow?' 'I wouldn't swear to it. *Si tu ne leur téléphones pas pour les prévenir, c'est la panique garantie!* If you don't phone them to warn them they'll panic, sure as eggs is eggs! **2** [in commercial contexts] guaranteed *fraîcheur garantie* guaranteed fresh
catégorique *adj* **1** [expressing an opinion with certainty] definite. *Je ne peux pas être catégorique là-dessus.* I can't be definite about it. **2** [leaving no room for doubt. Describes: answer, refusal] definite
formel, -melle *adj* positive *'Tu es sûr que c'est lui?' 'Formel!'* 'Are you sure it's him?' 'Positive!'

Exprimer une opinion convergente To concur
C'est certain! ALSO **C'est sûr!** quite right!
C'est sûr et certain! [stronger than **certain** or **sûr** on their own] absolutely right!
Certes! ALSO **Assurément!** [used in writing or in careful speech] (Yes) indeed!
Sans (aucun) doute! ALSO **Ça ne fait aucun doute!** Certainly!

92.7 *Verbes exprimant la certitude* Verbs for expressing certainty

assurer {6} *vt* [cause to believe in the certainty of] to assure *Il nous a assurés de sa bonne foi/qu'il était de bonne foi.* He assured us he was acting in good faith.
s'assurer *v refl* **1** [satisfy oneself that something is the case] to check *Je veux m'assurer que tout est en ordre pour la réunion.* I want to check that all is in order for the meeting. **2** [make sure that something will happen.

Slightly formal] to ensure *Assurez-vous que tous vos passagers portent une ceinture de sécurité.* You must ensure that every one of your passengers wears a seat belt.

garantir {19} *vt* [vouch for the quality of something. Often in commercial contexts] to guarantee *Vous garantissez la fraîcheur de cette viande?* Can you guarantee that this meat is fresh?

certifier {6} *vt* [in official contexts] to certify *Ce tampon certifie que toutes les bêtes ont été vaccinées.* This stamp certifies that all the animals have been vaccinated.

Locutions Idioms
J'en mettrais ma main au feu. I would bet my life on it.
Ça ne va pas faire un pli. [informal] It's a foregone conclusion.

92.8 *Incertitude* Uncertainty

incertain, e *adj* **1** [which cannot be known for sure but the implication is that it may be bad. Describes: future, result] uncertain *Le temps est incertain.* The weather's unsettled. **2** [a rather formal term. Hesitant] uncertain *Elle était incertaine des décisions à prendre.* She was unsure which decisions she should take.

incertitude *nf* uncertainty *être dans l'incertitude* to be uncertain.

douteux, -teuse *adj* [which may well not exist or not be true] doubtful *On dit qu'il s'est enfui en Palestine mais le fait est douteux.* He's said to have fled to Palestine but some doubt remains.

dubitatif, -tive *adj* [showing scepticism. Describes: e.g. answer, look] doubting

indécis, e *adj* [having not taken a decision] undecided

All the adjectives above belong to a slightly formal register and are used in writing or in careful speech.

doute *nm* **1** [state of mind] doubt *être dans le doute* to be in doubt **2** [doubting thought] doubt *D'un seul coup, j'ai eu un doute.* Suddenly I was doubtful.

douter {6} *vt* **1** [philosophical or religious] to experience doubt **2** (always + *de*) [suspect sb of not being as good or as trustworthy as they seem to be] *douter de qqn* to have doubts about sb *Je n'ai jamais douté de toi.* I have never doubted you.

Locutions Idioms
Dans le doute abstiens-toi. [proverb] When in doubt . . . don't do it.
ne pas savoir sur quel pied danser [rather informal] to be in a quandary

93 Necessity

93.1 *Nécessité et obligation* Necessity and obligation

see also **54.4 Sérieux**; opposite **92.3 Superflu**
nécessaire *adj* necessary
nécessité *nf* necessity *en cas de nécessité* if necessary
indispensable *adj* (often + *à*) [needed usu for practical reasons. Describes: e.g. gadget, tool] required *Pour se déplacer d'un bout de la ville à l'autre, la voiture est indispensable.* It's vital to have a car if you want to go across town. *Voici la liste des fournitures indispensables aux élèves du cours préparatoire.* Here is the list of school materials required by reception class pupils.

obligatoire *adj* [required by law or regulation] compulsory *La ceinture de sécurité est obligatoire.* Wearing a seat belt is compulsory.

avoir besoin de 1 [experience a need] to need *J'ai besoin de dormir.* I need to get some sleep. **2** [be subjected to a requirement] to need *Tu as besoin d'avoir tes papiers sur toi tout le temps.* Make sure you have your identity papers with you at all times. *La lettre n'a pas besoin de timbre.* The letter doesn't need a stamp.

incontournable *adj* [which cannot be avoided. Describes: e.g. obstacle, idea, principle] unavoidable *Pour un homme politique, savoir utiliser la télévision, c'est incontournable.* It is essential for a politician to be able to handle television appearances.

usage

il faut and **s'il le faut**
Il faut + infinitive is an extremely common phrase which expresses every nuance of necessity, from practical need to compulsoriness: e.g. *Nous sommes dans la mauvaise direction, il faut faire demi-tour* We're facing the wrong way, we have to turn round. Equally common is the construction *il faut que*: e.g. *Il faut que tu te dépêches si tu veux attraper ton bus.* You have to hurry up if you want to catch your bus. *S'il le faut* is the usual way of expressing 'if necessary'. *J'écrirai à ton professeur s'il le faut mais je saurai la vérité.* I'll write to your teacher if necessary but I will find out the truth.

Locutions Idioms
faire de nécessité vertu to make a virtue of necessity
Nécessité fait loi. [proverb] Needs must . . .
C'est forcé, ALSO **obligé!** [informal. The matter being discussed is considered to have an inevitable outcome] *Elle ne dort pas, alors elle ne sait plus ce qu'elle fait, c'est forcé!* She doesn't sleep, so she doesn't know what she's doing any more, no wonder!
Il/Elle ne peut pas s'en passer. He/she can't do without it.

93.2 *Superflu* Superfluous

see also **57.11 Négligeable**; opposite **93.1 Nécessité et obligation**
superflu, e *adj* [over and above what is required] superfluous
superflu *nm* [things which are over and above what we need] surplus *Donnez-nous votre superflu, et nous le vendrons au profit des sans-abri.* Give us things which you don't need and we'll sell them to get money for the homeless.
redondant, e *adj* [describes: words, sentences] superfluous
gratuit, e *adj* [added patently for effect alone] gratuitous *J'ai trouvé ses sarcasmes tout à fait gratuits.* I felt that there was absolutely no need for him to be sarcastic.
luxe *nm* [can be used ironically] *du luxe* luxury *C'est du luxe!* What luxury! *Va te laver la figure, ce ne sera pas du luxe!* Go and wash your face, it badly needs it!
n'avoir pas besoin de to be in no need of *Vous n'avez pas besoin de payer avant le 31 décembre.* There is no need for you to pay before the 31st of December.

94 Chance

94.1 *Chance et malchance* Luck and bad luck

see also **106 (Gambits)**

Hoping for good luck
These phrases are used when hoping for good luck:
Je touche du bois, ALSO **Touchons du bois.** Touch wood.
Je croise les doigts (pour vous/elle, etc). I'm keeping my fingers crossed (for you/her, etc).
Said in order to ward off ill-luck when someone is about to take an exam, attend a job interview, etc, sometimes ironically: **Je te dis 'merde'.** Break a leg!

hasard nm chance *un heureux hasard* a piece of good fortune *un hasard malheureux* a bit of bad luck
avoir la bonne fortune de 1 [good] to be fortunate enough to *J'ai eu la bonne fortune de la rencontrer en personne.* I was fortunate enough to meet her in the flesh. **2** [bad] to be unfortunate enough to *Elle a eu la mauvaise fortune de perdre son travail trois fois de suite.* She was unfortunate enough to lose her job three times in a row.
à la fortune du pot [used when impromptu lunch or dinner guests are welcomed but warned that the meal will be whatever is in the larder at the time] taking pot luck *Si, si, venez ce soir, mais ce sera à la fortune du pot, hein . . .* Yes, do come tonight, but it will be just pot luck, OK?
destin nm [implies that things are preordained throughout life] fate *Je vous prédis un destin glorieux.* I see a glorious fate awaiting you. *Elle a eu un destin tragique.* She had a tragic fate.

94.2 *Chance* Good luck

chance nf **1** [succession of favourable events, or absence of disasters] (good) luck *Quelle chance!* What luck! *Vite, le train n'est pas encore parti, on a de la chance!* Quickly, the train's still here, we're in luck! *Je n'ai jamais eu de chance dans ma vie.* I never had any luck in my life. **2** [opportunity] chance *C'est ta chance, ne la laisse pas passer.* It's your chance, don't miss it.
chanceux, -ceuse adj lucky
veine nf [informal] (good) luck *Il a eu de la veine de s'en tirer avec six mois.* He was lucky to get away with six months' imprisonment.
veinard, -narde adj [informal] lucky **veinard, -narde** n [informal] lucky sod
aubaine nf [implies a find of something very valuable, or a very good opportunity] windfall, godsend
porter chance to bring luck *Un trèfle à quatre feuilles! Peut-être que ça va me porter chance.* A four-leaved clover! Maybe it'll bring me luck.

94.3 *Malchance* Bad luck

malchance nf [any degree of intensity, from inconvenience to tragedy] bad luck *par malchance* through ill-luck
malchanceux, -ceuse adj unfortunate
pas de chance ill luck *C'est pas de chance!* What terrible luck!
Il/Elle n'a pas de chance. He's/She's unlucky. *Vous n'avez pas de chance, elle vient de partir.* Bad luck, you've just missed her.

mésaventure nf [implies inconvenience or a setback, but not tragedy] misfortune

Locutions Idioms
C'est (de) la faute à pas de chance. [informal] It's nobody's fault, just bad luck.
faire contre mauvaise fortune bon cœur to put a brave face on it
Il est né/Elle est née sous une mauvaise étoile. He/She was born under an unlucky star.

95 Usual and unusual

95.1 *Normal* Normal

normal, e adj, mpl **normaux 1** [in accordance with what the speaker expects things to be. Contains a strong value judgment] right, understandable *Les gens ne veulent pas payer un supplément, c'est normal.* People don't want to have to pay an excess charge, it's understandable. *Tu trouves ça normal qu'il soit tout le temps devant la télévision?* Do you (really) think it's right for him to be in front of the television all the time? **2** [unexceptional] normal *Vous faites des repas normaux ou vous grignotez beaucoup?* Do you eat normal meals or do you nibble a lot? *Sa température est normale.* His temperature is normal. *l'évolution normale de la maladie* the normal course of the illness **3** [routine] normal *Pour moi, une séance de travail normale dure trois heures.* For me, a routine work session lasts three hours.
normalement adv normally
en temps normal normally *En temps normal, nous demandons un préavis de quatre semaines, mais dans votre cas nous accepterons une quinzaine de jours.* Normally we ask for four weeks' notice but in your case a fortnight will be fine.
revenir à la normale to return to normal
naturel, -relle adj [which feels right, as nature intended] natural *Il a pleuré, c'est une réaction bien naturelle.* He cried, it's a very natural reaction.
ordinaire adj [which has nothing special about it. Can be slightly pejorative, or strongly pejorative if preceded by a modifying adverb] ordinary *Dans une semaine ordinaire je fais 45 heures de travail.* In an ordinary week I do 45 hours' work. *J'ai payé 320 francs pour un repas très ordinaire.* I paid 320 francs for a very average meal.
banal, e adj, mpl **banals** [without originality. Describes: e.g. script, story, reaction] banal, unoriginal *Un mari qui quitte sa femme pour une jeunesse, c'est malheureusement très banal.* A husband leaving his wife for someone younger, sadly it happens all the time.
caractéristique adj [representative] typical *paysage caractéristique de la Bretagne* typical Breton landscape
moyen, -yenne adj **1** [like the majority, often implying not quite good or interesting enough] average *À ce prix, vous avez une qualité moyenne.* For that sort of price, you get average quality. *le Français moyen* the average French person **2** [between two extremes] average *La note moyenne est 12.* The average mark is 12.
juste milieu nm happy medium *J'essaie de trouver un* ALSO *le juste milieu entre mes devoirs de mère et ma vie professionnelle.* I try to find a happy medium between my duties as a mother and my professional life.
médiocre adj [pejorative. Describes: e.g. pupil, performance, hotel] poor *un vin très médiocre* a very poor wine

95.2 *Inhabituel* Unusual

drôle *adj* strange *Swaadoyk, quel drôle de nom!* Swaadoyk, what a strange name! *C'est drôle, qu'il soit rentré si tôt!* How strange, for him to have come home so early!

rare *adj* **1** [which is difficult to find or not often found] unusual *C'est une maladie rare de nos jours.* That disease is rare nowadays.

unique *adj* [describes: e.g. opportunity, visit] unique

étrange *adj* **1** [slightly pejorative. Unusual and alarming] odd *Elle avait une étrange lueur dans les yeux.* Her eyes shone with an odd gleam. **2** [unusual, for good or bad] strange *Je me trouvais transporté dans un paysage étrange, plein de lumières et de couleurs.* I found myself transported to a strange land, full of light and colour.

bizarre *adj* [similar to **étrange 1**, though less alarming, and sometimes slightly amusing] unusual *Trouvant le comportement de cet élève un peu bizarre, j'ai demandé un rendez-vous à ses parents.* I thought this pupil's behaviour was rather unusual so I asked to see his parents. **2** [unusual and slightly unsettling] bizarre *J'ai cru voir une forme bizarre derrière ma fenêtre.* I thought I saw a weird shape outside my window.

extraordinaire *adj* [implies something greater than most others of its kind, good or bad] extraordinary *C'est une femme extraordinaire.* She's a very impressive woman. *Elle était d'une méchanceté extraordinaire.* She was extraordinarily nasty.

curieux, -rieuse *adj* [implies that the speaker is intrigued by the thing described] odd *Tiens, c'est curieux, pourquoi tourne-t-il ainsi autour de ma voiture?* Why is he going round and round my car, how odd!

exceptionnel, -nelle *adj* **1** [happening only once] exceptional, special *Les Octets donneront un concert exceptionnel samedi à la Salle Rouvet.* The Octets will give a special concert on Saturday at the Salle Rouvet. **2** [unusually good or interesting] exceptional *une année exceptionnelle pour les bourgognes* an exceptionally good year for Burgundy wines *Nous assistons à des événements exceptionnels.* We're witnessing something quite exceptional.

extravagant, e *adj* **1** [theatrical and extreme in behaviour. Can also apply to tastes, style, remarks, etc] eccentric *Elle organisait des soirées folles, où ses invités venaient dans des tenues extravagantes.* She held wild parties, to which her guests wore very eccentric clothes. **2** [pejorative. Implies exaggerating to the point of lying] wild *Il a raconté des choses extravagantes dans sa biographie de Marilyn.* He wrote some crazy things in his biography of Marilyn.

anomalie *nf* [slightly formal term] anomaly

anormal, e *adj, mpl* **anormaux** [often pejorative, implying too much or too little compared to the usual] abnormal *C'est une température anormale pour la saison.* [low] The temperature is way below the seasonal average. [above] The temperature is way above the seasonal average. *Le chien avait une soif anormale.* The dog was abnormally thirsty.

Locutions Idioms

L'exception confirme la règle. The exception proves the rule.

Ça ne se trouve pas sous le pas, ALSO **sous le sabot d'un cheval.** [can refer to any rarity, from stamps to stylish clothes, reliable friends, trustworthy politicians, etc] You don't come across this/those every day of the week.

tous les trente-six du mois once in a blue moon

96 Communicating with voice and body

96.1 *Parler* To speak

See also **96.8 Dire, 96.18 Discussion, 40.6 Converser**

parler {6} *vi* **1** [use one's voice] to speak *Parlez plus fort, je ne vous entends pas.* Please speak louder, I can't hear you. **2** [have a conversation or to have one's say] to talk, to speak *Tu as parlé au directeur?* Did you speak to the manager? *Laissez-moi parler!* Let me speak! *Ils parlent trop vite.* They're talking too fast. **3** (+ *de*) [put across as a message] to talk, to tell *Nous avons parlé du passé.* We talked about the past. *Parle-lui de moi.* Tell him about me

parler *vt* [have as a language] to speak *parler allemand/espagnol/hindi* to speak German/Spanish/Hindi

parole *nf* **1** [faculty] speech *Les humains sont dotés de la parole.* Human beings are endowed with speech. **2** [instance of this faculty] word

96.2 *S'exprimer* To express oneself

raconter {6} *vt* [explain something as a story] to tell *Viens me raconter ce qui t'est arrivé.* Come and tell me (all about) what happened to you. *raconter une légende à un enfant* to tell a child a folk tale *Le film raconte la guerre d'Algérie.* The film tells the story of the Algerian war. *Je vais vous raconter celle du croque-mort qui arrive au paradis.* I'll tell you the one about the undertaker who turns up at the Pearly Gates.

déclarer {6} *vt* [say in a definite way, often officially] to state *Il a déclaré n'avoir jamais eu connaissance de ce versement.* He stated that he'd never been aware of that payment.

déclaration *nf* statement *faire des déclarations devant les journalistes* to make statements to the press

exprimer {6} *vt* [put across] to convey *un poème qui exprime le désespoir de la jeunesse* a poem conveying the despair of youth *Je tiens à vous exprimer toute notre gratitude.* I'd like to convey our heartfelt thanks to you.

s'exprimer *v refl* [put one's message across, either in words only or in other ways] to express oneself *Elle sait parfaitement s'exprimer.* She's very articulate.

traduire {82} *vt* [a slightly literary synonym for **exprimer**] to express *Le film a su traduire l'angoisse de toute une génération.* The film succeeds in conveying the angst of a whole generation.

96.3 *Parler brièvement* To speak briefly

remarquer {6} *vt* to remark

remarque *nf* **1** [observation] remark *Je lui en ai fait la remarque.* I pointed it out to him. **2** [pejorative. Reproach] criticism *faire une remarque à qqn* to make a critical comment to sb

observation *nf* (passing) remark

mentionner {6} *vt* to mention (in passing)

mention *nf* (passing) reference *faire mention de* to mention (in passing)

96.4 *Parler en public* To speak publicly

discours *nm* [monologue] speech *faire un discours* to make a speech *Il fait toujours de longs discours.* He's always speechifying.

commentateur, -trice *n* [in journalism] commentator

porte-parole *nm inv* (often + *de*) spokesperson *Elle est le porte-parole des sans-abri.* She speaks on behalf of the homeless.

s'adresser à {6} *v refl* [direct one's words to. Often in a rally, classroom, television studio, etc] to speak (directly) to *Je m'adresse à vous ce soir pour pousser un cri d'alarme.* I'm speaking to you (directly) tonight to sound a note of warning.

96.5 *Parler à partir d'un texte* To speak from a text

lire {77} *vt* to read (out) *lire tout haut* ALSO *lire à voix haute* to read aloud

réciter {6} *vt* [subj: e.g. schoolchild, actor] to recite *Je vais vous réciter un poème.* I'll recite a poem for you.

citer {6} *vt* to quote

dicter {6} *vt* to dictate

dictée *nf* dictation *Les enfants font une dictée.* The children are doing a dictation. *J'ai noté les détails sous la dictée.* I took the details down verbatim.

96.6 *Façons individuelles de parler* Individual ways of speaking

voix *nf* voice *J'ai entendu des voix dans le jardin.* I heard voices in the garden. *à voix haute* aloud *à voix basse* quietly *parler d'une voix de fausset* to speak in a falsetto voice

accent *nm* **1** [in France] (local) accent *parler avec l'accent du Midi* to speak with a southern French accent **2** [outside France] (foreign) accent *Elle ne perdra jamais son accent anglais.* She'll never lose her English accent.

prononcer {7} *vt* **1** [articulate] to pronounce *Elle prononce bien l'allemand.* Her German pronunciation is good. **2** [make audible] to utter *A peine eut-elle prononcé ces mots qu'elle les regretta.* Hardly had she uttered the words when she began to regret them.

se prononcer *v refl* to be pronounced *Comment ça se prononce?* How do you pronounce it?

bégayer {16} *vi* and *vt* [through disability] to stutter, to stammer

bredouiller {6} *vi* and *vt* [through nervousness] to stutter, to stammer

ânonner {6} *vt* and *vi* [through inexperience or ill-preparedness] to read aloud laboriously *Apprends à mettre l'intonation au lieu d'ânonner.* Learn to use the right intonation when you read, instead of droning on.

grasseyer {16} *vi* [denotes a working-class Parisian accent, as in characters played by, e.g. Jean Gabin] to pronounce one's Rs the Parisian way

rouler les R to roll one's Rs

zézayer {16} *vi*, ALSO **zozoter** {6} *vi* to lisp

96.7 *Façons peu audibles de parler* Whispering

chuchoter {6} *vt* and *vi* [implies necessity to be discreet] to whisper
murmurer {6} *vt* and *vi* **1** [implies discretion or tenderness. Subj: person] to whisper **2** [poetic. Subj: e.g. brook, fountain] to babble
susurrer {6} *vt* [tenderly or hypocritically] to whisper

Locutions Idioms
couper la parole à qqn to interrupt *Ne coupe pas la parole à ton père!* Don't interrupt your father!
donner la parole à qqn 1 [informally] to let sb have a say **2** [formally] to give sb the floor
avoir un cheveu sur la langue to have a lisp
Ne perds pas ta salive! Don't waste your breath!
Tu parles!/Vous parlez! [expresses scepticism. Informal] You must be joking!

96.8 *Dire* To tell

The difference between **parler** and **dire**
While *parler*, to speak, is to make something known by means of speech, *dire* to tell, specifies the content of the message. The difference is illustrated in phrases like *parler pour ne rien dire*, literally: to speak and say nothing, to be full of hot air.
The two verbs also differ in construction. *Dire* is transitive, so the objects are expressed thus: *dire quelque chose à quelqu'un* to tell somebody something. *Parler*, on the other hand, is used intransitively, thus: *parler de quelque chose à quelqu'un* to talk to somebody about something. The English verbs 'to speak' and 'to talk' can often be used to translate *parler*.

dire {78} *vt* **1** [give as information] to tell *Dis à ma mère que je serai en retard.* Tell my mother that I'll be late. *Dis-moi ton nom.* Tell me your name. *Je vous ai déjà dit que je n'avais pas le temps de m' occuper de ce problème.* I told you before that I don't have time to sort out this problem. **2** [recite for effect. Obj: e.g. poem, lie] to speak, to tell *Pour dire son texte il faut se mettre dans la peau du personnage.* You need to get inside the character to speak your lines. **3** [order] to tell *Je vous ai dit de ne pas y toucher.* I told you not to touch it. *Tu lui diras qu'il vienne demain.* Tell him to come tomorrow.
informer {6} *vt* and *vi* [fairly formal] to inform *Il ne nous a pas informé de ses intentions.* He didn't inform us of his intentions. *La famille a-t-elle été informée de l'accident?* Have the next of kin been informed about the accident? *MGH 329, la radio qui vous informe 24 h sur 24!* MGH 329, the radio station that keeps you informed round the clock!
information *nf* **1** [individual item of public or private import] piece of news **2** [on TV and radio] *informations* news *écouter les informations* to listen to the news *Ils ont dit aux informations que le pape était gravement malade.* They said on the news that the Pope was very ill.
infos *nf pl* [informal synonym for **information 2**] news *Tu as pris les infos?* Did you catch the news?
message *nm* **1** [note] message *Je regrette, elle n'est pas là. – Alors, je peux laisser un message?* I'm sorry, she's not in. – In that case may I leave a message? **2** [substance of what is said] content *Il s'est exprimé très diplomatiquement mais son message est clair, il n'y aura pas de réductions d'impôts.* He spoke very diplomatically but the message was clear, there will be no tax cuts.
messager, -gère *n* messenger

annoncer {7} *vt* [state officially. Obj: e.g. results, death, appointment] to announce
annonceur, -ceuse *n* [on radio or TV] (commercial) sponsor

96.9 *Dire ce qui se passe* To report

témoigner {6} *vi* **1** [before a court of law] to be a witness **2** (often + *de*) [report in a semi-official capacity] to bear witness to *Je suis devant les caméras ce soir pour témoigner de la lâcheté de nos gouvernements dans cette guerre.* I stand in front of the cameras tonight to bear witness to the cowardice of our governments in this war.
rapporter {6} *vt* and *vi* **1** [convey information for official or technical purposes] to report **2** [pejorative. Subj: child] to tell, BrE to sneak AmE to snitch *Il a tout rapporté à la maîtresse.* He sneaked to the teacher.
rapport *nm* [information for an official body] report *rapport d'expert* expert report
reportage *nm* [in journalism] report

96.10 *Dire avec vigueur* To speak forcefully

apostropher {6} *vt* [shout to gain someone's attention and address the person forcefully] to shout at *Il m'a apostrophé pour m'accuser d'incompétence.* He shouted at me and accused me of being incompetent.
assener {9} *vt* [reveal something shocking. Obj: e.g. news, truth, judgment] *assener qqch à qqn* to let fly at sb with sthg *Il est convalescent, ce n'est pas le moment de lui assener la vérité.* He's convalescing, now's not the time to confront him with the truth.
râler {6} *vi* [informal] to moan, to grumble

Locutions Idioms
avoir le dernier mot to have the last word
parler d'or to talk good sense
en dire des vertes et des pas mûres [informal] to come out with some pretty strong language
sonner les cloches à qqn BrE to give sb a good telling off AmE to tell sb off good
Il va/Ils vont m'entendre! [informal] He hasn't/They haven't heard the last of this!

96.11 *Exprimer son opinion* To express opinions

d'après ALSO **selon lui/elle** according to him/her
à mon/son avis in my/his (or her) opinion
à mon/son point de vue in my/his (or her) view

96.12 *L'opinion publique* Public opinion

l'homme de la rue the man in the street
sondage *nm* **d'opinion** (opinion) poll
sondé, e *n* person surveyed *30% des sondés pensent que . . .* 30% of those surveyed think that . . .
sans opinion *nm* [in a poll] don't know *23% de sans opinion* 23% of people indicated 'don't know'

96.13 *Expliquer* To explain

see also **55.10 Spécifique**
expliquer {6} *vt* and *vi* to explain *expliquer qqch à qqn* to explain sthg to sb *Explique-moi pourquoi tu as menti.*

Explain to me why you lied. *Voilà, je vais vous expliquer.* Right, I'll tell you all about it.

explication nf **1** [clarification] explanation *L'explication est simple: je n'ai pas assez d'argent.* The explanation is a simple one: I don't have enough money. **2** [as a result of a quarrel] confrontation *Il va falloir qu'on ait une explication, nous deux!* We're going to have to have a little talk (together), you and I!

définir {19} vt to define *Le dictionnaire définit 'globe' par 'corps sphérique.* The dictionary defines 'globe' as a 'spherical object'. *Comment définissez-vous le bonheur?* How do you define happiness?

décrire {80} vt to describe *Le témoin a décrit l'homme avec beaucoup de précision.* The witness described the man in great detail. *Décrivez un paysage que vous aimez.* Describe a favourite landscape.

traduire {82} vt and vi [put into another language, in writing] to translate

traduction nf translation

traducteur, -trice n translator

interpréter {10} vt and vi **1** [convey someone's thoughts, with some modifications usu to ensure better understanding] to interpret **2** [put into another language orally] to act as interpreter

interprète n **1** [professional linguist] interpreter **2** [of songs] singer, performer **3** [of plays] actor, actress performer **4** *se faire l'interprète de qqn* to speak for sb

interprétariat nm [profession] interpreting

interprétation nf [putting someone's thoughts across] interpreting *Je récuse l'interprétation qui est faite de mes paroles.* I object to the interpretation that has been put upon my words.

Phrases utilisées pour expliquer Phrases used in order to explain

c'est-à-dire (que) that is to say (that)

il faut savoir que . . . what you have to remember is that . . .

il va sans dire que . . . it goes without saying that . . .

ce qui explique que . . . which accounts for the fact that

96.14 *Cris et exclamations* Shouts and exclamations

see also **96.8 Dire**

crier {15} vt and vi [in pain, in anger or as a warning] to shout

cri nm shout

s'exclamer {6} v refl, ALSO **s'écrier** {15} v refl [say something brief but forceful] to exclaim *'Pas possible!' s'exclama-t-elle*, ALSO *s'écria-t-elle* 'I don't believe it!' she exclaimed.

exclamation nf exclamation

appeler {11} vt and vi [raise one's voice to make contact] to call *Appelle ta soeur et venez manger.* Call your sister and come and eat. *J'ai eu beau appeler, le chien n'est jamais revenu.* I called and called but the dog never came back.

appel nm call

hurler {6} vt and vi [stronger and more emotional than **crier**] to yell, to scream *hurler de rage* to scream with rage *hurler de douleur* to scream with pain

hurlement nm yell, scream

rugir {19} vt and vi [in fierce anger] to roar

glapir {19} vt and vi [high-pitched and unpleasant] to screech

brailler {6} vt and vi **1** [cry. Subj: e.g. baby, toddler] to howl **2** [informal and pejorative. Shout] to yell one's head off *Pas besoin de brailler comme ça!* There's no need to make such a noise about it!

beugler {6} vt and vi [more inarticulate than **brailler**, often implies crying or slurring] to bawl

vociférer {10} vi [use words, fast and loud, in anger] to shout (abuse)

Using verbs for shouting in a narration
All the verbs listed below can be used as part of a narration, to convey what someone said and the forceful way in which they said it, e.g.: *'Voleuse, voleuse!' glapissait la vieille.* 'Thief, thief' screeched the old woman. *'Mon argent!' rugit-il en brandissant la boîte vide.* 'My money!' he roared, brandishing the empty box.

96.15 *Protester* To protest

protester {6} vi [speak against something which is perceived as unfair] to protest **protestation** nf protest

se plaindre {59} v refl **1** [address one's protest to an authority] to complain *se plaindre de quelque chose* to complain about something *se plaindre à quelqu'un* to complain to somebody **2** (always + de) [express as a symptom] to complain about *Elle se plaint de maux de tête.* She complains about headaches. **3** [pejorative. Express misery, not always truthfully] to moan *Arrête de te plaindre, ce n'est pas de ma faute s'il pleut!* Stop moaning, I can't help it if it's raining!

plainte nf **1** [official] complaint *déposer une plainte* to lodge a complaint *porter plainte contre qqn* to bring a lawsuit against sb **2** [gentle sound expressing pain] moan

critiquer {6} vt and vi [speak against something, analysing its faults] to criticize

jérémiades nf pl endless moaning *J'en ai assez d'entendre ses jérémiades sur l'injustice du sort.* I've had enough of his moaning on about how unfair life is.

hélas [used in everyday speech and in narration, to preface the announcement of bad news] alas, sadly *Les secours sont arrivés en quelques minutes, hélas il était déjà trop tard.* Help arrived within a few minutes, sadly it was already too late.

96.16 *Questions* Questions

see also **103, 108.6, 110.1, 115.1, 121, 127.2, 129.1, 130.1, 140.3 (Gambits)**

question nf *poser une question* to ask a question *C'est une bonne question!* That's a good question! *La question n'est pas là!* That's not the question.

questionner {6} vt [implies slight insistence] to put questions to

interrogation nf **1** [by police] interrogation **2** [doubt] question *Une interrogation subsiste: est-il aussi innocent qu'il le dit?* The question remains as to whether he is as blameless as he says.

demande nf **1** [question. Implies that the person asking stands to benefit from the question being answered positively] request *La demande avait de quoi surprendre: il voulait emprunter ma voiture pour un mois.* His request was somewhat unexpected: he wanted to borrow my car for a month. *à la demande* on request **2** [written document addressed to a department, an official] application *faire une demande* to put in an application *faire une demande d'emploi* to apply for a job **3** (often + de + noun) [psychological] emotional need *demande d'affection* need for love *Dans notre couple, c'était lui qui était en demande.* In our life together, he was the one with the greatest emotional need.

demander {6} vt to ask (for) *demander qqch à qqn* to ask sb (for) sthg *Demande du pain au garçon.* Ask the waiter for some bread. *demander l'heure à qqn* to ask sb the time *demander des nouvelles de qqn* to ask after sb

se demander *v refl* **1** [often implies scepticism] to wonder *Je me demande si elle a bien réfléchi à ce qu'elle va faire en l'épousant.* I wonder whether she's really thought through the consequences of marrying him. **2** [search one's heart or mind] to ask oneself *Demande-toi si tu as vraiment besoin de cet argent.* Ask yourself whether you really need this money.

solliciter {6} *vt* [formal. Seek to obtain: e.g. help, protection, interview] to ask for

se renseigner {6} *v refl* **1** (often + *sur*) [look for a specific piece of information] to make inquiries *Je vais me renseigner sur les formules de prêt proposées par ma banque.* I'll make inquiries about the loan schemes available from my bank. **2** [in a general way] to ask around

supplier {15} *vi* [strongly emotional] to beg *Je t'en supplie, ne me quitte pas!* I beg you, don't leave me!

réclamer {6} **1** *vt* [ask insistently for] to demand *Les employés réclament des horaires plus souples.* The employees are demanding more flexible working hours. **2** *vi* [make strong protests] to complain *Il n'y avait pas de chauffage dans la chambre d'hôtel, alors j'ai réclamé.* There was no heat(ing) in the hotel room, so I complained.

96.17 *Réponses* Answers

réponse *nf* answer *donner une réponse* to give an anwer *N'insiste pas, la réponse est non.* Not another word, the answer is no.

répondre {53} *vt* **1** [give as a reply] to answer *Il a répondu oui/non.* He answered yes/no. **2** (+ à) [make a response to] to answer *Répondez à la question qui vient de vous être posée.* Answer the question which has just been put to you. *Les candidats doivent répondre aux questions B et C en anglais.* Candidates must answer questions B and C in English. *Excuse-moi de n'avoir pas répondu à ta lettre.* I'm sorry I didn't answer your letter.

répondre *vi* **1** [act in response] to answer *Anne, répond au téléphone!* Anne, answer the phone! *Ça sonne mais personne ne répond!* It's ringing but there's no answer. **2** [pejorative. Reply rudely] to talk back *Ne réponds pas!* Don't talk back! *Elle répond à ses parents.* She is cheeky to her parents.

répondeur *nm* answering machine

permanence *nf* **téléphonique** **1** [for routine information] (24-hour) answering service **2** [for emergencies] hotline

répliquer {6} *vt* and *vi* [implies quick and sharp response] to answer, to retort

réplique *nf* **1** [in a conversation] sharp answer **2** [in the theatre, words given in answer] (next) line *J'oublie toujours cette réplique.* I always forget that line. *donner la réplique à qqn* to play opposite sb

rétorquer {6} *vt* and *vi* [stronger than **répliquer**] to retort

Locutions Idioms
Il/Elle a réponse à tout. He's/She's never at a loss for an answer.
répondre du tac au tac à qqn to answer sb tit for tat
C'est la réponse du berger à la bergère. [stresses appropriateness as well as finality of reply] There's no arguing with that, then.
faire une réponse de Normand [based on the supposed unwillingness on the part of the typical Normandy farmer to commit himself] to answer neither yes nor no *Il m'a fait une réponse de Normand.* I didn't get a straight answer out of him.
renvoyer la balle à qqn to put the ball back into sb's court

96.18 *Discussion* Discussion

see also **96.1 Parler**, **96.8 Dire**, **40.6 Converser**

discussion *nf* [implies a debate, issues, ideas, rather than simple chat] discussion, talk *Il va falloir que j'aie une discussion avec elle.* I'll have to have a talk with her.

discuter {6} *vi* (often + *de*) [speak with another or others. May imply debating, or simply chatting] to talk *Qu'est-ce que vous faites là vous deux? – Rien, on discute* What are you two doing here? – Nothing, just talking. *On a un peu discuté de ce qu'il y a à faire.* We talked a little about what has to be done.

discutailler {6} *vi* **1** [pejorative. Subj: one person] to be argumentative **2** [pejorative. Subj: two or more people] to argue (fruitlessly)

disputer {6} *vi* (+ *sur*) to debate *Nous disputions souvent sur des thèmes religieux.* We often discussed religion.

96.19 *Insistance* Insistence

insistance *nf* **1** [implies courteous determination to influence someone] insistence *avec beaucoup d'insistance* with great insistence *Elle a voulu que j'accepte son aide et elle y a mis beaucoup d'insistance.* She was determined that I accept her help and she was very insistent about it.

insister {6} *vi* **1** (with a negative) [convey something repeatedly or forcefully] to persist *Après cet échec, elle n'a plus insisté.* After that failure, she didn't persist. *Je t'ai dit que je n'irai pas, n'insiste pas.* I told you I wouldn't go, don't go on about it. **2** [used as a polite entreaty] to insist *Je n'ose pas venir, j'ai peur de vous déranger. – Si, si j'insiste!* I'm not sure I can come, I'm worried I might be in your way. – Not at all, please DO come! **2** [put the emphasis on] *insister sur* to stress *Ils ont insisté sur la nécessité d'un engagement écrit.* They stressed the need for a written commitment.

exagération *nf* [statement] *Ce serait une exagération de dire que . . .* It would be overstating the case to say that . . . *Sans exagération, il y avait bien 3000 personnes.* There were at least 3,000 people there, and that's no exaggeration.

exagérer {10} *vi* **1** to overdo it *Nous mettre de garde deux week-ends de suite, cette fois-ci ils exagèrent!* Put us on duty two weekends in a row, this time they've gone too far! **2** *vt* [make something seem more important than it is] to exaggerate *Il a exagéré son rôle dans l'histoire.* He gave an exaggerated account of the part he played in the story. *Oh 'du sang partout' . . . n'exagérons rien!* Come on there wasn't 'blood everywhere'; don't get carried away!

Locutions Idioms
mettre l'accent sur to put the emphasis on
Mets-toi/Mettez-vous bien ça dans le crâne. [used somewhat aggressively] Get this into your (thick) head.
T'exagères! [informal expression of frustration that someone is taking liberties] You're pushing your luck!

96.20 *Répétition* Repetition

répétition *nf* **1** [in a conversation, a text] repetition **2** [in the performing arts] rehearsal

répéter {10} *vt* **1** [obj: e.g. word, phrase, gesture, act] to repeat **2** [in the performing arts] to rehearse

refaire {62} *vt* to redo, to do again

redire {78} *vt* to retell, to tell again *Je te le redis, c'est moi qui paie!* I'm telling you again, I'm paying!

recommencer {7} *vt* [obj: e.g. piece of work, sentence] to start again *Je recommencerai!* I'll do it again!

radoter {6} *vi* [very pejorative] to repeat oneself *Tu me l'as déjà dit, tu radotes!* You've told me already, stop repeating yourself!

rabâcher {6} *vt* [pejorative] to keep harping on

écho *nm* [aural effect, also reiteration of an idea] echo *Je me ferai l'écho de ce que vous avez dit.* I'll echo what you said.

bis *nm* encore *Bis! Bis!* Encore! Encore!

bisser {6} *vt* to give an encore to *Le public a bissé l'"Hymne à la Joie'.* The audience encored the 'Ode to Joy'.

Locutions Idioms

C'est toujours la même chanson! [the same comment or complaint is always being expressed] It's always the same old story! *Oh, arrête, c'est toujours la même chanson!* Oh, for God's sake, change the record!

On efface tout et on recommence! Back to the drawing board!

96.21 *Blasphèmes et jurons* Profanity and swearwords

jurer {6} *vi* to swear

juron *nm* swearword

sacrer {6} *vi* to swear *sacrer et pester* BrE to eff and blind AmE to cuss and swear

pester {6} *vi* to curse *Je l'entendais qui pestait contre le patron/le mauvais temps.* I could hear him cursing the boss/the bad weather.

blasphème *nm* piece of blasphemy

blasphémer {10} *vi* to blaspheme

Some swearwords
con, -nne *n* bastard *sale con* dirty bastard
connard *nm* bastard
connasse *nf* bastard
la barbe! [very mild] drat!
nom de Dieu! [strong] (for) God's sake!
merde! [can cause offence] shit!
bordel (de merde)! [can cause offence] fucking hell!

Locutions Idioms

en entendre des vertes et des pas mûres [euphemism] to hear colourful language being used *Quand Papa s'est pincé le doigt dans la portière, on en a entendu des vertes et des pas mûres.* When Dad caught his finger in the car door, the air turned blue.

les cinq lettres, ALSO **le mot de Cambronne** [euphemism for **merde**] *Il lui a dit le mot de Cambronne.* He used the F word.

jurer comme un charretier to swear like a trooper

96.22 *Bavardages* Chatting

see also **96.1 Parler, 96.8 Dire, 96.18 Discussion**

conversation *nf* [socializing] conversation *participer à la conversation* to take part in the conversation

converser {6} *vi* [slightly formal term] to converse *Nous conversions ainsi le soir après notre journée de travail.* Thus we used to converse in the evening after our work was done.

bavarder {6} *vt* and *vi* [implies informality and more friend-liness] to chat

bavardage *nm* [friendly. Can be used pejoratively] chat(ter) *Arrêtez vos bavardages, au fond de la classe!* You at the back of the class, stop chattering!

papoter {6} *vi* [informal] to have a natter

Locutions Idioms

toucher un mot à qqn de qqch to have a word with sb about sthg

tailler une bavette avec qqn [informal] to have a chat with sb

Il/Elle a la langue bien pendue. ALSO **Il/Elle n'a pas sa langue dans sa poche.** He's/She's quite a talker.

une conversation à bâtons rompus [casual, and somewhat aimless] a general chat

tenir le crachoir ALSO **la jambe à qqn** [informal] to talk endlessly to sb

et patati et patata [indicates continuous talking] on and on *Elle m'a raconté son opération, les points de suture et patati et patata . . .* She told me all about her operation, the stitches . . . and so on and so forth . . .

C'est un vrai moulin à paroles. He's/She's a real chatterbox.

96.23 *Rumeur* Rumour

rumeur *nf* rumour *la rumeur publique* what people say *La rumeur enfle.* The rumour is spreading.

ragot *nm,* ALSO **cancan** *nm,* ALSO **potin** *nm* [informal. Idle and often malicious] piece of gossip

bruit *nm* (**de couloir**) [usu about politics or management] rumour, whisper

commérage *nm* [malicious rumour, often attributed to women] piece of (malicious) tittle-tattle

médisance *nf* slur

Locutions Idioms

Ce sont des 'on dit'. These are things that people are saying (but there is no proof that they are true).

apprendre quelque chose par le téléphone arabe to hear something on the grapevine

Les ragots ALSO **cancans vont bon train.** Tongues are wagging.

96.24 *Langage* Language

langage *nm* **1** [human faculty for using linguistic structures] language *Nous sommes des êtres doués de* ALSO *du langage.* We are creatures endowed with the ability to use language. **2** [any code for communicating. A human language may be thus described, if it is unfamiliar to the describer] language *le langage des abeilles* the language used by bees to communicate with one another. *Ils parlaient un langage que je ne connaissais pas.* They spoke a language which I didn't know.

langue *nf* [any one of the linguistic varieties spoken or written by humans] language *apprendre les langues vivantes* to learn (modern) foreign languages *les langues indo-européennes* Indo-European languages

96.25 Some major languages

Langues d'Europe European languages
allemand *nm* German
anglais *nm* English
basque *nm* Basque
bulgare *nm* Bulgarian
danois *nm* Danish
espagnol *nm* Spanish
finnois *nm* Finnish
français *nm* French
grec *nm* Greek
hollandais, ALSO **néerlandais** *nm* Dutch

hongrois *nm* Hungarian
italien *nm* Italian
norvégien *nm* Norwegian
polonais *nm* Polish
portugais *nm* Portuguese
roumain *nm* Romanian
russe *nm* Russian
suédois *nm* Swedish
tchèque *nm* Czech
turc *nm* Turkish

Autres langues beaucoup parlées dans le monde Other widely spoken languages
afrikaans *nm* Afrikaans
arabe *nm* Arabic
bengali *nm* Bengali
chinois *nm* Chinese
hindi *nm* Hindi
japonais *nm* Japanese
malgache *nm* Malagasy
panjabi *nm* Punjabi
persan *nm* (modern) Persian
somali *nm* Somali
swahili *nm* Swahili
urdu ALSO **ourdou** *nm* Urdu

96.26 *Termes grammaticaux* Grammatical terms

adjectif *nm* adjective *adjectif démonstratif* demonstrative adjective *adjectif possessif* possessive adjective
adverbe *nm* adverb
article *nm* article *article défini/indéfini* definite/indefinite article
auxiliaire *nm* auxiliary (verb)
conditionnel *nm* conditional
conjonction *nf* conjunction
conjugaison *nf* conjugation
conjuguer {6} *vi* and *vt* to conjugate
féminin *nm* feminine (gender)
féminin, e *adj* feminine
futur *nm* future (tense) *futur proche* near future
genre *nm* gender
grammaire *nf* grammar
grammatical, e *adj, mpl* **-caux** grammatical
imparfait *nm* imperfect (tense)
impératif *nm* imperative (mood)
indicatif *nm* indicative (mood)
infinitif *nm* infinitive (mood)
interrogatif *nm* interrogative form
interrogatif, -tive *adj* interrogatif
interrogation *nf* question form
inversion *nf* inversion *inversion du verbe et du sujet* subject-verb inversion
irrégulier, -lière *adj* irregular
masculin *nm* masculine (gender)
masculin, e *adj* masculine
mode *nm* mood
négatif, -tive *adj* negative **négatif** *nm* negative form
négation *nf* negation
nom *nm* noun
nombre *nm* number
objet *nm* object *objet direct/indirect* direct/indirect object.
participe *nm* participle *participe présent* present participle *participe passé* past participle
partie *nf* **du discours** part of speech
passé *nm* **composé** perfect (tense)
passé *nm* **simple** past historic
personne *nf* **(du verbe)** person

phrase *nf* sentence
pluriel, -rielle *adj* plural **pluriel** *nm* plural
plus-que-parfait *nm* pluperfect (tense)
préposition *nf* preposition
présent *nm* present (tense)
pronom *nm* pronoun *pronom relatif* relative pronoun
pronominal, e *adj, mpl* **-naux 1** [relating to pronouns] pronominal **2** [relating to verbs] reflexive *un verbe pronominal* a (French) reflexive verb
singulier, -lière *adj* singular **singulier** *nm* singular
subjonctif *nm* subjunctive
sujet *nm* subject
temps *nm* tense *les temps du passé* the past tenses *les temps composés* the compound tenses
verbe *nm* verb.

The form of words
The words *à* and *au* are used to talk about gender, number, tenses and moods of words, e.g.:
L'adjectif 'vertes' est au féminin pluriel. The adjective 'vertes' is in the feminine plural. *Mettez les verbes suivants au subjonctif présent.* Put the following verbs into the present subjunctive.

96.27 *Les sons des mots* The sounds of words

voyelle *nf* vowel
consonne *nf* consonant
syllabe *nf* syllable
rime *nf* rhyme
prononciation *nf* pronunciation
intonation *nf* intonation *lire un texte en mettant l'intonation* to read a text expressively

96.28 *Orthographier les mots* Spelling words

orthographe *nf* spelling *avoir une bonne/mauvaise orthographe* to be good/bad at spelling
orthographier {15} *vi* [more formal than **épeler**] to spell *Comment orthographie-t-on 'sympathique'?* How does one spell 'sympathique'?
épeler {11} *vt* [out loud] to spell *Peux-tu m'épeler ton nom?* Can you spell your name for me?
s'épeler *v refl* [out loud] to be spelled *Comment ça s'épelle?* How's it spelled?

> **usage**
>
> *Asking how to spell words*
> While *Comment ça s'orthographie ?* or *Comment ça s'épelle?* are both possible, an everyday way of asking this question is to use the verb *s'écrire*. e.g.: *Comment ça s'écrit?* How do you spell it?

alphabet *nm* alphabet
alphabétique *adj* alphabetical *par ordre alphabétique* in alphabetical order
alphanumérique *adj* alphanumerical
majuscule *nf* capital (letter)
majuscule *adj* capital *un A majuscule* a capital A
minuscule *nf* lower case (letter)
minuscule *adj* *un 'a' minuscule* a lower case 'a'
une minuscule ALSO **un A minuscule** a small a
un A en majuscules d'imprimerie an upper-case A
un a en minuscules d'imprimerie a lower-case a

96.29 *Ponctuation* Punctuation

point *nm* full stop **point d'interrogation** question mark
 point d'exclamation exclamation mark
virgule *nf* comma
point-virgule *nm, pl* **points-virgules** semi-colon
deux points colon
apostrophe *nf* apostrophe
accent *nm* accent *accent aigu* acute accent *accent grave*
 grave accent *accent circonflexe* circumflex accent
tréma *nm* umlaut
crochet *nm* square bracket *entre crochets* in square
 brackets
accolade *nf* curly bracket
parenthèse *nf* (round) bracket *entre parenthèses* in
 brackets

96.30 *Expressions utilisées lorsqu'on dicte un texte* Phrases used in dictation

plus loin new word
à la ligne new line, new paragraph
deux points colon
ouvrez les guillemets open inverted commas
ouvrez la parenthèse open brackets
paragraphe suivant new paragraph
point final full stop, end of text

Locutions Idioms
mettre les points sur les i (à quelqu'un) to spell it out
 (for someone)
point final and that's final *J'ai dit non, point final!* I said
 no and that's final!

96.31 *Signification* Meaning

vouloir dire to mean *Que veut dire le mot 'homme'?* What
 does the word 'homme' mean? *Qu'est-ce que tu veux dire
 par 'égoïste' exactement?* What exactly do you mean,
 'selfish'? *Il y a des nuages bas ce soir, ça veut dire qu'il va
 pleuvoir demain.* There are low clouds in the sky tonight,
 that means rain for tomorrow. *'Zrngjton', ça ne veut rien
 dire.* 'Zrngjton' doesn't mean anything. *Ils ont annoncé
 une amnistie mais ça ne veut rien dire.* They said there
 would be an amnesty, but it doesn't mean anything.
sens *nm* meaning *Le verbe 'faire' a des sens différents
 selon le contexte.* The verb 'faire' has different meanings
 in different contexts. *une phrase qui n'a pas de sens* a
 meaningless sentence *Dans son sommeil, il disait des mots
 qui n'avaient pas de sens.* In his sleep, he uttered
 meaningless words. *au sens figuré* figuratively speaking
signification *nf* [slightly more formal than **sens**] meaning
 Quelle est la signification du mot 'porte'? What's the
 meaning of the word 'porte'?
signifier {6} *vt* [slightly more formal than **vouloir dire**] to
 mean *Que signifie le mot 'girafe'?* What does the word
 'giraffe' mean? *Que signifie cette remarque?* What's the
 meaning of that remark?

Locutions Idioms
sans queue ni tête [describes: e.g. story, song] nonsensical
histoire à dormir debout [unlikely] tall story,
 [complicated] long, involved saga

96.32 *Écriture* Writing

see also **59.18 La littérature**
écrire {80} *vt* to write *Je lui ai écrit une lettre.* I wrote him a
 letter. *Je vais lui écrire pour le remercier.* I'll write him a
 letter of thanks.
écriture *nf* [a person's way of shaping letters] handwriting
 Elle a une belle écriture. She has beautiful handwriting.
inscrire {80} *vt* **1** [write for some official purpose] to
 register **2** [write on hard material other than paper] to
 inscribe
signer {6} *vt* to sign
noter {6} *vt* to jot down

96.33 *Façons d'écrire* Ways of writing

calligraphier {6} *vt* to write (out) in a beautiful hand
gribouiller {6} *vt* to scrawl
gribouillis *nm* scrawl *faire des gribouillis* to scrawl
lisible *adj* legible
illisible *adj* illegible
pattes *nf pl* **de mouche** illegible scrawl
en script in block letters

97 Mailing and sending

97.1 *Communications* Communications

see also **142 (Gambits)**
communiquer {6} **1** *vi* to communicate *C'est quelqu'un qui
 sait communiquer.* She's a good communicator. *Nous
 communiquerons par messagerie électronique.* We'll
 communicate by electronic mail. **2** *vt* (often + *à*) [obj: e.g.
 message, letter, data, passion] to give *Lui avez-vous
 communiqué notre adresse?* Have you given him our
 address? *Sa mère lui a communiqué son amour de la
 musique.* His mother passed on to him her love of music.
toucher {6} *vt* [get in touch, usu for reasons connected
 with work] to contact *Où peut-on vous toucher pendant la
 semaine?* Where can you be contacted during the week?
contacter {6} *vt* [synonym for **toucher**] to contact
 Contactez-moi au numéro suivant. Call me at the
 following number.

97.2 *Choses que l'on envoie* Mail, parcels

lettre *nf* letter *une lettre d'amour* a love letter *une lettre
 de réclamations* a letter of complaint *une lettre
 d'embauche* a letter of appointment
pli *nm* [synonym for **lettre**, used in some official contexts]
 letter, cover *Je vous adresse copie de mes certificats sous
 pli séparé.* I'm sending copies of my certificates under
 separate cover.
paquet *nm* [packaged goods, for sending or other form of
 handling] parcel
colis *nm* [synonym for **paquet**, but for sending only]
 package, parcel
carte *nf* **postale** postcard

Poster des documents To post documents
enveloppe *nf* envelope
adresse *nf* address
timbre *nm* stamp
cachet *nm* **de la poste** postmark *Le cachet de la poste
 faisant foi.* The postmark indicates the date.
code *nm* **postal** BrE postcode AmE zip code

adresse nf address mon adresse
personnelle/professionnelle my home/work address
adresser {6} vt **1** [send. Obj: e.g. letter, document] to
address Cette lettre ne t'est pas adressée. This letter isn't
addressed to you. **2** [obj: e.g. envelope, label] to write an
address on
envoyer {18} vt to send envoyer une lettre à qqn to send
sb a letter
poste nf **1** [distribution system] post (office) privatiser la
poste to privatize the Post Office **2** [place] post office Tu
vas à la poste? Are you going to the post office? mettre
une lettre à la poste to post a letter
poster {6} vt to post Votre commande a été postée. BrE
Your order is in the post. AmE Your order is in the mail.
postal, e adj, mpl **-taux** postal camion postal (large) postal
van services postaux post office services
courrier nm **1** [letters etc] post, mail Le courrier arrive à 8 h
30. The post/mail is delivered at 8.30 a.m. J'ouvre mon
courrier dès que j'arrive au bureau. I open my mail as soon
as I get to the office. **2** [delivery] post au
premier/deuxième courrier in the first/second post par
retour de courrier by return of post/mail
coursier, coursière n **1** [motorized messenger] courier **2** [
delivery] courier Les plis urgents sont envoyés par courrier.
Urgent letters are sent by courier.
facteur nm postman la camionnette du facteur the postal
van
factrice nf postwoman
préposé, e n (des postes) [official term] postman,
postwoman
levée nf collection La dernière levée est à 17h. The last
collection is at 5 pm.
frais nm pl **de poste** postage plus 32 francs pour frais de
poste plus 32 francs for postage

97.3 *Documents* Documents

texte nm text
en-tête nm, pl **en-têtes** letterhead papier à en-tête
letterhead (stationery)
brochure nf [with several pages, often sewn or stapled]
brochure
dépliant nm [usu for tourists. Folded] leaflet
imprimé nm [printed on documents delivered by mail]
printed matter
formulaire nm form
tableau nm, pl **-x** table Remplissez toutes les colonnes du
tableau suivant. Fill in each column in the following table.

97.4 *Documents officiels* Official documents

certificat nm certificat
carte nf **d'identité** identity card
permis nm **de séjour** permit authorizing residence on
French territory
passeport nm passport
visa nm visa
carte nf **grise** vehicle registration document
permis nm **de conduire** BrE driving licence AmE drivers'
license
assurance nf BrE certificate of motor insurance AmE
auto(mobile) insurance
papiers nm pl [informal] (official) papers

Livret de famille
The *livret de famille* is a document given to each French
couple when they get married. In the *livret*, important
information is recorded, such as the dates of births and
deaths in the family.

Being asked to produce documents
A police officer asking a motorist *Vous avez vos papiers?*
wants to see the driver's licence, the vehicle registration
document and the insurance certificate. If no vehicle is
involved, that same question means that the officer
wants to see a document identifying the person, i.e. an
identity card, a passport, or a permit authorizing
residence on French territory. In France it is illegal to be
without at least one of these forms of identification.

98 Communicating electronically

98.1 *Informatique* Information technology

see also **77.2 Équipement**
informatique nf **1** [area of knowledge] computing
2 [practical skills in handling data] data processing
informaticien, -cienne n computer specialist
assisté par ordinateur computer-assisted enseignement
assisté par ordinateur computer-assisted learning
conception assistée par ordinateur computer-assisted
design
virus nm virus
mémoire nf memory Les nouvelles données sont en
mémoire. The new data is in the memory. Il a combien de
mémoire, ton ordinateur? What's your computer's
memory?

98.2 *Techniques informatiques* Data processing

charger {8} vt to load
visualiser {6} vt to display
modifier {6} vt to edit
sauvegarder {6} vt to save
formater {6} vt to format
survoler {6} vt [obj: e.g. text, document] to browse
through
défiler {6} vi [subj: e.g. text, document] to scroll faire
défiler un texte to scroll a text
sélectionner {6} vt to select
faire une copie to copy
faire un document de secours ALSO **faire une copie** to
make a backup for a document
faire une édition to printout
être en ligne/hors ligne to be on-line/off-line
conversationnel, -nelle adj interactive

98.3 *Le logiciel* Software

logiciel nm **1** [as opposed to hardware] software **2**
[product] software package
progiciel nm [same as **logiciel 2**] software package
ludiciel nm games package

programme *nm* programme
fichier *nm* file
menu *nm* menu *menu déroulant* scrolling menu
icône *nf* icon

98.4 *Télécommunication* Electronic communications

see also **142 (Gambits)**

téléphone *nm* telephone *Va voir à la porte, je suis au
téléphone!* Answer the door, I'm on the phone! *Je l'ai eu
au téléphone hier.* I spoke to him on the phone yesterday.
téléphone portable mobile phone *téléphone cellulaire*
cellular phone *téléphone de voiture* car phone
téléphoner {6} *vi* and *vt* to phone
combiné *nm* handset
communication *nf* [slightly formal] call *J'ai du mal à
obtenir la communication pour Miami.* I'm having trouble
getting through to Miami.
télécopie *nf*, ALSO **fax** *nm* fax
télécopier {15} *vt*, ALSO **faxer** {6} *vt* to fax
numéro *nm* number *numéro de téléphone* telephone number *numéro de télécopie* ALSO *de fax* fax number *faire un
faux numéro* to dial a wrong number
répondeur *nm* answer(ing) machine *Son répondeur est
branché.* His answering machine is on. *laisser un message
sur un répondeur* to leave a message on an answer
machine
Minitel *nm* information and network service accessible via
the telephone
courrier *nm* **électronique** e-mail (system)
message *nm* **électronique** e-mail message
Internet *nm* Internet *sur Internet* on Internet
charger {8} *vt* to download
moteur *nm* **de recherche** search engine
standard *nm* switchboard
standardiste *n* operator
communiquer *vi* {6} **en réseau** to network
communication *nf* **en réseau** networking
forum *nm* **télématique** teleconference

A Minitel system

99 *Présentations* Introductions

99.1 *Se présenter* Introducing oneself

When meeting somebody informally, the simplest way to introduce yourself is to offer your hand and just say your name. The other person will respond with a handshake, and will say his or her name. The other person may also say *enchanté*, or *enchantée* if a woman, meaning 'delighted (to meet you)'.

Phrases such as *Bonjour, je suis Claire Mounard . . .* ' Hallo, I'm Claire Mounard . . . ' can be used when you are introducing yourself to a group of people, e.g., when you are speaking at a conference. It is very rare to hear someone introducing themselves with *Je m'appelle . . .* When meeting people in a work situation, you may add your job or position after your name, e.g. *Alain Lombard, chef de marché* 'Hi, I'm Alain Lombard, the marketing manager'. In a family gathering, you might hear people introduce themselves by saying: *Alain, le frère de Bernard.* 'I'm Alain, Bernard's brother'.

99.2 *Faire des présentations* Introducing others

Vous vous connaissez? Do you know each other?
Vous vous êtes déjà rencontrés? Have you met before?
Je vous présente? May I introduce you?

[informal]
François, Robert. Robert, François. François, this is Robert. Robert, this is François.

[more formal]
François, je te présente Robert. François, let me introduce Robert.

[very formal]
François, puis-je vous présenter Robert? François, may I introduce Robert?

Beware of the difference between *Je vais te présenter Fernand.* 'I'll introduce Fernand to you' and *Je vais te présenter à Fernand.* 'I'll introduce you to Fernand'.

Je vous laise vous présenter tout seuls. I'll leave you to introduce yourselves.
Je laisse à Luc le soin de faire les présentations. I'll leave it to Luc to do the introductions.

100 *Formules de politesse* Forms of address

In France, forms of address and titles are often used in speech. *Monsieur, Madame* and *Mademoiselle* are used all the time when addressing strangers, in the street, in shops, on the telephone, or in meetings between people who have not yet been introduced to one another. It is also customary to use these forms when addressing people with whom the speaker maintains a formal relationship, often including colleagues at work.

Madame or **Mademoiselle**?
There is currently no easy way of rendering Ms in French as a written abbreviation. In conversation the word *Madame* is often neutral as regards marital status. But if the person looks very young, you may offend her by calling her *Madame*. Ask explicitly and wait for her to supply her preferred form *'Eh bien, alors à demain Madame . . . c'est Madame ou Mademoiselle?'*

Docteur may be used *without* the surname when addressing a doctor of medicine, but is not so used when speaking to people with academic titles.
[Medical] *'Docteur, excusez-moi, je voudrais vous parler un instant'.* 'Excuse me Doctor, can I have a word with you?'
[Academic] *'Monsieur Guierrot, pourrions-nous nous voir pour parler de ma thèse demain?'* 'Doctor Guierrot, could we discuss my thesis tomorrow?'
Other titles such as **Professeur** (i.e., medical consultant)**, Monsieur le Curé, mon Père, mon Capitaine**, etc. are also normally only used *without* the surname in ordinary conversation.

Monsieur, **Madame** and **Mademoiselle** are used *without* the surname just as often as they are used *with* it. The difference is not easy to gauge, but as a rough guide, the less well you know the person, the less likely you are to use their surname.

Bonjour Madame, c'est gentil d'être venue. Hallo Mrs (whatever the name is), nice of you to come.
When making a public address (e.g. a speech) it is normal to begin with **Mesdames, Mesdemoiselles, Messieurs** though in informal situations, people often simply begin with **Bonjour** or **Bonsoir**.

101 *Saluer et prendre congé* Greetings and leave-takings

101.1 *Saluer* Greetings

Bonjour, ça va? Hallo, how are you? Hallo, how are things?
When you want to say that things are going well, or when you simply want to be polite, you reply:
Bien, merci, et toi? Fine, thank you, and you?
When things are neither especially good nor bad, normally in informal situations:
Oui, pas trop mal. Not so bad, thanks.
When things are not good:
Pas très bien [followed by an explanation of what the problem is] Not so good, really.

101.2 *Souhaiter la bienvenue* Welcoming people

Phrases to do with welcoming are used in French only by people whose job it is to welcome you (hotel receptionist, doorman) or in the formal context of an introduction at, for example, a seminar or a presentation.

Voici votre clef, Monsieur, chambre 33. Passez un bon séjour. Here's your key, sir, room 33. I hope you enjoy your stay.

Mesdames et Messieurs, permettez-moi de souhaiter la bienvenue à nos collègues de Dijon, qui nous ont fait l'amitié de venir ce matin participer à nos débats. Ladies and gentlemen, permit me to welcome our colleagues from Dijon, who have come to join us for this morning's discussions.

101.3 *Saluer après une absence* Greetings after an absence

Ça fait longtemps qu'on ne s'est pas vus! It's been a long time!

Ça fait plaisir de vous revoir. (It's) nice to see you again. [If you know the person well, you might say *Ça fait plaisir de te revoir.*]

101.4 *Mots familiers pour saluer* Informal words for greeting

Salut! Hi!
Ça va? Hiya!

101.5 *Prendre congé* Leave-taking

Au revoir! Goodbye!
À bientôt! See you soon!
Bon, il faut que je m'en aille. Well, I have to go now. [If the person knows where you're going, you might say, more informally *Il faut que j'y aille*, literally 'I must go there']
Ravi(e) d'avoir fait votre connaissance. Nice to have met you. [This is rather formal, e.g. when taking leave of people in professional or public situations.]
Tout le plaisir est pour moi. It's my pleasure. [When responding to somebody who has just said that they were pleased to meet you. A rather formal response.]

101.6 *Mots familiers pour prendre congé* Informal words for saying goodbye

Salut! Bye!
À la prochaine! Be seeing you!
À tout à l'heure! See you later!

101.7 *Partir en voyage* People going away/travelling

Bon voyage! Have a good trip!
[to someone driving] **Sois prudent!** Drive carefully!
Fais attention en conduisant. Drive carefully.
Bon retour! Have a safe journey back!
Appelle-moi en arrivant. Call me when you get there.

102 *Entamer une conversation* Opening a conversation

102.1 *Attirer l'attention* Attracting attention

[In a street or public place] **Pardon!** Excuse me!
Pardon Monsieur/Madame! Excuse me!
Vous pouvez me renseigner, s'il vous plaît! Could you help me please?
[If you need to attract the attention of a waiter or waitress, or to be noticed by an official]
S'il vous plaît! Excuse me!
Using **Garçon!** to attract the waiter's attention is now a little old-fashioned. If you want to be more polite, raise your arm briefly and say **(Monsieur) s'il vous plaît!** to a waiter and **(Mademoiselle or Madame) s'il vous plaît!** to a waitress.

102.2 *Faire la première approche* When you want to engage someone in conversation

On peut se voir un instant? Could we have a brief chat?
J'ai quelque chose à vous demander. There's something I wanted to ask you about.
J'ai besoin de vous parler. I need to have a word with you.

102.3 *Pour introduire un sujet de conversation* Introducing a topic of conversation

Il s'agit de . . . It's about . . .
Voilà, c'est . . . Well, it's about . . .
Le problème est le suivant . . . The problem is as follows . . .

103 *Au cours d'une conversation* During a conversation

103.1 *Amplifier un thème/changer de thème* Developing/Changing the topic

À propos, . . . By the way, . . .
En parlant de . . . Talking of . . .
Ça me rappelle . . . That reminds me . . .
[more formal] **Allons un peu plus loin . . .** Let's take this a bit further . . .

103.2 *Revenir sur un sujet précédent* Referring back to some earlier point in the conversation

Comme je disais (tout à l'heure), . . . As I was saying (before), . . .
Comme vous (le) disiez . . . As you were saying . . .
Pour revenir à . . . Going back to . . .
Pour en revenir à ce que je disais, . . . Anyway, as I was saying, . . .

103.3 *Pour soutenir l'argumentation de quelqu'un* Supporting someone's point of view

Comme tu dis As you say
Je suis d'accord avec ce que tu dis/avec toi. I agree with what you're saying/with you.
[more formal] **Je partage votre opinion.** I share your views.
Non seulement cela, mais . . . Not only that, but . . .
J'ajouterais que . . . I'd also say that . . .

103.4 *Interruptions* Interrupting

Désolé(e) de vous couper la parole . . . Sorry to butt in . . .
[rather formal] **Excusez-moi de vous interrompre.** Sorry to interrupt you.
[When you feel you cannot get a word in, or someone is dominating the conversation] **(Vous) permettez!** Hang on (a minute)!
Laissez-moi parler! Let me speak!
Laissez-moi terminer! Let me finish!
[when a child is trying to interrupt you] **Je parle!** I'm talking!
Vous n'avez pas répondu à ma question! You didn't answer my question!

103.5 *Hésitations* Hesitating

C'était . . . voyons . . . en 1994. It was . . . let's see . . . in 1994.
Je l'ai rencontré . . . (voyons . . .) que je me rappelle . . . à Toulouse. I met him . . . let me think . . . in Toulouse
Je suis libre . . . attends . . . mardi I'll be free . . . wait a minute . . . on Tuesday

104 *Terminer une conversation* Ending a conversation

Bon . . . Right . . .
[very informal] **Bon, allez, c'est pas tout ça . . .** Right, got to get on . . .
[slightly more formal] **Bon, je crois qu'on s'est tout dit.** Well I think that about covers it.
[When matters can be left till another occasion. Formal] **Restons-en là.** Let's leave it at that, shall we?

105 *Demander quelqu'un* Asking for someone

[These phrases are appropriate for face-to-face and for telephone inquiries]
Bonjour, est-ce que Philippe est là s'il vous plaît? Hallo, is Philippe there, please?
Bonjour, pourrais-je parler à Marc? Hallo, could I speak to Marc?
[more informal] **Salut, il est là, Joseph?** Hi, is Joseph in, please?
Je cherche Adeline, tu sais où elle est? I'm looking for Adeline, do you know where she is?
[very informal] **T'as pas vu Adrien?** Seen Adrien anywhere?

105.1 *À la réception* At the reception desk

Pourrais-je parler à Monsieur Berne? Could I speak to Mr Berne, please?
J'aimerais parler au directeur/à la directrice. I'd like to speak to the Manager, please.
Bonjour, je voudrais voir Mademoiselle Scott. Hallo, I'm looking for Miss Scott.
J'ai rendez-vous avec Monsieur Demesle. I've got an appointment with Mr Demesle.
Madame Verdier doit me voir ce matin. Mrs Verdier is expecting me this morning.

106 *Souhaiter quelque chose à quelqu'un* Expressing good wishes

106.1 *Pour l'avenir* For the future

[formal, eg. when making a speech, at retirement party]
Tous mes vœux pour une retraite heureuse I'd like to offer you my best wishes for a happy retirement.
[at a wedding] **Tous mes vœux de bonheur.** May I offer you my very best wishes for your future happiness.
Use **Tous nos vœux** if you're speaking on behalf of others.

106.2 *Pour encourager quelqu'un avant une épreuve* To give someone your support before an exam, test or interview

Bonne chance pour ton (test/examen, etc). Good luck with your (test/exam, etc).
Bonne chance pour mardi! Best of luck for next Tuesday!
Je croise les doigts pour toi. I'll keep my fingers crossed for you.
It is customary to wish people luck by saying *Merde!*, often in a stage whisper, to indicate that, reluctant though one might be to use such words, the occasion warrants it. Using an insult instead of a wish is a way of warding off bad luck. There is an equivalent superstition in the English phrase 'Break a leg!'

106.3 *Quand quelqu'un est dans une situation difficile* When someone is facing a difficult situation or an ordeal

J'espère que ça va bien se passer. I hope everything turns out well for you.
[more confident] **Tu vas voir, tout va bien se passer.** You'll see, everything will turn out all right.
[even more confident] **Ne t'inquiète pas, tout se passera pour le mieux.** Don't worry, everything's going to be (absolutely) fine.

106.4 *À un ou une malade* To someone who is sick

J'espère que ça va aller mieux. I hope you get better soon.
[formal, in writing] **Je vous souhaite meilleure santé.** Get well soon!

106.5 *Vœux à l'occasion de fêtes* Seasonal greetings

Joyeux Noël! Merry Christmas!
Bonnes Fêtes! Have a nice Christmas and New Year!
Bonne année! ALSO **Tous mes vœux pour l'année nouvelle!** Happy New Year!
[in print, on cards] **Joyeuses Pâques!** Happy Easter!
[in speech] **Bonnes vacances de Pâques!** Have a nice Easter break!
You may reply informally to the above greetings with *Merci, toi/vous aussi!* or *Merci, toi/vous de même!* 'Thanks, the same to you!'

106.6 *Anniversaires et fêtes* Birthdays and celebrations

Bon anniversaire! Happy birthday!
[to somebody on their Saint's day] **Bonne fête!** Happy Saint's day!
Bon anniversaire de mariage! Happy (wedding) anniversary!

107 *Compatir* Expressing sympathy

107.1 **Commisération** Commiserating

[To someone who has experienced a failure] **Quel dommage!** What a pity!
Vous devez être déçu(e). You must be disappointed.
Je suis désolé(e) ALSO **navré(e) pour vous.** I really am sorry (about what happened to you).

107.2 *Condoléances* Condolences

Toutes mes condoléances. Please accept my deepest sympathy.
[formal. At funeral] **Je suis de tout cœur avec vous.** I share in your grief.

108 *Dans les magasins* In shops/stores

108.1 *Entamer le dialogue* Beginning a conversation

The standard form is to use *Monsieur/Madame/Mademoiselle*, to which the assistant will reply in the same way.
Bonjour Madame, vous avez des ampoules de cent watts?
Hallo, have you got any 100-watt bulbs?
Ah, non Monsieur, nous devons en recevoir demain. Sorry, no, but we're getting some in tomorrow.
Vous désirez (Madame/Mademoiselle/Monsieur)? Can I help you (Madam/Miss/Sir)?
[informal] **À nous!** Yes! (how can I help?)
Pardon, (Madame/Mademoiselle/Monsieur), est-ce que vous avez du . . . ? Excuse me, have you got any . . . ?
S'il vous plaît, est-ce que je pourrais avoir du . . . ? Could I please have some . . . ?
Je cherche du . . . I'm looking for some . . .
On s'occupe de vous? Are you being served?
[Customer/client, etc, unsure whose turn it is.] **C'est à moi?** Is it my turn?
[more impatient] **Je pourrais être servi(e), s'il vous plaît?** Could somebody serve me, please?
[more formal] **J'aurais besoin d'aide, s'il vous plaît.** I wonder if you could help me?
In a village café or shop or a neighbourhood café in town the informal *Messieurs-dames!* is a friendly greeting used by customers and staff alike, providing people of both sexes are present. You may say *Bonjour Messieurs-dames!* (Morning!) on entering the premises. The assistant may say *Ces Messieurs-dames désirent?* (What would you like?) to a couple or to a mixed group of customers.

108.2 *Demander si des produits/services sont disponibles* Enquiring about the availability of goods/services

Vous vendez (des pellicules/blocs-notes)? Do you sell (film/paper)?
Vous avez (des calendriers/lacets)? Do you have any (calendars/shoelaces)?
Je cherche (une brosse à habits/une carte d'Espagne) I'm looking for a clothes brush/a map of Spain).
Vous réparez les (appareils-photos/poupées)? Do you repair (cameras/dolls)?

108.3 *Refuser un service* Declining the offer of service

Non, merci, je regarde. I'm just looking, thank you.
Oui, on s'occupe de moi. I'm being served, thanks.

108.4 *Difficultés pour obtenir ce que l'on veut* Difficulty in obtaining what you want

Je suis désolé(e), nous n'avons plus de (papier/vinaigre). I'm sorry, we're out of (paper/vinegar) at the moment.

Je suis désolé(e), nous sommes en rupture de stock.
I'm sorry, we haven't got any in stock at the moment.
**Je suis désolé(e), nous ne faisons pas les (CD/bottes
en caoutchouc)** I'm sorry, we don't do (CDs/wellington
boots).
Non, nous n'en avons pas, essayez [name of another
shop]. No, we haven't got any, try [name of another
shop].

108.5 *Expliquer ce que l'on veut* Specifying what you want

Vous en avez en (bleu/rose)? Do you have it in
(blue/pink)?
Vous en avez en (taille 40/42)? Do you have it in (size
40/42)?
Ça se fait en (plus grande/petite taille)? Do they come
in (a larger/smaller size)?
[informal] **Vous avez moins cher?** Do you have anything
cheaper?
Vous avez quelque chose dans une autre qualité? Do
you have anything of slightly better quality?

108.6 *Demander le prix d'une marchandise/d'un service* Asking the price of goods and services

C'est combien? ALSO **Combien ça vaut?** ALSO **Il/Elle
coûte combien?** How much is it?
Ça fait combien en tout? How much is it altogether?
Vous pouvez me donner une gamme de prix? Can you
tell me what sort of price range it is/they are in?

108.7 *Décider de ce que l'on va acheter* Deciding what you are going to buy

Je vais prendre celui-là/celle-là. I'll take this one, please.
Bon d'accord, je le/la prends. OK, then I'll take it
Non merci, je vais réfléchir ALSO **je vais voir.** No thanks,
I'll leave it (for the moment).
C'est exactement ce que je cherchais. This is exactly
what I was looking for.

108.8 *Payer* Paying

Vous payez comment? How would you like to pay?
Je peux payer par chèque? Can I pay by cheque?
Je peux payer avec ma carte de crédit? Can I pay by
credit card?
Vous prenez ALSO **acceptez la Visa?** Do you accept/take
Visa?
Je paie en liquide. I'll pay cash.
Mettez-le sur ma note. Put it on my account.
Je libelle le chèque au nom de qui? Who do I make the
cheque out to?
Je vais vous demander des arrhes. I'll have to ask you to
leave a deposit.
Vous n'avez pas de monnaie? Do you have any change?
Je n'ai qu'un billet de 200 francs. All I have is a 200-
franc note.
Je n'ai que des grosses coupures. I haven't got anything
smaller.

108.9 *Livraisons et transport des marchandises* Collecting and transporting goods

Je viens chercher (mon magnétophone/ma veste). I've
come to get (my video-recorder/my jacket).
Ça sera prêt quand? When will it be ready?
Vous pouvez me l'envelopper? Can you wrap it up for
me?
Est-ce que vous faites les livraisons? ALSO **Vous livrez?**
Do you deliver?
Je peux passer le prendre tout à l'heure? Can I pick it
up later?
On peut commander par correspondance? Do you have
a mail-order service?

108.10 *Se présenter dans un lieu et quitter un lieu* Checking in and out of a place

[at a conference or similar gathering]
**C'est pour le séminaire 'Environnement et planète',
où faut-il s'inscrire?** Hallo, I'm here for the
'Environment and planet' conference. Where do I register?
[at a hotel, if you haven't made a reservation]
Je voudrais une chambre s'il vous plaît. I would like a
room, please.
[if the room has already been reserved for you] **Je suis**
[your name], **j'ai une réservation.** I'm [your name], I
have a room booked.
Je voudrais régler la chambre, s'il vous plaît. I'd like to
settle my bill, please.

108.11 *Terminer la conversation* Ending a conversation

Vous êtes bien aimable, merci. Thanks for your help
[informal]**Bon, eh bien au revoir et merci.** Well, goodbye and thanks a lot.
[more formal] **Je vous remercie, au revoir.** Thank you
very much, good bye.

109 *Remercier* Thanking

Merci is acceptable in most situations, but if you want to
be a little more polite you could say **Merci beaucoup,
Merci bien,** and even stronger, **Merci mille fois** or
Merci infiniment. In any case, when thanking somebody
whose name you don't know, make sure you always use
Monsieur, Madame or *Mademoiselle*, e.g. **Merci
Madame, Merci beaucoup Monsieur, Merci bien
Mademoiselle.** If you're on title and surname terms with
somebody, say **Merci Monsieur Lambert, Merci
beaucoup Madame Favet.** For friends and relatives,
Merci Danielle, Merci Papa, etc. Saying thank you
without these forms of address may sound slightly abrupt.
For a very formal way of thanking, use **Je vous remercie
infiniment.** I'm very grateful to you.
Merci pour tout. Thanks for everything.
Merci pour lui/elle. I'm sure he/she'd like to thank you.
When refusing e.g. a cup of tea, some sugar in their coffee,
people will sometimes say **merci.** Beware, as this, in the
context, means **Merci, non** No, thank you. Thus:
Vous prenez du sucre? – Merci. Do you take sugar? – No,
thank you.

The latter is usually accompanied by an unambiguous movement with the hand emphasizing refusal.
[Polite formula for thanking someone, e.g. in a letter] **Je vous suis très reconnaissant(e) de tout ce que vous avez fait.** I am very grateful for everything you have done.
[To express thanks in anticipation] **Je vous serais reconnaissant(e) de bien vouloir . . .** I'd be extremely grateful if you would . . .

110 *Permission* Permission

110.1 *Demander la permission* Asking permission

Generally, permission may be asked for by saying **Je peux . . . ? Est-ce que je peux . . . ? Puis-je . . .** or **Pourrais-je . . . ?** in increasing order of formality.
Je peux me garer ici? Can I park here?
Est-ce que je peux prendre une photo? Can I take a photograph?
Puis-je vous demander de signer notre livre d'or? May I ask you to sign our visitors' book?
In public situations:
On peut fumer ici? Is smoking allowed here?
Je peux garder deux bagages avec moi dans l'avion? Am I allowed to take two bags onto the plane?
[for more sensitive requests] **Cela vous dérange si (je fume/j'amène un ami)?** Do you mind if (I smoke/I bring a friend)?
[more formal/tentative; note the use of the verb in the past tense, which makes the request more polite] **Est-ce que cela vous ennuierait si (je ne venais pas demain/j'amenais un ami)?** Would you mind if I (didn't come tomorrow/brought a friend)?
[less formal] **Je préfère (partir tôt/ne pas venir demain), d'accord?** Is it okay if I (leave early/don't come tomorrow)?

110.2 *Donner la permission* Giving permission

When replying to **Est-ce que ça vous dérange(rait)?** you give permission by saying **Non, pas du tout!**

A: **Est-ce que ça vous dérange si je m'assieds ici?**
B: **Non pas du tout allez-y.**
A   Do you mind if I sit here?
B   Not at all, please do.
A: **Ça vous ennuie si je prend cette chaise?**
B: **Non, non, allez-y.**
A   Do you mind if I take this chair?
B   Not at all, go ahead.
[less formal]
A: **Je partirai tôt, d'accord?**
B: **Oui oui, aucun problème.**
A   I'll leave early, OK?
B   OK, no problem.
[less formal]
A: **Il peut venir, Robert?**
B: **Oui oui absolument!**
A   OK if Robert comes along?
B   Of course, fine!

[informal]
A: [choosing a seat] **Je me mets ici?**
B: **Oui oui allez-y.**
A   Can I sit here?
B   Please do.

110.3 *Refuser une permission* Denying permission

[polite]
A: **Ça vous ennuie si je fume?**
B: **Oui, je préfère que vous ne fumiez pas.**
A   Do you mind if I smoke?
B   Yes, actually, I'd rather you didn't.
[direct and very firm]
A: **Ça vous ennuie si je fume?**
B: **Oui à vrai dire ça m'ennuie beaucoup.**
A   Do you mind if I smoke?
B   Yes, I'm afraid I do mind.

111 *Propositions* Offers

111.1 *Offrir son aide* Making offers of help

Est-ce que je peux vous être utile? May I be of assistance?
[very informal] **Tu veux un coup de main?** Do you want a hand?
[more formal] **Puis-je vous porter votre sac?** May I carry your bag?
[less formal] **Attends, je vais (te) le faire.** Let me do that for you.
Si tu veux j'apporterai le café. If you like, I'll bring the coffee.
[at the end of a meeting in e.g. a school or office] **Ne vous inquiétez pas, je fermerai.** You can leave it to me to lock up.
[In contexts such as meetings, where people are offering to do things] **Je suis volontaire pour (vendre les billets/ranger les chaises).** I'll volunteer to (sell the tickets/put the chairs away).

111.2 *Proposer de payer* Offering to pay

[rather formal] **Je tiens absolument à vous offrir ce repas.** Please allow me to pay for the meal.
[less formal] **C'est moi qui offre le café.** Let me pay for the coffee.
[very informal] **C'est moi qui régale!** It's on me!
[when the other person is about to pick up the bill] **Non, non, (je t'en prie) c'est moi!** No, please, this is on me.

111.3 *Accepter une proposition* Accepting an offer

[when someone has volunteered to do something] **Merci, c'est très aimable à vous de vous proposer.** Thank you, it's good of you to offer.
[less formal] **Merci, c'est gentil.** Thanks, that's kind of you.
[polite or hesitant acceptance] **Surtout, ne vous y croyez pas obligé(e).** Oh, you really don't have to.

[when a person is offering to inconvenience himself/herself, e.g. offering a lift] **Merci, j'espère que cela ne vous dérange pas?** Thanks, I hope it's not putting you out in any way.

[when someone has offered something and time has elapsed since the offer, without it being accepted] **C'est toujours d'accord pour samedi prochain?** Still OK for next Saturday?

[more informal] **Alors, je compte sur toi mardi, comme convenu?** So, are we still on for Tuesday?

[more formal] **Vous aviez eu la gentillesse de proposer de l'aide pour samedi prochain, puis-je compter sur vous?** I wonder if I could take you up on your offer of help next Saturday.

111.4 *Refuser une proposition* Declining an offer

[informal. When someone has offered some practical help] **Non, merci, ça va aller.** No thanks, it's OK.

[informal, in reply to an offer of help with a chore] **Ça va, je vais y arriver, merci.** It's OK, I can manage, thanks.

[declining the offer of a lift, etc.] **Non (on vient me chercher/j'ai mon vélo) mais merci quand même.** Thanks anyway, but (someone is coming to pick me up/I have my bicycle].

[rather formal, when an offer of some magnitude is made, e.g. the loan of a large sum of money] **Non, merci, c'est quelque chose que je ne peux absolument pas accepter.** Thank you, but I couldn't possibly accept.

112 *Invitations* Invitations

112.1 *Inviter* Extending invitations

Venez donc déjeuner/dîner un de ces jours. Would you like to come to lunch/dinner one day?

[Inviting someone to an already arranged event] **Voulez-vous vous joindre à nous pour notre déjeuner de fin de trimestre?** Would you like to join us for our end-of-term lunch?

[formal] **Nous vous proposons de (devenir membre du comité/venir faire une conférence).** We'd like to invite you to (join our committee/give a lecture).

[fairly informal] **Viens donc prendre un verre, un de ces jours.** Why don't you come round and have a drink some time?

112.2 *Accepter une invitation* Accepting an invitation

Merci, avec grand plaisir. Thanks, I'd love to.

[formal] **Je vous remercie, cela me fait très plaisir.** Thank you, I'd be delighted to.

[less formal, when someone has just invited you to have a coffee, see a film, etc.] **Bonne idée, oui, merci.** Thanks, that sounds nice.

112.3 *Refuser une invitation* Declining an invitation

Ça m'aurait fait plaisir mais malheureusement je suis pris(e) (ce soir-là/jeudi toute la journée) I'd love to, but I'm afraid I'm booked up (that evening/busy all day Thursday).

[more formal] **Je vous remercie de votre invitation mais malheureusement je ne suis pas libre ce jour-là.** Thank you for the invitation, but I'm afraid I'm not free that day.

[leaving room to negotiate an alternative] **Désolé(e), je suis pris(e) lundi. Nous pourrions convenir d'une autre date?** Sorry, I'm booked up on Monday. Could we fix another time?

[leaving it more uncertain, with a friendly smile] **Ce sera pour une autre fois . . .** Some other time, perhaps?

113 *Conseils* Advice

113.1 *Demander conseil* Requesting advice

Je voudrais louer un appartement, pourriez-vous me conseiller? I need some advice about renting an apartment, can you help me?

Je ne sais pas quoi faire (à propos de . . .), pouvez-vous me conseiller? Can you advise me as to what I should do (about . . .)?

Je voudrais m'inscrire à un séjour linguistique en Allemagne. Quels conseils pouvez-vous me donner? I want to take a language course in Germany. Can you give me any advice?

[informal] **Je voudrais louer une voiture en Espagne, vous avez des tuyaux?** I'd like to hire a car in Spain – do you have any tips?

113.2 *Donner des conseils* Offering advice

Le mieux, c'est (d'appeler la police/de réserver à l'avance). The best thing to do is (to call the police/ to book ahead).

[less formal] **Si j'étais toi, (je vendrais le piano/j'achèterais une voiture.** If I were you, I'd (sell the piano/buy a car).

[informal] **À votre place, je démissionnerais tout de suite.** If I were in your shoes, I'd resign straight away.

[formal] **Je vous conseille d'accepter cette offre.** My advice (to you) would be to accept this offer.

[very strong] **Si tu veux mon avis, tu devrais arrêter de sortir avec elle.** If you want my advice, you should stop seeing her.

[suggesting] **Tu pourrais essayer de (leur parler/trouver un autre poste).** You could try (talking to them/finding a new job).

[more tentative] **Ce serait peut-être une bonne idée de (faire une photocopie/commencer le yoga).** It might be an idea to (make a photocopy/start yoga lessons).

[polite but direct] **Pourquoi ne pas (lui téléphoner/les donner au teinturier)?** Why not (phone him/have them dry-cleaned)?

113.3 *Accepter un conseil* Accepting advice

Merci du conseil. Thanks for the advice.
[more formal] **Je vous remercie de votre conseil** or **vos conseils.** Thank you for your advice.
Merci, je ne manquerai pas de suivre votre conseil or **vos conseils.** Thank you I'll certainly follow your advice.
[informal] **Merci pour le tuyau.** Thanks for the tip.
Merci, j'y penserai. Thanks, I'll bear that in mind.

114 *Renseignements* Information

114.1 *Demander des renseignements* Requesting information

Pouvez-vous me renseigner? Can you help me?
Où est-ce qu'il y a (une cabine téléphonique/des toilettes/etc)? Where can I find (a phone/toilet/etc.)?
Où se trouve (la gare/la boulangerie/etc) la plus proche? Where's the nearest (station/bakery/etc.)?
Où se trouve (l'arrêt de bus/le marchand de journaux/etc) le plus proche? Where is the nearest (bus stop/news stand/etc.)?
Qu'est-ce que tu souhaites que je fasse de (cette clef/ces billets/etc)? What do you want me to do with (this key/these tickets/etc.)?
Pourrais-je connaître la raison de (ce supplément/ce retard/etc)? What's the reason for (this extra charge/the delay/etc.)?
Qui s'occupe (des remboursements/de la location des salles/etc)? Who is in charge of (refunds/room-bookings/etc.)?
Pouvez-vous m'indiquer comment remplir ce formulaire, s'il vous plaît? Could you explain to me how to fill/out in this form please?
Comment est-ce qu'on accède (à la rue/au sous-sol etc)? How can I get to (the street/the basement etc.)?
Comment m'y prendre pour (changer ma réservation/faire réparer mon talon de chaussure/etc)? How do I go about (changing my reservation/getting the heel of my shoe repaired/etc.)?
Où m'adresser pour (me faire rembourser/avoir des places gratuites/etc) ? Where do I go to (get my money back/pick up free tickets/etc.)?
Pouvez-vous m'indiquer où est le départ du bus? Can you tell me where the bus leaves from?
Pouvez-vous me donner son numéro? Can you tell me her number?
Pouvez-vous me renseigner sur (les horaires de bus/les hôtels)? Can you give me some information about (bus times/hotels)?
Est-ce que vous avez des renseignements sur (les cours de langue/la Turquie)? Do you have any information on (language courses/Turkey)?
Où est-ce que je peux me renseigner sur les assurances-voyages? Where can I get information about travel insurance?

114.2 *Dans l'impossibilité de renseigner quelqu'un* When you are unable to give information

Je suis désolé(e), je ne peux rien faire pour vous. I'm sorry, I can't help you.

Je suis désolé(e), vous n'êtes pas au bon endroit. Adressez-vous à la billetterie. I'm sorry, you've come to the wrong place. Ask at the ticket office.
Désolé(e), nous n'avons pas de brochures sur le Brésil en ce moment. Sorry, we haven't got any brochures on Brazil at the moment.
[informal] **Désolé(e), aucune idée.** Sorry, I haven't a clue.
In most situations, you can thank someone for giving information by just saying **Je vous remercie** or **Merci de votre gentillesse** or, more formally, **Je vous remercie de votre amabilité.**

115 *Instructions* Instructions

115.1 *Demander des instructions* Asking for instructions

Pouvez-vous (m'expliquer/me montrer) comment marche cette machine? Could you (tell me/show me) how to work this machine?
Y a-t-il un mode d'emploi pour la photocopieuse? Are there any instructions for the photocopier?
Comment faut-il faire pour changer la pellicule? What do I do if I want to change the film?
Comment faut-il faire pour installer ce projecteur? How do I go about setting up this spotlight?
Et qu'est ce que je fais (ensuite/maintenant)? And what do I do (then/now)?

115.2 *Fournir des instructions* Giving instructions

Tout ce qu'il y a à faire, c'est (appuyer sur le bouton/vérifier le niveau d'eau/etc) This is what you do, just (press the button/check the water level/etc.).
N'oubliez jamais de rabattre ce volet d'abord. You must always remember to close this flap first.
Vous rabattez ce contacteur et c'est tout. You just flick that switch down and that's it.
Conformez-vous aux instructions données sur le polycopié s'il vous plaît. Please follow the instructions on the handout.

116 *L'orientation* Directions

116.1 *Demander son chemin* Asking for directions

Pouvez-vous me dire comment aller à . . . ? Could you tell me the way to . . . ?
Excusez-moi, je suis perdu(e), pouvez-vous m'indiquer mon chemin? Excuse me, I'm lost, I wonder if you could help me?
Comment est-ce qu'on va à la gare, à partir d'ici? How do I get to the station from here?
S'il vous plaît, je cherche l'avenue Kennedy. Excuse me, I'm looking for avenue Kennedy.
[more formal] **Pourriez-vous m'indiquer où est l'avenue Kennedy?** Could you direct me to avenue Kennedy?

116.2 *Donner des indications à quelqu'un* Giving somebody directions

Vous y allez comment (en voiture, à pied, par les transports en commun)? How are you travelling (by car, on foot, by public transport)?
Prenez à gauche, puis à droite, et ensuite continuez tout droit. Turn left, then right, then go straight ahead.
Vous allez le voir (devant vous/sur votre gauche/etc). You'll see it (in front of you/on your left/etc.).
Vous pouvez prendre un raccourci par le parc. You can take a short cut through the park.
Si vous voyez une église, c'est que vous êtes allé(e) trop loin. If you see a church, you've gone too far.
Vous verrez la boulangerie sur votre droite. Look out for the bakery on your right.
Vous ne pouvez pas vous tromper. You can't go wrong.
Quand vous arrivez au feu, prenez sur votre droite. When you get to the lights, go off to the right

117 *Advertissements* Warnings

[These warnings can be mild or serious, depending on the tone of voice adopted]
Vous feriez mieux de ne pas vous garer ici, le quartier est plein de contractuels. You'd better not park there, the area's full of traffic wardens.
[very strong] **Je vous préviens, si vous vous garez là, j'appelle la police!** I warn you, if you park here I'll call the police!
[more indirect] **Si j'étais vous, je me tiendrais tranquille.** If I were you I wouldn't cause any trouble.
[more formal] **Sachez que si vous perdez de nouveau la clef, vous serez obligé(e) de payer le remplacement de la serrure.** I warn you that if you lose the key again you'll have to pay for a new lock.
Il est efficace, mais je vous préviens, il se met facilement en colère. He's efficient, but, be warned, he has a short temper.
[informal] **Je te préviens, elle ne va pas apprécier.** I'm warning you, she's not going to like it.
Attention (à ta tête/à la porte/à cette voiture)! Mind (your head/the door/that car)!
Attention en sortant, les marches sont glissantes. Take care when you leave, the steps are slippery.
Attention! Be careful!

118 *Promesses* Promises

Je te promets que je ne recommencerai pas. I promise you I won't do it again.
Je ne sortirai plus avec elle, je te le jure! I won't go out with her again, I promise!
[informal, childish language] **Juré, craché!** Cross my heart and hope to die!
[very formal] **Je déclare sous la foi du serment que . . .** I solemnly declare that . . .

119 *Prendre date* Agreeing to a date

119.1 *Prendre rendez-vous* Fixing times/dates, etc.

[rather formal] **Prenons date.** Let's make an appointment.
Est-ce que nous pourrions prendre rendez-vous? Could we arrange to meet some time?
[more informal] **On peut se voir bientôt?** Can we get together some time soon?
Vous êtes libre (jeudi/lundi)? Are you free (on Thursday/Monday)?
Et vendredi, vous êtes libre? What about Friday? Are you free then?
Êtes-vous disponible pour une réunion le 25? Could you make a meeting on the 25th?
Est-ce qu'on pourrait se voir bientôt pour parler (du recrutement/de la conférence)? Could we meet soon to discuss (recruitment/the conference)?
Êtes-vous libre le 15? Are you available on the 15th?
Disons 17 heures mardi, ça vous convient? Shall we say 5 pm on Tuesday, if that's suitable?
Lundi, je peux tout à fait. Monday suits me fine.
14 heures, c'est ce qui m'arrangerait le mieux. 2 o'clock would be best for me.
Je note le 23 au crayon, et on confirmera la date plus tard. I'll pencil in the 23rd, and we can confirm it later.
Disons le 18 pour le moment, et je vous recontacterai. Let's say the 18th for now and I'll get back to you.

119.2 *Difficultés à trouver une date/une heure, etc* Problems with times/dates, etc.

Je suis désolé(e) mais le 3, pour moi, c'est impossible. I'm afraid the 3rd is out for me.
Malheureusement, je suis pris(e) demain. I'm afraid I'm busy tomorrow.
Désolé(e), je n'ai pas un instant de libre cette semaine. I'm afraid I'm busy all this week.
Jeudi, ça n'irait pas, plutôt? Could we make it Thursday instead?
Désolé(e) mais j'ai pris deux rendez-vous en même temps pour vendredi. Est-ce que nous pourrions reporter? I'm afraid I'm double-booked on Friday. Could we rearrange things?
A Ça va être difficile pour 17 heures 30.
B 18 heures, ça irait mieux?
A: 5.30's a bit of a problem.
B: Would 6 be any better?
Est-ce que nous pourrions reporter la réunion de vendredi? Could we postpone Friday's meeting?
Désolé(e) mais nous allons devoir annuler la réunion de demain. Sorry, but we're going to have to cancel tomorrow's meeting.
Est-ce qu'on pourrait commencer à 15 heures 30, au lieu de 16 heures? Could we bring the time forward to 3.30 instead of 4?

120 *Plans et intentions* Plans and intentions

120.1 *Demander quelles sont les intentions de quelqu'un* Asking about someone's intentions

Qu'est-ce que tu vas faire? What are you going to do?
[more formal] **Qu'as-tu l'intention de faire?** What do you intend to do?

120.2 *Expliquer ses intentions* Explaining one's intentions

Je vais sans doute/je vais sûrement lui téléphoner. I'll most probably ring her.
[more tentative] **Je vais peut-être passer chez Paul.** I'll maybe drop round to Paul's place.
J'ai la ferme intention de lui dire ce que je pense de lui. I'm determined to tell him what I think of him.
[very formal] **Il n'entre nullement dans nos intentions de vous faire de la concurrence.** It is no part of our plans to enter into competition with you.

121 *Demander un service* Asking favours

[very polite] **Auriez-vous la gentillesse de me rendre un service?** I was wondering if you could do me a favour.
[rather direct but formal] **J'ai besoin de vous demander un service.** I need to ask a favour of you.
[less formal] **Vous pouvez me rendre un service?** Could you do me a favour?
[informal] **Tu peux me faire une fleur?** Can I ask a favour?
Polite and friendly replies when someone asks a favour include **Mais bien sûr, de quoi s'agit-il?** and **Mais certainement, avec plaisir.**

121.1 *Petits services* Small favours

Vous avez des allumettes, s'il vous plaît? Have you got a light, please?
Pourriez-vous me garder (mon sac/ma place) un instant, s'il vous plaît. Would you mind (my bag/my seat) for me for a moment, please?
[more informal] **Vous surveillez ma place une seconde, s'il vous plaît?** Would you keep an eye on my seat for a minute for me, please?
Vous avez un stylo à me prêter, je vous le rends tout de suite? Do you have a pen I could borrow for a moment?
Vous n'auriez pas la monnaie de ce billet, par hasard? Could you change this note by any chance?
Vous avez de la monnaie pour (le parcmètre/le téléphone)? Do you have any small change for (the parking meter/the phone)?
[in a queue] **Excusez-moi, vous me permettez de passer devant vous, je suis très très pressé(e)!** I wonder if you'd mind if I jumped the queue? I'm in a terrible hurry!

Cette place est libre/prise? Is this seat free/taken?
[In a restaurant or café where you notice acquaintances already seated] **Puis-je me joindre à vous?** Do you mind if I join you?
[In a restaurant or café where the only free seat is at a table already occupied] **Est-ce que ça vous dérange que je me mette là?** Do you mind my taking this seat?

122 *Excuses* Apologies

122.1 *S'excuser* Making apologies

[informal] **Excusez-moi, je suis en retard.** I'm sorry I'm late.
[more formal] **Veuillez m'excuser de vous avoir fait attendre.** I'm terribly sorry I've kept you waiting.
[rather formal, often used in writing] **Je vous prie de bien vouloir m'excuser du retard avec lequel je vous réponds.** I really must apologise for not having answered you earlier.
[very formal, often used in writing] **Veuillez accepter toutes nos excuses pour le dérangement que nous vous avons causé.** Our sincere apologies for the inconvenience we have caused you.
[rather formal] **Pardonnez-moi, vous êtes (Monsieur . . . /Madame . . . ?)** Forgive me, your name is . . . ?
[rather formal] **Je suis confus(e), mais j'ai oublié votre nom.** Forgive me, I've forgotten your name.

122.2 *Accepter les excuses de quelqu'un* Accepting apologies

Most common is **Mais je vous en prie, ne vous excusez pas. Je t'en prie, tu es tout(e) excusé(e)** is less formal. You can also use **Tout cela n'a aucune importance** or, less formally. **Aucune importance.**

123 *Rappeler quelque chose à quelqu'un* Reminding somebody of something

Vous n'oublierez pas de poster cette lettre, n'est-ce pas? Don't forget to post that letter, will you?
[less formal] **N'oublie pas de poster cette lettre, hein?** Don't forget to post that letter, OK?
[more formal] **Veillez à ne pas oublier d'apporter votre passeport.** Please remember to bring your passport.
[tactful but can be heard as slightly reproachful] **Tu n'as pas oublié que c'est l'anniversaire d'Anne demain?** You haven't forgotten it's Anne's birthday tomorrow?
[rather formal] **Puis-je vous rappeler qu'il n'y aura pas de réunion demain?** May I remind you that there will not be a meeting tomorrow?
[rather formal and tactful, when you suspect someone has forgotten something] **Si je peux me permettre . . . vous n'avez pas oublié que vous avez promis un séminaire, n'est-ce pas?** Can I jog your memory about the seminar you promised to give us?

If a reply is needed, you can say **Merci de me l'avoir rappelé.** If you want to apologize for forgetting something, you can say **Je suis désolé(e), j'ai complètement oublié** or **ça m'est complètement sorti de l'esprit.**

124 *Rassurer* Reassuring

Ne vous inquiétez pas, nous serons là avant 18 heures. Don't worry, we'll be there by six.
Il n'y a pas d'inquiétude à avoir. There's nothing to worry about.
[more formal] **Je vous assure qu'il n'y a aucun problème.** I can assure you that there'll be no problem.
[rather formal, typical of written style] **Soyez assurés de notre intention de contrôler les coûts.** I would like to reassure you that we intend to keep costs under control.

125 *Réclamations* Complaints

125.1 *Faire une réclamation* Making a complaint

Je ne suis pas satisfait(e) de la qualité du repas, pouvez-vous appeler le directeur de l'hôtel, s'il vous plaît? I'd like to complain about the meal; could you call the hotel manager, please?
Je viens faire une réclamation car je suis dérangé(e) par le bruit de la boîte de nuit. I've come to complain about the noise from the disco.
[more formal] **Je souhaite faire une réclamation concernant (ma chambre/le retard du vol/etc).** I'd like to make a complaint about (my room/the delay to the flight, etc.).
Pouvez-vous faire (arrêter ce bruit/accélérer le service), s'il vous plaît? Can you do something about (this noise/the slow service), please?
Je suis désolé(e), mais (ce réfrigérateur/cette tondeuse) ne marche pas comme il faut. I'm sorry but (this refrigerator/this lawn-mower) is not working properly.
[rather formal, typical of written style] **Je souhaite dénoncer de la façon la plus claire la médiocre qualité des services reçus.** I wish to complain in the strongest possible terms about the poor service I received.

125.2 *Recevoir des réclamations* Receiving complaints

Je suis désolé(e), je vais voir ce que je peux faire. I'm sorry. I'll see what I can do.
Écoutez, je prends note des détails, et je m'occupe personnellement de cette affaire. Leave it with me and I'll make sure something is done.
Je suis désolé(e), je vais faire en sorte que cela ne se reproduise plus. I'm sorry. I'll see to it that it doesn't happen again.
Je vais transmettre votre réclamation (au directeur/à la personne responsable du service/au service concerné) I'll pass your complaint on (to the manager/the person in charge of the department/the relevant department).

126 *Convaincre* Persuading

Pourquoi ne pas venir avec nous la semaine prochaine? Why don't you come with us next week?
[a little less formal] **Viens donc faire du parapente avec nous. Tu vas adorer, j'en suis sûr(e).** Why not come hang-gliding with us? You'll love it, I'm sure.
[more formal] **J'aimerais vous convaincre de vous joindre à nous ce soir.** Can I persuade you to join us tonight?
[less formal] **Venez donc passer Noël chez nous, ça nous ferait très plaisir.** Do come and stay at Christmas, we'd love to have you.
[informal] **Allez, prends un dessert, moi j'en prends un!** Go on! Have a dessert, I'm having one.
Je pense vraiment que vous devriez prendre quelques jours de congé. I really think you ought to take a few days off.

127 *Suggestions* Suggesting

127.1 *Faire des suggestions* Making suggestions

Prenons un taxi, d'accord? Let's take a taxi, shall we?
Et si on remettait cela à la semaine prochaine? Why don't we leave it till next week?
On pourrait peut-être changer la date? What about changing the date?
À mon avis, vous devriez annuler la soirée. I suggest you cancel the party.
[more formal] **Puis-je suggérer que nous reprenions la réunion demain?** May I suggest we continue with the meeting tomorrow?
J'ai une suggestion: organisons une vente aux enchères. I have a suggestion: let's hold an auction.

127.2 *Solliciter des suggestions* Asking for suggestions

Il faut absolument que nous fassions quelque chose: qu'est-ce que vous suggéreriez? We have to do something; what would you suggest?
Nous devons rassembler onze mille francs: y a-t-il des suggestions? We must raise eleven thousand francs: are there any suggestions?
[informal] **Tu vois ce que je dois faire pour réparer cette porte?** Have you got any suggestions as to how I can fix this door?
[informal] **Il nous faut douze mille francs immédiatement: quelqu'un a une idée?** We need 12,000 francs immediately; any bright ideas?
Tu aurais une idée de ce qu'il faut faire pour empêcher ce robinet de fuir? Can you think of a way of stopping this tap/faucet from leaking?

128 *D'acord, pas d'acord* Agreeing, disagreeing

128.1 *D'accord* Agreeing

A C'est fou
B Je suis bien d'accord
A: This is crazy
B: I entirely agree
Je suis d'accord avec tout ce que vous dites. I agree with everything you say.
[more formal] **Je partage entièrement votre opinion.** I am in complete agreement with you.
[informal] **Tu l'as bien dit!** Too right! You said it!

128.2 *Pas d'accord* Disagreeing

Je ne suis pas d'accord is a fairly strong way of expressing disagreement in French. Instead, people often partially agree before disagreeing. For example: **Je comprends ce que vous dites mais . . .** or **Oui, d'un côté vous avez raison mais . . .** I understand what you're saying but . . . or Yes, in a sense you're right, but . . .

[more formal] **Je suis désolé mais je ne suis pas du tout de votre opinion.** I'm afraid I can't agree with you.
Je ne suis pas du tout d'accord avec vous là-dessus. I have to disagree with you about that.
Tu dis que c'est un hypocrite, mais je ne le vois pas du tout comme ça. You say he's a hypocrite, but I don't see him like that at all.

129 *Opinions* Opinions

129.1 *Demander l'opinion de quelqu'un* Asking someone's opinion

Que pensez-vous de (la culture biologique/la politique du gouvernement)? What do you think of (organic farming/the government's policies) ?
[more formal] **Quel est votre point de vue sur . . . ?** What do you think about . . . ?
[informal] **Tu crois que (Robert va gagner/revenir/etc)?** Do you reckon (Robert will win/come back/etc.]?
[informal] **Tu vois la situation comment?** How do you see the situation?
[more formal] **Quelle est votre opinion sur la peine de mort?** What are your views on capital punishment?

129.2 *Donner son avis* Stating one's opinion

Je pense que . . . I think that . . .
[more formal] **Mon point de vue est le suivant . . .** My view is as follows . . .
[more formal] **À mon avis, nous avons attendu suffisamment longtemps.** In my view, we've waited long enough.
[informal] **Pour moi, il a un goût exécrable en matière d'habillement.** To my mind, his taste in clothes is appalling.

[informal] **J'ai l'impression qu'ils ne vont pas tarder à se marier.** I think they'll be getting married soon.
[very formal, in discussions, debates, etc.] **Si je peux émettre une opinion, je pense que . . .** If I may express an opinion, I think that . . .

130 *Préférences* Preferences

130.1 *S'enquérir des préférences de quelqu'un* Asking about someone's preferences

Qu'est-ce que vous préférez, une chambre à deux lits ou avec un grand lit? Which would you prefer, a twin-bedded or a double-bedded room?
[more informal] **Tu veux plutôt du thé ou du café?** What would you rather have, tea or coffee?
[fairly formal] **Avez-vous une préférence en ce qui concerne l'heure du vol?** Do you have any preference with regard to the time of the flight?
[informal] **On peut y aller vendredi ou samedi, comme tu veux.** We can go on Friday or Saturday, it's up to you.
Il y en a en rouge, bleu ou vert, au choix. They're available in red, blue or green; take your pick.

130.2 *Déclarer une préférence* Stating a preference

[slightly informal] **J'aimerais autant y aller lundi, si ça ne te fait rien.** I think I'd rather go on Monday, if you don't mind.
[more formal] **Je préfèrerais un siège dans le sens de la marche** I'd prefer a forward-facing seat, if possible.
[very formal, especially when you have not been asked your preference] **Si je puis exprimer une préférence, je souhaiterais ne pas avoir à venir en réunion vendredi prochain.** If I may express a preference, I would rather not have to come to a meeting next Friday.
[informal, in restaurants] **Bon, j'ai choisi, je prends le poulet.** I've decided, I'll go for the chicken.

131 *Degrés de certitude* Degrees of certainty

131.1 *Certitudes* Certainty

Nous nous sommes déjà rencontrés, j'en suis sûr(e) I'm sure we've met before.
[stronger] **Je l'ai laissé sur la table, j'en suis absolument certain(e).** I'm absolutely certain I left it on the table.
[informal] **C'est sûr que c'est le lecteur de compacts le moins cher que j'aie trouvé.** It's definitely the cheapest CD player I've found.
[more formal] **Elle est sans aucun doute/sans le moindre doute la femme d'affaires la plus connue du pays.** She's without doubt/undoubtedly the most famous businesswoman in the country.
[more formal] **Il faut faire quelque chose, il n'y a aucun doute.** There is no doubt that something must be done.

131.2 *Doutes et incertitudes* Doubt and uncertainty

Je ne pense pas pouvoir vous être utile. I'm not sure I can help you.

Je crois qu'il a dit 220 francs, mais je n'en suis pas sûr(e). I think he said 220 francs, but I can't be sure.

[stronger] **Je ne suis pas du tout sûr(e) que ça soit son numéro.** I'm not at all sure that this is his number.

[formal] **Nous avons actuellement quelques incertitudes quant à l'avenir.** At the moment we're a bit uncertain about the future.

Ça m'étonnerait qu'elle vienne avant mardi. I doubt whether she'll come before Tuesday.

Tout le monde trouve Pauline formidable, mais je suis sceptique. Everyone thinks Pauline is wonderful, but I have my doubts.

Sa réussite est loin d'être assurée. It's doubtful whether he will succeed.

Note that **sans doute** and **sans aucun doute** are used when you are reasonably sure of something, but would like confirmation that you are right:

Vous avez sans doute entendu parler de l'Opéra Bastille. You have doubtless heard about the Bastille Opera house.

However, **sans doute** can convey uncertainty, as in: **Elles sont sans doute parties à la plage.** Perhaps they went off to the beach.

131.3 *Approximations* Vagueness

Elle est, disons, entre deux âges. She's sort of middle-aged.

Ils ont besoin de vieilles boîtes, de colle, de carton et cetera. They need old boxes, glue, cardboard and things like that.

[informal] **Je ne comprends rien aux ordinateurs, CD Rom et tout ça.** I don't understand anything about computers, CD Rom and that sort of thing.

[informal] **Il a dit qu'il allait à Paris ou un truc de ce genre.** He said he was going to Paris or something.

When you don't want to be precise about a colour, the suffix **-âtre** can be used, though it is pejorative: **C'était une sorte de couleur grisâtre/verdâtre/jaunâtre/blanchâtre/noirâtre.** It was a grey-ish/greenish/yellowish/off-white/darkish sort of colour.

For quantities and ages, the suffix **-aine** can be used when you do not wish to be precise:

Elle a la trentaine. She's thirty-ish.

Une vingtaine de jours plus tard . . . Twenty or so days later . . .

131.4 *Hypothèses* Guessing and speculating

Je dirais qu'elle a à peu près la cinquantaine. I'd say she's about fifty.

[more informal] **Je pense que cet article fait environ 3.000 mots.** I would guess this article is about 3,000 words long.

[more formal] **J'estime qu'il nous faudrait environ 50.000 francs.** I would reckon that we would need about 50,000 francs.

[formal, when basing your speculation on calculations, experience, etc.] **Nous calculons que le projet s'étalera sur une durée de trois ans.** We estimate that the project will take three years.

[informal] **Je ne sais pas mais à vue de nez, je dirais qu'il y avait 10.000 personnes à la manifestation.** I don't know, but I would hazard a guess that there were about 10,000 people on the march.

[informal] **Devine qui j'ai vu aujourd'hui. Je parie que tu ne devineras pas!** Guess who I met today? I bet you can't!

Tu ne devineras jamais avec qui je dîne ce soir. I'll give you three guesses who I'm having dinner with tonight.

[informal] **Je (te) parie qu'elle sera encore là demain.** She'll be here again tomorrow, I'll bet.

Ne cherche pas qui je viens de voir, tu ne trouveras pas! Don't try to guess who I've just seen, you'll never get it!

132 *Obligation* Obligation

Il faut que je me lave les cheveux, ils sont dégoûtants. I must wash my hair, it's filthy!

[when the obligation is external] **Je dois faire/suis obligé(e) de faire renouveler mon passeport le mois prochain.** I have to renew my passport next month.

[as previous] **On nous a obligés à quitter le bâtiment.** We were forced to leave the building.

[stronger] **Les étudiants doivent impérativement s'inscrire une semaine avant le début des cours.** Students must make sure they register one week before the first day of term.

Il faudrait vraiment que tu remercies ta tante du cadeau qu'elle t'a envoyé. You really ought to say thanks to your aunt for that present she sent you.

[formal] **Devant ces témoignages, je suis contraint(e) de reconnaître que j'ai eu tort.** Faced with this evidence, I am forced to admit I have been wrong.

The word **Obligation** is very formal:

[formal] **Je suis dans l'obligation de vous demander de sortir.** I'm afraid I must ask you to leave.

Je suis désolé(e), mais je n'ai nullement l'obligation de vous fournir cette information. I'm sorry; I'm not under any obligation to provide you with this information.

Le jury a une obligation de réserve. Members of the jury must observe confidentiality.

133 *Exprimer sa surprise* Expressing surprise

Je suis étonné(e) que tu ne l'aies pas reconnue. I'm surprised that you didn't recognize her.

[stronger and more informal] **Je suis sidéré(e) que tu sois arrivé(e) si vite.** I'm amazed that you got here so quickly.

[informal] **Ça alors!** Well I never!

Ça alors, quelle surprise! Well! what a surprise!

Pour une surprise, c'est une surprise! Well! This *is* a surprise!

[said to someone to whom you are presenting a surprise gift or for whom you have arranged a surprise] **C'est la surprise!** Surprise, surprise!

Gina! C'est pas vrai! Qu'est-ce que tu fais là? Gina! I don't believe it! What are you doing here?

134 *Exprimer sa satisfaction/son mécontentement* Expressing pleasure/displeasure

134.1 *Exprimer sa satisfaction* Expressing pleasure

C'est vraiment agréable d'avoir la plage pour nous tout seuls. How nice to have the beach all to ourselves!
C'est formidable/merveilleux! This is wonderful/marvellous!
Quel plaisir de rentrer chez soi! What a pleasure to be home again!
[fairly formal, for example to a host] **Je suis vraiment ravi(e)/Nous sommes vraiment ravi(e)s d'être ici.** It's a real pleasure to be here.
C'est drôlement bien! Moi qui n'avais pas fait d'aviron depuis des années! What fun! I haven't rowed a boat for years!
C'est le bonheur parfait! Plus de travail pendant trois semaines! This is sheer delight! No more work for three weeks!
Je suis ravi(e) d'apprendre que vous avez résolu votre problème. I'm pleased to hear that you have solved your problem.
Vous vous mariez enfin: voilà une nouvelle qui me fait un immense plaisir. I'm delighted to hear that you're getting married at last.
Je suis content(e) que nous ayons eu l'occasion de nous rencontrer I'm happy that we've been able to meet.
[very formal, in speeches, etc.] **C'est avec le plus grand plaisir que je vous souhaite à tous la bienvenue ici ce soir.** It gives me great pleasure to welcome you all this evening.

134.2 *Exprimer son mécontentement* Expressing displeasure

The following phrases are all informal:
[about a town with no entertainment] **Quel trou!** What a terrible place!
[about a house with no charm or amenities] **C'est mortel, chez eux!** Their place is a terrible dump!
[about a very dull person] **Quel type sinistre!** What a terrible person!
[about a stupid person] **Quel crétin!** What a dope!
[about an interfering person] **Quel enquiquineur/enquiquineuse!** What a pest!
[about a job] **Quelle corvée!** What a pain!
Je ne suis pas très satisfait(e) de la façon dont les choses ont tourné. I'm not very happy with the way things have turned out.
Je ne suis pas ravi(e) d'apprendre que les prix ont augmenté. I wasn't at all pleased to hear that the prices are going up.
Je n'aime pas du tout la façon dont les choses se passent actuellement au bureau. I'm unhappy about what's going on at the office these days.
[strong] **Je suis atterré(e) de ce qui s'est passé.** I'm appalled at what has happened.

[formal and rather stern, e.g. when talking to a child] **Je suis extrêmement mécontent(e) de la façon dont tu t'es comporté(e)** I'm extremely displeased with your behaviour.
[formal, e.g. when talking to a subordinate] **Je dois vous dire que votre comportement d'hier est totalement inacceptable.** I have to tell you that your behaviour yesterday is quite unacceptable.

135 *Louanges/compliments/félicitations* Praises/compliments/congratulations

135.1 *Louanges* Praises

Bravo! Well done!
[informal. Used when someone has completed a difficult task] **Bravo.** ALSO **Bien joué!** Well handled!
[more formal, not limited to work] **Vous avez fait du bon travail.** You've done extremely well.
[informal] **Tu t'en es bien tiré!** You've done well!
J'admire votre savoir-faire/votre patience. I admire your skill/your patience.
[either to a person of lower status or, humorously, to someone of equal status] **Personnellement, je n'aurais pas pu!** I couldn't have done it!
[fairly formal] **Je dois vous féliciter pour le travail que vous avez fourni.** I think you deserve praise for all your hard work.

135.2 *Compliments* Compliments

Quelle jolie robe/quel beau jardin! What a beautiful dress/garden!
Elle te va très bien, cette veste. You look very nice in that jacket.
J'aimerais avoir une maison comme la vôtre, elle est vraiment formidable. I envy you your house, it's wonderful.
Je ne sais pas comment vous faites pour être aussi efficace. I don't know how you manage to be so efficient.
[more formal] **Je vous fais tous mes compliments pour votre dernier livre.** I must compliment you on your latest book.

135.3 *Félicitations* Congratulations

A **Je viens d'avoir une promotion/Je suis papa depuis hier.**
B **Oh, toutes mes félicitations!**
A: I've just been promoted/My wife had a baby yesterday.
B: Oh, congratulations!
[formal, eg. when making a speech] **J'ai/nous avons le plaisir de vous exprimer les félicitations de l'entreprise pour vos 25 ans de bons et loyaux services.** I/we'd like to congratulate you on 25 years of good and faithful service to the company

136 *Annonces* Announcements

[often precedes public announcements] **Votre attention s'il vous plaît?** Can I have your attention, please?
[about to explain something of practical importance] **J'ai une annonce à faire.** I'd like to make an announcement.
[more formal. About to announce important news] **J'ai une information à vous communiquer.** I have an announcement to make.
Je vais maintenant lire le nom de la personne qui a gagné le premier prix. I'm now going to read the name of the winner of the first prize . . .
Mesdames, Mesdemoiselles, Messieurs . . . Ladies and Gentlemen, . . .
Je vous remercie de votre attention. Thank you for your attention.

137 *Réagir à une information* Reacting to news

Formidable! How wonderful!
[informal] **Super!** Great!
C'est affreux! How awful!
[informal] **Non, c'est pas vrai!** Oh no!
[when the news is not good, and has been predictable] **Je m'en doutais!** I might have guessed!
[when the news is surprising] **Ça, je ne m'y attendais pas!** Well, I never thought I would hear that!
[informal. When the information is genuinely new for you] **Ah bon, première nouvelle!** Well, that's news to me!

138 *Parler de l'heure qu'il est* Talking about the time

Quelle heure est-il? What time is it?
Vous avez l'heure s'il vous plaît? Have you got the time, please?
[when you are not sure if you have the right time] **Vous avez l'heure exacte, s'il vous plaît?** Do you have the exact time, please?
[informal] **Il est dix heures pile.** It's exactly ten o'clock.
Il est trois heures et demie passé. It's just past half past three.
Il est presque six heures. It's approaching six o'clock.
Ma montre doit avancer/retarder. My watch must be slow/fast.
[more informal] **J'avance/Je retarde un peu.** I'm a bit slow/fast.
Ma montre s'est arrêtée. My watch has stopped.

139 *Raconter ce qui s'est passé* Describing and reporting

139.1 *Histoires et anecdotes* Stories and anecdotes

[all examples below are informal]
Tu as su ce qui s'est passé l'autre soir? Did you hear what happened the other night?
Tu as su, pour Juliette? Did you hear what happened to Juliette?
Je t'ai dit que . . . ? Did I tell you that . . . ?
Il faut que je te raconte . . . I must tell you . . .
Tu ne devineras jamais ce qui s'est passé! You'll never guess what happened!
[informal] **Figure-toi qu'on va avoir un nouveau chef!** Guess what? We're getting a new boss!
[something that happened a long time ago] **Je me rappellerai toujours/Je n'oublierai jamais . . .** I'll always remember/I'll never forget . . .

139.2 *Histoires drôles* Jokes

Tu connais celle de l'Allemand/du Français qui . . . ? Have you heard the one about the German/Frenchman who . . . ?
J'ai entendu une histoire très drôle l'autre jour . . . I heard a very funny story the other day . . .
[informal] **J'en ai entendu une bien bonne l'autre jour . . .** I heard a good one the other day . . .
[informal] **Je te l'ai racontée, celle de . . . ?** Did I tell you the one about . . . ?
Je vais vous en raconter une. Elle est tout à fait correcte/un peu osée. Do you want to hear a joke? It's quite clean/it's slightly risqué.
[When you do not see the point of a joke] **Désolé(e), je ne vois pas ce qu'il y a de drôle**. I'm sorry, I don't get it.

140 *Problèmes de communication* Problems of communication

140.1 *Malentendus* Misunderstandings

Désolé(e), je n'ai pas compris. I'm sorry, I don't understand.
Je pense que nous nous sommes mal compris(es) I think we've misunderstood each other.
[more formal or impersonal] **Je pense qu'il y a un malentendu.** I think there's been a misunderstanding.
[informal] **Je crois que tu n'as pas bien saisi.** I think you misunderstood.
Je crois que nous ne parlons pas de la même chose. I think we're talking at cross-purposes.

140.2 *Problèmes de volume et de vitesse* Problems with audibility/speed

Pouvez-vous parler plus lentement s'il vous plaît?
Could you speak more slowly, please?

Parlez plus lentement, s'il vous plaît, j'ai du mal à vous suivre. Could you slow down a bit, please? I find it difficult to follow you.

Je n'ai pas entendu ce que vous avez dit. Pouvez-vous répéter s'il vous plaît? I didn't catch what you said. Could you repeat it, please?

In French, the polite response when you do not hear what is said is simply to say **Pardon?**

140.3 *Demander de l'aide* Asking for help

Pouvez-vous m'aider, j'ai du mal à lire cette affiche. Can you help me? I'm having trouble understanding this notice.

Que veut dire 'contrevenant'? What does 'offender' mean?

[when you want to know precisely how someone is using a word] **Qu'est-ce que vous entendez par 'âgé'?** What do you mean by 'elderly'?

Comment épelle-t-on 'yoghourt'? ALSO **'Yoghourt', comment ça s'écrit?** How do you spell 'yogurt'?

Comment est-ce qu'on prononce le mot qui est écrit là? How do you pronounce this word here?

Où met-on l'accent tonique sur ce mot? How do you stress this word?

Pouvez-vous m'expliquer cette phrase? Can you explain this phrase for me?

[informal] **Aidez-moi, j'ai le mot sur le bout de la langue!** Help me! It's on the tip of my tongue!

Comment dire 'aimable' autrement? Is there another word for 'amiable'?

Pouvez-vous vérifier le français de cette lettre s'il vous plaît? Could you check the French in this letter, please?

140.4 *Corriger ses erreurs* Correcting one's mistakes

'Vite' est un adjectif . . . pardon, je veux dire un adverbe. 'Quickly' is an adjective . . . sorry, I mean an adverb.

Pardon, je voulais dire 'timoré', pas 'témérité'. Sorry, I meant to say 'timorous', not 'temerity'.

C'est à Laure . . . pardon à Linda qu'il faut demander ça. Laure . . . sorry, Linda rather, is the one you should ask about that.

[informal] **C'est le mardi, non . . . attendez, je me trompe, c'est le mercredi qu'ils ramassent les poubelles.** Tuesday . . . no, hang on a minute, I'm getting mixed up . . . Wednesday is the day they collect the bins.

[informal] **Angousson . . . Aubulême . . . ah, je vais y arriver . . . Angoulême vaut la visite.** Angousson . . . Aubulême . . . sorry, I'll get it right in a minute . . . Angoulême is well worth a visit.

[Correcting a mistake in a text] **Là où il y a '17 heures', il devrait y avoir '17 heures 30'.** Where it says '5 p.m.' it should say '5.30 pm'.

[more formal, often in written style] **Une erreur de la rédaction a substitué 'Nice' à 'Cannes' dans le troisième paragraphe.** 'Nice' should have read 'Cannes' in the third paragraph.

[correcting texts] **À 'carte bancaire' rayer 'bancaire' et mettre 'de crédit'** Where it says 'cheque card', cross out 'cheque' and put 'credit'.

141 *Communications écrites* Written communications

141.1 *Lettres personnelles: formules d'entrée* Personal letters: openings

Cher Michael, chère Dora Dear Michael and Dora

Merci de votre lettre. Thanks for your (last) letter.

Excusez-moi d'avoir mis si longtemps à vous répondre. I'm sorry I've been slow in replying.

[informal] **Quelques lignes pour vous dire que . . .** Just a few lines to let you know that . . .

[more informal] **Un petit mot pour vous dire bonjour.** Just a quick line to say hallo.

141.2 *Lettres personnelles: formules de fin* Personal letters: endings

[informal] **Voilà, c'est tout pour aujourd'hui.** Well, that's all for now.

(Mes) amitiés à . . . Give my regards to . . .

J'espère avoir de vos nouvelles bientôt. I hope to hear from you soon.

[Informal] **Écris-moi vite.** Write soon.

[for general use] **Bien à toi/vous, Jeanne.** Best wishes, Jeanne.

[rather formal] **Sincères salutations, Jacques Bonès.** Yours sincerely, Jacques Bonès.

[Informal, to a friend] **Amicalement, Nicolas.** All the best, Nicolas.

[To someone you are going to see soon] **À très bientôt, David.** Look forward to seeing you soon, David.

[to someone you really like a lot or are very close to] **Je t'embrasse (très fort), Thérèse.** Love, Thérèse.

[To a spouse, lover or boyfriend/girlfriend] **Je t'embrasse, Raoul.** All my love, Raoul.

p.s Céline vous fait un gros bisou. p.s.Céline sends love and kisses.

27, Chemin Grand
Crécy-Le-Vieil
49502 St Germain

Monsieur Pierre GOMEZ
Responsable export
Ets. Billard
Place Roberval
38000 GRENOBLE

Valence
Le 22 Mai 1999

Monsieur,

....

....

....

....

....

Je vous prie de croire, Monsieur, en l'assurance de mes sentiments les meilleurs.

Marie-Louise Rouet

Marie-Louise Rouet

141.3 *Correspondance commerciale*
Business letters: openings

How to address the recipient

<table>
<tr><td></td><td>Recipient's address</td><td>Opening line</td></tr>
<tr><td>You don't know their name but you know their title or function</td><td>Madame la Directrice,
Collège Bérard
La Pointe-Dieu
89239 Romilly</td><td>Madame la Directrice,</td></tr>
<tr><td>You know neither their name nor their title/function</td><td>Collège Bérard
La Pointe-Dieu
89239 Romilly</td><td>Messieurs,</td></tr>
<tr><td>You know their name</td><td>Madame Jacqueline Mairet,
Collège Bérard
La Pointe-Dieu
89239 Romilly</td><td>Madame,</td></tr>
<tr><td>You know their name and title/function</td><td>Madame Jacqueline Mairet,
Collège Bérard
La Pointe-Dieu
89239 Romilly</td><td>Madame la Directrice,</td></tr>
</table>

usage

Note that a woman holding a post referred to by a masculine name should be addressed as, e.g.:
Madame le Chef du Personnel
Madame le Maire

141.4 *Correspondance commerciale* Business letters: endings

The set closing formulae that follow are in order of increasing formality.

Recevez, M—, mes salutations distinguées.
ALSO
Agréez, M—, mes salutations distinguées.
Veuillez croire, M—, en l'expression de mes sentiments distingués.
ALSO
Veuillez agréer, M—, l'expression de mes sentiments distingués.
Je vous prie de croire, M—, en l'expression de mes sentiments respectueux.
ALSO
Je vous prie d'agréer, M—, l'expression de mes sentiments respectueux.

141.5 *Demandes de candidature* Applications

Je réponds à votre annonce parue dans [titre du journal]. **Je souhaite postuler à . . .** In reply to your advertisement in [name of source], I should like to apply for . . .
Merci de bien vouloir me faire parvenir tous renseignements complémentaires utiles ainsi qu'un formulaire de demande de candidature à . . . Please send me further details and application form for . . .
[Where there is no separate application form] **Par cette lettre, je souhaite faire acte de candidature au poste de . . .** In writing to you I wish to apply for . . .
J'espère que vous voudrez bien accorder votre attention à ma candidature. I hope you will give my application full consideration.
Je joins mon Curriculum Vitae. I enclose my curriculum vitae.
[Formal] **Veuillez trouver ci-inclus notre brochure.** Please find enclosed our (latest) brochure.

141.6 *Formulaires* Forms

Headings and phrases commonly found on forms:
Écrire en lettres d'imprimerie Please print
Remplir au stylo Please use a ballpoint pen
Prière de joindre une photographie récente Please attach a recent photograph
Cochez la case qui convient Please tick/check the appropriate box
Faites une croix dans la case Put an 'X' in the box
nil [a mark which you make on, e.g., a form when the rubric does not apply] n/a
Prénom(s) First name(s)
Nom (de famille) Last name
Nom de jeune fille Maiden name
Adresse/Domicile Address
Tel (personnel/travail) Tel.(home/work)
Profession Occupation
Nationalité Nationality
Âge/Date de naissance Age/Date of birth
Lieu de naissance Place of birth
État civil (célibataire/marié(e)/divorcé(e)) Status (single/married/divorced)
Niveau d'études Educational level
Diplômes obtenus Qualifications

Expérience professionnelle Work experience
Durée du projet/séjour Proposed duration/length of stay
Date d'arrivée/de départ Arrival/departure date
Signature/Date Signature/date

141.7 *Cartes postales* Postcards

Postcards are usually written in an abbreviated style, with subjects of verbs often omitted. Here are some typical phrases and expressions found in postcard messages.
Salut de Montjean-sur-Loire Greetings from Montjean-sur-Loire.
On passe de bonnes vacances. Having a lovely time.
Le temps est magnifique/épouvantable. Weather excellent/lousy.
La carte indique notre hôtel. This is the hotel where we're staying.
Amitiés à tout le monde Regards to everybody.
[informal] **Bises à tout le monde.** Love to everybody.

141.8 *Panneaux et affichettes* Signs and notices

Phrases and expressions commonly used in signs and notices.
Stationnement interdit No parking.
Accès interdit sauf riverains No entry except for local traffic
Accès interdit sauf livraisons No entry except for deliveries
Déviation Diversion
Hauteur max 5 m Max Headroom 5m
Interdit de fumer No smoking
Danger d'explosion No naked lights
Attention, travaux ALSO **Attention, chantier** Slow, men at work
Danger Danger
Attention enfants ALSO **Attention École** School crossing
Attention, passage de troupeaux Cattle crossing
La direction décline toute responsabilité en cas de perte ou de vol. The management does not accept liability for loss or damage.
Parking non surveillé Cars may be parked here at their owners' risk.
Entrée 50 francs Admission 50 francs
Réduction famille nombreuse 25 francs Reduced rate for families with more than three children 25 francs
Retraités 25 francs Senior citizens 25 francs
Fermé pour travaux BrE Closed during refurbishment AmE Closed for remodeling
Soldes de fermeture BrE Closing down sale AmE closeout sale
Soldes Sale
Sonnez SVP Please ring for service
Chambres d'hôte Rooms to rent
Camping interdit Camping prohibited

142 *Postes et télécommunications* Post and telecommunications

142.1 *Poster le courrier* Mailing letters

C'est combien un timbre pour l'Espagne, pour une lettre/une carte? How much is a letter/postcard to Spain?
Je voudrais l'envoyer par avion s'il vous plaît. Can this go airmail/express, please?
Quel est le moyen le moins cher pour envoyer ce colis? What's the cheapest way to send this parcel?
Ça arrivera dans combien de temps? How soon will it get there?
Où est la boîte à lettres la plus proche? Where's the nearest postbox/mailbox?
Vous avez un autocollant ALSO **une étiquette 'Par avion'?** Do you have an airmail sticker?

142.2 *Sur une envelope* On envelopes

À l'attention de For the attention of:
Urgent Urgent
Expéditeur Sender
Par avion Air Mail
Imprimé Printed matter
Fragile Handle with care
Ne pas plier Do not bend
[When you are not sure if someone is still at the address you have written on the envelope] **Faire suivre SVP** Please forward

142.3 *Au téléphone* Telephoning

Allô, je pourrais parler à Claire? Hallo, can I speak to Claire?
Est-ce que Thomas est là? Is Thomas there, please?
Allô, qui est à l'appareil? Hallo, who's calling?
Pourriez-vous me passer M. Rouget s'il vous plaît? Can you put me through to Mr Rouget please?
A   Pourrais-je parler à Madame Lincet?
B   C'est moi-même
A: Can I speak to Mrs Lincet?
B: Speaking
Ne quittez pas s'il vous plaît. Hold the line, please.
[informal] **Attends une seconde.** Hang on a minute.
[Re-establishing contact after a technical interruption of the call] **Désolé(e), je crois qu'on a été coupés.** I'm sorry, we seem to have been cut off.
Pouvez-vous parler plus fort, la ligne est mauvaise. Could you speak up a little, it's a bad line.
Il y a quelqu'un d'autre sur la ligne. Je vous rappelle? We seem to have a crossed line. Shall I call you back?
Elle n'est pas là en ce moment. Pouvez-vous rappeler plus tard? She's not here at the moment. Can you call back later?
Puis-je laisser/prendre un message? Can I leave/take a message?
Mon numéro c'est le vingt-six trente quatre cinquante-neuf, poste vingt-huit cinquante-sept, et vous faites le 1 d'abord. My number is 26 34 59, extension 28 57, and you have to dial 1 first.
Appelez-moi sur le (téléphone) portable. Call me on the mobile (phone).

Fred, c'est pour toi! Fred, there's a call for you!
Martin, quelqu'un te demande au téléphone. Martin, you're wanted on the telephone.
[informal] **Denise! Téléphone!** Denise! Phone!

142.4 *Autres moyens de communication* Other means of communication

Pouvez-vous nous envoyer un fax. Notre numéro de fax est le vingt-cinq, trente-six, soixante-quinze. Can you fax us please? Our fax number is 253675.
Il y a une machine pour envoyer un fax, ALSO **une télécopie?** Is there somewhere I can send a fax from?
Vous êtes sur messagerie électronique? Do you use electronic mail?
Je laisserai un mot dans votre casier. I'll leave a note in your pigeon-hole.

Verb conjugations

1 Avoir

Indicative	present	j'ai, nous avons
	imperfect	j'avais
	past historic	j'eus
	future	j'aurai
Subjunctive	present	que j'aie, que nous ayons
	imperfect	que j'eusse
Imperative	present	aie, ayons
Conditional	present	j'aurais
Participle	present	ayant
	past	eu, eue

2 Être

Indicative	present	je suis, nous sommes
	imperfect	j'étais
	past historic	je fus
	future	je serai
Subjunctive	present	que je sois
	imperfect	que je fusse
Imperative	present	sois, soyons
Conditional	present	je serais
Participle	present	étant
	past	été

3 Être aimé

Indicative	present	je suis aimé
	imperfect	j'étais aimé
	past historic	je fus aimé
	future	je serai aimé
Subjunctive	present	que je sois aimé
	imperfect	que je fusse aimé
Imperative	present	sois aimé, soyons aimés
Conditional	present	je serais aimé
Participle	present	étant aimé
	past	aimé, ée

4 Se méfier

Indicative	present	je me méfie
	imperfect	je me méfiais
	past historic	je me méfiai
	future	je me méfierai
Subjunctive	present	que je me méfie, que nous nous méfiions
	imperfect	que je me méfiasse
Imperative	present	méfie-toi, méfions-nous
Conditional	present	je me méfierais
Participle	present	se méfiant
	past	s'étant méfié

5 Endings for the three main groups of verbs

Verbs in the **first** group end in -er in the infinitive. Verbs in the **second** group end in -ir in the infinitive and in -issant in the present participle. Verbs in the **third** group comprise:
- aller, see conjugation no. 22
- all verbs in -ir which end in -ant (as opposed to -issant) in the present participle. They are at nos. 23–37.
- all verbs in -oir, see nos. 38–52.
- all verbs in -re, see nos. 53–82.

6 Verbs ending in -er: Aimer

Indicative	present	j'aime, nous aimons
	imperfect	j'aimais
	past historic	j'aimai
	future	j'aimerai
Subjunctive	present	que j'aime, que nous aimions
	imperfect	que j'aimasse
Imperative	present	aime, aimons
Conditional	present	j'aimerais
Participle	present	aimant
	past	aimé, eé

7 Verbs ending in -cer: Placer

Indicative	present	je place, nous plaçons
	imperfect	je plaçais
	past historic	je plaçai
	future	je placerai
Subjunctive	present	que je place, que nous placions
	imperfect	que je plaçasse
Imperative	present	place, plaçons
Conditional	present	je placerais
Participle	present	plaçant
	past	placé, ée

8 Verbs ending in -ger: Manger

Indicative	present	je mange, nous mangeons
	imperfect	je mangeais
	past historic	je mangeai
	future	je mangerai
Subjunctive	present	que je mange, que nous mangions
	imperfect	que je mangeasse
Imperative	present	mange, mangeons
Conditional	present	je mangerais
Participle	present	mangeant
	past	mangé, ée

9 Verbs ending in e(.)er: Peser

Indicative	present	*je pèse, nous pesons*
	imperfect	*je pesais*
	past historic	*je pesai*
	future	*je pèserai*
Subjunctive	present	*que je pèse, que nous pesions*
	imperfect	*que je pesasse*
Imperative	present	*pèse, pesons*
Conditional	present	*je pèserais*
Participle	present	*pesant*
	past	*pesé, ée*

10 Verbs ending in é(.) er: Céder

Indicative	present	*je cède, nous cédons*
	imperfect	*je cédais*
	past historic	*je cédai*
	future	*je céderai*
Subjunctive	present	*que je cède, que nous cédions*
	imperfect	*que je cédasse*
Imperative	present	*cède, cédons*
Conditional	present	*je céderais*
Participle	present	*cédant*
	past	*cédé, ée*

11 Verbs ending in -eler or -eter: Jeter

Indicative	present	*je jette, nous jetons*
	imperfect	*je jetais*
	past historic	*je jetai*
	future	*je jetterai*
Subjunctive	present	*que je jette, que nous jetions*
	imperfect	*que je jetasse*
Imperative	present	*jette, jetons*
Conditional	present	*je jetterais*
Participle	present	*jetant*
	past	*jeté, ée*

12 Verbs ending in -eler or -eter: Modeler

Indicative	present	*je modèle, nous modelons*
	imperfect	*je modelais*
	past historic	*je modelai*
	future	*je modèlerai*
Subjunctive	present	*que je modèle, que nous modelions*
	imperfect	*que je modelasse*
Imperative	present	*modèle, modelons*
Conditional	present	*je modèlerais*
Participle	present	*modelant*
	past	*modelé, ée*

13 Verbs ending in -éer: Créer

Indicative	present	*je crée, nous créons*
	imperfect	*je créais*
	past historic	*je créai*
	future	*je créerai*
Subjunctive	present	*que je crée, que nous créions*
	imperfect	*que je créasse*
Imperative	present	*crée, créons*
Conditional	present	*je créerais*
Participle	present	*créant*
	past	*créé, ée*

14 Verbs ending in -éger: Assiéger

Indicative	present	*je assiège, nous assiégeons*
	imperfect	*je assiégeais*
	past historic	*je assiégeai*
	future	*je assiégerai*
Subjunctive	present	*que j'assiège, que nous assiégions*
	imperfect	*que j'assiégeasse*
Imperative	present	*assiège, assiégeons*
Conditional	present	*j'assiégerais*
Participle	present	*assiégeant*
	past	*assiégé, ée*

15 Verbs ending in -ier: Apprécier

Indicative	present	*je apprécie, nous apprécions*
	imperfect	*j'appréciais*
	past historic	*j'appréciai*
	future	*j'apprécierai*
Subjunctive	present	*que j'apprécie, que nous appréciions*
	imperfect	*que j'appréciasse*
Imperative	present	*apprécie, apprécions*
Conditional	present	*j'apprécierais*
Participle	present	*appréciant*
	past	*apprécié, ée*

16 Verbs ending in -ayer: Payer

Indicative	present	*je paie, nous payons*
	imperfect	*je payais*
	past historic	*je payai*
	future	*je paierai*
Subjunctive	present	*que je paie, que nous payions*
	imperfect	*que je payasse*
Imperative	present	*paye or paie*
Conditional	present	*je paierais or je payerais*
Participle	present	*payant*
	past	*payé, ée*

17 Verbs ending in -oyer and -uyer: Broyer

Indicative	present	*je broie, nous broyons*
	imperfect	*je broyais*
	past historic	*je broyai*
	future	*je broierai*
Subjunctive	present	*que je broie, que nous broyions*
	imperfect	*que je broyasse*
Imperative	present	*broie, broyons*
Conditional	present	*je broierais*

Participle	present	*broyant*
	past	*broyé, ée*

18 Envoyer

Indicative	present	*j'envoie, nous envoyons*
	imperfect	*j'envoyais*
	past historic	*j'envoyai*
	future	*j'enverrai*
Subjunctive	present	*que j'envoie, que nous envoyions*
	imperfect	*que j'envoyasse*
Imperative	present	*envoie, envoyons*
Conditional	present	*j'enverrais*
Participle	present	*envoyant*
	past	*envoyé, ée*

19 Verbs ending in -ir/issant: Finir

Indicative	present	*je finis, nous finissons*
	imperfect	*je finissais*
	past historic	*je finis*
	future	*je finirai*
Subjunctive	present	*que je finisse, que nous finissions*
	imperfect	*que je finisse*
Imperative	present	*finis, finissons*
Conditional	present	*je finirais*
Participle	present	*finissant*
	past	*fini, ie*

20 Haïr

Indicative	present	*je hais, nous haïssons*
	imperfect	*je haïssais*
	past historic	*je haïs*
	future	*je haïrai*
Subjunctive	present	*que je haïsse, que nous haïssions*
	imperfect	*que je haïsse*
Imperative	present	*hais, haïssons*
Conditional	present	*je haïrais*
Participle	present	*haïssant*
	past	*haï, ïe*

21 S'en aller

Indicative	present	*je m'en vais, nous nous en allons*
	imperfect	*je m'en allais*
	past historic	*je m'en allai*
	future	*je m'en irai*
Subjunctive	present	*que je m'en aille, que nous nous en allions*
	imperfect	*que je m'en allasse*
Imperative	present	*va-t'en, allons-nous-en*
Conditional	present	*je m'en irais*
Participle	present	*s'en allant*
	past	*s'en étant allé*

22 Aller

Indicative	present	*je vais, nous allons*
	imperfect	*j'allais*
	past historic	*j'allai*
	future	*j'irai*
Subjunctive	present	*que j'aille, que nous allions*
	imperfect	*que j'allasse*
Imperative	present	*va, allons*
Conditional	present	*j'irais*
Participle	present	*allant*
	past	*allé, ée*

23 Verbs ending in -enir: Tenir

Indicative	present	*je tiens, nous tenons*
	imperfect	*je tenais*
	past historic	*je tins*
	future	*je tiendrai*
Subjunctive	present	*que je tienne, que nous tenions*
	imperfect	*que je tinsse*
Imperative	present	*tiens, tenons*
Conditional	present	*je tiendrais*
Participle	present	*tenant*
	past	*tenu, ue*

24 Verbs ending in -érir: Acquérir

Indicative	present	*j'acquiers, nous acquérons*
	imperfect	*j'acquérais*
	past historic	*j'acquis*
	future	*j'acquerrai*
Subjunctive	present	*que j'acquière, que nous acquérions*
	imperfect	*que j'acquisse*
Imperative	present	*acquiers, acquérons*
Conditional	present	*j'acquerrais*
Participle	present	*acquérant*
	past	*acquis, ise*

25 Verbs ending in -tir: Sentir

Indicative	present	*je sens, nous sentons*
	imperfect	*je sentais*
	past historic	*je sentis*
	future	*je sentirai*
Subjunctive	present	*que je sente, que nous sentions*
	imperfect	*que je sentisse*
Imperative	present	*sens, sentons*
Conditional	present	*je sentirais*
Participle	present	*sentant*
	past	*senti, ie*

26 Vêtir

Indicative	present	*je vêts, nous vêtons*
	imperfect	*je vêtais*
	past historic	*je vêtis*
	future	*je vêtirai*

Subjunctive	present	*que je vête, que nous vêtions*
	imperfect	*que je vêtisse*
Imperative	present	*vêts, vêtons*
Conditional	present	*je vêtirais*
Participle	present	*vêtant*
	past	*vêtu, ue*

27 Verbs ending in -vrir or -frir: Couvrir

Indicative	present	*je couvre, nous couvrons*
	imperfect	*je couvrais*
	past historic	*je couvris*
	future	*je couvrirai*
Subjunctive	present	*que je couvre, que nous couvrions*
	imperfect	*que je couvrisse*
Imperative	present	*couvre, couvrons*
Conditional	present	*je couvrirais*
Participle	present	*couvrant*
	past	*couvert, te*

28 Cueillir

Indicative	present	*je cueille, nous cueillons*
	imperfect	*je cueillais*
	past historic	*je cueillis*
	future	*je cueillerai*
Subjunctive	present	*que je cueille, que nous cueillions*
	imperfect	*que je cueillisse*
Imperative	present	*cueille, cueillons*
Conditional	present	*je cueillerais*
Participle	present	*cueillant*
	past	*cueilli, ie*

29 Verbs ending in -aillir: Assaillir

Indicative	present	*j'assaille, nous assaillons*
	imperfect	*j'assaillais*
	past historic	*j'assaillis*
	future	*j'assaillirai*
Subjunctive	present	*que j'assaille, que nous assaillions*
	imperfect	*que j'assaillisse*
Imperative	present	*assaille, assaillons*
Conditional	present	*j'assaillirais*
Participle	present	*assaillant*
	past	*assailli, ie*

30 Faillir

Indicative	present	
	imperfect	
	past historic	*je faillis*
	future	*je faillirai*
Subjunctive	present	
	imperfect	
Imperative	present	
Conditional	present	*je faillirais*
Participle	present	
	past	*failli*

31 Bouillir

Indicative	present	*je bous, nous bouillons*
	imperfect	*je bouillais*
	past historic	*je bouillis*
	future	*je bouillirai*
Subjunctive	present	*que je bouille, que nous bouillions*
	imperfect	*que je bouillisse*
Imperative	present	*bous, bouillons*
Conditional	present	*je bouillirais*
Participle	present	*bouillant*
	past	*bouilli, ie*

32 Dormir

Indicative	present	*je dors, nous dormons*
	imperfect	*je dormais*
	past historic	*je dormis*
	future	*je dormirai*
Subjunctive	present	*que je dorme, que nous dormions*
	imperfect	*que je dormisse*
Imperative	present	*dors, dormons*
Conditional	present	*je dormirais*
Participle	present	*dormant*
	past	*dormi*

33 Courir

Indicative	present	*je cours, nous courons*
	imperfect	*je courrais*
	past historic	*je courus*
	future	*je courrai*
Subjunctive	present	*que je coure, que nous courions*
	imperfect	*que je courusse*
Imperative	present	*cours, courons*
Conditional	present	*je courrais*
Participle	present	*courant*
	past	*couru, ue*

34 Mourir

Indicative	present	*je meurs, nous mourons*
	imperfect	*je mourais*
	past historic	*je mourus*
	future	*je mourrai*
Subjunctive	present	*que je meure, que nous mourions*
	imperfect	*que je mourusse*
Imperative	present	*meurs, mourons*
Conditional	present	*je mourrais*
Participle	present	*mourant*
	past	*mort, te*

35 Servir

Indicative	present	*je sers, nous servons*
	imperfect	*je servais*
	past historic	*je servis*
	future	*je servirai*

Subjunctive	present	que je serve, que nous servions
	imperfect	que je servisse
Imperative	present	sers, servons
Conditional	present	je servirais
Participle	present	servant
	past	servi, ie

36 Fuir

Indicative	present	je fuis, nous fuyons
	imperfect	je fuyais
	past historic	je fuis
	future	je fuirai
Subjunctive	present	que je fuie, que nous fuyions
	imperfect	que je fuisse
Imperative	present	fuis, fuyons
Conditional	present	je fuirais
Participle	present	fuyant
	past	fui

37a Ouïr

This verb has only one conjugated form:

| Participle | past | ouï (and tenses based on it, such as j'ai ouï dire que) |

37b Gésir

This verb has only three conjugated forms:

Indicative	present	je gis, nous gisons
	imperfect	je gisais, nous gisions
Participle	present	gisant

38 Verbs ending in -cevoir: Recevoir

Indicative	present	je reçois, nous recevons
	imperfect	je recevais
	past historic	je reçus
	future	je recevrai
Subjunctive	present	que je reçoive, que nous recevions
	imperfect	que je reçusse
Imperative	present	reçois, recevons
Conditional	present	je recevrais
Participle	present	recevant
	past	reçu, ue

39 Voir

Indicative	present	je vois, nous voyons
	imperfect	je voyais
	past historic	je vis
	future	je verrai
Subjunctive	present	que je voie, que nous voyions
	imperfect	que je visse
Imperative	present	vois, voyons
Conditional	present	je verrais
Participle	present	voyant
	past	vu, ue

40 Pourvoir

Indicative	present	je pourvois, nous pourvoyons
	imperfect	je pourvoyais
	past historic	je pourvus
	future	je pourvoirai
Subjunctive	present	que je pourvoie, que nous pourvoyions
	imperfect	que je pourvusse
Imperative	present	pourvois, pourvoyons
Conditional	present	je pourvoirais
Participle	present	pourvoyant
	past	pourvu, ue

41 Savoir

Indicative	present	je sais, nous savons
	imperfect	je savais
	past historic	je sus
	future	je saurai
Subjunctive	present	que je sache, que nous sachions
	imperfect	que je susse
Imperative	present	sache, sachons
Conditional	present	je saurais
Participle	present	sachant
	past	su, ue

42 Devoir

Indicative	present	je dois
	imperfect	je devais
	past historic	je dus
	future	je devrai
Subjunctive	present	que je doive, que nous devions
	imperfect	que je dusse
Imperative	present	dois, devons
Conditional	present	je devrais
Participle	present	devant
	past	dû, ue

43 Pouvoir

Indicative	present	je peux or je puis, nous pouvons
	imperfect	je pouvais
	past historic	je pus
	future	je pourrai
Subjunctive	present	que je puisse, que nous puissions
	imperfect	que je pusse
Imperative	present	——
Conditional	present	je pourrais
Participle	present	pouvant
	past	pu

44 Mouvoir

Indicative	present	*je meus, nous mouvons*
	imperfect	*je mouvais*
	past historic	*je mus*
	future	*je mouvrai*
Subjunctive	present	*que je meuve, que nous mouvions*
	imperfect	*que je musse*
Imperative	present	*meus, mouvons*
Conditional	present	*je mouvrais*
Participle	present	*mouvant*
	past	*mû, ue*

45 The impersonal verb Pleuvoir

Indicative	present	*il pleut*
	imperfect	*il pleuvait*
	past historic	*il plut*
	future	*il pleuvra*
Subjunctive	present	*qu'il pleuve*
	imperfect	*qu'il plût*
Imperative	present	——
Conditional	present	*il pleuvrait*
Participle	present	*pleuvant*
	past	*plu*

46 The impersonal verb Falloir

Indicative	present	*il faut*
	imperfect	*il fallait*
	past historic	*il fallut*
	future	*il faudra*
Subjunctive	present	*qu'il faille*
	imperfect	*qu'il fallût*
Imperative	present	——
Conditional	present	*il faudrait*
Participle	present	
	past	*fallu*

47 Valoir

Indicative	present	*je vaux, nous valons*
	imperfect	*je valais*
	past historic	*je valus*
	future	*je vaudrai*
Subjunctive	present	*que je vaille, que nous valions*
	imperfect	*que je valusse*
Imperative	present	*vaux, valons*
Conditional	present	*je vaudrais*
Participle	present	*valant*
	past	*valu, ue*

48 Vouloir

Indicative	present	*je veux, nous voulons*
	imperfect	*je voulais*
	past historic	*je voulus*
	future	*je voudrai*

Subjunctive	present	*que je veuille, que nous voulions*
	imperfect	*que je voulusse*
Imperative	present	*veuille, voulons*
Conditional	present	*je voudrais*
Participle	present	*voulant*
	past	*voulu, ue*

49 Asseoir

Indicative	present	*j'assieds, nous asseyons or j'assois, nous assoyons*
	imperfect	*j'asseyais or j'assoyais*
	past historic	*j'assis*
	future	*j'assiérai or j'assoirai*
Subjunctive	present	*que j'asseye, que nous asseyions or que j'assoie, que nous assoyions*
	imperfect	*que j'assisse*
Imperative	present	*assieds, asseyons, or assois, assoyons*
Conditional	present	*j'assiérais ou j'assoirais*
Participle	present	*asseyant or assoyant*
	past	*assis, ise*

50 Seoir

This verb is only conjugated in the third person, and is mostly encountered in the singular. It has no past historic.

Indicative	present	*il sied*
	imperfect	*il seyait*
	future	*il siéra*
Subjunctive	present	*qu'il siée*
Conditional	present	*il siérait*
Participle	present	*seyant*

51 Surseoir

Indicative	present	*je sursois, nous sursoyons*
	imperfect	*je sursoyais*
	past historic	*je sursis*
	future	*je surseoirai*
Subjunctive	present	*que je sursoie, que nous sursoyions*
	imperfect	*que je sursisse*
Imperative	present	*sursois, sursoyons*
Conditional	present	*je surseoirais*
Participle	present	*sursoyant*
	past	*sursis, ise*

52 Déchoir

This verb has no imperfect of the indicative.

Indicative	present	*je déchois, nous déchoyons*
	past historic	*je déchus, nous déchumes*
	future	*je déchoirai, nous déchoirons*
Subjunctive	present	*que je déchoie, que nous déchoyions*
	imperfect	*que je déchusse, que nous déchumes*

| Conditional | present | je déchoirais, nous déchoirions |
| Participle | past | déchu, ue |

53 Verbs ending in -dre: Rendre
Verbs ending in -andre, -endre, -ondre, -erdre, -ordre

Indicative	present	je rends, nous rendons
	imperfect	je rendais
	past historic	je rendis
	future	je rendrai
Subjunctive	present	que je rende, que nous rendions
	imperfect	que je rendisse
Imperative	present	rends, rendons
Conditional	present	je rendrais
Participle	present	rendant
	past	rendu, ue

54 Prendre

Indicative	present	je prends, nous prenons
	imperfect	je prenais
	past historic	je pris
	future	je prendrai
Subjunctive	present	que je prenne, que nous prenions
	imperfect	que je prisse
Imperative	present	prends, prenons
Conditional	present	je prendrais
Participle	present	prenant
	past	pris, prise

55 Battre

Indicative	present	je bats, nous battons
	imperfect	je battais
	past historic	je battis
	future	je battrai
Subjunctive	present	que je batte, que nous battions
	imperfect	que je battisse
Imperative	present	bats, battons
Conditional	present	je battrais
Participle	present	battant
	past	battu, ue

56 Mettre

Indicative	present	je mets, nous mettons
	imperfect	je mettais
	past historic	je mis
	future	je mettrai
Subjunctive	present	que je mette, que nous mettions
	imperfect	que je misse
Imperative	present	mets, mettons
Conditional	present	je mettrais
Participle	present	mettant
	past	mis, ise

57 Verbs ending in -eindre: Peindre

Indicative	present	je peins, nous peignons
	imperfect	je peignais
	past historic	je peignis
	future	je peindrai
Subjunctive	present	que je peigne, que nous peignions
	imperfect	que je peignisse
Imperative	present	peins, peignons
Conditional	present	je peindrais
Participle	present	peignant
	past	peint, einte

58 Verbs ending in -oindre: Joindre

Indicative	present	je joins, nous joignons
	imperfect	je joignais
	past historic	je joignis
	future	je joindrai
Subjunctive	present	que je joigne, que nous joignions
	imperfect	que je joignisse
Imperative	present	joins, joignons
Conditional	present	je joindrais
Participle	present	joignant
	past	joint, te

59 Verbs ending in -aindre: Craindre

Indicative	present	je crains, nous craignons
	imperfect	je craignais
	past historic	je craignis
	future	je craindrai
Subjunctive	present	que je craigne, que nous craignions
	imperfect	que je craignisse
Imperative	present	crains, craignons
Conditional	present	je craindrais
Participle	present	craignant
	past	craint, ainte

60 Vaincre

Indicative	present	je vaincs, nous vainquons
	imperfect	je vainquais
	past historic	je vainquis
	future	je vaincrai
Subjunctive	present	que je vainque, que nous vainquions
	imperfect	que je vainquisse
Imperative	present	vaincs, vainquons
Conditional	present	je vaincrais
Participle	present	vainquant
	past	vaincu, ue

61 Traire

Indicative	present	je trais, nous trayons
	imperfect	je trayais
	past historic	
	future	je trairai

Subjunctive	present	*que je traie, que nous trayions*
	imperfect	
Imperative	present	*trais, trayons*
Conditional	present	*je trairais*
Participle	present	*trayant*
	past	*trait, aite*

62 Faire

Indicative	present	*je fais, nous faisons*
	imperfect	*je faisais*
	past historic	*je fis*
	future	*je ferai*
Subjunctive	present	*que je fasse, que nous fassions*
	imperfect	*que je fisse*
Imperative	present	*fais, faisons*
Conditional	present	*je ferais*
Participle	present	*faisant*
	past	*fait, te*

63 Plaire

Indicative	present	*je plais, nous plaisons*
	imperfect	*je plaisais*
	past historic	*je plus*
	future	*je plairai*
Subjunctive	present	*que je plaise, que nous plaisions*
	imperfect	*que je plusse*
Imperative	present	*plais, plaisons*
Conditional	present	*je plairais*
Participle	present	*plaisant*
	past	*plu*

64 Verbs ending in -aître: Connaître

Indicative	present	*je connais, nous connaissons*
	imperfect	*je connaissais*
	past historic	*je connus*
	future	*je connaîtrai*
Subjunctive	present	*que je connaisse, que nous connaissions*
	imperfect	*que je connusse*
Imperative	present	*connais, connaissons*
Conditional	present	*je connaîtrais*
Participle	present	*connaissant*
	past	*connu, ue*

65 Naître

Indicative	present	*je nais, nous naissons*
	imperfect	*je naissais*
	past historic	*je naquis*
	future	*je naîtrai*
Subjunctive	present	*que je naisse, que nous naissions*
	imperfect	*que je naquisse*
Imperative	present	*nais, naissons*
Conditional	present	*je naîtrais*

| Participle | present | *naissant* |
| | past | *né, née* |

66 Paître

Indicative	present	*je pais, nous paissons*
	imperfect	*je paissais*
	past historic	
	future	*je paîtrai*
Subjunctive	present	*que je paisse, que nous paissions*
	imperfect	
Imperative	present	*pais, paissons*
Conditional	present	*je paîtrais*
Participle	present	*paissant*
	past	

67 Verbs ending in -oître: Croître

Indicative	present	*je croîs, nous croissons*
	imperfect	*je croissais*
	past historic	*je crûs*
	future	*je croîtrai*
Subjunctive	present	*que je croisse, que nous croissions*
	imperfect	*que je crûsse*
Imperative	present	*crois, croissons*
Conditional	present	*je croîtrais*
Participle	present	*croissant*
	past	*crû, ue*

68 Croire

Indicative	present	*je crois, nous croyons*
	imperfect	*je croyais*
	past historic	*je crus*
	future	*je croirai*
Subjunctive	present	*que je croie, que nous croyions*
	imperfect	*que je crusse*
Imperative	present	*crois, croyons*
Conditional	present	*je croirais*
Participle	present	*croyant*
	past	*cru, ue*

69 Boire

Indicative	present	*je bois, nous buvons*
	imperfect	*je buvais*
	past historic	*je bus*
	future	*je boirai*
Subjunctive	present	*que je boive, que nous buvions*
	imperfect	*que je busse*
Imperative	present	*bois, buvons*
Conditional	present	*je boirais*
Participle	present	*buvant*
	past	*bu, ue*

70 Clore

Indicative	present	je clos
	imperfect	
	past historic	
	future	je clorai
Subjunctive	present	que je close, que nous closions
	imperfect	
Imperative	present	clos
Conditional	present	je clorais
Participle	present	closant
	past	clos, se

71 Verbs ending in -clure: Conclure

Indicative	present	je conclus, nous concluons
	imperfect	je concluais
	past historic	je conclus
	future	je conclurai
Subjunctive	present	que je conclue, que nous concluions
	imperfect	que je conclusse
Imperative	present	conclus, concluons
Conditional	present	je conclurais
Participle	present	concluant
	past	conclu, ue

72 Verbs ending in -soudre: Absoudre

Indicative	present	j'absous, nous absolvons
	imperfect	j'absolvais
	past historic	
	future	j'absoudrai
Subjunctive	present	que j'absolve, que nous absolvions
	imperfect	
Imperative	present	absous, absolvons
Conditional	present	j'absoudrais
Participle	present	absolvant
	past	absous, oute

73 Coudre

Indicative	present	je couds, nous cousons
	imperfect	je cousais
	past historic	je cousis
	future	je coudrai
Subjunctive	present	que je couse, que nous cousions
	imperfect	que je cousisse
Imperative	present	couds, cousons
Conditional	present	je coudrais
Participle	present	cousant
	past	cousu, ue

74 Moudre

Indicative	present	je mouds, nous moulons
	imperfect	je moulais
	past historic	je moulus
	future	je moudrai
Subjunctive	present	que je moule, que nous moulions
	imperfect	que je moulusse
Imperative	present	mouds, moulons
Conditional	present	je moudrais
Participle	present	moulant
	past	moulu, ue

75 Suivre

Indicative	present	je suis, nous suivons
	imperfect	je suivais
	past historic	je suivis
	future	je suivrai
Subjunctive	present	que je suive, que nous suivions
	imperfect	que je suivisse
Imperative	present	suis, suivons
Conditional	present	je suivrais
Participle	present	suivant
	past	suivi, ie

76 Vivre

Indicative	present	je vis, nous vivons
	imperfect	je vivais
	past historic	je vécus
	future	je vivrai
Subjunctive	present	que je vive, que nous vivions
	imperfect	que je vécusse
Imperative	present	vis, vivons
Conditional	present	je vivrais
Participle	present	vivant
	past	vécu, ue

77 Lire

Indicative	present	je lis, nous lisons
	imperfect	je lisais
	past historic	je lus
	future	je lirai
Subjunctive	present	que je lise, que nous lisions
	imperfect	que je lusse
Imperative	present	lis, lisons
Conditional	present	je lirais
Participle	present	lisant
	past	lu, lue

78 Dire

Indicative	present	je dis, nous disons
	imperfect	je disais
	past historic	je dis
	future	je dirai
Subjunctive	present	que je dise, que nous disions
	imperfect	que je disse
Imperative	present	dis, disons
Conditional	present	je dirais
Participle	present	disant
	past	dit, ite

79 Rire

Indicative	present	*je ris, nous rions*
	imperfect	*je riais*
	past historic	*je ris*
	future	*je rirai*
Subjunctive	present	*que je rie, que nous riions*
	imperfect	*que je risse*
Imperative	present	*ris, rions*
Conditional	present	*je rirais*
Participle	present	*riant*
	past	*ri*

80 Écrire

Indicative	present	*j'écris, nous écrivons*
	imperfect	*j'écrivais*
	past historic	*j'écrivis*
	future	*j'écrirai*
Subjunctive	present	*que j'écrive, que nous écrivions*
	imperfect	*que j'écrivisse*
Imperative	present	*écris, écrivons*
Conditional	present	*j'écrirais*
Participle	present	*écrivant*
	past	*écrit, ite*

81 Confire

Indicative	present	*je confis, nous confisons*
	imperfect	*je confisais*
	past historic	*je confis*
	future	*je confirai*
Subjunctive	present	*que je confise, que nous confisions*
	imperfect	*que je confisse*
Imperative	present	*confis, confisons*
Conditional	present	*je confirais*
Participle	present	*confisant*
	past	*confit, ite*

82 Verbs ending in -uire: Cuire

Indicative	present	*je cuis, nous cuisons*
	imperfect	*je cuisais*
	past historic	*je cuisis*
	future	*je cuirai*
Subjunctive	present	*que je cuise, que nous cuisions*
	imperfect	*que je cuisisse*
Imperative	present	*cuis, cuisons*
Conditional	present	*je cuirais*
Participle	present	*cuisant*
	past	*cuit, uite*

A (musical note) 82.14
abandon 4.2
abandoned 35.11
abandonment 66.11
abhorrence 45.21
ability 59.2
able seaman 39.4
able to 59.2
abnormal 95.2
abortion 33.3
abroad 6.4
absence 87.5
absenteeism 87.5
absent-minded 64.6
absorbed 54.3
abstruse 51.7
absurd 57.2
absurdity 57.2
abundance 58.3
abuse (insult, v) 43.8
abuse (overuse, n & v) 32.1
abuse (sexual, n & v)) 64.19
accelerate 7.6
accent (in punctuation) 96.29
accent (in speech) 96.6
accept 40.7
acceptance 40.7
accessory 25.13
accommodation 24.8
accompaniment 82.9
accompany 82.9
according to 96.11
account (at the bank) 84.1
account (in a shop) 84.9
accountant 84.15
accounting 84.15
accounts (budget) 84.15
accumulate 29.5
accuracy 60.2
accurate 57.9
ace (playing card) 81.6
ache 66.5
achievable 92.1
achieve 00.0
achievement 00.0
acid (adj) 73.2
acorn 18.8
acquaintance 45.9
acquire 41.14
act (general term, n & v) 52.5
act (law) 37.5
active 52.4–52.5
activity 52.5

actor 82.4, 96.13
actress 82.4
adapt 89.2
adaptor 27.7
add 58.9
add up (be cumulative) 58.9
add up (in arithmetic) 58.17
adder 16.1
addition 58.9
address 97.2
adipose 20.2
adjective 96.26
adjoining road (on highway) 7.9
adjust 10.3, 89.2
adjustable spanner 27.5
administer 37.1
administrative region 3.4
administrator 37.2
admiral 39.4
admiration 45.16
admire 45.16
admit 40.7
adolescence 35.2
adolescent 35.2
adopt 33.4
adoption 33.4
adorn 49.2
advance (of an army) 39.6
advanced (of an army) 39.6
advance payment 59.19
advanced (in education) 57.8
adventure 59.15
adverb 96.26
advice 40.8
advise 40.8, 41.3
adviser 40.8
aerial (on a car) 7.2
aerial (on a house) 24.10
aeroplane 8.11
affair 45.7
affection 45.3
affectionate 48.4
Afrikaans 96.25
aftershave 69.5
age (of a person) 33.6
age (period) 9.9
age limit 2.1
age of reason 66.13
aggressive 48.5
aggressiveness 48.5
agile 59.2
agility 44.6
agnostic 38.18

ago 9.10
agree 40.5
agree to 40.7
agreement 40.5
agricultural 79.1
ahead (direction) 3.2
ahead (in position) 57.8
ahead of schedule 13.1
aid 46.1–46.2
ailment 66.2
air 20.10
airborne 8.13
air commodore 39.3
aircraft 8.11–8.15
aircraft carrier 5.4
aircraftman 39.3
air force 39.3
air freighter 8.11
airman 39.3
air marshal 39.3
airplane 8.11
airport 8.14
airspace 8.14
air taxi 8.11
air terminal 8.14
air traffic controller 8.15
air vice marshal 39.3
aisle 38.13
ajar 31.2
alarm-clock 9.8
alas 96.15
album (disc) 82.15
album (for photos) 59.17
alcohol 75.2
alcoholic (adj) 75.2
alcoholic (n) 75.8
alcoholism 75.8
alder 18.10
alert 45.24
algebra 58.16
alike 58.16
alive 53.4
Allah 38.12
allergic 66.1
allergy 66.1
alley cat 15.2
alligator 16.1
allow (give authorization for) 37.13
allow (make possible) 92.1
allowed 37.13
allow oneself 37.13
alloy 19.2
All Saints' Day 9.5

curve 1.5
curves (woman's body)1.1
curving 1.5
cushion 24.16
custody (of a child) 63.7
custom 38.1
customer 84.9
customs 6.4
customs officer 6.4
cut (hairdressing) 69.3
cut (in prices) 58.12
cut (n & v: general term) 91.11–91.14
cut (of meat) 72.6
cute 49.1
cutlery basket 32.2
cutlet 72.6
cutting board 24.17
cut up (in food preparation) 74.2
cylinder 1.3
cylindrical 1.3
cymbal 82.10
cymbalist 82.10
cypress 18.11
Czech 96.25

D (musical note) 82.14
dad(dy) 34.1
daily (everyday) 10.3
daily (newspaper) 82.1
dairy (on a farm) 79.3
dairy (shop) 72.1
dairy (shop) owner 72.1
dairy product 72.1
daisy 18.2
dam 51.9
damage (v) 91.6–91.15
damp 20.2
dampness 20.2
dance (n & v) 82.5
dancer 82.5
dandelion 18.2
danger 39
Danish 96.25
daredevil 39.11
daring 39.15
dark 21.1, 63.13
darkness 21.1
darkroom 83.4
darling 45.8
dashboard 7.4
dash off 44.5
data processing 98.1–98.2
database 77.2
date (calendar) 9.1, 9.5
date (fruit) 70.6
dated 12.4
daughter (child) 34.2, 35.10
daughter-in-law 34.4

dawdle 13.10
day after tomorrow 9.2
day before yesterday 9.2
daydreamer 54.3
dazed 59.4
dead 67.4
dead on (exactly) 60.2
deaf 66.3
deafening 63.16
deafness 66.3
deaf person 66.3
deal 68.6
dealer (drugs) 68.6
dealer (general term) 84.7
dealer (on the Stock Exchange) 84.10
dearness 84.17
death 67.4
death penalty 67.8
death sentence 67.8
debate 96.18
debris 20.7
debt 84.3
decade 9.9
decaf 75.4
decapitate 91.12
December 9.3
decent (good enough) 57.4
decent (moral) 43.1
decent (not sexually offensive) 57.9
deciduous 18.10
decigram 58.25
decilitre 58.37
decimate (diminish) 58.12
decimate (destroy) 91.7
deck 8.2
declare (at customs) 6.4
decline (v) 91.15
decompose 67.4
decorate 49.2
decorating 27.6
decoration (interior decor) 52.12
decoration (medal) 27.6
decrease (n) 58.12
deep 58.13, 63.13
deeper, to become 58.10
deer 14.2
deface 91.8
defeat 39.6
defence 37.11
defend 39.6
defendant 37.11
deficiency 74.13
define 96.13
definite 92.6
dehydrate 20.5
delay (lateness) 13.2
delay (postponement) 13.6
delete 59.21

delicatessen 78.2
delicious 73.4
delighted 47.8
delirious 66.11
delirium 66.11
deliver 5.1
demand (n) 36.7
demand (v) 96.16
demo 36.7
democracy 36.5
democratic 36.5
demolition 91.7
demonstration 36.7
demonstrator 36.7
dense 58.13
dent 91.9
dental 65.4
dental care 69.4
dental floss 69.4
dental hygiene 65.4
dental surgeon 65.4
dented 1.6
dentist 65.4
deodorant 69.2
depart 4.2
department (in a hospital) 65.2
department (in a store) 78.5
department store 78.4
departure 4.2
depraved 37.16
depreciation 85.1
depth 58.13
derision 7.2, 47.14
descendant 34.6
descended from 34.6
describe 96.13
desert 20.5, 22.10
deserted 90.4
design 1.4
desk 59.7
despair 47.19
despairing 47.19
desperate 47.19
despise 57.1
despondent 54.3
dessert 74.6
dessert spoon 24.19
destitute 84.19
destroy 91.7
destruction 91.7
detached house 24.1
detail (general term) 55.10
detail (precise circumstance) 87.3
detain 41.11
detergent 30.9
deterioration 91.15
determination 51.3
determined 51.3

faith (trust) 38.6
fall (drop) 5.12
fall (occur) 87.2
fall (autumn) 9.4
fall asleep 64.8
fall out 39.9
Fallopian tube 62.18
fallow deer 14.2
false (fake) 89.4
false (lying) 88.3
false (not correct) 60.3
false beard 89.4
false bottom 90.4
falsely 88.3
false teeth 65.4
fame 52.1
family 34.6
family ties 34.6
family tree 34.6
famine 74.13
famous 52.1
fan (for the face) 25.13
fan (supporter) 45.4, 45.13
fanciful 88.8
fang 14.6
fanny pack 84.14
fantastic 57.5
far 3.7
farm (converted farm) 24.5
farm (working farm) 79.1
farm building 79.3
farmer 79.1
farmhouse 79.1
farming 79
farmland 79.2
farm machinery 79.4
farm worker 79.1
farmyard animal 14.1
Far North 3.4
fascism 36.5
fascist 36.6
fashion (n) 12.3
fashion (v) 1.7
fast (general term) 13.7
fast (of clock) 13. 1
fasteners 31.7
fastening 31
fast-food restaurant 74.3
fast-forward 82.3
fat (adj & n: in food) 72.3
fat (adj: obese) 62.1
fat (n: fatty tissue) 62.2
fat (n: in meat) 72.6
fatal 67.10
fat-free 62.6
father 34.1
father-in-law 34.4
fatness 62.1

fatten (in cattle-rearing) 79.7
fatty 72.6
faucet 24.22
fault 60.1
fauna 14.3
fawn 14.2
fax 98.4
fear (n & v) 45.22–45.25
fearful 45.22
fearless 39.15
feather 14.6
feather duster 30.7
feature 64.1
February 9.3
feeble 48.3
feed (v: eat) 16.7
feed (v: give as food) 74.10
feel (have as an emotion) 42.4
feel (understand) 53.2
feel (when touching) 63.22
feeler 14.6
feeling (emotion) 42.3 190,
feeling (impression) 88.9
feel pain 66.5
feel passionately 50.1
feel sick 66.2
feel sorry 43.16
feel stiff 66.5
fellow-guest 74.12
fellow human being 35.1
felt 26.2
female 35.7
feminine (female) 35.7
feminine (in grammar) 96.26
feminine hygiene 69.7
femininity 35.7
fence 24.10, 51.9
fennel 73.3
ferocious 48.5
ferociously 48.5
ferret 15.5
ferry 8.8
fertilization 33.3
fertilize 79.7
fertilizer 79.7
festival 9.5
fiasco 52.10
fib 88.3
fiction 59.15
fidget 62.23
field 79.1–79.2
field marshal 39.2
fierce 48.5
fig 70.6
fig-leaf 18.3
fight 39.6–39.8
figure (in arithmetic) 58.20
figure (shape of body) 64.1

file (document) 77.3
file (in computing) 98.3
file (put away) 56.1
filing cabinet 77.3
fill 90.1–90.3
fill out 1.7
fill up 90.1
filling (in tooth) 65.4
filly 14.1
film 82.2
filth (dirt) 30.2
filth (term of abuse) 57.10
filthy 30.2
fin 14.6
final 11.2
finally 11.2
find 50.7
find out 53
finger 64.1
fingernail 64.1
finish 11.2
finish off (kill) 67.6
Finnish 96.25
fir 18.11
fire 20.6–20.9
fire (piece of apparatus) 24.23
fire engine 20.9
fire extinguisher 20.9
firefighter 20.9
fire hydrant 20.9
fireplace 24.16
firm (convinced) 38.7
firm (to the touch) 63.25
first aid 68.3
first aid kit 32.2
first-aid worker 68.3
first name 55.14
first night 82.2
fiscal 86.2
fish (n) 17.1
fish (v) 72.11, 81.2
fish bone 72.11
fishbowl 17.4
fish course 74.6
fish dealer 78.6
fish farm 17.4
fisherman, fisherwoman 72.11
fishing 72.11
fishing rod 81.2
fishmonger 78.6
fish shop 78.2
fish tank 17.4
fist 64.1
fit (healthy) 48.1
fit (seizure) 66.1
fit of the giggles 47.9
fit out 8.5
fix 2.3 7

goal 81.10
go around 5.15
go away 4.2
go back (up) 5.14
go bad 70.8
go black 30.3
gobble gobble 14.8
go cold 23.7
god 38.12
goddaughter 38.3
goddess 38.12
godfather 38.3
godmother 38.3
go down 5.13
godson 38.3
go in 4.1
go in for 81.10
gold 19.2
goldfish 15.4
good (rewarding) 52.7
good 43.1–43.2, 57.3
good-for-nothing 32.4, 59.6
good-humoured 47.8
goodie 82.4
goodness 43.1
goose (animal) 14.1
goose (insult) 59.5
gooseberry 70.4
go out (with) 45.7
go overboard 8.6
gorilla 14.2
go round 5.15
gosling 14.1
Gospel 38.15
gossip 96.23
gossipy 47.4
go through (live through) 87.1
go through (pass through stages)
    16.3
go up 5.14
gourmet 74.12
government 36.3
governor 37.2
GP 65.1
grab (hold of) 41.13
graceful (harmonious) 49.1
graceful (svelte) 62.7
gracefulness 49.1
grammar 96.26
grammatical 96.26
gramophone 82.15
grandad/grandpa 34.3
grandchild 34.3
granddaughter 34.3
grandfather 34.3
grandmother 34.3
grandparent 34.3
grandson 34.3

granny/grandma 34.3
grape 70.2
grapefruit 70.3
grape-picking 79.5
grass (drug) 68.6
grass (turf) 80.1
grasshopper 16.3
grass snake 16.1
grate (in a fireplace) 24.16
grate (in cooking) 74.2
gratuitous 93.2
grave 38.5
gravestone 38.5
gravy 73.6
graze 91.12
great (big) 58.1
great (excellent) 57.5
greatness 52.2
greedy 74.12
Greek 59.8, 96.25
green 63.12
greengrocer 78.6
greengrocer's shop 78.2
greenhouse 80.1
greet 45.12
greetings 45.12
grey 63.12
grievous bodily harm 67.1
grill (n) 24.17
grill (v) 74.1
grocer 78.6
grocer's (shop) 78.2
groom 38.4
grotesque 57.2
ground 80.3
ground floor 24.12
group (of musicians) 82.9
group (crowd) 35.8
group (form a crowd) 35.9,
group (put together) 29.5
group captain 39.3
groupie 5.10
grove 18.9
grow (become taller) 58.2
grow (crops) 79.5
grow (increase in prosperity) 58.9
growl 14.7
grown-up 35.1
growth 58.9
grow up 58.2
grub 74.5
grudge 39.10
grumble (be in a bad mood) 47.24
grumble (protest) 96.10
grumpy 47.24
grunt 14.7
G-string 88.6
guarantee 92.6–92.7

guaranteed 92.6
guard (for protection) 39.13
guard (on a train) 8.21
guard (tour of duty) 63.9
guardian angel 38.12
guess 53.3
guide 41.3
guide book 41.3
guilder 84.13
guillotine 67.8
guilt 37.15
guilty 37.15
guinea fowl 72.9
guinea pig 15.4
guitar 82.10
guitarist 82.10
gulf 22.2
gullible 38.8
gum (in anatomy) 64.2
gum (rubber) 26.3
gum shield 39.14
gunfire 39.6
gust 23.4
gutter (in the street) 7.11
gutter (on a building) 24.10
guy 35.4
gymnastics 81.9
gym shoe 25.9

haberdasher 78.6
haberdasher's (shop) 78.3
habit 10.3
hack at 91.14
hailstorm 23.2
hair (of an animal) 14.6
hair (of people) 64.1
hair band 25.10
hairbrush 69.3
hair care 69.3
hair colour 62.20
haircut 69.3
hairdresser 69.3
hair dryer 69.3
hairspray 69.3
half 58.18
half a dozen 58.23
half a pint (of beer) 75.2
half-brother 34.4
half-light 21.1
half-sister 34.4
half-starved 62.8
hall 24.13
hallway 24.11
halogen lamp 24.16
halve 58.12
ham 72.8
hamburger 74.3
hammer 27.5

leisure 81.1
lemon 70.3
lemonade 75.3
lemon sole 17.3
lend 84.4
length 58.13
leniency 43.17
lenient 43.17
lens 83.4
lentil 70.13
Leo 38.19
leopard 14.2
leotard 25.8
lesbian 64.22
lesson 59.1
lethal 67.10
let off 43.18
letter (of the alphabet) 59.14, 56.28
letter (written communication) 97.2
letterbox 24.10
letterhead 97.3
lettuce 70.14
level 24.12
level crossing 7.8
level out 63.29
liar 88.3
liberation 37.12
Libra 38.19
librarian 59.20
library 59.20
license plate 7.2
lid 31.4
lie (falsehood) 88.3
lie down 62.12
lieutenant 39.2, 39.4
lieutenant colonel 39.2
lieutenant commander 39.4
life 87.1
life assurance/insurance 39.12
lift 5.14
light (adj: clear) 63.13
light (adj: not heavy) 00.0
light (n) 21.2, 21.3, 21.5
light (v) 20.8
light up 21.3
lighter 68.5
lightning 23.6
like (v) 45.3
liked 45.5
likely 88.7
lily 18.6
lily-of-the-valley 18.6
limb 64.1
lime (fruit) 70.3
lime (substance) 26.3
limit 91.2
limited 91.2
limp (n) 66.3

limp (not firm) 62.23
limp (v) 5.6
line (drawing) 1.5
line (of a poem) 59.18
line (railway) 8.18
line (v: border) 2.1
linen 26.2
liner 8.8
linesman 81.11
linger 5.6
lion 14.2
lion cub 14.2
lioness 14.2
lip 64.1
lipstick 25.14
liquid 20.2
lira 84.13
lisp 96.6
listener 63.14
listen to 63.14
lit 21.4
literary 59.18
literature 59.18
lithe 44.6
litheness 44.6
litre 58.37
litter 32.5
little 58.4
live (be alive) 87.1
live (reside) 24.7
lively 53.4
liver (food) 72.7
liver (in anatomy) 62.17
livestock 79.8
living room 24.16
lizard 16.1
load (in computing) 98.2
load (weight) 58.25
loads of 58.3
loafer 44.3
lobby 24.13
lobe of the ear 64.1
lobster 72.12
lobster farm 17.4
local (near) 3.6
lock 31.1
locker 32.2
locomotive 8.17
lodge 24.2
logical 66.13
loiter 5.6
lollipop 73.8
loneliness 35.11
lonely 35.11
loner 48.5
long 58.13
long johns 25.6
long-haul 8.11

look (appearance) 88.9
look (scrutinize) 63.1, 63.3
look after (maintain) 30.4
look after (watch over) 63.8
looking after 63.7
look through 63.2
loose cover 31.4
loot 43.26
looting 43.26
Lord Chancellor 36.3
lorry 7.12
lose weight 62.9
loss 84.8
lot of 58.3
lottery 81.8
loud 63.19
loudhailer 63.18
loudspeaker 63.18
lout 43.7, 48.5
love 45.3, 45.6–45.8
love (lovemaking) 64.17
lover 45.7
love story 45.6
loving 45.6
lower 58.12
lower case 96.28
loyal 45.11
loyalty 45.11
lozenge 68.2
luck 94.1
luggage 6.3
luggage rack 5.4
lukewarm (indifferent) 45.14
lukewarm (not hot) 23.8
lump (shape)1.6
lumpy 63.27
lunch 74.4
lung 62.17
luxurious 45.1
luxury hotel 24.24
lychee 70.5
lying down 62.12
lyrics 59.18

machine (general term) 28.1
machine gun 39.5
machine tool 28.1
machining 28.1
macho 35.6
mad 66.10
madam 17.3
made up of 91.4
madman 66.10 339
madness 66.9–66.10
madwoman 66.10
maestro 37.2
magazine 82.1
maggot 16.3

relax 64.13

relaxation 64.13

relaxing 64.13

release 37.12

relevant 57.9

reliability 44.1

reliable 44.1

religion 38.9

religious (believing) 38.6

religious (non-secular) 38.9

relish 74.11

rely on 44.1

remark 96.3

remarkable 45.16

remember 64.5

remind 64.5

reminiscent of 55.5

remorse 43.19

remove 41.12

rendering (on brickwork) 24.10

rent (v) 24.9

reopen 31.2

repair (n: in car maintenance) 46.2

repair (n: in DIY) 27.4

repair (v) 46.3

repatriate 6.4

repay 84.4

repayment 84.3

repeat 96.20

repeat oneself 96.20

repent 43.19

repetition 96.20

replace 89.1

replica 89.4

report 96.9

repossession 84.3

reprieve 43.18

reproduce 89.4

reproduction 89.4

reproductive system 62.18

reptile 16.1

repulsion 45.21

repulsive 45.21

reputation 52.1

repute 52.1

request 96.16

required 93.1

reschedule 84.3

rescue 46.3

rescuer 39.12

reservoir 22.5

reside 24.7

residence 24.8

resort 6.2

respect 45.16

respectable 57.3

responsibility 37.15

responsible (guilty) 37.15

responsible (serious-minded) 54.4

rest 64.13

restaurant 74.8

result 61.3

resuscitation 68.4

retell 96.20

retirement 4.2

retort (v) 96.17

reverse (v) 7.6

revolt 36.7

revolution (rotation) 5.15

revolution (uprising) 36.8

reward 52.12

rewind 82.3

rhinoceros 14.2

rhyme 96.27

rhythm 82.8

rib (cut of meat) 72.6

rib (in anatomy) 62.16

ribbon 25.13

rib cage 62.16

rich 84.18

rickshaw 7.12

ride 81.3

ride (on horseback) 81.20

ridicule 57.2

ridiculous 57.2

riding breeches 81.25

rifleman 39.6

right (appropriate) 57.9

right (correct) 92.6

right (direction) 3.2

right (normal) 95.1

right of access 38.4

rigid 40.3

rind 70.7

ring (jewellery) 25.13

ring (v) 63.17

ringing 63.17

rinse 30.5

rinsing 30.5

rip (out) 27.3

rip off 43.22

rip-off 43.22

ripe 70.8

ripen 70.8

ripple (move) 5.16

rise (go up) 5.14

rise (n & v: increase) 58.9

rise (swell) 1.7

risk 39.11

risky 39.11

ritual 38.0

road (local) 7.10

road (main) 7.10

roadblock 51.9

road sign 7.8

roar (animal noise) 14.7

roar (shout) 96.14

roast 74.1

roast beef 72.5–76.6

robber 43.24

robe (nightwear) 25.7

robin 16.5

robust 48.1

rock 22.4

rock face 22.3

rock 'n' roll 82.7

rocky 22.4

rodent 14.4

rogue 43.23

roll (of fat) 62.2

roll (of film) 83.4

roll (one's rs) 96.6

roll over 5.12

roller 80.2

roller (for paint) 27.6

Romanian 96.25

roof 24.10, 31.4

roof contractor 24.6

roof-rack 7.2

room 24.24

roost 16.7

rooster 14.1

root 18.3

root vegetable 70.12

rope 31.7

rosary 38.14

rot 67.4

rotary press 28.2

rotation 5.15

rotten 70.8

rough (to the touch) 63.27

roughly (speaking) 58.23

round (shape)1.2

roundabout 7.8

route 6.2

routine 10.2–10.3

row (line) 1.5, 29.4

row (quarrel) 40.2

rowboat 40.2

rowing boat 8.7

royal 36.9

rubber blade (on windshield) 7.3

rubber (eraser) 59.21

rubber (material) 26.3

rubbish 32.5

rubbish bin 32.2

rubbish chute 32.5

rubbish collection 32.5

rubbish dump 32.5

rub out 59.21

ruby 19.1

rucksack 25.12

rudder 8.2

rude 43.7–43.8

rudely 43.8
rudeness 43.7
rug 24.16
ruin (financially) 84.19
ruin (spoil) 91.10
ruined 84.19
rule 37.5
ruler 59.21
rum 75.5
rumble strip 7.8
rumour 96.23
run (flow) 20.4
run (move fast) 5.7
run (manage) 37.1, 37.4
run after 5.7
run along 4.2
run away 4.2, 5.2
runny 20.2
run off 4.2, 5.6
run one's eye over 63.2
run over 91.9
runway 8.14
rush 13.8
rush (up) 5.7
Russian 96.25
rust 19.2
rusty 19.2
rye 79.6

sabotage 91.10
sacred 38.15
sad 47.17
sadden 47.17
saddlebags 62.2
sadism 45.17
sadistic 45.17
sadly 96.15
sadness 47.17
safe 39.12
safety 39.12
safety belt 7.3
safety pin 33.5
Sagittarius 38.19
sail 8.2
sail boat 8.7
sailing 8.3
sailing ship 8.7
sailor 8.9
saint 38.12
saint's day 38.2
salad 70.14
sale 84.9
salesperson 84.9
sales rep 84.7
saliva 64.2
salmon 72.11
saloon (car) 7.5
salt 73.3

salt and pepper 62.20
salt cellar 24.18
salt mill 24.18
salt shaker 24.18
salty 73.2
sample (n) 41.5
sample (v) 51.4
sample page 41.5
sand 22.7
sandal 25.9
sandbank 22.7
sand dune 22.7
sandpit 81.3
sandy 22.7
sanitary towel/napkin 69.7
sanity 66.13
sap 18.8
sapphire 19.1
sarcasm 47.14
sardine 72.11
Satan 38.12
satin 26.2
satisfaction 47.16
satisfy 47.16
Saturday 9.2
Saturn 22.14
sauce 73.5–73.6
saucepan 24.17
saunter 5.6
sausage 72.8
savage 48.5
savagely 48.5
savagery 48.5
save (in computing) 98.2
save (put money by) 84.2
save (retain) 41.11
savings 84.2
saviour 39.12
savoury 73.2
savoury food 73.6
saw (v: cut off) 91.14
saw (tool) 27.5
saxophone 82.10
saxophonist 82.10
scale (in music) 82.14
scale (of a fish or snake) 14.6
scale (on a map) 58.14
scales (for weighing) 58.26
scallion 70.14
scan (look quickly) 63.2
scan (ultra-sound) 33.3
scandal 43.19
scapegoat 37.18
scared 45.25
scarf 25.11
scatter 5.5
scene 82.2
scent 25.14

scheme 51.2
schizophrenia 66.11
schizophrenic 66.11
school 37.3, 59.1
schoolbag 24.12
schoolchild 59.1
school report 59.7
schoolteacher 59.9
science(s) 59.8
scissors 27.5
scorching 23.8
score 81.10
Scorpio 38.19
scrap 39.7
scratch 91.8
scrawl 96.33
scrawny 62.8
scream 96.14
screech 96.14
screen (of computer) 77.2
screen (television) 82.2
screw (n) 27.5
screw (v) 64.17
screwdriver 27.5
scroll 98.2
scrub 30.5
scrubland 18.10
scruffy 44.4
sculpt 83.5
sculpting 83.5
sculptor 83.5
sculpture 83.5
sea 22.5
seafood 72.12
seal 17.2
sealed 31.1
sea-lion 17.2
seam 83.6
search engine 98.4
seasick 8.6
season 9.1
season (in cooking) 73.6
seasoning 73.6
season ticket 6.1
seat (in a car) 7.3
seat (on a bus, on the underground)
     62.12
seat (on a train, a plane) 8.20
seaweed 22.7
secateurs 80.2
second 9.8
secondary 59.1
second floor 24.12
second home 24.1
secret 88.5
secret police 37.9
secretary (of a committee) 37.4
Secretary of the Interior 36.3

tense (not relaxed) 47.1
tenseness 47.1
tension 47.1
tent 81.2
term 59.1
term of endearment 45.8
terminal (inside airport) 11.2
terminus (of a railway line) 8.19
terrible 45.20
terrific 57.5
terrify 45.23
territory 22.11
terror 45.23
test (at school) 59.10
test (medical examination) 65.1
test (out) 51.4
test-tube baby 33.3
testicle 64.1
text 97.3
textbook 59.7
textile 26.1
theatre 82.2
theft 43.24, 43.26
theory 53.3
therapy 68.1
therefore 61.3
thermometer 68.4
Thermos flask 32.2
thick 62.1
thief 43.24
thigh 64.1
thin 62.6
thin (out) 80.1
thing 55.1
thingumabob 55.1
thingummy 55.1
think 54.1–54.2
thinker 54.1
thinking 54.1
thinness 62.6
third 58.18
thirst 75.1
thirsty 75.7
thorn 18.3
thorough 29.1, 44.2
thought 54.1
thousand 58.23
thrashing 52.10
thread (n) 26.1
thread (v) 83.6
threatening 48.5
three-dimensional 1.3
threshold 24.10
thrifty 86.1
thrill 47.2
throat 66.2
throne 36.9
throw 5.5

throw around (spend lavishly) 85.3
throw away 32.6–32.7
throw oneself 5.13
throw out 32.7
thrush 16.5
thumb 64.1
Thursday 9.2
thyme 73.3
ticket 6.1
ticket collector 37.2
tickle 63.22
tidal power 28.3
tidal wave 22.7
tide 22.7
tie 25.13
tie up 27.1
tiger 14.2
tights 25.6
tigress (animal) 14.2
tigress (woman) 14.5
tile 24.10
till (in shop) 00.0
timber 26.3
time (at work) 76.4
time (duration) 9.7–9.10
time (for resting) 64.14
time (off work) 64.14
time (period of) 9.9
time (telling the) 9.8
timely (opportune) 57.9
timely (punctual) 13.3
times (of trains, etc) 6.1
timetable 6.1
timid 48.5
timpani 82.10
timpanist 82.10
tin (container) 32.2
tin (metal) 19.2
tin opener 24.17
tin plate 19.2
tiny 58.5
tip (edge) 1.2
tip (money) 41.8
tiptoe 5.6
tire (become weary) 64.10
tire (on wheel) 7.2
tired 64.10
tiredness 64.10
tiring 64.10
title (of a book) 59.14
title (of a noble) 36.11
title (status) 55.14
tittle-tattle 96.23
toad 15.5
toady 37.17
tobacco 68.5
tobacconist 78.6
toe 64.1

toenail 64.1
toffee 73.8
toilet 24.22
toilet paper 24.22
toiletries 69.2
toilet paper roll 24.22
toilet seat 24.22
toilet tank 24.22
tolerant 43.17
toll 7.9
tom (cat) 15.2
tomato 70.14
tommyrot 57.2
tomorrow 9.2
ton 58.25
tone 63.15
toneless 10.2
tongue 64.2
tonne 58.25
tonsil 62.17
tool 27.5
tool bag 27.5
tool box 27.5
tooth 65.4
toothbrush 69.4
toothpaste 69.4
top 2.2
top (best) 57.8
top (of bottle) 75.6
topical 12.3
topple over 5.12
torch 21.5
tortoise 15.4
torturer 45.18
total (complete) 91.1
total (sum) 58.17
touch 63.22
tough 63.25
tour (on a bicycle) 81.20
tour (trip) 6.25
tour of duty 63.7
tour operator 6.2
tour organizer 6.2
tourism 6.2
tourist 6.2
tournament 81.12
tow 5.3
towelling 26.1
towel rail/rack 24.22
tower block 24.3
town 22.2
town house 24.4
toy 81.5
trachea 62.17
track (follow) 5.8
track (in athletics) 81.13
track (railway) 8.18–8.19
track suit 25.8

unharmed 91.1
unimportant 57.11
union (of workers)
union member 76.5
unique 95.2
unit 58.24
universe 22.14
university 59.1
university teacher 59.9
unjustly 43.13
unknown 52.3
unlikely 92.5
unload 90.4
unmarried person 38.4
unoriginal 95.1
unpleasant 51.5
unreal 88.8
unrecognizable 55.14
unripe 70.8
unshakeable 38.7
unthinkable 92.5
untidiness 29.3
untidy 29.3
untrue 88.3
unusable 32.4
unusual (rare) 95.2
unusual (surprising) 47.5
unwell 66.8
unwind 64.13
upper case 96.28
upright 2.2
upside down 2.2
upstairs 24.14
Uranus 22.14
Urdu 96.25
use 32.1
useful 32.3
useless 59.6
user-friendly 32.3
uterus 33.2
utility room 30.9
utter 96.6

vacuum cleaner 30.6
vagina 62.18
vain 43.12
vainglory 52.2
valley 22.3
valuable 85.1
value 85.1
van 7.12
vandalize 91.10
vanish 58.12
vanity 43.12
variety 55.2
variety show 82.2
various 55.7
vary 89.2

vase 24.16
vassal 57.12
veal 72.5
vegan 18.1
vegetable 70.10
vegetarian 18.1
vehicle 7.12
veil 88.4
vein 62.15
velvet 26.2
venison 72.9
venture capital 39.11
Venus 22.14
verb 96.26
verdict 37.11
vertical 2.2
vessel 8.1
vest 25.4
veto (v) 40.4
viable 92.1
vice 37.16
vice admiral 39.4
victim 37.18
victorious 52.7
victory (in war) 39.6
victory (overcoming sthg) 52.7
video game 98.1
view 63.11
village 22.2
vinegar 73.3
vine leaf 18.3
vineyard 79.2
viola 82.10
viola player 82.10
violence 48.5
violent 48.5
violently 48.5
violet 18.2
violin 82.10
violin case 32.2
violin concerto 82.13
violinist 82.10
virgin 64.17
virginity 64.17
Virgin Mary 38.12
Virgo 38.19
virile 35.6
virtue 43.1
virtuoso 59.3
virtuous 43.1
virus 98.1
visa 97.4
viscount 36.11
viscountess 36.11
visibility 63.11
visible 63.211
visibly 63.11
vision 63.11

visit (general term) 4.3
visit (to the doctor) 65.1
visual art 83
viva 59.10
vixen 14.2
vocal (music) 82.11
vocational 59.11
vodka 75.5
voice 63.19, 96.6
volcano 22.3
volume 58.24
volume (of alcohol) 75.2
vomit 66.2
vote 36.4
voter 36.4
voting 36.4
vowel 96.27
vulcanization 26.3
vulcanize 26.4
vulgar 43.7
vulnerable 48.3
vulture 16.6
vulva 64.1

wader 16.5
waist 64.1
waistcoat 25.4
wait 13.11
wait-and-see 52.6
waiter 74.9
waiting (general term) 13.11
waiting (parking a car) 7.5
waiting room 13.11
waitress 74.9
wake (for the dead) 38.5
wake (up) 64.12
walk 5.6
wall 24.10
wallet 84.14
wallpaper 27.6
wall-to-wall 24.16
walnut 70.9
walrus 17.2
want 51.1
war 39.1
ward 65.2
warden 63.9
wardrobe 24.20
warehouse 84.7
warlike 39.1
warm (friendly) 45.11
warm (not cold) 23.8
warmth 23.8
warning 37.15
warrant officer 39.1
warranty 92.6
warrior 39.1
warship 8.1

woof 14.8
wool 83.6
word 96.1
word processor 77.2
work (book) 59.14
work (v: exploit) 32.1
work (v: function) 28.3
work (labour) 76.3–76.6
workaholic 76.7
work out 53.3
worker 76.6
working class 36.2
workload 76.6
work of art 83.3
works committee 76.3
work surface 24.17
world 22.2
worm 16.3
worm-eaten 16.3
worried 45.2
worry 45.24
worse 57.10, 91.15
worsen 91.15
worsening 91.15
worship (admire) 45.3

worship (in religion) 38.14
worth (in terms of money)
    85.1
wound 66.1
wrap 31.3
wrap (up) 31.3
wraparound helmet 25.10
wrath 47.22
wrathful 47.22
wreath 38.5
wreck (v: ruin) 91.7
wrecker 8.4
wren 16.6
wrench (tool) 27.5
wring 1.7
wring dry 20.5
wrist 64.1
wristwatch 9.8
write 96.32
writing 96.32
wrong 60.3
wrongly 60.3

xylophone 82.10
xylophonist 82.10

yacht 8.7
yard 24.10
yawn 64.9
yell 96.14
yellow 63.12
yesterday 9.2
yew 18.11
yoghurt 72.2
young (adj) 33.2, 33.9
young (n) 58.4
younger (in a family or group) 33.8,
    33.9
youth 33.9
youthful 33.9

zany 57.2
zebra 14.2
zigzag 51.9
zip code 97.2
zodiac 38.19 171
zucchini 70.13

blindé (n) 39.5
blocage 51.12
bloc-note 59.20
bloc opératoire 65.3
blocus 51.12
blond, e 62.20 310
bloquer 51.12
blouse 25.4
blues 82.7
bluff 43.10
bluffer 43.10
bob 81.21
bobard 88.3
bobine de fil 83.6
bobsleigh 81.21
bocage 79.2
bocal (pour aliment) 32.2
bocal (pour poisson) 17.4
body 25.8
boeuf 14.1
bogie 8.17
boire (alcool) 75.1
boire (terme général) 75.7–75.8
bois (arbres) 18.9
bois (d'animal) 14.6
bois (de construction) 26.3
boisson 75.1–75.4
boîte (à lettres) 24.10
boîte (à outils) 27.5
boîte (bureau) 76.6
boîte (discothèque) 82.5
boîte (pour boire) 75.6
boîte (terme général) 32.2
boiteux, -teuse 66.3
boiter 5.6 20
bol 24.18
bon (de bonne qualité) 57.3
bon (exact) 60.2
bon (gentil) 43.1
bon à rien 32.4
bonbon 73.8
bon marché 84.16
bon mot 47.13
bon point 52.12
bon sens 66.13
bonde 24.22
bondé, e 90.3
bondir 5.11
bonheur 47.8
bonne (gentille) 43.1
bonne à rien 32.4
bonne femme 35.5
bonne humeur 47.8
bonne idée 54.5
bonne mémoire 64.5
bonne santé 66.7
bonnet d'âne 59.4
bonté 43.1

bord (à b.) 8.6
bord (bordure) 22.6
bordel (exclamation) 96.21
bordel (maison de prostitution) 64.20
bordure 2.1
borgne 66.3
borne (d'autoroute) 7.9
borne (distance) 2.5
bosquet 18.9
bosse 1.6
bosselé, e 63.27
bosser 76.6
botte (chaussure) 25.9
botte (de foin) 79.6
bouc (animal) 14.1
bouc (émissaire) 37.18
bouche (d'incendie) 20.8
bouche (partie du visage) 64.1
bouche à bouche 68.4
bouche bée 47.7
boucher, -chère 78.6
boucher (remplir) 90.2
boucherie (magasin) 78.2
boucherie (viande, métier) 72.4
bouchon (de bouteille) 75.6
bouchon (sur une route) 51.9
boucle (accessoire) 25.9
boucle (bijou) 25.13
Bouddha 38.12
bouddhisme 38.10
Bouddhiste 38.10
bouddhiste 38.10
boudin 72.8
boue 30.2
boueux, boueuse 30.2
bœuf 72.5
bouffe 74.5
bouffer 74.11
bouger 62.23
bougie 21.5
bouillant, e 23.8
bouillir 74.1
bouillon-cube 73.6
bouillotte 24.21
boulanger, gère 78.6
boulangerie 78.2
bouleau 18.10
boule (jeu) 81.24 392
boule de neige (augmentation) 58.11
boule de neige (jeu) 23.7
boulon 27.5
boulot (petit b.) 76.1
boulot (terme général) 76.6
boum 63.17
bouquet 38.4
bouquin 59.14
bouquiner 59.14
bourg 22.2

bourgeoisie 36.2
bourgeon 18.8
bourrasque 23.4
bourré, e 90.3
bourreau 45.18
bourreau de travail 76.7
bourrelet 62.2
bourrer, se bourrer 90.3
bourse 84.10
bousculer 13.8
bout 91.3
bouteille 32.2
bouteille Thermos 32.2
boutique 78.3
bouton (de manchette) 25.13
bouton (d'or) 18.2
bouton (pour vêtement) 25.2
bouton (sur la peau) 64.3
bovins 79.8
boxe 81.18
boxeur 81.18
bracelet 25.13
bracelet-montre 9.8
braguette 25.2
braiement 14.7
brailler 96.14
braire 14.7
branchage 18.8
branche 18.8
branchie 14.6
bras 64.1
bras d'honneur 62.22
brasier 20.6
brasse 81.16
brasserie 74.8
break 7.1
brebis 14.1
bredouiller 96.6
bretelle (d'autoroute) 7.9
bretelle (pour vêtement) 25.13
bricolage 27.4
bricoler 27.4
bride 81.25
brigade 68.6
brigand 43.24
brillant, e 21.4
briller 21.3
brin (de laine) 83.6
brin de (petit peu de) 58.7
brindille 18.8
brio 59.2
brioche (gâteau) 71.3
brioche (ventre) 62.2
briqué 29.2
briquet 68.5
brise 23.4
briser 91.6
broccoli 70.11

cour (espace) 24.10
cour (tribunal) 37.11
courant 22.8
courant d'air 23.4
courbatu, e 66.5
courbature 66.5
courbaturé, e 66.5
courbette 62.14
coureur (de dot) 84.18
coureur, -reuse (en sport) 81.15
courge 70.13
courgette 70.13
courir (aller vite) 5.7
courir (en sport) 81.15
couronne (de roi) 36.10
couronne (en dentisterie) 65.4
couronne (mortuaire) 38.5
couronnement 36.10
courrier 97.2
courrier électronique 98.4
courroucé, e 47.22
courroux 47.22
cours (du marché) 84.10
cours (leçon) 59.1
cours d'eau 22.8
course (de chevaux) 81.26
course (en athlétisme) 81.15
course-poursuite 5.9
courser 5.7
courses (dans les magasins) 78.1
coursier 97.2
court 81.13
courtier 84.8
courtoisie 43.6
couru, e 45.5
cousin, e 34.5
coussin 24.16
coût 84.11
couteau 24.19
coûter 84.11
coûteux, -teuse 84.17
coutume 38.1
couture 83.6
couvent 38.13
couvercle 31.4
couvert (de table) 24.19
couvert, e (nuageux) 23.1
couvert, e (protégé) 31.3
couverture (de lit) 24.21
couverture (pour protéger) 31.4
couvre-chef 25.10
couvre-lit 24.21
couvreur 24.6
couvrir 31.3
crabe (en cuisine) 72.12
crabe (animal) 17.2
crachin 23.3
crack 68.6

craie 26.3
craindre 45.24
crainte 45.24
crampe 66.5
crâne 62.16
cranté, e 63.27
crapaud 15.5
crasse 30.2
crasseux, -sseuse 30.2
cravate 25.13
crawl 81.16
crayon 59.20
créancier 84.3
crécelle 63.17
crédule 38.8
crème (fraîche) 72.2
crème à raser 69.5
crémerie 72.1
crémier, -mière 72.1
créneau (en voiture) 7.6
créosote 27.6
crêpage de chignon 40.2
crêpe 74.3
crépi 24.10
cresson 70.14
crétin, e 59.5
creuse 90.4
creuser 80.1
creux 90.4
crevaison 7.5
crevasse 31.6
crevé, e 64.10
crever 67.3
cri (animal) 14.8
cri (humain) 96.14
criard, e 63.13
crier 96.14
crime 37.7
crise (mauvaise santé) 66.1
crise (en économie) 86.3
crispant, e 47.1
crispé, e 47.1
crisper se 47.1
critiquer 96.15
croassement 14.7
croc 14.6
crochet (d'art) 83.6
crochet (en ponctuation) 96.29
crochet (pour attacher) 31.7
crocheter 83.6
crocodile 16.1
croire 38.6, 38.8
croisement 7.8
croiser 7.6 28
croissance 58.9
croître 58.9
croque-madame 74.3
croque-monsieur 74.3

croquis 83.3
crotté, e 30.2
croûte 71.1
croyance 38.6
croyant, e (adj & n) 38.6
CRS 37.8
cru (en équitation) 81.25
cru, e (non cuit) 74.1
cruauté 45.17
cruche 24.18
cruel, cruelle 45.17
cube 58.27
cubique 58.27
cuiller 24.19
cuillère 24.19
cuir 26.2
cuire 74.1
cuisine (activité) 74.1
cuisine (pièce) 24.17
cuisiner 74.1
cuisinier 74.9
cuisinière (personne) 74.9
cuisinière (appareil) 24.17
cuisse 64.1
cuisson 74.1
cuit, e 74.1
cuivre (jaune) 19.2
cuivre (rouge) 19.2
cuivré, e 62.20
cuivres 82.10
culot 43.9
culotte 25.5
culotté, e 43.9
culotte de cheval (graisse) 62.2
culotte de cheval (vêtement) 81.25
culpabilité 37.15
culte 38.14
cultivateur, -trice 79.1
cultiver 79.1
culture (agriculture) 79.1, 79.5, 79.6
culture (éducation) 59.1
culture (façon de vivre) 38.1
cupide 50.4
cupidité 50.4
cure (en médecine) 68.4
cure (de désintoxication) 75.8
cure (par les plantes) 18.5
curé 38.13
curieux, -rieuse (cherchant à
    découvrir) 47.4
curieux, -rieuse (étrange) 95.2
curiosité 47.4
curseur 98.1
cyclisme 81.19
cycliste 81.19
cygne 16.6
cymbale 82.10
cymbalier, -lière 82.10

fruité, e 70.1
fruits de mer 72.12
fruits exotiques 70.5
fuir 5.2
fuite 4.2
fulminer 47.24
fumer 68.5
fumier 79.7
furet 15.5
fureter 50.5
fureur 47.22
furie 47.22 230
furieux, -rieuse 47.22
fusain 83.2
fuselage 8.12
fuselé, e 62.7
fusible 27.7
futé, e 59.13
futur (avenir) 9.10
futur, e (en grammaire) 96.26

gabarit 64.1
gâcher (gaspiller) 85.2
gâcher (saboter) 91.10
gâchis 85.2
gadget 55.1
gaffe 60.1
gag 47.13
gaga 66.12
gagner 52.7
gai, e 47.8
gaieté 47.8
galaxie 22.14
galerie 7.2
galet 22.4
galoper 81.25
gamme 82.14
gant 25.11
gant de boxe 81.18
gant de toilette 69.2
garage 24.10
garanti, e 92.6
garantie 92.6
garantir 92.7
garçon d'honneur 38.4
garde (légale) 33.4
garde (personne, activité) 63.7, 63.9
garde à vue 37.8
garde des sceaux 36.3
garde-chiourme 37.2
garde-malade 63.9
garder (retenir) 41.11
garder (surveiller) 63.8
gardien (d'immeuble) 24.9
gardien (surveillant) 63.9
gardien de la paix 37.8
gare (pour trains) 8.19
garer, se garer 7.6

gaspillage 85.2
gaspiller 85.2
gâteau 71.3
gâteau sec 71.2
gâter 91.10
gâteux, -teuse 66.12
gauche 44.7 205,
Gaullisme 36.5
gaz (émanation) 20.1
gaz (ressource) 28.3
géant, e 58.1
gel (froid) 23.7
gel (pour la douche) 69.2
gelée (salée) 73.6
gelée (sucrée) 73.7
geler 23.2–23.7
gélule 68.2
Gémeaux 38.19
gencive 64.2
gendarme 37.8
gendre 34.4
gène 62.15
gêner (mettre mal à l'aise) 45.2
gêner (rendre inconfortable) 66.5
général, e (d'ensemble) 55.11
général (militaire) 39.2
général de brigade aérienne 39.3
général de l'armée de l'air 39.3
généralement 55.11
généralisation 55.11
généraliser 55.11
généraliste 65.1
généralité 55.11
génération 34.6
généreux, -reuse 43.15
générique 55.11
générosité 43.15
génial, e 57.5
génisse 14.1
genou (en anatomie) 64.1
genoux (posture) 62.13
genre (en grammaire) 96.26
genre (sorte) 55.2
gens 35.1
gens du voyage 6.2
gentil, -tille (amical) 45.11
gentil (dans une fiction) 82.4
gentil, -tille (généreux) 43.15
gentil, -tille (obéissant) 43.2
gentillesse 43.15
gentiment 45.11
géo 22.1
géographe 22.1
géographie (discipline scolaire) 59.8
géographie (science) 22.1
géographique 22.1
géologique 22.1
géologue 22.1

géomètre-expert 24.6
géométrie 58.16
gérant, e 37.2
gerboise 15.4
gérer 37.1
geste 62.21
gesticuler 62.21
gibier 72.9
giboulée 23.3
gicler 20.4
gifle 67.1
gifler 67.1
gigot 72.6
gilet 25.4 107, 25.5
gingembre 73.3
girafe 14.2
girafeau 14.2
girafon 14.2
glace (dessert) 73.7
glace (miroir) 24.20
glacer 23.7
gland 18.8
glapir 96.14
globe (planète) 22.2
globe oculaire 64.1
gloire 52.2
glorieux, -rieuse 52.2
gloriole 52.2
glou glou 14.8
gnome 88.11
gober 38.8
godasse 25.9
gogo 38.8
golfe 22.2
gomme 59.20
gommer 59.20
gonfler 1.7
gorille (animal) 14.2
gorille (garde du corps) 14.5
goudron 26.3
goudronner 26.4
goujat 43.7
gourmand, e (adj & n) 74.12
gourmet 74.12
goût (raffinement) 43.7
goût (saveur) 73.1
goûter 74.10
goutte 68.2
goutte (de pluie) 23.3
gouttière 24.10
gouvernail 8.2
gouvernement 36.3
gouverneur 37.2
grâce (pardon) 43.17
grâce (beauté) 49.1
gracier 43.18
gracieux, -cieuse 49.1
gradé 39.1

Orient 3.4
orient 3.3
orifice 31.6
original, e (adj & n) 12.2
originalité 12.2
orme 18.10
orner 49.2
orphelin, e (adj & n) 35.10
orteil 64.1
orthodoxe 38.11
orthographe 96.28
orthographier 96.28
os 62.15
osseux, -sseuse 62.15
otarie 17.2
ôter 58.17
ouah 14.8
oubli 64.6
oublier 64.6
oubliettes 64.6
oublieux, -lieuse 64.6
Ouest 3.4
ouest 3.3
ouïe 63.14
ouragan 23.6
ourdou 96.25
ourlet 25.2
ours, e 14.2
ourson 14.2
outil 27.5
ouvert, e (amical) 45.11
ouvert, e (non fermé) 31.2
ouverture (en musique) 82.13
ouverture (terme général) 31.2
œuvre (en littérature) 59.14
œuvre (peinture, sculpture) 83.3
ouvrage 59.14
ouvre-boîte 24.17
ouvrier, -rière 76.6
ouvrier, rière agricole 79.1
ouvrir, s'ouvrir 31.2
ovaire 62.18
ovationner 45.15
ovins 79.8
oxygène 20.1

Pacifique 22.2
pack (de bière) 32.2
pagaille 29.3
page 59.21
paiement 84.9
paillasse 24.17
paille 79.6
pain 71.1
pair, e (adj) 58.20
pair (nm) 55.4
paire (de lunettes) 63.10
paire (terme général) 29.4

paisible 47.3
paisiblement 47.3
paix 39.12
paix 47.3, 63.20
palace 24.24
pâle 63.13
palette 83.2
palier 24.14
palourde 72.12
palper 63.22
pamplemousse 70.3
panaché 75.2
panais 70.12
panaris 66.2
pancréas 62.17
panda 14.2
panier 32.2
panique 45.23
paniquer 45.23
panjabi 96.25
panneau (indicateur) 7.8
pansement 68.4
pantalon 25.4
panthère (animal) 14.2
panthère (femme) 14.5
pantoufle 25.9
paon 16.5
papa 34.1
Pape 38.13
papé 34.3
papeterie 59.21
papier (terme général) 26.3
papier hygiénique 24.22
papier peint 27.6
papiers (document) 97.4
papiers (ordures) 32.5
papier toilettes 24.22
papillon 16.3
papillon de nuit 16.3
papoter 96.22
papy 34.3
papyrus 26.3
paquebot 8.8
Pâques 9.5
paquet (emballage) 32.2
paquet (pour poster) 97.2
par conséquent 61.3
par inadvertance 60.3
par mégarde 60.3
par ordre de 56.1
par suite 61.3
parachute 81.22
parachutiste 81.22
paradis 38.17
paragraphe 96.30
paraître 88.9
parallèle (adj) 1.5
parallèle (nf) 1.5

parallèle (nm) 22.2
parano 66.11
paranoïa 66.11
paranoïaque 66.11
parapluie 25.11
paravent 88.6
parcelle 91.3
parcmètre 7.11
parcourir 63.2
parcours 6.2
pardessus 25.4
pardonner 43.18
pare-brise 7.2
pare-choc 7.2
parenthèse 96.29–96.30
parer 49.2
paresse 44.3
paresser 44.3
paresseux, -sseuse 44.3
parfait, e 57.3
parfaitement 57.3
parfois 10.1
parfum 25.14
parier 81.8
parlementaire 36.4
parler 96.1–96.7
parole 96.1
parole d'honneur 40.9
paroles (d'une chanson) 59.18
parquet (au tribunal) 37.10
parquet (plancher) 24.15
parrain 38.3
partage 27.2
partager (donner) 41.10
partager (séparer) 27.2
partenaire 84.5
partenaires (sociaux) 76.5
partenariat 84.5
parti (politique) 36.5
parti (prendre son p.) 00.0
partial, e 43.13
participe 96.26
particulier (individu privé) 35.1
particulier, -lière (spécifique) 55.10
particulièrement 55.10
partie (faire p. de) 91.4
partie (jeu) 81.6
partie (match) 81.12
partie (morceau) 91.3
partie du discours 96.26
partielle, e (nf) 36.4
parties (génitales) 64.1
partir (s'en aller) 4.2
partir (mourir) 67.3
partisan 45.4
pas (au p.) 81.25
pas mal 57.4
passable 57.4

pousse-pousse 7.12
pousser (propulser) 5.1-5.3
pousser (provoquer) 46.6
poussette 33.5
poussette-cane 33.5
poussin 14.1
pouvoir (nm) 37.1
pouvoir (v) 92.1
pouvoir d'achat 84.9
prairie 79.2
pratique 32.3
pratiquer 81.10
pré 79.2
prêcher 38.14
précieux, -cieuse 85.1
précipitation (hâte) 13.8
précipitation (pluie) 23.3
précipiter (propulser) 5.5
précipiter se (se hâter) 13.8
précipiter se (se jeter) 5.13
précis, e 60.2
précisément 60.2
préciser 55.10
précision 55.10
prédicateur 38.14
prééminence 57.8
préjugé 43.13
prélèvement automatique 84.2
prélude 64.18
préliminaires 64.18
première (au cinéma) 82.2
premier étage 24.12
premier ministre 36.3
premier plan 83.3
premiers secours 68.3
premiers soins 68.3
prendre (être à la mode) 45.5
prendre (saisir) 41.12–41.14
prénommer 55.13
préparer, se préparer 13.4
préposé, e (des postes) 97.2
préposition 96.26
prénom 55.14
près (approximativement) 58.23
près, près de (proche) 3.6
présence 87.1
présent (dans le temps, nm) 9.9
présent, e (dans le temps, adj) 9.10
présent (en grammaire) 96.26
présent, e (non absent) 87.1
présentations 45.12
présenter 45.12
présenter se (à une élection) 36.4
préservatif 64.21
président, e 37.4
présidentielles 36.4
présider 37.4
presse (dans le journalisme) 82.1

presse (machine) 28.2
pressé, e 13.8
presser 5.3
prêt, e (adj) 13.4
prêt (n) 84.3
prêt à l'emploi 32.1
prêt-à-porter 13.4
prêter 84.4
prêtre 38.13
prêtrise 38.13
preuve 37.11
prie-Dieu 38.13
prier 38.14
prière 38.14
primaire 59.1
primeur (nf) 54.4
primeur (nm) 78.2
prince 36.11
prince charmant 50.3
printemps 9.4
pris 52.4
prise 27.7
prison 37.9
prisonnier, -nnière 37.9
prix (d'achat) 84.9
prix (de vente) 84.9
prix (récompense) 52.12
prix (valeur) 85.1
probable 92.4
probablement 92.4
probe 43.20
probité 43.20
problème 51.6
procédé 56.2
procédure 56.2
procès 37.11
processus 56.2
prochain (autrui) 35.1
prochain, e (adj) 9.10
prochainement 9.10
proche (ami) 45.09
proche parent 34.6
proche (peu distant) 3.6
procréer 64.17
procurer se 41.14
productivité 79.7
produire 27.8
produire se 87.2
produit (à vaisselle) 30.8
produit (de beauté) 25.14
produit (terme général) 27.9
produit après-rasage 69.5
produit laitier 72.1
professeur 59.9
professionnel 59.3
profond, e (intense) 63.13
profond, e (qui descend loin) 58.13
profondeur 58.13

progéniture 34.6
progiciel 98.3
programme (en informatique) 98.3
programme (spectacle) 82.2
progrès (amélioration) 89.3
progrès (marche de la science) 57.7
prohiber 37.14
projectile 5.5
projet 51.2
projeter 5.5
prolétariat 36.2
prolongation 13.6
prolonger 13.6
promesse 40.9
promettre 40.9
promotion 84.7
pronom 96.26
pronominal, e 96.26
prononcer, se prononcer 96.6
prononciation 96.27
propagande 36.5
propension 45.3
propension à faire qqch 45.3
prophète 38.12
prophétique 38.12
proposer 40.8
proposer de, se 51.1
proposition 40.8
propre 30.1
propre à 57.9
propreté 30.1
propriétaire (non locataire) 24.9
propriétaire (terme général) 41.14
propriété 41.14
proprio 24.9
propulser 5.5
prose 59.18
prostitué, e 64.20
prostitution 64.20
protège-cahier 31.4
protège-slip 69.7
protéger (couvrir) 39.13
protestant, e (adj & n) 38.11
protestation 96.15
protester 96.15
prouver 41.1
province 22.11
provincial, e 22.11
provoquer 61.2
prudence 44.2
prudent, e 44.2
prud'hommes 76.3
prune 70.2
pruneau 70.6
prunier 18.12
psaume 38.14
pseudonyme 55.14
psy 66.10

psychologique 66.10
psychologue 66.10
psychose 66.11
psychotique 66.11
pubère 35.2
puberté 35.2
public 82.2
publication 59.19
puce (insecte) 16.3
puce (terme affectueux) 45.8
puceau 64.17
pucelle 64.17
puceron 16.3
puissant, e (adj) 48.1
puissant (n) 37.1
puits 31.6
pull 25.5
pullover 25.5
pulvériser 91.7
pupille 64.1
pur, e 43.1
pureté 43.1
purgatoire 38.17
purin 79.7
putain 64.20
pute 64.20
putois 15.5
pyjama 25.7
pyramidal, e 1.3

quadruple 58.9
quadruplés, quadruplées 33.1
quai (pour bateaux) 8.3
quai (pour trains) 8.19
Quai d'Orsay 36.3
quarantaine (exclusion) 91.5
quarantaine (quantité) 58.23
quart 58.18
quartette 82.9
quartier (de lune) 91.3
quartier (d'orange) 70.7
quatuor 82.9
quelquefois 10.1
querelle 40.2
question 96.16
questionner 96.16
queue (d'animal) 14.6
queue (de billard) 81.24
queue (file) 2.2
quincaillerie 78.3
quincaillier, -llière 78.6
quintal 58.25
quintuple 58.9
quinzaine (deux semaines) 9.2
quinzaine (quantité) 58.23
quitter 4.2
quotidien, -dienne (de tous les jours)
    10.3

quotidien (journal) 82.1

rabâcher 96.20
rabais 84.8
rabbin 38.13
race 55.2
rachat 84.9
racheter 84.9
racine 18.3
racisme 43.13
raciste 43.13
radiateur 24.23
radio 82.3
radio-réveil 9.8
radis 70.14
radoter 96.20
radoub 8.5
radouber 8.5
rafraîchir, se rafraîchir 23.7
ragaillardir 48.2
rage 47.22
ragot 96.23
raide (en pente) 1.5
raide (peu souple) 63.26
raie (ligne) 1.4
raie (poisson) 72.11
rail 8.18
raisin 70.2
raisin de Corinthe 70.6
raisin sec 70.6
raison (cause) 61.1
raison (sagesse) 66.13
raison de Smyrne 70.6
raison sociale 84.6
raisonnable 66.13
raisonner (penser) 54.2
raisonner, se raisonner (modérer)
    66.13
raisonneur, -nneuse 66.13
ralentir (en voiture) 7.6
ralentir (terme général) 13.10
ralentissement 13.10
ralentisseur 7.8
râler 96.10
rallonge 27.7
Ramadan 9.5
ramassage des ordures 32.5
rameau 18.8
Rameaux 9.5
ramener 5.1
ramolli, e 63.23
rampe 24.14
ramper 5.6
rançon 43.26
rancune 39.10
randonnée 81.20
randonneur, -nneuse 81.20
rang 29.4

rangée 1.5
rapatrier 6.3
râpe à fromage 24.18
râper 74.2
rapetisser 58.6
râpeux, -peuse 63.27
rapide 13.7
rapidement 13.7
rapidité 13.7
rappeler, se rappeler 64.5
rapport (entre personnes) 45.9
rapport (information) 96.9
rapporter (apporter) 5.1
rapporter (raconter) 96.9
rapporteur 58.19
rapports 45.9
rapports sexuels 64.17
rapprocher 40.5
rare 95.2
rasage 69.5
rasoir (électrique) 69.5
rasoir (ennuyeux) 10.2
rassemblement 35.8
rassembler (faire se grouper) 35.9
rassembler (remettre ensemble) 27.1
rassembler se 35.9
rat, e (animal) 15.5
rate (en anatomie) 62.17
rateau 80.2
rater 52.11
raton 15.5
rattraper 41.13
ravager 91.7
ravi, e 47.8
ravisseur, -sseuse 43.26
rayé, e 1.4
rayer 91.8
rayon (dans un magasin) 78.5
rayon (de soleil) 21.5
rayon (en géométrie) 1.2
rayonnage 24.16
rayure 1.4
raz-de-marée 22.7
ré 82.14
réacteur 28.2
réalisable 92.1
réaliser 53.2
réalité 88.7
rébellion 36.7
rebondir 5.11
rebord de fenêtre 24.10
rebutant, e 10.2
réception 38.4
réceptionniste 77.4
réchauffer 23.8
recherche d'emploi 76.2
rechercher 50.5
récit de voyage 6.2

salive 64.2

salle (d'attente) 13.11

salle (d'exposition) 41.4

salle (d'hôpital) 65.2

salle de bain 24.24

salle de séjour 24.16

salle des pas perdus 8.19

salon 41.4

salopette 25.4

saluer (dire bonjour) 45.12

saluer (s'incliner) 62.14

salutation 45.12

samedi 9.2

sandale 25.9

sandalette 25.9

sang 62.15

sanglier 14.2

sanglot 47.20

sangloter 47.20

sanguinaire 48.5

sanitaire 24.22

sans plomb 7.7

sans-domicile-fixe 24.9

santé mentale 62.19

saoûl, e 75.8

saphir 19.1

sapin 18.11

sarcasme 47.14

sardine 72.11

Satan 38.12

satin 26.2

satisfaction 47.16

satisfaire 47.16

Saturne 22.14

sauce 73.6

saucisse 72.8

saucisson 72.8

sauf 91.5

saule 18.10

saumon 72.11

saumure 73.6

saut (d'une rivière) 22.9

saut (en athlétisme) 81.15

saut (en équitation) 81.26

sauter (bondir) 5.11

sauter (séduire) 64.17

sauterelle 16.3

sautiller 5.11

sauvage 48.5

sauvagement 48.5

sauvagerie 48.5

sauvegarder 98.2

sauver se 4.2

savant, e 59.12

saveur 73.1

savoir 53.1

savon 69.2

savonnette 69.2

savourer 74.11

savoureux, -reuse 73.4

saxophone 82.10

saxophoniste 82.10

scandale 43.19

scellé, e 31.1

scène (au théâtre et au cinéma) 82.2

scène (de ménage) 40.2

schizophrène 66.11

schizophrénie 66.11

scie 27.5

science(s) 59.8

sciences nat 59.8

scier 91.14

scintillant, e 21.4

scintiller 21.3

scolaire 59.1

score 81.10

Scorpion 38.19

scotch 75.5

script 96.33

scruter 63.2

scrutin 36.4

sculpter 83.5

sculpteur 83.5

sculpture 83.5

SDF 24.9

seau à glace 75.6

sec, sèche 20.5

sécateur 80.2

sèche (cigarette) 68.5

sèche-cheveux 69.3

sécher 20.5

sécheresse 20.5

séchoir (à cheveux) 69.3

séchoir (à tambour) 30.9

secondaire 59.1

seconde 9.8

second maître 39.4

secouer (s. la tête) 62.22

secouer (terme général) 5.3

secourir 46.3

secourisme 68.3

secouriste 68.3

secours (aide) 46.2

secours (document de s.) 98.2

secret 88.5

secrétaire (au bureau) 77.4

secrétaire (d'un parti) 37.4

section 91.3

sectionner 91.12

séducteur 50.3

séduction 50.2

séduire 50.2

séduisant, e 50.2

seigle 79.6

sein 64.1

sel 73.3

sélection 56.3

sélectionner (en informatique) 98.2

sélectionner (terme général) 56.3

selle 81.25

selon 96.11

semaine 9.2

sémaphore 8.18

semblant (faire s.) 88.8

semblant (n) 9

sembler 88.9

semelle 25.9

semer (en jardinage, agriculture) 80.1

semer (perdre) 50.9

semestre 59.1

sens (direction) 3.1

sens (signification) 96.31

sensation 47.2

sensibilité 42.3

sensible 42.3

sensiblerie 42.3

sentiment 42.3

sentimental, e 42.3

sentir (avoir un sentiment) 42.4

sentir (par l'odorat) 63.30

séparation (entre époux) 38.4

séparation (terme général) 27.2

séparer 27.2

séparer se 38.4

septembre 9.3

sept familles 81.6

serein, e 47.3

sérénité 47.3

sergent 39.2

sergent-chef 39.2, 39.3

série (succession) 29.4

série télévisée 82.3

sérieux, -rieuse 54.4

seringue 68.4

sermon 38.14

serpent 16.1

serpillière 30.6

serre (de jardinier) 80.1

serre (d'oiseau) 14.6

serrement de coeur 47.18

serrer (la main) 45.12

serrer (retenir) 41.11

serre-tête 25.10

serrure 31.1

sérum anti-venin 68.4

serveur (au restaurant) 74.9

serveur (en informatique) 77.2

serveuse 74.9

serviable 46.1

service (dans un hôpital) 65.2

service (de table) 24.19

serviette (de bain) 69.2

serviette (périodique) 69.7

serviette (pour documents) 25.12

servir se (au repas) 74.5
servir se (utiliser) 32.1
seuil 24.10
seul, e 35.11
sève 18.8
sexe 64.15
sexisme 43.13
sexiste 43.13
sextuple 58.9
sexuel, -xuelle 64.15
sexuellement 64.15
sexy 64.16
shampooing 69.3
shit 68.6
shooter se 68.6
si 82.14
sidérurgie 19.2
sidérurgiste 19.2
siècle 9.9
siège (chaise) 24.16
siège (de voiture) 7.3
siège (des toilettes) 24.22
siège (d'une organisation) 37.4
siège (d'une ville) 39.6
sieste 64.9
sifflement 14.7
siffler (chanter) 14.7
siffler (émettre un son aigu) 63.17
siffler (respirer mal) 64.4
signal de détresse 46.4
signaler 41.1
signe (astrologique) 38.19
signe (de la main) 45.12
signe (de tête) 45.12
signer 96.32
signification 96.31
signifier 96.31
silence 63.20
silencieusement 63.20
silencieux, -cieuse 63.20
silhouette 64.1
silo 79.3
simple 43.5
(simple) soldat 39.2
simplement 43.5
sincère 88.1
sincérité 88.1
singe 14.2
singulier (en grammaire, nm) 96.26
singulier, -lière (en grammaire, adj) 96.26
sinistre 20.6
sirène 63.17
sirop (médicament) 68.2
sirop (pour dessert) 73.7
situation 87.4
ski 81.21
slip 25.5

sobre 75.8
sobriété 75.8
social, e 36.1
socialisme 36.5
société (entreprise) 84.6
société (population) 36.1
sœur (dans une famille) 34.2
sœur (religieuse) 38.13
sofa 24.16
soie 26.2
soif 75.1
soigné, e 29.2
soigneusement 44.2
soigneux, -gneuse 44.2
soin (attention) 44.2
soin (médical) 68.1
soins dentaires 65.4
soins des cheveux 69.3
soit . . . soit 56.3
soixantaine 58.23
sol (dans un bâtiment) 24.15
sol (en musique) 82.14
sol (terre) 80.3
soldat 39.1
soldat de l'armée de l'air 39.3
solde 84.2
solder 84.9
solder se 61.3
soleil 22.14
solfège 82.14
solidaire 45.10
solidarité 45.10
solide 48.1
soliste 82.9–82.10
solitaire 35.11
solitude 35.11
solliciter 96.16
solo 82.9
somali 96.25
sombre 21.1, 63.13
sombrer 8.4
somme 58.16
sommeil 64.7
sommet 22.3
somnambulisme 64.11
son 63.15
sondage d'opinion 96.12
sondé, e 96.12
songer 54.2
songeur, -geuse 54.3
sonner 63.17
sonnerie 63.17
sonnette 24.10
soprano 82.11
sorbet 73.8
sorcier, -cière 88.11
sort 88.10
sorte 55.2

sortie (d'autoroute) 7.9
sortie (d'un lieu public) 24.11
sortie (excursion) 6.2
sortie (porte) 24.11 99
sortir 45.7
sortir s'en 52.7
sosie 55.6
sot, sotte 59.4
souche 18.8
souci 18.2
soudain, e (adj) 13.9
soudain (adv) 13.9
soudainement 13.9
souffle 64.4
souffler (respirer mal) 64.4
souffler (technique du verre) 26.4
souffrance 66.5
souffre-douleur 37.18
souffrir 66.5
soulager 68.1
soulier 25.9
soumettre se 37.17
soumis, e 37.17
soumission 37.17
soupçon (petite quantité) 58.8
soupçon (suspicion) 37.8
soupçonner 37.8
souper 74.4
souple (agile) 44.6
souple (pliable) 63.24
souplesse 44.6
source 22.8
sourcil 64.1
sourd, e 66.3
sourd-muet, sourde-muette 66.3
souriceau 15.5
sourire 47.11
souris (animal) 15.5
souris (en informatique) 77.2
sous-bois 18.8
sous-classe 36.2
sous-fifre 57.12
sous-lieutenant 39.2
sous-marin 8.8
sous-marinier 8.9
sous-officier 39.1
sous-sol 24.12
sous-vêtement 25.6
soustraction 58.17
soustraire 58.17
soutenir (aider) 46.6
soutenir (porter) 5.4
soutien-gorge 25.6
souvenir, se souvenir 64.5
souvent 10.1
spécialiste (médecin) 65.2
spécialiste (terme général) 59.3
spécifier 55.10

spécifique 55.10
spécifiquement 55.10
spécimen 41.5
spectacle (au cinéma, au théâtre) 82.2
spectacle (vue) 63.11
spermatozoïde 62.18
sperme 62.18
sphère 1.3
sphérique 1.3
spirale 1.3
spirituel, -tuelle 38.17
spiritueux 75.5
sport 81.9
sportif, -ive 81.11
sports d'hiver 81.21
sprinter 81.15
squelettique 62.8
stade 81.13
stage 59.11
stagiaire 59.11
standard 98.4
standardiste (dans une entreprise)
    77.4
standardiste (des Télécommunications)
    98.4
station 6.2
station service 7.7
stationnement 7.5
stationner 7.5
statue 83.5
steak 72.6
stère 58.27
stéréo 82.15
steward 8.15
stock 84.7
stocker 84.7
strophe 59.18
studio (appartement) 24.2
studio (de théâtre, cinéma, TV) 82.2
stup 68.6
stupéfait, e 47.7
stupéfiant 68.6
style 55.2
stylo 59.20
subalterne 57.12
subjonctif 96.26
subordonné, e 57.12
substituer 89.1
substitution 89.1
succès 52.7
sucer 74.11
sucette 33.5
sucette 73.8
sucre 73.8
sucré, e 73.2
sucre d'orge 73.8
sucrer 73.8
Sud 3.4

sud 3.3
suédois 96.25
suer 64.3
sueur 64.3
suffire 91.2
suffisamment 91.2
suffisant, e 91.2
suggérer 40.8
suggestion 40.8
suicide 67.5
suicider se 67.5
suinter 20.4
suite (conséquence) 61.3
suite (entourage) 5.10 21
suiveur 5.10
suivre 5.8–5.9
sujet 96.26
sumo 81.18
super 7.7
super 57.5
supérette 78.4
superficie 58.14 283
superflu, e 93.2
supérieur (dans l'enseignement, nm)
    59.1
supérieur, e (dans l'enseignement, adj)
    59.1
supérieur, e (dominant) 57.8
supériorité 57.8
supermarché 78.4
supersonique 8.13
supplier 96.16
supporter (d'une équipe) 45.4
supporter (endurer) 37.17
supporter (fan) 45.4
supporter (porter) 5.4
supposer 53.3
supposition 53.3
suppositoire 68.2
supprimer (enlever) 32.6
supprimer (tuer) 67.6
sûr, e (certain) 92.6
sûr, e (fiable) 44.1
suranné, e 12.4
surdi-mutité 66.3
surdoué, e 59.12
sûrement 92.4
surexcitation 47.2
surface de réparation 81.10
surmenage 76.7
surmener se 76.7
surnaturel 88.12
surnom 55.14
surnommer 55.13
surprenant, e 47.5
surprendre, e 47.5
surprise 47.5
surveillance 63.7

surveillant, e 63.9
surveiller 63.8
survenir 4.1
survêtement 25.8
survoler 98.2
survolté 47.2
suspect, e 37.8
suspecter 37.8
susurrer 96.7
svelte 62.7
sveltesse 62.7
swahili 96.25
syllabe 96.27
sympa 43.15
symphonie 82.13
symptôme 66.5
synagogue 38.13
syndical, e 76.5
syndicaliste 76.5
syndicat 76.5
syndiquer se 76.5
systématique 29.1
système 56.2
système reproducteur 62.18
système solaire 22.14

tabac 68.5
tabagisme 68.5
table (de billard) 81.24
table (meuble courant) 24.16
tableau (dans une gare) 8.19
tableau (document) 97.3
tableau (en classe) 59.7
tableau (peinture) 83.1
tableau de bord 7.4
tableur 77.2
tabou 37.14
tache 30.3
tache (d'huile) 58.11
tacher 30.3
tâcher 51.4
tacle 81.10
tacler 81.10
taie 24.21
taille (dimension) 58.14
taille (en anatomie) 64.1
tailler 80.1
tailleur 25.4
taillis 18.9
taire, se taire 63.21
talc 69.2
talé, e 70.8
talon (de chaussure) 25.9
talon (de chèque) 84.2
talon (en anatomie) 64.1
tambour (à broder) 83.6
tambour (instrument) 82.10
tampon (périodique) 69.7

tank 39.5
tante 34.5
tantôt . . . tantôt 56.3
tapage 63.15
tape 67.1
taper 67.1
tapir se 62.13
tapis 24.16
tapis de bain 24.22
tapoter 67.1
taquiner 47.14
taquinerie 47.14
tard 13.2
tardif, -dive 13.2
tarif 84.11
tarte 71.3
tas (pile) 29.4
tas (quantité) 58.3
tasse 24.18
tata 34.5
tâter 63.22
tâtonner 51.4
taudis 24.1
taule 37.9
taupe 15.5
Taureau 38.19
taureau 14.1
taxation 86.2
taxe 86.2
taxi 7.12
tchèque 96.25
teinturerie 78.7
télé 82.3
télécommunication 98.4
télécopie 98.4
télécopier 98.4
télé-enseignement 3.5
téléobjectif 83.4
téléphone 98.4
téléphone de voiture 7.3
téléphoner 98.4
téléscope 22.13
télévision 82.3
témoigner 96.9
témoin (à un mariage) 38.4
témoin (au tribunal) 37.11
tempérament 42.1
tempête 23.6
temple 38.13
temps (à t.) 13.3
temps (en grammaire) 96.26
temps (il y a quelque t.) 9.10
temps (météo) 23.2
temps (partiel) 76.4
temps (plein) 76.4
temps (tout le t.) 10.1
tenailles 27.5
tendance 10.3

tendre (gentil) 48.4
tendre (savoureux) 63.23
tendrement 48.4
tendresse 48.4
tendu, e 47.1
ténèbres 21.1
tenir compte de 54.1
tenir de 55.5
tenir, tenir se 41.11
tennis (chaussure) 25.9
tennis (sport) 81.14
ténor 82.11
tension 47.1
tentative 51.4
tente 81.2
tenter 51.4
terminal 11.2
terminer, se terminer 11.2
terminus 11.2
terrain (de sport) 81.13
terrain (d'une propriété) 80.3
terrain à bâtir 27.10
Terre 22.14
terre (champs) 79.7
terre (domaine) 22.11
terre (maraîchère) 79.2
terre (sol) 80.3
terre glaise 83.5
terreau 80.1
terreur 45.23
terrible 45.20
terrifier 45.23
territoire 22.11
Testament (Ancien, Nouveau) 38.15
testament 38.5
testicule 64.1
tétine 33.5
tête 64.1
têtu, e 51.3
texte (sacré) 38.15
texte (terme général) 97.3
textile 26.1
TGV 8.20
thé 74.4
thé 75.4
théâtre 82.2
thérapie 68.1
thermomètre 68.4
thèse 53.3
thon 72.11
thym 73.3
tibia 64.1
ticket (de caisse) 84.11
ticket (terme général) 6.1
tiède (indifférent) 45.14
tiède (ni chaud ni froid) 23.8
tiers 58.18
tigre 14.2

tigresse (animal) 14.2
tigresse (femme) 14.5
timbale 82.10
timbalier, -lière 82.10
timbre 97.2
tir (au combat) 39.6
tir (en sport) 81.23
tire-bouchon 75.6
tirelire 84.14
tirer (au combat) 39.6
tirer (déplacer) 5.3
tirer (en sport) 81.23–81.24
tirer au sort 56.4
tireur 39.6
tiroir 24.20
tisane 18.5, 75.4
tisser 26.1
tisserand, e 26.1
tissu 26.1
tissu-éponge 26.1
titre (de noblesse) 36.11
titre (d'une oeuvre) 59.14
titre (en journalisme) 82.1
titre (état-civil, rang) 55.14
tituber 5.6
toboggan 81.3
toile (d'araignée) 16.4
toile (peinture) 83.2
toile (tissu) 26.2
toilette 69.2
toiser 63.4
toit 24.10
tomate 70.14
tombe 38.5
tomber (coincider) 87.2
tomber (diminuer) 58.12
tomber (trébucher) 5.12–5.13
tomber sur 50.7
ton 63.15
tondeuse 80.1
tondre (t. un animal) 79.8
tondre (t. une pelouse) 80.1
tonne 58.25
tonneau (accident) 5.12
tonnerre 23.6
tonton 34.5
topimambour 70.13
topologie 22.11
toqué, e 66.12
torchon (à vaisselle) 30.8
torchon (texte) 44.4
tordre 1.7
tordu, e 1.5
torrent 22.8
torride 23.8
tort 37.15
tortillard 8.20
tortiller 1.7

tortionnaire 45.18
tortue 15.4
tôt 13.1
total, e (complet) 91.1
total (en mathématiques) 58.17
totalement 91.1
touche 82.10
toucher (avoir un contact physique avec) 63.22
toucher (contacter) 97.1
toujours 10.1
tour (aux échecs) 81.7
tour (bâtiment) 24.3
tour (d'honneur) 81.15
tour (de potier) 83.5
tour de contrôle 8.14
tour de cou 58.14
tourisme 6.2
touriste 6.2
tourne-disque 82.15
tourner 5.15
tournevis 27.5
tourniquet 81.3
tournoi 81.12
tourte 71.3
tourteau 72.12
tourterelle 16.6
Toussaint 9.5
tousser 66.2
T.S.V.P. 59.14
tout à coup 13.9
tout à l'heure 9.10
tout bas 63.20
tout de suite 13.5
tout haut 63.19
tout le temps 10.1
toute vitesse 13.8
toutou 15.3
toux 66.2
toxico 68.6
toxicomane 68.6
trac 82.4
trachée(-artère) 62.17
tracter 5.3
tracteur 79.4
tradition 38.1
traducteur 96.13
traduction 96.13
traductrice 96.13
traduire (d'une langue à une autre) 96.13
traduire (exprimer) 96.2
tragédie 82.2
tragique 82.2
train 8.20
train (électrique) 81.5
train d'atterrissage 8.12
train-train 10.2

traînée 30.3
traîner (s'attarder) 5.6
traîner (tirer) 5.3
traire 79.8
trait 1.5
traite bancaire 84.2
traitement 68.1
traitement de texte 77.2
traiter 68.1
traître 57.10
traîtresse 57.10
traits (du visage) 64.1
trajet 6.2
tram(way) 7.12
trancher 91.12
tranquille 47.3
tranquillement 47.3
tranquillité 47.3
transformation 89.2
transformer 89.2
transistor 82.3 395
transparence 43.20
transpiration 64.3
transporter 5.1
travail 76.3–76.6
travail (de bureau) 77.1
travail (de l'accouchement) 33.2
travailler 76.3–76.6
travailleur, -lleuse 76.6
travail manuel 83.1
travaux d'aiguille 83.6
traveller 6.2
trébucher 5.12
tréma 96.29
trempage 30.5
tremper (mettre dans un liquide) 20.3
tremper (pour laver) 30.5
trentaine 58.23
trésor (objets précieux) 85.1
trésor (terme affectueux) 45.8
tri 56.1
triangle 1.2
triangulaire 1.2
tribunal 37.11
tricher 43.22
tricheur 43.23
tricot (activité) 83.6
tricot (vêtement) 25.5
tricoter 83.6
trier 56.1
trimestre 59.1
trio 82.9
triomphal, e 52.7
triomphe 52.7
trip 68.6
triperie 78.2
tripier 78.6
triple 58.9

triplés, triplées 33.1
tripler 58.9
tripoter 63.22
triste 47.17
tristesse 47.17
trognon 70.7
trois-pièces 24.8
trombone (de bureau) 31.7
trombone (en musique) 82.10
tromboniste 82.10
trompe 62.18
tromper 43.22
tromper se 60.1
tromperie (sur la marchandise) 43.22
tromperie (terme général) 43.22
trompette 82.10
trompettiste 82.10
tronc 18.8
tronçon 91.3
tronçonner 91.14
trône 36.10
trophée 52.12
troquer 41.10
trot 81.25
trotter 81.25
trottoir 7.11
trou 31.6
trou d'air 8.13
trou noir 22.13
troué, e 31.6
trouer 31.6
troufion 39.1
troupeau (d'animaux) 79.8
troupeau (foule) 35.8
trousse 32.2
trousse 59.7
trouvaille (chose trouvée) 50.7
trouvaille (idée) 54.5
trouver (acquérir) 41.14
trouver (découvrir) 50.7
trouver se 87.2
truc (chose) 55.1
truc (en magie) 88.10
truie 14.1
tuba 82.10
tubercule 70.12
tuer 67.5
tueur, tueuse 67.6
tuile 24.10
tunique 25.8
turban 25.10
turbine 28.2
turboréacteur 8.12
turc 96.25
turf 81.26
turfiste 81.26
tuteur 80.1
tutu 25.8